PRACTICE
of
BANKING 1

To all my former students
and especially
Athenoula, Christos, Louis and Stavros

PRACTICE
of
BANKING 1

Second Edition

J. E. Kelly

FCIB, ACIS

*Senior Manager, National Westminster Bank plc
Securities and Recoveries Department,*

*Chief Examiner of the Chartered Institute of Bankers
in Practice of Banking 1*

Pitman

PITMAN PUBLISHING
128 Long Acre London   WC2E 9AN

© J. E. Kelly 1984, 1987

First published in Great Britain 1984
Second edition 1987
Reprinted 1988, 1989

British Library Cataloguing in Publication Data
Kelly, J. E.
Practice of banking 1
1. Banks and banking – Great Britain
I. Title
332.1' 0941   HG2988

ISBN 0-273-02739-5

Printed and bound in Hong Kong

Contents

SECTION A   BANKER – CUSTOMER RELATIONSHIPS, BANKING OPERATIONS AND TYPES OF ACCOUNT HOLDER

redemption; Remedies in the event of failure to repay – legal mortgages; Remedies of equitable mortgagee; Remedies of a second or subsequent mortgagee; Banks' mortgage forms; Unregistered land; Discharge of mortgages over unregistered land; Registered land; The use of solicitors' undertakings

Advantages and disadvantages; Types of policies; Duplicate policies; The bank's form of legal assignment over life policies; Taking a first legal assignment; Second or subsequent assignments; Assignments by limited companies; Equitable assignment of life policies; Realizing the security; Releasing the assignment

Advantages and disadvantages; Problems with equitable charges; Problems with legal charges; The charge form – memorandum of deposit; Taking a legal mortgage over registered shares; Taking an equitable mortgage over registered shares; Shares charged by a limited company; Mortgage over bearer securities; American and Canadian securities; Unit trusts; Allotment letters; Gilt-edged securities; National savings certificates and premium savings bonds; Unquoted shares; Release of shares from security; Realization of shares as mortgagee

Advantages and disadvantages; Definition and features; Obligations to intending guarantor; Common law rights and protection of a guarantor; Clauses in bank guarantee forms; Special types of guarantee; Joint and several guarantees; Guarantees by partnerships; Guarantee for a partnership; Guarantee by a minor; Guarantees for the borrowing of a minor or unincorporated body; Guarantees by women; Guarantee by a limited company; Taking the security; Determination of guarantee; Guarantor's rights of subrogation and contribution; Discharge of the guarantee document; Repayment by principal debtor; Preferences

Agricultural charges; Goods and produce as security; Charges over interests in wills, trusts and settlements; Assignments of debts and contracts

Past examination questions set by the Chartered Institute of Bankers

A Student's Guide to Land Mortgage Analyis

Preface to the Second Edition

Although the first edition of this book appeared as recently as 1984, there have been so many changes in statute law and new case law since then that it has become necessary already to offer a second edition.

In 1985 we saw a consolidation of all the previous Companies Acts into the Companies Act 1985 and in May of that year the Consumer Credit Act 1974 became wholly operational, affecting all lendings up to £15 000 to non-corporate persons. This Act can be very confusing and creates complex areas for all involved, and will be particularly so for students and bankers abroad; hence I have devoted a separate chapter to it in this new edition in the hope that the explanations and procedures set out will prove of help.

At the end of last year the Insolvency Act 1986 became law, this being the first major review of insolvency for over 70 years. This too is complex legislation and has caused major amendments to many banking practices. The Act has introduced the new administrator procedure for insolvent companies and offers a means whereby individuals and companies can avoid the full rigours of bankruptcy or liquidation through voluntary arrangements. Additionally, bankruptcy has itself changed greatly, with acts of bankruptcy being abolished and the various stages of bankruptcy now being fewer in number. With new areas such as transactions at undervalue, preferences, and wrongful trading, the student and the branch banker has much to learn. As the Act and Rules are unfortunately unclear in places it will probably not be long before the courts are hyperactive, interpreting them!

At the time of writing already waiting in the wings for enactment are a new Banking Bill and a Minors' Contracts Bill, references to which are made in the text in case they should become law before publication.

Ahead lies the possibility of legislation amending procedures on land mortgages, securitization and the abolition of the ultra vires doctrine for companies, but here students will be relieved to know that at least for the moment they can relax and merely await developments.

March, 1987   JEK

Preface to the First Edition

The Institute of Bankers' subject Practice of Banking 1 in its examinations for Associateship is one of the most interesting and challenging in the syllabus for the aspiring banker and student. It seeks to build on the knowledge acquired in Law Relating to Banking, and calls for the candidate to demonstrate a firm understanding of those principles which have fashioned banking procedures over the years. Yet it is also a practical and up-to-date subject, calling for comment on how a banker would act in a problem situation in his or her own branch. It is therefore very relevant to any banker's daily work.

For some thirteen years I had the privilege in evening classes of guiding students through the subject, and for a slightly shorter period I was a revision course tutor within my own bank, National Westminster. In those years my own knowledge widened immeasurably, not least from those questions put to me in my classes, and in this way I came to understand more of a student's difficulties and of those areas of the syllabus which regularly prove a stumbling block. In particular, in teaching overseas students of many nationalities, I realized the special difficulties which they face in having to learn about English banking practices, often without any real personal experience of areas such as securities in their own careers to date.

For the past few years I have been the Institute's Chief Examiner in Practice of Banking 1, and in order to be entirely neutral I can of course no longer lecture in the subject. I have therefore turned to writing, and in this book I have set down much of the content of those lectures which I formerly delivered around the United Kingdom and abroad. In doing so I have attempted throughout to keep the student reader and young trainee banker in mind, seeking to amplify those points which from experience I know to prove difficult of understanding, and to place emphasis on what is actually done within a branch bank. It is therefore a book not only for the examinee but also for newcomers into the profession and especially for practising security clerks and officers.

Parts of the text are based on a correspondence course which I wrote for the School of Banking some years ago, which I understand has proved successful. I am therefore very appreciative of their ready agreement to release to me the copyright of such material. Throughout I have linked the text by the use of footnotes to recent questions in the Institute of Bankers' Papers, thus enabling the technical points to be illustrated by imaginary situations posed in the examination room. For permission to use those questions I express my warm appreciation to the Institute.

I am also very grateful to Bank of Cyprus (London) Ltd and to their Assistant General Manager Mr C. C. Pascalides for their kind permission to reproduce several of the forms in use within that bank. I know that these will be especially welcomed by readers, particularly those overseas, as for many years they and others have been advised to study common forms and security papers, but have been unable to obtain them readily. Now their preparation for the examination and for their future careers will be greatly enhanced. These forms are reproduced here without responsibility on the part of the author or Bank of Cyprus (London) Ltd, as to their effect in law or practice, and in any event must not be copied or reproduced in any way without the specific written permission of that bank beforehand.

A book on Practice of Banking cannot proceed far without reference to case law, for this is not dull legal decision, but an examination of past banking events which have caused difficulties and a guide as to the way in which we bankers should carry out our duties to our customers in the future. Nevertheless I am conscious that it can become tedious to illustrate every point with reference to cases and I have therefore sought to 'retire' some of these older ones which historically have been associated with a text book on this subject. In doing so, I have hoped to make room for more recent decisions and I have examined some of these in depth, for they well illustrate the changing environment and attitudes in and according to which banking is conducted, and to which it must adapt, in the late twentieth century.

Finally, I have of course been assisted by many friends who have made valuable comments and suggestions, and to Mr John Stephens, Assistant General Manager of Lloyds Bank plc, Mr Malcolm Glover, and Mr Robert Johnson, both solicitors, I express my thanks. I also thank and acknowledge the permission granted by the Controller of Her Majesty's Stationery Office, the Land Charges Department, and the Land Registry to reproduce forms and papers in respect of which copyright is held by them.

To my wife Ann I am especially grateful, for her patience and accuracy in typing and retyping several drafts of the material, while also looking after the daily needs of our family.

My hope and aim therefore is that this book will prove helpful to students far and near, yet will also be a ready reference point for all bankers in their daily work. Such is the vastness of the subject, however, that all points may not have been covered adequately, and where that may be so, I trust that the reader will feel able to let me know, so that any future edition may incorporate his point and also those amendments which will become inevitable in this changing world. Indeed, I recall that I was once told by one of my overseas students that 'Practice of Banking is a whole world in itself'!

1984   JEK

List of Figures

page

List of Tables

page

Table of Cases

Table of Statutes

BANKER—CUSTOMER RELATIONSHIPS, BANKING OPERATIONS AND TYPES OF ACCOUNT HOLDER

CHAPTER 1

Banker–Customer Relationships

Banking has to do with people and their money – or their lack of it, either temporary or permanent! The people who use banks are called 'customers', a term which implies something slightly different from a 'client', which is the noun used by accountants and solicitors to describe persons who employ them. Perhaps the term 'customer' emphasizes the need for service, as in a shop, and certainly in the present age banking is thought of as a service industry rather than as a profession, although it is that too, calling for the highest integrity and skills from those who engage in it. It seems right in beginning our study of the Practice of Banking that we should remember, whatever the problems and technicalities we shall meet, that real people are concerned with and affected by our procedures at all times.

THE CUSTOMER

There is no statutory definition of a 'customer' and one must turn to case law if any legal guidance is required as to what features need to be present to constitute a person a customer of a bank. Among other aspects, it can be most important to be able to decide whether or not a person or other body is a customer, when cheques to which he is not entitled are collected for him, for the protection for the bank in such circumstances under s. 4 Cheques Act 1957 applies only when the work is carried out on behalf of a customer.

At one time it was assumed that the existence of an account was an essential feature of the banker-customer relationship and in *Great Western Railway Co.* v. *London and County Banking Co. Ltd* (1901) it was said that there must be some sort of account, either a deposit or current account or some relation, to make a man a customer of a banker. More recently, however, where a bank gave investment advice to a person who was not in account at the time, the court held that nevertheless the bank had incurred responsibilities to him, as to a customer (*Woods* v. *Martins Bank Ltd* (1959)). It may be said therefore that a person becomes a customer as soon as an account is opened, and probably as soon as a business relationship is established. It is not necessary for the account to have been open for a long period, or for the business to have been conducted over a regular period (*Commissioners of Taxation* v. *English Scottish and Australian Bank Ltd* (1920)).

A bank can even be a customer itself, where it has an account with another bank (*Regina* v. *Grossman* (1981)).

THE BANKER

Similarly, there is no one clear descriptive definition of a bank in either statute or case law, although the use of the word 'bank' or 'banker' in various pieces of legislation is some help. For example, s. 2 Bills of Exchange Act 1882 says a banker is 'any body of persons whether incorporated or not, who carry on the business of banking'; and s. 5(7) Agricultural Credits Act 1928, states: ' "bank" means any firm, incorporated company or society, carrying on banking business and approved by the Minister'. Neither of these can be said to be definitive!

In 1986 the Deputy Chairman of one of the United Kingdom's largest banks expressed the view to the Institute of Bankers' Cambridge Seminar that to call his bank a bank was probably now anachronistic. 'A more appropriate title would be financial services conglomerate', he said.

However, under the Banking Act 1979 supervision of deposit-taking institutions is exercised by the Bank of England, and there are three classes of such institutions: recognized banks, licensed deposit-taking institutions, and exempt bodies. In this latter category come the Bank of England itself, the National Savings Bank, the Trustee Savings Bank, the building societies, the insurance companies and, lastly, local authorities.

Recognized banks

To be accorded recognition a bank must satisfy the Bank of England as to its standing and reputation in the financial community, with special reference to the ability and competency of its management. It must have an issued capital and reserves of at least £5 million, and an adequate level of solvency for the extent of its operations. The Bank of England will also take into account the extent of the banking service offered and the degree of specialization. Among the basic services required are the acceptance of deposits, lendings, foreign exchange transactions and bill finance, investment management and corporate financial services, although the Bank of England has discretion not to insist upon the provision of all of the last named. The first two, however, are essential. Such a body is authorized to use the words 'bank', 'banking' and 'banker' in describing itself.

Licensed deposit-taking institutions

These are smaller undertakings and in order to obtain a licence a deposit-taking institution must satisfy the Bank of England that its business is conducted in a prudent manner and that the directors and management are fit and proper persons. Such a body must have an issued capital and reserves of at least £250,000, coupled with a good trading record. In deciding whether to grant a licence or not, the Bank of England will take account of balance-sheet ratios, liquidity, and the matching of liabilities and assets. Upon obtaining its licence the institution may trade and accept deposits from the public, for whose protection this legislation was enacted following the secondary-banking crisis in the United Kingdom in the mid-1970s. A licensed deposit-taking institution cannot call itself a bank, although there will be occasions when it will, in the context of other legislation and case law, be deemed to be a bank or it will wish to set itself up as a bank to bring itself within those other wider definitions, as seen for instance in the *United Dominions Trust Ltd* v. *Kirkwood* (1966) decision.

At the time of writing (January, 1987) a new Banking Bill is before Parliament which, if enacted, will make changes to the Banking Act of 1979. Inter alia this will give statutory backing to the Bank of England's Board of Banking Supervision and the distinction between recognized banks and licensed deposit takers will end. To be able to call itself a 'bank' an institution will require a paid up capital of over £5 million.

RELATIONSHIPS

The basic and perhaps most common relationship between a banker and his customer is that of debtor and creditor, as was demonstrated in *Foley* v. *Hill* (1848). In that case a depositor had sought to show that the banker was a trustee of funds which he had lodged, and that, accordingly, the banker should account to him for the profits made with the money, but this proposition was not accepted by the court. The court stated that the banker simply owed the funds deposited to the customer; or, had he been overdrawn, the customer would have been indebted to the bank.

More recently in 1986 when the Trustee Savings Bank was preparing to go public and issue shares, some depositors objected and sought an answer to the question, as seen by Lord Keith in the House of Lords 'whether depositors in a trustee savings bank had any interest in its assets other than the right to receive back their deposits together with the interest contractually agreed'. His answer, and that of the other members of the House of Lords was 'No'. (*Ross* v. *Lord Advocate & others: Trustee Savings Bank Central Board and Others* v. *Vincent and others* (1986)). (An unrelated but coincidental matter at this point is the fact that it was the same Rev. J. J. Vincent who officiated at the author's wedding to his wife Ann, 25 years previously!)

In *Joachimson* v. *Swiss Bank Corporation* (1921) a most important statement on the banker–customer relationship was made in the judgment. Atkin LJ said:

> The bank undertakes to receive money and collect bills for its customer's account. The proceeds so received are not to be held in trust for the customer, but the bank borrows the proceeds and undertakes to repay them. The promise to repay is to repay at the branch of the bank where the account is kept, and during banking hours. It includes a promise to repay any part of the amount due against the written order of the customer, addressed to the bank at the branch, and as such written orders may be outstanding in the ordinary course of business for two or three days,

it is a term of the contract that the bank will not cease to do business with the customer except upon reasonable notice.

The customer on his part undertakes to exercise reasonable care in executing his written orders so as not to mislead the bank or to facilitate forgery. I think it is necessarily a term of such contract that the bank is not liable to pay the customer the full amount of his balance until he demands repayment from the bank at the branch at which the current account is kept.

The Judge therefore identified obligations and rights on both sides of the relationship.

The range of banking services is now more extensive, however, and indeed is expanding all the time, so it must be expected that other relationships will arise besides that of debtor and creditor. For instance, that of principal and agent is present when the customer instructs his bank to buy or sell stocks and shares on his behalf, and when items are held in safe-custody the relationship is that of bailor and bailee. Where the bank's executorship service takes on the administration of a deceased's estate the relationship is that of trustee and beneficiary. Duties akin to a trusteeship might also happen when a branch comes into possession of funds or property which belongs to a third party, as when the bank has sold property in mortgage, and has a surplus to pass to the subsequent mortgagee. Obviously the relationship with the customer in that situation is that of a mortgagor with a mortgagee. However, if the security had been given by a third party then another state of affairs would exist between the lender and his surety. There, duties and obligations would arise irrespective of the banker–customer relationship with the borrowing customer.

Finally, where a banker gives general, or specific advice, he must exercise great care, for if he is careless or reckless his negligence could leave him open to an action for damages.

These special relationships are examined more closely in specific banking situations later in the book.

Bank's duties and rights

These may be summarized as follows:

(a) Provided the customer's cheques are properly drawn, and there are no legal bars preventing payment, the bank must honour the cheques to the amount of the balance, or if the account is overdrawn, to within the agreed limit.

(b) The bank is entitled to charge interest and commission, except where special arrangements have been made. It is entitled to debit the account with charges, usually quarterly, or half-yearly by its own custom, without specific advice to the customer.[1] A charge for an item such as the stopping of a cheque or dishonour of a cheque would usually be advised, however, if made separately at the time.

1 See Appendix I, Q. 18 (April 1982).

(*c*) A bank must maintain strict secrecy about its customer's affairs, both while the account is open and even after it has been closed. (There are however, certain exceptions to this rule which are examined later.)

(*d*) A bank must always follow its usual course of business when acting for its customers, who can expect transactions to be dealt with in a consistent manner.

(*e*) A bank acquires a general lien over its customer's negotiable documents which come into its possession, unless an express contract has been made which would be inconsistent with a lien (*Brandao* v. *Barnett* (1846)).

(*f*) The bank must give reasonable notice to its customer, before closing an account, which is maintained in credit. However, overdrafts are repayable on demand, unless there is an implied or actual agreement to the contrary.

(*g*) The bank must repay the whole or part of the balance, if and when there is demand by the customer during banking hours, provided the demand is made at the branch where the amount is kept, or at a branch where prior alternative arrangements have been made, such as under credit-opened encashment facilities.

(*h*) A bank has no obligations to third parties, arising out of the duty to pay its customer's cheques, and the payee of cheques issued by a customer cannot sue the paying banker.

Customer's obligations to his bank

(*a*) The customer is under a duty to exercise reasonable care when drawing his cheques, to help prevent fraud or forgery, and so that the bank will not be misled (*London Joint Stock Bank Ltd* v. *Macmillan and Arthur* (1918)). This duty extends only to ordinary precautions and a customer has no duty in the general course of his business to prevent his servants forging cheques. Indeed in *Tai Hing Cotton Mill Ltd* v. *Liu Chong Hing Bank Ltd* (1985) the court felt that the risks of forgery in offering a banking service were such that the banks should either contract in express terms with customers or seek protection by statute.

(*b*) The customer must go to his bank when he requires payment; it is not incumbent on the banker to seek out the customer. However in practice, where a credit account has been dormant for a long time, a bank will usually take steps to trace and re-establish contact with the customer before making any internal entry transferring the funds to a Central Account of Dormant Balances. As far as the customer is concerned in those circumstances however, the account is still open and the Statute of Limitations is not running against him.

(*c*) Before drawing a cheque, the customer must ensure his account is put in funds to meet it. Alternatively, he must make arrangements for overdraft facilities to be available from his bank.

(*d*) A customer must pay reasonable interest and commission, and other charges for banking services, and this is implied when he opens his account.

Often specific terms, such as interest rates linked to a formula, are agreed.

The Barnes case

The most important case in recent years on banker-customer relationships and duties was that of *Williams & Glyn's Bank Ltd* v. *Barnes* (1980),[2] and in view of its importance we will examine it in detail.

Mr Derek Barnes was the chairman and managing director of a group of housebuilders, Northern Development Holdings Ltd, which was one of the largest such concerns in the United Kingdom in the early 1970s. The business had been built up since the late 1950s when profits of almost £0.5 million were made. By October 1972 the company was making profits of £7 million per annum and in that month Mr Barnes in his personal capacity borrowed £1 million from the bank in order to acquire more shares in the company. Repayment was eventually to come from loan monies which Mr Barnes had in the company but intended to recover, and in the meantime he lodged the shares which he had just bought with the bank as security.

At this time the bank was also lending about £6.5 million to the company and to its subsidiaries. In 1973 the company raised further finance from other banks, and then a further £3 million from Williams & Glyn's Bank to enable the company to settle its borrowing of £1.5 million with another finance house, Cornhill, which had failed.

Around that time, following a rapid inflation in house prices and other costs, business problems escalated when Middle East oil prices were raised substantially and the government had to introduce a three-day working week. This brought the property euphoria to an end and a severe financial crisis arose in the City. In June 1974 a rescue operation was put together for the Northern Development Homes Group and Williams & Glyn's Bank and others entered into a moratorium, although in that it was provided that all bank lending would be 'repayable on demand'. The moratorium was to be for twelve months, although there was provision for it to be ended by five banks acting together, at any time before then. The financial crisis deepened, property prices collapsed and in June 1975 Williams & Glyn's bank made demand upon the company and appointed a receiver. The bank also called upon Mr Barnes to repay the monies which he had borrowed personally and in 1976 it brought proceedings to recover £1.7 million and interest.

Mr Barnes proved himself to be a formidable defendant and while he admitted an inability to pay, he alleged that this inability had been caused by the bank's actions in that it had brought down his companies; therefore his position had been adversely affected and his income had ceased. He counterclaimed against the bank in the sum of £32 million, as damages arising out of its action in calling in the borrowing of the companies prematurely and putting them into receivership. He alleged that the bank owed a duty to him

2 See Appendix I, Q. 25 (April 1983).

not to damage his interests as a shareholder, particularly as the shares were held by the bank as security. Moreover, he claimed that the bank had a duty not to lend unwisely.

Mr Barnes said that the bank should have advised him not to borrow the £1 million lent to him personally in 1972, with which he bought further shares in Northern Development Holdings Ltd.

In particular Mr Barnes's case was that the bank should not have called in the company overdraft, for it had said in a facility letter that it would review the facility at the end of six months, although the loan was also said to be 'on the usual banking terms'.

In pursuance of his case Mr Barnes had attempted to persuade the company, through its receiver, to sue the bank but he was unsuccessful in those attempts and brought proceedings himself.

The case lasted 104 days and the judgment extended to 700 pages. Basically the judge found against Mr Barnes on the basis that the claim that he was putting forward was the company's claim and not a personal claim of Mr Barnes. However, because of the possibility of an appeal, the judge dealt in detail with all Mr Barnes's arguments.

He held in favour of the bank on all points apart from its point that one loan which had been made to the company subject to review after six months was, nevertheless, still repayable on demand even within the six-month period specified in the facility letter, because it had been said to be granted 'on the usual banking terms'.

On Barnes's main personal point (that the Bank should have cautioned against his borrowing £1 million to buy shares in Northern Development Holdings Ltd in 1972) the judge ruled that the bank was not Mr Barnes's personal financial adviser.

The other points mainly concerned the companies:

Whether the overdraft was repayable on demand Mr Justice Gibson said:

'Where money is lent on overdraft by a bank, and there is no agreed day for repayment, and no special terms which require implication of a further term as to the date of repayment, then it is clear to me that the overdraft is repayable on demand.'

Repayment of loan facility Mr Justice Gibson said:

'A loan is repayable on demand unless the terms and circumstances of the contract of lending show that, as a matter of necessity to give business efficacy to the contract, the term must be implied, requiring the lender to give notice over a reasonable period of time before his right to repayment arises.'

The facility letters were then examined and it was said that in one instance where an indication had been given that the facility would be reviewed at the end of six months, it was not sufficient merely to use the phrase 'on the usual banking terms' even though reserving the right to call in at any time. The judge said that

> 'A reference to "the usual banking conditions" without stating what they are, and without clear language showing that such conditions are to prevail over any other terms as to duration of termination, whether express or necessarily derived from the language used, cannot negative a term which is otherwise part of the agreement.'

That repayment depended upon fulfilment of the purpose of the advance   Mr Justice Gibson said:

> 'When a bank lends money to a customer there is no reason to suppose that, in the absence of agreement to that effect, the bank must regard the fulfilment of the customer's known purpose as the agreed, or only, source of repayment. Borrowing from a bank may be replaced by borrowing from another bank or moneylender. If the borrowing cannot be replaced, because of the parlous state of the borrower's business, or of the market generally, I know of nothing in the ordinary contract of lending which requires the lender to share the borrower's misfortune.'

That the bank had lent imprudently   One of Barnes's arguments had been that the bank should not have lent Northern Development Homes the £6 million in 1972 as a short-term facility and that the bank had owed a duty to the company to advise a long-term or other financial arrangement which would have covered the period over which the sites would have been developed. It was held that the bank owed no such duty of care, as it was not a financial adviser to the company. As the company had requested an overdraft, or short-term lending, and that had been granted, that was the company's wish. If the company, having assessed its requirements, albeit with external financial advice, had decided that a medium- or long-term facility was required, then it should have asked for one.

That the bank should have lent more   Despite the argument above, Mr Barnes had argued that the bank had been wrong to decline to lend more in 1973. His point was that over the years the bank had increased its lendings to the company as profits had grown and there was an implied term that the bank would continue to do so. It was held that the bank was under no such duty.

That the bank was under a duty to advise the company in respect of the transaction, involving the payment to Cornhill of £3 million   Barnes's point was that the company had only paid the money because the bank had lent it. He alleged that the advice which he had taken from other parties was inadequate and that only Williams & Glyn's Bank knew all the facts; in consequence it should have advised him not to pay £3 million. He alleged the bank had made him borrow this sum to discharge the other debt and to give additional security.

It was held that the bank had not acted improperly as the company could have refused the bank's offer to lend £3 million and that it made repayment to Cornhill on the advice given by its own solicitors and merchant bankers.

That there was a fiduciary relationship Mr Barnes sought to bring in the principle seen in *Lloyds Bank Ltd* v. *Bundy* (1975), alleging that in January 1974 when the facility letter was given the company was so weak and the bank was so strong that the bank was under a special responsibility through its fiduciary relationship not to take advantage for itself through its strong bargaining power. The court did not accept this argument.

That the moratorium agreement was contrary to public policy Mr Barnes alleged that when the bank supported the company in the moratorium arrangements which were negotiated in the summer of 1974 it was contrary to public policy that the monies which were not then called in should be repayable 'on demand' in the future. He developed his argument by saying that it was wrong for the company to be allowed to continue trading and running up trade credit when it could be brought down at any time by the banks calling in their lendings. This argument, too, was rejected, and the judge said that it was the directors' responsibility to determine whether or not trading was being carried on properly or improperly and that if they thought the latter, having the provisions of s. 332 Companies Act 1948 in mind (fraudulent trading) (now s. 213 Insolvency Act 1986) they should cease to trade.

Conclusions The court decision, that in the absence of an agreement to the contrary an overdraft is repayable on demand, was very reassuring to banks, but it is clear that care must be taken to ensure that when facilities have been made available, nothing is done directly or by implication to waive the bank's rights to call for repayment on demand.

Usually an overdraft is granted repayable on demand, but subject to review or renewal at the expiry of, say, twelve months. Thus the bank's ability to call in the debt is preserved for those occasions when, during the currency of the facilities marked, the trading situation deteriorates or events happen which mean the bank needs to take steps to protect its own position. Normally, however, the step of calling in an overdraft will have been preceded by correspondence and/or interviews with the customer, and the notice finally crystallizing the liability will not come as a surprise. When an overdraft has been called in, no further cheques should be paid on the account, and provided the liability is repaid, together with bank charges, the account can be closed.

Loan accounts may be conducted by oral agreement, or by a specially negotiated facility with an exchange of documents. It follows that in these cases, provided the loan instalments are up to date, and that there is no default in any ancillary covenants by the borrower (for example, to maintain insurance of property acquired with the monies lent, or to use the monies lent for the specific purpose mentioned in the application), then the bank cannot call for repayment of its loan. Where, however, loan instalments are in default, or there is a breach of covenant, the loan can be called in, and, upon repayment, the banker-customer relationship ceases.

STATUTE OF LIMITATIONS

The relationships between a banker and his customer can be affected by the Limitation Act 1980 and the provisions of this statute extend also into security situations. Basically this Act provides that proceedings in law cannot be brought after certain periods of time have elapsed, these varying from one situation to another. On a simple contract, for example, no action can be brought unless it is instigated within a period of six years from the date when the cause of action first arose (s. 5). However, under a specialty contract, that is one under seal, the time limit becomes twelve years (s. 8(i)). Also, where a sum of money is secured by a mortgage or a charge on real or personal property, no action can be brought to recover the principal sum outside a period of twelve years from the date when the cause of action first arose (s. 20(i)). From the point of view of security, this means that actions on guarantees, which are not personal property, must be brought within six years where the guarantee is under hand, but if it is sealed, a twelve-year period applies. Mortgages and charges on personal property fall within the twelve-year rule and personal property includes stocks and shares and life policies.

Occasionally it is very important for a bank to show when the time running under a limitation period began, this being particularly so with a debit account. Any action to recover an overdraft, or loan without a determinable repayment date, becomes statute-barred six years after demand for repayment has been made, although this period is extended where there is a subsequent acknowledgement within the six years (s. 6 Limitation Act 1980). If the loan has a fixed repayment date, the period of six years commences from the promised date of a repayment instalment, and can be extended by an acknowledgement within the six-year period. The acknowledgement should be in writing, or by way of a payment of interest or capital. However, in *Jones* v. *Bellegrove Properties Ltd* (1949) it was held that, where a debt outstanding was included in the 'sundry creditors' total in a balance sheet of the company, that was a sufficient acknowledgement to renew the time limit.

If a loan account or overdrawn current account is secured by direct security from the borrower, invariably the bank's form of charge will provide that repayment should be 'on demand', and with such a clause the question of when the Limitation Act begins to apply is put beyond doubt (*Lloyds Bank*

Ltd v. *Margolis & Others* (1954)). A clause with similar effect in a guarantee document was held to be effective against the guarantor in *Bradford Old Bank Ltd* v. *Sutcliffe* (1918).

Understandably, banks need not concern themselves with the effect of the limitation period upon a credit account, apart from remembering that an unclaimed balance in the customer's name can still be demanded after any number of years have elapsed since the last transaction.[3] The technical position is that the limitation period begins to run from the time when the customer has demanded payment (*Joachimson* v. *Swiss Bank Corporation* (1921)) and one cannot foresee a situation in which a bank refuses to pay its customer monies for a period of six years! All this means of course that credit balances taken into the bank's central accounting records as dormant balances do not become the property of the bank and they must be paid over when demanded. Of course, before making internal entries in this way, banks take steps to seek out their customer and to remind him that the account is still open, or to get him to withdraw the funds. It is only after such steps have proved abortive because the customer has not answered letters, or is untraceable without great difficulty, that the internal transfer to dormant balances is made. It is important at that stage for the branch to mark its records carefully, so that if a transaction ever arises in the future it can be handled properly.

Finally, it should be noted that following the passing of the Limitation Act 1980, which consolidated previous Limitation Acts, any right of action, once it has become statute-barred, cannot be revived by a subsequent acknowledgement or payment (s. 29(7)). A payment of part of the interest due does not extend the period for claiming the balance then due, but a payment of interest is treated as a repayment of the principal debt and as such it will start the limitation period running again against the principal debt (s. 29(6)).

THE DUTY OF SECRECY

While the main relationship between a bank and its customer is that of debtor and creditor, there are in addition other relationships and duties which do not normally exist between such parties. The most important of these is the duty of secrecy, and it is one which every customer expects his bank to maintain at all times. This duty is implied when the account is opened, and there is no need for a prospective customer to ask that the bank will keep his affairs confidential.[4] The implied duty extends not only to the account itself and the information that could be gained from it, but also to any other particulars of the customer's affairs which come into the bank's knowledge from conducting the account or in carrying out any other transactions or financial dealings on

3 See Appendix I, Q. 6 (September 1980).
4 See Appendix I, Q. 9 (April 1981).

behalf of the customer.[5] The duty must be maintained both while the account is open and even subsequently after it has been closed, and one of the first impressions which a new employee will gain on his first day in the bank is of the need to maintain this secrecy. All employees are asked to sign a declaration that they will not disclose any matters concerning the bank's customers' affairs to any party outside the bank.

Where records regarding a customer are maintained by computer, the Data Protection Act 1984 requires these to be accurate and provides an individual with the right to compensation if he suffers damage or distress arising out of loss of the records or their unauthorized disclosure to a third party. The individual has a right of access to any personal data about himself and may call for it to be corrected if necessary.

In practice however it would be impossible to conduct the bank's business unless some disclosure were made to outside parties, and while one may start with the basic concept it will soon be realized that this duty of secrecy is a qualified duty and not an absolute one. This was recognized in the leading case on secrecy of *Tournier* v. *National Provincial and Union Bank of England Ltd* (1924).

The Tournier case

Tournier had an overdrawn account, and because reductions to this were not being made as he had promised, the bank manager telephoned Tournier where he worked, but, being unable to speak to him in person, he discussed the position with Tournier's employer. Because of this conversation, the employer learned that Tournier's account was overdrawn and that his employee had been gambling with bookmakers. As a result Tournier was dismissed and later brought an action against the bank for damages. Not unexpectedly, he succeeded, thus illustrating how easy it is for a bank officer to forget his responsibilities and to incur a loss for the bank. The case gave the judge an opportunity to examine the bank's duty of secrecy and he held that this is a qualified duty and disclosure is justified in four circumstances.

As he saw it, where the bank has been authorized by its customer, either expressly or by implication, then the customer could not complain later. Similarly, it was right that the bank should be able to disclose its knowledge where, in order to look after its own interests, it needed to inform another party of matters relating to its customer's affairs and his account.

Again, a bank would also have to comply with any demand which would involve 'disclosure', where it was under some compulsion of law.

Finally, where there was a duty in the public interest, then the bank need not hesitate in revealing matters to the appropriate outside parties.

Disclosure with consent Few problems are likely to arise for the bank where the customer authorizes it to inform other parties of the state of his

5 See Appendix I, Q. 29 (September 1983).

account, and clearly there can be no grounds for alleging a breach of the duty of secrecy in those circumstances. The bank, however, will nearly always wish to obtain the written authority of the customer, so that if necessary its ability to disclose can be demonstrated to the court, should matters turn out differently. Obviously, much will depend upon the particular circumstances and there will be occasions when an oral authority might be acceptable, although no doubt even in those instances it would be helpful for the bank to make a record of the authority at the time, in its interview or telephone notes, as this would strengthen its hands if an action were brought unexpectedly.

A common example of where the bank discloses the customer's affairs is where the customer's auditors write to the bank calling for a note of the balance in the accounts at a certain date.[6] The bank will seek the customer's written authority to disclose the information, and this may well extend to giving details of safe-custody or security items held. Not infrequently the authority is drawn to cover not only the one annual audit, but also future occasions, although the bank must be careful to ensure that the customer does not change his auditors, for if so then another authority should be taken.

Where a limited company customer is concerned, there is an arrangement between the Auditing Practices Committee, representing the accountancy profession, and the Committee of London Clearing Bankers that the request for audit information will be sent to the bank well before the audit date. Standard questions will be asked, and because of the advance warning the banks are able to program their computers to abstract the necessary information as to the balances of the account(s) on the appropriate date. Details of any direct security held may be given, but it is usual only to refer briefly to third-party security without naming a chargor or guarantor. Should the customer have any contingent liability to the bank, such as a guarantee, the amount and nature can be described.

As will be appreciated, it is unlikely that any real problems will be encountered in situations similar to those mentioned above, but clearly there is a greater area of risk where the customer is only presumed to have given his consent, although in practice even here banks rarely experience trouble. A good example of the customer's implied consent is that concerned with the giving of replies to status enquiries. When a new customer opens his account, he is presumed to know that this regular practice exists between the banks and certain recognized credit information bureaux and that the bank will answer any enquiries received about him, although in general terms. Certainly, balances will not be disclosed nor will security, but the way in which an answer is framed will show the enquirer something of the financial standing of the customer as it appears to his bank.

Also, in looking at the question of implied consent, we can examine the taking of guarantee security. Here, the bank might be lending or about to lend

6 See Appendix I, Q. 9 (April 1981).

money to the customer, who has introduced a guarantor for his liabilities. The bank is then under no obligation or duty to inform the intending guarantor of the state of the customer's account, its conduct, or the customer's business, but equally, to ensure that his security cannot be upset later, he must not mislead the intending guarantor. This could arise where the guarantor is under a misunderstanding, and it would be just as misleading for the bank to remain silent then as to tell him untruths. Thus the bank would put its security at risk if it allowed the guarantor to sign without correcting the misunderstanding, and herein lies the bank's dilemma, for if it corrects the misconception, it could, by so doing, be in breach of its duty of secrecy to the customer. In such cases, the prudent banker will obtain the written authority of his customer to disclose matters and to discuss the account with the intending guarantor, although frequently matters are solved on a practical level by arranging an interview at which the customer and the intending guarantor can be present so that the customer's oral authority to answer any questions can be obtained at the outset of the interview, and any misunderstandings corrected at once.

Cases in which the bank has been sued for breach of secrecy are fairly few, but that of *Sunderland* v. *Barclays Bank Ltd* (1938) is well known. Here the bank had to defend an action brought by its customer for breach of duty of secrecy, and it did so on the grounds that she had impliedly consented to its disclosing her affairs by telephone to her husband. During the course of that conversation the bank mentioned that Mrs Sunderland was drawing cheques payable to a bookmaker. The telephone conversation had arisen because the bank had dishonoured cheques drawn on the account and was seeking to demonstrate why it had not been prepared to allow an unauthorized overdraft to Mrs Sunderland. The bank failed with its argument that Mrs Sunderland had given her implied consent, as the evidence presented to the court conflicted, but succeeded on the grounds that the disclosure had been in the bank's own interest. In other words, the court accepted that the bank had been trying to establish with the customer's husband that what it had done had been reasonable in all the circumstances.

It only remains to be said that naturally great care should be exercised in answering telephone calls and in disclosing balances or information over the telephone. The bank officer concerned must ensure that it is the customer who is making the call, and he must ask the customer to identify himself satisfactorily before providing any information that is required.

Disclosure in the bank's interests   There can be no doubt that the bank must of necessity disclose its customer's affairs when it takes steps to recover monies owing. Then, it may need to instruct solicitors and a writ or summons will be issued. Such papers will be seen by clerks, process servers, and officers of the court. Again, if the bank is considering selling a property as mortgagee then it will instruct estate agents, and it may be necessary to inform the estate agent of the customer's name and the reason why the bank requires a valuation, particularly if the co-operation of the occupant will not be forthcoming when the estate agent calls to value. Also, when legal proceedings are started against the bank by a customer or a third party, the bank must, in order to defend itself satisfactorily, be able to disclose its customer's affairs without limitation or hesitation.

By way of further example, when it appoints a receiver under a debenture, the bank will need to discuss its customer's affairs with the accountant who is the receiver designate, before he will be prepared to say that he is willing to accept such an appointment.

Disclosure as a duty to the public   In the *Tournier* case the judge indicated that the bank would be justified in disclosing its customer's affairs if there was a clear duty to the public so to do. It is the extent of that duty which was not defined and from time to time pressure is put on banks to disclose their customers' affairs, because it is said that they have such a duty. Most bankers are wary, however, of relying on this Tournier exception too readily, and even if a police officer is pursuing his enquiries into crime it is doubtful if many bankers would feel able to supply confidential information. Generally it is felt that the situations under which disclosure is justified because there is a duty to the public must not be construed too widely, and it would need to be a very serious matter before the banker would proceed without first of all seeking his customer's written authority. Thus, in wartime, if it were known that a customer were trading with the enemy, then clearly, because of the seriousness of the nature of the offence, disclosure would be justified. Also, in more modern times, if certain information on terrorist activities came within the bank's knowledge then this should be disclosed to the appropriate authorities.

Disclosure under compulsion of law   In pursuance of their investigations police officers may sometimes feel that information about a suspect's financial dealings or bank account could be helpful, and they might approach the bank. This can place the bank in an invidious position, for while it will not wish to impede the investigations, it will be concerned that if it helps the police by disclosing private information, it could expose itself to an action by the customer for unauthorized disclosure. Great care is necessary, and usually the bank will suggest that the police officer seek an inspection order under the Bankers' Books Evidence Act or a witness summons. Occasionally an unsigned statement may be provided on the basis that the police will hold it in confidence and give an undertaking not to use it in any legal proceedings unless and until a witness summons is served upon the bank.

Under the Bankers' Books Evidence Act 1879, any party to legal proceedings is able to obtain a court order enabling him to inspect entries and take copies of those entries in the bank's books. By these means investigating police officers can obtain the information they need in criminal proceedings, although a magistrate will not usually grant them the authority to inspect until he has been adequately assured that there are already good grounds in existence for such further investigation. In other words, the procedure cannot be used simply as a 'fishing expedition'.

The provisions of the Bankers' Books Evidence Act 1879, enable the bank to produce certified copies of book entries in court instead of actual books of record. When served with a section 7 inspection order (Fig. 1.1) the bank must comply. In *Barker* v. *Wilson* (1980) the court allowed microfilm to be admissible evidence as a 'bankers' book', and it was said that this term included any form of permanent record made by modern technology.

When a bank is served with a witness summons or subpoena (Fig. 1.2) to attend court it is under the same duty as any other member of the public, and the bank's evidence, which must be strictly factual, is protected from an action for unauthorized disclosure. Sometimes the witness summons or subpoena will call upon the bank to produce originals or copies of its records and if so then the witness summons will extend to those items which are not, strictly speaking, covered by the Bankers' Books Evidence Act, such as correspondence (*Regina* v. *Dadson* (1983)). Usually bank evidence is by way of a written statement, although occasionally bank officers are required to be cross-examined in evidence. In all cases they must ensure that they do not give expressions of opinion and that they merely supply the facts as they are known to them.

Disclosure under compulsion of law also arises under certain financial legislation. Under s. 17 Taxes Management Act 1970, the Inland Revenue are empowered to obtain details of any stock registered in the name of the bank or its nominee company on behalf of a customer, and by virtue of this same Act banks now have to make returns to the Inland Revenue disclosing interest credited to a customer's account exceeding £400 per year. Under s. 57 Finance Act 1976, referring to s. 20 Taxes Management Act 1970, the Inland Revenue is also granted wide powers to seek information from banks relevant to any taxation liability. The procedure is used comparatively rarely, and the Inland Revenue may not use it for 'general fishing' enquiries. However, where the procedure is invoked, with a view to limiting tax avoidance, all aspects of the banker-customer relationship are open to scrutiny.

Section 434 Companies Act 1985 empowers a Department of Trade and Industry Inspector to obtain information concerning a limited-company customer, where an investigation is being carried out, and a bank when served with such an order must always comply with it. Invariably it will take its own legal advice in such circumstances either from its own in-house or external solicitors.

Under the provisions of the recent Financial Services Act (1986) the Trade and Industry Secretary can appoint inspectors with power to examine on oath any person thought to be able to supply information on suspected insider

Bankers' Books Evidence Act, 1879, S-7

The   7th   day   March   19

In the matter of criminal proceedings against

John Young

IT IS HEREBY ORDERED on the application of   Martin Smith, Detective Sergeant attached to Town Police Station   a party to the

said proceedings, that he be at liberty to inspect and take copies of entries in the

books of the   Practice Bank plc.,
                Kings Road,
                Town

relating to the banking account of the said   John Young
                                      Account Number 01-764398

AND THE COURT HEREBY DIRECTS that this Order be obeyed forthwith

upon service of the same

J. Taylor

Justice of the Peace for   Town

sitting at the   Town   Magistrates' Court.

To the Manager of

Practice Bank plc
Kings Road
Town

Order to inspect
bank books

Fig.1.1   *Bankers' Books Evidence Act order*

In the Crown Court

at 1 High Street Town

To Mr Mark Peters

of Manager
    Practice Bank plc
    Palatine Road
    Town

YOU are summoned to attend and give evidence (at the trial)

of John Smith

before the CROWN COURT

at Town

on a date and at a time of which you will be notified

and on subsequent days until the court releases you.

and to produce the bank statement
                and record of returned cheques
                in relation to the bank account of
                John Smith A/C number 12345678

An Officer of the Crown Court

Date:

NOTE:

1. Under Section 3 of the Criminal Procedure (Attendance of Witnesses) Act, 1965, any person who without just excuse disobeys a witness summons requiring him to attend before any Court, shall be guilty of contempt of that Court, and shall be liable to a term of imprisonment not exceeding three months.

2. You should not attend until you are told to do so by either the solicitor concerned or the police officer in charge of the case.

Fig.1.2   *Witness summons*

dealings. Witnesses may be compelled to produce any relevant documents.

The Drug Trafficking Offences Act 1986 is the latest weapon in the authorities' armoury against crime and it is expected that the banks will have an important part to play in this new area.

Under s. 24 it is a criminal offence for anyone to hold or control the proceeds of drug trafficking or to assist in investment of the proceeds, or even to lend to a drug trafficker. However, it will not be an offence if the person concerned discloses his knowledge or suspicion, and such disclosure by a bank is not a breach of its duty of secrecy to a customer.

Under s. 27 the court may order that a bank must give access to its records to the authorities, who are empowered to retain any records or documents. These orders are known as Production and Access Orders and a customer must not be advised of their service on the bank, as to prejudice the investigation would be a criminal offence. Usually a bank would have 7 days in which to comply with service of such an order. Section 28 allows the court to grant a Search Warrant and this enables the authorities to enter and search the bank's premises and to seize and hold any documents or records which could assist their investigation.

MENTAL INCAPACITY

The Mental Health Act 1983 governs the conduct of a person's affairs when he becomes incapable of managing and administering them himself by reason of his mental disorder. Where it is clear that the customer has become incapable, any mandate which the bank has to operate his sole or joint account is terminated and in consequence no further cheques can be paid. Moreover any delegation he has granted is revoked and if a third party previously could draw cheques, this can no longer be allowed as the authority of the agent is also determined (*Drew* v. *Nunn* (1879)). Cheques drawn should be returned with the answer 'Insufficient mandate'.

Sometimes it is difficult for the bank to decide whether or not it should stop the customer's account, for there may be doubt about the actual state of his mental capacity. In some cases, while a customer might act in a strange manner it might not be sufficient to justify the dishonour of his cheques, and if the bank did so without adequate reason it could leave itself open to an action for damages. The prudent banker will, in these difficult circumstances, usually make enquiries of the customer's doctor, or a hospital where he might be a patient. Technically, this might be regarded as a breach of secrecy, but the circumstances could be said to be in the bank's own interests, and on those grounds to be fully justified. If the medical opinion is that the customer is incapable of managing his affairs, then the account can be safely stopped, and it is advisable for the bank to speak with the customer's relatives. If they have not already done so, it is best if they apply to the Court of Protection for the appointment of a receiver under the Mental Health Act and invariably this person is a near relative or friend. However, if the patient executed an Enduring Power of Attorney whilst of sound mind, then the Attorney can proceed under that (see page 31).

When the bank is shown the Court of Protection Order, whether or not it knew of the customer's state of affairs beforehand, there can then be no doubt about his inability to manage his own affairs and the account can and must be stopped. The receiver will probably open his account at the same branch as that of the patient,[7] and, if he is unknown, references should be taken before the account is opened.

The terms of the sealed order of the Court must be very carefully interpreted and complied with. The banker should look to see which accounts of the patient are to be transferred into the receiver's name, if any. However, following a change of procedure in 1981, if the Court of Protection Order makes no reference to a cash account, it is the intention that this amount should remain in the name of the patient. The bank should of course then stop that account. If interest is allowed, then the receiver will be able to receive this under his general powers or he can allow it to accumulate. The bank should then look to see if the receiver has access to safe-custody or security items. If the Court of Protection Order fails to refer to items which are held by the bank then the existence of these, such as safe custody, should be mentioned to the receiver, and then he can return to the court to obtain a further order, which can be exhibited to the bank giving it its instructions and power to deliver these items to the receiver, or elsewhere. If any safe custody or security is held in joint names, then it will be necessary for the written authority of the receiver and the other party to be obtained before delivery can be made.

A receiver has no power to borrow unless he is specifically authorized by the Court of Protection. Also, it should be remembered that a licence granted to the customer under the Consumer Credit Act 1974 is terminated when a receiver is appointed by the Court of Protection, although in certain instances the termination can be deferred for any period up to one year.

The authority of the receiver ceases upon the death of the patient,[8] and thereafter his affairs are managed either by the executor appointed under the patient's will, or the administrator(s) who must take out separate letters of administration. The bank should then seek the written authority of the receiver so that any balance in his account can be transferred into the new account which would be opened for the executor or administrator.

The danger of trying to conduct matters outside a formal appointment of a receiver under the Court of Protection was seen in two cases which are warnings to bankers.

In *Beavan, Davies, Banks & Co.* v. *Beavan* (1912), the customer became unable to manage his own affairs, and his family arranged between themselves

7 See Appendix I, Q. 3 (April 1980).
8 See Appendix I, Q. 3 (April 1980).

that his son would operate the account, and the bank fell in with this proposal. For two years the account was operated on this basis, and monies drawn out were used to maintain the household. At that point the father died, and under his will four executors were appointed, but two objected to the informal arrangement which had operated between the family and the bank. The account in fact was now overdrawn, and the executors would not accept any liability in the estate for this borrowing. Matters came before the court, which fortunately took the view that cheques which had been drawn by the son to pay for household necessities could represent a good claim against the father's estate. It reached this decision by reference to the doctrine of subrogation, whereby the bank was entitled to stand in the shoes of the parties who had benefited. However, the bank was also claiming in the estate for interest charges on the overdraft, and commission, and the court disallowed these, on the grounds that they were not 'necessities'.

A further warning of the problems that can arise if matters are not followed strictly is seen in the case of *Scarth* v. *National Provincial Bank Ltd* (1930). Here the customer became incapacitated when his balance was £194. This was transferred into an account in his wife's name, and the monies were then used to pay Mr Scarth's debts, after the wife and another member of the family had given an indemnity to the bank. However, the customer then recovered from his illness and, learning of what had happened, sued the bank for the recovery of the balance of his account. In this he failed – again because the court took note of the equitable doctrine of subrogation.[9] Thus the ruling in *B. Liggett (Liverpool) Ltd* v. *Barclays Bank Ltd* (1928) was followed, namely 'under which those who have in fact paid the debts of another without authority, are allowed in such an action as this to take advantage of that payment'.

Partnership accounts

Should one partner in a firm become mentally incapable of managing his affairs, this is usually grounds for the dissolution of the partnership by the other partners, and the bank will wish to interview them as soon as possible so that their intentions can be discovered. The remaining partners have power to continue a creditor account for the purpose of winding up the partnership, and usually they will wish to open a new partnership account for themselves, possibly introducing fresh partners to the firm. A creditor account can be continued therefore, although if any cheques are presented drawn by the patient then the bank should refer to the other partners to see whether they should pay these or not, and confirmation in writing is desirable.

In cases where the partnership account is overdrawn the bank will wish to preserve its rights against the estate of the sick partner, so the account must be stopped for otherwise the operation of the Rule in *Clayton's Case* will work against the bank, so that ultimately any claim will be extinguished by credits paid in.

9 See Appendix I, Q. 14 (September 1981).

Guarantee or third-party security

As soon as the bank receives notice that a guarantor or surety is suffering from mental incapacity, the account which is secured must be stopped, if all rights are to be preserved. If the customer's account is operating in credit, it may of course continue. As to any further action, much will depend upon the borrower's circumstances, and the nature of the other security if any. The bank ultimately might have need to look to the guarantor or surety, and if so it would call up the security. Meanwhile, if any new advances are made to the customer, clearly the patient will have no liability in that respect.

Where one of two or more joint and several guarantors suffers from mental incapacity, the guarantee remains valid in respect of the liability of the other. (*Bradford Old Bank Ltd* v. *Sutcliffe* (1918)). Some banks make a practice, however, of interviewing the customer and the remaining guarantor at an early date, and take a new guarantee.

CHAPTER 2

Types of Account Holder

OPENING THE ACCOUNT

While all banks are anxious to increase their business and draw in deposits, it is necessary to exercise a degree of caution before opening an account and affording full banking facilities. No prudent banker would open an account immediately on the mere request of a stranger, as there would be many risks in conducting an account for a rogue. For common-sense reasons therefore the most important requirement upon opening an account is that the banker should have a satisfactory introduction to his new customer, and this is commonly called a 'reference'. The importance of an adequate reference can be seen very readily when we look at cases in which actions have been brought against banks for conversion of cheques collected through a customer's account, although it has subsequently transpired that they belonged to someone else. We shall see later that in certain instances there is statutory protection for the bank in such a situation, but to qualify for this a bank must have acted without negligence – that is, without a breach of its duty to take care: this breach can take place not only at the time when the cheque is tendered for collection, but also can date back to the time when the account was opened. This is termed antecedent negligence, and would include the omission to take a reference.

Recently, however, some banks have surprisingly decided to dispense with the taking of references and are prepared to open accounts for new customers, provided the stranger satisfactorily 'proves' his identity and provided that upon carrying out a credit reference bureau search an adverse reply is not received. Presumably those banks which have reduced their standard of care in this way have been prepared to do so on reasoning that the new procedures will reduce the costs of opening a new account and will be less inhibiting to prospective customers. They have no doubt examined the extent of their losses over the years in conversion claims, and understand there is no law as yet to show whether such steps as they now take would be sufficient to satisfy a court that they act 'without negligence'.

Historically the courts have always laid stress on the need for a satisfactory personal or written reference.

In *Ladbroke* v. *Todd* (1914), a bank opened an account for an unknown person, and collected cheques made payable to the stranger who claimed to be the payee. There had been no introduction, and no reference was taken up. Shortly after the account was opened the funds were withdrawn, and the stranger disappeared. When an action was brought against the bank for conversion by the true owner of the cheques, it is not surprising that the courts took the view that there had been a breach of the duty to take care, and that, in consequence, the statutory protection then available under the Bills of Exchange Act 1882 was not to be granted.

Some nine years later in *Guardians of St John's Hampstead* v. *Barclays Bank Ltd* (1923) an account was again opened for a stranger, but this time excellent references were received but unfortunately from 'another' stranger. It later transpired that the new customer had in fact written the references for himself, and again the bank was found to have been negligent, as it had failed to check the facts, and the evidence showed that if the bank had attempted to verify the fictitious address given by their new customer, or if it had made reasonable enquiries to prove his identity, the fraud would have been discovered earlier. Where a proposed referee is unknown to the bank, it is common practice now for the new banker to obtain a status reply from the bankers to the referee as to whether he is a fit person to introduce a new account holder. This obviously means that it is necessary to ascertain the name and address of the referee's bankers, a step which can cause delay.

Yet a further nine years on, in *Lloyds Bank Ltd* v. *E. B. Savory & Co.* (1932), an account was opened for a married woman, but the bank failed to take a note of her husband's occupation and the name of his employers. Later, cheques were misappropriated from the husband's employer and were collected through the wife's account. The court ruled that the bank was guilty of conversion, and could not claim that it had acted without negligence (but *see* pp. 27, 41, 104).

In *Marfani & Co. Ltd* v. *Midland Bank Ltd* (1968) the bank took no steps to identify a new customer, and made no enquiries regarding his past occupation or previous bank accounts. The names of two referees were obtained, but only one replied, and a cheque was collected before that referee answered the enquiry. Later the true owner of the stolen cheque sued the bank for conversion, and it was alleged that the bank had been negligent in that only one referee had replied and the bank had taken inadequate steps to identify its new customer, for instance by asking for his passport, as he was a Pakistani.

In an important judgment the decision was given for the bank, during which it was said:

> Where the customer is in possession of a cheque at the time of delivery for collection and appears upon the face of it to be the holder, i.e. the payee or endorsee or the bearer, the banker is entitled to assume that the customer is the owner of the cheque unless there are facts which are known or ought to be known which would cause a reasonable banker to suspect that the customer is not the true owner. What factors ought to be known to the banker, i.e. what enquiries he should make, and what facts are sufficient to cause him reasonably to suspect that the customer is not the true owner, must depend upon *current banking practice* and change as that practice changes. Cases decided thirty years ago, when the use by the general public of banking facilities was much less widespread, may not be a reliable guide to what the

duty of a careful banker, in relation to enquiries and as to facts which should give rise to suspicion, is today.

It may well be this 'dictum' upon which reliance is placed by those banks which have recently changed their account-opening procedures and dispensed with formal references.

The *Savory* case presents an interesting situation for the bankers of today, in that to be consistent with its ruling, and to ensure that there is no sex discrimination, when opening an account for a man they should presumably make enquiries as to the name of his wife, and the identity of her employers. Some banks are therefore today regarding the Savory case as out of date, and ignore the need to enquire into the other spouse's background.

Invariably the bank will wish to see the prospective new customer personally and it would be dangerous to open an account merely at the request of some third party, although depending on the background and circumstances some flexibility might occasionally be necessary. In *Robinson* v. *Midland Bank Ltd* (1925) the dangers of opening an account in the name of a new customer without meeting him were highlighted, when a sum as large as £150 000 was credited to open the account by a dishonest solicitor's clerk, who later forged the signature of the account holder, 'C. Robinson', and absconded with the money. Even though the real Mr Robinson had not been entitled to the funds he later, upon learning of what had happened, sued Midland Bank for recovery of the monies said to have been lodged in his name, and withdrawn without his authority!

The main point that must be understood from the above cases is that no current account should be opened without a satisfactory reference or enquiry, the extent of which will depend upon the circumstances. This rule applies also to a deposit account or savings account, through which cheques are to be collected. However, where deposit accounts or savings accounts are to consist merely of cash credits then clearly there is little risk for the bank in agreeing to operate the account without a reference. Nevertheless, the bank must be careful not to be lulled into a sense of false security, and allow cheques to be collected at a later date, or to allow a current account to be opened subsequently without a reference, unless very adequate knowledge has been acquired about their customer over a sustained period.

Another important formality when an account is opened is the completion of a form or card upon which the customer's full names will be given, also his address and his specimen signature. Where the account is other than a sole account, in addition to the specimen signature card, a mandate appropriate to the nature of the account will be taken and signed by all parties, setting out, among other things, who can operate the account.

Where the new customer is in business and using a name other than his surname, with or without his first name or initials, it used to be necessary for him to register at the Business Names Registry, but this requirement was abolished in 1982. A bank can therefore no longer ask to see the Registration of Business Names Act certificate, and may need to satisfy itself in some other way, such as by seeing a letter heading, evidencing that the prospective customer is trading in the manner he claims to be.

Upon a satisfactory reference being obtained, a cheque book may be issued to the current-account customer, usually without charge, although if specially printed cheques are required a quotation for the cost of producing these may be obtained and given.

Quarterly or half-yearly bank charges are presumed to be payable, but the tariff may vary from one customer to another by special agreement, or prior general arrangements made to fit a certain class of customer. For the avoidance of doubt and later complaint, no element of uncertainty should be allowed to exist in this area of discussion, for new customers are very cost- and charge-conscious in the present consumer-protected society.

Finally, new customers should be asked how frequently they require to see a statement of the account, and they are often introduced to many of the other services of the bank at this time.

STATEMENTS AND PASS BOOKS

Except for regulated agreements under the Consumer Credit Act 1974 where the duty is a statutory one, it is part of the implied contract between the banker and his customer that the banker will provide a statement of the account from time to time, or when asked to do so by his customer. The modern practice is to issue computerized statements, and pass books are seldom used, except for savings accounts and occasionally deposit accounts. In the latter instances it is usual for the pass book to be retained by the customer and produced when a withdrawal or lodgement is taking place. In the case of savings accounts, some banks have arrangements whereby on production of the savings account pass book a withdrawal up to a certain figure may be allowed at a branch not holding the account, and without prior arrangement. Usually a specimen signature appears in the pass book, and the amount which can be encashed in this way is restricted to low figures.

Paget in his *Law of Banking* contended that the proper function of a pass book 'is to constitute a conclusive, unquestionable, record of the transactions between the banker and customer, and it should be recognized as such'. This statement reflects an ideal state of affairs, and the position encountered in practice, from time to time, may not be so straightforward. The receipt of a pass-book or statement, and its return without comment by the customer, does not prevent the customer from later disputing the accuracy of an entry. Even the fact that he had made marks against entries, e.g. ticks, suggesting that the entries had been checked, is not binding on him *(Chatterton* v. *London and County Bank* (1890). In *London Intercontinental Trust Ltd* v. *Barclays Bank Ltd* (1980) Mr Justice Slynn made a reference to the customer's bank statement, saying that the customer had no obligation to check the statement but that if he did so, and then failed to inform his bankers of a breach of mandate, this was a representation that the transactions shown in the statement were valid. In this case the bank had paid cheques drawn on one signature, although two were required by the mandate. The company was therefore estopped from reclaiming the funds later through its liquidator, particularly as the bank had been deprived of the opportunity of recovering the monies when it might still have been able to do so.

This view has not been followed subsequently however, and in *Wealden Woodlands (Kent) Ltd* v. *National Westminster Bank* (1983) and in *Tai Hing Cotton Mill* v. *Liu Chong Hing Bank Ltd* (1985) both banks failed in their defences of estoppel on actions brought when they had paid cheques on forged signatures, and statements of account had been sent out to the companies concerned.

Pass book entries in the customer's favour (i.e. a credit entry to his account) are prima facie evidence against the banker, but they are not conclusive evidence, and the banker may prove that any entry is an erroneous one. However the bank cannot recover money wrongly credited to the account, if the customer can show that, in good faith and relying upon the accuracy of the entry, he has been induced to alter his position.[10]

This was the situation in *Lloyds Bank Ltd* v. *Brooks* (1950) where the bank overcredited its customer, an old lady, and it was held that the bank had a duty not to induce her by its representations to draw more than she was entitled to.

The problems have been examined more recently in *United Overseas Bank* v. *Jiwani* (1976) and here it was held that for a customer to be able to lay claim to an amount credited in error he must establish all of the three following points:

(*a*) that the bank has misrepresented the state of the account,
(*b*) that he has been misled by that misrepresentation, and
(*c*) that as a result he has changed his position in a way which would make it inequitable for him to be required to repay the money.

It should be noted that the onus of proof is on the customer.

Further problems can arise where the dishonour of cheques becomes involved, because, say, the bank has corrected a previous erroneous entry in the customer's statement, but the customer has drawn a cheque in reliance on the statement, before the correction was made or notified to him. Also, if the credit wrongly applied to one customer's account has not been applied to the correct customer's account, then the customer who should have had the funds might well find that he has drawn cheques which have made his account overdrawn. In such a case, interest charged must be refunded, and an apology

10 See Appendix I, Q. 8 (September 1980).

must be made at the earliest possible opportunity. Clearly, again, if cheques drawn by that customer are dishonoured wrongly then the bank could be open to a claim for damages. This aspect, and the extent of damages, is considered in Chapter 3.

Pass book or statement entries which are to the customer's detriment need also to be considered. The main areas involved here will be those situations where the drawer's signature has been forged, or where debits have been applied without authority. Upon the true facts coming to light, the bank will have to correct the account, and any interest charged. However, in *Greenwood* v. *Martins Bank Ltd* (1933) it was held that a customer who is aware that his cheques have been forged has a duty to communicate this knowledge to the bank straight away. The bank is thereby put on its guard and it should not pay further cheques drawn in the same manner.

In *Brown* v. *Westminster Bank Ltd* (1964), the drawer, an old lady, confirmed, on being asked by the bank specifically, that signatures on cheques were hers. She was later estopped from bringing an action for restitution based on forgery.

POWERS OF ATTORNEY

Where a customer wishes to authorize another person to sign on his account without becoming a party to it, it will be necessary for a special written authority to be provided by the customer to the bank. This third-party mandate, sometimes referred to as a 'per-procuration authority', will include a clause stating that the customer will be liable for any overdraft created or increased by the operation of the account, and the mandate will show the name and give a specimen signature of the agent.[11] The authority becomes void upon the death, bankruptcy or mental incapacity of the customer, and any cheques drawn by the third party should then be returned unpaid by the bank with the answer 'Account holder deceased' or 'Refer to drawer' as appropriate.

The situation is slightly different, however, where cheques drawn by the third party are presented and the banker has notice of the agent's death or bankruptcy. These may be paid, although in the case of the mental incapacity of the agent it is wiser for the bank to refer to the principal for authorization, and if this is not forthcoming then to return the cheques with an answer such as 'Agent's authority terminated'.

An authority enabling another party to operate the account is frequently given by power of attorney, and if this is provided in the unamended form prescribed by the Powers of Attorney Act (1971) it may be accepted as giving full power to the agent to do all those things which the grantor himself could

11 See Appendix I, Q. 12 (April 1981).

do – for example borrowing, or lodging or withdrawing security. The form of such a power of attorney is as follows:

> This General Power of Attorney is made this . . . day of . . . ., 19. . . by . . . . of . . . . I appoint . . . . of . . . . (or . . . . of . . . . and . . . . of . . . . jointly, or jointly and severally) to be my Attorney(s) in accordance with section 10 of the Powers of Attorney Act 1971. In witness etc.

To operate an account under a power of attorney, the bank will ask for production of the original sealed power of attorney, and if it is not drawn pursuant to s. 10 it should be examined carefully to ensure that it is adequate for all the acts which the attorney wishes to do.[12] A power of attorney can be expressly revoked by the donor, or it can lapse upon the expiry of the period for which it was given. If it was given for a specific purpose, and that purpose has been accomplished, it becomes obsolete. As with third party per-procuration authorities, it is also determined by the death, mental incapacity, or bankruptcy of the donor.

However, under the Enduring Powers of Attorney Act 1985 an attorney can now be appointed with the intention and power to carry on acting in the event of the donor's mental failure. This type of power must be in the form laid down by the Act and must of course be given by the donor when he is in full possession of his mental faculties. It must be signed by the donor and the attorney, but not necessarily at the same time, and may be general or limited in its scope. An enduring power of attorney may be used by the attorney before the mental incapacity of the donor occurs, provided there is no restriction in the document, but when the donor becomes mentally incapable of managing his affairs, or the attorney suspects that this is the case, he must apply to the Court of Protection for the power to be registered, after giving notice of his intention to the donor and certain relatives specified in the Act.

The attorney may not then act until the court has registered the power and at this stage a bank will wish to see the power of attorney again, when it should bear the court seal authenticating the donee's powers.

Confusingly, if a power of attorney is drawn expressed to be 'irrevocable', it can nevertheless be cancelled, and thus if cheques are presented drawn by the attorney after the bank has had notice from the donor of revocation they should not be paid unless the donor so authorizes.

Where the bank is unaware that the power of attorney has been revoked, as for example where the donor has died, acts by the attorney remain valid, by virtue of s. 5(2).

It should be noted that the attorney, as an agent, need not himself have contractual powers, and consequently it is possible for a minor to be appointed. An attorney cannot himself delegate his powers, except under

12 See Appendix I, Q. 24 (September 1982).

special provisions, the old legal maxim of *'delegatus non potest delegare'* applying.

It is common practice for a bank to take its usual form of third-party mandate, as well as having sight of the power of attorney, whenever it is asked to operate an account by an attorney so appointed. This guards against any possible defects in the power of attorney, and prevents difficulties should the customer dispute any transactions or refuse to repay any borrowing created.

CLOSING A CREDIT ACCOUNT

Readers will recall from the *Joachimson* v. *Swiss Bank Corporation* (1921) case that it was said that it is a term of the contract between the bank and the customer that the bank will not cease to do business with the customer 'except upon reasonable notice'. What is 'reasonable notice' has never been decided by the courts, and consequently in daily practice each situation must be examined upon its merits. Clearly, a customer can close his account when he wants to, by withdrawing the funds and paying his bank charges to date, but where the bank wishes to sever the relationship and the customer's account is in credit then care is necessary.

Fortunately the circumstances under which the bank would wish to lose a credit account are relatively few, and are likely to arise only where there is concern on the bank's part that the continuation of the relationship or account would leave the bank open to risk, and perhaps even to criticism. Such a situation might arise where the customer did not provide funds before drawing his cheques, and had not made arrangements for overdrafts or had had his request declined. The bank then might take the view that the continual dishonour of cheques and the possible consequential losses to local traders was such that the bank's own reputation was suffering. Also, in such circumstances, there would be a risk that a cheque might be paid inadvertently, leaving the bank with an unsecured and unagreed overdraft.

In *Prosperity Ltd* v. *Lloyds Bank Ltd* (1923), the customer became the subject of bad publicity, and the bank decided that it wished to sever its relationship. However, the account was maintained in credit, and the bank therefore gave the customer one month in which to make alternative banking arrangements.[13] The customer sued the bank for breach of contract and, unhappily, it was held that the bank had not given adequate notice. The facts of this case were very special, however, as the customer was engaged in selling insurance contracts and the bank had agreed to receive applications from new subscribers; prospectuses had been issued to that effect. It had been following press criticisms of this scheme, which was similar to modern pyramid selling operations, that the bank had decided to disassociate itself from the business.

It could well be therefore that under other more normal circumstances one month might be regarded as perfectly adequate notice, and if the bank were

13   See Appendix I, Q. 25 (April 1983).

dealing with a private individual then there would seem to be little risk in giving one month's notice or even less.

It is worth looking for a moment at the unfortunate situation in which the bank could find itself, if the customer refuses to take heed of the notice, and continues to operate his account. At the expiry of the time given in the written notice, the bank could, if it wished, send the balance of the account to the customer and would be entitled to dishonour any cheques drawn and presented subsequently. However, no doubt it would have taken careful steps beforehand to obtain the return of unused cheques, and would probably have timed the service of its notice, so as to ensure that the customer had few unused cheques in his possession when matters came to a head. If the customer continued to pay in for the credit of his account, possibly even at other banks using the credit clearing, then such monies could be collected into a suspense account, the balance of which could be remitted to the customer from time to time. By these means, it would not be long before the customer lost patience and complied with the notice!

DEATH OF A SOLE ACCOUNT HOLDER

After it has received *notice* of a sole account holder's death, the bank should not honour any cheques presented, drawn prior to his death, as the mandate is determined (s. 75 Bills of Exchange Act 1882). The cheques should be returned with the answer 'Drawer deceased'.

Upon receipt of notice, therefore, all operations on the account should be stopped and bank charges should be calculated up to the date of death. If there is an overdraft this will include interest accrued to this date. Any credits, such as dividends received after notice, but before probate or letters of administration have been produced, can be placed to the account or to a suspense account for the time being, unless they represent monies which are known to cease to be payable upon the customer's death such as under an annuity. Such monies should be held apart and the remitter and/or executor should be informed.

In the case of credit balances, the bank will in due course obtain a valid discharge for the payment away of any sum standing to the credit of the deceased person, but this is done only after production of probate if the deceased has left a will, or after production of letters of administration if he died intestate. These documents give the executors or administrators the right to administer the deceased's estate.

Items in safe custody, and security not required by the bank, can be released only after production of probate, which is the document issued with an official copy of the will by the Probate Office to the executor.[14] Similarly, letters of administration are granted to the next of kin in an intestacy. Most branches

14 See Appendix I, Q. 27 (April 1983).

have a probate register in which is recorded particulars of all probates and letters of administration exhibited to the bank. To obtain probate, the named executors must be in possession of the will, but if this is held in safe custody then strictly they are not entitled to it before probate – a state of 'stalemate'! However, provided the bank knows the executors personally and can rely on them, or obtains an entirely satisfactory report on them by a solicitor acting on their behalf, the will may safely be released, although even then preferably to the solicitor himself, upon whom a good report is held and against his receipt. The retention of a photocopy of the will is desirable if this is possible. Meanwhile, as there is inevitably a delay before probate is produced, any matters which were in course before the customer's death – such as the purchase of stocks and shares – can be carried through, as for example by debiting the deceased customer's account on settlement day to complete the bargain.

If the estate is small and the customer has died intestate, that is without leaving a will, it may not be worth while for his next of kin to incur the expense of taking out letters of administration. However, under the provisions of the Administration of Estates (Small Payments) Amendment Act 1976 and the Increase of Limit Order 1984 most banks will be prepared to pay away the credit balance – provided the estate does not exceed £5000 gross – to and against an indemnity from such near relative, provided the latter is adequately identified and a good 'report' on him is obtained, but of course only after sight of the death certificate.[15]

In the case of a principal and agent, where the principal dies, the authority granted to the agent, whether by power of attorney or on a 'per-procuration' authority, is determined, and cheques signed either by the principal or the agent and presented after notice has been received of the customer's death should be returned with the answer 'Drawer deceased'. On the other hand, if the agent dies and the cheques are subsequently presented having been signed by him, they may be paid.

Where the customer's account is overdrawn at the time notice is received that he has died, it is stopped and the executor or administrator will be advised in due course of the bank's claim in the estate, which will include charges accrued to the date of death and subsequently. Details of any direct security held should be given and the personal representatives may be able to pay off the bank borrowing and obtain its release. Alternatively, they may give the bank instructions to sell items such as stocks and shares; or arrangements, under the bank's control, can be made to collect the maturity proceeds of a life policy.

JOINT ACCOUNTS

When opening a joint account the bank should take up references or have a satisfactory introduction to all the parties named in the account, and only

15 See Appendix I, Q. 10 (April 1981).

when these are received should the account become operative. Joint accounts may be run by two or more parties, although the most common type encountered is that opened by a husband and his wife. Obviously, where one party is already known to the bank he can introduce the other satisfactorily for banking reference purposes.

The mandate

A joint account might be opened and operated without a special form of mandate, but the bank would need to act with more than its usual care, and in certain instances its position would be very much weaker. All parties would need to sign for withdrawals, and joint and several liability would not exist.

Thus in the bank's standard form of joint account mandate (Fig. 2.1) a clear

To PRACTICE BANK plc

_____ 19 __

We request you to open a Joint Account(s) in our names, which are given below. We authorize you to honour the signature(s) of *any _____ of us/all of us jointly and to debit the account(s) with all cheques, bills or orders or other instructions so signed notwithstanding that thereby the account(s) may become overdrawn or may increase in overdraft.

We agree that in respect of any indebtedness to the bank on any account(s) in our names our liability shall be joint and several.

We authorize you to accept the signature(s) of *any _____ of us/all of us jointly by way of instructions to deliver or release any item lodged with you for safe-custody or by way of security or any other purpose.

We agree and authorize you that on the death of any one or more of us the balance of any monies standing to the credit of the account(s) and anything held by way of safe custody or security should be held to the order of the survivor(s) of us, subject to any lien mortgage or charge you may have thereon.

Full Names of all Parties	Address	Signatures of all Parties to the Account

*delete/complete as required

Fig.2.1   *Joint account mandate*

authority is given as to who can make withdrawals from the account.[16] The choice lies with the customers, and they can authorize the bank either only to accept transactions authorized on the signatures of all parties to the account or to make payments upon the signature of only one party, or, say, on two signatures out of the three parties to the account. If a bank debits its customer's account outside the scope of its mandate it can be liable for damages to the injured party (*Catlin* v. *Cyprus Finance Corporation (London) Ltd* (1982)). Many joint accounts are of course operated on one signature, with the mandate stating 'either to sign', and transactions then hold good until such time as, by countermand or by operation of law, the mandate is revoked.

The mandate will often recite whose authority is required to countermand payment of cheques, and some banks incorporate a clause dealing with the delivery of items in safe custody, while others deal with that by separate documentation. By common practice it is, however, accepted that any party to a joint account can stop payment of a cheque, even if this has been drawn by another party to the account. In the event of there being a disagreement between the parties to a joint account about a cheque issued, then this situation should be regarded as revocation of the mandate, and thereafter the bank should only accept the authority of all parties before paying a cheque.[17]

An essential clause is that whereby all parties to the joint account undertake to be jointly and severally liable for any borrowing, or indebtedness, and the bank's position is much improved by this clause in risk situations, particularly where it holds security lodged by one party for his own liabilities, as it is then available for the joint account debt. In the absence of this special agreement, the liability of parties to a joint account would only be joint.

With joint and several liability established the bank will be able to exercise its right of set-off over a credit balance in one party's sole name, against the indebtedness of the joint account – a step not possible if the account holders only assumed joint liability. Clearly, these rights of set-off can be very valuable in a bankruptcy situation.

Of equal importance is the somewhat strange legal situation that if only joint liability has been assumed, upon the death of one party to the account that party's estate is freed from any liability, and the bank can then only look to the survivor or the survivors for the monies which might be owing.

Death of one party

An important clause is that dealing with the way in which matters should be handled upon the death of one party to a joint account. The mandate almost invariably will include a clause stating that the survivor or survivors can give a satisfactory discharge to the bank, and this clause in fact reinforces the common law situation. Consequently when the account is in credit it need not be stopped, and the bank only requires the instructions of all the other parties

16 See Appendix I, Q. 2 (April 1980).
17 See Appendix I, Q. 12 (April 1981).

to deal with the balance. This means that where the account is, for example, that of a husband and wife, the surviving spouse has access to funds immediately upon the death of his or her partner, without waiting for probate to be obtained.

When the death certificate has been exhibited and entered into the bank's records the name of the deceased party can be deleted from the title of the account and future statements will be issued in the name of the survivor or survivors only. New arrangements should be made in respect of any correspondence which was formerly addressed to the deceased at his own address, if that was different from that of the other party or parties to the account.

However, although the bank obtains a satisfactory discharge, it is up to the remaining parties to account to the executors of the deceased's estate for his share of the balance, but this is of no concern to the bank. Very occasionally, situations arise whereby the bank receives competing claims for monies left in a joint account, following the death of one party. Strictly speaking, the bank can, on such an instance, obtain an adequate discharge from the survivor, and it should not become involved in any dispute, and should inform the executors of the deceased party that their claim is against the survivor.

Cheques presented, drawn on a joint account by a person who has died subsequently, should be returned unpaid with the answer 'Drawer deceased', unless the survivor is prepared to authorize the bank to pay the cheques, either by a general letter of authority scheduling the cheques drawn by the deceased, or by countersigning the cheques.

Upon notice of the death of one party to a joint account which is overdrawn, the bank should stop the account, if it wishes to preserve its claim against the deceased's estate for if not then the Rule in *Clayton's Case* will come into operation, whereby fresh credits will repay earlier borrowings and new withdrawals will only be reclaimable from the survivors. Again, each situation needs to be looked at carefully, and it could be that the bank will be quite happy to release the estate of the deceased party from liability and look only to the survivors. In that case it is desirable for a new mandate to be taken from survivors, if more than one.

Where the account is stopped, to preserve the bank's rights against the deceased, the bank should offer new facilities to the survivor or survivors and an authority should be taken to debit any cheques drawn by the survivors to this new account. The new account should operate in credit, unless arrangements are made for a fresh borrowing, and it may be that the bank will require further securities.

Problems can arise upon the death of one party to a joint account, where items are deposited in safe custody in joint names, as in this case the item deposited may not be jointly owned property, and in consequence title will not pass to the survivor; such securities should not be released without reference to the executors or administrators of the deceased. Such items would be locked deed-boxes, or jewellery, deposited in joint names, and in these instances the bank must act with caution, and seek an authority from the executor or administrator.

Bankruptcy

Where a bankruptcy order is made against one party to a joint account, then the mandate is revoked. It follows therefore, if the account is in credit, that whereas earlier one party may have been able to authorize a withdrawal, now the signatures of all parties to the account will be required, although in the case of the bankrupt party, the authorizing signature will be that of his trustee in bankruptcy. Thus the joint account should be stopped upon notice of the making of the bankruptcy order, and instructions in writing should be taken in due course from the appointed trustee in bankruptcy and the solvent account holder or holders as to how the bank should deal with the credit balance. Meanwhile cheques should be dishonoured with the answer 'Refer to drawer' or 'Refer to drawer – joint account holder in bankruptcy'. In appropriate circumstances, the bank may be prepared to open a new account for the solvent party and take an authority to debit that account with cheques drawn on the joint account by him.

Where a joint account is overdrawn, and a bankruptcy order is made against one party, and if the bank wishes to preserve its rights against the bankrupt's estate, the account should be stopped at once. This prevents the operation of the Rule in *Clayton's Case*. A new account, to operate in credit, should be opened for the remaining party or parties, to be overdrawn by prior agreement and maybe against the deposit of new security.

With joint and *several* liability assumed by the bankrupt, the bank is able to prove in his estate for the full amount of the debt, and it is able to look to each or all of the survivors for the full amount due also. In this way were it to recover, say, only twenty pence in the pound, from the bankrupt's estate it is nevertheless able to obtain that dividend on the full debt due at the date of the bankruptcy order, and need not give allowance for any monies repaid by the solvent parties. Equally it can sue the solvent parties for the full amount due. Thus the bank maximizes its recoveries of monies lent, although naturally it cannot retain more than one hundred pence in the pound.

Mental incapacity

Where the bank learns that one party to a joint account is suffering from mental disorder, which makes him incapable of dealing with his own affairs, the mandate is revoked, and the account, whether debit or credit, must be stopped, until such time as an authority is received from the receiver, appointed under the Court of Protection order, and the other joint account holders. Again, however, under special circumstances, if the bank is happy to release the estate of the mentally disordered person, then the account, if overdrawn, can be allowed to continue under the signature of the remaining party, who will be liable for any future borrowing.

Garnishee

Where the bank receives a garnishee order or summons, naming one judgment debtor only, but the account is in his name and that of other party(ies), the credit balance is not attached (*Hirschorn* v. *Evans* (1938)). However, if the garnishee order or summons names all the parties to a joint account as judgment debtors then the credit balance in the joint account will be attached, as also will be any credit balance in a separate account in a sole name.

Lending on joint account

Although in signing the mandate joint account customers each agree to be severally liable for any borrowing, whether created by themselves or the other account holder(s), it is wise for the bank, when it agrees facilities, to ensure that all parties understand and agree the terms, whether the borrowing is on overdraft or loan. This prevents any argument or dispute later about the bank's rights, and the obligations of the debtors.

MINORS

Under the provisions of the Family Law Reform Act 1969, a minor is a person under the age of eighteen. As such he or she has limited contractual powers, and while no problems should arise if the account is operated in credit, this is not the case where borrowings are allowed.

The age at which a young person will be considered suitable to operate a bank account will depend upon bank policy and the individual's circumstances. Few problems should be encountered with savings accounts, operated in the minor's own name after, say, the age of ten, but the facility of a current account and a cheque book should not be offered until a minor is a little older and more responsible.

A minor can be an agent,[18] and is able to be a director of a limited company if the articles so allow, and in drawing cheques on the company's account can cause the company as principal to be liable for any borrowings it takes from the bank.

However, a minor cannot be appointed as a trustee, or as an executor, nor can he make a valid will except where he is on active service as a soldier, sailor or airman. Also a minor cannot hold a legal estate in land.

The law concerning minors' contracts is in course of change at the time the author is writing, and if the bill currently before Parliament is passed the position which has obtained for over a century will be quite different. Both the old and proposed new law are set out in the following paragraphs and the student should check to see which applies at the time he is reading this book.

18 See Appendix I, Q. 12 (April 1981).

Old law:

Where debts are incurred, other than debts for necessities, by virtue of s. 1 Infants Relief Act 1874, any contract for the repayment of money lent or to be lent is absolutely void and irrecoverable. Moreover, because of s. 2, no legal action can be brought in repect of any promise made by the minor after he has attained his majority to repay a debt contracted during his infancy.

Consequently, a bank is unable to recover monies lent to a minor, even if it was unaware that its customer was a minor at the time the lending was agreed. Moreover, the infant cannot be sued on a cheque, or bill of exchange, even though that has been given for necessities, as the courts take the view that such an action would simply be a means of avoiding the provisions of the Infants Relief Act.

From this basic concept, it follows that any third-party security given for an infant's debts will also be void. This situation was considered in *Coutts & Co.* v. *Browne-Lecky* (1946), where the bank lent monies to a minor, taking a joint and several guarantee from two adults. When the bank sought to recover the monies lent from the guarantors, the courts took the view that there was no enforceable debt, and no default, and that it was impossible for the guarantors to make themselves liable by way of guarantee for an irrecoverable lending. Following this case, banks have amended their guarantee forms, and guarantors now enter into not only a contract of guarantee but also a contract of indemnity, whereby they accept primary responsibility for the bank advance. With such a clause in the charge form, a bank should safely be able to lend to a minor against third-party securities if it so wishes.

Minors are however able to become partners in a partnership, and in that position they are able to bind their co-partners, although they will not themselves become liable for any borrowing on a partnership account. In due course they will become personally liable for partnership debts incurred after they have attained their majority.

New law:

The Minors' Contracts Bill (1986) disapplies the Infants Relief Act 1874 and s. 5 of the Betting and Loans (Infants) Act 1892, and if it becomes law will allow a minor to ratify an otherwise unenforceable contract on attaining majority.

Clause 2 provides that where a guarantee has been given in respect of an obligation of a party to a contract made after the commencement of the Act and the obligation is unenforceable because that party was a minor when the contract was made, the guarantee shall not for that reason alone be unenforceable against the guarantor.

Clause 3 will allow the court, where it thinks it just and equitable to do so, to order the return of property acquired by a minor under an unenforceable contract. This clause would clearly give some protection to a bank which had lent money to a person under the age of 18 and who was refusing to repay.

To summarize the situation, the bank should exercise prudence and common sense in any dealings with a minor. While it may well wish to foster a good relationship because of family connections or with an eye to a good account in the future, the extent to which it will be prepared to treat a minor as an adult will depend upon the circumstances of each case, bearing in mind the legal dangers.

MARRIED WOMEN

Married women have free contractual capacity, and no special considerations are necessary when opening or conducting the account, apart from (perhaps) the need when opening the account to enquire as to her husband's name and the name of his employers (*Lloyds Bank Ltd* v. *E. B. Savory & Co.* (1932)), although, as has been mentioned, some banks now regard this requirement and case as out of date. By virtue of the Law Reform (Married Women and Tortfeasors) Act 1935, a married woman may contract exactly as though she were single, and she can sue and be sued in her own name, and is subject to bankruptcy. Indeed it would be an offence under the Sex Discrimination Act 1975 if a banker discriminated against a married woman (or for that matter a single woman or any man) on grounds of sex alone.

However, the one area in which care should be exercised is where a married woman is to deposit security for the liabilities of a third party. This is particularly so where that third party is her husband, or a business or limited company with which her husband is closely associated, perhaps as director. In such situations there may be a possibility of undue influence by the husband on the wife, endangering the security at realisation time. The wife as surety might be able to establish, then, that the contract of guarantee is voidable, and so avoid liability. Consequently, when there is any doubt in the banker's mind he should afford the married woman the opportunity of taking independent legal advice from her own solicitors before she signs the charge form, and in this way the bank will guard against problems at a later date. However, there will be many instances where a wife is a business woman or professional person in her own right, and where the banker will be entirely satisfied· that she fully appreciates the implications of all the obligations she is taking on, and the question of undue influence is irrelevant. In those cases independent legal advice is unnecessary.

Occasionally, a husband who is an undischarged bankrupt, prevented from operating a bank account in his own name, will arrange for his wife to open or continue an account in her name, through which he will pass his own transactions.[19] In such a situation, the bank should inform the trustee in

19 See Appendix I, Q. 10 (April 1981).

bankruptcy or the official receiver. Naturally, if there is any doubt then a prior interview with the wife would be desirable before taking such a step.

When a single woman informs her bank that she is now married, or a married woman remarries, the bank will need to re-style the account name heading and issue a new cheque book. Some banks call for sight of the marriage certificate, and ask for details about the customer's husband, but others are now prepared simply to accept a letter addressed to the bank informing it of her change of name and situation. Obviously a new specimen signature will be required.[20]

EXECUTORS AND ADMINISTRATORS

An executor derives his title from the will of a deceased person, but he is unable to deal with the estate and any balance in the deceased's bank account until such time as he has obtained probate, a prerequisite of which will be the payment of any inheritance tax arising.

An administrator is appointed to act in a deceased person's estate, when the deceased has died intestate, that is without making a will, or where the executor named is unable or unwilling to act. Usually, a near relative will apply to the probate court for letters of administration in such a situation.

An account can be opened for an executor or administrator in the usual way, references being taken up if the person is unknown. Commonly the account is styled, by way of example: John Smith, executor of James Smith, deceased. Where two or more executors are to act, a mandate similar to that for a joint account will be signed, and the executors/administrators will accept joint and several liability for any borrowing; they will instruct the bank whether the account is to be operated on one or more signatures. This is because executors and administrators are empowered to delegate, but this position should be contrasted carefully with the lack of such powers held by trustees, who all must sign cheques.

Where an executor or administrator himself dies, the remaining executor or administrator may continue to act under the original will and on production of his death certificate the name of the deceased executor can simply be deleted from the bank's records. Where the last surviving or sole executor dies, then his executors, on obtaining probate on his will, can take over the executorship, if they wish. Otherwise, parties interested in the estate of the original deceased person will need to apply to the court for letters of administration.

Frequently the account for the personal representatives is opened at the same branch as that where the account of the deceased was maintained. However there is no right of set-off between the credit balance in the name of an executor and a debit balance in the name of the deceased person, or vice versa. The size of the balance in the deceased's account will, of course, be a

20 See Appendix I, Q. 23 (September 1982).

factor taken into account when the bank is arranging the terms upon which it will charge for an advance to the executors to assist with the payment of inheritance tax.

When probate or letters of administration are exhibited to the bank the opportunity should be taken at that time to obtain a suitable authority from the executor or administrator for any credit balance in the deceased's account to be transferred to the executor's or administrator's account. Items in safe custody may then be released against a receipt.

Borrowings for Inheritance Tax

Before an executor or administrator can obtain probate or letters of administration he will need to meet the inheritance tax payable on the deceased's estate. Frequently, therefore, banks are approached by executors or administrators to bridge that period of time during which the personal representative is unable to deal with and realize the assets of the deceased, but needs the proceeds of these assets to pay the inheritance tax. Provided the executor or administrator has been satisfactorily introduced to the bank, for instance by a solicitor, or is already known to the bank as a good customer, the bank will look favourably upon a request for short-term lending facilities. The bank will then be interested in the estate of the deceased, the gross and net positions, and the amount of tax payable. More importantly, however, it will be anxious to know the source of repayment, and as this will usually flow from realization of property in the deceased's estate, it will be keen to see that there are assets there which will be readily realizable once probate or letters of administration have been obtained. If there are life policies, or quoted stocks and shares, or credit balances in building society accounts, or bank accounts, the bank will be assured that repayment of its lending will follow quickly. When however the assets in the estate consist of real property, or interests in other estates and trusts, it could be that the advance will not be self-liquidating in the short term. Occasionally, a bank will be prepared to shade the interest rate charged for inheritance tax advances, and it may take into account the worth of credit balances seen in the deceased's account, if that is maintained at the same branch. The advance should be granted on a loan account, and the bank will invariably charge an arrangement fee for its work in making the facility available, as the remuneration obtained merely by interest can be inadequate.

The executors themselves will look to sales of the assets in the deceased's estate for clearance of the borrowing, but the legal position is that they are personally liable to the bank, and in the rare event of default a bank would be able to sue the executor or administrator in his own name and to take action against their private assets.

If the will gives the executors no express authority to carry on the deceased's business, or there is no will, then the personal representatives may only borrow in order to carry on the business for the purpose of winding it up, or pending a sale in the short term. There is a risk here that the personal representative could trade on and incur losses, and that the assets in the deceased's estate could become inadequate for the purpose of paying off both the creditors at the date of death and the bank. In such a case the creditors could have priority over the bank. Where the bank is requested to lend to the personal representatives to carry on a business, therefore, it should make careful enquiries beforehand to see whether the creditors have assented to the bank having priority or to see whether they have already been paid off.

Even where the will gives the executors express power to carry on the business, it is desirable that the deceased's creditors have already been paid off, or that they have agreed to grant the bank priority in respect of its lending.

While, as mentioned, the executors or administrators are personally liable for any borrowing where their action is approved by the creditors and beneficiaries, they are indemnified out of the assets of the deceased. For security the bank can accept items owned by the personal representatives in their own right, without risk, but the latter have no authority to charge the deceased's assets employed outside the business. If the will allows, however, they can give a good security by way of a charge over assets utilised in the business. Clearly, the situation can become complex, and the bank should not hesitate to take legal advice; if in doubt, and wherever possible, it should lend by way of loan accounts to prevent the operation of the Rule in *Clayton's Case*.

In the case of *Morton* v. *Marchanton* (1930) the executors were empowered by the will to carry on the business and employ the assets of the estate for this purpose. They paid off the deceased's overdraft by a transfer from their account against a charge on the assets of the estate. Within two years the estate was insolvent, and a creditor of the deceased's estate who had assented to the continuation of the business tried to get priority over the bank's charge. The bank argued that their charge took priority over the creditors of the deceased, and it was held that, in view of the fact that the creditor had acquiesced in the continuation of the business, the bank had priority.

Executors becoming trustees

We have seen that executors have the power to delegate among themselves, but it is possible that with a complex estate their duties will in due course take on the role of trusteeship, and in that event, as trustees, they are unable to delegate and all of them must act. Consequently, in operating an executor's account the bank should beware of the administration becoming a trusteeship, particularly where the mandate is for any one executor to sign alone on the account. After about twelve months, if an estate has not been wound up, the executors should be interviewed to see if they are now really trustees, and in that event a new mandate should be obtained, whereby all will sign in the future; the account should be restyled 'Trustees of . . . deceased' in the bank's records.

TRUSTEES

A trust has been defined as

> an equitable obligation imposing upon a person (who is called a trustee) the duty of dealing with property over which he has control (which is called the trust property), for the benefit of persons (who are called the beneficiaries or *cestuis que trust*) of whom he may himself be one, and any one of whom may enforce the obligation [Underhill].

A banker can become involved in trust situations in varying ways. For instance he might have direct notice of the trust, as where an account is opened in the name of two parties described as trustees, or he might be presumed to know that executors have effectively become trustees simply by the passage of time and the nature of their duties.

It is sometimes difficult to decide the point of time at which executors have become trustees, but comments made in the case *Re Smith, Henderson-Roe* v. *Hitchins* (1889) help to define the position. There it was said:

> It is the duty of the executor to clear the estate – to pay the debts, funeral and testamentary expenses, and the pecuniary legacies, and to hand over the assets specifically bequeathed to the specific legatees. When all this has been done, a balance will be left in the executor's hands and I think it is plain that this balance will be held by him in trust.

Where an executorship account has been opened for a period longer than is compatible with pure executorship, the banker should make enquiries as to whether or not a trust has begun. If so, the heading of the account should be altered and fresh instructions taken; in particular, all parties should sign cheques on the new account in future. An administrator is in the position of a trustee under the same circumstances. Twelve months is often regarded as a suitable period for an executorship to be concluded, but each case will depend on its own facts and the bank should not act hastily.

Also, a bank might have indirect notice of a trust, as for example when an account is opened in the style 'John Smith re James Smith', or 'John Smith, Treasurer of Hill Top Club'. These may not be trust accounts in the strict sense but the banker should always be careful in their conduct, and be alive to any transactions which could be a misappropriation of funds. The guiding principle for a banker in conducting accounts in the name of trustees, or where there is any trust element, is that he must not become a party to any breach of trust, for if he is then he may become liable in damages to the beneficiaries.

Breach of Trust

The judgment in *Gray* v. *Johnston* (1868) is old but explains the banker's position relating to a breach of trust. When Johnston died, he had an overdraft with Gray, his banker, which was secured by life policies. Johnston's widow was his executrix, and after obtaining probate, which was seen by the bank, the bank obtained the death maturity proceeds of the life policies, which were used to repay the overdraft, and a credit balance resulted. The executrix withdrew the credit balance and used the funds to continue her husband's former business. She drew a cheque made payable to the firm name and a new account was opened with the bank. Later, one of Johnston's sons alleged that there had been a breach of trust by his mother, in which the bank had taken part. It transpired that the deceased had in fact only left a life interest to his widow of his estate, and on these grounds damages were sought from the bank. In judgment it was said:

> On the one hand, it would be a most serious matter if bankers were to be allowed, on light and trifling grounds – on grounds of mere suspicion or curiosity – to refuse to honour a cheque drawn by their customer, even although that customer might happen to be an administrator or an executor. On the other hand, it would be equally of serious moment if bankers were to be allowed to shelter themselves under that title, and to say that they were at liberty to become parties or privies to a breach of trust committed with regard to trust property, and, looking to their position as bankers merely, to insist that they were entitled to pay away money which constituted a part of trust property at a time when they knew it was going to be misapplied, and for the purpose of its being so misapplied . . . the law on that point is clearly laid down . . . In order to hold a banker justified in refusing to pay a demand of his customer, the customer being an executor, and drawing a cheque as executor, there must, in the first place, be some misapplication, some breach of trust, intended by the executor, and there must in the second place . . . be proof that the bankers are privy to the intent to make this misapplication of the trust funds . . . if it be shown that any personal benefit to the bankers themselves is designed or stipulated for, that circumstance, above all others will most readily establish that the bankers are in privity with the breach of trust which is about to be committed.

Thus judgment was given for the bank, as it had no knowledge of the breach of trust, and this will always be a relevant and important principle, although in recent years there have been attempts to draw banks into liability in situations where it has been claimed that they 'should have known' that a breach was occurring.

The circumstances of each particular case must be viewed carefully, and we can now look at *Foxton* v. *Manchester and Liverpool District Banking Company* (1881). In this case there were two executors by the name of Hardman, and both had overdrawn private accounts with the bank. They misappropriated monies from the deceased's estate, and transfers were made from their executorship account to each of their private accounts. Later the beneficiaries sued the bank and succeeded, it being said:

It appears to be plain that the bank could not derive the benefit which they did from that payment, knowing it to be drawn from a trust fund unless they were prepared to show that the payment was a legitimate and proper one, having reference to the terms of the trust. That appears to me, I confess, to be immaterial, because those who know that a fund is a trust fund cannot take possession of that fund for their own private benefit, except at the risk of being liable to refund it in the event of the trust being broken by the payment of the money

Similarly, in *Midland Bank Ltd* v. *Reckitt & Others* (1933), when an agent, acting under a power of attorney granted by a Sir Harold Reckitt drew cheques on Barclays Bank and paid them into his own account at Midland Bank, which has been pressing for his borrowings to be reduced, the Midland Bank was held to have been guilty of conversion. It was unable to shelter behind a clause in the power of attorney (which incidentally it had not seen) stating that the principal would ratify all of the attorney's acts.

The judgment in *Selangor United Rubber Estates Ltd* v. *Cradock and others* (1968) was very disconcerting for banks. Here, District Bank Ltd conducted an account for the company which was maintained in credit. It paid a cheque for £232 500 in favour of a company called Woodstock Trust Ltd, it being explained to the bank that this was a loan. The cheque was endorsed in Cradock's favour and was paid into his personal bank account at the same branch. Later, after Selangor had been placed in liquidation an action was brought against the bank, and the transaction was held to have been a breach of s. 54 Companies Act 1948, (now s. 151 Companies Act 1985) under which it was illegal for a company to give financial assistance for the purchase of its own shares. The court held that because of the special knowledge which the bank had or *should have had* it was liable as constructive trustee and that it should not have paid the company's cheque without making further enquiries.

The decision in *Karak Rubber Co. Ltd* v. *Burden and others* (1972) was based on similar principles.

In *Baden Delvaux* (1983) the court examined the extent to which 'knowledge' and the circumstances in which the trustee 'ought to have had knowledge' apply. Five categories were set out, viz:

(1) actual knowledge,
(2) wilfully shutting one's eyes to the obvious,
(3) wilfully and recklessly failing to make such enquiries as an honest and reasonable man would make,
(4) knowledge of circumstances which would indicate the facts to an honest and reasonable man, and
(5) knowledge of circumstances which would put an honest and reasonable man on enquiry.

Opening the account

Generally, a banker is quite safe in opening an account for persons professing to be trustees and does not need to see the trust deed or a copy of the will, although some authorities recommend that where the banker knows there is a trust he should ask for, and file, a copy of the trust deed. If not known, the trustee(s) should be satisfactorily introduced, and where more than one is appointed then a mandate will be required. This will take the form of a request to open and conduct the account, showing the full names of the trustees, and giving specimens of their signatures. All trustees will be required to sign cheques and other authorities, so the choice of who is to sign will not be present, as in the case of executors. However, each trustee will agree to be personally liable for any borrowing, both jointly and severally (Fig. 2.2).

Delegation

With certain wide exceptions, trustees are not allowed to delegate their duties to others, even to one of themselves, unless authorized to do so in the will or deed establishing the trust. As noted, if there is more than one trustee then all should join in opening the account, in signing cheques and in authorizing the withdrawing of trust securities out of safe custody or security. There is thus considerable danger if a banker acts on the instructions of one trustee only where there are two or more. This gives rise to certain difficulties in relation to bank accounts, as for instance where a trustee has gone abroad for a short period. However the Trustee Act 1925, as amended by the Powers of Attorney Act 1971, provides that a trustee may, by power of attorney, delegate, for a period not exceeding twelve months, the execution or exercise of all or any of the trusts, powers and discretions vested in him as trustee, either alone or jointly with any other person or persons. Under s. 9 of the 1971 Act the absent trustee may delegate his powers and duties by means of a power of attorney to any person or trust corporation, but not to his only other co-trustee, unless the latter is a trust corporation such as a bank or other body acting as trustee. In special circumstances and for undoubted customers, a bank might be prepared to allow one trustee alone to operate an 'income account', in which the turnover will be small. This will be on the basis that the other trustees indemnify the bank, and ratify the transactions on the account from time to time, perhaps by signing and returning a copy of the bank statement. However, the main trust 'capital account' through which large transactions will pass should not be operated outside the laid down rule that all trustees must sign.

Borrowings

If a trustee wishes to borrow then the trust deed should be examined to see if specific powers exist for the purpose requested, as there is no implied power to borrow. If there is no power to borrow in the trust deed, the powers of trustees to borrow on the security of the assets of the estate are determined by ss. 16 and 17 Trustee Act 1925. Section 16 covers borrowings for capital purposes and s. 17 provides that no purchaser or mortgagee, paying or advancing money on a sale or mortgage purporting to be made under any trust

APPLICATION BY TRUSTEES FOR THE OPENING OF AN ACCOUNT.

_____ 19 _____

The Manager,

BANK OF CYPRUS (LONDON) LTD

Dear Sir.

We the undersigned:—

_____

_____

_____

being the trustees of _____ hereby
request you to open an account in our names as trustees of _____
and we authorize you from time to time until we shall give you notice to the contrary in writing under our hands to pay and honour all cheques that may be drawn
on our said account by all of us and to charge the amount of all such cheques to
the debit of our said account whether it is in credit or overdrawn at the time such
cheques are presented for payment any overdraft which may from time to time be
created on our said account being at our Joint and several responsibility.

Yours faithfully,

_____

_____

_____

Fig.2.2   _Trustees' mandate_

or power vested in trustees, need be concerned to see that the money is
wanted, or how it is used.

The most frequent occasion when trustees will need to borrow from a bank
will arise where the trustees are carrying on the business of a deceased's estate
and it will usually be found that the will gives the trustees power to borrow
and mortgage or charge any of the assets of the estate as security for such
borrowings. In such a situation the banker should peruse the will to ascertain
the trustees' powers. A trustee should not be allowed to charge trust property

to secure a borrowing on his own private account and it should be noted that when a trustee mixes trust money with his own money it is presumed that he has drawn out his own money in priority to the money he holds in trust; hence the Rule in *Clayton's Case* does not apply (*Re Halletts Estate* (1880)).

Death

When a trustee dies, the remaining trustees may continue to operate the account, and act, under the provisions of s. 18 Trustee Act 1925. The trustees should then consult the instrument under which they were appointed to see whether they must seek the appointment of an alternative replacement trustee. If the trust account is overdrawn then the bank might wish to stop the account to preserve its full claim against the estate of the deceased trustee, which will be personally liable under the joint and several liability clause to the bank, albeit with a right of indemnity out of the trust estate assets.

In the case of the death of a sole trustee, or where all the trustees have died and no new ones have been appointed, the executor or administrator of the last trustee may take over until such time as a new trustee is appointed (s. 18 Trustee Act 1925).

Bankruptcy

Perhaps surprisingly, the bankruptcy of a trustee is not automatic grounds for his resignation, and he may continue to act. However, an interested party such as a co-trustee or beneficiary can apply to the court for his removal and the appointment of a new trustee, and often that would seem a wiser and safer way to proceed.

UNINCORPORATED ASSOCIATIONS, CLUBS AND SOCIETIES

Unincorporated associations have no separate identity of their own in law, and their business affairs are usually conducted by the members in a general meeting, although many powers are delegated to a committee, upon which will be the main officers of the association such as the chairman, secretary and treasurer. Frequently such asssociations will be formed with a set of rules, and the conduct of its affairs must thereafter be in accordance with those rules until such time as they are changed in the manner laid down at the outset.

Banks often open accounts for sports clubs, or local hobby clubs, or for an organization which may have been set up for a short period to run an event such as an agricultural show. When such an organization requires a bank account, it will be found that the committee of management, acting within their powers under any rules which may exist, will usually delegate to certain of their number the power to conduct and operate the bank account. It is better if an account is then opened in the name of the club or society, although occasionally the account is styled in the name of the treasurer or secretary re the club, e.g. 'Gordon Ruscoe re Northenden Tennis Club', in which case the bank is at once on notice that a trust element is present in the funds on that account. Moreover, the individual concerned is then personally liable for any overdraft on the account. It will be important to separate the affairs of this account from the treasurer or secretary's private account and care should be taken to ensure that any cheques payable to the association or society are accepted only for the credit of the trust account. Monies should not be transferred from the trust account to the private account without a satisfactory explanation. In all such cases there is the possibility of conversion, and the bank might not be able to show that it had acted without negligence, enabling it to obtain the protection of section 4 of the Cheques Act 1957, if the club or association later brought an action for conversion.

Mandate

The more usual and safer method is for the acount to be opened in the name of the club, and a mandate (Fig. 2.3) should be obtained referring to the passing of a resolution by the club members, or their committee, appointing the bank as the club's bankers. The chairman of the meeting and its secretary should certify that this resolution was passed, and should also verify the authority resolved upon as to which officials can operate the bank account. It is better if this authority is drawn in such a way that it refers to 'The treasurer and secretary for the time being' or whoever. In this way, whenever there is a change in one person holding office all that will be necessary will be for another copy resolution, on the bank form, to be certified by the chairman and secretary, stating that Mr A has resigned as a treasurer and that Mr B has been appointed in his place. A specimen signature of the original officers, or the new officer, will be supplied on the original mandate, or the change of mandate form, on each occasion.

Occasionally the rules of the association are lodged with the bank, but if the account is to be conducted in credit then the bank frequently does not concern itself with these. However, if there is ever any conflict within the organisation, and changes in the operation of the bank account are mooted, it might be wise for the bank to peruse the rules, and to ensure that the authority given to it is not in conflict with anything within the rules.

Very occasionally a club is incorporated and registered under the Companies Acts, and if so will then be a legal entity. This type of club will be in the form of a private company and in some cases the liability of the shareholders may be limited by guarantee. The bank will then obtain a copy of the memorandum and articles of association, a suitable minute governing operations on the account, and specimen signatures of those authorized to sign, and matters will proceed much as with any other limited company. With the sanction of the Department of Trade and Industry, the word 'Limited' may be dispensed with, subject to the provisions of the Companies Acts.

Societies, Clubs and Associations.

_____ 19_____

To **BANK OF CYPRUS (LONDON) LTD.**

(1) Insert name of Society, Club or Association

(¹) _____

(Address or) _____
(Office   )

(2) Insert "Committee," or as the case may be

My (²) _____ request you to open an account

with the above-mentioned (³).

(3) Insert "Society," "Club" or "Association." or as the case may be

In pursuance of this request I hand you herewith :

   I. Copy of the Rules.

   II. Certified Copy of a Resolution of the (²) _____ (overleaf).

   III. Specimen signatures of the persons authorized to sign (overleaf).

Yours faithfully,

_____ Secretary.

(¹) _____

Insert Committee." or as the case may be.

(2) Insert name of the Society, Club. or Association

We hereby certify that the following Resolution of the (¹) _____

of the (²) _____

was passed at a Meeting of the (¹) _____ held on the

_____ and has been duly recorded in the Minute Book :—

   R E S O L V E D — That a Banking Account for the

(¹) _____

be opened with Bank of Cyprus (London) Limited at their

(3) Insert name of Branch

(³) _____

Branch and that the Bank be and is hereby empowered to honour Cheques, Orders for Payment, Bills of Exchange and Promissory Notes drawn, signed, accepted or made on behalf of the said

(¹) _____

_____

(4) Insert "any two members of the Committee for the time being and countersigned by the Secretary." or otherwise as may be required.

by (⁴) _____

and to act on any instructions given by the persons so authorised with regard to any accounts whether in credit or overdrawn or any transactions of the said _____

Chairman of the Meeting.

Secretary.

PERSONS AUTHORIZED TO SIGN

FULL NAME	OFFICIAL POSITION	SPECIMEN SIGNATURE

Fig.2.3   *Club mandate*

Borrowings

If the account is maintained always in credit, the banker need not concern himself about locating responsibility for debts incurred on behalf of the society, but if an overdraft is required then it is essential that the banker should be able to fix the liability for repayment upon some definite person or persons. Because the club or society has no separate legal entity, it cannot itself be sued for the recovery of debt, and nor will the members be liable for any debts incurred on the club's behalf by either the committee or the officers unless the members have personally agreed to be liable.

As to the possible liability of the officers, the situation is not entirely clear, but under the principles set out in *Bradley Egg Farm Ltd* v. *Clifford and others* (1943) it is possible that the appointed officers could be liable for any borrowing which has been authorized by the committee, acting within the rules, if there are any.

Usually the bank will be happy to lend provided third-party security is given in the form of a guarantee incorporating an indemnity clause, under which the person signing will assume primary responsibility. If this clause of indemnity were not in the charge form then the guarantee or third-party charge could be worthless to the bank, as seen in *Coutts & Co.* v. *Brown-Lecky* (1946), which case, while referring to the borrowing of a minor, showed that where a debt is irrecoverable from the principal debtor, legal action will not be successful against a surety.

Occasionally a club or society will have acquired property such as a club house and this will be held in the name of trustees. There will therefore be a trust deed, and if this property is offered as security it will be necessary for the bank to give consideration to the rules of the society and to the provisions of the trust deed. It will be important that all trustees should act and sign the forms of charge, and that care should be taken to ensure that there is no breach of trust. If the situation is complex then the bank should take legal advice from a solicitor.

Death of an officer

Where a person signs a cheque in an official capacity as treasurer, secretary or chairman, either by himself or with others, his death does not determine the banker's mandate to pay that cheque, even though it is presented after his death. However, early steps will need to be taken in such a situation to appoint a new official, and notice of the new appointment and a specimen signature of the new officers must be given to the bank, usually by means of a printed form supplied by the bank, which incorporates a suitable resolution which the chairman or secretary can say has been passed by the appropriate meeting. It should of course be remembered that the executors or personal representatives of a deceased person do not take over and act in any of his official appointments, whether these were honorary or not.

SOLICITORS' ACCOUNTS

Solicitors frequently handle large sums of money on behalf of their clients, and under special rules under the various Solicitors' Acts every solicitor who holds or receives money on behalf of a client must, without undue delay, pay that money into a current or deposit account at a bank, in the name of the solicitor, although the title of the account must include the word 'client'. These provisions are known as the Solicitors' Accounts Rules. The solicitor may have as many such accounts as is necessary, and as he wishes, but if he holds monies for a client in excess of £500 for over two months he must place them in a separate deposit account, for the benefit of the client.

Banks prize these clients' account balances and to have a solicitor in account is itself desirable, as the relationship built up between solicitor and banker can be helpful in local business affairs, and the bank has a ready friend to turn to should it need legal advice. Moreover, the solicitor may well from time to time be able to direct clients to the bank to open an account. There is, in consequence, strong competition between the banks to obtain a solicitor's business.

In addition to his client accounts, the solicitor will usually also have an 'office' account for running the day-to-day accounting side of the practice. Also, solicitors are frequently appointed trustees under settlements or wills of their clients, and the Solicitors' Trust Account Rules provide that such accounts should be styled with the bank in such a way that the name of 'executor' or 'trustee' appears. Because of the nature of the client account or trustee account overdrafts should not arise, but if they do then it should be a cause of concern for the bank, as either there has been an error in the bookkeeping at the bank or in the solicitor's office, or there is evidence of the misappropriation of clients' funds. It is in fact a breach of the Solicitors' Accounts Rules for a solicitor to overdraw a clients' account.

Transfers between the clients' accounts and the solicitor's office account will be seen from time to time, and while these do not directly concern the bank, the bank might regard itself as put on enquiry if anything of an obviously irregular nature is noticed. Under the Solicitors' Accounts Rules, payments out of the clients' account to the office account should be by way of a cheque drawn in favour of the solicitor, or by way of a transfer to the solicitor's office account but there is no obligation upon the bank to verify the propriety of such a transaction. However, if the solicitor's office account has been irregularly overdrawn, or pressure has been applied by the bank for repayment, then the bank should very much bear in mind the possibility of misappropriation of clients' monies, for in such an instance, and if conversion is taking place, the bank may not be able to show that it acted in good faith in debiting the client account. Much would depend upon the amount involved in such a situation.

Generally, however, there is no onus on a bank to enquire into individual transactions and it is protected by the provisions of s. 85 Solicitors Act 1974, although this protection will not apply in the case of a blatant breach of trust.

This was clearly seen in the recent case of *Lipkin Gorman* v. *Karpnale and Another* (1986), where a partner (Cass) in a firm of solicitors misappropriated monies from the firm's clients' account to fund his compulsive gambling activities. Upon matters being discovered the other members of the firm succeeded in an action against Lloyds Bank for breach of duty as constructive trustee, basing their claim on the fact that the bank manager knew of Mr Cass's gambling and on suspecting that the clients' account was being misused preferred not to look. The court accepted the categorization of 'knowledge' for a constructive trustee set down in *Baden Delvaux* (1983) and said that points (2) and (3) at least applied.

That case had recognized the possibility of five possible different mental states:

(1) actual knowledge,
(2) wilfully shutting one's eyes to the obvious,
(3) wilfully and recklessly failing to make such enquiries as an honest and reasonable man would make,
(4) knowledge of circumstances which would indicate the facts to an honest and reasonable man, and
(5) knowledge of circumstances which would put an honest and reasonable man on enquiry.

There is no legal right of set-off between a clients' account and other accounts, for the monies are not held in the same right, and so if a bankruptcy order is made against a solicitor, the funds in the clients' account do not vest in the trustee, for they are not part of the bankrupt's estate (s. 283 Insolvency Act 1986). Nor can they be taken by the bank as reduction to any borrowing in the solicitor's office account or private account.

Similarly, upon the death of a solicitor, the clients' account balances are not part of his estate, and they may only be paid away by the bank to an executor solicitor, appointed to wind up the deceased's practice, or by a solcitor appointed by the Law Society to take charge of the practice. Usually another qualified local solicitor will be authorized to act, either on the death of a solicitor practising on his own, or in the event of a bankruptcy order being made against him.

Remembering the trust element of the clients' account, one would not expect a garnishee order naming a solicitor as judgment debtor to attach balances in the clients' account, but this is not the case. In accordance with the rule in *Plunkett and another* v. *Barclays Bank Ltd* (1936) the clients' accounts must be stopped upon receipt of a garnishee order or summons. However, the nature of those balances will be explained to the court, and the court will then rule as to whether any part of the balance should be paid over to the court, or whether all or any is free to be paid away by the solicitor.

ACCOUNTS OF LIQUIDATORS

Only a licensed insolvency practitioner may act as a liquidator. He is appointed by the court in a compulsory winding up, by the creditors in a creditors' voluntary liquidation, and by a resolution of the members in a members' voluntary winding up.

In the case of a compulsory winding up, the liquidator is required to pay all monies into an insolvency services account at the Bank of England, but if the liquidation committee can obtain dispensation from the Department of Trade and Industry then the liquidator may be empowered to open an account with another bank and in such a case, when opening the account, the local bank should ensure that it sees the court order appointing the liquidator, and also the Department of Trade's authority allowing the account to be operated locally. The account should be styled 'Alan Brown, liquidator of Long's Tools Ltd'.

In the case of a members' voluntary winding up, or a creditors' voluntary winding up, the rule requiring the account to be with the Bank of England does not apply, and frequently the liquidator will choose either the branch of the bank where his firm conducts its practice account or the branch of the bank where the company did its business. When opening an account for a liquidator appointed by the creditors or members, the bank should see a certified copy of the resolution passed, appointing the liquidator.

In a creditors' voluntary liquidation it should be remembered that it is the creditors choice which prevails, and whilst a company is placed into this type of liquidation by the resolutions of the company acting by its members in general meeting, a meeting of creditors must then be held within 14 days. Pending that second meeting, any liquidator appointed by the members has limited powers. (See Chapter 9.)

The funds on a liquidator's account should be regarded by the banker as trust funds, and there is no right of set-off with any other balances in the liquidator's name.

Liquidators rarely need to borrow, but if they do they have no personal liability, unless they agree to accept liability, and almost certainly this would be a requirement of the bank, before lending.

In the case of a compulsory liquidation, the liquidator is empowered to borrow and charge the assets of the company, and he may do so without the authority of the court. It will be usual, however, for him to act in liaison with the liquidation committee representing the creditors, and where he wishes to carry on the business the authority of the court and the committee of inspection is mandatory for the borrowing and the provision of the security.

In the case of a members' voluntary winding up, or creditors' voluntary winding up, the liquidator may borrow and may give security, although he will invariably obtain the authority of the liquidation committee before doing so.

Where a liquidator charges company assets as security, unless those assets are already in mortgage to a creditor of the company, then the new lender has priority over the claims of any unsecured creditors in the liquidation. However, the position can become complex, and, in the unusual event of a liquidator wishing to borrow and charge security, legal advice should be taken by the bank.

RECEIVERS OF LIMITED COMPANIES

A receiver of a limited company may be appointed by the court or the holder of a floating charge under a debenture. In the first instance he is known simply as a receiver. In the second, where he is the receiver or manager of the whole (or substantially the whole) of a company's property appointed by holders of any debentures secured by a charge which, as created, was a floating charge, he is known as an administrative receiver for the purposes of the Insolvency Act 1986 (s. 29 defines).

An administrative receiver must hold a current licence as an insolvency practitioner.

It is of course possible to appoint two or more receivers to act jointly or separately.

The administrative receiver's job is to realize the assets of the business, and to use realizations to repay the debenture holder, although out of floating-asset realizations he will firstly have to meet all the claims of preferential creditors (s. 40 Insolvency Act 1986). In some instances, before realizing assets, the administrative receiver may trade on for a period, while he assesses the situation, and indeed it might be that in an exceptional case he will be able to return the business to profitability and repay the debenture holder from trading profits or by hiving off certain parts of the company's ongoing activities, without redundancies or selling assets piecemeal. Such cases are rare, however, and the administrative receiver's prime duty is to the debenture holder, and he is not appointed as 'rescuer'.

The powers of an administrative receiver are set out in Schedule 1 of the Insolvency Act 1986 but may be restricted by the debenture, although this would be unusual. He is appointed by the debenture holder by being handed an instrument of appointment, often in letter form, signed under hand or sealed. An appointment is of no effect unless it is accepted before the end of the first business day after the one on which he receives the appointment, or it is received on his behalf. Subject to that requirement (s. 33 Insolvency Act 1986) it takes effect at the time it was received. Before opening an account for an administrative receiver, the bank should see this evidence of his appointment, be satisfied that he is a licenced insolvency practitioner and has accepted the appointment, after which the account can be opened in the style 'John Smith, Administrative Receiver of ABC Ltd'.

It is possible that a receiver will need to borrow, and if he has been appointed by the court it will be necessary for the bank to see a court order giving authority for him to borrow and to charge the company's property as security. However, where an administrative receiver has been appointed by a holder of a floating charge debenture, the appointer's attitude need not be known, and the lending banker should simply obtain sight of the debenture document to ensure that his power under the Insolvency Act has not been withdrawn. The receiver will be personally liable for any borrowing but he will have a right of indemnity out of the assets of the company. It will also be important for the bank to know the purpose of the borrowing, for it will be conscious that an administrative receiver will probably have been appointed in a failing business, and there must be a strong chance therefore that if he continues trading he too will incur losses similar to those incurred prior to his appointment. The bank will also wish to see the statement of affairs produced by the directors in the early days of his appointment, which will show the assets of the company and its liabilities. The extent of preferential creditors will be important, for an administrative receiver should not put their rights, such as repayment from floating-asset realizations, at risk by trading on at a loss.

These considerations will apply whether the administrative receiver is appointed by an outside debenture holder, or by the bank itself under the terms of a debenture securing a limited company's account, and they apply even though the administrative receiver appointed by a debenture holder is deemed, usually, to be the agent of the company and not the agent of the persons appointing him. This position of agency is terminated, however, if the company is placed into liquidation.

AN ADMINISTRATOR (OF A COMPANY)

Part II of the Insolvency Act 1986 empowers the court to appoint a licenced insolvency practitioner as an administrator of a company, upon the presentation of a petition by the company, its directors, or creditors. Notice of the petition must be given to the holder of a floating charge at least five days before the hearing and if he then appoints an administrative receiver before the hearing the court will not appoint an administrator unless there are doubts about the validity of the security. An administrative receiver cannot be appointed after an administrator has been appointed.

An administrator has the same powers as an administrative receiver, and these are set out in Schedule I; Insolvency Act 1986.

The purposes and ramifications of the making of an Administration Order are discussed fully in Chapter 9, but at this stage it should simply be appreciated that the administrator is there to control, and perhaps to save a company in dire financial straits, or at least achieve a better realization of its assets than in liquidation. When a bank is asked to open an account for an administrator it should see the court order appointing him and style his account 'John Smith, Administrator of XYZ Ltd'.

An administrator is the agent of the company and is not liable on any contract unless he so agrees, and hence, if he wishes to borrow, the bank should ensure that this point is covered by written documentation. He may pledge company assets as security and has a right of indemnity to the company assets in respect of his liabilities incurred and his costs. If the assets pledged are the subject of an earlier floating charge, where the debenture holder has not appointed an administrative receiver, the lender's charge will take priority over the earlier floating charge.

SUPERVISORS UNDER VOLUNTARY ARRANGEMENTS

The Insolvency Act 1986 has introduced two new methods of dealing with financial difficulties outside of the extremes of bankruptcy or liquidation. In the case of an individual, the scheme is called an *individual voluntary arrangement* and in the case of a limited company a *company voluntary arrangement*. Both are discussed fully in Chapters 7 and 9.

In both, a licenced insolvency practitioner is appointed to look after the affairs of the individual or the company and he takes his powers from the terms of the arrangement agreed by the creditors (in the case of an individual) and by the creditors and members of the company (in the case of a company).

If a bank is asked to open an account for a supervisor under a voluntary arrangement it should see that the person nominated holds a current licence as an insolvency practitioner and should examine the arrangement which will show in particular whether the supervisor is entitled to have any credit balance, safe custody or unrequired security on the customer's account paid or handed to him, as whilst this is likely, it may not be automatic as in bankruptcy or liquidation.

The arrangement may allow the supervisor to borrow against the security of the assets in the free estate. Again it would seem advisable for a bank to ensure that he accepts personal liability for any borrowing that is agreed.

PARTNERSHIP ACCOUNTS

The law relating to partnerships is found in the Partnership Act 1890, and in s. 1 a partnership is defined as 'the relationship which subsists between persons carrying on a business in common with a view to profit'.

In England a partnership has no legal entity although the partner may sue and be sued in the firm's name, but the partnership really consists of the individual partners.

A partnership may not consist of more than twenty persons in an ordinary business, or ten in the case of a banking business.

There is no limit on the number of partners in a firm of solicitors, accountants, stockbrokers or other bodies which may be specified by the Department of Trade and Industry. If the appropriate number is exceeded, the firm is an illegal association and for as long as it remains so it cannot enforce contracts which it has entered into. At the same time, outside parties can, as a rule, enforce their contracts against the firm. In practice, if the specified numbers were to be exceeded then the business would be formed into a limited company.

Liability

Every partner is an agent of the firm for the purpose of the partnership business. The powers of a partner may be limited or restricted in the contract of partnership, but a person in dealing with a partner is under no obligation to examine the deed of partnership and can assume that a partner has full power to do everything usual and necessary within the scope of the business of the firm. However if a person is aware that the partner is exceeding his authority then the firm is not bound. Any act done by a partner outside the scope of the ordinary business of the partnership does not bind the firm only. The partner himself as an individual is personally liable for the consequence of such an act.

There is an implied authority for each general partner of a firm to use the firm name and bind the firm in all matters relating to the partnership business, but that does not necessarily mean that he has power to borrow money so as to bind the firm and his partners. There may be an implied power to borrow or not according to the nature of the firm. For example in a firm of accountants, where no trading is carried on, it is usually unnecessary to borrow money for business purposes and, accordingly, a partner has no authority to incur an overdraft in the name of the firm. If he does so, the other partners are not bound. It is therefore important to distinguish between a trading partnership and a non-trading partnership.

If an overdraft is desired by a non-trading firm, it is desirable for the bank to receive a letter stating the amount required from all the partners, but in the case of a trading concern this is generally dispensed with.

Where, as is usual, a partner is liable, this is to the full extent of his private means for the debts and liabilities of the firm. The debts of the firm are the debts of the partners and the liability is joint but not several and arises for all debts incurred while the individual is a partner. However, the bank mandate invariably establishes joint and several liability.

A person who becomes a partner of an existing firm is not liable to the creditors of the firm for anything done before he became a partner, unless the parties have agreed to substitute the liabililty of the new firm for that of the old. Banks usually have a form for use in that event.

If a partnership owes monies to the bank and a new partner is to be appointed, the safest course is to stop operations on the existing account until the new arrangements have been properly made. The new partnership may then agree to be jointly and severally liable for the debts of the old firm, and an authority signed by all the new partners will enable the bank to repay the old debt, should the bank be prepared to release its claim against the retiring partner.

A partner is not liable for debts of the firm after he has ceased to be a partner provided he gives due notice of his retirement. If a partnership account is overdrawn at the time of the retirement of a partner, the bank, if it wishes to preserve its right against the retiring partner, should stop operations on the account to prevent the operation of the Rule in *Clayton's Case,* and ask the continuing partners to open a new account. A person who retires from a firm does not thereby cease to be liable for partnership debts or obligations incurred before his retirement. To free him creditors must agree to accept the new firm as the debtor in substitution.

Every partner in a firm is jointly liable with the other partners for all debts and obligations of the firm incurred while he is a partner; and after his death his estate is also severally liable for such debts as remain unpaid, subject, in England, to the prior payment of his private debts.

At one time, in law, only one action used to be possible, where joint liability only had been taken on (as, for example, where the bank did not take a mandate) and if only one party was sued and judgment was not obtained against him, it was not possible then to sue the others who had been omitted from the action (*Kendall* v. *Hamilton* (1879)). Now, under s. 3 Civil Liability (Contribution) Act 1978, it is possible to sue any party to a joint account or a partner whose name was omitted from the first set of proceedings.

The account

An account should be styled in the name of the partnership, and when it is opened all the partners should sign the mandate showing who is to sign on behalf of the firm (Fig. 2.4). Each partner who is to operate on the account should give a specimen of the signature he intends to use in all operations of the firm's account. For instance a partner in the firm of 'Epsom Paints' may sign

'per pro Epsom Paints
Alan Jones'

or just 'Epsom Paints', as any cheque signed in the firm's name by one of the partners is equivalent to the signature by the partner so signing of the names of all persons liable as partners in that firm (Bills of Exchange Act 1882, s. 23).

The bank mandate for the account will incorporate a clause whereby each partner accepts joint and several liability for any overdraft or borrowing created or increased by any partner. This is extremely valuable to the bank, as otherwise partners are only jointly liable and in the event of the insolvency of

To PRACTICE BANK plc

_____19____

We, the undersigned, are individual partners in the firm of

_____

We request you to ‡ open and conduct/continue to conduct an account or accounts in our firm's name, until such time as we or any of us shall give you notice to the contrary.

You are authorized to accept the signature of ‡ either/any of us/any two of us/all of us in respect of any or all transactions with the bank, and in particular in respect of the drawing of cheques, endorsement or acceptance of bills of exchange and/or promissory notes, and the withdrawal of items for safe-custody and/or security.

We agree that in respect of any indebtedness of the firm to the bank at any time howsoever arising we shall each of us be jointly and severally liable to you.

Full Names of Partner	Private Address	Signature*	Signature † (Firm Name)

Partnership Name	Partnership Address

‡ delete as required
* Partner's own signature
† Partner's signature in firm name, if his intention is to sign in that form.

Fig.2.4   *Partnership mandate*

the partners only one right of proof would be possible. With several liability established there are separate rights against each partner and through the joint liability clause there is also a right against the firm and any assets held jointly.

It would also be possible to set off a credit balance in a partner's private account against the debt in the partnership account under rights in the several liability clause.

As a partnership can be formed orally or by implication, there need not necessarily be a written agreement or deed. Most professional partnerships are formed by deed but, even then, bankers may not ask for sight of the partnership deed when opening the account. They will however be more concerned on that aspect if borrowing facilities are required.

The need for partners to register under the Registration of Business Names Act 1916 was abolished by the Companies Act 1981, and banks can no longer ask for sight of the certificate of registration, as the register no longer exists.

Now, any individual or partnership using a trade name or a name not consisting solely of his, her or their surname or surnames must disclose the name of the proprietor or proprietors and his, her or their business (or another) address located within the UK. These facts must be shown on all business correspondence, orders, invoices and receipts and written demands for payment of monies due, and must be supplied on request to anyone with whom business is being transacted. Also, the relevant information must be on display in all business premises. Partnerships of twenty or more persons (e.g. solicitors, accountants and stockbrokers) are exempted from scheduling all the names and addresses on documents, provided a list is kept at the main place of business. (Business Names Act 1985).

The change in law has meant that banks can no longer rely on the protection under s. 4 Cheques Act 1957 in a situation of conversion where previously they were able to demonstrate that they had acted without negligence by seeing the Registration of Business Names Act certificate (*Smith and Baldwin* v. *Barclays Bank Ltd* (1944)).

It should be noted that the amended rules in the Business Names Act 1985 apply not only to partnerships but also to any person (including corporations) trading under a name other than his own real name. If, for example, a new customer should state that he is a freelance author using a *nom de plume* to which cheques will be made payable, the prudent banker should ask for sight of his business letter heading, or require confirmation from his publishers.

Fraud arising from the conversion of cheques by a partner occurred in *Baker* v. *Barclays Bank Ltd* (1955).[21] In this case Barclays Bank were conducting an account for a Mr Jeffcott who was considered to be a good customer. He paid cheques into his account in favour of 'Modern Confections' which were endorsed in favour of Jeffcott by one of the partners or the proprietor. The bank made enquiries of their customer Jeffcott, who claimed that the person endorsing the cheques, Bainbridge, was the sole proprietor of the firm, and Jeffcott said that he was helping with the accounting side of the business, and would enter into a partnership later. He said that Bainbridge owed him money. In fact, there were two partners in the firm of Modern Confections, a Mr Baker and Mr Bainbridge, and Bainbridge was defrauding his co-partner. When Baker found out about the frauds, he sued Barclays

21 See Appendix I, Q. 7 (September 1980).

Bank for conversion of the cheques but that bank pleaded that it was protected under s. 82 Bills of Exchange Act 1882, as it had collected the cheques in good faith and without negligence for a customer. (This section is now enacted in s. 4 Cheques Act 1957.) The court found against the bank, on the grounds that the enquiries made by the collecting banker had not been detailed enough. The Judge said: 'The explanation which the manager received when he asked for one, was not one which should have satisfied a bank manager'. However, the interesting facet of the case was that although Barclays was found to be guilty of conversion, it was held that as partners shared profits equally, and as Bainbridge, one of the partners, had been guilty of a fraud which had led the bank into this position, Mr Baker his co-partner was entitled to judgment in money terms for only half the value of the cheques which had been collected.

Should a partner have a private account, it is not incumbent upon the bank to question the validity of transfers from the partnership account to the private account, unless the amounts and circumstances are such as to make the bank suspicious of fraud. A bank must not permit any partner to pay into his private account cheques drawn in favour of the firm unless all the partners expressly authorize it to do so, for the chance of defending an action for conversion successfully would not be high.

Occasionally a dispute arises between partners and then clear instructions to the bank from *all* partners must be obtained, to prevent the bank being drawn into claims and litigation. It should be noted that a bank must comply with a notice from one partner stopping payment of a cheque drawn on the partnership account.

Death

In the event of the death of a partner, his representatives are not liable for debts later contracted by the firm. Usually the bank will wish to look to the representatives of a deceased partner to repay any private debt and, if overdrawn, the partnership account should be stopped and a claim lodged in the estate, if the bank wishes to preserve its rights, and does not intend to look only to the other partners. If the account is not stopped the Rule in *Clayton's Case* applies; the first item on the debit side is discharged or reduced by the first item on the credit side, and eventually the old debt is repaid by credit turnover and the claim in the deceased's estate becomes extinguished.

In regard to cheques issued before the partner's death, the bank should return them marked 'Partner deceased' if it decides to stop the account to preserve its claim against the estate. Otherwise, it may honour cheques, although it may well consider it advisable to obtain confirmation beforehand from the remaining partners. If the account is maintained in credit, the other partners are entitled to deal with the balance and can give a valid discharge for it, as they may continue the business in order to wind it up. If they need to borrow for this purpose, they are entitled to charge partnership property, or the bank can rely on partnership property charged before the death of their other partner. Often a new partnership is formed by the remaining partners and if so a new mandate should be obtained.

New partner joining the firm

When a new partner joins an existing firm, he must complete a bank mandate (Fig 2.5), which will give the bank identical rights to those it had against the former partners. It is desirable for the former partners to confirm that they have accepted the new person into partnership.

Should the old firm have had an overdraft or loan at the time when the new partner joins, it is important to know whether or not he accepts liability for that. The mandate he signs may well be drawn to cover the point. If not, and if the old account is continued, eventually by the operation of *Clayton's Case,*

To PRACTICE BANK plc

_____19___

We, the undersigned, being the individual partners in the firm of

_____

advise you that we have taken into partnership

_____of _____. ___

Name of Partner	Signature

I, _____ of _____
beg to advise you that I have been accepted into the above named partnership.
I agree to be bound by the terms of the mandate to the bank dated _____
19___ and in particular I agree that I shall be jointly and severally liable in respect of any existing indebtedness of the said firm to the bank and in respect of any future indebtedness, howsoever arising.

Signature of new partner_____
        and*
Signature of new partner (Firm Name)_____

*only to be completed if the new partner intends to sign in the firm name.

Fig.2.5   *Partnership – new partner admitted*

the old debt will be fully repaid and the borrowing will consist of monies drawn by the new partnership in respect of which the new partner will be fully liable. Alternatively the old partnership account may be stopped, and a new one opened. The new partner will then only be liable for debts on the new account.

Mental incapacity

The mental incapacity of a partner does not dissolve a partnership, but another partner may apply to the court to have the partnership dissolved. If the account is overdrawn the bank should stop the account when it learns of the mental incapacity if it wishes to preserve its rights against that partner's estate, which may then be administered by the receiver appointed by the Court of Protection.

Insolvency of a partnership

Under the old law (Bankruptcy Act 1914) the bankruptcy of a firm automatically involved the bankruptcy of each partner and the assets of the firm were applied firstly in payment of the partnership debts, and the private assets of each partner were applied firstly to the payment of his private liabilities. Any surplus on the private estates was then treated as part of the firm's assets, the joint estate, and any surplus on the partnership estate was dealt with as part of the respective private estates of the partners, in proportion to the rights and interest of each partner in the firm's estate. The partners were required to submit a statement of affairs for the firm and each partner had to file a separate statement in respect of his private affairs.

These provisions will still apply if under the Insolvency Act 1986 and the Insolvent Partnership Order 1986, a winding up order is made against the firm and a bankruptcy order against one or more of the partners.

However a petitioning creditor now has the choice of deciding whether or not to petition for the bankruptcy of the individual partner(s) when seeking an insolvency order, known as a winding up order, against the firm, which estate will in future be wound up as if it were an unregistered company. If the petitioner elects only to seek the winding up of the firm, the liquidator will be able, presumably, to call upon the members to contribute to any shortfall if the assets are insufficient to pay the firm's debts in full, but intitially, the estates of the individual partners are not affected.

As soon as a bank learns that a winding up order has been made against the firm all operations on the account must be stopped. However, the accounts of the individual partners may be continued, if the bank wishes, although it may prefer to call up any personal debt outstanding, or, if the partner's account is in credit, to appropriate the balance against its claim under the several liability obtaining through the bank mandate, which governs the partnership account.

Where the bank learns that a winding up order has been made against the firm and bankruptcy orders have been made against some or all of the partners, all operations on the accounts of the partnership and of the partners involved must be stopped, whether the accounts are in credit or overdrawn. In most cases, where a firm's account is overdrawn, the bank will have a mandate under which the partners will have undertaken joint and several liability, and so the bank can prove in the private estate(s) for the full amount of the partnership debt, as well as in the joint partnership estate.

Bankruptcy of one partner

If a bankruptcy order is made against only one partner and there is no winding up order against the firm then the other partners do not become directly involved in the bankruptcy proceedings. However, unless the partnership articles allow otherwise the partnership will be terminated, and the solvent partners will account to the trustee in bankruptcy for the bankrupt partner's interest. If the articles allow the firm to continue then the bankrupt partner will resign and a new partner may possibly be invited to join the firm. In both cases, if the partnership account was conducted in credit then it may continue to operate, although if a cheque drawn by a partner who is the subject of bankruptcy proceedings is presented it should not be paid without the consent of the other partners.

Where the partnership account was overdrawn, however, if the bank wants to preserve its claim in the bankrupt partner's estate and look to any security he has lodged for the borrowing, then the account must be stopped to prevent the operation of the Rule in *Clayton's Case*. A new account could then be opened for the remaining or new partners to operate in credit, or by agreement against existing or new security from the firm or solvent partners.

Security for a partnership

When taking a charge over partnership property it is usual for a bank to obtain a legal mortgage in the case of land and all partners should execute a direct form of charge. The mortgage will usually contain a clause stating that the security remains good despite any change in the future constitution of the firm; thus the bank is secured when a partner resigns or when a new partner joins the firm.

Where only one partner executes a legal mortgage form over partnership property without authority this may constitute an equitable charge, but difficulties with realisation are likely to be experienced, especially if there is a partnership dispute.

As, under the usual form of bank mandate, a partner will have undertaken several liability for partnership debts, he can give a charge over his private house, or other personal security, on the direct form of charge expressed to cover an individual's own liabilities however they arise. Such a mortgage would be available for a debt on the partner's private account or the partnership account. Alternatively, it could be taken as a third-party security expressed to be for the liabilities of the partnership only, in which case it would not be available for the partner's own borrowing on sole account.

Guarantees by partnerships

No partner can bind the firm by giving a guarantee, unless the giving of guarantees is a customary part of the firm's business. Preferably, such a guarantee should be signed by all the partners, although a written authority from all partners authorizing one partner to execute the form of charge may be acceptable, provided it clearly shows the transaction and refers to the nature of the guarantee involved.

A guarantee should never be taken from a partner for the partnership's liabilities, for of course there is no need as the partner is already fully liable, and to do so is superfluous and could be dangerous. Thus a guarantee, especially one limited in amount, could prejudice the bank's position. Surprisingly, however, the author has encountered such a situation several times in his banking career.

Limited partnerships

Limited partnerships are regulated by the Limited Partnerships Act 1907. At least one of the partners must be a general partner or an unlimited partner, liable for all the debts and obligations of the partnership, and the others are limited partners only to the extent of the capital they have contributed. Limited partners must not take part in the management of the business and the general view is that they have no powers to draw cheques. The Limited Partnerships Act does not require the firm's name to show that the partnership is a limited partnership. So, unless the information is volunteered a bank would need to find out from the Registrar of Companies whether there were limited partners or not. The importance of this is that the bank may be relying on a man of substance associated with the firm who may turn out to be a limited partner for a small amount only. Fortunately such partnerships are uncommon.

A limited partner, so long as he remains a limited partner, must not draw out any of his capital, because if he does so he will still be liable to the firm's creditors, up to the amount of the capital he has drawn out. Every limited partnership must be registered with the registrar of joint stock companies and if it is not registered the partnership is deemed to be an ordinary partnership in regard to its members, whether general or limited. The death, mental incapacity or bankruptcy of a limited partner does not dissolve the firm. The provisions of the Insolvency Act 1986 apply to limited partnerships just as to ordinary partnerships, and should a limited partnership be wound up, its assets vest in its liquidator.

ACCOUNTS OF ESTATE AGENTS

Under the Estate Agents Act 1979 an estate agent is required to keep any monies received from clients in a separate clients' account and this account is effectively a trust account. Monies paid into the account may be expected to represent pre-contract deposits, or contract monies, and there is an obligation on the estate agent to pay interest on such monies in excess of £500, where such interest would be £10 or more. It is possible, therefore, that an estate agent will ask his banker to open a client's deposit account so that the interest he has to pay is recouped from the bank.[22]

Under s. 23 Estate Agents Act 1979, it is not permissible for an undischarged bankrupt to act as an estate agent, although he may be engaged as an employee.[23]

Overall supervision is by the Director General of Fair Trading, who is empowered to ban any unfit person from carrying on work as an estate agent. Such instances, although presumably rare, could arise where a person has been convicted of dishonesty or fraud or where he has failed to comply with the requirements of the Estate Agents Act.

ACCOUNTS OF INSURANCE BROKERS

An insurance broker, whether a private individual or a limited company, must be registered with the Insurance Brokers Registration Council, a body set up under the Insurance Brokers (Registration) Act 1977. The Council has made strict rules relating to the control of monies coming into the hands of insurance brokers and unless the broker is a member of Lloyds he is required to have separate current or deposit accounts with a bank which has been approved by the Council to keep separate all monies which relate to insurance transactions. This account, which is similar to a clients' account maintained by a solicitor, has to be entitled 'Insurance Broking Account' and the bank can be asked from time to time to confirm in writing to the broker himself or his accountant that an account, so styled, has been opened and is still maintained. Specifically, the bank maintaining such an account may be asked to state that it has no rights of set-off, lien or charge over any monies in any account so designated, the object of this being to protect the clients' fund and to give statutory recognition to the trust nature of such monies. Consequently, where a bank seeks to recover an overdraft on an insurance broker's private account it cannot take into consideration any credit balance on the insurance broking account, nor, in bankruptcy proceedings, could the bank set off the balances to arrive at a net figure.

The insurance broking account is used for the receipt of premiums due on policies and the payment out of monies in respect of claims. Also, the bank

22 See Appendix I, Q. 26 (April 1983).
23 See Appendix I, Q. 26 (April 1983).

might expect to see transactions in the account relating to refunds of premium and brokerage payments and salvages. It is permissible for the insurance broker to overdraw on the account temporarily where short-term approved assets are to be acquired and monies to cover the purchase are awaited from another source. However, this is only allowed when the 'insurance transaction assets' are not less than the amount of the 'insurance transaction liabilities'. Fortunately there is no obligation on a bank to make any enquiries or to satisfy itself that these conditions are in existence.

CHAPTER 3

The Paying Banker

One of the major aspects of the daily work of a branch bank is dealing with the payment or dishonour of cheques drawn by its customers. These may be presented either over the counter, for cash or collection, or through the General In Clearing. They are also occasionally received by way of a special presentation made by the collecting bank.

In all these incidents, the cheque is the customer's mandate, or authority, to the bank to debit the account, although it is also a bill of exchange in its own right, and by virtue of which certain liabilities and rights arise and are acquired. Under s. 59(i) Bills of Exchange Act 1882 a bill is discharged by payment in due course by or on behalf of the drawee or acceptor. 'Payment in due course' means payment made at or after the maturity of the bill to the holder thereof, in good faith and without notice that his title to the bill is defective.

A busy branch of a clearing bank will have to deal with hundreds of cheques drawn on it by its various customers in any one business day, and while much of the tedium of the accounting side has now been made obsolete by the introduction of computer-generated entries, it is still essential that each cheque be examined carefully to see that it may safely be 'paid'. If not, any computer-generated entry, and bank charges incurred, must be reversed. It is usual for the officer who examines the cheque and who authorizes payment to place his own initials through the drawer's signature and/or to stamp the cheque with a 'paid' stamp using indelible ink.

If the cheque is dishonoured, the reason or 'answer' is written on the top of the face of the cheque and if it has been inadvertently cancelled or stamped 'paid' this should be mentioned, i.e. that it was so marked in error. Most banks retain record books in which are entered details of all cheques returned by the branch. (Often a similar record book is also maintained in respect of cheques returned inwards to the branch, covering those items which it has collected on behalf of its customers and which have been dishonoured.)

EXAMINING THE CHEQUE

In deciding whether to pay a cheque or not, it is necessary for the bank officer to examine the item to see that it is technically in order and also to consider other aspects. This work involves the consideration of:

The date

A cheque which is dated in the future should not be paid,[24] for until such time the account cannot legally be debited, and in the intervening period the funds could be withdrawn, or an event could take place, such as the death or bankruptcy of the drawer, which would prevent the entry on the due date. It is also possible that the cheque could be stopped. Moreover, if a postdated cheque were paid, and other cheques were to be dishonoured which would otherwise have been paid because there should have been covering funds, the bank could find itself sued for substantial damages. Any cheque therefore which is dated in the future after the day upon which is presented should be returned to the presenting bank or the presenter, with the answer 'Postdated'.

Conversely, a cheque can become 'stale',[25] but this is a matter of treatment and custom; most banks, however, allow a period of six months after the date of issue before dishonouring a cheque with the answer 'Out of date'. It might of course be possible to obtain the confirmation of the drawer that payment is in order, and if so then the return of the cheque can be avoided.

If a cheque is returned as stale, the drawer remains liable on the cheque for six years from its date, but any endorser will be discharged if there has been an unreasonable delay in the cheque being presented for payment.

Occasionally, in the early weeks of a new year bankers find themselves presented with cheques which prima facie have been in circulation for over a year, but where in fact the customer has inadvertently dated the cheque with the wrong year. Most banks take a practical view and pay such cheques, and little harm seems to come from this established practice.

The payee

If the cheque is not paybale to bearer, the payee must be named or otherwise indicated with reasonable certainty, although he may not be known to the drawee bank. The cheque may be payable to two or more payees jointly, or it may be made payable in the alternative to one of two, or to one or some of several payees, although this is unusual. A cheque or bill of exchange may also be made payable to the holder of an office for the time being, and if the payee is a fictitious or non-existent person it may be treated as payable to bearer.

Cheques are sometimes drawn payable to impersonal payees, such as 'Cash' and 'Wages' and it has been held that these are not strictly cheques, nor bills of exchange, as neither payee is 'a specified person' or 'bearer', as required by ss. 3 and 7(i) Bills of Exchange Act 1882. Banks generally will only encash such items for the drawer in person or his known agent. It is felt that it would be risky to treat the cheques with an impersonal payee as payable to bearer, although if the person whom the drawer actually intended receives the money then little harm is likely to come to the paying or collecting banker even if the

24 See Appendix 1, Q. 22 (September 1982).
25 See Appendix I, Q. 22 (September 1982).

cheque is not endorsed by the drawer himself (*North and South Insurance Corporation Ltd* v. *National Provincial Bank Ltd* (1936)).

The bank should not pay a cheque which has been altered from an 'order' cheque (e.g. 'Pay John Smith or order') to a 'bearer' cheque ('Pay John Smith or bearer') unless the drawer has signed the alteration. Some banks might be prepared to accept the drawer's initials, but of course, these are easier to forge than a full signature.

Occasionally the payee will be another customer of the same branch, and the cheque will be paid in over the drawee bank's own counter. In such a case, the drawee bank acts both as collecting and paying banker, and he has dual responsibilities to each customer.

The amount

To meet the requirements of the Bills of Exchange Act 1882 the amount must be in writing (words), but for practical and accounting purposes the amount in figures is likely to be the sum in which the cheque has been handled through the clearing system. To protect himself, the paying banker must ensure that there is no discrepancy beteen the amount in words and figures, and if there is then he may dishonour the cheque with the answer 'Words and figures differ'. Sometimes a bank may be prepared to pay the smaller amount on the cheque, if that is the amount claimed by the payee or the presenting bank.

One of the dangers encountered by the paying banker is where the amount on the cheque has been altered between the date on which it was signed and the time of presentation. Also, fraud can be facilitated where spaces have been left for the amount in words and figures and the cheque has effectively been blank when signed by the drawer. From the banker's point of view however the legal position is clear, as s. 20(i) of the Bills of Exchange Act 1882 gives the person in possession the authority to fill up any omission in any way he thinks fit, and where a banker is good faith pays such a cheque he may debit his customer's account with the amount, notwithstanding that the cheque has been filled in contrary to the intentions or instructions of the drawer. The drawer is then estopped from denying that the cheque represents his mandate as presented.

In drawing his cheques a customer is under a duty of care not to mislead the bank, or to facilitate fraud, and in the leading case on this aspect it was said that if a customer signs a cheque in blank, and leaves it to another person to complete it, then be becomes bound by the instrument as completed by his agent. The leading case of *London Joint Stock Bank Ltd* v. *Macmillan and Arthur* (1918) examined a situation where the drawer had signed a cheque for £2 (in figures) but the amount in words had been omitted. The cheque was payable to the firm itself, or bearer, and had been prepared by a clerk employed by the firm. This deceitful individual then inserted the figures '1' and '0' before and after the '2', and completed the amount in words as 'One hundred and twenty pounds'. He then cashed the cheque for that larger amount. Upon discovering the fraud, the customers sued the bank for overdebiting their account £118. The case reached the House of Lords, where it was held that the customer is under a special duty to the bank when drawing his cheques, and must take reasonable and ordinary precautions to prevent forgery. On the facts of the case the Law Lords found that there had been a breach of that duty, and the bank was therefore entitled to debit the account with the increased amount, i.e. £120.

It should be noted, however, that this decision was based on a non-apparent alteration. Where there is an alteration which is apparent, and which has not been authenticated, the bank would not be successful in pleading the Macmillan defence.

The decision in this case relating to the raising of the amounts on cheques was unsuccessfully invoked in *Slingsby* v. *District Bank Ltd* (1932), where a space had been left between the name of the payee and the words 'or order'. This had enabled a fraudulent solicitor to insert the words, 'per Cumberbirch & Potts', the name of his firm, and by these means he was able to obtain the proceeds of the cheque for himself. Upon trial, it was held that the form of the words 'pay A B per C D', which was unknown to the drawer, was not in sufficiently common usage as to make it unreasonable or negligent conduct on the part of the drawer in leaving such a space. In other words, it was not customary to draw a line after the name of the payee to prevent such a fraud; it may be noted however that some banks now recommend such a step, in their printed guideline notes on a cheque book cover. Strictly, and leaving aside the Macmillan decision, in cases where the amount in words and figures has been altered to increase the amount, the banker cannot debit his customer's account with the amount paid, because any material alteration without the authority of the drawer makes the cheque void. Additionally, the cheque is a mandate to pay a sum certain in money, and the banks have paid a different sum. The fact that no reasonable examination of a cheque could have revealed the alteration does not assist the bank's position, unless it can be proved that the drawer had been negligent. It would seem therefore that technically the banker cannot even debit his customer with the original amount of the cheque, although in practice few such claims are encountered. It may be noted also that where a cheque has been materially altered all parties cease to be liable on it, except the party who himself altered it or assented to or authorised the alteration, or unless that party is an endorser subsequent to the alteration (s. 64, Bills of Exchange Act 1882).

The crossing (if any)

If a cheque is not crossed, it is an 'open' cheque, and there is no restriction placed on it by the drawer as regards a holder being given cash by the drawee bank upon the cheque being presented. Crossed cheques should not be cashed unless the drawee bank is absolutely certain that the true owner is being paid, as for example where the drawer presents the cheque himself to make a withdrawal, or the withdrawal is made by his known agent, such as his wife, who calls regularly to obtain money from the bank and there is an established safe practice.

Section 76 Bills of Exchange Act 1882 enacts:

(1) Where a cheque bears across its face an addition of –

(a) The words 'and company' or any abbreviation thereof between two parallel transverse lines, either with or without the words 'not negotiable'; or,

(b) Two parallel transverse lines simply either with or without the words 'not negotiable',
that addition constitutes a crossing, and the cheque is crossed generally.

(2) Where a cheque bears across its face an addition of the name of a banker, either with or without the words 'not negotiable', that addition constitutes a crossing, and the cheque is crossed specially and to that banker.

Section 77 provides as to the party who may cross a cheque, or add to the crossing:

(1) A cheque may be crossed generally or specially by the drawer.

(2) Where a cheque is uncrossed, the holder may cross it generally or specially.

(3) Where a cheque is crossed generally the holder may cross it specially.

(4) Where a cheque is crossed generally or specially, the holder may add the words 'not negotiable'.

(5) Where a cheque is crossed specially, the banker to whom it is crossed may again cross it specially to another banker for collection.

(6) Where an uncrossed cheque, or a cheque crossed generally, is sent to a banker for collection, he may cross it specially to himself.

Thus a complete system of crossings can be built up by various persons – e.g. a holder of a cheque crossed 'generally' by the drawer may cross it 'specially'; the next holder may add the words 'not negotiable'; a cheque sent to a banker for collection, whether uncrossed or crossed generally, may be crossed by the banker specially to himself. Under the Act, any one of the crossings is a material part of the cheque, so that an obliteration, addition, or altertion will make the cheque void, unless the additions or alterations are authorized by the Act (s. 78).

It is a general rule that the liability of a banker is to his customer but under s. 79 there is liability to a third party, the 'true owner', as follows:

(1) Where a cheque is crossed specially to more than one banker, except when crossed to an agent for collection being a banker, the banker on whom it is drawn shall refuse payment therof.

(2) Where the banker on whom a cheque is drawn which is so crossed nevertheless pays the same, or pays a cheque crossed generally otherwise than to a banker, or if crossed specially otherwise than to the banker to whom it is crossed, or his agent for collection being a banker, he is liable to the true owner of the cheque for any loss he may sustain owing to the cheque having been so paid.

Provided that where a cheque is presented for payment which does not at the time of presentment appear to be crossed, or to have a crossing which has been obliterated, or to have been added to or altered otherwise than as authorised by this Act, the banker paying the cheque in good faith and without negligence shall not be responsible or incur any liability, nor shall the payment be questioned by reason of the cheque having been crossed, or of the crossing having been obliterated or having been added to or altered otherwise than as authorized by this Act, and of payment having been made otherwise than to a banker or to the banker to whom the cheque is or was crossed, or to his agent for collection being a banker, as the case may be.

If a cheque is presented crossed to two banks, the cheque should only be paid if one of the banks is the agent of the other. It is also clear from the provisions of s. 79 that a banker should not pay cash over the counter for a crossed cheque unless he is absolutely satisfied as to the identity of the payee, because where a crossed cheque has been paid to someone who has stolen it, the bank is liable to the true owner for the amount of the cheque and he cannot debit his customer's account because he has ignored the mandate of the customer. However, the paying banker is protected by s. 80, as follows:

Where the banker, on whom a crossed cheque is drawn, in good faith and without negligence pays it, if crossed generally, to a banker, and if crossed specially, to the banker to whom it is crossed, or his agent for collection being a banker, the banker paying the cheque and, if the cheque has come into the hands of the payee, the drawer, shall respectively be entitled to the same rights and be placed in the same position as if payment of the cheque had been made to the true owner therof.

Section 81 of the Act provides:

Where a person takes a crossed cheque which bears on it the words 'not negotiable', he shall not have and shall not be capable of giving a better title to the cheque than that which the person from whom he took it had.

To illustrate this let us imagine that a cheque to 'bearer' or one to 'order' bearing a genuine endorsement which is crossed 'not negotiable' is stolen. The thief has it cashed by a publican who has acted in complete good faith in doing so. Nevertheless the publican obtains no better title than the thief, and he cannot retain the cheque as against the true owner, and if payment of it is stopped he cannot sue the drawer. Thus the cheque has been deprived of its negotiability but it is still transferable.

Often a cheque is crossed 'Account payee' or 'Account payee only'. It should be remembered however that these words do not appear in the Bills of Exchange Act 1882 and the paying banker may ignore them so long as he pays a cheque in accordance with the protection afforded by s. 80 of the Act. The legal decisions show that the words 'Account payee' should be regarded as being addressed to the collecting banker, as it would be impossible for the paying banker to satisfy himself that the account of the payee had in fact been credited unless the same branch of the bank was both paying and collecting the cheque.

It can be seen therefore that the purpose in crossing a cheque is to afford proctection for the drawer and subsequent holders, and the fraudulent encashment of a cheque becomes less likely. A fraudster would have to pay a crossed cheque into a bank account, and this would provide a fuller record of the transaction, enabling the thief or fraudster to be traced. Because of the time taken to clear a cheque, the possibility of discovery before the proceeds are paid away is increased, and the drawer might be able to stop payment. The 'not negotiable' crossing is particularly useful in protecting the drawer himself from having or incurring any unexpected obligations on the cheque to a future holder.

The signature(s)

The bank officer paying the cheque should both recognize the signature(s) and know or ensure that there are sufficient signatures from the correct parties or officials, if the account is not simply in a sole name. If the cheque is drawn by a limited company, for example, the full name of the company should appear, and the bank must ensure that the mandate it holds, however amended from time to time, now authorizes the parties purporting to act, as being those whose signatures it may accept.

It will be understood therefore that a bank cannot debit its customer's account if it pays a cheque on which the customer's signature has been forged, as a forged cheque is not the mandate of the customer, and under the provisions of s. 24 of the Bills of Exchange Act 1882 is 'wholly inoperative'. If a bank has debited its customer's account wrongly then it is more than likely that it will have to refund the monies, and adjust any bank charges.

Any action against the bank for paying on a forged signature can be based on breach of mandate, conversion and negligence. The drawer's signature on the cheque must be his own or that of someone authorized by him, and if the bank is doubtful about the genuineness of the signature and is unable to obtain the drawer's confirmation or otherwise, then the cheque should be returned to the collecting banker with the answer 'Signature(s) differ(s)'.

However, certain defences may be possible if a bank is sued by the drawer for damages for payment of a forged cheque. The drawer may be estopped or precluded from asserting that his signature has been forged or made without his authority. This may arise from express representation by the customer that the signature on the cheque is his or her own, as where the paying banker, being in doubt, referred cheques to the customer, who informed him that all was in order. Later, when sued by the customer's son, acting under a power of attorney, for reimbursement of 329 cheques allegedly forged by his mother's servant, the bank admitted that 100 cheques were forged but succeeded in avoiding liability, as it had repeatedly asked the customer if the signature was her own and she had always 'confirmed' that it was. Thus she and the agent under the power of attorney were estopped in the action, not only in respect of those cheques drawn before the enquiries but also in respect of those paid afterwards (*Brown* v. *Westminster Bank Ltd* (1964)).

Again, estoppel may arise through the breach by a customer of his duty to his banker to inform him that he has discovered that his signature is being forged, with the result that the banker loses his right against the forger. If the customer fails in this duty, he represents, in effect, that subsequent signatures are genuine, although forged, and he will be estopped or legally barred from contending against the bank that payment should not have been made on such signatures. This is clearly illustrated in *Greenwood* v. *Martins Bank Ltd* (1933), which went to the Court of Appeal and later to the House of Lords. There it was emphasized that there was a duty on the part of the customer, if he became aware that forged cheques were being presented, to inform the bank in order that loss might be avoided in the future. The facts were that Mrs Greenwood had forged her husband's signature on cheques purporting to be drawn by him. Mr Greenwood discovered this, but did not tell the bank, simply warning his wife not to do it again. Later, after his wife had committed suicide, Mr Greenwood sought to obtain reimbursement from the bank, but failed because of his delay in informing the bank, which delay had prevented the bank from seeking redress from the forger, because of her subsequent death.

If a cheque is presented to a banker, and he returns it because it is forged, then the banker is under a duty to report this fact to his customer, to enable him to enquire into the matter and protect himself for the future. This corresponds with the duty of the customer that if he becomes aware that forged cheques are being presented to the bank he ought to inform the banker in order that the bank may avoid loss in the future.

Another possible defence available to the banker who has paid cheques on forged signatures is that of 'contributory negligence' on the part of the customer, although to date there has been no case decided on this point in a bank's favour. Everything will depend upon the facts, if and when the law is tested again, and at present the only precedent is not in favour of banks, viz. *Lewes Sanitary Steam Laundry Co. Ltd* v. *Barclay Bevan & Co. Ltd* (1906), where the company employed a known forger and had allowed him to sign with another person (whose signature he then forged!) on the company's account!! As recently as 1983 in *Wealden Woodlands (Kent) Ltd* v. *National Westminster Bank Ltd* the bank lost an action brought by its customer for reimbursement of cheques paid outside the mandate, where one director's signature had been forged by the other who also signed on the account. The monies had been paid to another business in which the forger had an interest, and the bank failed to persuade the court that the company itself had been negligent in failing to spot the forgeries after bank statements had been sent to it. Similar principles were followed in *Tai Hing Cotton Mill* v. *Liu Chong Hing Bank Ltd* (1985).

However, in certain circumstances a bank may still be able to charge its customer's account with cheques not properly drawn, if the court will accept, in any action brought by the drawer for reimbursement, that the drawer has not suffered as a result of payment of the cheques. For example, if X Ltd operates an account on which Mr A and Mr B should both sign as directors, but the bank, albeit wrongly, has paid cheques signed by Mr A alone, then provided the monies have been used genuinely to meet the company's liabilities, it would be wrong in equity for the company to succeed in its action. This is an example of the application of the principle seen in *B. Liggett (Liverpool) Ltd* v. *Barclays Bank Ltd* (1928).

It may be noted in passing that as the practice of having printed facsimile signatures on cheques is increasing, particularly in the case of dividend and interest warrants, before agreeing to this a bank should ensure it is given a suitable indemnity covering the bank against the risks involved.

Meanwhile, as we consider the drawer's signature to a cheque, it may be timely to note the recent flurry of activity in the Courts in connection with s. 349(4) Companies Act 1985.[26] Thus where the full name of a limited company is not correctly shown any officer or any person on the company's behalf who 'signs or authorizes to be signed on behalf of the company any bill of exchange, promissory note, endorsement, cheque, or order for money or goods in which the company's name is not mentioned . . . is personally liable to the holder . . . (unless it is duly paid by the company)' – see *British Airways Board* v. *Parish* (1979) and *Maxform SpA* v. *Mariani and Goodville Ltd* (1979). This means that if the bank dishonoured a cheque then a holder might be able to sue the signatories themselves if the company's full name did not appear as drawer. Perhaps of more concern to a bank is not the liability of the party who signs, but the risk that the bank itself could be drawn into any action if it had been careless in preparing printed cheques which did not accurately reflect the true name of the company customer.

Has the customer stopped payment?

This question, which the cancelling officer must be able to answer in the negative, is necessary because of the provisions of s. 75 Bills of Exchange Act 1882, which states that the duty and authority of a banker to pay a cheque drawn on him by his customer are otherwise determined.

From time to time banks have suffered losses by ignoring their customers' instructions to stop payment of cheques, usually because internal records on a 'stop' card have not been checked before payment of a cheque, although in more recent times it has been possible to program the computer which acts as a back-up.

The loss and danger to the bank arises not only because the customer's account must be refunded and charges adjusted but because it is usually too late to return the cheque unpaid. However, if goods have been acquired, the bank could insist on these being handed over to it, and then proceed to sell them to reduce its loss. Another danger to the bank is that, because of the depleted balance in the account,[27] other cheques presented subsequently might

26 See Appendix I, Q. 5 (September 1980).
27 See Appendix I, Q. 8 (September 1980).

possibly be wrongly dishonoured, and if so that would leave the bank wide open to an action for damages.

However, in *Barclays Bank Ltd* v. *W. J. Simms, Son & Cooke (Southern) Ltd and W. Sowman* (1979), a decision was reached which can, in appropriate circumstances, offer some hope of recovery for a bank which pays a stopped cheque.[28] A housing association, customers of Barclays Bank, drew a cheque for £24 000 in favour of Simms, Son & Cooke, a building company which was carrying out contract work for them. On the following day National Westminster Bank, bankers to Simms, Son & Cooke, appointed a receiver, under powers in their debenture, and the receiver received the cheque through the post and paid it into his bank account, asking for special clearance. However, by this time, the housing association had learnt of the appointment of the receiver, and was concerned that future work due under the contract would not be carried out; to protect its position it stopped the cheque by telephoning its bankers, Barclays. The telephone conversation took place on 15 September, but on the following day Barclays overlooked the stop instructions, despite having programmed their computer, and the cheque was paid.

Later, recognizing that they had no mandate from their customer to debit its account, Barclays reimbursed the housing association, but then, in a step which was new, called upon the receiver to repay. He refused, and Barclays then sued the receiver and the company in respect of which he was agent.

In giving judgment, the court examined the rights of parties involved in a situation where money had been paid under a mistake of fact and held that where a person has paid money to another under a mistake of fact he is entitled, prima, facie, to recover it, although his claims might fail on three grounds. These were that if the payer had intended that the payee should have the money whatever the circumstances then the payer could not recover. Secondly, if the payment were in respect of the discharge of a debt owed to the payee by the payer or by a third party who was authorized to discharge the debt, the payer could not recover. Thirdly, if the payee had changed his position in good faith, or in law was deemed to have changed his position, recovery would not be possible.

The court examined the bank's oversight in not acting upon its customer's stop order and recognized that it is an everyday hazard that customers' instructions may be overlooked. Moreover the court understood that modern technology had if anything increased the risk of overlooking a customer's instructions. In the circumstances of this case the court felt that the bank was entitled to recover unless the payee had changed his position in good faith. As neither the receiver nor the company had changed their positions, Barclays were able to recover the monies wrongly paid over.

In *Baines* v. *National Provincial Bank Ltd* (1927) the plaintiff, a customer of

28   See Appendix I, Q. 28 (April 1983).

the bank, sought reimbursement of the amount debited to his account by a cheque issued shortly before the bank closed for business, in the belief that the payee would not be able to obtain clearance that day. However the payee had paid in the cheque at a nearby sub-branch and the cheque was paid when the sub-branch clerk returned to the main office. Consequently, when on the next morning, the customer's messenger gave the bank instructions to countermand payment, it was already too late.[29] However the plaintiff claimed that in paying the cheque after its advertised closing time the bank had not paid 'in the ordinary course of business'. This argument was not accepted by the court which recognized that 'a reasonable period' is necessary after closing time for a bank to complete its work.

Often, the instructions for stopping payment are received by telephone and it is preferable that the customer should be asked to confirm in writing, giving the number and date of the cheque, the amount and the name of the payee. Some banks rely on the doctrine of estoppel however, and if the customer stops payment by telephone then they confirm the instructions to the customer in writing that day by post. On the basis that the customer does not object, he is then deemed to have prevented himself from claiming that he had not countermanded payment orally earlier.

It should be noted that one party to a joint account or partnership can stop payment of a cheque signed by another party but that removal of a 'stop' in such circumstances should be by all signatories, to prevent dispute.

One of the major cases on stopped cheques is that of *Curtice* v. *London City and Midland Bank Ltd* (1908). Here the facts were that the drawer stopped payment of his cheque by telegram, which, unfortunately, was delivered into the letter box of the bank after it had closed. Moreover, the next morning when the box was emptied, the telegram was not extracted, and upon the drawer suing the bank, after the cheque was paid, the court found in the bank's favour, on the basis that the notice had not effectively reached it when it paid the cheque. Also the judge said: '. . . I am not satisfied that the bank is bound as a matter of law to accept an unauthenticated telegram as sufficient authority for the serious step of refusing to pay a cheque'. Even so, today it would not be safe to pay a cheque after receiving any unauthenticated message and the best way ahead would be to return the cheque with the answer: 'Payment postponed; confirmation of countermand awaited'.

In any stop instructions the number of the cheque is very important. In *Westminster Bank Ltd* v. *Hilton* (1926) a simple mistake by the customer resulted in an action against the bank which went to the House of Lords, from which the legal position would appear to be that if there is ambiguity, and the banker reasonably and honestly interprets his customer's instructions contrary to the customer's intention, then the banker is not liable for any loss which may result.

---

29 See Appendix I, Q. 13 (September 1981).

Here Mr Hilton stopped a post-dated cheque which he had issued, but in error he gave number 117283, instead of 117285. When the cheque was presented, as the number differed, and as the other details were identical, the bank assumed that it was dealing with a duplicate issued later, as inferred by the numerical sequence; the bank therefore paid the cheque, as it had been unable to contact the customer to check on the facts. Later it returned other cheques for shortage of funds, and was then sued for alleged wrongful dishonour, and for paying more monies without mandate on the stopped item. As indicated, the action failed. Part of Lord Shaw's judgment is worth noting:

> When a banker is in possession of sufficient funds to meet such a cheque from a customer the duty of the bank is to honour that cheque by payment and failure in this duty may involve the bank in serious liability to its customers. This duty is ended and on the contrary when the cheque is stopped another duty arises namely to refuse payment. In a case of that character it rests upon the customer to prove that the order to stop reached the bank in time and was unequivocal to a cheque then in existence and signed and issued by the customer prior to the notice to stop.

Thus any countermand must be sent to the branch of the bank where the drawer keeps his account or it will be ineffective. Even so, if the wrong branch to which the stop order is sent knows the particular branch where the account is kept, it should immediately telephone that branch informing them of the stop and giving full details. In the same way, where other branches have been authorized to cash cheques for a customer it is advisable to inform them also of the countermand, especially where the payee regularly receives cheques from the customer and cashes them at a particular branch.

One of the first 'computer' cases to be considered was *Burnett* v. *Westminster Bank Ltd* (1965). Mr Burnett had two accounts, one at Borough branch and one at Bromley branch. He wished to draw a cheque on the Bromley branch and for this purpose he used a form from his Borough branch cheque book, altering the cheque by substituting the name and address of the Bromley branch and initialling the alterations. Later he wished to stop payment and he telephoned the *Bromley* branch and instructed it to stop payment of the cheque, giving the number of the cheque and stating that it was on a Borough cheque form altered to Bromley. These details were confirmed in writing. However, the clerk overlooked the implications of the background and as the bank's computer could not 'read' the alterations, which were in ordinary ink, the cheque passed through the clearing house to the *Borough* branch where it was paid. Mr Burnett sued the bank for a declaration that he was entitled to be recredited with the amount of the cheque and the court found for him, placing reliance on the customer's written authority and the absence of any warning to customers (such as on a cheque book cover, when a book was issued) not to 'interchange' cheques between branches and accounts.

The position is further complicated if the payee has negotiated the cheque to another party who can claim to be a holder in due course. While the bank would return the cheque in the ordinary way with the answer 'Orders not to pay', the holder in due course would be able successfully to sue the drawer for the amount. Of course no direct action is possible at the instance of a payee who is a holder for value, against the bank on which the cheque is drawn and which has refused payment because of the countermand. However, if the payee had paid the cheque into his bank account to reduce an overdraft, the collecting bankers may be holders in due course and entitled to sue the drawer for the amount, even if he has countermanded payment.

Has notice of the drawer's death been received?

Section 75 Bills of Exchange Act 1882 deals not only with the countermand of payment, but also with the bank's position on receiving notice of the customer's death. Put simply, the authority to pay a cheque drawn on the bank is then revoked. It is the *notice* of death which gives the bank authority to return the customer's cheques, so that cheques paid after the date of the death of the customer, but before notice of the fact had reached the banker, present no problem. 'Notice' is usually received in the form of a letter or telephone call from a near relative, or perhaps even from an article or entry in a newspaper. In all cases, it is effective notice and the bank should regard its mandate as cancelled, although in due course it will wish to see the death certificate. A suitable letter of condolence to the next of kin may be thought desirable. Cheques presented thereafter should be returned with the answer 'Drawer deceased'.

Has the bank notice of any other operation of law which would prevent payment?

In the main, events which will determine the bank's authority to pay further cheques are seen in bankruptcy and liquidation situations or when there is mental incapacity on the part of the drawer. For the sake of ease, these situations have been examined in detail elsewhere under the relevant sections of this book. Also, injunctions and their effect are examined in Chapter 5. A variety of situations can be encountered, and the question in our sub-heading is therefore an important one, for if cheques are paid when they should have been returned, eventually the customer will claim reimbursement and this will be costly to the bank.

Has the bank notice – direct or constructive – of a breach of trust?

The obligation of a banker in respect of trust funds had been stated by Hart in his *Law of Banking* in the following terms: 'A banker who receives into his possession, monies of which his customer has, to his knowledge, become the owner in a fiduciary capacity, contracts the duty not to part with them, *even at the mandate of his customer*, for purposes which he *knows* are inconsistent with the customer's fiduciary character and duty'. In 1978 this principle was seen clearly in the ruling against the bank in *Rowlandson* v. *National Westminster Bank Ltd*, where the court held that once a bank has opened what is clearly a trust account, it is under a fiduciary duty to the beneficiaries of the trust and is liable to them if it assists in a dishonest or fraudulent design on the part of the trustees. In this case the bank had failed to prevent or even question certain withdrawals which should have put them on enquiry and it was accordingly held accountable to the trust beneficiaries.

This was only one of a series of cases, and over the years bankers have lost money when they have paid cheques drawn by their customers which have involved transactions where the drawer has been acting in breach of the duty of trust imposed upon him. Actions for reimbursement by the bank, although not directly liable, have been brought by the beneficiaries or those on whose behalf the customer was acting as agent, presumably in the almost certain belief that the bank is a safer body to sue financially than the fraudulent trustee himself!

Several cases examined by the courts have seemed fairly simple and clear cut – as in *Foxton* v. *Manchester and Liverpool District Banking Co.* (1881), where an executor reduced his own personal overdraft by transferring funds from the executor's account. Clearly the bank itself derived some benefit from this transaction, and the circumstances were such that it could reasonably have been expected to know what was being done. However, a rather worrying development for bankers was the extension of this area of law seen in *Selangor United Rubber Estates Ltd* v. *Cradock & Others* (1968). In this case the bank derived no benefit, but became liable because it was held that even in a complicated situation it *should* have known that directors of a limited company were acting in breach of section of the Companies Act to the detriment of the company's creditors and the shareholders, i.e. they were behaving in breach of their fiduciary capacity as directors (see also in *Baden Delvaux* (1983) discussed on pages 47 and 55).

Are there sufficient funds or unused overdraft facilities to meet the cheque?

In the absence of an agreement to allow a customer to overdraw his account the banker is under no obligation to pay a customer's cheques, where the customer has insufficient funds to the credit of his account. Also, where an overdraft limit has been fixed, the banker need not pay cheques which would increase the amount of the overdraft beyond the agreed limit. If the balance is insufficient to meet the cheques and it has been decided to return them, the answer on the cheques should be 'Refer to drawer', or 'Refer to drawer – please re-present', if there is a possibility of monies being received in the short term which might facilitate payment of cheques drawn. However, care should be taken if cheques have been paid in the past which have in effect meant that the overdraft has from time to time risen to more than the strict amount of the agreed facility. By such a course of conduct it could be implied that the bank was prepared to pay cheques; and therefore to dishonour one later, without warning, could possibly lead to a difficult situation developing between the customer and the bank.

In determining the extent of funds available, care must be taken in examining credit balances on accounts other than those on which the cheque is drawn, for these may not be available for set-off, being held in trust or not solely in the name of the drawer.

It is also understood that a banker may return his customer's cheque where it is drawn against cheques paid in earlier but still in course of clearing, the answer being 'Effects not cleared'. Again, some difficulty may arise with the customer if the banker has been in the habit of allowing him to draw against uncleared cheques, and if this has been the practice the banker should give reasonable notice to his customer that the customer should not assume in future that such cheques will be paid until the cheques credited to the account have been cleared.

Sometimes banks fail to consider whether the monies in the account represent cleared funds, and unscrupulous customers engage in 'cross-firing', or 'teeming and lading', or 'kite-flying' as it is sometimes called. This means that to disguise the true state of the account, A, they pay in cheques specially drawn by themselves or their associates on another account, B, at another bank, to inflate the apparent balance. After three or four days they draw a cheque on account A and pay it into account B on which the first cheques were drawn. This operation takes advantage of clearing time, and they continually repeat the process before cheques are presented. Consequently to the unobservant banker who is relying merely on the *ledger* balance, and not the true *cleared* balance, the account appears to be operating in credit, or within an agreed borrowing facility. In fact, the proper position is quite different. If a non-clearing bank is involved the dangers can be increased, when clearing time takes more than the usual four days. With an extensive chain of persons operating, large uncleared positions can thus be built up, and sooner or later one bank will spot the danger and dishonour cheques; this can have a dramatic effect on the position of the banker to whom the cheques are returned. Cross-firing can be discovered by noticing the increased and unexpected turnover through an account, or by the alertness of a cashier who sees cheques being paid in for 'round amounts', often drawn by the same person. Cross-firing is a criminal offence, and over the years banks have lost large sums as a result of it.

There is, however, one set of circumstances when the bank is obliged to pay a cheque, even if the customer is short of funds, and that is when it has been drawn against a cheque guarantee card, and all the terms upon which the card has been issued have been met.[30] The extent to which this would be apparent to the paying banker will be by an examination of the front of the cheque to

---

30 See Appendix I, Q. 22 (September 1982).

see that it is technically in order, and the reverse to ensure that it bears a cheque card number written on by a hand, presumably the payee's, other than the drawer's. The bank is then under an implied contract to the payee to meet the cheque, whatever the state of the account and even, it appears, if an injunction has intervened (*Z Ltd* v. *A-Z and AA-LL* (1981)). Presumably on the same basis, even if a bankruptcy order has been made, the bank must pay the cheque, and hope that the trustee in bankruptcy will allow the bank to claim in the estate. (For a fuller discussion of cheque guarantee cards see p. 91f.)

Does the cheque require endorsement?

At this stage of our examination of the paying banker's role, the writer will presume that his readers already possess a good working knowledge of the Bills of Exchange Act 1882 as it applies to endorsements and as learnt in his previous studies for the Institute of Bankers' examinations in the Law Relating to Banking subject. What will therefore be discussed now are those practical situations where endorsement becomes a matter of importance for the paying banker: fortunately, since 1957 and the passing of the Cheques Act in that year, such occasions have become few. For sake of ease we shall look at cheques cashed over the counter and then those paid when presented through the clearing, or handed in for collection by another customer but drawn on the same branch.

CHEQUES ENCASHED

The Cheques Act 1957 was enacted to relieve bankers of the tedium of examining endorsements, which prior to that year were required on all cheques. Section 1 states:

> Where a banker in good faith and in the ordinary course of business pays a cheque drawn on him which is not indorsed or is irregularly indorsed, he does not, in doing so, incur any liability by reason only of the absence of, or irregularity in, indorsement, and he is deemed to have paid it in due course.
>
> Where a banker in good faith and in the ordinary course of business pays any such instrument as the following, namely –
>
> (a) a document issued by a customer of his which, though not a bill of exchange, is intended to enable a person to obtain payment from him of the sum mentioned in the document;
>
> (b) a draft payable on demand drawn by him upon himself, whether payable at the head office or some other office of his bank; he does not, in doing so, incur any liability by reason only of the absence of, or irregularity in, indorsement, and the payment discharges the instrument.

Section 3 enacts:

> An unendorsed cheque which appears to have been paid by the banker on whom it is drawn is evidence of the receipt by the payee of the sum payable by the cheque.

Despite the provisions of s. 1, the Committee of London Clearing Bankers decided that as some protection for the public and deterrent against frauds was desirable, its member banks would still continue to require endorsements on cheques encashed, in those cases where endorsements had been required prior to the passing of the Act. This meant that 'bearer' cheques, and, dependent on previous practice, cheques payable to 'cash', would still need signatures on the back of the cheque and which would purport to be in order. Such signatures need not necessarily be made in the presence of the cashier, although some banks might require their cashiers to see the presenter sign in the cashier's presence. However, as proof of identity is not necessary, little is achieved by that rule.

It follows therefore that provided the endorsement appears to be in order (e.g. a cheque payable to A. Smith is endorsed 'A. Smith' or if payable to Alan Smith is endorsed 'Alan Smith' or 'A. Smith') and the bank acts in good faith, then it is falling in line with established banking practices, and can rely on s. 1 Cheques Act 1957 which covers cases of no endorsements or an irregular endorsement. Also available is the protection of s. 60 Bills of Exchange Act 1882, if the bank pays money to a person who is not entitled to it, and it can debit its customer's account provided the requirements of that section are met. Section 60 states:

> When a bill payable to order on demand is drawn on a banker, and the banker on whom it is drawn pays the bill in good faith and in the ordinary course of business, it is not incumbent on the banker to show that the endorsement of the payee or any subsequent endorsement was made by or under the authority of the person whose endorsement it purports to be, and the banker is deemed to have paid the bill in due course, although such endorsement has been forged or made without authority.

Thus the bank is protected if the endorsement is forged or unauthorized. A charge of acting without 'good faith' is not one that is likely to be brought against a bank and it will be recalled that s. 90 Bills of Exchange Act 1882 states that a thing is done 'in good faith' where it is done honestly whether it is done negligently or not. What is 'the ordinary course of business' is a matter of fact and practice, but presumably the encashment of a cheque well outside normal opening hours would not fall in any definition. The protection of s. 60 is not available where the cheque has been altered in a material particular, as for example where a cheque payable to 'X' was altered by the addition of the words 'per Y & Co.' and paid on Y's endorsement (*Slingsby* v. *District Bank Ltd* (1931)). The Act would not apply where the bank cashed a crossed cheque for a person other than the drawer or his known regular agent.

It may be noticed here that s. 60 does not call for absence of 'negligence', which will be found to be so important when the legal position of the *collecting* banker comes to be discussed.

CHEQUES PRESENTED VIA THE IN GENERAL CLEARING

Nearly all cheques presented in the In General Clearing are unendorsed and the only cheques that a banker need concern himself with, as regards endorsement requirements, are those being a large letter 'R' on the face of the cheque, before the amount in figures. Such cheques incorporate a receipt form on the reverse of the cheque, which is a combined receipt and endorsement, and this must purport to be in order. Such cheques are few, however. Other items requiring endorsement are travellers' cheques, bills of exchange and promissory notes. The protection of s. 60 remains available for such cheques as does s. 80, which protects a bank paying a crossed cheque to a banker in accordance with the crossing in good faith and without negligence. It can be seen therefore that the importance of s. 60 has diminished because if there is no endorsement the question of a forged or unauthorized endorsement cannot arise. Section 80 has never been of great value to the paying banker but remains available, covering crossed cheques, in case of need.

CHEQUES PAID UPON COLLECTION FOR THE PAYEE AT THE DRAWER'S BRANCH

Except where they bear a large letter 'R', cheques collected for the payee who tenders them at the drawee branch need not be endorsed, although the bank should remember that in such circumstances it is both the paying and collecting banker, and has all duties which each of those two roles involves.

It is sometimes asked as to when a cheque paid in over the counter for collection is 'paid'. Fortunately the time is rarely critical, but for practical purposes most bankers agree that the cheque is only '*effectively* paid' when it is processed at the end of the business day and debited to the account, or sooner should its fate be communicated to the presenter. This raises the question of whether a payee can be given an answer, if he asks, when paying in a cheque drawn on the branch, if the cheque is paid, and of course such a cheque may be either open or crossed.

It is the writer's firm view that if asked the paying banker must give an immediate reply, and that, contrary to what is sometimes thought, it is wrong to say that the presenter must wait until the close of business for an answer. (However, it is known that some banks adopt that approach.) If the cheque were an open cheque then the presenter could be given cash, if he so wished, and the author's view is that the crossing is merely the instruction of the drawer to his bank not to pay cash; it is not an instruction to defer an answer. Indeed, to decline to reply or to delay a reply could cast doubt on the drawer's standing. In *Ringham* v. *Hackett & another* (1980) it was decided that it is a misconception that a crossed cheque can only be presented by passing it through a bank account and that the requirements as to presentation under s. 45 Bills of Exchange Act 1882 are met if the payee presents in person, as he is the holder who must present the cheque at the proper place and he is presenting it to the person designated as the payer in accordance with the requirements of the section.

For the same reasons as indicated above, if the cheque is presented specially by a collecting banker in person on behalf of his customer then an answer must be given, and if the cheque is paid then the drawee bank will usually settle by issuing a banker's payment.

However, in those circumstances where a payee merely hands in a cheque for collection and no question is asked, the cheque merely being accepted into the drawee bank's day's work, then, should an event intervene before the close of business, e.g. the making of a bankruptcy order, or the receipt of an injunction, the cheque may be returned unpaid to the payee.

WRONGFUL DISHONOUR

Before the bank dishonours a customer's cheque for shortage of funds, it should be absolutely certain that it is in order to do so, because substantial damages might be awarded against the bank if it wrongfully dishonours a cheque and thereby injures the customer's credit. The customer will be able to base his claim on a breach of the contract between himself and the bank under which the bank undertook to pay cheques properly drawn (*Joachimson* v. *Swiss Bank Corporation* (1921)).

It is wiser, therefore, before actually returning a cheque, to ensure in so far as is possible that a credit has not been misapplied to another account, or that other cheques have not been paid which have been stopped or which are postdated.[31]

In computing the balance available in a customer's account, the bank need not take into reckoning cheques paid in which are still in course of clearing (uncleared effects), unless in the past the bank has agreed specifically or by implication through its conduct to pay cheques so drawn. The implication could arise where previous cheques drawn against uncleareds have always been paid, without any warning to the customer that he must in future ensure that cleared covering funds are available (*A. L. Underwood Ltd* v. *Barclays Bank Ltd* (1924)).

However, if in error a cheque is dishonoured with the answer 'Refer to drawer' or 'Refer to drawer – please re-present' and the mistake is then discovered, the bank should at once take all possible steps to correct matters, both out of common sense, and also because in so doing it will help alleviate the extent of damages which might be awarded in any subsequent court action brought by the drawer. Steps to remedy the situation should include contacting the payee and the presenting banker as soon as possible, by telephone, and then by letter in confirmation. The message should state that

31 See Appendix I, Q. 8 (September 1980).

the cheque should have been paid and the fault lies wholly with the bank and that neither party should construe the events as being any reflection upon the creditworthiness of the drawer. The bank may prefer to obtain the customer's authority to disclose any details which are relevant, and should of course remember that in admitting the error it will be unable to defend an action brought by the customer against it later. However, it will hope to correct matters and limit any damages awarded, as the court will take the bank's conduct into account in assessing the actual loss to the customer.

We are talking here of a genuine error, and it would not be possible for the bank to act in this way if, say, the day after dishonour, the customer had provided covering funds and asked the bank to recall the cheque. In such circumstances, where the dishonour was correct, the drawer must himself explain matters to his payee.

If unhappily, however, an error is not discovered, and later the drawer sues the bank, if a prior settlement cannot be achieved then the court will need to assess the extent of damages.

The normal rule here is that established in *Hadley* v. *Baxendale* (1854) under which the party in breach must pay the amount of damage which flows directly and naturally from his failure to keep his contract, provided that such would reasonably have been within the contemplation of the parties at the time when they made their contract. It is of course difficult to apply this rule to a contract to honour a customer's cheques, because it would only be on very rare occasions that a bank has any knowledge as to the circumstances under which the customer came to be drawing his cheque. For instance, suppose by the wrongful dishonour of an engineering company's cheques the company lost a valuable two-year contract. Would the bank be liable for the whole of the loss of profits? There is little doubt that substantial damages would be awarded in such circumstances, particularly as the customer was a trader. The same would be true in the case of a business man. It is possible that in the case of a non-trading customer, however, only nominal damages would be awarded unless special damages were proved. The smaller the cheque the greater might be the damage to the customer's credit. In *Gibbons* v. *Westminster Bank Ltd* (1939) it was said in the judgment: '. . . a person who is not a trader is not entitled to recover substantial damages unless the damages are alleged and proved as special damages'.

Instead of claiming damages for breach of contract, the injured customer might raise a claim for damages for defamation, based on the words used when the cheque was returned with the answer 'Refer to drawer'. This claim is based on alleged injury to his reputation, by reason of the wording written on the cheque. It has in fact become common practice, in an action for wrongful dishonour and breach of contract, to add a claim for damages for libel. In some of the cases the two claims have been dealt with without differentiations (e.g. *Flach* v. *London and South Western Bank Ltd* (1915)), while in others there have been decisions on both claims. In the Flach case, the judge said the words amounted merely to a statement by the bank, 'We are not paying; go back to the drawer and ask why', or else 'Go back to the drawer and ask him to pay' and he felt that it was not possible to extract a libellous meaning from the words 'Refer to drawer'.

There is a tendency in the more recent cases, however, to regard the words 'Refer to drawer' as being capable of a defamatory meaning and this was seen in *Jayson* v. *Midland Bank Ltd* (1968). Mrs Jayson carried on business as a manufacturer and retailer in ladies' clothes and she claimed damages from the bank for alleged breach of contract and for libel, after her bank wrongfully dishonoured two cheques drawn by her, returning cheques with the answer 'Refer to drawer', thereby lowering her reputation. The bank had agreed an arrangement for an overdraft limited to a maximum amount of £500 and, in defence, maintained that their obligation to pay the cheques was only on condition that the limit was not exceeded and it would have been if the cheques in question had been paid. Mrs Jayson's case was that the bank had agreed to meet the two cheques against her undertaking to pay in £100 during the following week. In an action heard before a jury it agreed in reply to a specific question put to it that the bank's contract was to honour the two cheques, provided Mrs Jayson's net overdraft did not exceed £500 after paying these cheques and that, with regard to the claim for libel, the words 'Refer to drawer' did lower Mrs Jayson's reputation in the minds of right-thinking people. However, when the words were written on the cheques she would have exceeded her agreed limit of £500.

The claim against the bank therefore failed and the bank successfully defended when a appeal to the Court of Appeal was made. The jury's view that the words 'Refer to drawer' could be libellous or defamatory was important, however, and damaging for banking practice.

CHEQUE GUARANTEE CARDS

Cheque guarantee cards have entered into the banking service scene in fairly recent years and now most customers expect to be issued with one as soon as possible after opening an account, so that they will be enabled to issue cheques in payment for goods and services to retail outlets without question. However bankers must be cautious, for in the hands of untrustworthy persons overdrafts can be run up which might be irrecoverable. Consequently most banks have an in-house rule that unless the customer is of particularly high standing they need to have had personal knowledge of his account for six or twelve months before supplying a card. However, exceptions will be made, from time to time, in the interests of marketing, but these should be made in the knowledge of the risks.

A cheque guarantee card is usually made out of plastic and it carries a number which is unique to the holder. This card is signed by the customer when it is issued to him, and it guarantees to a payee of cheques that any cheque drawn by the customer in accordance with the terms printed on the reverse of the card and up to a stated maximum, which is usually £50 in any one transaction, will be paid by the drawee bank upon presentation. It can be seen therefore that the card is a move towards the cashless society and, as well as facilitating purchases for the cardholder, assures the retailer that he will be paid, for the risk of any dishonour of the cheque is obviated, and the cheque cannot be stopped, nor can it be returned for technical reasons. Another advantage to the holder is that he is able to present his own cheques for encashment at other banks and branches without making prior arrangements, as under credit-opened facilities.

When a cheque card is issued to the customer, the latter is asked to sign an agreement form, which states that the card is the property of the bank and will remain so. The customer undertakes to return the card to the bank when requested to do so, and also to advise the bank at once if it is lost or stolen. Usually the customer is advised to carry the card separately from his cheque book, to prevent fraud should both be lost together, and this might be part of the agreement between bank and customer. Again, the bank might wish the customer to agree that the possession of the card does not entitle him to overdraw the account without prior arrangement.

When the card is used it is the terms on the reverse of the card which form the contract between the bank and the payee. The bank therefore will only agree to pay the cheque, within the limit of the amount (£50), provided the cheque is signed in the presence of the payee and provided the signature on the cheque agrees with the specimen on the cheque card. The cheque card and cheque book must bear the same name. Also, the card must not be out of date, and the payee must ensure that the sorting code number on the card also appears on the cheque which is being used. There is then an obligation on the payee to write the unique cheque card number on the reverse of the cheque himself.

After issue, a cheque guarantee card is usually valid for a period of one or two years, and at the end of the time it will be renewed either automatically or upon request.

Understandably, over the years, banks have suffered considerable losses through the misuse of cheque cards, either because their customers have mislaid the trust put in them, or when cards have been lost and have fallen into the hands of fraudsters. As we have seen, great care is taken before a cheque guarantee card is issued for it must be remembered that with a book of thirty cheques a customer has available a credit line of up to £1 500 if he so wishes. If a customer misuses a card and so obtains an unauthorized overdraft, his action is in fact a criminal offence under the Theft Act 1968, following the ruling in *R.* v. *Kòvacs* (1974) and *Metropolitan Police Commissioner* v. *Charles* (1976). In this case it was held that the defendant had dishonestly obtained a pecuniary advantage for himself and that this was an offence under s. 16(1) Theft Act 1968, by misusing his cheque guarantee card when he had issued

twenty-five cheques totalling £750 without having co[...]
account. He had done this in settlement of debts incurre[...]
play at a gaming establishment. Nowadays, however, t[...]
wording on the back of the card, a paying branch will [...]
cheque as only one cheque up to £50 in any one [...]
guaranteed.

Apart from these cases there has been little case law [...]
cheque cards and position of the drawee bank. In consequence, there are
several technical situations which remain unclear regarding the drawee bank's
position. One example is that which obtains should a bankruptcy order be
made and advised to the bank before a cheque is presented drawn against a
cheque card. If the cheque is paid then strictly the amount is not provable in
the bankrupt's estate, but of course the bank must honour the cheque under
its agreement with the payee. Fortunately, the amounts involved in such
issues are small, and any problems are settled in a practical way, without
resort to litigation. A similar dilemma would be presented for the bank had
funds been frozen by receipt of a garnishee order or summons, and a cheque
then been presented guaranteed by a cheque card.

In a case concerning Mareva injunctions, *Z Ltd* v. *A-Z and AA-LL* (1981),
Lord Justice Kerr examined a bank's position when cheques drawn against a
cheque guarantee card were presented for payment after receipt of a Mareva
injunction freezing all monies in the account. He recognized that in such
circumstances there was a previous obligation on the part of the bank to the
third party and saw that this meant that there was an exception to the rule
that the account must remain inoperative; it was his view that the cheque
could be paid to the debit of that account as it related to a transaction carried
out by the customer before the date of the order which was served on the
bank. He commented, however, that normally, where a bank has been served
with a Mareva injunction, it would be advisable for it to withdraw the cheque
guarantee card forthwith.

BANK DRAFTS

Bank drafts are handled similarly to cheques, but because they are drawn by
the bank as drawer they are an attractive means of settling monies owing, as
they provide a near certainty that they will be paid upon presentation.
Consequently, drafts are popular where large sums of money are passing
between parties, particularly where delivery of goods or the transfer of title to
land is concurrent.

A customer requiring to be issued with a draft is usually asked to sign a
draft request form which he completes with details as to the amount and the
name of the payee. The request form will incorporate an authority by the
customer enabling the bank to debit his account. Thereafter the banker will
draw the draft, usually on itself, or another of its branches, as the drawee.

are payable on demand to the named payee or to his order. casionally, a draft will be drawn upon another bank, and an advice is then sent to that bank giving details of the draft issued, and placing it in funds. Drafts should not be made payable to bearer, but only to a specified payee, and usually, unless the customer requests otherwise, they are crossed with the words 'Not negotiable', as this provides further protection should the draft fall into the wrong hands. It is also common practice for a draft to be marked with the words 'Not exceeding . . . pounds', and this is a further attempt to prevent anybody obtaining more than they should, by fraudulently altering the amount of the draft as drawn.

Protection for bankers

In handling drafts, for collection and payment, banks are protected by the same statutes as when handling cheques. Thus, in collecting a draft for a customer who has no title to it, the bank is protected by s. 4 Cheques Act 1957 provided the collection is made in good faith and without negligence, as is the case with a cheque.

In paying drafts, s. 1 Cheques Act 1957 gives a good discharge, whether the draft is crossed or uncrossed and even if it is unendorsed or irregularly endorsed, provided payment is made by the drawee bank in good faith and in the ordinary course of business. Similarly, s. 80 Bills of Exchange Act 1882 protects the paying banker in respect of crossed drafts provided payment is made in good faith, without negligence, and in accordance with the terms of any special crossing. Additionally, s. 19 Stamp Act 1853 provides that a good discharge is obtained when uncrossed drafts are cashed over the bank counter, even should there be a forged endorsement, but provided the draft purports to be endorsed by the payee.

Lost drafts[32]

Occasionally a draft, after issue, is lost, either by the customer or by the payee. The bank could then be requested to stop payment, but usually it would be reluctant to refuse to meet its own paper as this could reflect adversely upon it. However, a practical view can be taken, where a draft has been issued crossed 'Not negotiable', for in such an instance any party in possession of it would have no better title than the payee who has either not received it or else lost the draft himself. A presenting party would in those circumstances almost certainly be involved in fraud. If a bank agrees, on the customer's request, to stop a draft then it is likely that it will first ask the customer to indemnify it against any possible loss which might occur, and in considering these matters the bank will need to know that the customer would be good for the amount involved in case of need.

The loss of a draft invariably means that a duplicate draft is required and

32 See Appendix I, Q. 28 (April 1983).

again the bank's attitude will depend upon the circumstances of the first issue and the loss, and the amount and standing of the parties involved. Probably the bank would prefer to wait for a brief period to see whether the first draft comes to light and is presented for payment and in any event it would need the customer's good indemnity if it were to issue the second instrument.

BANKERS' ORDERS AND DIRECT DEBITS

Bankers' orders, or standing orders, and the direct debit system embody a very helpful service for a customer, under which, having once given a clear written instruction to the bank, he need not thereafter concern himself with a series of regular payments which are then made on their due date to the debit of the account and for the benefit of third parties.

Items commonly seen as the subject-matter of a banker's order, or direct debit, are annual subscriptions to clubs and societies, the payment of rates, instalments due to hire purchase companies and premiums to insurance companies.

Bankers' order

The bank is given a mandate (Fig. 3.1), signed in accordance with the authority to operate the account, which states on which date the specific payments are to be made and in whose favour and to which branch of whatever bank. Care must be exercised by the customer in signing the authority, for if he facilitates fraud and his account is debited in a sum greater that that which he intended, he might not be able to recover the excess funds from the bank, should he have failed in the duty he owes, as demonstrated in the decision of *London Joint Stock Bank* v. *Macmillan & Arthur* 1918. This, while a case concerning the drawing of cheques, would undoubtedly extend into this mandatory area. The customer must ensure that the details are correct and must pay particular attention to avoid ambiguity in respect of the timing of the first and last payments. Some bankers' orders are drawn so as to be payable 'until further notice', while others terminate on a certain date, or after a specific number of payments. If the bank is in any doubt, it, in turn, should not hesitate to question the customer and seek his clarification. Sometimes the mandate is handed to the bank, but in many instances the standing order authority is sent by the customer to the beneficiary, who then inserts the necessary details and forwards it to the customer's bankers. It is in this area that fraud might arise, and this is why, when drawing the authority in the first place, the customer must exercise care, as with a cheque, so that the amount cannot be artificially raised, or the beneficiary's name fraudulently changed. Thereafter the customer's responsibility is to make sure that there are always adequate funds in the account on the due date, or that, alternatively, he has made prior arrangement for borrowing facilities, for if not then the bank will be justified in withholding payment.

ACCOUNT No. ....

STANDING ORDER FORM

The Manager,   Date:

Dear Sir,

I/We hereby authorize and request you to pay to:

CODE No.	BANK & BRANCH TITLE	ACCOUNT	AMOUNT
BY ORDER OF:			

as follows

DURATION
WEEKLY/MONTHLY/QUARTERLY/YEARLY Payments of £
1ST PAYMENT DUE ON
LAST PAYMENT OF £   DUE ON

Yours faithfully,

(CAPITALS) NAME...

CFS 19

Fig.3.1 *Bankers' order*

The bank's responsibility is to make the correct payment on the due date, and it is usual for the beneficiary's account to be credited by computer-generated entries or through the bank giro system. The risk to the bank is that it will make an error and pay the wrong amount, or omit a payment which could have damaging effects for the customer. Sometimes a new standing order authority is issued in the body of which a previous standing order is cancelled, and it is important that the bank should notice this and act accordingly, for if not then the customer's account will be over-debited and problems could arise in recovering the monies wrongly paid away.

Where the bank is unable to make a payment on the due date because of the lack of funds, it is usual to advise the customer by an advice note, which instructs him to make his own arrangements for payment of that instalment, for while banks occasionally are prepared to hold over a standing order for a day, and then to check whether covering funds have been provided, the extra work occasioned by this is not justified in the provision of the service. In *Whitehead* v. *National Westminster Bank Ltd* (1982) the customer's account occasionally had sufficient funds to enable a monthly mortgage payment to be made by banker's order, but often there were insufficient funds and the bank made no payment. However, if the account then subsequently reverted to credit, from time to time the bank agreed to make the last payment, but this was not always the position. Eventually, the arrears under the mortgage payments reached such a level that the building society took possession of Mrs Whitehead's property and sold it. She then brought an action against the bank, claiming that the bank had had a duty to ensure that each bankers' order payment had been made on the due date, or the next date on which her account had been in sufficient credit to enable the payment to be made. In this action she failed, as the court ruled that the bank's duty related simply to complying with the payment of the standing order on its due date each month, and that, if there were insufficient monies in the account on that date then the bank had no further obligations to its customer in respect of that instalment.

It should be remembered, of course, that a beneficiary has no authority to amend the customer's written instructions and the bank should refuse to accept any changes from that source. Moreover, if a payment is not made, the bank must not disclose to the beneficiary, or his bankers, the reason why not, and he should be referred to the customer. Similarly, a beneficiary cannot give instuctions to the remitting bank for the payment to be cancelled, and again the bank must take instructions from its customer.

Direct debits

The direct debiting system has similar advantages from the customer's point of view, as he benefits from the ease of administration and has no need to remember to make specified payments on due dates. The accounting procedures are different however, for it is the beneficiary who originates the entry, and his bankers credit his account and pass a debit, known as the direct debit, through to the paying customer's account, either through the debit clearing in voucher form, or by electronic entry.

Again, the customer must give a clear instruction to his bank, so that the latter is empowered to accept a direct debit entry when it is received.

However, there are specific requirements on the beneficiary creditor, now called the originator, who must execute an indemnity addressed to all the clearing banks and Scottish banks before he is admitted to the scheme. In this he agrees to indemnify them against all actions claims or damages which might arise, whether directly or indirectly, out of his use of the direct debit system.

Frequently the instruction given by the customer, now known as the payer, is worded so that the bank may accept variable amounts from the originator, the duty of care on the customer in all these instances being the same as with a standing order. The payer must also ensure that sufficient funds are available in the account to meet the direct debit when it is received. If funds are not sufficent, then the direct debit should be returned with the answer 'Refer to debtor'.[33] In other circumstances, answers could include 'No mandate', 'Debtor deceased', 'Mandate cancelled', 'Out of date' or 'Amount not yet due', as appropriate.

Where a bank receives cancellation instructions or an amendment from its customer, it should in turn advise the originator, to ensure that he does not originate an entry. Thus, if the originator thereafter originates an entry in error, the bank, should it accept the direct debit itself by mistake, will be able to claim reimbursement, under the general indemnity which the originator entered into when being accepted into the scheme.

---

33   See Appendix I, Q. 22 (September 1982).

CHAPTER 4

The Collecting Banker

Every day over the counters of the clearing and other banks many hundreds of thousands of cheques are paid in by customers to their accounts. In all these instances the banks are acting as their customers' agent, as, even though the account is credited immediately with the amount of the cheque, the banks in law are not then deemed to be collecting on their own behalf, except under certain special circumstances, as when they are a holder for value. In carrying out their duty of agency, banks must exercise their usual diligency and the expertise acquired and associated with their traditional role; should they fail to do so they will be liable in damages for any loss which the customer might incur. Most cheques are of course collected and presented for payment through the Clearing House, although in a few instances special presentations will be required, and for branches banking within the Town Clearing Area it will be necessary for cheques falling within certain special limits to be collected differently.

In a dispute in which the parties agreed to abide by an arbitration award (*Barclays Bank plc and others* v. *Bank of England* (1985)), the Judge said: 'Where bank A (the presenting bank) receives from a customer for collection a cheque drawn on bank B (the paying bank) by a person having an account at a branch of the paying bank and the cheque is dealt with through the inter-bank system for clearing cheques, the presenting bank's responsibility to its customer in respect of the collection of the cheque is discharged only when the cheque is physically delivered to the said branch for decision whether it should be paid or not'. There was 'a clear duty imposed on the collecting bank to present the cheque for payment and obtain an answer without delay'. Hence a collecting banker's duty is not discharged when a cheque is handed over in the Clearing House.

Fortunately, the number of instances where a breach of normal procedures has resulted in loss is few, particularly remembering that on average in 1983 6½ million cheques were daily passing through the Clearing House and that the total amount handled each day was on average £2155 million. We can, however, speculate on situations where a breach of duty would occur, as for example where a customer might pay in a cheque which is temporarily lost on the collecting banker's premises. As a result of this, because of delays the cheque does not reach the drawee bank until a day or so later than that upon which it would normally have arrived. In the meantime, however, the drawer has had a bankruptcy order made against him, and the cheque cannot be paid – whereas it would have been had it been presented within the normal time span.

Another example may be given of an associated breach of duty. If, after the cheque has been collected, it is returned unpaid then the collecting banker must notify his customer immediately, and this will usually be done by the cheque being sent to the customer with a covering letter indicating that his account has been debited. Receipt of this letter will enable the customer to give notice of dishonour to any party liable on the cheque in accordance with the provisions and rules of s. 49 Bills of Exchange Act 1882. Suppose, however, that the collecting banker was late in carrying out his duties of advice to the customer. The latter might then lose his rights against parties liable on the cheque, or be unable to take quick action to remedy his own risky position upon the drawer's default.

Usually the customer's rights will not have been lost against the drawer, even if notice of dishonour has not been given, for under the provisions of s. 50 Bills of Exchange Act 1882 delay in giving notice of dishonour is excused where the delay is caused by circumstances beyond the control of the party giving notice and is also dispensed with in a number of instances which may be summarized as when the drawer is aware or should already be aware that his cheque has not been paid (as for example when covering funds are not available, or when he has stopped payment of his own cheque).

CONVERSION

However, many more problems have been encountered in a different sphere – namely that of conversion, where a person, other than the customer, is entitled to the proceeds of the cheque, and has been deprived of these by the bank's action in collecting the cheque for the customer, who is not the true owner. Here is an example of how the bank can become liable to third parties, and it will be appreciated that a bank can then become, albeit unwittingly, embroiled in its customer's fraudulent activities, when the exposure risk can be large. In *Hiort* v. *Bott* (1874) conversion was defined as 'an unauthorized act which deprives another person of his property permanently or for an indefinite time'. This would happen when the cheque proceeds are made available for the wrong person; the thief will of course usually have made off with them by the time that the true owner realizes that he has been defrauded. If it is sued by the true owner the bank will have counter-rights against the customer, for what they are worth, but in the main it will need to rely on the statutory protection which is available, if it is to avoid loss.

Before we examine the conditions necessary to meet the statutory protection it is worth remembering that two other defences might possibly be available to the bank. These will be a plea of estoppel, and a plea that there was contributory negligence by the defrauded party. The defence of estoppel is rarely likely to be available, and indeed there are no reported cases of its successful use. In essence such a defence would be that the plaintiff had, by his own account, represented to the bank that it would collect the cheques on behalf of the person for whom it had done so. It is in fact difficult to see the circumstances under which this could apply.

Of more help in mitigating the extent of any loss is the defence in appropriate circumstances that the plaintiff has himself contributed to the difficulties in which the bank now finds itself. Section 1 Law Reform (Contributory Negligence) Act 1945 enacts that:

> Where any person suffers damage as a result partly of his own fault and partly of the fault of any other person or persons a claim in respect of that damage shall not be defeated by reason of the fault of the person suffering the damage, but the damages recoverable in respect thereof *shall be reduced* to such extent as the Court thinks just and equitable, having regard to the claimant's share in the responsibility for the damage.

A defence based on this principle was successfully pleaded in *Lumsden & Co. v. London Trustee Savings Bank* (1971) where it was shown that the plaintiffs had also conducted their affairs negligently, and the outcome of the case was that the bank was held to be liable only for 90 per cent of the amount of the cheques collected. It may be noted in passing, for the avoidance of doubt, that this defence is still available, s. 47 Banking Act 1979, restoring the position which had temporarily been destroyed by s. 11(i) of the Torts (Interference with Goods) Act 1977.

Protection under the Cheques Act 1957

By far the most important protection for the collecting banker, however, lies in s. 4 Cheques Act 1957 which re-enacts s. 82 Bills of Exchange Act 1882 and extends the provisions to open cheques as well as crossed cheques and whether the cheque is endorsed irregularly or unendorsed. The section provides:

(1) Where a banker, in good faith and without negligence,

(a) receives payment for a customer of an instrument to which this section applies; or

(b) having credited a customer's account with the amount of such an instrument, receives payment thereof for himself; and the customer has no title, or a defective title, to the instrument, the banker does not incur any liability to the true owner of the instrument by reason only of having received payment thereof.

(2) This section applies to the following instruments, namely:

(a) cheques;

(b) any document issued by a customer of a banker which, though not a bill of exchange, is intended to enable a person to obtain payment from that banker of the sum mentioned in the document;

(c) any document issued by a public officer which is intended to enable a person to obtain payment from the Paymaster General or the Queen's and Lord

Treasurer's Remembrancer of the sum mentioned in the document but is not a bill of exchange;

(d) any draft payable on demand drawn by a banker upon himself, whether payable at the head office or some other office of his bank.

(3) A banker is not to be treated for the purpose of this section as having been negligent by reason only of his failure to concern himself with absence of, or irregularity in, endorsement of an instrument.

A closer examination of sub-section (1) indicates that the requirements necessary to be satisfied if the banker wishes to avoid liability on an instrument which he has collected for a person not entitled to it are as follows:

(a) He must act in *good faith*. This is a requirement which, while understandable, rarely provides the banker with any difficulties in satisfying the court. No banker worthy of the name would knowingly become associated with his customer's fraud and the bank invariably is assumed to have met the requirements of s. 90 of the Bills of Exchange Act 1882 which states: 'A thing is deemed to be done in good faith, within the meaning of the Act, where it is in fact done honestly; whether it is done negligently or not'.

(b) The banker must *'receive payment'*. This requirement is naturally satisfied when the bank is acting as agent for collection, and the cheque is credited to the customer's account or in some other way the customer comes into receipt of the proceeds.

(c) Payment must be received *'for a customer'*. It will be recalled that a customer is someone who has opened an account with the bank, and that the length of time for which the account has been opened is not an important factor. Thus if a person opens an account by tendering a cheque for collection he becomes a customer from that moment, and the bank is brought within the requirements of the section. However, despite the arguments which could be advanced in present-day banking for the claim that a person can be a customer of the bank even though he does not have an account, because the bank carries out other services for him, it is most unlikely that a court would accept that a bank had acted in collecting a cheque 'for a customer', if it merely carried out a casual collection through a suspense account for someone who was unknown or only known to the bank because it had provided other services.

These last two requirements, namely 'receiving payment for a customer', present few problems today, but historically it is interesting to note that in the earlier part of this century it was necessary for another Act of Parliament to be passed, the Bills of Exchange (Crossed Cheques) Act 1906, to remedy the far-reaching implications of the decision in *Capital and Counties Bank Ltd* v. *Gordon* (1903). In that case the court had held that the bank was not enabled to plead the protection of s. 82 of the Bills of Exchange Act 1882, as it then was, because its bookkeeping process was such that it credited the customer's account immediately the cheque was tendered for collection and that in so doing the bank had given value for the cheque to the customer and was therefore collecting the cheque not on its customer's behalf but for itself.

These points are discussed later in this chapter, but the area is of no concern today as s. 4 of the Cheques Act 1957 is so worded that the banker is protected whether he receives payment for a customer or whether, having credited the customer's account, he receives payment for himself.

(*d*) The instrument must be one of those clearly set out in sub-section (2), the most important being cheques and drafts.

(*e*) The collection must be made 'without negligence', and it is in fact the two words embodied in this one phrase and their interpretation which have placed banks in difficulties from time to time. Indeed, the case law is extensive and needs to be examined in some depth for the reader to have a full appreciation of the circumstances in which it has been held that the bank has acted negligently. What, then, is negligence? It is a breach of a duty of care which, in this instance, is owed to the true owner of the cheque, albeit that his person or identity may be unknown to the bank. Negligence arises when the person owing that duty of care has by some act or omission failed to meet acceptable standards, as a result of which the person to whom the duty is owed suffers loss.

There is no statutory definition of negligence in the Bills of Exchange Act, or the Cheques Act, but in the *Commissioners of Taxation* v. *English, Scottish and Australian Bank Ltd* (1920) it was said that 'The test of negligence is whether the transaction of paying in any given cheque coupled with antecedent and present circumstances was so out of the ordinary course of business that it ought to have aroused doubts in the banker's mind and caused him to make inquiry'. This statement is helpful, and we can appreciate that while there is no duty in common law on the collecting banker to exercise care, the duty has been created by the relevant statutes. However, the test of negligence mentioned in the *Commissioners of Taxation* case is not entirely adequate, for, as we shall see, not only need the banker make enquiry, when doubts are aroused, but he must also be able to show that the answers he has received to his enquiries are satisfactory in the light of all the circumstances surrounding the transaction and the customer's account generally.

What is entirely clear is that the courts have shown in the decided cases that they require a high standard of care on the part of the bank, despite the volume of cheques processed for collection each day.

Where a bank is sued for conversion, clearly the prospects of success for the plaintiff will depend on the facts of his particular case, but over the years, because of the volume of litigation in this area, it has become apparent that the bank is particularly prone to loss through its inability to show that it has acted without negligence in situations where it has failed in one of the following three ways:

(*a*) It has not properly completed the account-opening formalities.

(*b*) It has not made enquiries when there has been a fiduciary relationship between the customer and the drawer of the cheque, or the customer and the payee.

(*c*) It has failed to enquire where the surrounding circumstances, generally, ought to have caused suspicion to arise.

These three broad headings will now be examined in more detail by looking at several of the cases involved.

In our first chapter concerning the opening of an account, we have already seen the need for a new customer to be satisfactorily introduced to the bank and we noted, in *Ladbroke* v. *Todd* (1914), that where the bank failed to take up a reference it was later unable to persuade the court that it had acted 'without negligence' in collecting a cheque. We can deduce therefore that even though a cheque may be collected some time after the account has been opened, the negligence of the bank can go right back to the beginning of the relationship with the customer, and this is sometimes termed 'antecedent negligence'.

It is also of course important to ensure that the reference is obtained from a person known to the bank, or that, if not, a reference is obtained on the referee, for in *Guardians of St John's Hampstead* v. *Barclays Bank Ltd* (1923) the new customer wrote his own reference, not unexpectedly speaking well of himself! However, it is interesting and reassuring to a degree to know that over the years the standard of care required by a court has changed in the light of the modern environment and in 1967, in *Marfani & Co. Ltd* v. *Midland Bank Ltd*, although the new customer had given the names of two referees, the bank was still held to have acted carefully even though it conducted the account after only one referee replied, and then only orally. The bank was able to show the court, from internal records, that this satisfactory oral reference had been obtained and the attempts by the plaintiffs to show that there had been negligence in that the new customer had not produced his passport (he was a Pakistani), failed. In fact, had the bank asked for the passport, the new account holder, who claimed to have the name Eliaszade, would not have been able to produce it. The fraudster was however able to obtain the satisfactory reference on 'himself', from another customer of the branch, because he was using a name known to that customer and the latter thought that he was speaking of the real Mr Eliaszade. The fraudster had come into possession of a cheque payable to Eliaszade, and after it had been collected the balance was withdrawn over a short period.

One of the best-known cases concerned with the opening of accounts is that of *Lloyds Bank Ltd* v. *E. B. Savory & Co.* (1932). This case is important for two reasons. First, it demonstrated the doctrine of split knowledge, which in the banking sense means that the law regards a bank as one entity, despite the fact that it operates through many branches, and it presumes that information which is available to the officers at one branch is also known by officers at another – a state of affairs which in practice is unlikely. Nevertheless, in 1932 the courts held that if the banks wished to transact their business through numerous outlets then they must accept the consequences. (It is interesting to note that some fifty years later, however, in a case concerning Mareva injunctions, *Z Ltd* v. *A-Z and AA-LL* (1981), the court seemed to take a more understanding view when laying down guidelines.) The second point of importance in the Savory case was that it was shown how important it is to obtain the details about a new customer's occupation and the name of his employers; moreover, because in this case the fraud was perpetrated on the fraudster's employer through the use of his wife's account, the court saw a need, when a married woman's account was being opened, for details of her husband's name and employment, and the name of his employers to be obtained. Presumably in more modern days, following the passing of the Sex Discrimination Act 1975, it would, conversely, be necessary to obtain details of his wife's employment, when opening an account for a married man. In practice, however, it seems that many banks do not go to the lengths of obtaining details of the other spouse's occupation and thus they carry the risk associated with the Savory judgment, in the interests of forming easier relationships with new customers.

An examination of the facts of this case will show how the fraud was committed and how a bank can become exposed to risk. There were two fraudsters, who were clerks working for a firm of stockbrokers E. B. Savory & Co. Both of them stole cheques drawn by the employer payable to various other firms or brokers or to 'Bearer'. All the cheques were paid in at City branches of Lloyds Bank for the credit of accounts in the suburbs. Perkins paid in cheques for his own account and Smith paid some cheques in for the credit of his wife's account, which at one time was at Redhill branch and then later at Weybridge branch. Lloyds Bank operated the 'branch credit' system to pass bookkeeping entries with their other branches, and the cheques were sent through the clearing for collection. The branch credit slips which were forwarded contained no detailed information of the cheques which had been paid in, and in consequences the account-holding branches were unaware of the identity of the drawers of the cheques or the payees; however, even if they had had that information they would not have appreciated the special relationship between the drawer and the account holder for they had not obtained details of who employed Perkins, or Mrs Smith's husband. When the fraud was discovered, the bank was sued for conversion by the stockbrokers, and in endeavouring to plead that it had acted 'without negligence', failed, because of its omissions when opening the accounts.

It might be asked then whether a branch bank needs continually to be updating its own knowledge as to a customer's employment, but fortunately this does not appear to be so, for in *Orbit Mining and Trading Co. Ltd* v. *Westminster Bank* (1962) the fraudster had changed his employment, without notifying the bank, and he then stole three cheques and paid them into his account. Had the bank known the new employer, it might have been suspicious and would probably have been in difficulty in showing that it had not acted without care. The cheques which had been stolen had been signed by the employer in blank and the fraudster made these payable to 'Cash or order'. This meant that the items, strictly speaking, were not cheques, under the definitions in the Bills of Exchange Act and Cheques Act, but nevertheless the court accepted that they were covered by the statutory protection and, to the Bank's relief, held that as it knew nothing of the customer's present employment, it had acted without negligence when collecting, for there had been nothing to arouse suspicion.

In turning to our second division of those situations in which banks have acted negligently we need to examine a number of cases dealing with positions where there was a fiduciary relationship between the various parties. In fact we have already seen this in the Savory case discussed above, which well illustrated the wide opportunity for fraud which can exist where an employee is in a position of trust with his employer.

Similarly, the fiduciary relationship is strong where an agent is employed by a principal, and one of the well-known cases illustrating the risks involved for a bank in this area is that of the *Marquess of Bute* v. *Barclays Bank Ltd* (1954). Here, Barclays collected cheques for their customer McGaw which were drawn 'Pay D. McGaw', with the words 'For Marquess of Bute' printed immediately outside the box for the payee's name. McGaw had been the manager of the Marquess of Bute's farm, and as such he received warrants as agent for his employer. it was held that the bank had been negligent in collecting these warrants for McGaw's private account, as there had been an indication that he was only to receive them as an agent for the true owner who was the Marquess himself, even though he was not named as payee on the cheque.

In *Morison* v. *London County and Westminster Bank Ltd* (1914) the bank collected cheques drawn by an agent on his principal's account, placing the proceeds to the credit of the private account of the agent. The bank had made no enquiries and thus was held to have been negligent in respect of most of the collections, although in respect of those carried out towards the end of the episode they escaped liability, as the principal had had an opportunity to discover what had been going on, and had failed to take precautionary steps.

It is particularly important when dealing with matters connected with limited companies to remember that they have their own separate identity in law and that this is quite separate from that of any director who might have a similar name. In *A. L. Underwood Ltd* v. *Bank of Liverpool and Martins* (1942), while Mr Underwood was the sole director of the company and held all but one of the shares, the court saw that it was quite wrong for the bank to collect cheques payable to the company for the credit of Mr Underwood's own private account. After Mr Underwood's death, the bank was sued for conversion by the company and failed to show that it had acted without negligence.

Indeed, it is invariably the practice of a limited company to pay cheques which it has received into its own bank account and the transfer of company cheques is rare.[34] (*London and Montrose Shipbuilding & Repairing Co. Ltd* v. *Barclays Bank Ltd* (1926).)

Before leaving this area we may also note that a bank would be put on enquiry if a member of a partnership drew a cheque on the firm's account payable to himself and it were collected for his private account, unless the amount was small or the circumstances were such that the transaction was clearly a regular drawing. Much would depend on the circumstances and the state of the partner's own account. Similarly, if an executor acting in a deceased's estate drew a cheque in his fiduciary capacity payable to himself, the circumstances would be such that the bank would need to make detailed enquires and to be satisfied with the answers before proceeding (*Foxton* v. *Manchester and Liverpool District Banking Co.* (1881)).[35]

Our third area of examination deals with suspicious circumstances, and while a bank cannot be an amateur detective agency in receiving cheques for collection it must take note of the customer's station in life, the knowledge of his financial affairs which has been acquired through the conduct of the account, and of any other surrounding circumstances which might put it on enquiry. It must then be entirely happy that answers in reply to its questions are satisfactory, at least for the needs of a reasonable man.

In *Nu Stilo Footwear Ltd.* v. *Lloyds Bank Ltd* (1956) the secretary of the company opened a personal account under a false name giving his real name as that of the referee. Not unexpectedly, the bank obtained a good reply to their enquiry as to their new customer, Mr Bauer, and the enquiry on the secretary's, Gerald Montague's, own bankers stated that he was suitable to act as a referee in introducing another account. When 'Bauer' had opened his account he had told Lloyds Bank that he was a freelance agent. The fraud then commenced and in his capacity as secretary Montague drew cheques on behalf of the company Nu Stilo Footwear Ltd, making them payable to 'Bauer', while some were payable to third parties who purported to have endorsed them over to 'Bauer'. Nine cheques were involved in the fraud, which upon its coming to light resulted in Nu Stilo Footwear suing Lloyds Bank for conversion. The bank pleaded the statutory defence of s. 82 Bills of Exchange Act 1882, as it then was, and succeeded in respect of the first cheque collected, which had been for £172 only. However, in view of the amounts of the second and subsequent cheques which totalled £4855, the bank was held to have been negligent, as it had failed to make enquiry and the amounts were too large to be consistent with the description which their new customer had given of his employment. At the time banks regarded this decision as a little harsh, but the warning remains.

The conduct of the past history of an account must also be taken into consideration, when cheques are collected, and which should put a banker on enquiry; this was well illustrated in *Motor Traders Guarantee Corporation Ltd*

34 See Appendix I, Q. 16 (September 1981).
35 See Appendix I, Q. 27 (April 1983).

v. *Midland Bank Ltd* (1937). The customer here was a Mr Turner, a car
trader, who got hold of a cheque payable to Welsh & Co. He then forged an
endorsement and paid the cheque into his account, although the cashier when
accepting the cheque made enquiries about the circumstances whereby it had
been negotiated to Mr Turner. Turner replied that the sum involved was
owed by Welsh & Co. to him and upon inspecting Turner's account the
cashier saw that there had been several previous transactions between the
parties who were both in the motor trade. The cashier was therefore satisfied
at this and did not refer to his manager, although the bank's internal
instructions were that all third-party cheques must be referred to him. In fact,
the customer's account had only been opened fairly recently, its conduct had
been unsatisfactory, and the manager had found it necessary to return a
number of cheques which Turner had drawn. When the fraud was discovered
Welsh & Co. sued the bank, who relied upon s. 82 Bills of Exchange Act,
claiming that they had acted without negligence, as they had made enquiries
and the reply was not unreasonable. However, this did not satisfy the court,
which, taking into account the unsatisfactory history of the account, was of
the view that more detailed enquiries should have been made. The fact that
the cashier had not referred to his manager, as instructed in the internal
branch instructions, was, however, not in itself said to be an act of negligence,
for a bank does not owe a duty to its customers to abide by its own rules.
Thus the test in every case of alleged conversion is whether the bank's
conduct in the light of the facts and particular circumstances of the
transaction are such as to discharge the duty of care which is placed upon it.
Here, the court was of the view that it had not been.

Cheques payable to third parties should always be treated with more care
than a cheque payable to the customer as payee, and if they are collected for
the account holder of another bank, we have seen how important it is from the
Savory decision to ensure that the account-holding branch is made aware of
the details. This is usually carried out by writing the information on the bank
giro credit or sending a separate paper of advice to that bank.

It is particularly important when collecting a third-party cheque to look to
see whether the cheque is crossed with the words 'Account payee only'.
Although these words have no statutory force and are not mentioned in the
Bills of Exchange Act, they are a direction indicating the wishes of the drawer
and if a collecting banker takes in a cheque for the credit of an account other
than that of the payee, he does so at his peril, should conversion be taking
place. All may not be lost, however, for in *Bevan* v. *National Bank Ltd* (1906)
cheques were collected payable to Malcolm Wade & Co. and were credited to
Malcolm Wade's private account. The cheques had been crossed 'Account
payee' but the bank was successful in defending the action for damages for
conversion by showing that in the light of all the facts it had been careful, had
made enquiries, and that it was not unreasonable for them to have accepted
their customer's reply that he was trading as Malcolm Wade & Co. The truth

of the situation was however that he was merely the manager of that firm, and he had misappropriated the cheques.

Cheques made payable to a named payee 'or bearer' and crossed 'Account payee' are not encountered so frequently in modern banking, as the purpose of adding the words 'or bearer' was to obviate the need for endorsements before the passing of the Cheques Act 1957. In *House Property Co. of London Ltd & Others* v. *London County and Westminster Bank Ltd* (1915), a dishonest solicitor obtained a cheque payable to a group of trustees 'or bearer' which was crossed 'Account payee'. He then paid the cheque in for the credit of his own account, and, when sued, the bank defended on the basis that the cheque was a bearer cheque they had collected for the payee, as directed by the drawer; they also contended that the 'Account payee' crossing was not material to their position. The bank lost, as the court took the view that the words 'Account payee' were an instruction which needed attention, and the owner of the cheque was the named payee, the trustees, F. S. Hanson & Others, and not any person in possession of it as 'bearer'. The circumstances were such that when collecting for the solicitor's private account the bank should have been put on notice that a misappropriation was in course.

At this stage, brief mention of the effect of a 'not negotiable' crossing may be appropriate. As we know, this crossing deprives a cheque of its negotiability, and means that the holder cannot obtain better title than that of the person from whom he takes it. It would seem, however, that such a crossing imposes no greater a duty upon a collecting banker than with any other cheque, whether crossed or open, and in *Crumplin* v. *London Joint Stock Bank Ltd* (1913) the bank successfully relied upon the protection of s. 82 Bills of Exchange Act 1882 where it had collected cheques crossed 'Not negotiable' for a customer who purported to take them by endorsement from the payee. The drawer of the cheques had been persuaded by his employee to sign cheques drawn in favour of a Mr Davies and the employee had then forged Mr Davies's endorsement and paid them into his own account. Mr Davies was not entitled to the monies, however, and the employee had merely been using his name as a cover for his own speculative stock exchange transactions, so that the employer, Crumplin, would not know. In giving judgment for the bank it was said that the 'Not negotiable' crossing was merely one factor among a series which needed consideration at the time of collection. 'The mere taking of a 'Not negotiable' cheque ought not to be held to be evidence of negligence.' Thus the court felt that what was of equal importance was the number of cheques paid into the account in relation to the total number of credits and the amount of those cheques; this, coupled with consideration as to the period over which the cheques were paid in, and all the other surrounding circumstances, needed to be considered, to judge whether the bank was put upon enquiry. The extent of such enquiries was not analysed, however, and while it was appreciated that if the collection banker had referred to the drawer then the activities of the employee would have come to light earlier, any suggestion that a bank should refer to the drawer when collecting a 'Not negotiable' cheque does seem extremely impracticable.

Collecting banker also acting as paying banker

Where the drawer of a cheque maintains his account at a branch of the bank where the party who pays in the cheque also maintains his account, the bank has two roles, that of paying banker and that of collecting banker, and, in the event of any conversion, it will be necessary for the bank to show that it meets the requirements of both sets of statutory protections which respectively cover the paying banker and the collecting banker, if it is to escape liability. In other words, it will not merely be sufficient for the bank to show that it has acted 'without negligence', in collecting the cheque, as while this would protect it under s. 4 Cheques Act 1957 as collecting banker, the circumstances may be such that it will not be able to obtain the statutory protection of s. 60 or s. 80 Bills of Exchange Act 1882 and it will thus be liable to the drawer.

This important point was seen in *Carpenters' Company* v. *British Mutual Banking Co. Ltd* (1938) where a fraudulent clerk who worked for the plaintiffs had an account at the same branch of British Mutual Banking Co. Ltd as his employers. He misappropriated funds, forging the endorsements of payees of cheques drawn by the company and then paid them into his own account. In the lower court, the bank failed to show that it acted 'without negligence', and so had no statutory protection as collecting banker under s. 82 Bills of Exchange Act 1882 (now s. 4 Cheques Act 1957). However, the bank had also sought the protection of s. 60 of the earlier Act, claiming that as paying banker the cheques had been paid 'in good faith and in the ordinary course of business' and while this point was accepted in the lower court, upon appeal it was not. In the course of the judgment it was said 's. 60 of the Bills of Exchange Act 1882 only protects a bank when that bank is *merely a paying bank,* and is not a bank which receives the cheque for collection'. (Emphasis added.) In the light of this statement, the bank's duties when acting for two customers are quite clear.

The collecting banker as a holder for value

Although a bank may not be successful in showing that it has acted 'without negligence', and therefore is not entitled to the statutory protection of s. 4 Cheques Act 1957 in a case levelled against it for conversion, it is possible that in certain circumstances it will nevertheless be able to avoid liability. This will be where the bank itself can show that it is a holder for value, or possibly even a holder in due course. Reference to the Bills of Exchange Act 1882, which defines these two types of holders, shows that under s. 27:

> (1)   Valuable consideration for a bill may be constituted by (a) any consideration sufficient to support a simple contract; (b) an antecedent debt or liability. Such a debt or liability is deemed valuable consideration whether the bill is payable on demand or a future time.

(2)   Where value has at any time been given for a bill the holder is deemed to be a holder for value as regards the acceptor and all parties to the bill who became parties prior to such time.

(3)   Where the holder of a bill has a lien on it, arising either from contract or by implication of law, he is deemed to be a holder for value to the extent of the sum for which he has a lien.

Section 29 defines a holder in due course. Thus:

(1)   A holder in due course is a holder who has taken a bill, complete and regular on the face of it, under the following conditions; namely:

(a)   that he became the holder of it before it was overdue, and without notice that it had been previously dishonoured, if such was the fact;

(b)   that he took the bill in good faith and for value, and that at the time the bill was negotiated to him he had no notice of any defect in the title of the person who negotiated it.

(2)   In particular the title of a person who negotiates a bill is defective within the meaning of this Act when he obtained the bill, or the acceptance thereof, by fraud, duress, or force and fear, or other unlawful means, or for an illegal consideration, or when he negotiates it in breach of faith, or under such circumstances as amount to a fraud.

(3)   A holder (whether for value or not) who derives his title to a bill through a holder in due course, and who is not himself a party to any fraud or illegality affecting it, has all the rights of that holder in due course as regards the acceptor and all parties to the bill prior to that holder.

A holder for value need not himself have given value, and value may have been given at some time prior to his becoming a holder by another party. If a person accepts a bill of exchange without giving value, then he acquires no rights against the party from whom he received the bill, but he can claim the rights of that party against all other parties liable on the bill. A holder for value, however, cannot obtain a better title than that of the person from whom he took the bill.

To be a holder in due course, which gives superior rights, the party so claiming must have no notice of any previous defect in the title of the person who negotiated it to him. Notice may be actual knowledge of a defective title or a disregard of suspicious circumstances which would operate against him. This means that the notice need not necessarily be a formal notice and a holder in due course can acquire and give a good title, remembering always of course that no title can be acquired through a forgery.

Before a person can become a holder in due course, the cheque must have been negotiated to him, and the original delivery of a bill of exchange or a cheque to the payee is not a negotiation (*R. E. Jones Ltd* v. *Waring and Gillow Ltd* (1926)). There is, however, a presumption regarding value and a presumption that matters have been transacted in good faith. Thus under s. 30 Bills of Exchange Act every party whose signature appears on a bill is 'prima facie' deemed to have become a party thereto for value. Moreover,

Every holder of a bill is 'prima facie' deemed to be a holder in due course; but if in an action on a bill it is admitted, or proved that the acceptance, issue, or subsequent negotiation of the bill is affected with fraud, duress, or force and fear, or illegality, the burden of proof is shifted, unless and until the holder proves that, subsequent to the alleged fraud or illegality, value has in good faith been given for the bill.

A holder is the person in possession of the bill, and he may sue on it in his own name and where he is a holder in due course, he can hold the bill free from any defect in title of any prior parties and he may enforce payment against all parties liable on the bill.

The circumstances under which a bank can set itself up as a holder for value are fairly limited but they include the following situations:

Encashment of cheques   Where a bank cashes a cheque which iş drawn on another bank for the convenience of the customer of that other bank, then it acquires the rights of a holder for value, and if, unexpectedly, the cheque is dishonoured then it may sue the drawer/payee.

Cheques collected in specific reduction or repayment of a borrowing   In these instances, the bank will be a holder for value in respect of the cheque, but it should be noted that the rights will apply only where the intention when the cheque is paid in is the specific reduction of the overdraft, and the bank would not be a holder for value if a cheque had simply been collected in the ordinary course of business and credited to an overdrawn account. So, if the bank had called in a borrowing, or were suing a borrower, and he produced a cheque drawn on another of his accounts at another bank, or provided monies in the form of a cheque drawn by a third party, the collecting banker would come within the necessary requirements and would be a holder for value if the cheque were dishonoured (*M'Lean* v. *Clydesdale Banking Co.* (1883)).

Payment of a customer's cheques against uncleared effects   If cheques have been paid in which are still in the course of clearing, but in specific reliance on them the bank is prepared to honour cheques drawn by the customer, then it will become a holder for value in respect of the cheques collected, should they be dishonoured. Similar rights will arise if the customer is impliedly permitted to draw against his uncleared cheques, but it should be noted that the bank's rights can be lost if they have said or done anything which might refuse a customer the right to draw against uncleareds. For instance, in *A. L. Underwood Ltd* v. *Barclays Bank Ltd* (1924) and *Westminster Bank Ltd* v. *Zang* (1965) the bank was unsuccessful in setting itself up as a holder for value, as in both cases the paying-in slips used by the customer had a warning to him preprinted by the bank saying that it reserved the right to defer payment of any cheques drawn by the customer against those which were being paid in. The Zang case was interesting, as the cheque which was collected was payable to an individual who himself paid it in to a limited company's account at the bank. The court saw that despite this he was a 'holder' and that he had delivered it to the bank for 'collection', the collection being within the meaning of s. 2 Cheques Act 1957. This states: 'A banker who gives value for, or has a lien on, a cheque payable to order which the holder delivers to him for collection whithout endorsing it, has such (if any) rights as he would have had if, upon delivery, the holder had endorsed it in bank'. The bank lost the case because, despite the argument that on the day when the cheque was collected it had permitted a considerable excess in the agreed overdraft and hence had given value, the court ruled in the light of the evidence that the bank had not charged interest on £1000 of the overdraft (the amount of the cheque paid in), but rather had charged it on the cheque itself. Moreover, it did not accept that, by crediting the cheque to the account and reducing the overdraft, the bank had in fact given value.

Although not material to the decision in this case, the *obiter dicta* of two of the appeal judges is also a warning as to how a bank should act in circumstances where a cheque has been dishonoured. They were of the opinion that as the bank had parted with the cheque subsequently, it had lost its lien and could not recover those rights after the cheque had been returned to it, because at the time it was not delivered for collection. The implication of this view is that where a cheque is dishonoured and the customer's account carries insufficient funds to allow it to be debited without creating an overdraft, the bank could lose its rights as a holder for value if the cheque were sent to the customer, as is in fact usual practice. Consequently, if the bank fears any future difficulties, the cheque should be retained, and the customer should be advised of the cheque's dishonour merely by letter or notice, reserving the bank's rights. It is indeed preferable for the cheque to be debited to a suspense account or dishonoured bills account where the entries will show that value has been given. However, all rights may not be lost if a suspense account is not used (*Midland Bank Ltd* v. *R. V. Harris Ltd* (1963)).

The bank's main object in setting itself up as a holder for value will be to preserve its rights against parties to the cheque other than their customer; usually the other party concerned will be the drawer. Upon the return of the cheque unpaid, notice of dishonour should be given without delay to all parties liable on the cheque, in accordance with the provisions of s. 49 Bills of Exchange Act 1882. However, if this is not done then the bank will not lose its rights where the circumstances are such that notice can be dispensed with under s. 50. These circumstances include situations where the other party concerned knows or is deemed to know of the dishonour – as will happen where the drawer's cheque is returned for lack of funds or he has stopped payment.

The occasions on which a bank will turn to the other parties will be rare, but are they useful in special situations where, say, the bank has been deliberately misled or defrauded, as in a cross-firing operation where the customer and the other party swap cheques to take advantage of clearing times and set out to paint a wholly misleading ledger balance in their accounts.

Where the bank has a lien on a cheque This applies in the circumstances outlined above, and also in those situtations where specific or implied arrangements have not been made for the customer to draw against uncleared cheques.

An interesting example in bankruptcy proceedings was seen in the case of *Re Keever* (1966). Mrs Keever had an account with the Midland Bank and paid in a cheque for £3000 on 15 November, the day before a receiving order in bankruptcy was made against her. Prior to that, an act of bankruptcy had been committed and a petition had been presented in the previous month. Mrs Keever's account had been overdrawn £1350 when the cheque for £3000 was paid in, and the trustee in bankruptcy sought to show that the bank could not apply the cheque in reduction of the overdraft. The court ruled, however, that the bank had a lien on the cheque and were protected under s. 45 Bankruptcy Act 1914 as they had dealt for value without notice of the act of bankruptcy and before the receiving order had been made. This was because under s. 27 Bills of Exchange Act value can be constituted by an *antecedent* debt and moreover the bank was in any event a holder in due course meeting the provisions of s. 29 Bills of Exchange Act.

In another case (*Barclays Bank Ltd* v. *Astley Industrial Trust Ltd* (1970)), the bank had allowed its garage customer to increase their overdraft on their assurance that they would pay in cheques for £2850 in two days' time issued by Astley, who were hire purchase financiers. The cheques were paid in, but when Astely realised that they had issued the cheques against hire purchase agreements which had been forged they stopped payment. Barclays were unable to recover the monies from their customer and sued Astley, claiming to be holders for value, having given value by way of the overdraft, and having a lien on the cheques collected. They succeeded in their reliance on s. 27(3) Bills of Exchange Act as it was held that they had not prejudiced their lien by being also an agent for collection contemporaneously.

CHAPTER 5

Legal Processes and Banking Operations

GARNISHEE ORDERS AND GARNISHEE SUMMONSES

Garnishee proceedings may be brought in either the High Court or the county court.

In the High Court they are known as garnishee orders (Fig. 5.1) and in the county court as garnishee summonses (Fig. 5.2).

The proceedings are brought by a party (A) who is owed money and who has already been to court and obtained judgment against his debtor (B), thus establishing in the eyes of the law that the debt exists. Thereafter, in an attempt to recover that judgment debt he (A) has taken enforcement proceedings by way of an application for a garnishee. The garnishee is a further 'ruling' (order or summons) of the Court (High or County) that a third party (C), who, it is known or claimed, owes monies to (B), should pay those funds not to (B) but to the court for the benefit of the party who is seeking to recover his debt (A).

A bank can become involved when it is named as a third party, and so is ordered by the court in the garnishee order or summons to pay monies it holds for its customer, the judgment debtor, to the court.

The parties involved therefore are:

(a) The judgment creditor: the creditor who is owed money, and who has already been to court, and obtained judgment against his debtor.

(b) The judgment debtor: the customer of the bank who owes the money, under the judgment, to the judgment creditor.

(c) the garnishee: the third party who owes money to the judgment debtor. In our example, this is the bank, although it could be any other person or party.

Without our going futher into the procedures associated with debt recovery, readers should understand that a garnishee order or summons is therefore an enforcement procedure taken after judgment, whereby the person who is owed money takes further legal steps to ensure that funds owing to his debtor are mandated to him, the creditor, via the court, so that they do not pass into the debtor's own hands, where they could be used for other purposes.

In the county court there is only one stage in garnishee proceedings and thus any monies in a bank account attached by the service of a garnishee can be paid into court immediately upon receipt of the garnishee summons.

In the High Court, the garnishee action is in two stages:

(a) the garnishee order *nisi*, followed some days later by

(b) the garnishee order *absolute*.

115

Garnishee Order
to show cause
(O. 49 r. 1)

IN THE HIGH COURT OF JUSTICE   19 .— .—No.
Queen's Bench Division

Master.   Master in Chambers.

Between

         ZETA LTD   Judgment Creditor

             AND

         JANE ELIZABETH JONES   Judgment Debtor

         PRACTICE BANK plc   Garnishee

Upon reading the affidavit   of   John Smith of Zeta Ltd

filed the   4th   day of   December   19 .

IT IS ORDERED by Master   TAYLOR   that all debts due or accruing
due from the above-mentioned Garnishee   to the above-mentioned Judgment
Debtor [in the sum of £ 1,119.50   ] be attached to answer [a judgment
recovered against the said Judgment Debtor   by the above-named Judgment
Creditor   in the High Court of Justice on the   15th   day of   October
19   , for] [an order made in the High Court of Justice on the   day of
         , 19   , ordering payment by the said Judgment Debtor
to the above-named Judgment Creditor of] the sum of £ 1,192.50
[debt, and £ 73.00   costs] (together with the costs of the garnishee
proceedings), on which [judgment] [order] the sum of £ 1,192.50
remains due and unpaid.

         AND IT IS ORDERED that the said Garnishee attend Master   TAYLOR
                       in Chambers, in Room No.   216   , Central Office,
Royal Courts of Justice, Strand, London, on the   20th
day of   January   19   , at 3.45 o'clock on an application by the
said Judgment Creditor   that the said Garnishee   do pay to the said Judgment
Creditor   the debt due from the said Garnishee   to the said Judgment Debtor ,
or so much thereof as may be sufficient to satisfy the said [judgment] [order]
together with the costs of the garnishee proceedings.

**Add where appro-
priate*

The   name   and
address of the branch
of the garnishee insti-
tution   at   which   the
debtor's   account   is
believed   to   be   held
is . . . . . . The number
of that account is
believed to be . . . . . .'

*

         Dated the   4th   day of   December   19

To the above-named Garnishee ⎫
    and the Judgment Debtor ⎬
                             ⎭

Fig. 5.1   *Unlimited garnishee order*

IN THE   WESSEX   COUNTY COURT

CASE NO. 98765

BETWEEN   ROSEMARY SMITH   PLAINTIFF

AND   ALAN THOMAS   DEFENDANT

AND   PRACTICE BANK plc   GARNISHEE

SEAL

Upon reading the affidavit of ROSEMARY SMITH filed on   7th
day of March 19..
IT IS ORDERED that the above-mentioned garnishee do attach so much of the debts owing or accruing from the said garnishee to the above-mentioned defendant as will satisfy a judgment or order obtained against the said defendant by the above-mentioned plaintiff in this court (or otherwise

on

for the sum of £ 956.97   including costs, of which the sum of £ 956.97
remains due and unpaid together with £ 10.00   the costs of these proceedings.

AND IT IS ORDERED that the garnishee do attend this court

at THE COURT HOUSE, PALATINE ROAD, WESSEX on
   WEDNESDAY THE 11TH DAY OF APRIL 19..

at   2.00   o'clock to show cause why an order should not be made that the garnishee do pay into the office of this court the debt due from the garnishee to the defendant or so much thereof as may be sufficient to satisfy the judgment or order, together with the costs of these proceedings.

The garnishee may, at any time before the return day, pay into court the amount required to satisfy the judgment or order and costs or such lesser sum as he admits to be owing by him to the defendant, and thereupon the proceedings against the garnishee shall be stayed.

	£	p
Amount remaining due under judgment (or order)		956.97
Court fee		10.00
Solicitor's costs		36.00
TOTAL		£1002.97

The name and address of the branch of the garnishee deposit taking institution at which the defendant's account (account no. 973519   ) is believed to be held is:

PRACTICE BANK plc
1, HIGH STREET
LONGCHESTER

The name and address of the defendant is:

ALAN THOMAS
14, ALBERT ROAD   DATED 8th March 19..
TOYTOWN

Address all communications to the Chief Clerk AND QUOTE
THE ABOVE CASE NUMBER

Plaintiff's solicitor's address for service:

YOUNG & YOUNG
19, UPPER HIGH STREET
WINKLE

Fig.5.2   *Limited garnishee summons*   117

The garnishee order nisi is an interim stage, freezing any debts due to the judgment debtor by the garnishee, pending the further court hearing, when the garnishee order absolute is made or the action is dismissed. Thus, a bank receiving a garnishee order nisi must ensure that it acts carefully and correctly, as otherwise it will be in contempt of court. It is only when the order is made absolute, however, that monies are paid over, or, if it is dismissed, that the frozen funds attached in the customer's account can be released again to the customer.

A garnishee order or summons may be:

(a) limited (Fig. 5.2) or
(b) unlimited (Fig. 5.1)

as to the amount attached, and if unlimited, all monies due at the time of service are caught, even though the judgment debt is for a lesser amount. It is more usual for limited orders or summonses to be made.

We have seen that the basic relationship between a banker and his customer is that of debtor and creditor, and it follows therefore that if the customer is a judgment debtor, but has a *cleared* credit balance in his account with the bank, then the bank in turn is indebted to him, and is a party on which a garnishee order or summons can be served. A judgment creditor being aware of the existence of the bank account swears an affidavit to this effect, and the court, on his application, makes the order or summons, which is served both at the head office of the bank concerned and at the branch where the account is kept.

As under the procedure the monies attached are only those which are due or accruing due *at the time of service*, the head office of the bank and the branch will always liaise quickly, as notice to the head office is effectively notice to the bank as a whole, including the branch concerned, for it could be embarrassing if the branch were unaware of the receipt of the garnishee order or summons at head office, and released funds in the period before it received its copy of the garnishee order or summons.

Problems can arise if the branch concerned is not recited in the garnishee application, and the order or summons is only served at head office, but usually the courts allow a reasonable period of time for liaison and reasearch, and real difficulties are rare.

Action to be taken on service – limited amount

(a) If the account is overdrawn, then clearly no funds are due to the customer at the time of service, and consequently no funds are attached by the garnishee order or summons. In these circumstances, the bank will simply inform the court that no monies are attached, and the account may continue in the ordinary way, although the bank will doubtless wish to inform the customer of the receipt of the garnishee order or summons, and call him for an interview to receive his explanation of the circumstances involved. This is because it has had evidence that its customer is a judgment debtor, and this can be regarded as a warning with regard to its own lending which may perhaps be at risk.

(*b*) If the account is in credit, and the order is for a limited amount, then:

(*i*) The amount recited in the order, or the balance of the account, whichever is the lesser, should be transferred to a suspense account, provided the funds are cleared monies.

Alternatively, the account(s) could be frozen and any surplus monies not attached could be transferred to a new account(s) in the name of the customer, which could operate as the stopped account used to.

(*ii*) The bank's solicitors should be instructed to represent the bank at the hearing for the garnishee order absolute, or, if the garnishee is a garnishee summons, the monies may be paid over at once to the solicitors for onward transmission to the county court.

(*iii*) The customer should be advised of the receipt of the garnishee, and of the action taken by the bank. Preferably, the customer should admit the existence of the judgment debt in writing, but this is not essential.

(*iv*) The bank will no doubt wish to call for the customer's explanation of the garnishee proceedings, and, in view of the evidence of financial stringency, steps may be taken inside the branch to ensure that no unauthorized overdrafts arise.

(*v*) The customer should be asked to make provision for any cheques which he has drawn, in reliance on the credit balance, so as to avoid the necessity for these being dishonoured.

(*vi*) If cheques have been received in the branch via the General In Clearing[36] or by special presentation at the time of service of the garnishee order or summons, and these have not been 'effectively paid', then they should be returned unpaid with the answer 'Refer to drawer' or 'Funds attached by garnishee order', assuming of course that there are no funds remaining on the account to enable payment. The term 'effectively paid' refers to those situations where the fate of the cheque has been communicated to another party, as for instance where the presenting banker has made a specific enquiry or where the cheque may have been presented specially, and its fate communicated by telephone immediately at the commencement of business for the day. Also, where a cheque has been presented over the counter, and a specific request has been made at that time as to whether it is paid or not and an affirmative answer has been given, then it has been effectively paid. However, where a cheque is simply in the General In Clearing, and has been debited to the customer's account by computer process, or has been tendered for collection over the counter, but no specific question has been asked as to payment, then it should be returned, unpaid, in the absence of surplus funds after sufficient monies have been transferred to the suspense account to meet the garnishee and costs.

36 See Appendix I, Q. 1 (April 1980).

It is possible that, under special circumstances, the branch might agree to pay the cheques and allow an overdraft, but this would only be in those instances where the customer provides adequate security, and/or is able to give the branch a reassuring explanation as to the reason for the garnishee. It could be, for instance, that the customer is in dispute with a supplier or contractor over the quality of goods supplied, or work done, and that although judgment has been obtained against him for non-payment of an account, he has been slow in settling, and garnishee proceedings have followed as enforcement of the judgment.

The question of the bank's position where cheques in the General In Clearing bear evidence of issue against a bank guarantee card is interesting, for there is no case law, as yet, on the subject, and it could be argued that they have been 'effectively paid' and the balance is not available for a judgment creditor under a garnishee order or summons. In such circumstances, as with any others where the situation is in doubt, it is recommended that legal advice is taken, and that the facts of the situation are brought to the court's attention for a ruling. In a case concerning Mareva injunctions, it was indicated that cheques presented bearing a cheque card number on the reverse should be paid, even though the bank had earlier received the injunction restraining it from parting with the balance.

Cleared funds

It should be noted that normally only *cleared* funds are attached,[37] unless there is an agreement with the customer either specifically or by a course of transactions leading to a general presumption that he may draw against uncleared funds in his account.

The most recent case illustrating this area is *Fern* v. *Bishop Burns* (1980) where the facts were as follows:

On 10 March 1980 Bishop Burns & Co. Ltd paid into their current account with Lloyds Bank a cheque for £4700 which brough the balance on their account to £4998. The cheque was sent for clearance in the usual way and at this time there was no agreement in existence between the bank and its customer that the company could draw against uncleared cheques.

The following morning at 11.35 a.m. the bank was served with a garnishee order nisi in the sum of £802. In accordance with its usual practice it transferred the uncleared balance in Bishop Burn's account to a separate account, and applied bank charges, leaving a balance of £218 in the original company account which it regarded as attached by the order. However, when the matter came before the district registrar, the order was made absolute in the full amount of £802, on the grounds that the current account itself showing a credit balance was evidence of a debt due by the bank to its customer, the judgment debtor, even though this contained an element of uncleared monies. The bank appealed against this decision. In the Court of

37 See Appendix I, Q. 1 (April 1980).

Appeal it was held that if it is to be attached, a debt or money must be due or accruing due at the time when the garnishee order is served. As regards cheques in course of collection, if the bank was a holder for value in respect of such items, then it was collecting for itself, and the balance in the account was due to the customer, and hence would be caught by a garnishee. If, however, the bank was not a holder for value then there was no debt owing by the bank to its customer in respect of those cheques in the course of collection.

Reference was made to the *A. L. Underwood Ltd* v. *Barclays Bank Ltd* (1924) case which illustrated the need to show an express or implied agreement between the banker and customer that the customer could draw against cheques before they were cleared, if it were sought to show that the bank was a holder for value. In this respect the judge felt that the statement in *Capital and Counties Bank Ltd* v. *Gordon* (1903), namely that 'It is well settled that if a banker before collection credits a customer with the face value of a cheque paid into his account, the banker becomes holder for value of the cheque', needed considerable limitation.

The question before him therefore, he said, was where the onus of proof should lie. It would be rare for express agreements between the bank and its customer enabling the latter to draw against uncleared cheques to be encountered, but where such situations existed there was a duty on the bank as garnishee to disclose this express agreement to the court. In those other situations where by implication from a course of conduct the customer was entitled to draw against uncleared cheques, the bank should not offer details of banking transactions. It was therefore up to the judgment creditor to seek an order for discovery if he so wished. In the case before him, this order had not been sought and on the evidence he accepted that the cheque for £4700 was uncleared as 'it takes four days for a cheque to be cleared in present day conditions'. In consequence the first order absolute was set aside and a new one was made in the sum of £218.

Accounts affected upon service[38]

Care should be taken to ensure that the name recited in the garnishee order or summons agrees accurately with that of the bank customer, as any discrepancy could give the bank grounds for claiming that no funds are attached. Indeed, the bank will wish to ensure that it does not freeze the account of a customer who has no connection with the proceedings! Conversely, although there might be a minor discrepancy in the name recited, the bank would need to exercise care so as not to be in contempt of court if there were good grounds for believing that the person (or persons) named in the order were one and the same person as the customer. In such circumstances, urgent enquiries should be made.

If the garnishee order or summons recites only one name for the judgment debtor, then a balance held in joint names by the judgment debtor and

38 See Appendix I, Q. 31 (September 1983).

another or other parties is not caught (*Hirschorn* v. *Evans* (1938)). Consequently, where the funds are in a partnership account, unless the garnishee order or summons recites the name of the partnership, or the order is made against all the partners, no funds will be attached.

However, if the garnishee order or summons recites the name of both the account holders to a joint account, then that balance is attached, as it also any balance in a sole account. Similarly, if the garnishee order or summons recites the names of two judgment debtors, but only one is in account, then that credit balance is caught.

Contrary to what might be expected, trust account balances are caught, as are balances on solicitor's clients' accounts, although under both circumstances the bank will explain the nature of the accounts to the court, and the court may dismiss the garnishee order or summons, or make an amended order, having analysed the funds, and being assured that some or all of them are a debt due to the customer in his own right.

Garnishees catch balances on current account, and, since the passing of the Administration of Justice Act 1956, monies on deposit account. Moreover, savings accounts are no longer exempt. Since 1 January 1982, under the provisions of the Supreme Court Act 1981, they too are available for the judgment creditor.

As regards foreign currency balances it was held in *Choice Investments Ltd* v. *Jeromnimon: Midland Bank Ltd Garnishee* (1980) that they are attachable. This type of account should therefore be stopped, and the balance should be notionally converted at the appropriate rate of exchange to equate with the sterling amount of the garnishee. The bank should then inform the court of the foreign currency balance attached and the rate of exchange. If the garnishee order absolute is made, the bank should convert so much of the foreign currency as equates to the sterling judgment debt and costs, and pay this to the court. Meanwhile the judgment creditor must carry the risk of exchange rate fluctuations between receipt of the garnishee nisi and the later hearing.

It should be borne in mind that any cash credits for the customer's account in the bank's hands at the time of service of the garnishee, although not yet placed to the account, are caught. It would seem therefore that a bank giro credit, received at another branch on the previous day, made up of cash or cleared funds, would be a debt due to the customer at the time of service, and would be caught. Similarly, proceeds of stock or share sales in the bank's hands but not actually yet in the account at the time of service would be caught.

Unlimited garnishee order or garnishee summons[39]
Even though the judgment debt may be recited in an unlimited garnishee order or summons, and may be less than the amount appearing on the

39 See Appendix I, Q.1 (April 1980).

customer's account, upon receipt of an unlimited garnishee order the whole cleared balance in the account(s) is frozen, and it is usual in such instances for the account to be stopped. Again, the customer is informed, and usually a new account is opened or the whole balance is transferred to a suspense account. Depending upon the customer's background, and the circumstances generally, it might be that in such an instance the bank would be prepared to allow an overdraft on the new account up to the extent of the apparent surplus funds attached by the garnishee.

Set off
Both upon receipt of a limited or unlimited garnishee order or summons, the bank is able to exercise its right of set off to arrive at the amount caught. Thus if No. 1 account is credit £200, and No. 2 account is overdrawn £50, then £150 is the maximum amount which can be caught by the garnishee.

However, where the debit balance is on loan account, and particularly where loan repayments are up to date, the view is taken that set-off cannot be exercised, presumably on the grounds that had the customer called at the branch to withdraw the balance of the current account, the bank would have been under an obligation to allow him to take the full extent of that balance. There is no modern case in a court of precedent on this matter, although some years ago a Mayor's Court in the City of London did in fact take a different view, and allowed set-off between a loan account and current account, but generally banks prefer not to rely on this decision.

INJUNCTIONS

An injunction is an order of the court restraining any person or body against whom it is made from doing some act. A bank can be the recipient of an injunction directly, when the injunction is addressed to the bank, or indirectly, when it becomes aware of an injunction addressed to its customer. In both instances, should the customer attempt to deal with any assets or property, such as the balance of his account, security, or items in safe custody, in breach of the injunction, the bank must refuse to assist. In order words, the customer's mandate is revoked.

However, not infrequently, matters are not as simple as that, particularly since the growth of the use of the Mareva injunction in recent years. Indeed, matters were becoming so difficult for banks a few years ago that one case was deliberately taken to the Court of Appeal, so that guide lines could be set attempting to establish some form of regular practice (*Z Ltd* v. *A-Z and AA-LL* (1981)).

A Mareva injunction (Fig. 5.3) is one obtained before or after the plaintiff has got judgment against the defendant in the action, and extends to those situations where assets could be dissipated both in the UK as well as outside its jurisdiction. In examining the Mareva injunction, Lord Denning, the

No. 1234 of 19..

IN THE TOWN COURT

UPON hearing Counsel for the Plaintiff, JESSIE GITTINS
AND UPON READING the draft Affidavits of BENJAMIN PRETTY
AND the Plaintiff by her Counsel undertaking:

1. to issue a writ of summons claiming relief similar to or connected with that hereinafter granted;

2. to serve this Order by a solicitor of the   TOWN   Court together with copies of draft or sworn affidavits substantially in the form of the said draft Affidavits read to the Court and the Exhibits thereto;

3. to abide by any Order this Court may make as to damages in case this Court shall hereinafter be of the opinion that the Defendant shall have sustained any by reason of this Order which the Plaintiff ought to pay.

1. THIS COURT DOTH ORDER that the Defendant ELIZABETH ANNIE LEWIS whether by herself her servants agents or otherwise howsoever be restrained until trial or further order from:

(1) instructing, assisting or participating in the disposal, parting with possession, charging, pledging or otherwise dealing howsoever without the Plaintiff's consent with:

   (a) any assets within the jurisdiction of this Court in England and Wales save and insofar as they may exceed   £100,000   in value in which she directly or indirectly has any interest, beneficial or otherwise, PROVIDED THAT she be at liberty to expend a sum not exceeding £100 per week for ordinary living expenses and such reasonable sum as may be necessary for the purpose of obtaining legal advice and assistance upon informing the Plaintiff's solicitors of the source or account from which such sum is to be withdrawn.

2. AND IT IS ORDERED that the Defendant do forthwith:

   (a) disclose to the person serving this Order the whereabouts of all assets records and documents of such assets in her possession or control;

   (b) deliver to the person serving this Order all documents or records referred to that are in her possession custody power or control and do all such acts as are necessary to ensure (insofar as she is able) the delivery to such person of such documents and records.

3. AND IT IS ORDERED

That the Defendant, Elizabeth Annie Lewis, by 5.00 p.m.
Monday, 10th November 19..   do swear and serve on the Plaintiff or her solicitors an affidavit:

   (1) identifying any asset whether within or without the jurisdiction of the   TOWN   Court of Justice exceeding £200 in value which is in the ownership, custody or possession or control of the said defendant, identifying that asset's whereabouts and if not in her possession identifying insofar as she is able any person having possession of it;

   (2) identifying any bank account:
      (a) of which she is a signatory or has since
          1st January 19..   had signatory powers;
      (b) in which she has an interest direct or indirect beneficial or otherwise giving the name and address of such account, the account number or other identifying code or symbol.

BY ORDER OF THE COURT

Fig.5.3   *Mareva injunction*

Master of the Rolls, said that a bank could be notified of the granting of a Mareva injunction by the applicant after he had obtained the injunction from the court, and at that stage the defendant customer might himself not be aware that the order had been made. In such circumstances, the customer might attempt to carry through transactions on the account, either deliberately to remove assets or in complete innocence. However, Lord Denning said that the principle involved was that

> As soon as the Judge makes his order for a Mareva injunction restraining the defendant from disposing of his assets, the order takes effect at the very moment that it is pronounced. . . . Every person who has knowledge of it must do what he reasonably can to preserve the asset. He must not assist in any way in the disposal of it. Otherwise he is guilty of contempt of court.

Consequently, this means that once a bank has notice, by whatever means, it must not dispose of any assets, except in accordance with the terms of the order, or with the authority of the court. Cheques presented for payment therefore should be dishonoured with the answer 'Refer to drawer – injunction in force', and if the bank were sued by the customer for wrongful dishonour, the bank's answer in those circumstances would be that it would have been unlawful for the bank to honour the cheque. A credit balance may be set off against a debit account.

Upon notice, a bank must freeze the account named, and the court indicated that if it were required that the injunction should catch funds in a joint account, the injunction should be worded in such a way as to cover such funds. The court also ruled that any items in safe custody that are covered by the terms of the injunction must be held pending any further court order.

It then went on to examine those situations that presented difficulty for the bank because it was already under a prior commitment to third parties, such as under a letter of credit or under a bank guarantee. Lord Denning felt that the injunction would not prevent payment under either of these, although if monies were received under a letter of credit for the benefit of the defendant then such funds should be frozen.

Similarly, the Mareva injunction would not affect the bank's duty to honour all cheques drawn against a cheque card or credit card, except where the card had been used fraudulently or wrongly.

Banks are put to much trouble and expense in dealing with injunctions and they are entitled to recover their costs from the plaintiff in the action, and to be indemnified by him in respect of any liabilities which the bank might leave itself open to as the result of complying with the injunction.

It is interesting to note that Lord Denning recommended that the injunction should be clearly worded and that it should tell the bank what it could or could not do. Thus the bank account and the branch where it was maintained should be identified, as should any other assets. Lord Denning said that if the plaintiff could not do that, then he could ask the bank to search whatever records it had, but must undertake to pay all the costs involved, and that if the bank found an account or assets as a result of the search it should not tell the plaintiff, but should freeze the assets which had been discovered. A later case recommended that the order should be clear about set-off rights, which normally would be preserved.

Frequently, nowadays, an injunction is drawn in such a way that it freezes assets only up to a certain amount and this presents difficulties for banks, as they do not know that other assets have been frozen elsewhere or what the value of those assets might be. Lord Denning recommended that injunctions be issued without restrictions, but that if limited injunctions were granted it was desirable for a special injunction to be made referring to the sum standing to the credit of the defendant in a specified bank account. However, despite this recommendation, banks still experience the receipt of Marevas which place much onus on them, as for example where the defendant is allowed to withdraw up to a specified amount each week 'for normal living expenses'. In such circumstances, the monitoring of the account and the decision whether to pay or dishonour cheques is quite out of proportion to the duties normally faced in the role of a banker.

Lord Justice Kerr examined the position of banks in respect of assets which came into their hands after the date on which a Mareva injunction was served, and he felt that while such events would be rare, the order should not apply to such assets, unless they are specially referred to. Almost certainly, in practice, a bank would take legal advice, if it found itself in receipt of sums or assets after an account had been frozen.

Lord Justice Kerr also dealt with currency accounts, and recommended that the same procedures should be adopted as with garnishee orders (see *Choice Investments Ltd* v. *Jeromnimon* (1981)). In other words, the credit currency balance should be converted into sterling at the then buying rate, and the account should be stopped to the extent necessary to meet the terms of the Mareva injunction.

Obviously, upon receipt of an injunction, a bank will read the terms most carefully, and will ensure that it abides by them, and if any are unclear or any circumstances arise which are doubtful it will take legal advice. The customer should of course immediately be informed in writing of the receipt of the injunction, and if necessary an explanation should be sought. The balance, and any assets frozen, must not be released until a further court order is made and received by the bank.

RESTRAINT ORDERS

Under the Drug Trafficking Offences Act 1986, the court can order a bank, and others, not to part with the property or assets of a customer, until further notice. Such an Order applies to balances, safe custody, or unwanted security items at the time of service and also to any property coming into the bank's hands afterwards. The court has power to appoint a Receiver and upon satisfactory evidence of his identity, and sight of the sealed Order, any credit balances, safe custody and unwanted security can be given up to him on request against his written receipt. Under s. 11 of the Act the Receiver can be appointed to deal with property over which the court has granted a Charging Order.

WRIT OF SEQUESTRATION

This is an order of the court appointing a person, usually an accountant or lawyer, as sequestrator with powers to seize and control the assets of a party who is in default of an earlier court ruling. In other words, it is a process of penalty imposed for contempt of court, and understandably is not often encountered. Banks become involved when their customer is the party in default, and upon learning of the issue of the writ of sequestration or upon being served with a copy they must freeze the account to the extent specified, if any, and retain items in safe custody or security or act as otherwise ordered by the court or the sequestrator.

Close liaison with the sequestrator will be necessary and disclosure of the customer's affairs is not a breach of the usual duty of secrecy. If the customer attempts to breach this further order of the court the sequestrator should be informed. Upon request the balance of the account (or the maximum sum involved) may be paid to the sequestrator against his receipt, and any unrequired securities or safe custody may be delivered to him. The bank's costs are usually recoverable, via the courts.

Somethimes the writ will allow the customer to carry out certain transactions and this can place the bank in a difficult position if and when a cheque is presented for payment, as it has no means of knowing the circumstances. The bank should then refer to the sequestrators by telephone for permission to pay the cheque, if it is in any doubt, or alternatively the cheque may be dishonoured with the answer 'Writ of sequestration obtained. Written confirmation of sequestration commissioners required'.

THE APPROPRIATION OF PAYMENTS

The general rule
If a person owes more than one debt to his creditor, there is a general rule that when he next pays the monies he has the right to say to which debt the monies should be applied, and which debt should be paid off or reduced. If, however, at the time when he makes the payment he does not make any specific appropriation, then the right to appropriate falls to the creditor, who can place the funds to any debt owing by the debtor, even to discharge a debt which has become statute barred under the Limitation Act. Applying these general rules to a banking situation, we can see as an example that if a

customer has more than one liability to the bank (perhaps a debt in his sole name, and a debt on a joint account), when coming to terms with the bank he can forward funds which he has the right to say must be taken in redemption of his sole debt. Naturally, that will not preclude the bank from looking to the customer for the joint debt, but at least, from the customer's point of view, it keeps alive the possibility that the bank will seek out the co-debtor on the joint account.

Clayton's Case

In practice, specific appropriation of funds is rare, but there are many fields which are affected by presumed appropriation, particularly in respect of a current or running account. In law, if there has been no specific appropriation either by the debtor or the creditor, then the presumption is that the first item on the debit side is extinguished or reduced by the first item on the credit side of the account. Conversely, it is presumed that the sum first paid in is the first sum to be drawn out. This is the well-known Rule in *Clayton's Case* which affects all current accounts whether overdrawn or in credit, although banks are much more concerned with the effect of the Rule when the account is in debit. In *Clayton's Case* (*Devaynes* v. *Noble* (1816)) it was said:

> Where all the sums paid in form one blended fund . . . neither banker nor customer ever thinks of saying, 'this draft is to be placed to the account of the £500 paid in on Monday, and the other to the account of the £500 paid in on Tuesday'. There is a fund of £1,000 to draw upon, and that is enough. In such a case there is no room for any other appropriation than that which arises from the order in which the receipts and payments take place, and are carried into the account. Presumably, it is the sum first paid in that is drawn out. It is the first item on the debit side of the account that is discharged, or reduced, by the first time on the credit side.

The application of the Rule was examined closely again in *Deeley* v. *Lloyds Bank Ltd* (1912), where Lord Shaw summed up the rule clearly and concisely. He said:

> According to the law of England, the person paying the money has the primary right to say to what account it shall be appropriated; the creditor, if the debtor makes no appropriation, has the right to appropriate; and if neither exercises the right of appropriation, one can look on the matter as a matter of account and see how the creditor had dealt with the payment in order to ascertain how in fact he did appropriate it. And if there is nothing more than a current account kept by the debtor, or a particular account kept by the creditor and he carries the money to that particular account, then the Court concludes that the appropriation has been made; and, having been made, it is made once for all, and it does not lie in the mouth of the creditor afterwards to seek to vary such appropriation.

Let us now take another example to see how the rights of appropriation will apply in practice. John Jones has debts to the bank on two accounts; No. 1 account is overdrawn £100 and No. 2 account is overdrawn £500; both are current accounts. John Jones also executed a guarantee for the liabilities of John Jones Ltd, and his guarantee has been called up in the sum of £200. The bank instructs solicitors to sue Jones, but before proceedings are commenced he calls to see his bank manager and hands over £80, promising further monies on a regular basis. He does not fill in a credit slip indicating which account the monies should be paid into and he makes no specific appropriation. In these cirumstances the bank may place these funds in reduction of the No. 1 or No. 2 account borrowing, and if it does so the monies will repay the liabilities which arose on those current accounts in accordance with the Rule in *Clayton's Case*. Alternatively, the bank can place the funds to a separate suspense account, where they will be held against Jones's guarantee liability.

To see how the borrowing on a fluctuating current account is affected by the operation of the Rule In *Clayton's Case* we can study a typical account:

Peter Taylor – Current Account

1987		Debit £	Credit £	Balance £
Jan. 1	Balance b/f	110		Dr. 110.—
2	0117	55		Dr. 165.—
4	0118	100		Dr. 265.—
7	Cash		(A) 200	Dr. 65.—
8	0119	40		Dr. 105.—
10	Cheques		(B) 62	Dr. 43.—

Observations:

(a) Item A repays those items which were brought forward in the balance at the turn of the year and £90 of the subsequent turnover (i.e. cheque 0117 for £55 and £35 of cheque for £100).

(b) Item B repays almost all of the remaining amount (£65) of the cheque (0118) for £100 not repaid by item A previously.

(c) At the end of the example the debit balance outstanding of £43 is made up of the last debit turnover on the account (0119–£40 and £3 of 0118–£100).

Adverse effects of the Rule in *Clayton's Case*

It can be seen therefore that on the current account the borrowing is turning over all the time, and is constantly being repaid and a new borrowing is being created. It is to overcome the effect of the operation of the Rule in *Clayton's Case* that all bank security forms have a 'continuing security' clause. Were this clause not present, the security would be available only for the lending which existed at the time the security was taken, or immediately thereafter; the lending would be repaid by the receipt of credits and a new borrowing would arise through subsequent withdrawals which would be unsecured. However, because the charge form is drawn to secure all past present and future borrowings, and to be of a continuing nature, this danger is avoided.

There are many other instances in the conduct of its ongoing business, where the operation of the Rule in *Clayton's Case* will work to the bank's disadvantage, and it is important to recognize these situations and to take action immediately, for the effect cannot be guarded against in the same way as in a security form.

For instance, upon the death, bankruptcy or mental incapacity of one party to a joint account which is overdrawn and where each party is jointly and severally liable under the usual bank mandate, the account must be stopped on the bank receiving notice. If the operations on the account are not stopped, the effect of credits subsequently paid in reduce the liability of the deceased or bankrupt party for the borrowing at the date of his death or bankruptcy, and subsequent cheques drawn by the surviving account holder (if he is allowed to continue to operate the account) will not become a liability in the deceased or insolvent party's estate. Consequently, through the operation of the Rule in *Clayton's Case*, the bank will eventually lose all its right to claim against the deceased or bankrupt party, and will only be able to look to the other party. It might be, of course, that in a practical situation the bank would be quite happy to do just that, but it must take the decision consciously and not merely by default.

Similarly, on the determination of a guarantee either by the operation of law, as in the bankruptcy liquidation administration or mental incapacity of the guarantor, or under the terms of the guarantee where the guarantor gives notice to determine his liability, it is important that the account secured is stopped. If the operations on the account are not broken, subsequent credits reduce the guarantor's liability at the date the determination takes effect, while further drawings are of no concern to the guarantor. Frequently in banks' guarantee forms there is a clause providing for the liability of the deceased's estate to continue for a certain period after his death and until the expiration of a prescribed period of notice, which must be given by the executors or personal representatives. Nevertheless, banks invariably stop the operations on the secured account upon receiving notice of the death of the guarantor, to prevent complications and disputes arising with the personal representatives. If the guarantee is supported by security, or if the security has been given by a third party directly to cover the customer's overdraft, it is not usual to find any provision in such a charge form extending the liability of his estate after his death and if advances were made subsequently in reliance on this security then payments to the credit of the account would reduce the debt secured at the date of the surety's death.

Naturally, when dealing with a partnership account, upon receipt of notice of the death or bankruptcy of one partner, the operation on the firm's account should be stopped if it is overdrawn and if the bank wishes to retain the liability of that partner or his estate.

We have already seen part of the judgment in *Deeley* v. *Lloyds Bank Ltd* (1912), and this case illustrates the danger to a bank when it holds security from its customer and receives notice of a subsequent mortage but fails to stop the operations on an overdrawn current account. If the account is not stopped then *Clayton's Case* operates and the bank's priority to its security is lost, by the turnover on the account, and the effect is that the later mortgagee eventually ranks in front of the bank. The bank is still secured, but the amount owing to the later mortgagee must be repaid out of the security first, and there is obviously a risk that the security might not cover both liabilities.

Another disadvantage of the Rule is seen in liquidation or receivership situations. When a limited company is placed into a compulsory or voluntary liquidation, lendings which the bank had made to facilitate the payment of wages or salaries can represent a preferential claim in the liquidation as under its rights of subrogation to the employees' claims under s. 175 and Schedule 6, Insolvency Act 1986 the bank can stand in their shoes. Such lendings must have been made within a period of four months before the liquidation, but, remembering *Clayton's Case*, it is possible that in some instances if the turnover in the current account has been substantial then some of the earlier cheques paid for wages might have been repaid by credits into the account subsequently, and the new debt outstanding at the date of the liquidation might not consist of all the cheques drawn for wages within the four-month period. Thus in those circumstances the bank's preferential claim would be reduced or extinguished, and if assets were few then the bank's recovery in the liquidation might be less than it would be otherwise. It is because of the effect of the rule in *Clayton's Case* that in such situations the prudent banker will open a separate wages and salaries account so as to maximize his claim. This is discussed in detail in Chapter 9.

Benefits from the Rule in *Clayton's Case*

Readers will begin to feel that the Rule is only disadvantageous to the bank, but this is not so, for there is one important situation where it operates in the bank's favour. This concerns the security of a floating charge given by a limited company. Under the provisions of s. 245 Insolvency Act 1986, a floating charge will be void if the company goes into liquidation within twelve months of the giving of the security, unless it can be shown that the company was solvent at the time. The security will also be good where it is given in consideration for a new borrowing and it will be appreciated that here *Clayton's Case* works in the bank's favour, even if, effectively, no increased lending is made, and the bank's commitment by way of overdraft simply remains at the former pre-security level. The effect was seen first in *Re Thomas Mortimer Ltd* (1925). In that case the company gave its bank a debenture for £50 000 incorporating a floating charge and at the time the company owed the bank £58 000. The company went into liquidation within three months of granting the floating charge, but during this short period the

company paid in £41 000 and drew out £51 000. Mr Justice Homer decided
that the floating charge contained in the debenture was valid to the full extent
of £50 000 and stated:

> I come to the conclusion that the £51 000 paid out by the bank to the creditors of
> the company in honouring the cheques of the company were payments in cash made
> since the date the debenture was issued and in consideration of the charge, and that
> no part of that £51 000 had been, by the date of the liquidation, . . . repaid to the
> bank.

In *Re Yeovil Glove Co. Ltd* (1964) this view was supported, and thus while a
floating charge may be invalid for debts existing at the time it is given, it can
become a good security for new advances by the operation of sufficient
turnover. This effect has been the subject of criticism in submissions to the
Review Committee on Insolvency Law and Practice and it remains to be seen
whether the holder of a floating charge, lending on current account, will
retain this advantage or whether legislation will be introduced to change his
position. In any event, it must always be remembered that in a cross-guarantee
situation, where the guarantees are secured by debentures incorporating
floating charges, the guarantee liabilities can only become secured by the
passage of twelve months' time, as turnover will not affect that situation.

To sum up, therefore, whenever at present a floating charge is taken as
security for an existing debt on a current account the Rule in *Clayton's Case*
operates in favour of the bank and the extent of the validity of the charge in
relation to s. 245 Insolvency Act 1986 depends upon the activity in the
account. All debts created by cheques paid after the date of the charge will be
secured and the existing unsecured balance will gradually be repaid by credits
paid in.

Appropriation of security proceeds

Finally, in concluding our examination of situations affected by the rules of
appropriation, we can note an instance where problems can sometimes arise
with the bank's security proceeds.

Occasionally in a bankruptcy or liquidation a bank will encounter a trustee
or liquidator who tries to insist that monies raised from a sale of the security
should be applied first of all to reduce or repay any preferential element in the
bank's claim. Clearly the bank will prefer to put the proceeds towards the
non-preferential element first, in order to maximize its recovery, especially
where there is a possibility that preferential creditors will not be paid in full.
Under the ruling in *Re William Hall (Contractors) Ltd* (1967) it can in fact do
so, for the court then reaffirmed the bank's common-law right to apply the
proceeds of its security to whichever debt is wished – a right which in any
event is often reinforced by a specific clause in the charge form. However, this
position is different where a regulated lending under the Consumer Credit Act
1974 is secured (see Chapter 8).

SET-OFF

Set-off arises when a debtor or his creditor wishes to arrive at the net figure owing between them when separate accounts or debts are involved. This is best seen by way of a simple example. If Jones owes his friend Smith £1000 for monies lent and then later Smith buys Jones's car for £400, Smith could refuse to pay Jones the £400 and could set off this sum against the loan due and settle simply in the net figure of £600.

The three requirements

There are three prerequisites before a right of set-off can be exercised, although these can be varied by special agreement between the parties. The sums involved must be certain and clearly ascertained; they must be due between the same parties, and they must be due in the same right.

Between a debtor and creditor there is an undisputed right of set-off, but between the bank and its customer the situation is not always so clear, and so bankers, when exercising set-off, must do so cautiously, so as to ensure that they do not leave themselves open to counter-claims by their customer, as, for example, to an action for the wrongful dishonour of a cheque.

Certain sums Looking first at the need for the sums to be clearly ascertainable and certain in amount, when the balances concerned in the action of set-off are in the bank accounts no problems arise as to the certainty of the sums in question, for the precise figures can of course be seen readily. However, unless a personal customer is made bankrupt, or a limited company goes into liquidation, or unless there is a special agreement between the bank and the customer, the bank cannot set-off a credit balance on its customer's account against that customer's contingent liabilities. For example, a credit balance cannot normally be set off against liabilities on discounted bills or indemnities given on a customer's behalf. In *Jeffryes* v. *Agra and Masterman's Bank* (1866) it was said: 'You cannot retain a sum of money which is actually due, against a sum of money which is only to become due at a future time'. However, where discount request documents or counter indemnities have been given to the bank it is usual for these papers to include clauses which would give the bank a right of lien and set-off, at any time, so strengthening the bank's position over and above the common-law rules.

Between same parties Turning to the second requirement to be met if set-off is to be exercisable, namely that the sums due must be owing between the same parties, it will be readily apparent why this is so, for if the bank is owed money by customer Brown then clearly it cannot transfer funds out of the account of customer Green to repay that debt! However, the situation can be different where the customer has executed a mandate undertaking joint and several liability, for then if there is a borrowing of £400 on the account of

Green and Brown, and a credit balance of £200 on the account of Green, as Green is severally liable for the joint account indebtedness, and as the bank owes money to him in his own right on the private account, a right of set-off exists, although, because separate types of account are involved, the bank will proceed with caution.

Also, a right of set-off will arise when there is a credit balance on a partner's private account and a debt on the partnership account and the bank holds a partnership mandate incorporating joint and several liability. Again, in those circumstances, if it wished to recover its borrowing, the bank could call in the full amount owing by the partnership, but serve a notice on the partner with the credit private account demanding the lesser sum, and notifying him that his credit private account balance had been set off against the partnership debt. We will consider the risks of such action later.

Frequently, the bank will strengthen its position by including a clause in its charge forms, particularly guarantee forms, giving it a right of set-off where normally one would not exist. Thus with a borrowing on the account of X Ltd secured by a guarantee by Mr X, the bank might have a right to appropriate monies out of the private account in support of the guarantee liability, although usually such funds would be held on a separate suspense account and not taken directly in reduction of the company debt immediately. These illustrations are, however, an example of special arrangements which can be made and they are separate from the common-law position.

In the same right   The final requirement for set-off to be exercisable is that the funds must be owed in the same right, so if the customer owes money to the bank, the bank may not set off the balance on a credit account if there is any indication of a trust element in respect of the creditor balance. It follows therefore that if, say, Ruscoe owes the bank £500 on current account, but has credit balances on accounts designated

(1) P. Ruscoe, Treasurer Northenden Tennis Club
(2) P. Ruscoe, Executor of A. Bradford deceased
(3) P. Ruscoe, Trustee of H. Slater deceased
(4) P. Ruscoe, Clients' Account

then set-off will not be exercisable, for ostensibly the balance on each of those accounts is held in trust. Occasionally, however, where the second account has simply been named with a title for accounting purposes, e.g. 'Value Added Tax Account' or 'Office Account' there is no element of trust, and the bank may exercise its rights over such monies.

It is appropriate here to mention again the accounts of certain customers who are required by law to maintain their clients' funds in a separate account. Thus solicitors must keep their clients' monies in an account designated 'Clients' Account' under the provisons of the Solicitors Acts, and obviously, if the bank sought to recover the borrowing in the solicitor's own name, he could not apply the balance in the clients' account in reduction.

Similarly, under the Insurance Brokers (Registration) Act 1977 registered brokers are required to maintain separate clients' insurance broking accounts. Moreover, the broker's bankers are required to write to the broker stating that they will exercise no right of set-off, lien or charge over monies in these accounts, other than where, exceptionally, a lending has been made on such an account and there is a credit balance elsewhere available.

Estate agents are also required by the provisions of the Estate Agents Act 1979 to maintain separate clients' bank accounts for monies received in respect of pre-contract deposits or contract monies, and these accounts are classed as trust accounts.

Of course, an account which is trust account may not always be specially so designated, but the circumstances under which the monies have come to be placed in the account can be known to the bank, and in such a situation it may be that the bank will be aware that these funds are subject to an overriding trust. In *Barclays Bank Ltd* v. *Quistclose Investments Ltd* (1968) a company owed money to Barclays Bank. It was in financial difficulties and did not have the funds to pay its dividend, so it borrowed from another bank to faciliate that payment to its shareholders. These monies were received by Barclays Bank and placed in a separate account, but before any cheques could be drawn on the dividend account the company was put into liquidation, and Barclays then sought to exercise a right of set-off by transferring the substantial credit balance in this dividend account against the borrowing on the company's current account. When matters came before the court it was held that this was not possible as the monies had been provided for a specific purpose. This purpose had failed, and there was consequentially a resultant trust for the lender. It may be noted that it was because Barclays were aware of the overall cirumstances and the purpose for which the monies had been provided that the court reached this decision.

Situations where set-off applies

Having examined the three pre-conditions which are necessary before set-off can be exercised, we can go back again and look at those circumstances in which thereafter the right of set-off is automatic and undoubted. The situations arise where the bank has notice of the death of its customer, or his mental incapacity. There is also no doubt that set-off is exercisable where the bank receives a garnishee order or summons, for in all these cases it is essential that the bank should be able to determine precisely how much it owes to or is owed by the customer. However, there is some debate about the position in respect of garnishees where a current account and loan account are maintained, as we saw earlier in this chapter.

Where an individual has a bankruptcy order made against him, or a limited company customer goes into liquidation, whether compulsorily or voluntarily, then there is no doubt that set-off must be exercised. The court held, in *National Westminster Bank Ltd* v. *Halesowen Presswork and Assemblies Ltd*

(1972) that set-off in a liquidation was more than a right, it was a statutory obligation (now covered in s. 323 Insolvency Act 1986 (for individuals) and Insolvency Rules 1986, 4.90 (for companies)).

In this case the company went into liquidation, and the court had to consider the arrangements between the company and the bank prior to the liquidation, and whether under those it had contracted out of the statutory requirements of set-off. The company owed money to the bank on an account which had been frozen, and the bank agreed to open another account, which the company said would be maintained in credit, and the agreement was that, except in materially changed circumstances, the bank would not exercise a right of set-off over the monies in this new account for a period of four months. The company went into liquidation sooner, when there was a credit balance on this new account; the bank therefore exercised its right of set-off and claimed a lesser figure in the liquidation than the balance outstanding on the frozen overdrawn account. The liquidator of course challenged the bank's action, but the court, in examining the dealings between the parties, accepted that these were all mutual and that while the circumstances had materially changed, so permitting set-off, in any event, in view of the liquidation, s. 31 Bankruptcy Act 1914 as then embodied in s. 317 Companies Act 1948 must apply; there was an *obligation* to set off the balances to arrive at a net sum due.

While we are examining the bank's position in the event of the liquidation of its customer, we should also look at the earlier case of *Re E. J. Morel (1934) Ltd* (1962), where the bank was required to set off a credit balance in a particular way. Here, because the arrangement with the customer had been that the overdrawn balance on the wages account would never exceed a credit balance on another active account, the court viewed the two accounts as one, and ruled that the bank must apply the credit balance in reduction of the wages account debt and not against the overdrawn balance on another account which had been stopped earlier upon the determination of a guarantee which secured it; this meant that the bank's preferential claim in the liquidation was reduced, for naturally the bank would have preferred to apply the credit balance against the non-preferential debt. However, this decision has been modified recently by that in *Re Unit 2 Windows Ltd* (1985), where it was said that in the absence of guidance, a credit balance should be set-off pro rata against preferential and non-preferential claims.

The banker's right to set-off one balance against another, even while accounts are active, is put beyond doubt where the bank holds a letter of set-off from the customer (Fig. 5.4); this is regarded as a security and is usually entered into the bank's security register. The letter of set-off will incorporate a right for the bank to transfer monies from the customer's account at any time at the bank's own discretion, whether before or after it has made a demand for repayment. Moreover, it excludes the need for the bank to give notice beforehand as to what it is doing; and, to protect the bank against any action for the wrongful dishonour of cheques, the bank is authorized to dishonour

LETTER OF SET-OFF
(Customer Only)

To : **BANK OF CYPRUS (LONDON) LIMITED**

In consideration of your granting time or making advances to, discounting bills of exchange or promissory notes for, or otherwise granting accommodation to, me/us to such extent as you may think fit:-

1.   I/We hereby agree that you may at any time without prior notice to me/us combine or consolidate all moneys now or at any time hereafter standing to the credit of my/our account(s) with you of whatsoever nature with all moneys that may now or at any time hereafter be owing from me/us to you on any account(s) or in any manner whatsoever and whether actually or contingently alone or jointly with any other(s) and whether as principal or surety and in whatever name style or form together with interest discount commission and all other charges and expenses.

2.   I/We hereby authorize you to refuse payment of any cheque, bill or other document the payment of which to the debit of my/our account would reduce my/our credit balance(s) with you below the amount so owing to you for the time being by me/us, whether actually or contingently.

3.   I/We hereby agree that you may without further notice or consent apply or transfer any money now or at any time hereafter standing to the credit of my/our account(s) with you in payment of any such moneys owing to you by me/us.

4.   I/We hereby undertake to keep at your Bank a balance on my/our   account at present numbered   (or such other account as may from time to time be substituted therefor) with you of not less that £   (say:
   pounds) so long as any advances granted or to be granted to me/us or any bills of exchange or promissory notes which shall be or have been discounted at any time by you for me/us shall be current or dishonoured.

Dated this   day of   19

Signature. . . . .

WITNESS

Signature. . . . .

Full name (block capitals). . . . .

Address. . . . .

. . . .

Occupation . . . .

S6/83

Fig.5.4   *Letter of set-off*

cheques drawn in reliance on balances on the appropriated accounts, even though such cheques may have been drawn before the monies were seized.

It might be wondered why the letter of set-off is necessary, but an examination of the cases where banks have set-off monies without such specific authority clearly indicates that they should always proceed with caution, because of the repercussions which can follow and because of slightly conflicting case law. Some of this case law puts the bank on notice that arbitrary action might be risky, for, as we know, the bank is under an obligation to honour any cheques properly drawn by its customer, and the implied right of set-off may often be subject to this overriding duty. Consequently, except where a bank is setting off a balance to arrive at a net figure when calling in its debt, and where it will feel free to dishonour cheques safely, where monies are to be appropriated in respect of a separate liability – say in respect of a guarantee liability – the prudent banker will invariably pay cheques which are presented after the appropriation, but which bear a date prior to the date of appropriation. Cheques presented bearing a date after the appropriation could safely be dishonoured, provided the bank has given written notice to the customer of the appropriation and warned him not to draw cheques in reliance on the balance or to provide covering funds for any further cheques which he may draw.

This is the modern view, although in 1877 in *Garnett* v. *McKewan* the court was quite happy to allow the bank to set off a credit balance in one account at one branch of a bank against an overdrawn balance in another account held at a different branch. Without notice to their customer the bank combined the balances and dishonoured cheques drawn against the credit account, and when challenged the court held that the bank had been entitled to do so.

Some fifty years later in *Greenhalgh and Sons* v. *Union Bank of Manchester* (1924) it was said.

> With regard to the question whether a banker, having two accounts open for a customer and having appropriated bills to one, is entitled to transfer their proceeds to the other without the customer's permission, I hold that the bank has no right, without the assent of the customer, to move either assets or liabilities from one account to the other. The very basis of his agreement with the customer is that the accounts shall be separate.

However, it must be remembered that this case did not call for consideration of a banker's duty to pay his customer's cheques, and although the words are strong, the judge in *National Westminster Bank Ltd* v. *Halesowen Pressworks and Assemblies Ltd* (1972) indicated that the dictum in the Greenhalgh case was incorrect.

Moreover, in *Barclays Bank Ltd* v. *Okenarhe* (1966) the bank was said to be justified in setting off a credit balance at one branch, A, against a debit balance at another branch, B, although here again special circumstances applied. A fraud had been committed and, unusually, the debit balance at B had arisen on a deposit account because of a cheque which had been returned to that bank as collecting banker, with payment countermanded. Branch B had earlier allowed a withdrawal from the deposit account against uncleared effects and these monies had been paid into an account in the name of the same customer at branch A.

Certainly, in an ongoing situation a bank cannot set-off a credit current account and a loan account, where repayments are up to date (*Bradford Old Bank Ltd* v. *Sutcliffe* (1918)).

The case of *Buckingham & Co.* v. *London and Midland Bank Ltd* (1895) illustrates the dangers where set-off is applied arbitrarily, and under circumstances which would seem not to justify it.[40] Here, a current account and loan account were involved, and payments on the loan account had been met. The branch manager revalued the security which he held for the loan account, and became concerned at its inadequacy for the borrowing. This security was a mortgage over the customer's house, and when he wrote down its value he unwisely decided that the lending was at risk. He then told the customer that his credit balance had been appropriated in reduction of the loan account, and that his current account had been closed. Upon hearing this the customer advised the manager that there were cheques outstanding but nevertheless these cheques were duly dishonoured when they were presented for payment. The customer then sued the bank, and the court held that he had been entitled to 'reasonable notice' before such action was taken; it therefore awarded damages for wrongful dishonour.

The moral of this long line of cases is that bankers must proceed with great care; much will depend upon the circumstances of each case, and the size of the balance which is to be appropriated. In the event of challenge the damages which might be awarded for the wrongful dishonour of a cheque could be far in excess of the apparent benefit of the credit balance seized, and clearly the prudent banker will be extremely cautious except where he holds a letter of set-off, or the right is undoubted through insolvency, or through determination by other legal processes.

Notice of later charge   Finally, under our examination of set-off, it is appropriate to examine the steps which the bank can take when it is lending against security to its customer who has more than one account, and it receives notice of a subsequent charge affecting its security. For example, the bank might hold a mortgage over the customer's house, and receive notice that another charge has been created. In those circumstances it is of course necessary for the ongoing overdrawn account to be stopped, for if not then the bank will lose its right of priority, as the Rule in *Clayton's Case* will come into operation. Usually the subsequent mortgagee will ask the bank how much is secured by its charge and the question then arises as to how a credit balance in

40   See Appendix I, Q. 46 (September 1981).

a separate account should be treated. Can the bank exercise a right of set-off and advise the subsequent lender of the net position between these two accounts? It is generally thought that this is the case, even though monies are not transferred between the accounts, but it may well be necessary to examine the basis on which the borrowing facilities were granted, and if they were specially allocated to the overdrawn account only, and the limit was not a 'net limit' between the accounts, then it is arguable that the credit balance should be ignored, and that the bank's priority should be fixed at the balance on the overdrawn account alone. This is the view taken by Paget where the lending is on loan account, and the current account is in credit.

LIEN

The right of lien may be defined as the right of one person to retain property belonging to another until such time as that other person has met certain outstanding obligations or legal demands. It, too, is perhaps best illustrated by a simple example: an owner takes his motor vehicle to his garage for repair, but when he calls to collect it later, the garage refuses to part with the vehicle until the work is paid for; in doing so it is exercising a lien.

From time to time banks will encounter similar situations, albeit fairly rarely. For instance, solicitors acting for their customers might be in possession of deeds or documents of title and, being uncertain as to whether they are going to be paid for their work, refuse to release the deeds until the fees are met. Or a bank may be pressing its customer for sight of audited accounts, but the customer's accountants will not make these available, or realease the customer's books, until they are paid for the work they have carried out. Such cirumstances can present difficulties for the bank, although if it holds an undertaking from the solicitors over the deeds it should be possible for these to be overcome fairly readily.

However, in this part of our book we are more concerned about examining the banker's own right of lien – that is, the right to retain property belonging to a customer in view of obligations which are outstanding.

A lien may be particular or general. If it is a particular lien it arises out of a specific transaction; if it is a general lien it is an ongoing right which is available should problems arise between the two parties, and one finds himself holding items belonging to the other which he can then retain.

Normally a lien does not give the person holding the property the right to sell the goods or items concerned, but a banker's lien which is a general lien is more like a pledge, and provided the bank gives adequate notice to the owner, affording him the opportunity to settle matters or redeem the goods before he exercises his rights, the banker can proceed to a sale. However, in practice, sales of items caught under a banker's lien are rarely carried out.

It should be noted that if items have been lodged with a banker for a specific purpose which would be inconsistent with a lien, as for example if property had been deposited for safe custody, then a lien does not arise. Similarly, if items come into the banker's possession as the customer's agent for the purpose of sale, as might happen with stocks and shares, then there can be no lien. Positions of this sort, inconsistent with lien, arise under a specific or an implied contract.

The most frequently quoted case on lien is that of *Brandao* v. *Barnett* (1846), and while the facts need not be examined it may be recalled that in the judgment it was said: 'Upon the facts found, there was no lien. . . . The right acquired by a general lien is an implied pledge. . . . In the present case there was an implied agreement on the part of the defendants, inconsistent with the right of lien they claim'.

How then does a banker acquire a lien? A good illustration is where he has collected a cheque on behalf of his customer and this has been dishonoured upon presentation at the drawee bank. The cheque is returned to the banker and because his customer's account is or will become overdrawn when he debits the returned item, he retains the dishonoured cheque by way of lien and sets himself up as a holder for value with rights against all parties to the cheque. Section 27(iii) Bills of Exchange Act 1882 states that 'where the

---

TO PRACTICE BANK plc

In consideration of your granting or continuing banking accommodation and facilities to me, I

_____

of _____

1) agree that all stocks, shares, securities, goods or other items now or at any future time in or coming into your possession in whatsoever manner and whether for safe-custody or otherwise may be held by you as a security for all or any indebtedness or liability, actual or contingent, joint or several, which I might have to you

2) this security is a continuing security and covers any such items or situation arising now, in the past, or at any time in the future

3) for the purposes of this security possession by any officer or employee of yours is to be deemed as possession by you at any time

4) these rights are in addition to any general lien or other right to which you are entitled either by law or Statute from time to time

SIGNED_____

WITNESS_____

ADDRESS _____ DATE _____

Fig.5.5   *Letter of lien*

holder of a bill has a lien on it, arising either from contract or by implication of law, he is deemed to be a holder for value to the extent of the sum for which he has a lien'.

It can be seen therefore that items over which is accepted that the banker has a general lien will clearly include promissory notes, bills of exchange, exchequer bills, coupons and bonds of foreign governments.

To ensure that there is no dispute about his rights, a banker, will frequently include a clause in his security forms, especially the guarantee form, under which the chargor or guarantor will agree to the bank having a right of lien over 'all or any items coming into the bank's possession. Sometimes this right is extended even to cover items deposited in safe custody, thus overcoming the ruling that those items would not be subject to lien when deposited simply under the normal contract of bailment. This type of security clause granting a lien might also be drawn to cover any credit balances which might be in the guarantor's account and will give the banker the right to set them off against crystallized or uncrystallized liabilities. Where clauses such as these are included in security forms given by limited companies it is important to ensure that they are not capable of being construed as charges over book debts, for, if so, to be good against a liquidator and creditors of the company it would be essential for them to be registered under s. 395 Companies Act 1985. To avoid this, they are invariably drafted in a different manner.

Sometimes a bank will use a specific form drawn to cover its right of lien and this clearly will put any argument beyond real dispute. An example of the type of clauses used can be seen in Fig 5.5.

CHAPTER 6

Banking Operations – Services

SAFE CUSTODY

Since their early days bankers have provided a most useful service for their customers in holding property for safe keeping in their safes or strongrooms. This aspect of their activities falls within that branch of the law known as bailment.

A contract of bailment only arises when the property is lodged for a specific purpose, in this case safe custody. The intention is that the property concerned should be preserved and returned to the bailor, in the same condition as it is deposited, upon demand, or should be delivered to another person on his instructions. The customer is the bailor, and the banker is the bailee.

The bailee's duty is to the bailor only, and except upon the operation of law, a good discharge can only be obtained from the depositor. Thus a banker, while perhaps taking note of a claim of a third party to items held on his customer's behalf in safe custody, should not be prepared to deliver those items to anyone else, even though, perhaps, they appear to belong to him. If we pause for a moment, by way of example, we can imagine a situation where customer Jones has lent money to Brown, and taken as security a share certificate showing Brown as the proprietor of the shares. Jones might deposit this share certificate for safe keeping at his bank, and although there is no evidence on the share certificate to indicate Jones's interest (as equitable mortgagee), clearly it would be prejudicial to him as customer if, upon a request from Brown, and because the shares seemed to belong to Brown, the bank delivered the certificate to the registered proprietor.

Degree of care

In law, bailment can be examined under two areas, paid bailment and gratuitous or free bailment.

We need therefore to look at each bank's own particular practice when considering which branch of the law governs the contract of safe custody, although, as we shall see, the distinction is mainly technical.

This is because some banks make a specific charge for their safe-custody services, and others include a charge in their quarterly or half-yearly commission or service charge where it is not identifiable. Others (the gratuitous bailees) make no charge at all.

A paid bailee, known as a bailee for reward, has imposed upon him the need to exercise the utmost degree of care, to ensure that loss is not occasioned to

143

the bailor. The standard of care must be that which can reasonably be expected from a person in the bailee's line of business. He is therefore liable for ordinary negligence.

The gratuitous bailee, on the other hand, is 'only bound to take the same care of the property entrusted to him as a reasonably prudent and careful man may fairly be expected to take of his own property of the like description' (*Giblin* v. *McMullen* (1868)).

However, the attempt to distinguish the two branches of bailment received a setback in the ruling in *Houghland* v. *R. R. Low (Luxury Coaches) Ltd* (1962) in which it was said that an attempt to put the bailment into a watertight compartment oversimplified the situation. It was held there that the standard of care demanded from a bailee, whether gratuitous or paid, must be that standard demanded by the circumstances of the particular case.

More recently in a Privy Council decision (*Port Swettenham Authority* v. *T. W. Wu & Co.* (1978)), while it was accepted that the degree of care imposed on a gratuitous bailee might be less than that on a paid bailee, it was also said that the line between the two was 'very fine, difficult to discern and impossible to define'. It was also felt that the onus of disproving negligence fell on the bailee, whether he was paid or gratuitous.

Having considered the distinction between the two types of bailment, a moment's reflection will indicate that, in practice, the standard of care imposed upon a banker will be almost identical, whether the bailment is gratuitous or paid. Clearly, as bankers exercise such care with their own property, holding cash and securities and valuables in safes and locked cupboards inside strongrooms, which themselves frequently have two locked doors, with combination locks, then they must be expected, even as gratuitous bailees, to do the same with their customer's property.

Of course, banks, when issuing a receipt to the depositor, will invariably disclaim liability for loss or damage to the item deposited, and while in a Trustee Saving Banks case (*Award Kesby* (1958)) this disclaimer was held to protect the bank, it is possible, in other circumstances, and where it can be shown that loss to the depositor has been occasioned by the negligence of the bank, that on commercial and ethical grounds the bank would not wish to seek to escape liability. Indeed, in view of the subsequent legislation in the form of the Unfair Contract Terms Act 1977, it is felt that the disclaimer might not now protect a bank as bailee, except in so far as the bank is able to show that it has met the test of 'reasonableness'.

Risks

The risks that a bailee incurs therefore include negligence. This is a breach of the duty to take care, and this is very high in the case of a bank that has accepted items for safe keeping. To be successful a claim in negligence would need to establish that the conduct of a bank had been such that, as a direct result, the depositor had suffered loss, and in some instances such a claim might need to show that the bank had specific knowledge as to the item deposited. For instance, if a valuable stamp collection were lodged, it would clearly be a breach of care if the bank left this in a strongroom which was known to suffer from damp, and the stamps lost their value because of the action of mildew. However, if the bank were not aware that the package contained valuable stamps, it could be argued in defence that as it had exercised reasonable care in looking after the package it had no liability in respect of the damage by damp to its contents.

The second risk is that of conversion. This is 'an unauthorized act which deprives another person of his property permanently or for an indefinite time' (*Hiort* v. *Bott* (1874)), and would arise, for instance, where items were delivered to the wrong depositor. It can be seen, therefore, that where there is similarity of names of account holders at a branch, great care should be taken to ensure that records, and delivery of safe-custody items, guard against possible wrongful delivery.

We can also consider robbery to be a real risk. Theft of items in safe custody could be either by a criminal bank employee, or by thieves breaking in. In the case of an employee, clearly an action lies against him, but the question as to whether the bank, as employer, is also liable in damages to a depositor, is questionable, and there is no legal decision on this point. Provided there is no negligence in the custody of the goods, then no legal liability will fall upon the bank if there is theft by an outside criminal.

There was, until it was abolished by the Torts (Interference with Goods) Act 1977, the risk of a claim of detinue. That was the wrongful retention of goods belonging to another person, but any action to recover the property would now be brought by way of a claim of interference with goods, covering conversion and trespass. On can, however, only imagine a bank retaining items, for a short period, in those special circumstances where the right to deliver to the depositor is questionable, or requires confirmation, or in a situation where a bank claims a lien itself over the items concerned. The normal situation is that items lodged in safe custody are not caught under the banker's lien, but this presumption can be rebutted by a specific contract between the depositor and the bank, where he has given the bank a letter of lien, or has given the bank equivalent rights by signing a security form which includes a clause to the same effect.

Method of deposit

Items for safe keeping are usually lodged either in a locked metal box, the customer retaining the key, or in a sealed parcel, the customer using his personal seal, or signing over sealing wax, or under Sellotape. Sometimes items like share certificates, bearer bonds or a will are lodged loosely.

Most banks will give the depositor a receipt for the item lodged (Fig. 6.1), and certainly should do so if requested, while others ask the depositor to sign

Nᵒ   200

BANK OF CYPRUS (LONDON) LIMITED

27/31 Charlotte Street
London W1P 4BH
Telephone
01-637 3961
Telegraphic Address
Cyprobank
London W1P 4BH
Telex
22114 Cybanc G.

The Items enumerated below have today been lodged on account of

....

....

....

....

....

Customers are requested to take note that the Bank take all reasonable steps to protect the boxes, parcels or securities lodged, but is not responsible for loss of or damage to such boxes, parcels or securities or their contents by reason of fire, burglary or other causes. They are advised to consider the desirability of insuring such items if they are not already covered by existing policies.

Date .... Manager

Registered Office
27-31 Charlotte Street
London W1P 4BH
Registered Number
652394 (London)

Fig.6.1   *Safe–custody receipt*

the counterfoil of a ledger referring to the transaction. The receipt will invariably include the disclaimer of liability clause, and also a note of advice to the depositor that he should insure against loss by fire or theft. Frequently insurance can be arranged on a householder's comprehensive insurance policy.

It is important when a receipt is made out, and when the item deposited is entered in the bank's records, that the description is entirely accurate. For instance, a sealed parcel, marked 'Deeds of Animal Farm, Ashford, Kent' should simply be recorded as 'A sealed parcel *marked* Deeds of Animal Farm, Ashford, Kent' and should not recorded as 'The Deeds of Animal Farm, Ashford, Kent'. The bank can have no knowledge of the contents, and the effect of giving a receipt in the wrong terms could have adverse repercussions.

Delivery

If a receipt was given at the time of deposit, then when the item is to be withdrawn the receipt should be produced by the customer who should then sign his part of the form as an acknowledgement of redelivery, and this will then be retained as a discharge in the bank's records. It is not absolutely essential, however, for the customer to produce the original receipt, and indeed if this referred to several items, only one of which is now to be redelivered, then clearly a separate form will be required. It is important that delivery is only made to the depositor, as we have seen, or to a third party, from whom a receipt should be obtained, on the depositor's written authority. It is only those circumstances where operation of law prevents delivery on the instructions of the depositor that are outside this rule.

Great care must be exercised where an authority signed by the depositor is produced by a third party which only gives him the right of *access* to the items lodged. This limited right must be strictly adhered to, and it will be necessary for a bank officer to remain with the third party, throughout the duration of the time when he has access to the contents of a locked tin box, to ensure that nothing is removed.[41] If the authority extends to the removal of any property, this must be adequately identified, and acknowledged by a receipt.

Mandates

When an item is deposited by one person, who is in account solely, and also jointly with others, it is important to ensure in whose names(s) the property is lodged and to whom delivery can correctly be made. Is the intention for the item to be held solely in the individual's own name, or is it lodged to be held jointly, and then in accordance with the existing or a new mandate? In the absence of any clear intention for the item to be held on behalf of all parties in a joint account, it is prudent for the bank to hold the deposit in the individual's sole name.

When a joint account, partnership account or limited company account is opened, the mandate then taken by the bank as to the conduct of the account may recite the terms upon which securities and safe custody can be delivered. Some banks do not include these clauses in the account-opening form, and a separate mandate is taken later, upon the first occasion when use is made of the safe custody service. It is of course important that any changes to the mandate are authorized to the bank in the manner and terms provided for in the original authority.

Determination of mandate

Upon the death of a sole depositor of safe custody, it will be necessary for his executors, or administrators, to produce probate before items in safe custody can be delivered to them. However, in the case of the customer's will lodged

41 See Appendix I, Q. 21 (September 1982).

in safe custody, an exception to this rule is necessary, for probate or letters of administration will not be obtainable without production of the will.[42] In these circumstances, as a practical matter, provided the bank is assured as to the identity of the persons acting, and that they are the named executors in the will, or the next of kin, where the executors are deceased or unwilling to act, then the bank will release the will against their adequate receipt. Invariably in such cases solicitors are already instructed, and provided the bank is satisfied on the points already mentioned, and also the standing of the solicitors concerned, it seems that little harm will result. Where the branch has copying facilities, it might be considered prudent for a photostat copy of the will document to be retained. A satisfactory banker's opinion on the standing of the solicitors should be obtained, if they are not already known.

Occasionally if a valuable item such as a diamond ring or other piece of jewellery is held in safe custody, the executors may ask the bank if they can withdraw it to have it valued for probate purposes. This type of request should be politely refused, and either arrangements should be made for the valuation to be made on bank premises, or it should be suggested that an estimate of the value be used for purposes of obtaining probate or letters of administration. Only when the executors are fully authorized to act and produce probate (or the administrators show their authority by producing the letters of adminstration) can withdrawal against their receipt be permitted.

Turning to the situation upon the death of one party to a joint account, although we have seen that in the joint account mandate the common law rule is reinforced and the bank is enabled to obtain a satisfactory discharge for a credit balance from the survivor, this does not apply to property lodged in joint names in safe custody. The reason for this is that only joint property vests in the survivor, and the item in safe custody might not be so owned. Thus while there might be a case for releasing deeds, or stocks and shares, in joint names, it is unwise to release property such as jewellery, locked boxes, and sealed parcels. To prevent legal problems most banks therefore call for a receipt from the survivor *and* the executor or administrator of the deceased to obtain a good discharge.

Where the banker has notice that a petition for bankruptcy has been presented against his customer, or that a bankruptcy order has been made, items in safe-custody should not be released.

Where a bankruptcy order is made against one party to a joint account, the mandate is revoked, and delivery of items in safe custody can be made only on the joint written instructions of the trustee in bankruptcy and the other party or parties to the account.

When a bankruptcy order is made against one partner in a partnership, as opposed to a winding-up order being made against the partnership itself, the solvent partners are able to give an effective discharge to the bank for

42 See Appendix I, Q. 39 (September 1980).

partnership safe-custody items, although usually the bank will take a new mandate, and in case of doubt would prudently refer to the trustee in bankruptcy first.

In the case of the mental incapacity of the customer, where a receiver is appointed by the Court of Protection, before safe custody items can be delivered to the receiver it is important that the bank examines the order carefully, and ensures that this extends to the delivery of such items specifically. In the absence of any reference to safe custody it will be necessary for the receiver to return to the court for a further order.

Night safe facilities

All clearing banks offer a special form of safe custody to their customers at selected branches, for the safe keeping of money overnight, such cash being deposited in the branch night safe, access to which is available from the street. The customer is provided with a key to the door which opens in the wall, and with a wallet in which the cash is to be secured, and locked with another key. A special agreement is entered into between the bank and the customer, whereby the customer agrees to be responsible for any loss, and the bank undertakes to hold the wallet simply under a contract of bailment (safe custody), and not under that of debtor – creditor. The latter relationship only arises when the monies are deposited in the bank account on the following business day. The deposit into the account is made by the customer when he calls at the branch and opens his wallet, and at that time he signs for the return of the wallet in a register maintained by the branch, the wallets having been extracted from the bank safe by two officers before the branch opened for business. Occasionally the agreement authorizes the branch bankers to open the wallet before the customer calls, and in such instances it is prudent for the wallet to be opened by two bank officers, who will check the contents against a credit slip already prepared. Also, occasionally the agreement enables the bank to hand the wallet, unopened, to a named person, on the following or subsequent business day, the monies not then being lodged in the account. Clearly, in such instances, the bank must be assured as to the identity of the named person, and must obtain his receipt, checking his signature against a specimen which will have been provided earlier.

CREDIT CARDS

Some banks issue combined cheque guarantee cards and credit cards, while others have separate items. Often, the issuer of the card is a finance house owned by the bank, although in such instances the contract entered into by the customer is with the bank and the finance house, and this means that any securities which the customer has lodged become available for any liability which might be outstanding and unpaid to the finance house.

As with the cheque guarantee card, upon issue the customer will sign an agreement form under which it is said that the card will remain the property of the the credit card company; the customer agrees to return the card upon demand. Also, if it is lost or stolen, he undertakes to advise the credit card company immediately. One difference with a credit card is that a credit limit is set and the customer is advised of this and then agrees that he will not exceed this ceiling. Where a card is issued to joint account holders they undertake joint and several liability and agree that in the event of the death or bankruptcy of either of them, or upon breach of the terms of issue, the whole amount outstanding shall be due.

The customer is thus enabled to pay for his goods in shops accepting the credit card and each month he is supplied with a statement showing his transactions. At that point, depending upon the agreement, he must either settle the outstanding amount in full or in a minimum figure leaving the balance outstanding upon which interest will be added. The interest rates involved are usually higher than those on normal bank overdrafts, and another feature of the credit card is that when the card is issued or renewed, usually annually, some companies charge a fee. From the retailer's point of view, the major advantage is that he is again guaranteed payment. The retailer must in this instance be a member of the scheme and for this he is charged a small percentage on the transaction by the credit card finance house, but he has the satisfaction of knowing that payment is assured. Where the amount is large, and where his floor limit set by the finance house is exceeded, the retailer will telephone the finance house and can obtain a quick sanction for the guaranteed transaction. Retailers display cards in their windows indicating that transactions to be settled by this and/or other cards are acceptable, and this attracts trade to a shop. At the time of the transaction, the retailer raises a voucher upon which the card details are imprinted, and the form is signed by the card holder. A copy is given to the customer, and the retailer retains the other parts of the voucher, paying one copy into his bank account just as he would pay in a cheque. This form is then collected through the clearing system for settlement.

When a customer requires a credit card, he will be asked to complete an application form giving details of his personal and financial position, and often his branch banker will add a recommendation, for the form is then sent to the finance company who will issue the card. Occasionally the form is sent direct to the finance house, and the branch is then asked to speak for their customer by way of a status report.

In one of the few cases yet heard on this area of money transmission services (in *re Charge Card Services Ltd* (1986)) the judge looked at the relationships arising upon the use of a charge card or credit card and saw three separate contracts coming into operation. These were:

(1) a contract of supply between the supplier of goods or services and the cardholder;

(2) a contract between the supplier and the company which issued the card

under which the card company undertakes to honour the use of the card;

(3) a contract between the card company and the cardholder under which the latter undertakes to reimburse the company for payment it makes to the supplier as a consequence of the cardholder's use of the card.

As to whether payment for goods or services by use of a credit card is absolute or conditional as when a cheque is tendered or an irrevocable letter of credit is used (i.e., as to who is liable if the card-issuing company fails) the court felt that it would be necessary to look at the precise terms of the contract when the goods were supplied to the card-holder.

The misuse of a credit card is an offence under s. 16 Theft Act 1968, as was upheld in the case of *R. v. Lambie* (1981). It follows, therefore, that where a bank has a customer who is misusing his cheque card or credit card, then, in the light of this decision and the cheque card decisions, it would be unlikely to be out of place if the bank warned the customer, albeit carefully, that the continued misuse of the cheque card or the credit card could lead to the customer becoming liable for possible criminal proceedings under the Theft Act 1968. The advantage of such a warning is that further losses to the bank might be avoided.

ADVICE ON INVESTMENTS

Bankers are occasionally asked to give advice to their customers on investments, perhaps with increasing frequency in view of their own advertisements which offer this service. However, it must be remembered that the service is a general one, and bankers should never become involved in the specific recommendation of a particular share or 'opportunity', for therein would lie considerable danger. Indeed, the whole area of what duty, if any, a professional person owes to his client, or even third parties who might be unknown to him but rely on his views (for example a lender relying on figures in a balance sheet certified by an accountant) is a highly sensitive one these days, and one of increasingly broadened claims.

Generally, as far as any investment is concerned the advice that can safely be given will only be on the nature of types of securities, the risks associated with different classes, and the returns which are available. This means that a banker is able safely to discuss the relative merits of such items as unit trusts, equities, government securities and building society accounts as well as local authority bonds and the returns on National Savings certificates.

If his customer requires specific advice on a particular security, the banker should seek the opinion of a stockbroker, and usually this will be forwarded to the customer with a disclaimer clause in the bank's covering letter indicating that it accepts no responsibility itself for what is said. It must be remembered however that the effectiveness of the disclaimer clause is now subject to considerable doubt following the passing of the Unfair Contract Terms Act 1977.

In calling for his broker's opinion, the banker will need to have questioned his customer beforehand, so that he is adequately briefed on the latter's financial position, and on his highest tax rate, which can be an important factor. Also, the banker will need to know whether the customer is looking for income in the short term, or can defer this, or simply wants capital appreciation of his investment. Perhaps he might prefer a mixture of both.

In giving advice, the main risk to both the bank and the officer concerned is that of negligence – in other words, a breach of the duty of care.

The bank carries the additional risk that responsibility for any fraudulent misrepresentation by the individual officer will fall upon the bank as employer, and this usually means that the officer has absconded when the fraud comes to light.

In order to succeed in a claim of negligence a customer would need to be able to demonstrate that it is part of the bank's business to give investment advice. He would then have to show that the advice which was given was careless, and that he had however acted upon it and thereby suffered loss. If the customer succeeded on all these points be would be entitled to damages.

It is now a well-established part of the bank's business to give investment advice, and while at one time there was a debate about this, it would not now be relevant. The view seen in the case of *Banbury* v. *Bank of Montreal* (1918), when it was thought that only on occasions would the relationship of banker and customer take the banker into an area where it was part of his ordinary business to provide specific advice, is now outdated.

In *Woods* v. *Martins Bank Ltd* (1958) it was held that where an official gave specific advice then there was no doubt that he owed a duty of care. If that care were not exercised then a customer, and possibly even a non-customer, for example a person not actually holding an account at the time, would be entitled to damages. However, the circumstances of the *Woods* v. *Martins* case were special, and no prudent banker would ever give the advice which was given in that case. Surprisingly there the bank advised its customer to invest his money in a private limited company requiring finance, and which had an account at the same branch. The customer acted on this advice and subsequently lost his money. Clearly, with hindsight it is possible to see that there was a conflict of interests for the bank at the time when it gave the advice, and there were certain similarities with the later case of *Lloyds Bank Ltd* v. *Bundy* (1975), which concerned guarantees. The moral to be drawn however is clear: No banker should involve one of his customers in another customer's affairs, and recommendations to invest in private shares must always be fraught with danger.

In conclusion it is worth stressing again the author's firm opinion that branch bankers, and perhaps others, should not stretch out into the field of financial or business advice without caution. Unhappily, it seems easier for a litigant to succeed these days in pursuing a claim against a bank, perhaps referring back to circumstances which years ago would have seemed entirely safe for the officer concerned. In one instance the writer saw a manager attacked by his customer for 'negligent advice and lending' some three years after the customer had bought a business which had subsequently failed. The manager was alleged to have said that the business would be a 'goldmine', although nothing was admitted of the customer's own ineptitude and mismanagement in the years when he had traded!

DISCOUNTING OF BILLS

The discounting of a bill of exchange may be likened to the sale by the customer of an accepted bill to the bank. By discounting the customer is able to obtain funds in advance of the due date of the bill, and thus his liquidity is improved. However, the value which he receives for the bill is less than the face value, and the difference represents the bank's interest. From the bank's point of view, therefore, the discounting of a bill is similar to a lending proposition and the bank's security is the bill itself, through which it acquires rights of recourse which, in the event of dishonour, it may rely upon against the drawer, drawee and all endorsers, if any.

This is because it becomes a holder for value, or a holder in due course, under the provisions of the Bills of Exchange Act 1882, provided it meets the requirements of s. 27 (holder for value) or s. 29 (holder in due course). These sections are quoted on pp. 110-111.

Before a bank will be prepared to discount a bill for its customer, it will wish to be assured that the bill is drawn in respect of a recognized trading transaction, and it will look particularly at the trade in which the customer is engaged. In certain trades the use of bills, and discounting, is common, while in others the appearance of such a transaction might be a warning factor. The timber trade is a good example of one in which the use of bill finance is common.

The bank will always be on its guard to ensure that any bill tendered for discounting is not an accommodation bill, that is one drawn by the customer on another party simply as a means of raising finance, and not in respect of a genuine trade settlement. If accommodation bills are met, the customer's solvency and liquidity might well be open to question, and the risks for the bank could be considerable. In each case, therefore, the bank will ask itself whether it is usual to encounter discounting in the particular trade, and whether this customer has engaged in such operations before, and if not, why not.

For the purpose of our examination of discounting, we are concerned only with inland bills, and the bank will usually make it a condition of any discount transaction that the bill is a short bill – that is one payable within, say, six months at the outside, and preferably sooner. A guiding general rule for the bank will be that there should be two good names on the bill. These should be the customer's as drawer or endorser, and the acceptor's. Frequently, the identity and standing of the acceptor will not be known to the discounting bank, and in consequence it will be necessary to obtain a status report, and for this to be renewed regularly, to monitor any possible change in his financial circumstances. Usually, the bank will prefer to discount a series of bills only when there is an acceptor of exceptionally high standing, or where there is a spread of acceptors, as this broadens the risk.

As with any lending proposition, the background of the customer will be all-important and the usual criteria associated with lending propositions should be employed. It may be noted here that if the customer is a limited company then it is not necessary to include the amounts of bills discounted in the calculation to ascertain the extent of the company's present borrowing, when considering this total with any limitation upon the borrowing powers of the company and its directors in the memorandum and articles of association.

Before taking a bill for discounting, the banker will wish to ensure that it is regular on the face of it, and has been endorsed by his customer, who usually will have drawn it in his own favour, or who may have taken it by way of endorsement from another party. The bill must be accepted, and must be payable at a recognized bank; it is prudent for the bill to be sent to that bank, so that the signature of the acceptor may be confirmed. If satisfied on these points the discounting bank will take the bill into its records, and the customer's account will be credited with the face value of the bill, less the discount factor, which is credited to an interest received account, and which is calculated at the going interest rate for such transactions over the period between the discounting operation and the bill's maturity. A bills discounted account will receive the corresponding debit entry, for the face value of the bill. Chreful diary notes should then be made to ensure that the bill is tendered for payment on its due date.

In the event of nonpayment, it is essential for the bank to give notice of dishonour to all parties liable on the bill, in accordance with the provisions of s. 49 Bills of Exchange Act 1882. In this way, the bank will preserve its rights as a holder for value and/or a holder in due course, and will be empowered to sue all parties liable. If the customer's account is in sufficient credit, the dishonoured bill may be debited to that account, and thereby the bank will recoup the monies advanced. However, if the account is overdrawn, or there is insufficient credit balance available, then the bill should be placed to the debit of a suspense account, possibly styled as 'dishonoured bills account'.

CLEARING SYSTEMS

The public tends to take the clearance of cheques by the banking system for granted, without thought as to the cost of the operation or the mechanics of the extensive work involved. It is often only when a bank talks to its customer about commission charges and the recovery of its costs that the work involved is appreciated. Undoubtedly the clearing of cheques and the processing of bank giro credits is a major service operated for customers and non-customers alike. However, in examining clearing systems for the purpose of the Practice of Banking 1 syllabus, we need only to look briefly at the mechanics of the credit and debit clearings as they affect operations in a branch.

Clearing of cheques

Almost all cheques paid in by a customer are cleared through the Clearing House, if the collecting bank is a member of the Association for Payment Clearing Services (APACS), the association set up by the banks in 1985 to oversee and manage the payment clearing and money transmission systems. If not, it may use a clearing bank as its agent. At the collecting branch office, after a cheque has been paid in for the credit of an account, it is crossed specially to that branch by means of a crossing stamp, and it is then forwarded, along with other cheques, daily, to the head office of the bank, or its clearing section, from where it is passed forward to the drawee bank, with all the other cheques for that bank, which are in the hands of the collecting bank. At the same time the drawee bank will pass over cheques which it wishes to exchange and, through the mechanics of the Clearing House, a net settlement takes place.

After exchange, each bank sorts its own cheques into branch order, and the cheques are then dispatched by mail, or, more usually these days, by the use of a security service. At the same time, accounting entries are passed through the computer so that the customer's account will be debited, and this entry takes place on the third business day after the cheque was paid in. The passing of entries by magnetic ink character recognition (MICR) is facilitated as the collecting branch encodes each cheque when it is paid in over the counter, taking the amount in figures on the cheque as its base, and inserting the amount in magnetic ink on the bottom of each cheque. It is therefore important when the paying bank receives its batch of cheques, together with a list of the amounts involved, that the amount in words is compared carefully either with the amount in figures on the cheque, or the amount on the listing which is derived from the magnetic ink encoding.

The cheque must therefore be paid on the third day, or dishonoured, and if dishonoured, the 'answer' must be written in the top left-hand corner of the cheque, which is then returned by first-class post to the collecting bank branch, as identified by the crossing stamp. Consequently, in the absence of delays in the post, the collecting bank should be aware on the fourth business day whether the cheque is paid or not. There is a presumption that if it has not been returned by then it has been cleared.

Late return of cheques

However, there is an agreement between the clearing banks that where a cheque has been paid inadvertently on the third day – that is, when it was not noticed on that day that a cheque should have been returned – then it may be returned on the next business day, i.e. the fourth day, provided the reason is not a technical irregularity – such as the cheque being 'postdated' or having insufficient signatures as drawer – but rather that there are insufficient funds in the account. This might only be noticed, on the fourth day, when a computer print-out is received of customers' balances and it is then realized that the cheque should not have been paid. Another reason for use of the late-return system is when payment of the cheque has been stopped, provided the stop authority is received by the drawee bank no later than the close of business on the third day – that is the day of first presentation. Also, a cheque may be returned late if the account has been closed, or if something has happened to revoke the mandate such as the death of the customer or his bankruptcy or the liquidation of a limited company. The arrangement between the clearing banks is that where a cheque returned late is more than thirty pounds in amount, then the drawee bank must telephone the presenting bank, but not later than mid-day on the day after presentation – that is day four. Details of the cheque must be given, and the officers concerned making and receiving the telephone call should exchange names so that records can be made at each branch as a concurrent verification of the matter. Thereafter, the cheque must be returned in the normal way, with the reason confirmed in writing. Where a cheque is £100 or less in amount it is not necessary for the telephone conversation to take place, and the written procedure alone is acceptable.

Special clearance

Sometimes a customer will wish his collecting banker to clear a cheque quickly so that he may know whether it is paid or not[43] and in such circumstances, on payment of a fee, the collecing banker will be happy to assist outside of the usual clearing system. Indeed, there will be occasions where the bank itself may wish to ensure that the funds in the customer's account represent cleared monies, and for its own protection it will clear the cheque specially.

Again, the cheque is crossed with a crossing stamp, and it may then be sent either by first-class post direct to the drawee bank or, if feasible, taken by hand by an officer of the collecting bank to the drawee bank during business hours. In either event, a specific request should be made as to whether the cheque is paid or not, and settlement can be affected by means of a banker's payment. If the post is used it should be first class, and the letter covering the cheque should be clear as to whether advice is required by return of post, or, as is more likely, by telephone. Usually, the collecting banker will telephone

43　See Appendix I, Q. 13 (September 1981).

the drawee banker on the following morning, just after the drawee branch has opened for business, and if a confirmatory answer is given that the cheque is paid then the drawee bank cannot later change its decision. However, should the cheque not be paid, by reason of shortage of funds, it is occasionally arranged for the drawee bank to hold the cheque briefly before returning it to the collecting bank. This is in case the drawer should place his account in funds, and to obviate the cheque passing backwards and forwards. However, if such special arrangements are made, the collecting banker must remember that the cheque has been dishonoured, and it is his duty to advise the customer at once.

The credit clearing

This has grown in size and importance in recent years and is now fully automated. It is possible for any person, using a bank giro credit form, to pay in for the credit of the beneficiary's account at a named bank and branch over the counter of any bank in the country. It is helpful if he knows the account number, and the sorting code number, but neither detail is essential. Some banks make a small charge for accepting bank giro credits from non-customers. The mechanics of the clearance of bank giro credits are similar to the much older debit clearing and the vouchers are separated into banks and passed forward to the head office or clearing system where they are exchanged and where a net settlement takes place. The time scale is that on the third business day after the credit has been tendered the beneficiary account is credited. No differentiation is made as to whether the items making up the bank giro credit are then cleared or uncleared funds and it would be necessary for the recipient bank to examine the voucher carefully if it wished to have some knowledge of that situation, although even upon examination the make-up of items might not be entirely apparent.

Occasionally, a customer or third party might wish to ensure that monies are remitted quickly to a beneficiary's account, not being prepared to wait three days. If both account-holding banks are settlement banks participating in CHAPS (Clearing House Automated Payments System) then through the use of computer-generated entries the funds can pass in a matter of minutes although the present minimum figure for use of CHAPS is £10 000 (February 1987). Some undoubted customers will be allowed to generate entries themselves.

In due course it is expected that this new system will make telegraphic transfers obsolete, but for the time being these remain in use and are the only other means of remitting monies speedily. They involve the processing of funds by the use of a code, through the intermediary of the respective banks' head offices. Effectively, however, provided the recipient of the message is satisfied that it is authentic, he can credit his customer's account upon receipt of the message and settle through inter-branch or inter-bank means.

If the person requiring quick settlement is not prepared to pay the fees incurred for CHAPS or a telegraphic transfer then his only other alternatives are the use of the normal postal system, remitting the monies to the account-holding branch, or a visit to that office by himself or by special messenger.[44]

INDEMNITIES

While some banks are prepared to be active in the field, it is not part of the general activity of a clearing bank to give guarantees or indemnities to third parties in respect of their customer's liabilities. But there are several instances where even a clearing bank will be prepared to help in this way. It must be remembered, however, that if it executes an indemnity it assumes a real liability, and all the circumstances must be examined most carefully before the commitment is undertaken. This means that the indemnity, bond, or guarantee document must be read in detail, and fully understood, and the extent of the maximum financial liability must be quantified. If the indemnity refers to a transaction or liability in foreign currencies, then there will be the added risks of exchange rate fluctuations, and currency premium variations which could adversely effect the bank's position at the time if and when it is called upon to pay.

It follows therefore that the bank will enter into indemnities only for good customers with sound financial backgrounds, and it may well be that even then the bank will call for security, or cash cover. A commission will be charged for entering into the agreement, and this may be a percentage rate or a flat charge levied at the outset, and perhaps again upon renewal, or upon specified dates. A look at a bank's balance sheet on both the assets and liabilities sides will show the extent of the engagements entered into on behalf of its good customers.

Common situations

Let us now look at some typical situations where indemnities are involved and where the nature of the liability and the transaction can be seen.

With a building customer invariably the developer will have to satisfy the local authority that he will be able to make up the roads and lay the drains before he commences work on an estate of houses, and such a customer is frequently asked by the local authority to provide a bond from his bank or another organization, protecting the local authority in the event of poor work or should the work not be completed because of the bankruptcy or liquidation of the builder. Such performance bonds to local authorities arise under s. 38 Highways Act 1980 and usually involve substantial sums of money. Frequently the bank is also lending to assist with the building development and in assessing its overall risk it should not forget that it might be called upon to pay under the performance bond.

Again, if the customer is a travel agent then the bank might be requested to

44 See Appendix I, Q. 13 (September 1981).

give a bond or indemnity on behalf of the customer to a holiday tourist organization, and such a document is virtually a guarantee, up to the sum specified, against their customer's failure or insolvency. If the customer is an importer of wines or spirits then he may be required to give a bank bond to HM Customs & Excise to cover any duty payable. Sometimes when a customer is temporarily exporting a car or caravan the Automobile Association or Royal Automobile Club require an indemnity from the bank to cover liabilities which they enter into on behalf of the customer.

A frequent example of the need for an indemnity is when a customer has lost a share certificate.[45] Usually then, when he applies to the registrars for a duplicate, he will not be issued with one, unless the bank will join with the customer in the request, and indemnify the company against any loss which may arise should the original certificate come to light. This is similar to an indemnity given in respect of missing or lost bills of lading as part of shipping documents.

Where a customer has died and there is a credit balance remaining in his account, if the estate is small then the bank might well be prepared to release the balance to the next of kin without letters of administration or probate being taken out, and provided the next of kin satisfactorily identifies himself and the estate in total is below the limit then in force, against that person's counter-indemnity the bank will usually be prepared to help.[46] This procedure is in line with the provisions of the Administration of Estates (Small Payments) Amendment Act 1976 which permits the disposal of certain property to persons entitled to the funds, without a grant of representation. Most clearing banks will release funds up to £5000 on this basis at the present time.

There are other situations in which a bank might be requested to give an indemnity and each one must be viewed on its own merits. Naturally, each bank has its own policy towards which items it will and will not become associated with, but in every case where it is prepared to help it is vital to assess the customer and to have complete trust in him. Many of the criteria used to judge lending propositions should and can be used when deciding whether or not to enter into an indemnity liability on behalf of the customer.

Counter-indemnity

Under common law the bank has a right to reimbursement when it has paid up under an indemnity, but invariably it will also have taken a written counter-indemnity at the outset from the customer, strengthening its position. This counter-indemnity may be either general or specific in nature (Fig. 6.2). A general counter-indemnity will cover all contracts of indemnity entered into by the bank on the customer's behalf, giving the bank recourse to the customer, and a right to debit his account or set off credit balances at will. A

45 See Appendix I, Q. 23 (September 1982).
46 See Appendix I, Q. 10 (April 1981).

To the

BANK OF CYPRUS (LONDON) LTD

WHEREAS on the _____19__, you issued to me
one Bankers Draft numbered_____for the amount of £ _____
(say: _____) on _____
_____ AND WHEREAS
such Bankers Draft has been lost or mislaid and I have requested you to refund to me
the amount of such Bankers Draft which you have agreed to do upon having the
Indemnity hereinafter contained:

NOW, THEREFORE, in consideration of your refunding to me the amount of such
Bankers Draft I hereby undertake and agree to indemnify you from and against all
losses, costs, damages, expenses, claims, and demands which you may incur or
sustain by reason thereof, and particularly in the event of the said Bankers Draft
being presented and paid, I agree to repay the amount of such Bankers Draft so paid
and further, that if such Bankers Draft shall at any time hereafter come into my
possession or control, I will forthwith deliver the same or cause the same to be
delivered to you.

Dated this _____day of _____, 19__

We join the above Indemnity

_____

Fig.6.2   *Counter–indemnity*

specific counter-indemnity will refer just to the one transaction, and it will be
necessary therefore to obtain a series of specific counter-indemnities relating to
each incident to give the bank the fullest cover.[47]

Sometimes difficulties can arise as to the interpretation of the terms of an
indemnity or counter-indemnity and this is why it is so important that the full
extent of the liability is understood at the outset. This is particularly so if the
indemnity is given in respect of foreign transactions, or is given abroad, and
its terms are subject to interpretation by the laws of an overseas country. Even
if drawn in English, the terms can be hard to understand at times and can
mean one thing to one party and another thing to someone else. The writer
was once involved with the problems which arose from an indemnity which
was called to be paid where the bank had thought its contingent liability had
been £x. However the beneficiary had genuinely regarded the document as
representing four bonds, each for £x, which arose in series of quarterly
cumulative amounts. It was necessary for the parties to go to court to obtain

47 See Appendix I, Q. 58 (April 1983).

the judge's ruling, based on his interpretation, as to whether £x or £$4x$ was payable!

Demand

If the bank receives a demand to make a payment under an indemnity it has given then it is preferable for it first to refer to its customer and to seek his written agreement to the payment being made. However, the counter-indemnity the customer has signed will include a clause to the effect that the bank is entitled to debit the customer forthwith, or set off credit balances that might be available in his account. If the customer's agreement is not received then the bank rarely has any option in the matter in any event, for under the indemnity it has assumed primary responsibility to the party secured, and it will be required to make payment of the monies due under the terms of the indemnity without delay. In *R. D. Harbottle (Mercantile) Ltd and another* v. *National Westminster Bank Ltd and others* (1977) the bank entered into a guarantee in favour of certain foreign banks and was called upon to pay. Before it could do so its customer, who had a dispute with his foreign buyers, suceeded in obtaining an injunction preventing National Westminster from meeting its obligation. This was embarrassing to the bank, as in the circumstances of the case it felt its international reputation on guarantees was at stake and it asked the court to remove the injunction. This the court was prepared to do, and the bank then made payment, recovering the monies from its customer's account because it held a counter-indemnity allowing the immediate debiting of the account by way of recourse.

BANKERS' OPINIONS AND REPLIES TO STATUS ENQUIRIES

While a banker has a duty to keep his customers' affairs secret, one of the exceptions whereby disclosure is possible is where the customer has given his consent. In the case of a banker replying to a status enquiry (Fig. 6.3), the practice is so well established that the customer is presumed to have given his implied consent when he opened the account. Of course, if he then expressly said to the bank that it must not answer any status enquiries made about him, then the implied consent would be revoked, but the circumstances would be very unusual, and the bank might then wonder about the advisability of conducting the account at all.

Businessmen and others value the status enquiry system, which is usually a free service, and there is no doubt that it is of considerable help in day-to-day commerce when dealing with an unknown or even a regular customer. The enquirer must approach his own branch, as bankers will only give opinions to other bankers, and certain recognized trade protection societies, and opinions will not be given direct to an individual. An exception to the latter rule, however, would be where the customer making the enquiry banks with the

---

BANK OF CYPRUS (LONDON) LIMITED 〔◉〕

BRANCH

Our Ref.: . . . .   Date 19

The Manager,

PRIVATE AND CONFIDENTIAL

Dear Sirs,

The Manager would be obliged by your opinion in confidence as to the business integrity and financial standing of:-

and whether . . . . may be considered trustworthy in the way of business
for £

Bank of Cyprus (London) Ltd. is registered in England No. 652394 Registered Office: 27/31 Charlotte Street, London W1P 4BH

FORM No. G 2

Fig.6.3   *Status enquiry*

---

same bank and branch as the subject of the research, in which event the banker has in effect two roles.

The enquiries made should always be for genuine trade or financial transactions, and the answer is usually given also in brief terms.[48] Over the years certain phrases have come into general use between banks, and their meaning is usually clear to the recipient banker or to an experienced trader.

Thus, in response to an enquiry as to whether a customer is good for £1000 trade credit, an answer might be given to the effect that he is considered 'Undoubted' or 'A respectable customer who maintains a satisfactory account.

48 See Appendix I, Q. 4 (April 1980).

We regret however that we have insufficient knowledge of his affairs to speak for your figure (£1000 trade credit)' (Fig. 6.4).

BANK OF CYPRUS (LONDON) LIMITED

B R A N C H

PRIVATE AND CONFIDENTIAL

Your Ref.:

Our Ref.:

London .... 19....

In reply to your enquiry, the information herein is given in strict confidence, for your private use only, without any guarantee or responsibility on the part of this Bank or its officials and where the information has been obtained from another bank or informant without responsibility on the part of themselves or of their officials

Your enquiry dated   Re

Reply :

This Bank is not a credit reference agency within the terms of Section 145 (8) of the Consumer Credit Act, 1974. Disclosure of the content and source of this opinion is NOT required by that Act.

FORM No. G18

Fig.6.4 *Status enquiry reply*

It is usual for the bank to keep a record of all opinions given, often in a card index, and this is of help in ensuring that a consistent view is taken. Also, when a customer's financial position changes it is then easier for the bank to decide how it should shade or improve its answer as against former expressions of opinion. A record will also help the account-holding bank to see if a customer is apparently attempting to raise too much by way of credit finance or whatever.

Disclaimer

All replies are unsigned, and the standard printed form used by the bank will bear a disclaimer clause, which might read 'Confidential, and for your private use and without responsibility on the part of the bank or its officials'. However, since the Unfair Contract Terms Act 1977 came into force it has been felt that such a disclaimer clause would not protect the bank if the recipient relied on the answer and suffered loss, where the answer would not meet the test of 'reasonableness' as described in s. 11 of that Act.

The printed reply also bears a statement to the effect that under the Consumer Credit Act 1974 the bank is not a credit reference agency.

When preparing his answer, the banker should give consideration to all matters relating to the customer's financial and business affairs which are known to him, but there is no onus on the banker to make enquiries outside as to the customer's solvency or otherwise, and all that is required is an honest opinion, which should give no details of the actual bank account or the security lodged. Where the bank holds a debenture from a limited-company customer, it is invariable practice to disclose that fact, the nature of the security being so all-embracing that the bank's special position is perhaps material to the enquirer.

Duty to enquirer

It can be seen therefore that the bank might well have a duty to the enquirer, for it could be that, acting on the opinion given, he might grant credit and later suffer loss. The drafting of a suitable reply can be particularly difficult where the customer is known to have financial problems. Clearly, in such circumstances a favourable reply cannot be given, but equally to suggest by inference that his business is about to collapse could in fact cause that very event. The bank must be neither too optimistic nor too pessimistic in its reply.[49]

The leading case which examined these matters is *Hedley Byrne & Co. Ltd v. Heller and Partners Ltd* (1963), which was taken to the House of Lords. The facts, briefly, were that Hedley Byrne & Co Ltd enquired through their own bankers, National Provincial, as to the respectability and standing of a company known as Easipower Ltd whose account was with Heller and Partners Ltd. The enquiry asked about their trustworthiness in business to the extent of £100 000 per annum. The answer given was:

> Confidential.
> For your private use and without responsibility on the part of the bank or its officials.
> Dear Sir, In reply to your enquiry of 7th instant. We beg to advise: Re E . . . Ltd. Respectably constituted company, considered good for its ordinary business engagements. Your figures are larger than we are accustomed to see. Yours faithfully, . . . Per pro. Heller & Partners Limited.

Hedley Byrne & Co. relied on this opinion, entered into a contract with Easipower Ltd, and lost some £17 000 when that company went into

49 See Appendix I, Q. 32 (September 1983).

liquidation. They then sued Heller & Partners Ltd, on the grounds that the opinion had been given negligently and in breach of a duty owed to them to exercise care.

In the court of first instance it was held that there was no contract between the bankers giving the opinions, Heller & Partners Ltd, and Hedley Byrne & Co. Ltd. Thus there could be no duty of care and so there could be no breach. Moreover, there was no fiduciary relationship between the enquirer and the bank giving the opinion. The plaintiffs appealed, but the judgment was affirmed. Still dissatisfied, however, Hedley Byrne & Co. Ltd took matters to the House of Lords, where the decision was still in favour of the bankers, although for different reasons. Here, it was felt that if it could be shown that the circumstances whereby information and/or opinions were given established a form of relationship, which was equivalent to, but did not actually constitute a contract, then there was a duty on the maker of the statement to exercise care. One view was expressed that a banker's opinion could well fall in that category. However, the decision in favour of the bank was made because of the disclaimer clause, whereby the bank had at the outset declined to accept any responsibility, and never therefore established such special relationships.

It can be seen from this decision that the use of standard forms, with the disclaimer clause, is most important, and also that where opinions are given orally (a practice which is unusual and which requires special care) the giver of the opinion should always preface his remarks with the disclaimer.

As we have noted, however, the passing of the Unfair Contract Terms Act 1977 has thrown some doubt upon the worth of this practice, and it may be that a court in the future will take a different view. Bankers will of course continue to maintain the disclaimer clause in their answers to status opinions, but it is necessary to exercise even greater care in framing the answer in the present day.

Fraudulent misrepresentation

We can now go on to examine that aspect of this subject which deals with fradulent misrepresentation. Naturally, one would not expect a banker to give a fraudulent opinion, but an examination of the definition of that phrase seen in *Derry* v. *Peek* (1889) will demonstrate the risk area. In that case it was said: 'Fraudulent misrepresentation consists of a false statement of fact which is made knowingly, or without belief in its truth, or *recklessly*, without caring whether it is true or false, with the intention that it should be acted upon, and which is in fact acted upon'.

From these words it can be seen that the careless banker could bring himself within the terms of that definition. However, since the passing of the Statute of Frauds Amendment Act 1828, s. 6, it has always been thought that a fraudulent misrepresentation must be signed before the giver will become liable in damages. It is perhaps for this reason that the practice has grown up for bankers' opinions not to be signed.

Nevertheless, the law can change, and English Law may take note of decisions in other jurisdictions, where principles similar to our own form the basis of judicial decisions. Consequently, the decision in the Australian Court of Appeal in *Commercial Banking Co. of Sydney Ltd* v. *R. H. Brown & Co.* (1972) could be relevant. There the court took the view that an unsigned opinion had been given fraudulently, and that, despite the disclaimer clause, the bank was liable. In other words, it applied the Rule in *Derry* v. *Peek* (1889) and gave recognition to the relationship established between the banker giving the opinion and the enquirer. It accepted that there was a duty of care, and that there had been a 'fraudulent' breach of that duty when the opinion had been given recklessly.

In conclusion therefore we can see that there is a degree of present-day uncertainty; because of this practising bankers should not treat the giving of status opinions lightly, and managerial involvement is recommended. Indeed it is an area where, increasingly, outside parties seek to blame banks for losses they have incurred, after entering into contracts or continuing to trade with the bank's customer, in the light of a favourable reply. Bearing in mind that banks do not charge for giving opinions, and yet expose themselves to risk, one does just wonder whether the service will continue to be provided in the longer term in its present form.

CHAPTER 7

Insolvency of the Customer

BANKRUPTCY

The law governing bankruptcy is very detailed and still somewhat complex despite its revision by the Insolvency Act 1986, but a thorough knowledge of certain important sections and their repercussions is essential for bankers, so that in their daily work they are able to recognize those situations where the failure, or impending failure, of the customer affects the normal banker-customer relationship. The risks must be recognized as soon as they appear, and the banker must be aware what his rights and obligations are. In this connection it is important to know the actual point which has been reached in bankruptcy proceedings, for the situation varies according to the stage reached and a bank becomes more exposed at certain times than at others.

Bankruptcy law is now governed by the Insolvency Act 1986, as the Bankruptcy Act 1914, the Bankruptcy (Amendment) Act 1926 and the Insolvency Act 1976 have been repealed. In general terms, the procedures concerned with the bankruptcy of an individual, are now similar to those applicable for the compulsory liquidation of a limited company. To assist student readers who might have studied the old provisions which applied until 29 December 1986 when the Insolvency Act came into force the undermentioned table of changes may be helpful. However, bankers and others involved in bankruptcy proceedings should remember that if an individual had a receiving order made against him before 29 December then the old provisions will still regulate his estate and its administration. Moreover, if a bankruptcy order is made against a customer under the new Act, his trustee will only be able to apply the provisions of the Insolvency Act in so far as any offence or transaction occurred after the date the Act came into force, or to the extent that it would have been relevant under the old law. (See Table 7.1.)

The object of bankruptcy

Bankruptcy is a legal process whereby when an individual is unable to pay his debts as they fall due, statutory protection is afforded for him and his creditors. The debtor's assets are called in and realized by an independent person who is either the official receiver or, more likely, a licensed insolvency practitioner appointed as his trustee in bankruptcy. The trustee has wide powers under statute to investigate the debtor's affairs, to realize his assets, and to distribute the monies realized, after costs, to creditors in accordance with the priorities laid down in the Insolvency Act. For the individual debtor

New terms and procedures	Old terms and procedures
BANKRUPTCY	
—	Acts of bankruptcy (3 months availability)
Statutory demand	Bankruptcy notice
—	Doctrine of relation back
—	Doctrine of reputed ownership
—	Interest claims restricted
Bankruptcy order	{ Receiving order Adjudication order }
Preference	Fraudulent preference
Transactions at undervalue	Fraudulent conveyance
Income payment order	—
Banks can be preferential creditors by subrogation for wages advanced	—
INDIVIDUAL VOLUNTARY ARRANGEMENT	
Nominee	Individual voluntary arrangements did not exist
Supervisor	
Debtor's proposal	
Creditors' meeting	
Approval – voting by value	

Table 7.1   *Table of Changes – Personal Insolvency – Insolvency Act 1986*

himself, the advantage of bankruptcy proceedings is that he is freed from the weight of his debt and pressure by his creditors, so that in due course, despite the disabilities which will fall upon him in the short term, he is able to make a fresh start.

The bankruptcy process
To enable bankruptcy to be considered from a banker's point of view it will be useful to run briefly through the various stages, for should a banker's

customer be involved in bankruptcy proceedings, it is important for the banker to know the precise stage reached, if he has to make a decision as to what to do in connection with his customer's affairs.

The stages in bankruptcy are:

(*a*) The presentation of a petition to the court by a creditor (or possibly the debtor himself).

(*b*) The hearing of the petition by the court.

(*c*) The making of a bankruptcy order by the court (or the dismissal of the petition).

(*d*) The advertising of the bankruptcy order in the *London Gazette*.

(*e*) The circularization of the debtor's statement of affairs to creditors.

(*f*) The meeting of creditors, if one is held.

(*g*) The appointment of the trustee in bankruptcy, possibly with a creditors' committee.

(*h*) The public examination of the debtor (if held).

(*i*) The payment of dividends to the creditors.

(*j*) The discharge of the debtor from bankruptcy.

The petition to the court   The bankruptcy process begins when there is an unsecured debt of at least £750 and a petition is presented to the court seeking the making of a bankruptcy order. The grounds for presenting a petition can be

(1) the failure of an execution or other process attempted by a judgment creditor;

(2) the failure of the debtor to respond satisfactorily to the service of a statutory demand upon him by a creditor, either before or after judgment;

(3) the failure of an individual voluntary arrangement, which allows the supervisor to petition;

(4) grounds for a criminal bankruptcy under the Criminal Justice Act 1972, when the crown court has ruled that the defendant should be made bankrupt in addition to his sentence for a crime which has caused loss or damage of £15 000 or more. Similar provisions apply under the Criminal Courts Act 1973. In both cases only the official receiver may be the trustee in bankruptcy.

(5) upon an inability to pay his debts, a person may present his own petition.

In this latter case the total amount of the unsecured debts must exceed the 'small bankruptcies level' (currently £20 000) and the value of the assets in the estate must be equal to or more than 'the minimum amount' (currently £2000), unless the debtor has been bankrupt within the preceding five years or made a composition with his creditors in that time. In these instances the court appoints an insolvency practitioner to report on the debtor's financial position and to comment as to whether the debtor would be willing to make a proposal for a composition in satisfaction of his debts or for a scheme of arrangement of his affairs. The object behind these procedures is to try and limit actual bankruptcy cases to the larger and more complex insolvencies and to encourage voluntary arrangements for non-serious cases.

Where a creditor presents a petition this is usually sworn by his solicitor and a copy is served on the debtor and filed in the court for hearing in due course. Where the petition is based upon the failure to respond satisfactorily with cash or security in response to the service of a statutory demand, twenty-one days must have elapsed, and the petition must be presented within four months of the date of service of the statutory demand, although that period has no relevance for any other party.

Normally there is a delay of about four or six weeks before the court can hear the petition, although where the debtor presents his own petition and the case does not fall within the small bankruptcy procedures, the bankruptcy order is invariably made simultaneously.

The hearing of the petition   At the hearing, unless the small case procedure is invoked or the debtor has been able to arrange to settle with his creditor or supply security, perhaps from a third party, the facts are heard and a bankruptcy order will usually be made. If not, the petition is dismissed, although possibly the hearing might be adjourned if the debtor pleads for further time, so that he can raise funds to deal with the petitioning creditor.

The bankruptcy order   The bankruptcy order is the equivalent of the former receiving order and adjudication order merged into one. It is not a temporary order as the receiving order used to be and the bankruptcy takes effect on the day the order is made and continues until the debtor is discharged, which is likely to be after any period of between three and fifteen years later, although where summary administration applies, a two-year period is applicable.

As a result of the making of the bankruptcy order, the official receiver becomes the debtor's trustee in bankruptcy and he holds the office until the creditors meet and appoint their own trustee in bankruptcy, who must be a licensed insolvency practitioner.

Gazetting of the bankruptcy order   When the bankruptcy order has been made, the Department of Trade and Industry advertises it in the *London Gazette* and a local newspaper, and this is deemed to be notice to the whole world. It is therefore important for bankers to peruse the *Gazette*, and to see whether the names of any of their customers appear, for if the account is allowed to continue then the bank will be exposing itself to unnecessary risk. Usually, however, immediately the bankruptcy order is made, the official receiver will question the debtor, and if he learns, or is aware from other sources, of the name and branch of the debtor's bank, he will immediately telephone the bank to inform them and later write by way of confirmation. It is frequently therefore by telephone that banks receive the first indication that a bankruptcy order has been made against their customer, and this helps avoid those considerable dangers in respect of transactions which could be made after the making of the bankruptcy order and before the branch had notice from a perusal of the *Gazette*.

Simultaneously with the making of the bankruptcy order, an entry is made on the Land Charges Register against the debtor's name, and automatically the entry is then applied to the Land Register, should any registered title be owned. These steps protect the rights of creditors in respect of any interest in the land which is owned by the debtor, particularly as against a bona-fide purchaser for value who could acquire a good title if he had no notice of the petition, or of the making of the bankruptcy order. Usually, the petition will earlier have been recorded on the Land Charges Register and again it will automatically have been transferred to the Land Register where any title to registered land is held.

The statement of affairs   One of the first duties of a debtor is to prepare his statement of assets and liabilities, showing what he owns and giving an indication of the likely realizable value. The debtor has to list the names of all his creditors, preferential and non-preferential, and he will be questioned by the official receiver and will give an indication of the reasons, as he sees them, for his bankruptcy. He must do this within 21 days of the making of the bankruptcy order.

The bankrupt's assets include all property belonging to or vested in him at the time of the commencement of the bankruptcy, and also any property which he acquires or which devolves upon him at any time up to the day on which he is discharged from bankruptcy. However, he is entitled to retain tools, vehicles and other equipment which he may need to carry on his employment personally, and he may also keep his household property necessary for his family's basic needs. If the bankrupt holds any property on trust, that property is exempt from his estate and no complications now arise under the Insolvency Act 1986, in respect of property which he might be in possession of at the time of his bankruptcy and which formerly would have been caught as part of his estate under the doctrine of reputed ownership.

The statement of affairs is published and supplied to all creditors and from this they will be able to judge whether there is any likelihood of a dividend being paid in the debtor's estate. The statement of affairs includes a short history of the debtor's business affairs which is prepared by the official receiver, and it will include the official receiver's observations upon the matter, and comment upon the debtor's explanation for his downfall. Not infrequently and not surprisingly, the official receiver sees different reasons from those given by the debtor himself. Common causes of failure in business are those of expanding or trading without adequate capital, speculating, excessive drawings and failure to keep proper books of accounts.

Proof of debt Shortly after the bankruptcy order is made the bank will receive a form of proof of debt (Fig. 7.1), for lodging with the trustee, to enable it to receive dividends in the estate. The bank will also be entitled to attend and vote at meetings of creditors when it has submitted its proof of

Date of Bankruptcy Order   8th July 19...   No 23 of 19...
RE: John Smith

1	Name of Creditor	Practice Bank plc
2	Address of Creditor	Palatine Road Town
3	Total amount of claim, including any Value Added Tax and outstanding uncapitalised interest as at the date of the bankruptcy order	£ 17,723-14p
4	Details of any documents by reference to which the debt can be substantiated. [Note: the official receiver or trustee may call for any document or evidence to substantiate the claim at his discretion]	Bank Statement of Account
5	If the total amount shown above includes Value Added Tax, please show:— (a) amount of Value Added Tax (b) amount of claim NET of Value Added Tax	£ £
6	If total amount above includes outstanding uncapitalised interest please state amount	£ 214-46p.
7	If you have filled in both box 3 and box 5, please state whether you are claiming the amount shown in box 3 or the amount shown in box 5(b)	
8	Give details of whether the whole or any part of the debt falls within any (and if so which) of the categories of preferential debts under section 386 of, and schedule 6 to the Insolvency Act 1986 (as read with schedule 3 to the Social Security Pensions Act 1975)	Category Amount(s) claimed as preferential £ NIL

9	Particulars of how and when debt incurred	Fluctuating Overdraft on Current Account
10	Particulars of any security held, the value of the security, and the date it was given	Legal Second Mortgage by the debtor over 14 Green Way Town, dated 17-12-83. Value: £7,100
11	Signature of creditor or person authorised to act on his behalf	*Gudgin.*
	Name in BLOCK LETTERS	SIMON SIMPLE
	Postition with or relation to creditor	Bank Manager

Fig.7.1   *Bankruptcy – proof of debt*

debt, but not often does the bank concern itself with these matters, except where the circumstances are special and it wishes to influence proceedings. A more simple form of proof is now used, and this no longer requires swearing in the presence of a solicitor. However, the trustee in bankruptcy has the power to call for a sworn proof of debt if he so wishes.

Proof of debt where direct security is held   Where the bank holds security lodged by the bankrupt, in respect of its proof of debt, it has four options. These are as follows:

(a) The security may be surrendered to the trustee, and the bank can prove as an unsecured creditor for the whole debt.

(b) The bank may estimate the value of the security in the proof of debt, and claim as an unsecured creditor for the resultant balance.

(c) The bank may realize its security, and if a shortfall arises then it can prove for the residual debt.

(d) The bank may realize its security, and if it is repaid then it will lodge no proof, and will pay any surplus proceeds over to the trustee in bankruptcy.

It is rare for a bank to surrender its security to the trustee, for naturally if there is any likelihood of realizing value, the bank will wish to do that and then lodge a proof of debt for the residual liability. However, the security held by the bank can occasionally have liabilities, as for example where a lease is held and quarterly rentals are payable. It might be that in these circumstances, if the outgoings are heavy, and the bank is unlikely to see any benefit from a sale at a premium, then it will surrender the security. Usually, the trustee in bankruptcy himself is quick to disclaim onerous property or contracts which he too feels could saddle him with liabilities under the provisions of ss. 315–319 Insolvency Act 1986.

It is clearly easier for both the trustee and the bank if the bank is able to realize its security before dividends are declared, for then it can lodge its proof of debt for the residual outstanding debt. However, it could be that the security is difficult to realize, as for example where perhaps a domestic property is in mortgage, and the bank might need to take legal proceedings to obtain possesion before it can sell. If the trustee declares a dividend before the bank had realized its security then the bank will have to estimate the value of its security and prove for the balance. The valuation placed on the security will be carefully assessed, and professional advice from estate agents and valuers will be taken if property is concerned. It will also be necessary to take into account the anticipated expenses relating to the sale, for it is the net proceeds which will be shown in the proof of debt. When a secured creditor places a value on his security, however, the trustee in bankruptcy can if he wishes take over the security at that figure, and it is for this reason that the bank will wish to ensure that it does not place too low a valuation on its security. Conversely, if the bank were to place too high a figure it would receive low dividends on its claim.

Understandably, when the security is realized, it invariably produces a figure different from the estimated figure, and at that stage the bank is entitled to advise the trustee of the true value, and to receive its dividend on the amended figures, but only if subsequent dividends are payable. Naturally, if a surplus arises from the receipt of dividends and the proceeds of the security then this must be paid over to the trustee. The bank is under a statutory duty to advise the trustee of all the items of security which it realises and how much it has obtained for them.

Security lodged by solvent third parties Section 383(2) Insolvency Act 1986 states that '. . . a debt is secured for the purposes of this Group of Parts to the extent that the person to whom the debt is owed holds any security for the debt (whether a mortgage, charge, lien or other security) over any property of the person by whom the debt is owed'.

The important words of this section are 'the property of the person by whom the debt is owed', and consequently any security lodged by a solvent third party does not affect the bank's position in the bankruptcy proceedings of the borrower. Thus third-party security may be ignored for purposes of lodging the proof of debt, and no reference to that security should be made nor its value when lodging a claim in the bankruptcy of the customer. Consequently, the bank can realize the proceeds of third-party security, and place these to a suspense account or realized-security account, and still receive all the dividends in the customer's estate as if it were an unsecured creditor, which technically it is for bankruptcy purposes.

The situation is best illustrated by the well-known case of *Re Sass* (1896). Mr Sass had an overdraft of £755 when he was made bankrupt. The bank held a guarantee from a third party which was couched in usual banking terms, and the guarantee was therefore expressed to be for the whole of the debt, although with a monetary limitation upon the amount recoverable, namely £300. The bank made demand upon the guarantor, who paid £300, and these funds were lodged in a suspense account. Thereafter the bank lodged its proof of debt in Mr Sass's bankruptcy in the sum of £755. The trustee in bankruptcy rejected this proof and claimed that the £300 paid by the guarantor should be deducted from the amount of the bank's proof. If he had been right in this, the bank would have received a smaller dividend out of its customer's estate. However, the court held in the bank's favour, taking note of the fact that the guarantee was expressed to be available for the whole of the debt; therefore it saw that a guarantor who has paid has no right himself to lodge claim in the estate by way of subrogation, until such time as the bank has been paid in full.

Subrogation rights of paying surety   Where a guarantor or depositor of thrid-party security has paid suffcent monies to enable the bank to be paid in full, then under s. 5 Mercantile Law Amendment Act 1856 that party has the right to stand in the bank's shoes, by way of subrogation. This means that the guarantor can take over, by way of transfer, any security which the bank holds from its customer, and also that the guarantor or depositor of the security is entitled to receive all the dividends which would have been payable to the bank. Sometimes matters proceed on the basis that by arrangement with the trustee in bankruptcy the guarantor or third-party surety lodges his own proof of debt. More usually, the bank will lodge its proof of debt and then pay over any dividends received to the guarantor or third party; this method is usually more acceptable to the other party as the bank then deals with the formalities.

The creditors' meeting   Where a bankruptcy order has been made and no certificate of summary administration has been issued the official receiver must decide within 12 weeks whether to call a meeting of creditors to appoint a trustee in bankruptcy. If he decides not to call a meeting he must so inform all known creditors. However, any creditor with the support of not less than one quarter in value of the total creditors may request a meeting, and if so one must be called. If a meeting is not held the official receiver may remain as trustee in bankruptcy or the Secretary of State may make an appointment.

If the official receiver remains as trustee a creditors' committee cannot be formed, but if an insolvency practitioner is appointed either at a meeting or otherwise, he may be supported by a creditors' committee. Generally speaking, except in special cases, banks seem to prefer not to involve themselves with creditors' meetings or creditors' committees, but they may vote for the appointment of a trustee of their own choice, if the background is such that they wish to be assured that certain matters or transactions will be fully investigated.

The job of the creditors' committee is to supervise the work of the trustee in bankruptcy, and to approve his actions when he reports to them at future meetings. In some instances the trustee will need their authority before pursuing certain courses of action.

The debtor's public examination   Not every debtor is now examined, and in small bankruptcies the public examination is dispensed with, so as to save costs and time. A public examination must be held, however, if one is applied for by the official receiver or a creditor supported by at least half in value of all creditors, including himself. However in larger cases the examination is in court under oath, and any creditor can put questions to the debtor on his statement of affairs, or his conduct, or any other matter related to his business or financial affairs.

Order of payment   The monies which the trustee in bankruptcy realizes from the sale of the debtor's assets are used firstly to pay the costs of the bankruptcy proceedings, which include the legal expenses and also the remuneration of the trustee in bankruptcy. The costs of the petitioning creditor are pre-preferential, and following the settlement of this liability the preferential debts are the next to be paid. These include taxes and national insurance contributions and the wages and salaries of any employees which have accrued but which have been unpaid in the four months before the bankruptcy order was made. The amount in respect of wages and salaries which can be claimed as a maximum is £800 for each person. A bank can now be a preferential creditor, by way of subrogation in respect of monies advanced to enable the payment of wages or salaries, just as in the liquidation of a limited company, although this is unlikely to be the case often, in personal insolvency. It follows therefore that if there are heavy preferential liabilities and few assets, there may be little left available to distribute on a *pro rata* basis between the unsecured creditors.

If unsecured creditors are paid in full, then a bank as an unsecured creditor will be entitled to a dividend on interest as this continues to accrue on the borrowing at the greater of the rates agreed with the customer, or the rate specified in s. 17 of the Judgments Act 1838 (Judgment Rate – currently 12% January 1987). Other creditors are entitled similarly, and in their case, interest accrues at Judgment Rate. The last class of creditors to be paid are the deferred creditors, which will include a bankrupt's spouse.

Discharge from bankruptcy   The earliest time after the making of a bankruptcy order when a bankrupt can be discharged is two years, this applying in summary cases. In other cases the period may be between three years and fifteen years, in most cases the earlier three-year period applying unless the bankruptcy occurred within less than fifteen years of an earlier bankruptcy or unless the bankruptcy had been brought about by a criminal bankruptcy order. In cases other than summary cases, a bankrupt can apply to the court for his discharge at any time after five years have elapsed. Upon receiving his discharge, because creditors have not opposed it and the court has made the order, the bankrupt is released from his liabilities although his creditors can continue to receive dividends or realize their security. The court may, if it wishes, lay down conditions for the discharge which could involve the receipt of contributions by his trustee in bankruptcy from future earnings.

Occasionally, it is important for a branch to ascertain whether a person with whom it has dealings is an undischarged bankrupt or not. In those circumstances, the branch should search in the Bankruptcy Register against the name of the person concerned, although the search is not necessarily conclusive because, understandably, similarities of names arise, and also because unscrupulous debtors can use more than one name, thus hiding their real identity.

Having examined the various stages in bankruptcy proceedings, we can now move forward and look at those areas in which banks become particularly involved, and see how these effect different classes of customers and their transactions.

Transactions between petition and bankruptcy order

A debtor's bankruptcy commences on the day on which the bankruptcy order is made. However, it must be remembered that bankruptcy law is now parallel with company law relating to compulsory winding up, and there is therefore an intention to prevent the estate being dissipated in the period between the presentation of the petition for bankruptcy and the making of a bankruptcy order. However, whereas in the case of a company the petition is advertised, this is not so in bankruptcy proceedings, and third parties could be in the course of transactions with a person who has had a petition presented against him and where, shortly, the court will make a bankruptcy order based on that petition. In particular, a bank could be in course of conducting an account for a customer who is about to be made bankrupt and unless the bank learns of the presentation of the petition from its customer, or another source, problems could arise were it not for statutory protection.[50]

The relevant section is s. 284 of the Insolvency Act 1986. This states

(1) 'Where a person is adjudged bankrupt, any disposition of property made by that person in the period to which this Section applies shall be void except to the extent that it is or was made with the consent of the Court, or is or was subsequently ratified by the Court.

(2) Subsection (1) above applies to a payment (whether in cash or otherwise) as it applies to a disposition of property and, accordingly, where any payment is void by virtue of that Subsection, the person paid shall hold the sum paid for the bankrupt as part of his Estate.

50 See Appendix I, Q. 20 (April 1982).

(3) This Section applies to the period beginning with the day of the presentation of the petition for the bankruptcy order and ending with the vesting, under Chapter IV of this Part, of the bankrupt's estate in a trustee.

(4) The preceding provisions of this Section do not give a remedy against any person –

(a) in respect of any property or payment which he received before the commencement of the bankruptcy in good faith, for value and without notice that the petition had been presented, or

(b) in respect of any interest in property which derives from an interest in respect of which there is, by virtue of this Subsection, no remedy.

(5) Where after the commencement of his bankruptcy a bankrupt has incurred a debt to a banker or other person by reason of the making of a payment which is void under this Section, that debt is deemed for the purposes of any of this Group of Parts to have been incurred before the commencement of the bankruptcy unless –

(a) the banker or person had notice of the bankruptcy before the debt was incurred, or

(b) it is not reasonably practicable for the amount of the payment to be recovered from the person to whom it was made.'

In looking at this section the first thing which must be said about Subsection (1) is that a person is not now 'adjudged bankrupt' and this wording is an error on the part of the draftsman and parliament. The section only makes sense if these words are presumed to apply to when a bankruptcy order is made against a person. The section attempts to deal with transactions between the time when a petition is presented and the time when the bankrupt's assets vest in his trustee (a time which may not be the same day as when the bankruptcy order is made). In practice it is highly unlikely except where the circumstances are special and a debtor is receiving legal advice, that he will ever consider applying to the court for consent to deal or dispose of his property. Moreover, it seems likely that instances where transactions in this period require ratification by the court will be limited to those where there is dispute between creditors or against third parties.

As far as banks are concerned, it is quite possible that a customer will continue operating his account after the presentation of the petition against him and the bank will usually have no knowledge of this state of affairs. The protection for the bank if a bankruptcy order is made subsequently lies in Sections (4) and (5). Subsection (4)(a) protects a bank dealing in good faith, for value, and without notice that a petition has been presented when property or payments are received either as security or as payments into the bank account. Subsection (5) specifically mentions a banker and this again refers to 'the commencement of his bankruptcy', which is of course the day of the making of the bankruptcy order. However, possibly the draftsman had in mind here the presentation of the petition but as it stands the subsection must be read as referring to borrowings granted by the banker or taken by the customer without arrangement after the day on which the bankruptcy order was made. In those instances, provided the bank had no notice of the making of the bankruptcy order, the debt which has arisen is deemed to have been incurred before the bankruptcy commenced and presumably therefore becomes a provable debt in the bankruptcy. However, subsection (5)(b) brings in a proviso that it must not be reasonably practical for the payment to be recovered from the person to whom it was made, but the subsection does not say who should made the effort to recover the monies. Should it be the trustee in bankruptcy, or the bank? An interpretation that it is the bank would seem to make more sense.

Overall the position now seems to be that if a bank has notice of a petition it should stop all the accounts affected. However, where, usually, a bank has no notice and continues to operate its customer's account, it will be protected from claims by a later trustee in bankruptcy in respect of any credits received provided it has acted in good faith and for value. In respect of any cheques paid in the period between the petition and the bankruptcy order matters are not clear but if a bank is challenged by a trustee in bankruptcy it is hard to see how any court would fail to ratify the payment of those cheques where they had been paid by the bank in good faith and in total ignorance of the proceedings in train. There must be doubt as to what constitutes 'value' under the provisions of Subsection (4)(a). Presumably payments in will be deemed to have been received 'for value' if withdrawals are allowed against them and a good argument could be made for the point that as value under the Bills of Exchange Act 1882, Section 27, can be constituted by any antecedent debt or liability, such credits would constitute 'value' as repayment of all or part of an existing lending.

Preferences

Although the protection afforded by s. 284 is wide, it does not seek to cover any transaction which was a preference of one creditor over another and such a transaction may be set aside by the court upon the application of the trustee in bankruptcy. In that event the court may make such order as it thinks fit for restoring the position to what it would have been if the bankrupt had not given the preference. A preference is given to a person who is one of the bankrupt's creditors, or a surety or guarantor of any of his debts or liabilities, if the bankrupt does anything or allows anything to be done which has the effect of putting the other party into a position which, in the event of the individual's bankruptcy, will be better than the position he would have been in, if that thing had not been done. However, the court is not empowered to make an order unless the individual who gave the preference was influenced in deciding to give it by a desire to produce 'in relation to that person the effect mentioned' i.e. being in a better position in the event of bankruptcy. In the case of an associate of the bankrupt, however, it is presumed, unless the contrary is shown, that the bankrupt was influenced in deciding to give the preference by the desire to place his associate in a better position (s. 340 Insolvency Act 1986).

The court will not make an order unless the preference occurred at 'a relevant time' and this is defined under s. 341, which covers both preferences and transactions at an undervalue. In the case of bankruptcy the time is a 'relevant time' if the preference, not being a transaction at an undervalue, was given at some point in the period of six months before and ending with the day on which the bankruptcy petition was presented. In the case of a preference given to an associate, however, the relevant time is two years. In addition to the periods involved, the time of the transaction is not 'a relevant time' unless the individual was insolvent at the time of the transaction or became insolvent as a consequence of the preference. This applies whether the creditor preferred was an associate or not. In order to establish whether an individual was insolvent, Subsection (3) states that an individual is insolvent for these purposes if:

(a) he is unable to pay his debts as they fall due, or

(b) the value of his assets is less than the amount of his liabilities, taking into account his contingent and prospective liabilities.

Section 342 sets out what the court may order to restore the position to what it would have been. Property transferred may be vested in the trustee of the bankrupt's estate, as may the proceeds of sale of property or money. The court may order any security to be released or discharged, wholly or in part, and it may require any person to pay money to the trustee for the bankrupt's estate. Section 342(1)(e) is important for bankers. It provides that any surety or guarantor whose obligations to any person were released or discharged (in whole or in part) may be ordered to be under a new or revived obligation to that person. The court may also provide for security to be provided for the discharge of any obligation imposed by its order and this may be charged on any property and that security may have the same priority as the security which was released or discharged earlier. Where obligations are resurrected by the court order because the preference is reversed, the creditor is entitled to prove in the bankruptcy for the debt or other liability.

Section 342(2) empowers the court to make an order or impose an obligation on any person whether or not he is the person with whom the individual in question entered into the transaction or the person to whom the preference was given. In that event the order must not prejudice any interest in property which was acquired by another person in good faith, for value and without notice of the relevant circumstances. Nor can the order require a person, who received a benefit from the transaction or preference in good faith, for value, and without notice of the relevant circumstances, to pay a sum to the trustee of the bankrupt's estate, except where he was a party to the transaction, or a payment is to be in respect of a preference given to that person at a time when he was a creditor.

All this is very complicated and at the time of writing, in the early days of the Act, there have been no actual bankruptcies and no instances of reference to the courts for interpretation of these provisions. In summary, however, the situation would seem to be that as a banker will rarely be an 'associate' of the bankrupt the 'relevant time' as far as he is concerned can only be some time within the six months preceding the presentation of the bankruptcy petition.

The two-year provision applying to associates is designed to give greater protection to creditors and to extend the arm of the trustee in bankruptcy to reverse transactions which the bankrupt is more likely to have made with parties close to him. Hence s. 435 defines an associate as an individual's husband or wife, or relative, or the husband or wife of a relative or any person with whom he is in partnership, or the husband or wife or relative of any individual with whom he is in partnership. A person is also an associate of any person whom he employs or by whom he is employed.

It should be noted that it is no longer necessary for the trustee in bankruptcy to show 'a dominant intent' in the mind of the bankrupt to prefer and hence the escape route by which banks once used to claim that they had exerted pressure on the customer to reduce the level of the overdraft or loan, may no longer be as relevant as previously. The state of mind of the bankrupt has simply to be that of wishing to place the bank in a better position than it would be if the customer were made bankrupt.

Most customers of course, when in financial difficulties, are unlikely to have the bank in mind as a creditor which they wish to see 'better placed', but the complication arises where the payment is made when the bank holds a guarantee or security lodged by a third party. The debtor, knowing that there is a possibility of his failure, can in those circumstances reduce his borrowing, or perhaps repay it completely, and then a request can be made to the bank to release the security to the depositor, or to agree to the guarantee being set aside. If the bank should accede to these requests, and should their customer later become bankrupt, and a successful preference claim be brought, the bank could find itself with the borrowing reinstated, but with the security gone.

Although a company law case, that of *re M. Kushler Ltd* (1943) illustrates a preference situation clearly. Lloyds Bank were lending money to this company, whose only shareholders and directors were Mr and Mrs Kushler. Mr Kushler guaranteed the company's borrowing and supported this by charges over life policies. Realizing that the company was insolvent, Mr Kushler ceased to draw cheques in favour of the company's creditors, but continued paying in receipts into the credit of the company's account. By these means, soon, the bank account reverted to a credit position and the guarantee was no longer relied upon. Shortly afterwards, the company went into liquidation, and the liquidator brought an action against the bank claiming that all the payments into the account had been a preference. It was possible for the liquidator to demostrate to the court that the director, who was the guarantor, had had the intention in mind of preferring himself, particularly as the bank had not been pressing for repayment of the company borrowing. In these circumstances, the bank lost the case and had to refund the monies to the company's liquidator.

It will be appreciated that in a situation such as this, if the bank has already given up the security lodged by the third party it could be in an invidious position. It was to attempt to guard against the worst of such a situation, that some banks introduced into their third-party charge forms and guarantee forms clauses which attempt to preserve the right for the bank to retain any security for six months after the account has returned to a credit balance. This enables the bank to refuse any requests made by a guarantor or third-party depositor of security for the return of his security or the setting aside of the guarantee, until the six-month period has elapsed. Another way the problem is dealt with is to include a clause in charge forms stating that any settlement in respect of the guarantee or security can be avoided by the bank, if subsequently the bank finds itself facing a claim in bankruptcy or liquidation proceedings, such as a preference. The difficulty with having given up the security already, however, is that, while technically the bank might under this clause still have rights to the security, in the meantime, if the owner has dealt with and lodged it in good faith with somebody else, there is no way in which the bank will be able to recover the security for itself. The safest way to proceed in these situations therefore is to examine the account carefully, and to consider whether there is any possibility of a preference claim arising. If there is, and if the charge form includes the clause for the bank to retain the security for six months, then reliance on that clause, by refusing to release the security for the time being, is the only safe way to proceed.

If such clauses are not present in a charge form, all is not now lost for the bank, however, as it will be recalled that under s. 342 the court can make an order restoring the position to what it was previously. The only difficulty with this is that the order must not prejudice any interest in the property which has subsequently been acquired in good faith, for value, and without notice of the relevant circumstances. Hence, for instance, if customer A preferred the bank, and the bank released the deeds security mortgaged by surety B, who then went on to sell the property to Mr C, the bank would not be able to obtain an order from the court in respect of that property if Mr C had acquired it from B in good faith, for value, and without notice of the relevant circumstances. However, if B were still in possession of the cash or consideration, or other assets of equivalent value, or some value, the court would have the power to make an order over those assets making them security for the bank in respect of customer A's borrowing which would have to be reconstituted. In this situation the bank would also have a right to prove in A's bankruptcy as the security is third party security.

One final point may be discussed. In a preference situation the bank is vulnerable for six months but if the surety, B in the above example, is an associate of the bankrupt then as far as he is concerned the transaction can be attacked by the trustee in bankruptcy if it occurred within a period of two years of the petition.

Of course, in the majority of cases, where the debtor repays his borrowing, the bank will feel perfectly safe in releasing security lodged by a third party when it is asked to do so. The bank should always therefore look at the overall surrounding circumstances of any transaction in which it is involved, and should take a practical approach with the use of sound judgment.

Transactions at an undervalue

Under the old Bankruptcy Acts a trustee in bankruptcy was empowered to recover certain property which used to belong to the bankrupt but which he had transferred or settled on another person.

The object was to recover for the benefit of all creditors any assets which used to belong to the bankrupt and which, with an eye to the future and his possible failure, he had attempted to put out of reach of his creditors. This same intent and effect is brought into the new Act by s. 339 which deals with transactions at an undervalue and which is headed 'Adjustment of Prior Transactions, etc.' It provisions are such, however, that the range of transactions capable of reversal by application to the court of the trustee is somewhat wider.

Again the transaction must occur at a 'relevant time' and here too the trustee must apply to the court for an order for the position to be restored to what it would have been if the transaction had not been entered into. Section 339(3) enacts

'. . . an individual enters into a transaction with a person at an undervalue if –

(a)   he makes a gift to that person or he otherwise enters into a transaction with that person on terms that provide for him to receive no consideration,

(b)   he enters into a transaction with that person in consideration of marriage, or

(c)   he enters into a transaction with that person for a consideration the value of which in money or money's worth, is significantly less than the value in money or money's worth, of the consideration provided by the individual'.

For example, suppose John Smith held the title to the matrimonial home, but, realizing his possible financial failure was imminent, he transferred the deeds into the name of his wife eighteen months before a bankruptcy order was made against him. This transaction was not a preference, for nothing passed to one of his creditors; nevertheless, his creditors are worse placed because this asset was moved out of his estate. Under the provisons of s. 339 Mr Smith's trustee in bankruptcy would be able to upset this transaction as one at an undervalue for no consideration. Similarly, if Mr Smith had sold his property, worth £50 000, to his wife for £10 000, the transaction would be capable of reversal as a transaction at an undervalue.

The powers of the court are similar to its powers in respect of transactions which are preferences, and it can make orders restoring the position to what it would have been but for the transaction. However, a transaction at an undervalue must have occurred at a 'relevant time' and the period is different to that applying for a preference. In the case of a transaction at an undervalue

s. 341(1)(a) enacts that the time is a 'relevant time' if the transaction occurred in the period of five years which end with the day of the presentation of the bankruptcy petition. Again, however, the time is not a 'relevant time' (unless it is a time less that two years before the presentation of the bankruptcy petition), unless the individual was insolvent at that time or became insolvent in consequence of the transaction. In other words, a transaction at undervalue can be attacked within two years of the petition, whether the bankrupt was insolvent or became insolvent in consequence of the transaction, or not. Outside of the two-year period it is necessary for the trustee to show insolvency, which is defined as for preference transactions and as mentioned earlier as s. 341(3).

Once more, however, the trustee's powers are stronger where the transaction was entered into by the bankrupt with a person who was an associate of his, other than by reason only of being his employee, and the bankrupt is presumed to have been insolvent or become insolvent unless the contrary is shown where the transaction was with the associate.

Banks need not be too concerned about s. 339, for it should not in ordinary circumstances present dangers to them, and moreover it is rare for a trustee in bankruptcy to meet situations where he needs to use such powers. However, perhaps in a situation where the bank is a large creditor, and knows that substantial assets have been transferred in the years prior to the bankruptcy, it will be keen to see the trustee taking whatever steps he can to recover monies for the estate. Indeed, it might have been part of a creditor's intention, when presenting a petition, to recover such assets, for bankruptcy proceedings are the only way in which property moved out the debtor's hands can be attached by a creditor.

A bank need not be concerned where property has been charged to it by another person, and the chargor has acquired title through a settlement of this nature. In these situations, provided the bank has acted in good faith for value and without notice of the relevant circumstances, then the security which it takes from the third party is good, and it will be able to refute any claim to the property brought by a trustee in bankruptcy. Table 7.2 summarizes the preferences and undervalue transactions.

Bankruptcy order against a sole account holder

As soon as the bank is telephoned by the official receiver, or receives notice through the post, to the effect that a bankruptcy order has been made against its customer, all accounts held in that customer's name should be stopped. Similarly, if the bank, when perusing the *Gazette*, sees that its customer's name is shown as being the subject of a bankruptcy order, then provided the bank is entirely certain that the person named is the customer the same action must at once be taken.

Any cheques presented for payment after notice of bankruptcy order should be dishonoured with the answer 'Refer to drawer, bankruptcy order made'. If,

	Preference	*Transactions at undervalue*
ORDINARY CREDITOR	Within 6 months of petition Trustee to prove insolvency Trustee to prove debtor was 'influenced by a desire to place creditor in a better position'.	Within 2 years of petition whether solvent or not, i.e. years 1 and 2 Within 5 years of petition, trustee must prove insolvency in years 3, 4 and 5.
ASSOCIATE	Within 2 years of petition Trustee to prove insolvency Desire to 'place in a better position' presumed.	Within 5 years of petition insolvency presumed (unless contrary is shown)

Table 7.2   *Summary of Preferences and Transactions at an Undervalue in Bankruptcy*

exceptionally, credits are received after the bankruptcy order, these may be accepted, but they should be credited to a suspense account, and held to the order of the trustee in bankruptcy.

The letter which the bank receives, advising it of the making of the bankruptcy order, will also include enquiries asking for the bank to state the balance of the account, its preferential claim (if any) and to give details of any securities held (Fig. 7.2). The official receiver will want a list of any items held in safe custody, and he will also wish to know if the customer has any guarantee liabilities or has lodged any security in support of the liabilities of others. There is no need for the customer's authority to answer these enquiries and short answers are usually given. Shortly afterwards the official receiver, or trustee, will ask for any credit balance to be paid to him and, provided the bank does not wish to exercise any right of set-off or lien, the balance of the account may be remitted, after taking interest to date and any bank charges.

Bankruptcy order against a party to a joint account
As soon as the bank has notice that a bankruptcy order has been made against one or more parties to a joint account, the joint account must be stopped, even if there is a credit balance, and certainly if it is overdrawn. The effect of the bankruptcy order is to determine the bank's mandate, and it is not possible thereafter for the solvent party to continue the account, even though it is in

Dear Sir

RE:

I hereby give you notice that a Bankruptcy Order was made on the   day
of   against the above-named debtor who is described as

I understand that the debtor's account is held by you, and in connection therewith should be obliged if you would please:-

a   State for what period the account has been in existence and
     forward a statement of the account to date, together with the
     relative paid cheques, and hold any credit balance to the
     order of the Official Receiver or Trustee subsequently
     appointed in these proceedings.

b   Furnish details of all securities, whether direct or collateral,
     deposited with you at any time for safe custody or otherwise.

c   Furnish certified or photostat copies of all outstanding
     guarantees given by the debtor and, if applicable, details of
     any guarantees given in favour of the debtor.

d   In the case of a joint, or partnership account, furnish copy
     of the mandate.

e   Supply a list of all cheques returned unpaid at any time.

f   Supply details of all overdraft facilities, viz: amount, when
     given, and in what circumstances, e.g. representations. Also
     furnish copy loan applications where applicable.

g   State whether you are aware of any other accounts operated by
     the debtor at any of your branches, or with other banks.

Yours faithfully

Official Receiver

Fig.7.2   *Bankruptcy – Official Receiver's advice of bankruptcy order*

credit and even though the joint and several mandate might allow any one
person to sign. The situation is best understood as being similar to the
situation if the bank had not taken a mandate. In that situation both parties to
the account would have to give instruction to the bank, and so it is here,
although the trustee in bankruptcy stands in the place of the party who has
had the bankruptcy order made against him. In other words, the bank seeks

the joint written instructions of the trustee in bankruptcy and the other party or parties to the account as to how any credit balance should be dealt with. The trustee may be prepared to allow all monies (or part of them) to pass to the solvent party, but as far as the bank is concerned the division of the funds is a matter between themselves and all the bank requires is their written instructions. Similarly, if any items are held by the bank in safe custody, in joint names, they may only be delivered on the joint written instructions of the trustee in bankruptcy and the other solvent party or parties.

As soon as possible the bank will interview the solvent party and he will be offered the opportunity to open a new account in his own name. To be able to deal with any cheques drawn by the solvent party on the joint account, which would otherwise need to be dishonoured with the answer 'Refer to drawer – joint account holder in bankruptcy proceedings', a written authority could be taken from the solvent party that any such cheques presented should be debited to his new sole account. Any cheques drawn by the party against whom the bankruptcy order was made must be returned and the answer used is 'Refer to drawer – bankruptcy order made'.

If, when the bank receives notice of the bankruptcy order, a joint account is overdrawn, the bank will be anxious to preserve all its rights against all parties to the account, and as it will usually hold a joint and several mandate entitling it to look to each party for the full extent of any borrowing, the account will be stopped to prevent the operation of the Rule in *Clayton's Case*. This would work to the bank's disadvantage if the account were not stopped, and the solvent party were allowed to continue operations. Under the Rule, any credits paid in would serve to reduce the debt at the date of the bankruptcy order, and cheques drawn would create a new debt in respect of which the bank would not be able to look to the bankrupt. By stopping the account, the bank has a full claim in his estate in respect of the debt outstanding at the date of the making of the order, and it will be empowered to lodge a proof of debt and receive all dividends. The bank will also have rights to call upon the solvent party for proposals for dealing with the borrowing, and if any monies are paid, these should be held in a separate account so that the claim in the bankrupt's estate is not reduced and the bank's dividend is maximized.

Similarly, if the bank holds security lodged by the solvent party then this can be realized either with the co-operation of that party, or by the bank under its own power of sale. The proceeds of the security should be credited to a realized security account or a suspense account, and again these monies need not be shown in the bank's proof of debt. However, if the security was lodged by the bankrupt, then the bank will have several courses of action which it can follow, and the same rules apply as with the holder of a sole account.

Bankruptcy order against one member of a partnership

When one partner has a bankruptcy order made against him and the partnership bank account is in credit, the operation of the partnership account need not be affected, although any cheques drawn by that partner will need to be adopted by the other partners or returned with the answer 'Refer to drawer – bankruptcy order made against X'. Usually, however, it will be a term of the agreement between the partners that upon the bankruptcy of any one of them, the partnership is to be dissolved, and in those circumstances the other partners are empowered to wind up the partnership with the object of realizing the insolvent partner's interest in the partnership, so that this can be paid over to his trustee in bankruptcy. The partnership account, in credit, can then be allowed to continue, operated by the remaining partners, and ideally a new mandate should be taken from these, although quite frequently, if any one partner has been allowed to sign on the account previously, this practice is merely continued, with the authority of the bankrupt partner being withdrawn.

The bank will wish to take a different approach where the account is overdrawn, for again it will be anxious to preserve all its rights and particularly against the estate of the bankrupt partner. Consequently, the partnership account should be stopped to prevent the operation of the Rule in *Clayton's Case*, as explained for a joint account, which situation is identical here.

Sometimes, however, in a special situation, where the financial standing of the remaining partners is such that the bank is prepared to waive its rights against the estate of the bankrupt partner, the account can be allowed to continue and the bank in this way will be looking simply to its rights against the remaining solvent partners. However, if security has been provided by the bankrupt partner, then the account must be stopped, and the bank will have the same rights as explained for a joint account. Consequently, the bank will need to see the remaining partners at an early date to determine their approach and attitude and, as normally the account is stopped, a new partnership account will be opened and new arrangements made for any borrowing, together with a new mandate showing how the account is to be operated.

Obviously, if the one partner involved in these bankruptcy proceedings also has other accounts, these should receive the appropriate treatment upon notice of the making of the bankruptcy order.

Winding up order against a partnership

When a creditor is owed money by a partnership, under the provisions of the Insolvency Act 1986 and the Insolvent Partnership Order 1986 he has a choice of either petitioning for the winding up of the partnership alone or concurrently seeking the winding up of the partnership and the individual bankruptcy of one or more of the partners. In the future it will not be possible for a bankruptcy petition to be presented against a partnership or against the partners in the name of the firm. An insolvent partnership is wound up as if it were an unregistered company, and in that event, without a petition involving the bankruptcy of the individual partners, they are not *ipso facto* affected immediately by the winding up of the partnership. However, the liquidator of the partnership will be able to call upon them to make contribution to the partnership estate if the partnership assets are insufficient to meet all claims in full. If at that point the individual partners fail to make a contribution, then presumably the insolvency practitioner acting will be able to take steps to present bankruptcy petitions against the individual partners, or take such other remedies as he thinks fit.

When a winding up order is made against the partnership, the bank must stop the partnership account. It appears that under the new legislation it may allow any account conducted by a partner in his own name to continue, whether credit or debit. However, a bank might well prefer in such circumstances to exercise its right of appropriation in respect of any credit balance and where the account is overdrawn, the warning signs of financial difficulties could be sufficient to justify the bank calling in any personal borrowing.

Winding up order against partnership and bankruptcy order(s) against member(s)

Where a partnership is the subject of a winding up order and *also* bankruptcy orders are made against one or more of the individual members, the firm's account and the accounts of any individual partners(s) named in the bankruptcy order must be stopped, whether in credit or overdrawn. In this event the liquidator of the partnership will realize the partnership assets and will use the proceeds to pay dividends to the creditors of the partnership. Meanwhile, private assets belonging to each partner's private estate will also be realized, and the partner's private creditors will be paid their dividends out of these realizations. However, when creditors of the partner's separate estate have received a dividend of one hundred pence in the pound, if there is any surplus then the monies are taken from the separate estate into the partnership estate where they are available to pay partnership creditors further dividends.

As far as the bank is concerned, it will be able to lodge a proof of debt in the partnership account, and also in the separate estate of each partner in respect of the partnership liability. This is because the partnership mandate, taken when the partnership was opened, will have a clause whereby the partners accepted joint and several liability. This places the bank in a superior position to other creditors of the partnership, who can only look to the partners under their joint liability and the partnership estate. In this way the bank is able to maximize its return, although of course it must not recover more than the total amount owing.

Where the bank holds security lodged by one partner, clauses in the charge form will enable it to apply the proceeds of any realisation to either that partner's sole liabilities or to the joint liabilities. Thus the bank will be able to use the proceeds to reduce the partner's separate debt for the partnership liability, or take the monies in reduction of the partnership borrowing. The bank will decide where to apply the proceeds in the light of what it is told by the liquidator and the trustee in bankruptcy as to where the maximum rate of dividends is to be declared, and, armed with this information, the bank will apply the proceeds to that estate where the dividends will be least.

This applies only to private assets charged, and if the partnership has lodged security held in the name of the partnership then the proceeds of this must be deducted from the claim in the partnership estate.

Should any partner have a credit balance on a private account, when notice is received of the making of the winding up order against the partnership, and a bankruptcy order against that partner, because of the joint and several liability clause the bank may exercise its right of set-off either against any other private account debt or against the several liability of that partner for the partnership borrowing.

Guarantor's or surety's own bankruptcy

As soon as the bank becomes aware that a guarantor or a third party who has lodged security is involved in bankruptcy proceedings, it will be necessary for the customer's account to be stopped. This applies when the notice the bank receives is of the presentation of a petition against a guarantor or surety. More usually, the advice will come when a bankruptcy order is made, and if the account is not stopped in all these circumstances the operation of the Rule in *Clayton's Case* would reduce, or lose, for the bank its rights to claim against the third party. By stopping the customer's account, the third party's liability is fixed at that point in time and at the balance then due by the customer.

Looking at the development from the customer's point of view, clearly this will be inconvenient, and the bank must interview him immediately, so that the situation can be explained, and steps taken for a new account to be opened. It might be necessary to renegotiate the lending arrangements, and possibly the borrower will be able to provide additional security of his own, or if not then to introduce a different third party. Each situation will need to be carefully assessed on its merits, and the bank will be anxious to preserve its secured position, while on the other hand it will want to be as helpful as it can be to the customer.

When the bank hears from the official receiver it can disclose the extent of the third party's guarantee liabilities, or the reliance which the bank places on the security which he has lodged.

The bank's options in the bankruptcy proceedings will be the same as those when its customer has a bankruptcy order made against him. Where the third party is simply a guarantor who has lodged no other security in support, the bank will be able to lodge a proof of debt in his estate for the full amount of the guaranteed liability, as determined by the stopping of the customer's account. This will be the balance of the accounts secured, up to any limitation in the amount of the guarantee. Any dividends received should be placed to a realized security account, or suspense account, where effectively they become cash security as collateral cover for the customer's borrowing. In due course, should the customer repay his own debt then the funds in the realized security account should be refunded to the trustee in bankruptcy.

Dealings with undischarged bankrupts

Under the provisions of s. 360 Insolvency Act 1986, a person who is an undischarged bankrupt must never obtain credit of more than £250 without disclosing to the other party that he is an undischarged bankrupt. Moreover, he is prohibited from trading under a name which is different from the name under which he was adjudicated bankrupt, unless, again, he discloses his status as a bankrupt to the person with whom he is dealing. If therefore a person who is undischarged from bankruptcy proceedings opens an account with a bank, and borrows money in excess of £250, without disclosing that he is an undischarged bankrupt, he commits a criminal offence. The first that a bank knows of the situation may be when the truth has been discovered by the official receiver, and it is asked to state whether an account is held in that name and whether it is overdrawn. For its own part, should the bank ever suspect that a customer might be an undischarged bankrupt, it is necessary to search in the Bankruptcy Register.

The form of prohibitions on an undischarged bankrupt operating a bank account without the permission of his trustee have been omitted from the Insolvency Act 1986, and it seems that it will be up to a banker to make up his own mind as to whether he wishes to conduct an account for an undischarged bankrupt. The onus will be on the bankrupt to keep his trustee advised as to his financial affairs and under s. 333 the banker has an obligation to give his trustee any information which the latter may reasonably require. Moreover, where an undischarged bankrupt acquires property subsequent to the date of his bankruptcy or his income increases, he must inform his trustee in bankruptcy and should he not do so he could be liable for contempt of court.

Sections 307 and 309 Insolvency Act 1986 give the trustee in bankruptcy power to claim property by giving notice in writing or to seek an Income Payments order under s. 310. Under this the court would make an order that so much of the bankrupt's income should pass to his trustee in bankruptcy for the benefit of the creditors.

Under the provisions of s. 307(3) the title of property after-acquired by the bankrupt vests in his trustee in bankruptcy at the time when the property was acquired or when it devolved upon the bankrupt. Understandably the situation could have very dangerous consequences for a bank or another party who, say, had acquired a mortgage or security over that property and lent against it. Hence s. 307(4) offers protection. This states:

'Where, whether before or after the service of a notice under this Section –

(*a*)   a person acquires property in good faith, for value and without notice of the bankruptcy; or

(*b*)   a banker enters into a transaction in good faith and without such notice, the Trustee shall not in respect of that property or transaction be entitled by virtue of this Section to any remedy against that person or banker, or any person whose title to any property derives from that person or banker'.

Again a banker is mentioned specifically and in order to meet the requirements of the subsection need only have acted in good faith and without notice of the bankruptcy, both conditions appearing to present little difficulty in practice.

Occasionally, a bankrupt who wishes to hide his present business transactions, uses an account which has been opened in the name of his wife. The bank might notice this if there is substantial turnover, and if this does not seem to be consistent with what was told them by the wife, when the account was opened. If it becomes suspicious, the bank should interview the lady customer, and if she admits that the account is being used for her husband's activities and he is an undischarged bankrupt, then it seems that the bank should stop the account at once, and that the trustee in bankruptcy should be informed.

An undischarged bankrupt is also prohibited by ss. 11 and 13 Company Directors Disqualification Act 1986 from being a director of a limited company, except with the dispensation of the court. In consequence, the bank might learn that a director signing on a company account is an undischarged bankrupt and each situation will need to be reviewed on its merits. The bank probably would not wish to stop a company account immediately, and as there will be other officials, directors or secretary, they should be interviewed at once, and their observations and instructions should be taken as to the future operations on the company account. It is really a matter for them as to how the company affairs are conducted, and as the undischarged bankrupt will need to resign, a new director or secretary will need to be appointed and a new bank mandate given as soon as possible. In the meantime, provided the transactions are not unusual, there is probably little risk in allowing a company account to continue.

INDIVIDUAL VOLUNTARY ARRANGEMENTS

Part VIII of the Insolvency Act 1986 introduced a new procedure to avoid all the rigours of bankruptcy for small personal debt, under which an individual can make a proposal as to how he will deal with his various liabilities, and his creditors can vote at a meeting on whether they will accept his proposals or not. The Insolvency Act and the Rules are not comprehensive in setting out the procedures and it seems that this new insolvency process will develop slowly by usage. Initially, however, the debtor must make an application to the court, whereupon an interim order is made which will be in force for fourteen days or such longer period as the court may order. A trustee in bankruptcy or the official receiver can also make an application for an interim order if he wishes to seek a less formal process than bankruptcy. The result of the interim order is that all enforcement proceedings against the debtor and his estate are suspended and a petition for bankruptcy may not be presented or, if it has already been presented, it will not be heard.

At the time when the interim order is made, a licensed insolvency practitioner is appointed as the nominee, and it is his job to try and establish a workable voluntary arrangement. The debtor has to give the nominee full details of his assets, income and liabilities, and must set out his proposals for dealing with his liabilities. The nominee, the insolvency practitioner, then expresses his own views on the debtor's proposal to the court and if he thinks it appropriate a meeting of creditors is called to consider, amend, and vote on what the debtor has proposed. In all cases, however, the creditors' meeting cannot interfere with the rights of preferential or secured creditors and if the creditors wish to vary the debtor's proposal the debtor himself must agree to what they suggest. Creditors may also change the identity of the nominee if they so wish and appoint a different licensed insolvency practitioner.

The Rules have built-in safeguards to prevent a debtor arranging matters to his own advantage through the presence of connected parties as creditors. Firstly a resolution will only be carried if it is passed by a majority in value of at least three-quarters of those present in person or by proxy and voting. Under a second count, associates are not included and the resolution will not be carried if those voting against it include more than half in value of all the creditors to whom notice of the meeting was sent. In other words, the first count requires a 75 per cent majority and the second a 50 per cent majority excluding for the latter purpose the votes by value of connected persons from both the vote figure and the total value of creditors.

In all cases when establishing the right to vote, value is determined by reference to unsecured debt, and where a creditor holds security he must estimate the value and agree this sum with the nominee.

If the resolution is passed the individual voluntary arrangment will bind all the debtor's creditors who had notice of the meeting even if they did not attend or vote by proxy. At this point the nominee reports back to the court and he is then appointed the supervisor of the arrangement. His powers as supervisor are derived from the terms of the arrangement, although he may always apply to the court for directions if necessary. Hence whenever a banker deals with a supervisor in respect of a customer's account which is subject to an individual voluntary arrangement, the banker should ask to see a copy of the arrangement to ensure that the supervisor is entitled to delivery of any credit balance, safe custody items, or unwanted security which fall into the arrangement.

Usually the bank will have heard of the proposal earlier and it will have been entitled to attend in person or vote by proxy at the meeting of creditors.

When the notice of the meeting of creditors is received, any overdrawn account in the debtor's name or any account secured by him or his security should be stopped, to prevent the operation of the Rule in *Clayton's Case*, just as in bankruptcy proceedings. However, if the debtor's account is not overdrawn, it can be allowed to continue to be used by the debtor until the arrangement is approved by the meeting of creditors and the supervisor is appointed. At that stage, the bank would be able to see whether the credit balance was caught under the arrangement.

Joint accounts and partnership accounts

Where notice is received of the calling of a meeting of creditors or the making of an interim order in respect of a customer who is a party to a joint account and/or a member of a partnership, and those accounts have no liabilities to the bank, those accounts need not be stopped. If, however, they are overdrawn, and if the bank wishes to preserve its claim, the overdrawn account should be frozen under notice to the other account holders, for whom new accounts may be provided if the bank wishes.

Once a supervisor is appointed, similar considerations apply, but a credit balance, if mentioned in the arrangement, should only be paid to the supervisor upon the joint written instructions of the supervisor and the other parties to the account.

If all the parties wish to continue to operate the joint account or the partnership account in credit, upon the appointment of the supervisor, the opinion of the supervisor should be obtained, if it is proposed that the debtor remain as a party to the account.

Where the account is overdrawn and the bank is prepared to waive its claim in the individual voluntary arrangement against the debtor the joint account or the partnership account may be continued. It must of course be stopped if the bank wishes to retain its rights for any borrowing against the party subject to the individual voluntary arrangement or if it needs to look to any security for the account which that party may have charged.

DEEDS OF ARRANGEMENT

A deed of arrangement, sometimes referred to as a deed of assignment, covers a procedure similar to bankruptcy, but the debtor hopes under this slightly different procedure to avoid the stigma associated with bankruptcy and the disabilities attached to being an undischarged bankrupt. However, while the debtor's assets are assigned to a trustee for the benefit of creditors generally, and statutory provisions under the Deeds of Arrangement Act 1914 regulate matters carefully, from the creditor's point of view there are nevertheless certain disadvantages.

Under a deed of arrangement, the debtor is not subject to a public examination, and his trustee does not have the same statutory powers to investigate and research the debtor's financial background, to discover assets which might have been hidden away out of the reach of creditors; in particular the ability to upset preferences and transactions at an undervalue is not available.

Frequently, however, under a deed of arrangement the debtor will undertake to pay a proportion of his future earnings to his trustee, or perhaps sums are introduced into the estate by a friendly third party. Usually the costs of realization and administering the estate under a deed of arrangement are less than under bankruptcy proceedings, and there is therefore attraction for creditors in that the prospects of higher dividends are present.

Usually, to initiate matters the debtor will approach an insolvency practitioner and a carefully worded letter will be written to creditors proposing a meeting at which his financial position can be assessed. It is intimated that a deed of arrangement is proposed, and a statement of affairs is often included, showing the debtor's assets and liabilities and his proposals to his creditors. The receipt of this letter may be the first that the bank knows of the customer's financial problems.

It will be necessary for a majority in number and value of creditors to assent to the deed of arrangement, if it is to become effective, and it is registered within seven days of its execution at the Department of Trade and Industry under the provisions of the Deeds of Arrangement Act. Sometimes a creditor will refuse to assent, and he can threaten to petition for bankruptcy, if, for example, he serves a statutory demand to which the debtor does not respond.

If the bank is prepared to go along with the proposals in the deed of arrangement, it will need to quantify its debt, and if it holds direct security then this must be valued so that the unsecured portion of the liability can be mentioned in its assent. Frequently the co-operation of the bank is necessary, if the bank's lending is large in relation to the total extent of the debtor's liabilitities, in view of the need to obtain a majority in value. However, depending on the circumstances, the bank might prefer not to agree to the proposals, and to await developments generally, and should it do so, and matters proceed as proposed so that the deed is executed and registered, then the bank will be able to assent later, should it wish, and lodge claims for its dividend. The same options for security exist as in bankruptcy proceedings, and third-party security proceeds may be disregarded for the purposes of assent. The trustee must be a licensed insolvency practitioner, and the bank might be asked to open an account in the name of the trustee in respect of the estate of the debtor. The usual account-opening facilities are necessary, and the account will be styled 'John Smith, Trustee for James Jones'.[51] As Acts of Bankruptcy no longer exist, there need be no concern by the bank as to the operation of this account at once.

---

51 See Appendix I, Q. 20 (April 1982).

CHAPTER 8

Consumer Credit Act 1974

Many of the duties and responsibilities of a bank have been modified by the Consumer Credit Act where there is provision of credit up to £15 000 in amount to a non-corporate borrower. In consequence, banking procedures have had to change, for otherwise lendings would become irrecoverable if the precise requirements of the Act were not met.

The Consumer Credit Act protects individuals either in a private capacity, as sole or joint traders, as trustees or executors, or when acting in any capacity for an unincorporated club or society, or as partners in a professional partnership. In particular, for banks this means that special forms must be used for regulated agreements, which must draw the debtor's attention to his rights, and copies of all the forms used must be supplied to the borrower and any surety, both in respect of the loan agreement and any security. Moreover, guarantees and other forms of third party security must be in a form prescribed by the Act. The Act prevents banks from canvassing for credit except when they do so within criteria specifically laid down and in certain situations it calls for cooling off periods, being periods of time for the borrower to consider the proposed contract coupled with an ability for him to cancel the agreement under certain circumstances. In every case the true cost of the credit supplied must be told to the borrower and to the surety, and lenders are not allowed to vary the terms of an agreement except as prescribed by the Act.

If the bank omits in its agreement any of the general information required by the Consumer Credit Act, or any financial particulars or statement of the debtor's rights, the agreement will subsequently not be capable of enforcement except with a court order. Moreover if the agreement is not completed when presented to the debtor the same provisions apply, and if the minimum information required under the Act has been omitted the agreement will be completely unenforceable.

CONSUMER CREDIT LICENCE

The Act states that a person engaged in one or more of the following categories of consumer credit activity must hold a licence, these being: lenders of money, credit reference agencies, debt counsellors, debt collectors, debt adjusters, providers of consumer hire, and credit brokers.

Each bank must therefore hold its own licence and when dealing with a customer in the credit industry must ensure that the customer is licensed, for otherwise an agreement of an unlicensed customer may be unenforceable. It is possible for the Public Register of Consumer Credit Licences, which is open for personal inspection, to be examined by way of search but normally the customer will be asked to show his licence when he opens the account, and again if the bank is asked to lend money; for in the event of an unlicensed trader entering into an agreement with the bank it is possible that monies lent might be irrecoverable.

The Director General has wide powers enabling him to suspend or revoke a licence where he is of the opinion that the licence holder is not a fit person to have one.

Banks should therefore remember that if a borrower is introduced by a broker it is essential to check that the broker himself is licensed, for if not, the lending, albeit to another party, will be unenforceable without a special order from the Director General.

A licence is also revoked by bankruptcy, mental incapacity, or the death of the holder.

CONNECTED LENDER LIABILITY

Where a bank is introduced to its customer by a supplier of goods and it has financed the contract between the customer and the supplier, should the customer later have any claim against the supplier in respect of misrepresentation or breach of contract, the customer also acquires a similar right of action against the bank which becomes jointly and severally liable with the supplier. If the bank suffers any loss, it is then entitled to be indemnified by the supplier, although these provisions do not apply to items costing £30 or less or more than £10 000. Connected lender liability extends to the provision of credit on overdraft, loan, or where a credit card advance is made.

CANVASSING

Canvassing is an oral attempt by a lender to encourage a third party to avail himself of the lender's services, and under s. 49(i) it is an offence to canvass a debtor–creditor agreement (a regulated agreement) off 'trade premises', without a prior invitation. Trade premises are the bank's normal premises, or any temporary premises such as a branch in a show ground, or the *business* premises of the customer. As private customers do not have business premises, it would be an offence to canvass that class of customer off the bank's business premises, without a prior written invitation. Canvassing involves inducing the third party, by personal contact, to enter into an agreement with the bank, or with any of its subsidiary finance companies. However, it is permitted for general discussion of financial matters to take place off trade premises provided the discussion is commenced by the third party and not by the banker, and provided the banker has not gone along to the meeting for the purpose of canvassing. Also, communication by telephone or in writing is permitted and the canvassing of overdrafts for existing customers is exempt from the regulations.

CIRCULARS TO MINORS

Under s. 50, it is an offence to send a minor any document which invites him or her to borrow or seek information or advice on borrowing, or to obtain credit for purchases or in respect of services.

ADVERTISING AND QUOTATIONS

Advertising services for limited companies is exempt from the requirements of the Act, but any advertisement of credit to the personal sector must meet the requirements laid down. The advertising is classified into 'simple, intermediate, or full' categories, and any advertisement which falls between these definitions constitutes an infringement, carrying potential fines or imprisonment for the individual concerned.

Each borrower is enabled to request a 'quotation' and the bank, as lender, must then reply in writing. It is necessary for it to include all aspects of charges in its quotation. Thus, interest, arrangement fees for setting up the lending, charges for taking the security, legal costs, and any other applicable charges directly related to the lending must be totalled. This enables the total charge for credit (TCC) and the annual percentage rate (APR) to be assessed, although of course there is no commitment to lend at this stage. The provision of the quotation enables the prospective borrower to compare the prices of credit offered by different lenders. If necessary, certain assumptions can be built into the projected quotation or advertisement in respect of certain categories of borrowing. This means that a bank's base rate can be quoted at its current rate, but a note can be appended that this is subject to variation from time to time. Any inclusion of front-end fees should state whether these are based on reasonable estimates or whether they are fixed fees, and once they have been quoted such fees are not subject to variation. Banks, when quoting for overdrafts (not fixed-sum lendings), must quote an 'effective rate of interest', based on the actual rate charged, and calculated in the same way as the APR. In this case, fees should be shown separately and should not be included in the calculation.

It should be noted that these 'Truth in Lending' Regulations also extend without restriction as to amount in respect of any advertisements and quotations in respect of credit for individuals which is to be secured by a charge over land.[52] In other words, the £15 000 maximum is immaterial and the quotation must be given.

52 See Appendix I, Q. 63 (September 1983).

BANKERS' OPINIONS

The Office of Fair Trading has expressed the view that banks are not subject to the provisions of s. 145(8) Consumer Credit Act 1974 when giving replies to status enquiries. This means that there is no obligation on them to make their opinions available for inspection and, if necessary, correction by the customer who could otherwise exercise such rights. In consequence, all status reply forms now include a printed mention that the bank is not a credit reference agency pursuant to the section.

A REGULATED AGREEMENT

Under the Act, in general, any agreement to grant credit up to and including £15 000 to a non-corporate body is regulated. The credit may be provided in sterling or in a foreign currency, but the provision of finance for foreign trade purposes is not affected. Clearly therefore ordinary banking loans, personal loans, business development loans, home improvement loans, or whatever phraseology is used by the bank concerned, all become regulated agreements. Also credit provided by way of a credit card, hire purchase, or leasing, or credit sale agreement is caught.

As regards the amount, the relevant sum is determined by the principal amount lent, but interest and commission charges are excluded. Also, if the finance is granted on more than one account then each must be regarded separately.

Overdrafts are caught by the Consumer Credit Act but by virtue of a dispensation under Section 38 Banking Act 1979 the Director General of Fair Trading has exempted banks from the documentation relating to the provision of the finance but not the security.

The form and content of a regulated agreement will usually therefore include reference to the following matters. In the case of the first four mentioned items if the agreement is silent, it will be totally unenforceable.

(a) The amount of credit granted or available
(b) The timing as to when repayments are to be made
(c) The amount of each repayment
(d) The rate of interest chargeable
(e) A heading to the agreement e.g. 'Credit Agreement regulated by the Consumer Credit Act 1974'
(f) The borrower's and lender's names and addresses
(g) The annual percentage rate (APR)
(h) A description of the item, property, services, the purchase of which, if applicable, is to be financed
(i) The total charge for credit (TCC), applying in the case of fixed interest agreements only

(*j*) The total amount repayable, capital, interest, and any other charges, applicable to fixed interest agreements only

(*k*) Reference to any variable rates of interest or other charges used in calculating the annual percentage rate

(*l*) Any security arrangements and requirements

(*m*) Certain prescribed statutory notices advising the borrower of his rights under the Act

(*n*) Charges applicable, if any, in the event of default.

When an agreement form has been completed it must be signed by all borrowers in the signature box on the form, and by the bank. A copy of the agreement must be given to each borrower and if an unexecuted agreement already signed by the bank has been given to the borrower personally for his signature it is necessary for a copy of the executed agreement to be given to him after he has signed. Similarly, if the bank has not signed when a copy of the unexecuted agreement is given to the borrower then a copy of the executed agreement after it has been signed by the borrower and the bank must be sent to the borrower within 7 days of the borrower signing.

Whenever an unexecuted agreement is sent to the borrower a copy must be sent at the same time and a further copy within 7 days of the agreement being executed, unless the borrower brings the form into the bank and signs there, or unless the borrower signs and returns an agreement form which has already been signed by the bank.

In every case the copy of the agreement must always be accompanied by a copy of any other document of which mention is made in the agreement and this applies particularly to security forms.

Types of regulated agreements

The Consumer Credit Act refers to debtor–creditor–supplier agreements, debtor–creditor agreements, credit-token agreements, consumer-hire agreements, exempt agreements, small agreements, and multiple agreements, but in branch banking for practical purposes the types of regulated agreements break down into four principal categories. These are:

(*a*) *A non-cancellable agreement*   This is one which has been signed by the bank officer and all the borrowers on the bank's own premises. A copy of the completed form(s) will have been given to each of the borrowers and the finance can then be made available immediately. Whenever an agreement is made secured on land it will always be classed as a non-cancellable agreement wherever it is signed.

(*b*) *A non-cancellable bridging loan, or loan for purchase of land*   Where the finance is provided by way of a bridging loan for the purchase of land or is finance for the purchase of land which will be mortgaged to the bank as security, the agreement form may be signed on or off the bank's premises and a signed copy must be given or sent to each borrower, who will have no cancellation rights.

(*c*) **Cancellable agreements** In the banking context cancellable agreements usually arise where there have been face to face negotiations between the banker and the borrower(s) and where the agreement form has not been signed by all the borrowers on the bank's business premises.

This might arise, for instance, where the loan is made to joint account holders and where one party to the account calls at the branch and signs the agreement form and then takes the form away for the other party to sign, or where the bank sends the form to the other party for signature and return. Also, it could happen where forms are sent out by post for signature and return after the customer has telephoned or written to the bank requesting a loan, previously having called at the branch to discuss matters.

Section 67 and 69 of the Act apply in all the cases giving the borrowers the right to cancel and under the provisions of s. 64 the bank must send out a notice by post within 7 days of the agreement being signed, advising the borrower(s) of his right to cancel. This notice will say that cancellation must be in writing and must be within 5 days, which start with the day after the notice is received. Only after this period has expired can the bank safely make the finance available.

(*d*) **Land agreements** Leaving aside the non-cancellable agreements discussed in (*b*) above, where the provision of credit for any purpose is to be secured wholly or partically by a charge over land, special provisions apply.

Firstly the borrower must be given a 'consideration period' during which he must not be approached by the lender in any way, unless he requests advice. This consideration period begins when the advance copy of the land agreement is sent to the prospective borrower marked 'Copy of Proposed Credit Agreement containing notice of your rights to withdraw. Do not sign or return this copy'.

Next, and not earlier than 7 days later, the regulated agreement form is sent by post, together with the borrower's copy of the agreement, and completed copies of the security documents mentioned in it. The consideration period ends when 7 days have elapsed after the agreement has been sent by post for signature, or upon the return of the agreement duly signed, whichever event takes place first. The customer may sign at the bank or elsewhere but it will be seen from the above that normally the consideration period extends to about 15 days.

If the bank has not signed the agreement form when it is sent to the borrower, then when the borrower returns his copy the bank needs to send him another copy of the agreement duly signed together with further copies of the mortgage forms mentioned in the regulated agreement. Also if there is more than one borrower, then each party must receive his own copy of the agreement form and his own copy of the security form mentioned.

MODIFICATION OF A REGULATED AGREEMENT

The terms of a regulated agreement may be changed and in that event the bank must enter into a modifying agreement or an entirely fresh agreement must be entered into with the customer. Modification will arise when the amount of the original loan is increased or when, for example, a new security is taken.

Even if the customer has defaulted and the bank has called up the original loan and then agrees to extend the period or vary the repayment terms or take new security, a modified agreement or a new agreement form must be signed, unless the customer consents to judgment in the county court, after legal proceedings have been started.

Modified agreements involve cumbersome procedures but they can be avoided if the change is made to accommodate the borrower and there are no benefits to the bank as a result of the change.

DIRECT SECURITY FOR REGULATED AGREEMENTS

Where a borrower(s) charges his own item of security, the Consumer Credit Act has occasioned no changes to the bank charge form, and any security lodged with the bank before the Act became wholly operational in May 1985 is sound. However, it is essential that that security be scheduled in the regulated agreement and that a copy of the agreement and a copy of the charge form be given to each borrower. If new security is being pledged a copy of the new charge form must obviously be supplied.

Some banks have amended their security forms so that they incorporate a clause stating that the security will be available for a liability arising under a regulated agreement only if the security is scheduled in the agreement form, this being done, to avoid any possible problems with the usual covenant which states that a security is available for 'all monies'.

THIRD-PARTY SECURITY FOR REGULATED AGREEMENTS

The Consumer Credit (Guarantees and Indemnities) Regulations 1983 provide that any agreement or indemnity in respect of a regulated lending must be in a form meeting certain requirements. These regulations apply whether the finance is provided by way of loan or overdraft. The regulations state that the form must include a description of the regulated agreement secured, a statement of the third parties' rights, a note of the names and addresses of all parties to the security and a prescribed box for the signature of the guarantor, referred to as the indemnifier. The form must also have a prescribed heading and if it is a guarantee which is to be supported by another item of security, the supporting security must be described in the guarantee form. All third-party securities carry prominent warnings such as 'sign only if you want to be legally bound'. 'Important – you should read this carefully' and, 'you may have to pay instead'.

A consequence of these requirements is that banks have introduced new forms of guarantee for regulated lendings and some banks have introduced new third-party security forms for mortgages over land, assignments of life policies and charges over stocks and shares. Other banks, however, have simply amended their existing security forms, deleting the 'all liability' clause and referring to the availability of the security only for the regulated lending specified.

All third parties pledging their security for the liabilities of the customer must receive a copy of the agreement form and a copy of the security form. Should the agreement be signed after the security is executed, the copy of the executed agreement has to be sent to the third party surety within 7 days.

Whenever a regulated lending goes into default, it is necessary for the bank to serve a copy of the default notice on the surety as well as on the borrower, the surety's copy being headed 'Surety's Copy of a Notice Served on the Debtor'.

NEGOTIABLE INSTRUMENTS

One unexpected result of the Consumer Credit Act, is that negotiable instruments should not be charged as security for a regulated agreement. However, if, surprisingly, that situation is encountered, it would be possible for the bank to go to court to seek an order that the agreement and the security were enforceable, but at the time of writing, there is no case law on this area.

RIGHTS OF THE BORROWER AND SURETY

At any time a borrower is entitled to ask for a statement of the amount due and repayments he has made on any fixed sum agreement. He must pay a small fee, but he is also entitled to further copies of the regulated agreement and any security forms, if he wishes (s. 77). The bank then has 12 working days to supply the information, but if it fails, the agreement becomes unenforceable until the request has been met. If the bank fails to deal with matters for one month or more it becomes liable to penalties.

As regards overdrawn current accounts, the bank must send out regular statements of account including the opening date and the last date covered by the statement, the opening and closing balances and details of all payments to the credit and debit of the account. The statement must also mention that details of interest calculations can be obtained.

In the case of a joint account each party is entitled to his or her own separate statement but in many instances banks have now made use of the dispensation procedure whereby it is only necessary to supply one statement to a named party. This situation is arrived at by the other party agreeing in writing to waive his or her rights to a separate statement.

Third-party sureties are also entitled to information and under s. 107 for a fixed sum agreement a surety may apply in writing. After payment of a small fee he is then entitled to a further copy of the executed agreement and any security document and a statement signed on behalf of the bank showing as far as is practicable the total sum paid by the debtor and the total sum remaining unpaid under the agreement. He may also be informed of the various amounts comprised in the total figures and the dates when each instalment became due.

In respect of overdrafts a third-party surety must be supplied with a signed statement which refers to the state of the account, the amount, if any, currently payable under the agreement, and the amounts and due dates of any payments which, if no further drawings are made, will become payable later (s. 108). These are wide-ranging information provisions and are a clear exception to the banker's usual duty of secrecy.

APPROPRIATION OF PAYMENTS

If a borrower has more than one regulated agreement then when making a payment he is entitled to choose the agreement to which the monies should be placed. Should he make no appropriation, the bank may do so, unless there is a secured agreement, in which case the monies must first be placed in reduction of that liability. If there is more than one secured agreement, and the debtor does not make any appropriation, then the bank must appropriate the funds proportionately between them. All this is, of course, quite different from a creditor's rights outside the Act (see earlier).

DEATH OF THE BORROWER

Whereas outside of Consumer Credit Act situations upon the death of a borrower, his executors or administrators meet the liability when they have realized assets in the estate, different considerations apply where the deceased had a regulated agreement with a liability outstanding at the time of his death. In general terms, the provisions mean that the executors or administrators do not necessarily need to pay off the debt in one sum, and their position will depend upon whether the regulated agreement was fully secured, partially secured, or unsecured. In the case of a fully secured regulated agreement the executors or administrators may continue to make the payments at the rate and times specified in the agreement. However, where the agreement is only partially secured or is unsecured that right is not absolute and the provider of credit can apply to the Court for the rate of repayment to be accelerated.

In practice, it seems likely that bank overdrafts will not be treated in this way, even if they are under £15 000, unless the agreement with the deceased was that the overdraft was available for a specific period, and this is, of course, unlikely.

REPAYMENT BEFORE THE DUE DATE

Section 94 of the Act gives every debtor the entitlement to repay his debt whenever he wishes. Upon enquiry, in writing, albeit free of charge, he is entitled to be informed of the amount required to repay early and he must be told how this sum has been calculated. This means that in the case of a structured loan he is entitled to receive a rebate on the total interest charge which would have been applied if the loan had run its full period (s. 95).

TERMINATION OF THE AGREEMENT

A regulated agreement may include a provision whereby the lender or the borrower may terminate the agreement after giving a period of notice. This is called termination. Usually, however, the most likely cases where the agreement will come to an end before its scheduled date will be where the borrower defaults in meeting one or more terms of the agreement, most commonly in failing to make a scheduled repayment instalment. The borrower might also have a bankruptcy order made against him, and in the event the whole amount due under the regulated agreement becomes repayable.

Where there has been a default by a borrower in meeting an instalment, unlike with non-regulated lendings, it will be necessary for a bank to serve a warning notice on the borrower, before calling in the full amount outstanding. This warning notice must set out the consequences of his failure to make the instalment and state that if the situation is not corrected the total lending will be called up after a specified period has elapsed, which period must be a minimum of seven days. This warning notice must show the amount in which demand will be made, and the date on which that will happen. Thereafter if the debtor fails to correct matters the bank may proceed as indicated. If, however, the debtor restores matters to the state which they should be in under the regulated agreement, then the bank's right to call in the total amount outstanding cannot then be exercised. The warning notice must state that it is required under s. 87 (1) Consumer Credit Act 1974.

It is not clear where banks wish to call in an overdraft of £15 000 or less, whether it is necesary to use the dual notice procedure, but to prevent difficulties arising in court should they need to sue, several banks are using both the default notice and the call up notice later. The first warning notice may well in practice start to replace the correspondence which usually was a forerunner of call up, when the bank was seeking to obtain the customer's co-operation towards dealing with his liabilities.

RECOVERY OF AMOUNT DUE UNDER REGULATED AGREEMENT

If the agreement is enforceable and the security steps have been carried out correctly, then after serving a separate default notice for each loan or overdraft and call up notices on all the borrowers and all third-party sureties, the bank is entitled to sue in the county court for recovery of the monies due or for an order enabling it to realize its security. It is not correct simply to serve notices on one borrower, when there is more than one and not to serve notices on third-party sureties concurrently. The object of the legislation at the time of recovery is the same as at the outset, namely to ensure that every party liable is fully aware of the stage reached. Also, it should be noted, that even though the agreement might be secured by a mortgage over a property which is not occupied, it is still necessary to obtain a court order before the property is sold.

CHAPTER 9

Limited Companies

Limited companies probably constitute one of the most important types of customers encountered by bankers, and since the creation of limited liability towards the latter part of the nineteenth century they have grown in number and size so that nowadays the majority of a bank's lendings will almost certainly have been made to such organizations. Because of their importance, and in view of the complexity encountered in lending and security situations, it is most important for a banker to have a good knowledge of that part of company law which impacts upon his banking practice.

The limited company is a separate legal entity quite different in law from its shareholders or directors. It has its own existence which is perpetual, until it goes into liquidation, or it is struck off the register of limited companies by the Registrar. When formed, it takes powers to itself and these are set out in its memorandum and articles of association, although these powers are to some extent restricted by the various Companies Acts and in particular the Act under which it is incorporated.

The leading case concerning the complete separateness in legal identity between the company and its director or shareholder is that of *Salomon* v. *Salomon & Co. Ltd* (1897). Here the similarity in names can be seen, which can be confusing for the uninitiated. However the warning to bankers is clear. Mr Salomon was the major shareholder, holding also £10 000 worth of secured debentures in the company. The company was placed into liquidation, and its unsecured creditors claimed the assets in the company which were encompassed by Mr Salomon's debentures. Their argument was that he, Mr Salomon, and the company, were one person, and that he had no priority over them. However, the court held that the company was a separate legal unit quite different from its shareholders, and as Mr Salomon had entered into a legal contract with the company in his own right he was perfectly entitled to rank as a secured creditor by virtue of his debenture secured by company assets.

This separate legal identity, despite similarity of names, must always be borne in mind by bankers when cheques are being collected, for to collect for one or other account which is not the payee's could result in conversion (see Chapter 4).

When it has been created, and meets the requirements of the Companies Act, a limited company is issued with a certificate of incorporation and until that stage has been reached the company does not exist legally. Consequently,

207

up to that point, the company has no contractual powers and should it purport to enter into any contract beforehand, that contract will not be binding against the company, even if the certificate of incorporation is subsequently issued. It is therefore important for bankers to ensure, when dealing with a situation involving the incorporation of a company, that everything is watertight before obligations are entered into.

Some companies are limited by guarantee, and there are others where the liability of the shareholders is not restricted in any way in respect of the company's debts, known as unlimited companies, and there are a few companies created by their own Act of Parliament and known as statutory companies. However the most usual types of companies met by a bank are the private company and the public company.

PUBLIC LIMITED COMPANIES

The Companies Act 1985 makes the following requirements of a public company:

(*a*) It must be limited by shares capable of being transferred without restrictions, or limited by guarantee and have a share capital. The share capital must be for a minimum authorized amount of £50 000, all of which must have been issued. It must have at least two members.

(*b*) The company's memorandum must state that it is a public company, and it must have a name ending with the words 'public limited company', although the abbreviation 'plc' is permitted; the Welsh equivalent, or 'ccc', is used where the company's registered office is in Wales.

(*c*) The company must have been registered or re-registered as a public company.

The Act also lays down more stringent requirements for a public company than for a private company in respect of the manner in which profits available for distribution are calculated, and states the steps necessary should the directors become aware of a deficit of an amount of 50 per cent or more of the called-up capital in respect of the net assets of the company (s. 142 Companies Act 1985).

A public company must have a minimum of two directors and one secretary and all companies quoted on the Stock Exchange are public companies, although the converse does not apply, for there are many public companies without a quotation. Before a public company is able to commence business, in addition to its certificate of incorporation it must also obtain a trading certificate, or a certificate to commence business from the Registrar, by filing certain documents required under the Companies Acts with the Registrar. Should a public company purport to enter into any contract after incorporation, but before it is issued with its trading certificate then the contract is only provisional and will depend for its validity upon the issue of the certificate to commence business. Thus the difference is that whereas the absence of the certicate of incorporation will render the contract void, the absence of the trading certificate will not necessarily do so.

PRIVATE LIMITED COMPANIES

All other companies are private companies, although, because of earlier requirements relating to private companies in the Companies Act 1948, it is likely that for many years private companies will exhibit certain common characteristics, such as a restriction in the articles of association as to the right of a member to transfer his shares, and a limitation on the number of members to a maximum of fifty. Previously, private companies also prohibited any invitation to the public to subscribe for any shares or debentures.

A private comany must have at least one director and a secretary, and does not require a trading certificate to commence business, as is the case with a public company, so a private company is able to start business as soon as it has been incorporated.

MEMORANDUM OF ASSOCIATION

Each company has a memorandum of association, in which will be found its name, the location of its registered office, and, of great importance to bankers, its objects clause. The company has no power to contract beyond the limits set out in this objects clause, and any transaction outside the limitation will be *ultra vires*.[53] As such, the contract will be void, and cannot later be ratified. However, it is possible for the objects clause to be amended by a special resolution being passed by the members of the company in a general meeting. It is clearly most important for a banker to ensure that any dealings which it has with its company customer will not fall foul of this legal requirement and this is particularly so when lendings are made to enable the company to carry out certain activities, or when security is taken from the company for its own or third-party obligations. It is, for instance, essential to ensure that specific powers exist in the objects clause of the memorandum for a company to give a guarantee.

Limitations on borrowing powers in the memorandum are not often encountered, and if with a trading company there is no mention of borrowing powers then the right to borrow and give security is implied. It is more usual to restrict any borrowing powers by way of limitation on the directors and this is effected in the articles of association. However, should the bank lend monies which are *ultra vires* the company, then as retrospective amendment of the memorandum is not possible, the position can only be changed for future borrowings by an amendment to the memorandum by the company in general meeting. As soon as this resolution has been passed, future borrowings would

53 See Appendix I, Q. 17 (April 1982).

be *intra vires*, and to that extent, *Clayton's Case* will work in favour of the bank in that, as turnover passes through the current account, old *ultra vires* lendings will be repaid, and new drawings will constitute new monies which are *intra vires* following the amendment to the memorandum.

There is of course nothing to prevent the bank asking the company to return the monies lent which were *ultra vires* and such transaction is effective (*Sinclair* v. *Brougham* (1914)). In practice, this is an area in which problems are rarely encountered, although a liquidator might take the point if the company failed.

One remedy available to a lender in an *ultra vires* situation would be to trace the use to which the unauthorized loan had been put. *Sinclair* v. *Brougham* (1914) was a case involving the unauthorized banking activities of the Birkbeck Building Society. Here, the House of Lords was asked to decide upon competing claims by shareholders and depositors, and it was held that where a fund exists to which there are rival claimants, the claimants are entitled to a *pro rata* division of assets. In this case, the deposits consisted of unauthorized borrowings by the society. Later, in the case of *Re Diplock* (1948), the principle was extended by the Court of Appeal. In this case, the assets in the estate of a deceased person had been distributed wrongly to a number of charities and the court was asked to determine the extent to which the proper beneficiaries of the estate could benefit by the tracing and recovery of the payments made in error. The court saw two guiding principles, namely that where the proceeds of monies are traced only to parties who have themselves given value for the monies then recovery cannot be achieved. However, where the monies are traced into the hands of a third party who knew or was on notice of the irregular nature of the transaction, the third party would not be able to resist the tracing claim. Again, where monies have been mixed with other monies, or part of them has been used to buy an asset, then the lender and beneficiary must share, *pari passu*.

Another remedy available to a lender arises under the doctrine of subrogation whereby he can step into the shoes of the creditor where an unauthorized lending has been used to pay off the legitimate debts of the company, even if such debts had been incurred before the time the monies were lent. However, the lender has no priority and does not acquire any rights to any securities that the paid creditor may have held.

If the bank considered it worth while, in such a situation it could sue the directors of the company for damages for breach of their warranty of authority. However, the bank would need to prove that the directors had held out that they had authority to contract a loan which purported to be binding upon the company, and it seems likely that the bank would not be able to rely on such a remedy where it knew or should have known that the loan was in fact *ultra vires*. In the majority of instances such circumstances would apply, for the bank, in accordance with its normal practice, would have a copy of the memorandum of association in its own records.

It is for this last reason that doubt has been expressed as to whether the protection afforded by s. 35 Companies Act 1985 is effective as far as banks are concerned.

ARTICLES OF ASSOCIATION

The articles of association govern the internal management of the company, which on a daily basis falls into the hands of its directors. The articles invariably appear in the same booklet as the memorandum, at the back, and the banker should consult these to learn of the powers and duties of the directors and to see if there are limitations which would effect the bank's dealing.

A specimen set of articles of association appears in each of the major Companies Acts, 1929, 1948, 1985, and is referred to as Table A. Frequently Table A is adopted by a company with the exclusion of certain numbered articles and special articles are substituted to meet the wishes of the particular company. The most important part of the articles as far as a bank is concerned is any restriction on directors' borrowing powers and the requirements necessary in respect of any security to be given on behalf of the company by the directors.

Examination of memorandum and articles of association

When a company is incorporated, a copy of its memorandum and a copy of the articles of association are filed at Companies Registration Office, and they can be examined by the public on payment of a small fee. Additionally, all extraordinary or special resolutions passed by the company are registered at Companies Registration Office, and the company is bound by law to file annual returns there, including copies of its audited figures. It is therefore possible for a bank to search at Companies Registration Office, and to learn much about a limited company with which it will have dealings. Usually, however, such searches are merely protective in special circumstances, and in a normal satisfactory banker–customer relationship the bank is able to obtain all the information it requires by talking to the directors of the company and by obtaining a certificate that the copy of the memorandum and articles which it holds is up to date.

OPENING A COMPANY ACCOUNT[54,55]

Most new company accounts are introduced to the bank by persons already known, such as the directors, accountants or solicitors. Occasionally, accounts are obtained from competitor banks, and in all these circumstances no difficulties will arise in taking up adequate references, which are as necessary with a company as with a private individual.

54 See Appendix I, Q. 19 (April 1982).
55 See Appendix I, Q. 5 (September 1980).

Additionally, certain other steps are essential before opening and conducting a limited company account:

(a) The certificate of incorporation must be seen, and usually a note of the company's registered number is entered in the bank's records, following which the certificate can be returned to the directors (Fig. 9.1)

If the company is in fact never formed then any liability purported to be entered into by the company, or by a person as its agent, becomes the personal liability of that person, unless there is any agreement to the contrary. This ruling under s. 9(2) of the European Communities Act 1972 was upheld in *Phonogram Ltd* v. *Lane* (1981).

(b) The company's memorandum and articles of association must be seen, and usually, a copy is retained so that the bank can refer to this when taking securities in the future, although even so it is then desirable for this to be certified by the directors as being up to date.

(c) The bank will require a copy of a resolution passed by the directors appointing the bank as the company's bankers. Quite often this copy resolution is embodied in the form of a mandate which the bank takes, as in that way the bank is certain that a correct resolution has been passed and recorded in the minutes (Fig. 9.2). All this is achieved by the bank delivering a blank form of mandate incorporating the resolution to the representatives of the company when they first call to discuss the opening of the company account.

(d) The mandate governing the operation of the company account (Fig. 9.2) will provide space for the name of the directors and company secretary and will incorporate the necessary authority as to who has power to draw cheques or transact other banking operations such as the negotiation of bills of exchange, endorsement of cheques or withdrawal of items in safe custody. It is preferable for the mandate simply to refer to the number and capacity of officers who are authorised so to act, for in this way, when there are changes in personnel all that is then needed is a copy of the resolution and a specimen signature referring to the new person.

(e) If the company is a public limited company the bank will need to see the trading certificate, for without this the company is unable to commence business or borrow money. This certificate is also known as a certificate to commence business, and after being exhibited and entered into the bank's records it is usually returned to the directors.

Most newly incorporated companies are formed as private companies, and are converted into public limited companies at a later date. However, where a new account is being opened for a public limited company it must be remembered that the company will not be able to start up in business without obtaining its trading certificate. Without sight of this certificate, the bank should not allow any withdrawals on the company's account, although the account can be opened, and monies can be received into it. Possibly these

SPECIMEN

CERTIFICATE OF INCORPORATION

OF A PRIVATE LIMITED COMPANY

No.   987654

I hereby certify that

ZETA LIMITED

is this day incorporated under the Companies Acts 1948 to 1981 as

a private company and that the Company is limited.

Given under my hand at the Companies Registration Office,

Cardiff the   11TH MARCH 19..

an authorised officer

C.173

Fig.9.1   *Limited company – certificate of incorporation*

To

BANK OF CYPRUS (LONDON) LIMITED

At a Meeting of the Directors of . . . .

Company Limited, ... held on . . . . 19 . . . . .

it was resolved:

1.   That an account be opened at the . . . .
     branch of Bank of Cyprus (London) Limited.

2.   That the Bank be instructed:
     a) to honour and debit to the Company's account or accounts whether in credit or overdrawn or
         becoming overdrawn in consequence of any such debit, all cheques or other orders signed,
         bills accepted and promissory notes made on behalf of the Company
     b) to accept any other instructions from the Company, except in so far as this resolution may
         specifically provide otherwise, provided they are signed, accepted or made by

     . . . .

     . . . . *

3.   That bills of exchange and promissory notes payable to the Company be endorsed on behalf of

     the Company by . . . .

     . . . . *

4.   That this resolution be communicated to the Bank and remain in force until an amending
     resolution shall be passed by the Board of Directors, and a copy thereof, certified by the
     Chairman of the meeting, shall be communicated to the Bank.

5.   That the Bank be informed of any changes which may occur from time to time in the directors
     and other officers of the Company.

     Persons authorized to sign on behalf of the Company:

                    Name in full   Signature

     . . . .

     . . . .

     . . . .

(*Insert eg "any one director," "any one director together with either one other director or the secretary" or "any two directors"
or as desired)

We hand you herewith:
a)   A copy of the Company's Memorandum and Articles of Association

b)   A full list of the present Directors and Secretary, and any signatories who are not either Directors
     or the Secretary, together with specimens of their respective signatures.

c)   A copy of the last Balance Sheet, Trading and Profit and Loss Accounts of the Company or the
     Opening Statement.

d)   The Original Certificate of Incorporation which please return to us.

e)   (In the case of a public limited company only) The original Trading Certificate which please
     return to us.

Dated . . . . 19 . . . . .

. . . . Secretary . . . . Chairman

Form No. C.28/83
(Company Mandate)

Fig.9.2   *Limited company – resolution appointing bankers and mandate*

might be in the form of share subscription, and in that event, if there is an over-subscription, the return of the unrequired monies can be allowed, but no other transactions should take place. If, however, there is a special situation, perhaps brought about by a mere technical delay in the issue of the certificate to commence business, with an entirely sound background, the bank might be prepared to allow a few entries on the account provided these were monitored closely, and perhaps with the support of an indemnity from the directors, providing of course that the bank could regard them as being of high integrity. As far as the company is concerned however, any transactions before the issue of the certificate to commence business are only provisional. Under the provisions of s. 117 and s. 118 Companies Act 1985, the certificate will not be issued unless the capital of the company is at least £50 000.

Whenever a new company account is opened, the first interviews with the directors should be used to ensure that a good relationship is founded at the outset. This is helpful from both points of view, and the banker will naturally wish to learn as much as possible about his new company's business and its financial position. With companies which are already incorporated, sight of existing balance sheets will be helpful, even if borrowing facilities are not required, and where they are then balance sheets will almost certainly be a prerequisite of the granting of facilities. With a newly incorporated company, an opening statement of affairs should be sought, and companies should be encouraged to bring in their audited accounts whenever they are produced, so that a good relationship can be built up between the bank and the company, and so that the bank may be able to offer its services in the various areas which become apparent from the conduct of the account and the nature of its operations.

Occasionally a limited company account is opened when the business in the name of a sole proprietor or a partnership is being converted into that of a limited company. The usual documentation, as indicated above, must of course be supplied, and if the balance on the former sole business account or partnership account is to be transferred into the name of the new limited company account, then appropriate written authorities should be taken enabling monies to be moved across. For instance, if the partnership account is in credit then the authority should be signed in accordance with the partnership mandate, while if it is overdrawn, and is to be repaid by the company, then any transfer must be made by way of a debit to the company's account, in accordance with the company's mandate. The banker should also ensure that he has adequate authority to deal with any cheques which might thereafter be presented drawn on the old account. It should not be presumed that the company will wish to adopt these, although normally this is the case, and the bank should safeguard itself by taking an adequate written instruction from the company so that cheques presented on the old account can be debited to the company account.

If the newly formed limited company wishes to borrow from the bank and offers security which was formerly in the name of the partnership or the sole trader, the bank should excercise caution to avoid a situation similar to that which occurred in the well-known case of *Re Simms* (1930). In that instance, the bank took a debenture from the newly incorporated limited company, which caught company assets which had been transferred to it by Mr Simms himself. Shortly after these events, a receiving order in bankrupty was made against Mr Simms and his trustee in bankruptcy succeeded in tracing the assets which had been transferred and in recovering them from the limited company, on the basis that the transfer has been a fraudulent conveyance. The result of this was that the bank found itself in a situation where the debenture was worthless, because the assets has gone.

Under the provisions of the Insolvency Act 1986, it would seem that a trustee in bankruptcy might be able to attack such a transaction as one at an undervalue if the conditions of ss. 239 and 240 were met.

To safeguard itself against such a risk, if there is any possibility of the insolvency of the sole proprietor or partnership, before the banker lends to the limited company against former personal assets he should make careful enquiries to ensure that the personal creditors of the former proprietor or business have been paid off, or that they have agreed to the formation of the limited company and the transfer of the private assets to it. Naturally, if the background of the individuals concerned is entirely sound, the considerations are not ones which should worry the bank, and it should not then go to the lengths of calling for such confirmations, for to do so could create ill-will and difficulties.

COLLECTING CHEQUES FOR A LIMITED COMPANY'S ACCOUNT

A bank owes the same duty to its limited company customer as to a private individual when collecting cheques, and exposes itself to the usual risks of an action for damages should it fail to act in accordance with established practice and thereby occasion loss to the company. The risk of conversion is no more, nor no less, than with a private individual's account, but what must be remembered is that the company is an entirely separate legal entity in law and must be treated as such. Most problems in collection have arisen from a failure to apply this strict rule.

One of the best-known cases is that of *A. L. Underwood* v. *Bank of Liverpool and Martins Ltd* (1924). Cheques were received payable to the limited company, and were handled by Mr Underwood, who was the company's sole director. Moreover, he held all but one of the issued shares. However, in his capacity as director he endorsed the cheques and then tendered them for collection for his own private account with the Bank of Liverpool and Martins. Subsequently, the bank was sued for conversion and in trying to set up a defence failed to show that it had acted 'without negligence', as was necessary to obtain the protection of s. 82 Bills of Exchange Act 1882, being provisions now seen in s. 4 Cheques Act 1957. The bank had failed to make any enquiries as to why the cheques payable to the limited company had been endorsed and paid into Mr Underwood's private account, as it should have done. It is in fact rare for limited companies to negotiate cheques, and therefore if enquiries had been made it may be presumed that the answer would have had to be entirely satisfactory to protect the bank. The judgment in a later case of *United Australia Ltd* v. *Barclays Bank Ltd* (1941) is helpful in this respect, for there it was said: 'In these days every bank clerk sees a red light (a warning) when a company's cheque is endorsed by a company's official and paid into an account which is not the company's'.

The importance of this dictum must be remembered not only when cheques payable to the company are paid into the director's account but also when, as might happen, they are tendered for collection for the amount of a subsidiary company or another company in a group of companies, or even the holding company.[56] Occasionally, with 'blue chip' companies, where perhaps one company acts as banker to the group, the bank might be prepared to operate such a system provided there were no risk of imminent insolvency. Undoubtedly a bank would require satisfactory indemnities from all the companies concerned enabling transactions to proceed in such a way, so that it could defend any claim by one or other company that its own monies had been converted. Even so, the worth of such an indemnity could be questioned, in the event of a situation where claims arose.

PAYMENT OF CHEQUES

The bank's authority to pay cheques flows from the mandate and it should ensure that they are drawn by a sufficient number of the authorized officials, and that the full name of the company appears in the drawer's space, followed by the known signature and designation of the authorized official or officials. In preparing a cheque book for the use of a limited company, great care is necessary in ensuring that the company's registered name appears correctly; usually this is in the bottom right-hand corner above the place where the directors and/or secretary sign in that capacity. This is because under the provisions of s.349(4) Companies Act 1985 a director can be held personally liable if the company's whole name on a bill of exchange does not appear.[57] For instance, in *British Airways Board* v. *Parish* (1979) the Court of Appeal held that a director of Watchstream Ltd was personally liable on a cheque which had been dishonoured, and which he had signed on behalf of a company, where the company's name above his signature had only appeared as 'Watchstream'. Again, in *Maxform SpA* v. *Mariani and Goodville Ltd* (1979) a director of Goodville Ltd was held to be personally liable on three bills of exchange which he had accepted drawn in the name of Italdesign which was

56 See Appendix I, Q. 16 (September 1981).
57 See Appendix I, Q. 5 (September 1980).

the company's trading name. These bills of exchange were subsequently dishonoured, and as the company's name, as it has been registered at Companies Registration Office, had not appeared on the bills of exchange, the director, when sued, was unable to escape personal liability.

These cases have involved problems for the directors concerned, but it is no great step to see that there could be an argument, in an appropriate situation, that the problem and liability had come about through the bank's negligence in preparing cheque forms inaccurately.

The payment of any cheque can be stopped by any one of the authorized signatories, but the removal of the stop must always be in accordance with the mandate; that is, if two or more signatories are required to draw the cheque in the first place then they must all authorize payment after it has been countermanded. When the bank pays a cheque, it should not be aware of any legal bar to payment, and while in some instances this bar might be apparent in others the situation might not be entirely clear, leaving the paying banker in some doubt. Company directors' responsibilities have been likened to those of trustees. They owe fiduciary duties to their company and shareholders, and in consequence, if they act outside their stewardship, it is possible that the bank is not empowered to debit the company's account with cheques drawn and it might have to refund monies debited.

Where cheques are clearly paid outside the authority of the mandate, then the bank is open to a claim for the wrongful debiting of the account, conversion, restitution and damages. However, if sued, the bank might be able to defend itself by showing that despite the technical irregularity the monies were still used for the legitimate purposes and objects of the company, and the company has benefited. On this basis, under the equitable doctrine 'under which those who have in fact paid the debts of another without authority are allowed in such an action as this to take advantage of that payment', damages might be avoided (*B. Liggett (Liverpool) Ltd* v. *Barclays Bank Ltd* (1928)).

Two cases which have caused bankers considerable concern are *Selangor United Rubber Estates Ltd* v. *Cradock* (1968), and *Karak Rubber Company Ltd* v. *Burden and others* (1972). In both instances the company's account was debited in accordance with the mandate and against cleared credit balances. Large cheques were involved, in one instance £232 500 and in the other £98 900. In both instances the transactions in which the directors were engaged were breaches of s. 54 of the Companies Act 1948. Now embodied in ss. 151 and 152 Companies Act 1985, these enact that it is not lawful for a company to give, either directly or indirectly, and whether by a loan, guarantee, security, or otherwise, any financial assistance for the purpose of, or in connection with, a purchase or subscription to be made by any person of or for any shares in the company or, where the company is a subsidiary company, in its holding company except in certain exceptional instances. In both cases the chain of events, and transactions, particularly in the second, were very complex, but the court decided that in the Selangor case the bank had had notice of, and had paid away money contrary to, the terms of the trust, and had acted negligently. It held that the bank itself had been a constructive trustee, for it had known or should have known what was involved. Barclays Bank were held to have failed in their contractual duty of care, and their duty as constructive trustees.

If therefore a company's bankers are in any fear that a transaction involves a possible breach of trust, legal advice should be sought and payment of the cheques involved should be postponed. Such a step will not be taken lightly, of course, and the author does not disagree with those who feel that these judgments impose an almost impossible burden of duty on bankers in the modern world, where the volume of transactions, and the manner in which funds are moved about by transfers, electronic and otherwise, are such that entries can pass without coming to the attention of busy senior officals. Where amounts are large, however, clearly great caution is necessary, and members of staff should be trained to refer to their managers.

LENDING TO LIMITED COMPANIES AND TAKING SECURITIES FROM THEM

The lending criteria which need to be considered when a limited company wishes to borrow are beyond the syllabus of the Practice of Banking 1 paper covered by this volume. However, there are in addition many legal considerations concerning the borrowing and any security offered which require attention, with special considerations applying only to limited companies. This is because of the restrictions placed upon a company by the various Companies Acts, and also by the limitations which the company may take upon itself in its memorandum of association. Additionally, the articles of association may restrict the ability of the directors to borrow and/or give security, even though the memorandum (on behalf of the company itself) gives wide powers. We shall examine these various aspects in a moment, but first it will be helpful to deal with developments arising out of s. 35 Companies Act 1985. This section states that:

(1) In favour of a person dealing with a company in good faith any transaction decided on by the directors shall be deemed to be one which it is within the capacity of the company to enter into, and the power of the directors to bind the company shall be deemed to be free of any limitation under the memorandum or articles of association;

(2) A party to a transaction so decided on is not bound to enquire as to the capacity of the company to enter into it or as to any such limitation on the powers of the directors, and is presumed to have acted in good faith unless the contrary is proved.

In the light of this it might then be asked why bankers concern themselves with possible *ultra vires* acts. However, a close reading of the section will show that the *ultra vires* doctrine has not been abolished, but only restricted, and in fact the position now ruling will not be entirely clear until there are judicial decisions based on actual cases, for as yet, the courts have not been asked to pronounce. It is felt, however, that where a bank has actually seen the memorandum and articles of association (and in most cases it will have a copy which has been retained in its files), if the transaction is outside the powers set out in them then it might be difficult to plead that an *ultra vires* transaction was entered into 'in good faith'. Bankers therefore have in fact continued to ask for copies of the memorandum and articles of association when opening accounts for limited companies, and the opportunity which presented itself at the time for a change in systems was not taken, the risks involved being considered too great.

As banks do not rely on this section to protect them it means that they are thrown back on the earlier position which obtained, although, if they are called upon in an alleged *ultra vires* situation to state a defence, they may well bring in s. 35 additionally. The section should be regarded in that light only, and not as giving the banker rights to proceed with entire disregard to the *ultra vires* doctrine in his daily dealings with a company and its officers.

Seven criteria need to be examined therefore before the banker proceeds to lend or take security, namely:

(a) Does the company have power in its memorandum to borrow?

(b) Is there any limitation on that amount?

(c) Is the purpose of the borrowing or security consistent with the objects clause in the memorandum?

(d) Is the borrowing or the giving of security for the benefit of and to promote the prosperity of the company (i.e., is there commercial justification)?

(e) How and by whom can the power be exercised according to its articles?

(f) Is there any limitation on the amount of such parties' borrowing powers in the articles?

(g) Was any meeting of directors in respect of the transaction validly formed in accordance with the articles?

The company's power to borrow

A trading company has an implied power to borrow money, although express powers may also be taken in the memorandum of association. Express or implied powers to borrow give an implied power to give security, although the power to give securities is also occasionally given specifically. Any limitation on the amount which can be borrowed is unusual in practice.

It follows therefore that a non-trading company is not entitled to borrow money in the absence of express powers.

The first step is always for the bank to examine the memorandum to see if an express power appears in the objects clause. If these are silent, but the company is a trading company, then this aspect need not be taken further. However if the memorandum makes no reference to borrowing powers and the bank is dealing with a non-trading company then an amendment to the objects clause must be put in hand by the company. This must be by a special resolution of the members in general meeting and the amendment should be effected before the borrowing is taken.

Is there any limitation on the amount which can be borrowed by the company?

It is in fact rare to find any limitation in the memorandum, but a check is necessary, for if the limitation of the company is exceeded, any excess will be *ultra vires* and the bank's position could be at risk. Again, if there is a need to amend the memorandum this must be done by the shareholders of the company acting in a general meeting of the company and passing a special resolution, which must be exhibited to the bank.

Problems concerning limitations on borrowings arise far more commonly with the director's powers, however.

Is the purpose consistent with the objects clause in the memorandum?

The objects clause will usually be a long and extensive clause, under which the company takes upon itself many powers. These may appear to be divided into principal objects and subsidiary objects, and in the latter case subsidiary objects must be read in conjunction with the prime object or purpose of the company. However, provided the primary object is being furthered, and if the act is thought incidental to the primary object, then the secondary act will be *intra vires* (*Ashbury Railway Carriage and Iron Co.* v. *Riche* (1875)).

Any other act is void and banks should not therefore knowingly lend monies for purposes inconsistent with the company's objects. The danger of doing so was highlighted in *Introductions Ltd* v. *National Provincial Bank Ltd* (1969). The company was incorporated in 1951 with the object of offering services and information to overseas visitors in connection with the Festival of Britain which was held in that year. The memorandum of association contained a variety of powers and objects and concluded with a clause stating that each preceding sub-clause should be interpreted independently of, and in no way linked by reference to, any other sub-clause. It was stated that the objects set out in each sub-clause were independent objects of the company. Power was also given to the company to borrow in such manner as it thought fit. Between the years 1951 to 1953 the company provided accommodation and services to overseas visitors, but thereafter for five years its only business was the provision of deck chairs and amusement machines at a holdiday resort. Then, in 1960, the company started pig breeding as its only business. It borrowed from its bankers, and gave debentures as security. The business failed and subsequently the company was placed in liquidation owing the bank money. The question arose as to whether the bank could recover its loans and whether it was entitled to realize its security. The bank argued that as the power to borrow was given under a sub-clause, which enabled the company to borrow or raise money in such manner as it thought fit, this should be regarded as an independent object irrespective of how the money was to be used. Unfortunately, the court rejected this argument, and held that on a true construction of the sub-clause of the memorandum of association (which was a sub-clause that was incapable of being a wholly independent object), notwithstanding the final provision in the memorandum declaring all objects to be independent, the power of borrowing was to borrow *for the legitimate purposes of the company*. As the borrowing from the bank was for a purpose which was *ultra vires*, i.e. carrying on the business of pig breeding, the borrowing and the creation of the debentures was *ultra vires* and void. The Court of Appeal later affirmed this decision.[58]

Should the bank find it has lent money in a situation which is *ultra vires* the company, as mentioned above, its only sources of comfort are those rights and remedies covered earlier.

Is the borrowing for the benefit of and to promote the prosperity of the company?

At first sight it might be thought that this question is the same consideration as the one just discussed above, but here more relevant is the question of security given in respect of the liabilities of other parties and any borrowing on their behalf. Thus although, for example, power to give a guarantee may appear in the memorandum, further consideration is necessary before A Ltd can guarantee B Ltd.

The answer to the question may not always be an easy one to decide without full knowledge of the entire background, and where necessary bankers should not hesitate to take legal advice. A clear danger can be seen where the answer is 'No', as where there is no subsidiary or holding company relationship between two companies. The only connection may be that the identity of the directors or shareholders is the same, which would probably be inadequate. To illustrate this, if Mr Brown holds the majority of shares and is a director of Browns Clothes Ltd, which company is engaged in the clothing manufacturing trade, and he is also a shareholder and director of Seaview Hotels Ltd, which is engaged in running a hotel business at a seaside resort, then if the bank is asked to lend to Seaview Hotels Ltd against security given by Browns Clothes Ltd it is very difficult to see how the giving of that security could be said to promote the prosperity of Browns Clothes. The common shareholding and common directorship is irrelevant, and while both companies might even maintain accounts at the same branch, where it is common for Mr Brown to discuss his own and all the companies' borrowings at the same time with his bank manager, the bank must not be led into treating matters, in law, as a group of companies.

58 See Appendix I, Q. 17 (April 1982).

Commercial justification must exist for the giving of a company security. In *Charterbridge Corporation Ltd* v. *Lloyds Bank Ltd* (1969) the question of commercial justification was considered in respect of the validity of a guarantee supported by a legal charge given by Pomeroy Developments (Castleford) Ltd to Lloyds Bank. Both companies were part of a large group trading as property developers, and all the companies had a common shareholding, common directors and shared the same office. In 1960 the accounts of the group's leading company, Pomeroy (which was not a holding company), and of some other companies in the group were overdrawn and Castleford gave Lloyds Bank the guarantee to secure the overdrafts; later it executed a legal charge in favour of the bank.

The memorandum of Castleford stated that the purposes of the company were to acquire lands for investment with a strictly qualified power of realisation. Another clause gave the company power to grant guarantees. In court it was argued that the guarantee and legal charge were not created for the benefit of Castleford and were therefore *ultra vires*.

It was held that, when deciding on whether an *ultra vires* situation existed, the only relevant issue was whether in accordance with its objects clause a company had acted in an authorized manner, and that the 'state of mind of the directors of Castleford and of the bank officers was irrelevant upon this issue of *"ultra vires"*'. The judge also considered whether only the question of benefit to the particular company giving the security had to be taken into account, or whether the benefit of the whole group, to which the company belonged, could be considered. He said that the first view was correct:

> Each company in the group is a separate legal entity and the directors of a particular company are not entitled to sacrifice the interests of that company. This becomes apparent when one considers the case where the particular company has separate creditors. The proper test, I think, in the absence of actual separate consideration, must be whether an intelligent and honest man in the position of a director of the company concerned, could, in the whole of the existing circumstances, have reasonably believed that the transactions were for the benefit of the company.

On the facts, the judge concluded that the transactions were for the benefit of the company giving the security, and he said that, in the circumstances, Castleford depended upon the continued existence of Pomeroy for its day-to-day operations.

It is likely therefore that in a situation where security is being given by a subsidiary for the liabilities of a fellow subsidiary or its holding company it will not be hard to find commercial justification and some benefit accruing for the company giving the security, although it must not be presumed too readily.

In the example given earlier, however, one cannot see any justification for Browns Clothes Ltd giving the security for Seaview's liabilities.[59]

The court took this view in *Rolled Steel Products (Holdings) Ltd* v. *British*

59 See Appendix I, Q. 54 (September 1982).

Steel Corporation (1984), where, although the company giving security acted within its powers, the transaction was set aside as the directors were acting for their own purposes and not in the interests of the company. Moreover the court said that if the person dealing with the company was on notice that the directors were exercising their powers for a purpose other than the company's purposes, he could not rely on the directors' ostensible authority, nor on ordinary agency principles could he hold the company liable.

This problem area has similarities to the 'transactions at an undervalue' provisions in the Insolvency Act 1986 and is a difficult one. A lending proposition and the security offered should always be referred to the bank's solicitors if there is any doubt or if large sums are involved. Some banks have established a system, as an added precaution, whereby they ask the board of directors to consider the commerciality of the transaction and then to pass a resolution authorizing the giving of the security or borrowing with the interests of the company in mind. However, there is some reassurance in the Charterbridge judgment, in that even if the transaction had not been for the benefit of 'Castleford', the judge took the view that in the absence of knowledge on the part of the bank officers concerned the plaintiff would have lost.

How and by whom can the power to borrow be exercised?

The answer to this question lies in the articles of association. These might be special ones, or the company might have adopted the specimen set of articles in Table A of the Companies Act under which it is incorporated. Quite often, only certain articles of Table A are adopted, and the company has it own rules in certain areas.

Many companies that are in existence today were incorporated under the 1948 Companies Act, but increasingly, new companies are being registered and the 1985 Companies Act will apply for them.

Article 80 of Table A of the Companies Act 1948 provides that 'the business of the company shall be managed by the directors who . . . may exercise all such powers of the company as are not by the Act or by these regulations required to be exercised by the company in general meeting. . . .'

Article 70 of the Companies Act 1985 provides 'Subject to the provisions of the Act, the memorandum and the articles and to any directions given by special resolution, the business of the company shall be managed by the directors who may exercise all the powers of the company. . . . The powers given by this regulation shall not be limited by any special power given to the directors by the articles and a meeting of directors at which a quorum is present may excercise all powers exercisable by the directors'.

Specially adopted articles may be more specific, and may extend or limit the powers of the directors. Happily, restrictions on the borrowing by directors, without reference back to the company in general meeting, are not encountered very frequently and usually the directors are able to exercise the borrowing powers of the company, although often with a limitation as to the amount in total (see below)

Is there any limitation on the amount which can be borrowed by the directors?

Companies Act 1948 As regards the directors' borrowing powers, one of the following alternative situations could exist, where the company was registered under the Companies Act 1948:

(*a*) *Unlimited borrowing powers.* Specimen article 79 of Table A is excluded, and a new clause is substituted in the articles of association stating that the directors can exercise in full all the borrowing powers of the company.

(*b*) *Unlimited borrowing powers.* Article 79 of Table A is adopted, but with the exclusion of the 'proviso' clause (see below). This enables the directors to exercise the borrowing powers of the company in full.

(*c*) *Unlimited borrowing powers.* Article 79 of Table A may have been excluded in full, but with no other clause substituted. In this case, article 80 applies, and the directors are empowered to exercise the full borrowing powers of the company.

(*d*) *Limited borrowing powers.* The articles may allow the directors to borrow but only up to a certain expressed figure, e.g. £100 000. Thereafter reference to the company in general meeting is necessary.

(*e*) *Limited borrowing powers.* The articles may allow the directors to borrow an amount which is the equivalent of the issued share capital of the company. This can be achieved by article 79 of Table A being adopted in full.[60]

(*f*) *Limited borrowing powers.* The articles may restrict the directors to a borrowing limitation based on a formula linked to the issued share capital and the company's reserves. Often this occurs with public limited companies quoted on the Stock Exchange, as it is a condition then that there should be a restriction on the directors.

Article 79 in Table A of the Companies Act 1948 This is obviously a key item and it states:

The directors may exercise all the powers of the company to borrow money, and to mortgage or charge its undertaking, property and uncalled capital, or any part thereof, and to issue debentures, debenture stock, and other securities whether outright or as security for any debt, liability or obligation of the company or of any third party:

Provided that the amount for the time being remaining undischarged of monies borrowed or secured by the directors as aforesaid (apart from temporary loans obtained from the company's bankers in the ordinary course of business) shall not at any time, without the previous sanction of the company in general meeting, exceed

60 See Appendix I, Q. 17 (April 1982).

the nominal amount of the share capital of the company for the time being issued, but nevertheless no lender or other person dealing with the company shall be concerned to see or enquire whether this limit is observed. No debt incurred or security given in excess of such limit shall be invalid or ineffectual except in the case of express notice to the lender or the recipient of the security at the time when the debt was incurred or security given that the limit hereby imposed had been or was thereby exceeded.

Thus it can be seen that the directors have their borrowing powers limited to the amount of the *issued* share capital of the company. If Table A applies, therefore, the banker must ascertain the amount of the issued share capital and the total of borrowings from the bank *and elsewhere* at the relevant date, to which will be added the maximum new advance now required from the bank. The issued capital will of course be shown in the company's latest balance sheet, and enquiries may need to be made to learn if this has been increased since then.

The source of information with regard to other borrowings, apart from existing bank accommodation, will again be the latest balance sheet. The items which should be included in the 'borrowings', as abstracted from the balance sheet, include debentures, mortgages and other loans. It is often banking practice to obtain a certificate from the chairman or secretary confirming that the proposed advance is in fact within the actual unexhausted borrowing powers of the directors, and while this is useful it is no protection against dishonesty, and helps more to draw attention at the right time to any technical irregularity which exists and which needs correction.

The discounting of bills drawn by the company and accepted by third parties should not be included in the calculation of the 'borrowing', but accommodation bills must be included. In the assessment any security given to third parties must be included, e.g. a guarantee.[61,62] Naturally, share capital and amounts due to trade creditors are excluded. Care is necessary where a fixed asset has been mortgaged, and where a net figure is, perhaps, shown in the balance sheet. In this case, the mortgage should be included as a 'borrowing'. However, amounts owing in respect of hire purchase transactions do not enter into calculations, nor are leasing transactions included.

It is sometimes said that the additional provisions of article 79 in Table A of the Companies Act 1948 mean that the limitations on the director's borrowing powers do not apply to bank advances because of the words 'apart from temporary loans obtained from the company's bankers in the ordinary course of business'. It is difficult, however, to define accurately 'temporary loans', and in the absence of a legal decision the exact meaning of 'temporary loans' is not certain. While, in theory, bank overdrafts are changing all the time, and if taken on current account are subject to the operation of *Clayton's Case*, in practice many borrowings remain outstanding for many years. This is

61 See Appendix I, Q. 17 (April 1982).
62 See Appendix I, Q. 64 (September 1983).

particularly so in the modern age where banks are not averse to medium-term loan facilities which cannot by any stretch of the imagination be classed as 'temporary'.

Also banks are reluctant to rely on the last sentence of article 79, which seems to give protection, in that no lender, it is said, need be concerned to see whether the limit has been observed, unless he had express notice at the time of his advance. Banks are advised by their lawyers that as they have such close financial knowledge of their customers' affairs it would be unwise to rely on this clause.

Companies Act 1929 If the company customer is registered under the earlier Companies Act 1929 and has adopted the specimen article in that Act then it is article 69 which applies. This states: 'The amount for the time being remaining undischarged of monies borrowed or raised by the directors for the purpose of the company (otherwise than by the issue of share capital) shall not at any time exceed the issued share capital of the company, without the sanction of the company in general meeting'.

In practice, for banks this means that the situation is similar to article 79 of Table A of the Companies Act 1948 but the 'fall back' clauses are absent. Understandably, the number of situations where a bank has dealings with a company registered under the Companies Act 1929 is becoming less frequent.

Companies Act 1985 What then is the position for a company registered under the Companies Act 1985 and which has adopted the specimen Articles of that Act? Happily the situation is more straightforward, as, if the company has adopted Table A in full, or just Article 70 on its own, then the directors are able to exercise all the powers which the company has.

For the banker, this means that he must check to see that any meeting of directors was quorate and he must then look to the Memorandum of Association to see if there is any restriction on the company's borrowing powers there. If the Memorandum is silent and the company is a trading company then it will be presumed to have the power to borrow and the directors may exercise that power in full.

Remedies when a borrowing is ultra vires *the directors* The position of the bank is not so serious when it has lent *ultra vires* the directors, as when it is in a situation outside the borrowing powers of the company. Nevertheless, the borrowing will be void and the bank may not be able to sue the company, unless the company ratifies the transaction. For example, where a company's borrowing powers are unlimited but the directors' powers are restricted to, say, one half of the company's paid-up capital, if a borrowing in excess of this limit is allowed then it may not be possible to sue for recovery of the excess from the company. However, the position can be remedied by taking one or other of the following steps:

(a) The company may alter its articles of association by its members passing a special resolution in general meeting removing any restrictions.

(*b*) The members of the company in general meeting may pass an ordinary resolution ratifying the irregular borrowing, and if so then the effect is retrospective and an enforceable debt arises.

(*c*) The bank might be able to rely upon the doctrine of ostensible authority as shown in *Royal British Bank* v. *Turquand* (1856). In effect this means that where anyone deals with a company having satisfied himself that the proposed transaction is not inconsistent with the memorandum and articles, he is not bound to enquire further into the internal proceedings of the company. Thus if an official of a company carries out acts on behalf of the company which the articles permit him to do when duly authorized, then the bank, or for that matter anybody conducting business with the company, is entitled to assume that the authority has actually been granted by the company. The facts in the Turquand case were that the directors had power to issue bonds if authorized by a general resolution of the company, and they issued a bond to the Royal British Bank. Subsequently it was claimed that no such resolution had been passed, but nevertheless the court held that the bank could sue on the bond and was entitled to assume that the resolution had been passed. It was said: 'Persons dealing with a company are bound to read the registered documents, and to see that the proposed dealing is not inconsistent therewith. But they are not bound to do more; they need not inquire into the regularity of the internal proceedings'. The Rule in *Royal British Bank* v. *Turquand* is an extremely important one, not only in company law, but also in banking law, although there is a possibility that in recent years the limitations to the Rule have become so extensive that the basic object seems to have been lost sight of. Care is therefore necessary in relying on this doctrine which has been modified by later decisions. For instance, the Rule might not apply where the transaction is unusual.

(*d*) If article 79 of Table A of the 1948 Act applies then the bank might be able to rely on the protective clauses contained in the Article. It will be remembered that this concludes by stating that 'temporary loans obtained from the company's bankers in the ordinary course of business' are excluded from the limitation, but whether or not this will provide protection to the lending banker has not yet been the subject of a ruling by the courts. It will also be recalled from article 79 that 'nevertheless no lender or other person dealing with the company shall be concerned to see or enquire whether this limit is observed'. The article goes on to show that the limiting feature is whether or not the lender had express notice of the irregularity when it granted the loan. It is very doubtful whether this would give much protection to the banker, as the company's memorandum and articles will be available in the branch along with the company's latest balance sheet. On the other hand, this article might protect a lending bank where the directors borrowed from another source in excess of their powers, after the bank accommodation had been agreed and before the information was disclosed in a balance sheet.

(e) Finally, as with an *ultra vires* situation appertaining to the company, the bank might be able to rely on s. 35 Companies Act 1985. The reasons why the section is not relied on at the outset have already been examined.

Quorums and interested directors[63]

As well as ensuring that any resolution is passed by a properly constituted quorate board, the bank must also always consider the legal position in respect of directors who are interested personally in a particular transaction, and see whether the articles of association allow them to be counted for quorum purposes in those present at the meeting of directors, and if so whether they can vote on the resolution. Under s. 317 Companies Act 1985 it is the duty of every director who is in any way, whether directly or indirectly, interested in a contract or proposed contract with the company, to declare the nature of his interest at the board meeting at which the contract is considered. The articles of many companies contain a clause prohibiting directors from voting at board meetings in relation to contracts in which they have a personal interest, unless their interest is disclosed to the board, meaning to a disinterested quorum of directors, a rule that is sometimes difficult to apply.

Thus, where the company is giving security to a bank after the director himself or his wife have guaranteed the company's account or, perhaps where the company itself may be giving a guarantee to a bank and a director may be interested because he is a director or shareholder of the company whose account is to be guaranteed, then the matter must be carefully considered.

It is not sufficient merely for the director to disclose that he is interested, and he must go on to state the nature of his interest.

For companies which were registered under the 1948 Act and which adopted the relevant part of Table A, Article 84(2) contains a general prohibition against voting by a director in respect of any contract or arrangement in which he is interested and provides that he shall not be counted in the quorum present at the meeting when this item is discussed. If it is not possible to obtain an independent quorum, the transaction must be sanctioned by the company in general meeting after a full disclosure of the director's interest. If a security which ought to have been sanctioned by a general meeting has already been granted by the directors and accepted by a bank, the transaction can be ratified at any time by the shareholders. However, Article 84 of Table A of the 1948 Act goes on to state that the prohibition on voting shall not apply to any arrangement for the giving by the company of any security to a third party in respect of a debt or obligation of the company for which the director himself has assumed responsibility in whole or in part under a guarantee or indemnity or by the deposit of security.

One of the leading cases in this area is that of *Victors Ltd (in liquidation)* v. *Lingard and Others* (1927). The articles of that company had provisions

---

63 See Appendix I, Q. 37 (September 1980).

regarding disclosure, and prohibited the directors from voting on contracts and other transactions in which they were personally interested. Midland Bank lent the company money and took the guarantee of the directors as security. A year later, on its own initiative the board resolved that debentures should be issued to secure the bank in place of the directors' guarantees and these were accordingly issued to Lingard and Mare as nominees for the bank. Some time afterwards, when the company had gone into liquidation, the liquidator attacked this security and at a trial the court held that the directors had been personally 'interested' in the arrangement which had been made with the bank in regard to the issue of the debenture within the meaning of the company's article, and that the resolution was a nullity. The bank's defence was based on the principle in *Royal British Bank* v. *Turquand* (1856), already discussed, but did not claim that it was justified in assuming that the resolution for the issue of the debentures had been validly passed, as it was aware of the provisions of the company's articles; it contended that when it received debentures bearing the company's seal, it was justified in assuming that the seal had been properly affixed, as could have been done if the company in general meeting had duly affirmed the action of the directors, or had otherwise approved the security. The judge ruled that this extended the principle of the Turquand case further than was justified. The bank knew that it was not the company but the directors who had resolved on the issue of the debentures, and that in fact they had made certain stipulations regarding the form of the board resolution. There was no justification, then, for any assumption that the issue had been sanctioned by the company in general meeting. However, the judge held that as a result of the subsequent history of the case, the company was estopped by its behaviour from enforcing the claim now brought on its behalf by its liquidator. An important aspect was that the liquidator had for a considerable time treated the debentures as good and allowed the receiver appointed under the debenture to dispose of the assets, without taking active steps to secure the proceeds for the general creditors.

The dangers in the *Victors* v. *Lingard* case may not be present where the bank agrees to lend to a company on condition that it will receive both a guarantee from the directors and direct security from the company. The giving of the company security is really then contemporaneous with the giving of the guarantee by the directors. Even so, it is the practice of some banks to take the direct company security first, and when this has been completed, to take the directors' guarantee, or if there is any doubt, to have the company pass a resolution covering the giving of the direct security to the bank. Happily, those companies which adopted Table A of the Companies Act 1948 in its entirety, or which did not exclude article 84, do not present banks with the difficulties of the *Victors* v. *Lingard* case.

Turning to the new consolidating Companies Act of 1985 we find that similar provisions to those of the 1948 Act apply. Thus a director may not vote on a matter in which directly or indirectly he has a material interest which conflicts with the company's interests, unless

'(*a*) the resolution relates to the giving to him of a guarantee, security, or indemnity in respect of money lent to, or an obligation incurred by him for the benefit of, the company or any of its subsidiaries;

(*b*) the resolution relates to the giving to a third party of a guarantee, security, or indemnity in respect of an obligation of the company or any of its subsidiaries for which the director has assumed responsibility in whole or part and whether alone or jointly with others under a guarantee or indemnity or by the giving of security.'

(Table A. Article 94)

The new feature here is the provision enabling the director to vote on a matter in respect of which his interest is related to one or more of the company's subsidiaries. To cite an example: if Mr B, a director of companies X and Y, parent and subsidiary, has given a guarantee to company Y's bankers, he may later vote at a board meeting of company X resolving to give a debenture or other security covering the liability of company Y.

REGISTRATION OF SECURITIES GIVEN BY LIMITED COMPANIES

Individual securities will be examined in later chapters, but it will be helpful now to look at certain features in respect of securities taken by banks when they lend to limited companies. The most commonly taken securities are mortgages over freehold and leasehold land and properties, debentures which may be secured by specific or floating charges, or both, and assignments of contracts and debts. All these securities must be registered at Companies Registration Office to be enforceable against the company's liquidator or its creditors (s. 395 Companies Act 1985). There are a few types of security which can be taken without this registration but most company securities are void against creditors and/or a liquidator, unless they are registered in compliance with that Act, within twenty-one days of their creation.

Failure to register a charge within the necessary time period can lead to dire consequences, but some protection is afforded under s. 404 of the Companies Act 1985. This states:

'(*1*) The following applies if the court is satisfied that the omission to register a charge within the time required by this Chapter or that the omission or mis-statement of any particular with respect to any such charge or in a memorandum of satisfaction was accidental, or due to inadvertence or to some other sufficient cause, or is not of a nature to prejudice the position of creditors or shareholders of the company, or that on other grounds it is just and equitable to grant relief.

(*2*) The court may, on the application of the company or a person interested, and on such terms and conditions as seem to the court just and expedient, order that the time for registration shall be extended or, as the case may be, that the omission or misstatement shall be rectified.'

Naturally banks do not like to rely on this safeguard, and if other considerations do not enter into the matter (e.g. turnover in respect of a floating charge) then they will almost certainly take a fresh charge from the company, and register that within twenty-one days of its execution.

It should be noted that the contract to repay the lending is not prejudiced, but failure to register at Companies Registration Office means that there is no good security for the bank, if a creditor or liquidator intervenes.

Section 396 of the Companies Act 1985 calls for registration of the following charges:

(a) a charge for the purpose of securing any issue of debentures;

(b) a charge on uncalled share captital of the company;

(c) a charge created or evidenced by an instrument which, if executed by an individual, would require registration as a bill of sale;

(d) a charge on land, (wherever situated) or any interest in it, but not including a charge for any rent or other periodical sum issuing out of land;

(e) a charge on book debts of the company;

(f) a floating charge on the company's undertaking or property;

(g) a charge on calls made but not paid;

(h) a charge on a ship or aircraft or any share in a ship;

(j) a charge on goodwill, on a patent or a licence under a patent, on a trademark or on a copyright or licence under a copyright.

The prescribed particulars of the charge, together with the actual instrument (if any) by which the charge is created or evidenced, must be delivered to the registrar for registration within twenty-one days after the date of its creation (Fig. 9.3). Thus if the bank in unusual circumstances obtains an equitable mortgage by a mere deposit of the title deeds, the charge can still be registered by furnishing the prescribed details to the Registrar, although taking security from limited companies in this way is not to be recommended.

Charges which do not require registration are:

(a) a charge on documents of title to goods;

(b) a charge over life policies, where the company is the beneficial owner;

(c) guarantees by a company;

(d) a charge on stocks and shares;

(e) a charge of negotiable instruments;

(f) a rent charge.

The following important cases dealing with late or defective registration show the problems which have been encountered.

In *Esberger & Son Ltd* v. *Capital & Counties Bank* (1913) a company lodged the deeds of its property as security and executed a formal legal mortgage but the bank unwisely held this undated, until the accommodation was actually required. Several months later the bank manager inserted the then current date and registered the charge, because the company's account

M

COMPANIES FORM No. 395

Particulars of a charge

Pursuant to section 395 of the Companies Act 1985

395

Please complete
legibly, preferably
in black type, or
bold block lettering

* insert full name
  of company

To the Registrar of Companies

For official use

Company number

Name of company

*	EXAMPLE Ltd.

Date of creation of the charge

20th May 19...

Description of the instrument (if any) creating or evidencing the charge (note 2)

Mortgage and Debenture

Amount secured by the charge

> All liabilities of Example Ltd. past present and
> future actual and/or contingent to the charge-holder

Names and addresses of the chargees or persons entitled to the charge

Practice Bank plc	
High Street	
Town	Postcode

Presentor's name address and
reference (if any):

For official Use

Mortgage Section | Post room

Time critical reference

Fig.9.3   *Limited company – Form 395: registration of charge*

Short particulars of all the property charged

Please do not
write in
this margin

Please complete
legibly, preferably
in black type, or
bold block lettering

1) A charge by way of legal mortgage over : MAGNUM FACTORY,
                                           117-119 KINGSWAY, TOWN.
2) A specific equitable charge over the company's estate of
interest in all freehold or leasehold properties for the time
being belonging to or charged to the Company other than the
property described above.
3) A specific charge over its goodwill patents and licenses and
any stocks shares or other securities in any subsidiary company
or companies.
4) A specific charge over all book and other debts in respect of
which the Company shall pay into the Company's account with the
Bank all monies which it may receive in respect of such debts and
without the prior consent in writing of the Bank will not factor
discount sell or otherwise charge or assign in favour of any
other person.
5) A floating charge over the undertaking and all other property
and assets present and future of the Company in respect of which
the Company has covenanted that it will not without the Bank's
consent create any mortgage or charge ranking in priority to or
pari passu with this charge.

Particulars as to commission allowance or discount (note 3)

Signed   Date

On behalf of [company][chargee]†

Notes

1   The original instrument (if any) creating or evidencing the charge, together with these prescribed
    particulars correctly completed must be delivered to the Registrar of Companies within 21 days after
    the date of creation of the charge (section 395). If the property is situated and the charge was created
    outside the United Kingdom delivery to the Registrar must be effected within 21 days after the date on
    which the instrument could in due course of post, and if dispatched with due diligence, have been
    received in the United Kingdom (section 398). A copy of the instrument creating the charge will be
    accepted where the property charged is situated and the charge was created outside the United
    Kingdom (section 398) and in such cases the copy must be verified to be a correct copy either by the
    company or by the person who has delivered or sent the copy to the registrar. The verification must be
    signed by or on behalf of the person giving the verification and where this is given by a body corporate
    it must be signed by an officer of that body. A verified copy will also be accepted where section 398(4)
    applies (property situate in Scotland or Northern Ireland) and Form No. 398 is submitted.

2   A description of the instrument, eg "Trust Deed", "Debenture", "Mortgage" or "Legal charge", etc, as
    the case may be, should be given.

3   In this section there should be inserted the amount or rate per cent. of the commission, allowance or
    discount (if any) paid or made either directly or indirectly by the company to any person in
    consideration of his;
        (a) subscribing or agreeing to subscribe, whether absolutely or conditionally, or
        (b) procuring or agreeing to procure subscriptions, whether absolute or conditional,
    for any of the debentures included in this return. The rate of interest payable under the terms of the
    debentures should not be entered.

4   If any of the spaces in this form provide insufficient space the particulars must be entered on the
    prescribed continuation sheet.

Fig.9.3   *(contd)*

had become overdrawn. Later the company was put into liquidation, and the liquidator claimed that the charge was void, as it had not been registered within twenty-one days of its creation. He succeeded, as the court held that the date of creation of the charge had been the actual date of execution, when the seal was applied and the mortgage had been delivered to the bank and not the date when the advance had been first taken. Sensible banking practice would be to rely on the date of sealing and not the date of delivery if the two dates are different.

However, in *Re C. L. Nye Ltd* (1970) National Westminster Bank lent money to the company to enable it to buy some land, the intention being that the land should be charged as security by the company when it was conveyed. Delays occurred in the solicitors' offices and the transfers of the land by the vendors and the mortgage by the company to the bank were undated, with registration being omitted. These events took place in February, but in the following June the omissions were noticed, whereupon a date in June was entered, and registration took place within twenty-one days of the June date. Very soon afterwards the company went into creditors' voluntary liquidation, and the liquidator sought to set aside the bank's charge. In its defence the bank sought to rely on s. 98(ii) of the 1948 Act, now s. 401(2) Companies Act 1985, which states that a certificate of registration issued by the Registrar of Companies is conclusive evidence that the requirements of the Act as to registration have been complied with. On this point the bank won its case in the Court of Appeal. However, banks would not wish to rely on this safeguard as a regular feature and the proper course for security clerks is clear: Securities registrable under s. 395 Companies Act 1985 must be so registered within twenty-one days of being executed. Where the formalities in respect of company security are left to solicitors who do not normally act for the bank, it is wise to ensure that they are reminded of this necessary early registration, and that a suitable check is done to see that the task has been properly carried out.

This will avoid the problems which arose in *R* v. *Registrar of Companies ex parte Esal (Commodities) Ltd* (1985), where the solicitors had not completed the form of registration correctly and overlooked the need to send the original form of charge, not just a copy. The Registrar returned the copy and the form without registering the charge, but later issued a certificate of registration dated 29 February 1984 of the charge executed on 9 February. Meanwhile a petition for winding up the company had been presented. Ultimately in the Court of Appeal the security was allowed to stand on grounds that the Registrar's certificate was conclusive evidence of registration and met the requirements of the Companies Act. However the Registrar's procedures were carefully examined and it is clear that in future he will simply return inaccurate documents and that the risk in those circumstances will lie with the mortgagee or his solicitors.

In *Re Kent & Sussex Sawmills Ltd* (1947) the facts were as follows. The company entered into a contract with the Ministry of Fuel and Power to supply thirty thousand tons of cut logs, and asked its bankers, Westminster Bank, to help in financing the contract. The bank granted an advance against authorities in letter form which it later claimed were informal assignments of the amounts due under the contract. The method used was that the company sent a short letter to the Ministry asking them to remit the amount due under the contracts to their bankers, whose receipt would be a sufficient discharge. The instructions were to be regarded as irrevocable unless the bank consented to their cancellation in writing. The Ministry acknowledged the authority and confirmed that they would act upon it. A year later a further contract covering the supply of seventy thousand tons of logs was agreed and the bank increased its financial help to £70 000 against a further letter sent by the company to the Ministry which it acknowledged. In February 1946 the company went into a creditors' voluntary liquidation, at a time when there was £30 000 due to the company from the Ministry under the two contracts, and the company owed the bank £38 000. The liquidator contended that the two letters were in effect assignments of the book debts of the company and as they had not been registered under s. 79 Companies Act 1929 (corresponding to s. 395 of the 1985 Act) they were void. The court agreed and gave judgment in his favour!

Earlier, in *National Provincial & Union Bank of England* v. *Charnley* (1924), the position arising from a partial omission of the registration details in the completion of Form 395 was considered. The company had granted the bank a fixed charge on its leasehold property and on the plant situated there. The reference in the Form 395 made mention of the fixed charge only. Later, a creditor attempted to levy execution against some of the plant which was movable but the bank claimed that it had priority in view of its charge. Upon matters being heard in court, it was held that the bank's claim prevailed, despite the irregularity of the registration, because the Registrar's certificate was conclusive evidence of the registration of the entire charging instrument.

On the same point, in *Re Mechanisations (Eaglescliff) Ltd* (1964) the court held that the whole terms of a charge granted by a limited company are binding on the world, provided registration of the charge has been effected even though all the terms do not appear on the register. Nevertheless, care should be taken by security clerks to ensure that complete registration of all particulars of any charge are recorded on Form 395.

More recently, in *Siebe Gorman & Co. Ltd* v. *Barclays Bank Ltd* (1978) the question of whether an absolute assignment of a book debt was registerable under the Companies Act was examined, and the court took the view that here the assignment was an absolute assignment and the authority was couched in irrevocable terms. The assignment was not by way of security, but was created with the intention for the full title to the debts to pass outside the company's rights to exercise its right to redeem the charge. Registration was therefore not necessary. Despite this, in practice banks invariably continue to register these types of charge.

Summary of procedures in respect of company securities

The steps involved in taking securities from a limited company present a branch securities officer with a special challenge, for many aspects need attention, and the ramifications of failure to attend to matters properly can be disastrous. In the next part of this book we shall be looking at individual securities in depth, but wherever a company is the chargor, the following areas should always be considered carefully:

(a) First, the memorandum should be perused to ensure that the company has power to borrow and give security, if it is not a trading company, and that there are no limitations. The purpose for which the security is required must be one within the objects of the company.

(b) Thereafter the articles of association must be examined to ensure that the directors have sufficient power to charge securities for borrowings up to the amount of what will be the total after this new advance. If any special authorities are called for, then these should be obtained to ensure that the directors are acting *intra vires* their delegated authority.

(c) The whole transaction should then be considered and the bank should be satisfied that it is one which is in the interests of and for the benefit of the company giving the security: in other words that commercial justification exists.

(d) The register of charges at Companies Registration Office should be searched to ensure that there are no prior charges, or that, at least, no prior charges appear other than those which the bank has been told about by the directors.

(e) The company should execute the security, either under seal or (if appropriate) under hand by the directors, with a supporting resolution from the board of directors.

(f) If the particular security requires registration at Companies Registration Office under s. 395 Companies Act 1985, then this should be carried out within twenty-one days, using Form 395.

(g) The bank should ensure that the certificate of registration (Fig. 9.4) is received from the Registrar of Companies, and that the charge form has been returned, bearing the Registrar's stamp, which notes the registration.

These procedures summarize the basic areas, but they are not fully comprehensive and other aspects will be looked at later. However, the first three items of the procedures have already been reviewed closely and we may now look briefly at possible problems which might be encountered with the others.

The search at Companies Registration Office should not reveal any prior charges that are unknown to the bank, unless there has been an oversight by the directors, or the solicitors acting for the company. Sometimes, however, a security which has been charged in the past to another lender, and which has later been released, is still shown outstanding on the register of charges at

CERTIFICATE OF THE REGISTRATION

OF A MORTGAGE OR CHARGE

Pursuant to section 401 (2) of the Companies Act 1985

I hereby certify that a mortgage or charge dated the 26th January 1987

and created by   ZETA LIMITED

for securing all moneys now due, or hereafter to become due, or from time

to time accruing due from the company to   PRACTICE BANK PLC

on any account whatsoever

was registered pursuant to Chapter I Part XII of the Companies Act

1985, on the 11th February 1987

Given under my hand at the Companies Registration Office,
Cardiff the   16 FEB 1987

No.   1234567

an authorised officer

C.69a

Fig.9.4   *Limited company – certificate of registration of charge*

Companies Registration Office. This is because a memorandum of satisfaction, Form 403a, had not been lodged by the company following the release of the security. It is a matter which can easily be corrected, as time is not of the essence.

As to the manner in which company security is to be charged, reference to the articles of association will show whether this must be under seal, although legal charges over land must always be executed under seal. The articles should indicate how many directors are to attest the affixing of the seal, and of course in these cases the bank's charge form is not witnessed by a bank officer, or a solicitor, as is the normal rule. If the articles of association allow the directors to charge company security under hand, the bank may accept security in that way, although in such cases the signature of the directors/secretary should be witnessed.

As regards registration at Companies Registration Office, any interested party may complete and submit Form 395. Bearing in mind the importance of the time scale however, it is often the practice of bankers to carry out that task for themselves, or to request their solicitors to perform the duty, and not to rely on the company itself to do so. When the security is released, however, invariably the memorandum of satisfaction is lodged by the company. All registrations of charges by limited companies appear in due course in the *London Gazette*, and other trade gazettes, and the lending banker should always examine these, as he can learn of later charges created by the company which may be relevant to his security or to his overall lending situation. Satisfactions of earlier charges are seen also in these gazettes, as also are petitions, winding up orders, and the appointment of a receiver.

GUARANTEES FROM LIMITED COMPANIES

It is very common in a group situation for the holding company, and the subsidiary companies, to give guarantees for each other's liabilities. We have already seen the need to ensure that commercial justification exists, and another possible problem in this area could be encountered in a breach of ss. 151/154 Companies Act 1985 (restrictions on financial assistance to buy company's own shares).

These considerations apart, the power to give a guarantee must of course always be authorized in each company's memorandum of association. The wording of the objects clause should be quite clear to prevent later problems, and many banks also like to see a specific power to give security in support of a guarantee obligation.

In *Re Friary, Holroyd and Healy's Breweries Ltd* (1922) it was held that the words 'to subsidize or otherwise assist' in the objects included the giving of a guarantee, but even so, cautious bankers today faced with such wording would prefer to see the memorandum of association changed by a special resolution of the company in general meeting, to incorporate a specific authority to give a guarantee.

Any form of company guarantee must be executed in accordance with the company's articles of association. It should be given under the company seal, or by hand, signed by officials authorized to do so, on a resolution of the board of directors. The bank usually retains a certified copy of this resolution with the guarantee document.

DIRECTORS HOLDING TITLE TO COMPANY PROPERTY

Occasionally, with a land certificate, or with deeds where title is unregistered, the title to a company property is vested in a director's or the directors' names(s). This arises where a business formerly in a sole proprietor's name, or partnership name, has been converted into a limited company. However, although the land has been transferred to the company, to avoid conveyancing costs and transfer fees a full conveyance did not take place, and a trust deed was executed by the former proprietors to the effect that henceforth they would hold the property in trust for the beneficial interest of the company. The trust deed may not have been placed with the packet of deeds, or with the land certificate in the case of registered title. Consequently, any lender examining the deeds or land certificate may not be on notice that the security is company property. In such a case, it is possible that the wrong form of charge could be used, e.g. the third-party form where it should have been a direct one. Worse, registration under s. 395 Companies Act 1985 will be omitted. Should the company go into liquidation the risk will then be present that a liquidator will upset the security, for want of registration. Even if the bank then tries to show that it had no notice that the property was company security, the liquidator will doubtless point to the negotiations and discussions with the lender, and may well be able to establish that the lender had sight of a company balance sheet in which the property appeared. In such a situation, the bank would find it very difficult to prove that it had not been on notice that the property was company property, and consequently, might fail in an action brought by the liquidator based on non-registration at Companies Registration Office.

The bank should therefore be alert to such possibilities existing, when directors charge property in their own names, particularly where this is commercial property, and if, after suitable enquiries, it is ascertained that the property does belong to the company then the charge should be executed, not only by the parties in whom the legal estate in the land is vested, but also by the company, in accordance with its memorandum and articles of association. The direct form of charge is considered preferable in such circumstances and registration under s. 395 at Companies Registration Office must be carried out within twenty-one days.

LIQUIDATIONS

Apart from being struck off the register after it has become defunct, the most usual way in which a company is brought to the end of its existence is by being placed in liquidation. Such a development is obviously serious for the company's bankers.

There are three types of liquidation, with important differences in procedures applicable to each. They are:

(a) A compulsory winding up, upon a winding up order by the court.

(b) A creditors' voluntary liquidation.

(c) A members' voluntary liquidation.

Winding up by the court

There are several grounds upon which a company may be compulsorily wound up by the court, but the most common is when a creditor who is owed £750 or more presents a petition on grounds that the company is unable to pay its debts, failure to satisfy a statutory demand within 21 days being common evidence of this.

Usually a period of about four to six weeks elapses between the actual presentation of the petition and the hearing at which the court examines the facts and makes its decision. All petitions are advertised in the *London Gazette* and this is notice to the world. Bank lending officers and security officers should therefore regularly peruse the *Gazette* without delay to ensure that there are no proceedings against one of their company customers of which they are not aware from other sources. The date of the presentation of the petition is very important, for if a winding up order is made by the court the liquidation will be deemed to have commenced at the date of the presentation of the petition (s. 129 Insolvency Act 1986). Consequently, any dispositions of the company's property in the period between the petition and the hearing will be void against the liquidator appointed by the court, and in view of the period which elapses between the two events, it can readily be understood that transactions through the bank account in that period might be challenged by the liquidator, and that he might claim reimbursement for the benefit of the creditors. The safest think for a bank to do, upon learning of the presentation of a petition, is to stop all accounts, whether credit or debit, and to refuse to do further business.[64] However, such a course of action has many undesirable effects, if the company is unable to continue its business, in consequence.

Section 127 Insolvency Act 1986 enacts that: 'In a winding up by the court, any disposition of the company's property and any transfer of shares, or alteration in the status of the company's members made after the commencement of the winding up, is, unless the court otherwise orders, void'.

The commencement of the winding up is the presentation of the petition, but provision is made for the court to authorize any disposition, whether

64 See Appendix I, Q. 30 (September 1983).

between the petition and winding up order or subsequent to the winding up order.

At one time some banks took it upon themselves to monitor the situation, and to continue to operate the bank account after the presentation of the petition, albeit with risk, provided that transactions were unexceptional, in order to enable the company to continue trading. They did so in the belief that the liquidator subsequently appointed would understand their situation and not challenge them. However, following the decision in *Re Gray's Inn Construction Co. Ltd* (1980) against the bank, there has been a change in approach.

The problem was seen earlier in the case of *D. B. Evans (Bilston) Ltd* v. *Barclays Bank* (1961), where there was an internal dispute in the company, and a petition was presented to the court. Barclays Bank allowed the company to pay in cheques to its account, but refused to allow any withdrawals, until the petition was dismissed. The company needed access to its bank account and to its money to pay wages and buy materials, and it brought an action against the bank, claiming that the bank was under a legal duty to honour cheques drawn on the credit balance. However, both parties reached a compromise solution outside the court and no legal decision was then reached.

Now, however, the banks' position has been made quite clear by the judgment in *Re Gray's Inn Construction Co. Ltd* (1978). The facts of this case clearly illustrate the risk to a bank. The company was engaged in building contracts and borrowed from the bank on current account. Also, they were indebted to a loan creditor and on 3 August 1972 that creditor presented a petition to the court for the winding up of Gray's Inn Construction Co. Ltd. The petition was advertised on 10 August but the branch of the bank where the account was maintained did not learn of the petition until 17 August, when an internal circular from the bank's head office, prepared from a perusal of the *Gazette*, was seen at the branch. In the court hearing it was apparent that the precise date on which the bank head office had first become aware of the advertisement was not known, although they were certainly aware of it on 15 August.

At that time the bank's internal rules allowed a branch to continue a company's account after the presentation of the petition, provided the branch made sure that any cheques drawn were in the ordinary course of the company's business. At that time the bank took the view that, in the interests of its customer and the trading community generally, it was helpful to allow a company to continue its banking account. In this case, the bank was assured by the company that the petition, when heard, would be dismissed, and it continued operating the account in good faith, accepting payments into the account and honouring cheques drawn by the company. The company's overdraft fluctuated beween £7000 and £3600, having been overdrawn £5322 on the date when the petition was presented, and being overdrawn £4464 on the date when the winding up order was made. Between those two dates, the bank had received credits into the account totalling £25 313, and had paid cheques totalling £24 129.

The court did not dismiss the petition, and a winding up order was made on 9 October. Subsequently, the liquidator appointed claimed against the bank that all credits and all debits in and out of the account since the date of the petition, 3 August 1972, were void, being dispositions made after the commencement of the liquidation. However, as the case proceeded, the liquidator did not press his claim in full, and in the lower court his demand was limited to reimbursement of the amount which he alleged the company had lost by remaining in business after the petition had been presented. This figure was £13 260, but the judge held that while it was difficult to assess the true loss, he saw the figure as £5000. Upon appeal, the liquidator did not oppose that assessment. However, in the Court of Appeal, the ruling of the lower court was reversed, and it was held that any payments in and out of an account, whether debit or credit, were 'dispositions', and that it was not just the net position arising between the credit turnover and debit turnover that needed to be examined. Nor was it the extent of losses. The Court of Appeal felt that it must protect the interests of unsecured creditors and ruled that it was not proper to validate transactions which would result in debts being paid which had arisen before the presentation of the petition.

It is clear from this decision that to continue operating the account after knowledge of the presentation of a petition is extremely risky, and it is general practice now to stop the account and return cheques presented with the answer 'Refer to drawer – petition presented'. The company should be informed by the bank that until the petition is dismissed no transactions can be allowed; moreover it should be advised to take legal advice with a view to obtaining a validation order, under s. 127 Insolvency Act 1986, which could be produced to the branch as authority for paying any cheque or dealing in any transaction while the petition is outstanding. If and when such a validation order is produced, and its meaning is entirely clear and relevant to the transaction before the bank, then, if the bank wishes, it may deal with the company without risk.

The situation following the making of a winding up order is equally clear. Whether overdrawn or in credit the account must be stopped, and the power of the directors ceases. The bank should ask for the copy of the order to be exhibited and may then inform the liquidator of the balance of the accounts, and give details of all security lodged by the company. Contingent liabilities can be disclosed and items held for safe keeping may be handed to the liquidator against his receipt. Any cheques presented for payment should be returned with the answer 'Refer to drawer – winding up order made' and the credit balance, if any, should be sent to the liquidator.

If there is more than one account, consideration will of course be given to the bank's possible right of set-off, for under the Insolvency Rules 1986 (4.90), where there are mutual debits, and credits, or dealings between the company and the creditor, all the debits and credits must be set off, and only the net amount due is to be claimed or paid (see *National Westminster Bank Ltd* v. *Halesowen Presswork and Assemblies Ltd* (1972)). However, sums due from the company to another party must not be included if that other party had notice at the time when they became due that a petition for the winding up of the company was pending (and, in the case of voluntary liquidation, if a meeting of creditors had been summoned).

If the account is overdrawn, the bank will lodge its claim in the liquidation, having considered whether any of its claim can be classed as preferential.

Generally, the bank's rights in respect of its security are the same as in bankruptcy, and it will invariably either itself realise security charged by the company, or allow the liquidator to carry out sales, accounting to the bank for the realisation monies, less his expenses. Occasionally, if a security is difficult to realize, it may have to be valued for purposes of lodging the proof of debt, so as to quantify the bank's unsecured debt, upon which dividends can be paid. Subsequently, after a sale, the liquidator must be given a detailed account, and the bank's claim can then be either increased or decreased.

Voluntary liquidation

A voluntary liquidation is a common form of liquidation[65] and is usually initiated if the company resolves by extraordinary resolution that it cannot by reason of its liabilities continue its business and that it is advisable to wind up (s. 84 Insolvency Act 1986). This resolution must be advertised in the *Gazette* within 14 days and the liquidation commences at the time of the passing of the resolution. The company must then cease to trade except to the extent that that is necessary for its beneficial winding up. There is no problem with dispositions in this case, and the bank account may safely be continued until the company resolves to go into liquidation, whether it is overdrawn or in credit.

There are two types of voluntary liquidation, members' and creditors'. The type will depend upon whether or not the directors at a directors' meeting within five weeks immediately preceding the date of the passing of the resolution for winding up, make a statutory declaration to the effect that they have made full enquiry into the company's affairs and believe that the company will be able to pay its debts in full, together with interest at the official rate, within 12 months of the start of the liquidation (s. 89). The directors' declaration must include a statement of the company's assets and liabilities and the declaration must be filed at Companies House within 15 days following the date of the resolution to wind up voluntarily. If all this can be done the liquidation is a members' voluntary winding up. If not it will be a creditors' voluntary winding up (s. 90).

65 See Appendix I, Q. 11 (April 1981).

Members' voluntary liquidation

Liquidations of this type should, in theory, give the bank less cause for concern as by their title it is implied that all creditors will be repaid. This liquidation commences on the date of the passing of the resolution by the members, and the effect of the calling of the meeting is not such as to concern the bank in the conduct of the account. There is no relation back to the time of the calling of the meeting and the directors' powers cease only when the resolution is passed. Problems with dispositions do not arise, and s. 127 considerations do not enter into the bankers' decisions.

The members therefore choose the liquidator who must be a licensed insolvency practitioner. If at any time he comes to the opinion that the company will not be able to pay its debts in full he must call a meeting of creditors and the liquidation will then become a creditors' voluntary liquidation, and they can choose and elect a different liquidator if they wish. Other than this, a dissatisfied creditor could petition the court for the making of a winding up order.

Creditors' Voluntary Liquidation

It is not often that a members' voluntary liquidation is encountered and even more rarely that, when one is, it becomes a creditors' voluntary liquidation subsequently.

Usually a creditors' voluntary liquidation occurs at the outset of the liquidation because the directors cannot pass a resolution that they believe that the company will pay all its debts in full. In that event the company must call a meeting of creditors to be held not later than the fourteenth day after the day on which the company meeting (members meeting) is to consider the resolution to wind up voluntarily. Creditors must receive notice at least 7 days before the date of their meeting which must also be advertised in the *Gazette*.

A statement of affairs must be presented to the meeting of creditors. The liquidator in a creditors' voluntary liquidation is the person nominated by the creditors but if they do not choose it is the person nominated by the company. The liquidator may be supported by the election of a creditors' committee to which he will report from time to time. On the appointment of the liquidator all the powers of the directors cease except in so far as the liquidation committee of creditors sanction their continuance.

If there is a time gap between the passing of the resolution by the company and the meeting of creditors then the liquidator appointed by the company has only limited powers until his position is confirmed or the creditors appoint the insolvency practitioner of their own choice (s. 166). In this period the liquidator may protect and preserve assets but cannot sell or dispose of any, unless they are of a perishable nature, or unless he has obtained the sanction of the court.

Occasionally, whilst the directors are preparing to go into liquidation and call a meeting of creditors, and therefore before the company has resolved to go into liquidation, banks are approached by the intended liquidator, and are asked to hold any monies received by the company, in a separate account, and in trust for creditors generally. If they are willing to waive their right of set-off and regard the monies as trust funds then there is no reason why such a procedure should not be followed, although understandably the bank would be unlikely to agree to this, if this meant increasing its own commitment by additional facilities on the old current account to which cheques drawn by the company would be debited. Some prospective liquidators prefer to open a 'holding' account at another bank to prevent any possible problems with set-off.

Where a bank agrees to hold, in a separate account, deposits lodged with the customer by its customers as monies 'up front' before goods are delivered or work is done, then such funds are imbued with a trust element and cannot be set off or appropriated against the borrower's own debt, nor will a liquidator or trustee in bankruptcy of the customer be entitled to the funds (*Re Kayford Ltd* (1974)).

Action to be taken upon Notice of Voluntary Liquidation

Upon learning that one of its company customers has held a meeting of members and passed a resolution to go into voluntary liquidation, the bank should ascertain whether this is a members' or creditors' voluntary liquidation. In the latter case it should be remembered that the liquidator will have only limited powers until the meeting of creditors is held and his position is confirmed or another liquidator is chosen.

In a creditors' voluntary liquidation therefore a credit balance, safe custody or unrequired security should not be delivered to the liquidator until a copy of the creditors' resolution has been seen. In a members' voluntary liquidation the bank can act immediately upon seeing a copy of the resolution of members.

In both instances the liquidator must of course hold a current licence as an insolvency practitioner and some banks make a practice of seeing this, if the individual is unknown. Often, however, he will be an insolvency specialist partner in one of the large accountancy practices, already known to the bank. The liquidator should be advised of the balance(s) of the account(s) which will have been stopped immediately upon notice of the passing of the company's resolution to go into voluntary liquidation. Any cheques presented have to be returned marked 'Return to drawer – company in voluntary Liquidation'. Details of all security lodged by the company should be given and safe custody can be delivered against the liquidator's receipt, as can also the balance of the account if credit. If there is more than one account, the bank must exercise its right of set-off and only the net amount claimed in the liquidation or the net credit balance paid over. The liquidator must be told of any contingent liabilities. If the net balance is debit, the bank will lodge its claim, quantifying as much as possible as preferential. Its rights over security from the company will be the same as in a compulsory winding up or bankruptcy and usually the bank will realise the security itself or come to an arrangement for a fee with the liquidator whereby he sells it and accounts to the bank.

Alternatively, the security may be valued for the purpose of lodging proof, so as to quantify the bank's unsecured claim in order to obtain any dividend declared. In that event when the security has been sold, the bank must give the liquidator a detailed account, whereupon its unsecured claim will be adjusted in respect of any future dividends to be paid.

Preferential claims

Under ss. 175, 386 and Schedule 6 of the Insolvency Act 1986, all wages and salaries in respect of services rendered during the four months prior to the liquidation rank as preferential, up to a maximum of £800 per employee. Additionally, holiday pay accruing due at the date of the liquidation is preferential. However, directors' fees are not preferential, nor are payments to sub-contractors (*Re C. W. and A. L. Hughes Ltd* (1966)).

By virtue of Schedule 6, if any of the wages, salary payments or holiday pay has already been paid, out of money advanced by any person for that purpose, then the lender can stand in the employee's place and subrogate to his position, ranking preferentially. An examination of the overdrawn bank account for the four months prior to the liquidation (the date of the making of the winding up order in a compulsory liquidation) is therefore most important, to ascertain and add up all wages, salary and holiday pay cheques debited in that period.[66] It will probably be impossible for the bank to decide whether the maximum of £800 per employee has been exceeded, and the bank will usually simply compute its claim, and rely on the reputable accountant appointed as liquidator to examine the company's books, and to see whether the amount of the bank's claim needs to be reduced by the application of the monetary limit. In carrying out these duties, the liquidator may also find that some monies drawn in the form of 'cash' or 'wages' were used for other purposes such as petty cash, and these amounts of course cannot be admitted by the liquidator as preferential.

Unfortunately, in an active current account the factor most likely to reduce the bank's preferential claim is the Rule in *Clayton's Case*, for where there has been substantial turnover the liquidator may be able to show that monies lent to pay wages in the early part of the four-month period have effectively been repaid by subsequent credits to the account. Consequently, in examining the current account the banker should note the final overdrawn balance and then work backwards in date order through the debit turnover to see the point at which this equals the debit balance: this might be in the middle of one particular item. It is these cheques which have gone towards making up the debit balance outstanding at the liquidation. A further examination of all these

66 See Appendix I, Q. 59 (April 1983).

items should then be made, and if any wages cheques paid in this group of debit entries can be identified, and provided they are not outside the four-month time limit, then they constitute a preferential claim. Wages paid prior to this point on the account, however, even though within the four-month period, will be disallowed (Fig. 9.5).

It follows from the impact of *Clayton's Case* that where the bank fears that failure of the company could be imminent, and that liquidation or receivership is a real possibility, there can be an advantage to the bank, and to the company (for the bank will possibly agree to continue its support), in operating a *separate* wages and salaries account, so as to maximize the bank's preferential claim and prevent the operation of *Clayton's Case*, should the company be placed in liquidation or receivership.[67,68] (By virtue of s. 40 Insolvency Act 1986, the provisions of s. 175 apply in a receivership situation also.) With the authority of the directors, a separate account will be opened, to which all wages and salary payments will be debited for a period of four months, and this account will show the bank's preferential claim at any one time. A separate cheque book is given to the company for use on this account. Overall, no increased lending need be allowed, and the purpose of the account is merely to maximize the potential preferential claim. The company's current account will operate alongside, but at reduced lending levels, as the wages cheques are being debited to the wages and salaries account and not to the current account. For sixteen weeks, the new wages and salaries account debit balance builds up, but in week 17, the cheque which was debited in week 1 (which will not now be eligible for a claim under s. 175, being time-expired) is removed from the account by a transfer to the credit side of the wages and salaries account, at the debit of the current account. Week 17 will, of course, also carry a debit for the wages encashed in that week. The account will now continue with debits in respect of wages for the week in question, and transfer credits from the current account in respect of those wages paid sixteen weeks earlier, which have become time-expired.

Over the years, the bank's right to claim as a preferential creditor has been challenged by liquidators, especially when a separate wages and salaries account has not been opened, although the existence of such an account is irrelevant to the right to claim by way of subrogation. In *Re Primrose (Builders) Ltd* (1950) the liquidator alleged that the bank, in coming to an agreement with the company whereby it would not make wages payments from a current account until such time as the company produced credits to ensure that the overall borrowing did not rise, was appropriating such credits against the wages encashed, and thus the normal operation of *Clayton's Case* was not to apply. The court took the view that this was not the case and found for the bank, as it had found in an earlier case, *National Provincial Bank Ltd v. Freedman and Rubens* (1934).

67   See Appendix I, Q. 50 (April 1982).
68   See Appendix I, Q. 59 (April 1983).

PREFERENTIAL CLAIM IN LIQUIDATION

Example of the Operation of the Rule in Clayton's Case

Winding up order/resolution to place company in creditors' voluntary liquidation on 3.4.84.

What is the Bank's Preferential Claim?

———Ltd — Current account

			Debit	Credit	Balance	Preferential claim	Debit turnover
			£	£	£	£	£
1983							
July	1	Balance b/f			Dr. 30,312.–		
	2	Gas Board	210.17		Dr. 30,522.17		
	4	Rates	2,008.29		Dr. 32,530.46		
	17	Cheques		8,010.98	Dr. 24,519.48		
	28	Wages and salaries	8,016.42		Dr. 32,535.90		
Aug	9	Electricity	507.19		Dr. 33,043.09		
	28	Wages and salaries	8,102.19		Dr. 41,145.28		
Sep	1	Transfer from Zeta Bank		15,000.–	Dr. 26,145.28		
	28	Wages and salaries	8,016.42		Dr. 34,161.70		
Oct	10	Long Transport Ltd	3,814.76		Dr. 37,976.46		
	28	Wages and salaries	7,810.50		Dr. 45,786.96		
	30	Cheques		7,248.10	Dr. 38,538.86		
Nov	11	Gas Board	529.18		Dr. 39,068.04		
		Transfer Zeta Bank		15,000.–	Dr. 24,068.04		
	28	Wages and Salaries	7,606.03		Dr. 31,674.07		
Dec	10	Cheques		3,111.14	Dr. 28,562.93		
	28	Wages and salaries	➤ 8,010.54		Dr. 36,573.47	768.78	768.78
		Interest	4,002.18		Dr. 40,575.65		4,002.18
		Commission	50.–		Dr. 40,625.65		50.–
1984							
Jan	10	Transfer Zeta Bank		15,000.–	Dr. 25,625.65		
	17	Electricity	1,637.39		Dr. 27,623.04		1,637.39
	28	Wages and salaries	7,648.28		Dr. 34,911.32	7,648.28	7,648.28
Feb	10	Mays Computer Co.	4,310.43		Dr. 39,221.75		4,310.43
	28	Wages and Salaries	6,582.94		Dr. 45,804.69	6,582.94	6,582.94
March	3	Cheques		5,804.69	Dr. 40,000.00		
	10	Transfer Zeta Bank		15,000.–	Dr. 25,000.00		
						15,000.00	25,000.00

METHOD Examine debits (backwards in time) for a maximum period of four months from date of Winding Up Order or Resolution, or for a lesser period if the total turnover (backwards) reaches debit balance earlier. It will be seen that in date order the debit balance of £25,000 is comprised of all debit turnover starting in the middle of the cheque drawn for wages on 28th December. Only part of that cheque is eligible for claim, and to this are added all other subsequently paid wages items.

See also Appendix I, Q. 59.

Fig.9.5   *Current account wages claim –* Clayton's Case *effect*

In *Re Rampgill Mill Ltd* (1967) the bank had paid cheques for wages, without considering the possibility of a preferential claim if the company failed, and without the special intention of lending money for wages. Nevertheless, the judge took the view that the bank's overall *purpose* was to support the company in its trading, and he said that this was all that was necessary to justify a preferential claim, when liquidation subsequently ensued.

In *Re William Hall (Contractors) Ltd* (1967) the bank had a total claim in the liquidation of £8000, of which £2280 was preferential and £5720 non-preferential. It held security, and realized approximately £5780 from this, appropriating the money firstly to repay the non-preferential debt, with security proceeds of £60 being used to reduce the preferential claim. The liquidator rejected the bank's proof of debt, which it had submitted on this basis, taking the view that the bank should have applied the security proceeds firstly to the preferential debt, thus clearing this completely and leaving the bank with only an unsecured, non-preferential claim in the liquidation. The matter came to court where it was held that the bank was entitled to appropriate its security proceeds to the non-preferential part of the company's debt, in the first instance, if it wished. It was said that the general principle of law was quite clear: 'A creditor who has a security which he has a right to apply to one or other of two debts due to him, can exercise that right in any way he thinks fit'.

Apart from this general principle of common law, most bank forms of charge contain a clause allowing the bank to appropriate its security proceeds in whichever way it wishes, which can usefully be quoted to a difficult liquidator if necessary.

However, there is one case decision which should put a banker on his guard when operating a wage and salaries account. This is *Re E. J. Morel (1934) Ltd* (1962), where, although the facts were special, the bank was made to set off a credit balance in a company's No. 2 account against its preferential claim arising through the wages and salaries account, and could not set off the credit balance against a debit balance in a stopped No. 1 account.

The balances at the date of liquidation were:

E. J. Morel (1934) Ltd No. 1 account	Dr. £1839 (stopped on crystallization of a guarantee)
E. J. Morel (1934) Ltd No. 2 account	Cr. £1545
E. J. Morel (1934) Ltd Wages & salaries account	Dr. £1624

Thus the bank claimed to be a preferential creditor for £1624, and non-preferential creditor for £294 (£1839 − £1545), but was made to be a preferential creditor for £79 (£1,624 − £1,545) and a non-preferential creditor for £1,839. While the total claims were the same, the dividend benefit was quite different.

However, this decision has been modified recently by that in *Re Unit 2 Windows Ltd* (1985), where it was said that in the absence of guidance, a credit balance should be set-off pro rata against preferential and non-preferential claims, and this is clearly an improvement for a bank finding itself in this position.

THE ADMINISTRATOR

In the review of insolvency law which preceded the passing of the Insolvency Act 1986, the value of appointing a receiver under a floating charge and debenture was well recognized, albeit that the receiver acts for the debenture-holder. The Review Committee felt that where there was no floating charge, and hence a situation where a receiver could not be appointed, liquidation was not always appropriate and other schemes under the previous Companies Acts were slow to set up and costly. Hence the new administrator procedure was introduced.

An administrator of a company is appointed after a petition is presented to the court by the company or its directors, or its supervisor under a scheme of arrangement or by one or more of the company's creditors. It must be shown that the company is unable to pay its debts or is likely to become unable to pay and the proposal presented in the petition to the court must seek to achieve one or more of four objectives specified in the Act (s. 8(3)). These are:

(*a*) the survival of the whole or part of the company's undertaking as a going concern;

(*b*) the approval of a composition in satisfaction of the company's debts, or a scheme of arrangement of its affairs;

(*c*) the sanctioning of a compromise or scheme of arrangement under s. 425 Companies Act 1985;

(*d*) a better realization of the company's assets than would be likely to be achieved in a liquidation.

The petition must seek to appoint a licensed insolvency practitioner as the administrator, but where a bank or other party holds a floating charge and has appointed an administrative receiver before the hearing, the court will not appoint an administrator unless there are grounds for believing that the security under which the administrative receiver was appointed is defective.

A petition to appoint an administrator is not advertised, but notice must be given to any party who is entitled to appoint an administrative receiver under a floating charge; this notice must be at least five days before the date of the hearing, but the court has power to shorten this period. For banks this means that if they wish to avoid the appointment of the administrator they must appoint their own administrative receiver quickly. However, where they do not hold a floating charge they may not hear of the petition and in such a case their first notice may be after the hearing when the administrator has been appointed. They will then have the same rights as other unsecured creditors, being entitled to attend and vote at a meeting of creditors upon the administrator's proposals, but they will need to value their security for this purpose and it will only be the unsecured element of their lending which will be taken into account when voting takes place and when decisions are made by a majority in value of the creditors present or voting by proxy. A bank might decide, in certain instances, not to appoint an administrative receiver under its floating charge debenture, and in that case it would only be entitled to vote at meetings of creditors to the extent that its security did not fully secure the bank. If the bank were fully secured by its floating charge debenture but had not appointed an administrative receiver it would to all intents and purposes be allowing the control of matters to fall into the hands of outside parties.

However, in that event, the administrator would have an obligation to account to the bank upon realizing fixed charge assets. Hence if the administrator sells a factory, or collects book debts secured by a fixed charge, he must account to the bank when the proceeds of sale or collection come into his hands. In the case of floating charge assets, however, this is not the case and the administrator may retain the use of those for the purposes of the administration. In that event the Act provides that the floating charge holder will have the same priority in respect of any property of the company directly or indirectly representing the property disposed of, as he would have had in respect of the property subject to the security. (s. 15(4)). There is a further worry for a bank in respect of its fixed charge security, whether charged under a debenture where it has not appointed an administrative receiver or where charged separately by way of legal or equitable mortgage. It is possible that the administrator, in order to achieve the object of his appointment, might wish to dispose of the property secured by the fixed charge, but that the price being obtained is less than would be obtained by a sale of the property in the open market by a willing vendor. This situation might arise where the administrator is selling the business as a going concern, to preserve its entity and jobs and where the purchaser is acquiring stock and work in progress etc. but where the consideration placed upon, say, a factory, is less than might be expected if that factory were sold separately in the open market. In that instance the administrator must have applied to the court, for the order for sale may only be made if the interests of the fixed charge mortgagee are protected by an order that sums be made available to make good the deficiency. Unfortunately the Act does not say where those funds should come from, but in reality, the only source is the floating charge assets or assets not in mortgage to other parties. Hence, if there is no floating charge debenture, and other realizations are sufficient to pay the cost of the administration then a source for compensation for the fixed charge mortgagee exists. Where however, for example, a bank might not have appointed an administrative receiver under its debenture, and the property is sold by the administrator at less than open market value, the only source of compensation will be the realisations of the floating charge assets which are due to the bank anyway and hence in effect there is no source of compensation available. It is for this and other reasons that where banks hold debentures they are most likely to appoint an administrative receiver when a petition is presented to the court for the appointment of an administrator.

Presentation of the petition protects the company from action by its creditors and executions or other legal processes may not be continued, nor may a creditor with a reservation of title right over goods claim those goods back from the company. Also, a mortgagee may not enforce his security without the sanction of the court.

If and when he is appointed, the administrator is empowered to do everything necessary to achieve the objectives for which he was appointed. Clearly, because creditors do not need to be paid immediately his efforts to enable the company in whole or part to survive are much easier to achieve.

At the hearing of the petition, if an administration order is made, and should any winding-up petition for liquidation be pending, that winding-up petition is dismissed. Moreover, if an administrative receiver has been appointed he must vacate office, but of course if the security under which he was appointed was sound, the court will not be able to make the administration order. During the course of an administration a company may not resolve to go into liquidation, nor may an administrative receiver be appointed, and secured creditors are not able to take any steps to enforce their security except with the consent of the court or the administrator.

After he has been appointed, the administrator is under an obligation to present his proposals to the creditors at a meeting held within three months, and the directors of the company must produce a statement of affairs to him for that purpose. At the meeting of creditors, approval or modification of the proposals takes place by a vote carried by simple majority based on value of unsecured debt.

The extent to which the administration procedure will be used is unknown at the time of writing but clearly a new weapon has been placed in the armoury for dealing with insolvent companies and where there is no debenture and the company is of substantial size it could well be that its use in a crisis will be valuable, as the ability to grip the situation quickly and to preserve the assets and undertaking as a whole will be superior to liquidation. In the case of smaller companies, however, its use, at this stage, appears limited.

COMPANY VOLUNTARY ARRANGEMENT

The Insolvency Act 1986 also introduced a new procedure known as the Company Voluntary Arrangement, under which a proposal can be put to the company's creditors or members by the company's liquidator, administrator, or the company's directors. A meeting of creditors is held, but in this instance whilst voting is again calculated on value, the approval of any proposal must be by three-quarters in value of unsecured debt of those voting in person or by proxy. Also, to prevent dishonesty on the part of the directors a resolution will not be carried unless there is another count of votes excluding the votes of connected persons and then the resolution will not be carried if those voting against it include more than half in value of all the creditors to whom notice of the meeting was sent. In other words, the first count requires a 75 per cent majority and the second count a 50 per cent majority excluding for the latter purpose the votes by value of connected persons both from the voting figure and the total value of creditors. A connected person is a director, shadow director, an associate of either, or an associate of the company, such as an officer of the company or of another company under the same control or with controlling shareholders.

A company voluntary arrangement is initiated when proposals are put to an insolvency practitioner, who at this stage is called 'the nominee'. He will then submit a report to the court stating his view as to whether a meeting of the company and its creditors should be held. The nominee will be the chairman at the meeting, and it will be necessary for a secured creditor, such as a bank, to agree the value of its security with the chairman beforehand, if it wished to be counted in any vote.

Whatever is agreed at the meeting, the rights of the secured creditors and the preferential creditors must be preserved, unless they consent to any variation. If the meeting approves the proposal the nominee becomes known as the supervisor, and he may apply to the court for directions if necessary. Meanwhile the court may discharge the administration order or stay any winding up procedures which are in train. Dissatisfied creditors also have a right to apply to the court for redress.

The difference between a company voluntary arrangement and a petition for the appointment of an administrator lies in the fact that there is no petition and no protection for the company at the stage when the insolvency practitioner is acting merely as the nominee. Hence creditors with reservation of title rights could at this time be reclaiming goods supplied, and creditors could be taking action by way of execution or other process. It is possible therefore that the company voluntary arrangement may not be a feasible proposition, except where a petition to the court has been presented for the appointment of an administrator. Readers should note that the individual voluntary arrangement procedure differs in that when a nominee is appointed for individuals, protection for the debtor from the actions of his creditors automatically ensues.

Transactions at an Undervalue and Preferences[69]

Just as in bankruptcy proceedings, so there are provisions for the protection and benefit of creditors in company liquidations or administrations to claw

69 See Appendix I, Q. 37 (September 1980).

back assets or funds which a company has disposed of prior to its collapse in an unfair manner.

The old term 'fraudulent preference' has now disappeared and has been replaced simply by the term 'preference' in the Insolvency Act 1986. This is because it is not necessarily fraudulent for a debtor to repay one of his creditors ahead of other creditors, although in certain circumstances there could be such intentions in the background. Slightly different considerations apply to the circumstances necessary to enable a liquidator or administrator to attack a transaction as a preference successfully.

Transaction at an undervalue The 'transaction at an undervalue' is a new concept created by the Insolvency Act, although there are similarities to those transactions which were classed as voidable conveyances under previous insolvency legislation.

A transaction at an undervalue is one where the company makes a gift to a person or otherwise enters into a transaction on terms that provide for the company to receive no consideration, or a consideration, the value of which, in money or money's worth, is significantly less than the value, in money or money's worth, of the consideration provided by the company. If such a transaction has taken place at 'a relevant time' (which is later defined in s. 240 as being at a time in the period of two years ending with the onset of insolvency), the officeholder, being the liquidator or the administrator, may apply to the court for an order to be made for the position to be restored to what it would have been if the company had not entered into the transaction (s. 238 Insolvency Act 1986). When attacking a transaction with an ordinary creditor the office holder must be able to prove insolvency, which is an inability by the company to pay its debts at the time, or in consequence of, the transaction at the undervalue. However where the transaction was with a connected person, insolvency is presumed, unless the contrary is proved by the connected person.

A company is deemed to be unable to pay its debts under s. 123 if it fails to comply with a written demand made in the sum of £750 or more at its registered office, an execution by a creditor is unsatisfied, it is proved to the court that the company cannot pay its debts as they fall due, or it is proved to the court that the value of its assets is less than its liabilities, taking into account its contingent and prospective liabilities.

In all instances the court may not make an order if it is satisfied that the company had entered into the transaction in good faith and from a purpose of carrying on its business, and that at the time it did so there were reasonable grounds for believing that the transaction would benefit the company.

The court has wide powers to rearrange matters and it may require any propety transferred to be revested back into the name of the company, or, alternatively, order that the application of the proceeds of sale of the property or of money transferred be returned to the company. Security given may be ordered to be released or discharged and the court may even order security to be provided for the discharge of any obligation imposed by the order. The order may be made against any person, whether or not he was the person with whom the company entered into the transaction, but the interests of any person who acquired property in good faith, for value, and without notice of the relevant circumstances will not be prejudiced.

It has been suggested in certain areas that bankers lending to companies in a group situation might need to be more cautious when taking cross guarantees from the holding company and the subsidiary companies for each other's liabilities. All these companies would of course be connected persons and hence the two-year period would be applicable if the transaction could be attacked as one being 'at an undervalue'. Probably the area concerned is little different from the considerations of 'commercial justification', which have always needed to be examined and which were discussed in this book with reference to the *Charterbridge Corporation Ltd* v. *Lloyds Bank Ltd* (1969) decision and *Rolled Steel Products (Holdings) Ltd* v. *British Steel Corporation* (1984). The important words in the Insolvency Act in this connection seem to be in s. 238 where the transaction may not be set aside if it was entered into in good faith, for the purpose of carrying on the company's business, at a time when there were reasonable grounds for believing that the transaction would benefit the company giving the item in security.

Preferences   Preference transactions, too, may be attacked by a liquidator or administrator but in the case of a preference to an ordinary creditor, the period involved is only six months from the onset of insolvency, although where a connected person has been preferred the period is two years. In respect of a preference of both ordinary creditor or connected person, the officeholder must be able to prove insolvency, as discussed above, and in the case of an ordinary creditor there is a further need for him to demonstrate that the company has done something or allowed something to be done which has had the effect of putting the creditor or surety or guarantor into a position which, in the event of the company going into insolvent liquidation, will be better than the position which that person would have been in if that thing had not been done. However, the court may not make an order unless the company which gave the preference was influenced in deciding to give it by a desire to place that person in the better position (s. 239). This section goes on to say that where a connected person receives a preference the court shall presume, unless the contrary is proved, that the company was influenced by such a desire at the time.

Most companies will be unlikely to want to prefer their bankers, but a bank can become embroiled in a preference claim where monies have been lent to a company, and then repaid with the objective of getting the bank to release security lodged by a third party. If that third party is a director, and therefore a connected person, the preference of him will be open to attack for two years from the onset of insolvency, but for the bank, as an ordinary creditor, the period of risk will be six months. Thus, if one of the directors is a guarantor, or has charged personal assets in support of the company borrowing, it can obviously be to his advantage to attempt to reduce any potential claim upon him by the bank, if, looking ahead, he foresees the imminent collapse of the business. Bankers must always take care, therefore, if an account which has been unsatisfactory suddenly relies less heavily on bank borrowing, or is repaid completely, and there is then a request for the release of security lodged by a third party. In such cases it could well be desirable only to release the security after six months has elapsed. If not, should the bank later receive a claim from a liquidator appointed in that period to refund the credits to the company's account, the bank could then find itself with the borrowing restored but its security gone.

The case of *Re M. Kushler Ltd* (1943) illustrates the points in question. One of the directors of this company was a guarantor of the bank account and he was advised by his accountants that the company was insolvent. He therefore arranged for the company's borrowing of £600 to be repaid, although other trade creditors were pressing. Shortly afterwards the company went into a creditors' voluntary liquidation and in due course it was accepted by the Court of Appeal that there had been a preference of the bank and the guarantor.

Under the old law pressure by the bank to repay the borrowing helped to show that the company itself had not had a dominant intent to prefer the bank, but this area of consideration has now changed and all the officeholder needs to show is that in entering into the transaction the company was influenced by a desire to produce in relation to the creditor, surety or guarantor the effect that he would be better placed if the company went into insolvent liquidation.

It will be noted in the chapter on guarantees that through their charge forms banks seek to retain a degree of protection in respect of released security in circumstances such as these, but once a security such as property has been released there can be no certainty that the owner will not use it for other purposes which effectively will place it beyond the attempts of the bank to reclaim it. Under the Insolvency Act 1986, in theory a bank's position is now better in that the court has power, even in the absence of such a clause, to make an order for the position to be restored to what it was before the transaction took place. Hence a guarantee obligation might be restored, but where tangible security has been transferred and taken in good faith, for value, and without notice of the relevant circumstances, that property would not be capable of being returned to the bank. Nevertheless, if there is available other free property of similar monetary worth then presumably the court would order that that should be charged to the bank for the increased debt which the bank would be facing. In these circumstances where a bank does suffer through a court order, it will be enabled to prove in the liquidation for the extra obligation which is imposed upon it.

Table 9.1 summarizes the position in respect of transactions at an undervalue and preferences.

	Preference	*Transactions at undervalue*
ORDINARY CREDITOR	Within 6 months of onset of insolvency Officeholder to prove insolvency Officeholder to prove company influenced by desire to place in better position.	Within 2 years of onset of insolvency Officeholder to prove insolvency*
CONNECTED PERSON	Within 2 years of onset of insolvency Officeholder to prove insolvency 'Desire to better' is presumed (unless contrary shown)	Within 2 years of onset of insolvency Insolvency presumed but *still applies
		N.B. *No court order if satisfied transaction was in 'good faith' and for 'purpose of carrying on its business' and reasonable grounds for believing 'benefit to company'.

Table 9.1   *Summary of preferences and transactions at undervalue in company insolvency*

LOANS TO DIRECTORS

The Companies Act 1985, s. 330, lays down stringent rules preventing companies from giving financial assistance to directors of the company and persons associated with them. Thus no company, whether public or private company, may make a loan to a director, nor give any security, whether by way of guarantee or otherwise, to secure the director's personal liabilities.[70]

70 See Appendix I, Q. 16 (September 1981).

Moreover, relevant companies, being public companies or private companies which are part of a group containing a public company, are prohibited from making loans or quasi-loans to a director of the company or its holding company or to any person connected with such a director. Again, it is not permissible to provide security or enter into any guarantee covering such a loan or quasi-loan made to such a person by a third party such as a bank.

Quasi-loans refer to situations such as where a director might use a credit card for his own purposes but where the company pays, or has promised to pay, in settlement. Quasi-loans must not exceed £1,000 in aggregate over a period of two months, and by the end of that time the director must have reimbursed the company.

However, there are exceptions, and lendings between a holding company and its subsidiary are allowed, as are also legitimate short-term loans made by a company to its director to cover expenses, pending reimbursement by the company. Understandably, where the company's ordinary business is that of lending money as in the case of a bank, any loans made in the ordinary course of business are permitted, provided the amount of the transaction and its terms are not more favourable than would normally be expected to apply to a lending to a third party of similar financial standing. There is a monetary limitation of £50 000 in respect of any one director in the case of a recognized bank – that being a bank which has been recognized by the Bank of England under the Banking Act 1979.

If s. 330 Companies Act 1985 is breached, the transaction is voidable at the option of the company, and the director must reimburse the company. Moreover, the director and the company are open to criminal proceedings.

It follows from all the above that care and research is necessary where an individual wishes to borrow from the bank and offers company security in support. It is more than likely that most propositions put in such way will not be acceptable to the lending banker.

Occasionally, a customer who is a director of a company and who may be its principal shareholder, offers repayment of his own borrowing by transfers from the company account. Unless the monies emanating from the company are in the form of a salary or repayment of fees or a loan, an area of risk would again be opening up for the bank, if it were prepared to proceed on that basis. Obviously much would depend upon the amounts involved and the general background. If the bank is prepared to agree it would probably be safer if the cheques drawn on the company account were signed by other directors, as this might enable the bank to rely on *Turquand's Case* in case of extreme need later.

DEATH OF A DIRECTOR

As a director is an agent for the company, any cheques drawn by him either alone or jointly with another officer may still be paid by the bank after it has received notice of his death. The bank should, however, check its mandate to see if any changes will be necessary for the future operation of the company account and, as necessary, an approach can be made to the other officer(s) to ensure that steps are taken to appoint a new director. The bank must be informed of this and authorized on its usual form to accept his signature in lieu of that of the deceased director.

INSOLVENCY OF A DIRECTOR

When a company director has a bankruptcy order made against him, certain matters require attention, although the continued legal existence of the company is not affected.

First, it would not be possible for the bankrupt to continue acting as a director without the consent of the court, and if the company has adopted article 88 of Table A of the Companies Act 1948 then his office as director is automatically vacated. He must also vacate office if he makes an arrangement or composition with his creditors generally, e.g. as under the new Insolvency Act procedures relating to an individual voluntary arrangement. Similar provisions apply under Article 81, Table A, of the Companies Act 1985. This can present problems for the bank, depending upon the number of other directors remaining and the terms of the company's mandate, and steps may be necessary to encourage the board of directors to meet at an early date to pass a resolution to amend the mandate terms. It may be necessary to appoint a replacement director, and if insufficient directors remain to form a quorum at a board meeting then the remaining directors may act under article 100 of Table A of the Companies Act 1948 and Article 90 of Table A of the 1985 Act. In an extreme situation, where there are no directors remaining, it will be necessary for an application to the court to be made by a member, or for the court acting on its own to make directions as it thinks expedient.

DISQUALIFICATION OF A DIRECTOR

The Insolvency Act 1986 and the Company Directors Disqualification Act 1986 place much more responsibility on directors of limited companies than was formerly the case. Hence a director can be disqualified from holding office without the leave of the court for a minimum of two years and a maximum of 15 years. Moreover, he must not in that period be concerned or take part in any way in the promotion, formation or management of a company without the leave of the court.

Every liquidator in a voluntary liquidation, every administrator and every administrative receiver has to file a report with the Secretary of State on each person who has been a director or shadow director of the company in the three years immediately preceding its insolvency.

The grounds on which the court may disqualify the person concerned, in the light of that report and other evidence, are when the person is deemed responsible for fraudulent or wrongful trading, unfitness to be concerned in the management of a company or a persistent default in relation to duties to file returns and documents at Companies House.

A shadow director is a person 'in accordance with whose directions or instructions the directors of the company are accustomed to act', but a person is not deemed to be a shadow director by reason only that the directors act on advice given by him in a professional capacity (s. 741(2) Companies Act 1985).

Hence a company's auditors, solicitors or bankers cannot be a shadow director if they act in their usual professional way. In appropriate instances, however, possibly a holding company giving directions to a subsidiary could be classed as a shadow director.

The purpose of identifying shadow directors is to be able to establish the liability of rogues, who in the past have been able to operate in the background for their own safety through the medium of other persons or companies, causing considerable loss to creditors who have supplied goods, etc. on credit, only to find that the company has failed.

WRONGFUL TRADING

Wrongful trading is a new concept introduced by s. 214 Insolvency Act 1986, applicable only in liquidations. Under these provisions the company's liquidator may apply to the court for a director or shadow director to be ordered to contribute to the assets of the company (i.e make a monetary payment into the company's estate to enable creditors to be paid a higher dividend than would otherwise be the case). The grounds for the application must be that the company is insolvent and that at some time before the start of the liquidation the person knew or ought to have known that there was no reasonable prospect of avoiding insolvent liquidation. However, the person involved will not be liable if he can show that he took every step to minimize the potential loss to the company's creditors that he ought to have taken.

The object therefore is to penalize any stupid, incompetent, lazy, or fraudulent director, or one who trades on, increasing the losses of those with whom the company deals, at a time when it should be taking steps to prevent such losses, for example, by applying for the appointment of an administrator or by going into liquidation forthwith.

FINANCIAL ASSISTANCE FOR THE PURCHASE OF A COMPANY'S OWN SHARES

Sections 151-154 of the latest Companies Act, that passed in 1985, prohibit a company from giving either direct or indirect assistance to a third party facilitating the purchase of shares in the company or shares in a holding company. (These provisions were formerly included in s. 54 Companies Act 1948 and s. 42 of the Companies Act 1981.) The prohibitions extend to financial assistance given before, or at the time of, or after the acquisition has taken place, but the Act excepts several situations from the general rule. Now, provided the company's purpose is made in good faith and in the interests of the company, and provided certain criteria set down in the section are met, then, whether the company is a public or private company, assistance can be given.

Financial assistance includes gifts, loans, security, guarantees, indemnities and waivers, and the assistance can be given by way of bonus shares, the payment of dividends or the distribution of assets upon the liquidation of a company.[71] In all cases the principal purpose of the transaction must not be the acquisition of shares by the giving of that assistance, which must be an incidental part of some larger purpose.

Section 155 of the 1985 Act exempts a private company even further. In their case, however, the rules are that the company's net assets must not be reduced by the transaction, unless the amount of the reduction is equal to a figure which would have been available for distribution from profits earned in the past. This means the capital reserves are retained in the business for the benefit of its creditors.

The Department of Trade and Industry has defined net assets as 'the amount by which the aggregate amount of a company's assets exceed the aggregate amount of its liabilities taking the amount of both assets and liabilities to be stated in the company's accounting records immediately before the financial assistance is given'.

There are stringent rules governing the procedure involving the passing of a special resolution by the shareholders in a general meeting and a statutory declaration by the board of directors which must be advertised naming the person to whom the assistance is given and the amount and nature of that financial assistance. The directors are required to swear that the company is solvent and will continue to be so, even should the company be placed in liquidation within the next twelve months. (In theory, a very demanding obligation!) Moreover, the company's auditors are brought into the proceedings and their report must support the directors' statutory declaration. Finally, the transaction concerned must be brought to fruition within eight weeks of the date of the directors' statutory declaration. However, where the lending of money is part of a company's ordinary business, such as in the case of a bank, it may give financial assistance, as by lending to its customers to enable them to buy shares in the bank.

The purpose behind these relaxed requirements is to facilitate management buy-outs and take-overs where private companies are concerned, but the technicalities are such that it will be difficult for a banker to follow matters through closely himself and almost certainly the banker will need either his own legal advice or an assurance from the solicitors acting for the company

71 See Appendix I, Q. 48 (September 1981).

that all matters appertaining to these new procedures have been satisfactorily performed.

Schemes to acquire shares with financial assistance have, historically, met with difficulties under the less relaxed requirements of s. 54 of the Companies Act 1948 and it remains to be seen how the new procedures develop. The decision in *Selangor United Rubber Estates Ltd* v. *Cradock and others* (1968) was a very disturbing one for banks, as we saw earlier. However, for the purposes of this book and by way of illustration, the following very simple example is given:

Company X borrows from its bank and offers as security a mortgage over a factory by Company Y. However, X requires the money to take up shares in Y and uses it for that purpose. In this situation company Y is clearly indirectly facilitating the purchase of its own shares by X and the security it has given to the bank could well be at risk. Indeed, it seems from the decision in *Heald and Another* v. *O'Connor* (1971) which reversed that in *Victor Battery Co. Ltd* v. *Curry's Ltd* (1946) that the security would be void, even if the bank had acted without direct knowledge of a breach of the Companies Acts prohibitions. Unfortunately, situations involving breaches of the section are rarely simple, and the bank should take legal advice in complex situations so there can be no doubt, for many devious schemes and arrangements have been drawn up in an attempt to circumnavigate the provisions of the Companies Acts.

Having read this far, readers will readily appreciate the pecularities and complexities of matters relating to limited companies.

These features will continue to be seen when we study a type of security which is unique and which only limited companies are empowered to grant – the debenture incorporating a floating charge. However, we must now pass from Section A of the Institute syllabus to Section B which covers this and other types of securities.

SECTION B

SECURITIES FOR ADVANCES

CHAPTER 10

Debentures and Floating Charges

Technically, any document acknowledging an indebtedness is a debenture, but the term is used generally to mean an instrument sealed by a limited company which makes provision for the repayment of a sum of money at some future time. Usually it will include a covenant that interest will be paid pending repayment and more often than not the debenture is secured by a charge over the company's property or undertaking. If no security is given, the debenture is termed a 'naked' debenture.

The debenture may be a security for all sums owing by the company to the chargee or it may be limited in the amount it secures. These are known as 'all monies' debentures and 'fixed sum' debentures respectively. As far as banks are concerned, fixed sum debentures are rarely taken these days, although old forms of security drawn in that way may still be held. Where debentures are issued as a means of raising loan capital, they may be redeemable or perpetual, and in the latter case there is no obligation on the company to repay the borrowed money except when the company is placed into liquidation, or if and when it defaults in a provision on the debenture document, as would happen if it failed to make interest payments on the due date. Such debentures can be bearer debentures or registered debentures and they may be issued in a single form or in a series of debentures for specified amounts. Usually when the debenture has been issued to raise loan capital and the borrowing is secured on the assets and undertaking of the company, a collateral trust deed is executed by the company in favour of known trustees of standing, such as a reputable insurance company, to whom the company's assets are charged for the benefit of the debenture holders. The charge may be by way of either a fixed charge or a floating charge.

A limited company is empowered to redeem issued debenture stock by purchasing it itself, and when the market price of a quoted debenture falls below face value this may be attractive to the company. As, however, it is possible for the company to reissue redeemed debentures under the Companies Act, except where there is a provision in the articles of association of the company preventing this, or where the company has redeemed the debentures and stated that it is its intention to cancel them and set them aside, there is a risk that debentures might be reissued and, if so, they would have the same priority as if they had never been redeemed. Understandably, such an action could have very serious repercussions for a person who has lent money subsequently and taken a charge over the company's assets. Thus, where there is any possibility that the company might reissue redeemed debentures, it is usual for the subsequent lender to ask the company to pass a resolution cancelling the redeemed debentures.

BANK DEBENTURES

The usual form of bank debenture will be an all-monies debenture and will give a fixed charge over the company's real property, goodwill, uncalled capital and possibly fixed plant and machinery. Recently, it has become the practice to charge debtors by way of fixed charge.[72] The debenture will also usually be drawn to give the bank a specific equitable charge over any real property which the company might acquire at any time in the future. Thereafter, the charge will give the bank a first floating charge over all the other assets and undertakings of the company whatsoever and wheresoever situated.

FIXED CHARGE

The fixed charge given in the debenture is similar to the legal mortgage or equitable mortgage which the company could have given as an alternative over those assets. Thus the company's land, factories and offices can be legally mortgaged in the debenture and in this way they are not subject to the disadvantages of the floating charge which are discussed later.

The specific equitable mortgage in the debenture is usually drawn to cover any other company land or property which is not actually scheduled and charged by way of legal mortgage in the debenture, and, as we have seen, it also gives the bank an equitable charge over any future property which the company might acquire.

In recent years banks have started to include a clause in their debenture forms whereby the company creates a fixed charge over its book and other debts. Prior to this, there had been a long legal debate as to whether it was possible for a company to create a fixed charge over an asset which was regularly changing, but in *Siebe Gorman & Co. Ltd* v. *Barclays Bank Ltd* (1979) the bank's fixed charge over debts was accepted and thus debts are no longer subject to the disadvantages which they would be if only charged by way of a floating charge (see below). It is usual for the debenture creating the fixed charge over book debts to include a clause whereby the company covenants to pay all monies collected into its bank account, and in this way it is felt that the freedom of use of an asset which the company would have under a floating charge no longer exists. This clause is registered at Companies House, and it is notice to the world that debts are charged by way of fixed charge.[73] In *in re Brightlife Ltd* (1986) it was decided that a credit

72 See Appendix I, Q. 50 (April 1982).
73 See Appendix I, Q. 50 (April 1982).

balance in a bank account was not itself included in the phrase 'all book debts and other debts', although in that case the debenture had been given to a party other than a bank.

Dangers exist, however, with book debts, whether they are charged by way of fixed charge or floating charge, because not infrequently the company may decide to factor its debts with a factoring company to increase its liquidity and to ease its cash flow. In such an event, a factor company usually buys the debts or acquires an outright assignment over them, or if it advances only a certain percentage then it may reserve the right to a charge over the balance of the debt. Where the bank has a debenture, the factoring company will ask the bank to agree to it having priority, and to that extent the bank's security will be reduced in value and will need to be written down in its books. It is better for the bank not to release its charge entirely, but simply to agree to the factoring company having priority, for in this way, if any equity in the debts ever arises, after the factor has been repaid, then the bank in a receivership will be enabled to collect the balance of money available.[74,75]

FLOATING CHARGE

Only a limited company can create a floating charge, although under the Agricultural Credits Act 1928 a farmer, not being a limited company, can give a similar type of security to his bankers (see Chapter 16). The floating charge is drawn to create a security over all the company's assets other than those which have been charged by way of a fixed charge, and this in practice means that all assets which are employed in the course of the company's business are part of the security. It is the nature of a floating charge, however, that the company remains free to deal with those assets until such time as the floating charge crystallizes and becomes a fixed charge by the occurrence of a specific event, which will have been named in the debenture. The floating charge is not used in some countries, and there it is necessary for a limited company to create a fixed charge over any asset it wishes to mortgage. However, when the company wishes to sell that asset in the course of trade, much documentation is necessary to release the charge from the bank's security and a new charge has to be given over new assets which are acquired. This cumbersome procedure is avoided in the United Kingdom and those Commonwealth countries which possess the floating charge.

Assets usually caught under a floating charge are the company's stock, work in progress, and loose plant machine and tools. If a fixed charge has not been given over debtors then these will be caught under the floating charge.

The nature of a floating charge has been considered in several legal decisions. In *Re Yorkshire Woolcombers' Association* (1903) three characteristics

74 See Appendix I, Q. 48 (September 1981).
75 See Appendix I, Q. 53 (September 1982).

were noted. It was accepted that the charge was on both present and future assets and that the assets could change in the ordinary course of the company's business which could be carried on until an event occurred in the future. In *Evans* v. *Rival Granite Quarries Ltd* (1910) it was said:

> A floating security is not a future security; it is present security, which presently affects all the assets of the company expressed to be included in it. On the other hand, it is not a specific security; the holder cannot affirm that the assets are specifically mortgaged to him. The assets are mortgaged in such a way that the mortgagor can deal with them without the concurrence of the mortgagee. A floating security is not a specific mortgage of the assets, plus a licence to the mortgagor to dispose of them in the course of his business, but is a floating mortgage applying to every item comprised in the security, but not specifically affecting any item until some event occurs or some act on the part of the mortgagor is done which causes it to crystallize into a fixed security.

The events which cause a floating charge to crystallize and become fixed are usually specified in the debenture document and include such matters as the company going into liquidation, whether compulsorily or voluntarily, or a bailiff seizing and selling any company asset under a levy of execution on behalf of the company creditors, or a landlord distraining to recover arrears of rent. Sometimes there is a clause to the effect that if the company disposes of its assets in such a way which is not in the normal course of business, then the debenture holder can step in. The most usual event, however, in the bank's form is when the company is called upon to repay its borrowings and defaults. The floating charge then crystallizes and in such circumstances the bank usually appoints an administrative receiver to obtain repayment of the borrowing by the realization of the company assets caught by the security. Prior to the Insolvency Act, 1986 the person(s) appointed was known simply as a receiver, but now, most unfortunately, there is this new term the administrative receiver which serves more to confuse than to clarify.

In *re Woodroffes (Musical Instruments) Ltd* (1985) it was held that a floating charge crystallizes automatically on a company ceasing business or ceasing to be a going concern. Also, if the debenture holder serves notice on the company converting the floating charge to a fixed charge, then this is effective.

ADVANTAGES OF THE FLOATING CHARGE

The floating charge developed in the United Kingdom in the late nineteenth century, with the increase in numbers of limited-liability companies, although it was not until 1961 that it was introduced into Scotland. The floating charge has the advantages of 'simplicity, convenience, and, above all, flexibility' according to the Review Committee on Insolvency Law and Practice which reported in 1982, for it creates an 'effective and comprehensive' security which can cover the entire undertaking of a company, while leaving the company and its officers free to deal with those assets in ordinary day-to-day affairs and business. The need therefore, as abroad, to be continually charging assets and then seeking their release by the mortgagee is avoided.

From a lender's point of view the security is all-embracing and has the attraction that in the necessary circumstances a receiver can be appointed to take immediate control of the business, and to continue trading, if appropriate. Thus, unnecessary time is not lost in legal processes and problems can be gripped quickly. The receiver is able to sell the entire business as a going concern, or he can hive profitable parts down to a new company, and preserve employment. A management 'buy-out' or investment by an interested party can be facilitated after the weight of debt in the receivership company has been dropped, as unsecured non-preferential creditors have no rights.

Understandably, unsecured creditors have occasionally commented unfavourably on the advantage derived by the holder of a floating charge and some critical evidence was placed before the Insolvency Law Review Committee on that issue. The Committee, however, firmly recognized the desirability of retaining the floating charge concept, as it had 'become so fundamental a part of the financial structure of the United Kingdom that its abolition cannot be contemplated'. Certainly, if it ever ceased to exist, it is hard to see the banks being prepared to advance monies to the extent that they now do, or to see them supporting companies in difficulties for as long as they have done, as in the recession of the early 1980s.

DISADVANTAGES OF THE FLOATING CHARGE

However, common as it is as a bank security where large lendings have been made, the floating charge does suffer from several major disadvantages and possible problems. These are:

The hardening period[76]
Under the provisions of s. 245 Insolvency Act 1986 a floating charge will be invalid where it is given within twelve months of the commencement of the winding up of the company or a petition for an administration order, if the company is at the time when it is given unable to pay its debts or becomes unable to pay them as a consequence of the transaction.

Where the floating charge is given in favour of a person connected with the company the period involved is two years and the question of solvency is irrelevant. However, in both instances the charge will be valid to the extent of the aggregate of –

'(a) the value of so much of the consideration for the creation of the charge

76 See Appendix I, Q. 37 (September 1980).

as consists of money paid, or goods or services supplied, to the company at the same time as, or after, the creation of the charge,

(*b*) the value of so much of that consideration as consists of the discharge or reduction, at the same time as, or after, the creation of the charge, of any debt of the company, and

(*c*) the amount of such interest (if any) as is payable on the amount falling within paragraph (*a*) or (*b*) in pursuance of any agreement under which the money was so paid, the goods or services were so supplied or the debt was so discharged or reduced.'

For bankers in effect this means that a floating charge will be invalid where it was given within twelve months of the commencement of the winding up of the company or the presentation of a petition for an administration order unless it is *proved*:

(*a*) that the company was solvent *immediately after* the giving of the charge, or

(*b*) monies were paid to the company, when the security was given or subsequently on the basis that the security was given for that new advance.

It will be a question of fact as to whether or not the company was solvent at the time of the creation of the charge, with the inability to pay its debts being defined in s. 123 Insolvency Act 1986, which states:

(1) A company is deemed unable to pay its debts –

(a) if a creditor (by assignment or otherwise) to whom the company is indebted in a sum exceeding £750 then due has served on the company, by leaving it at the company's registered office, a written demand (in the prescribed form) requiring the company to pay the sum so due and the company has for three weeks thereafter neglected to pay the sum or to secure or compound for it to the reasonable satisfaction of the creditor, or

(b) if, in England and Wales, execution or other process issued on a judgment, decree or order of any court in favour of a creditor of the company is returned unsatisfied in whole or in part, or

. . . .

(e) if it is proved to the satisfaction of the court that the company is unable to pay its debts as they fall due.

(2) A company is also deemed unable to pay its debts if it is proved to the satisfaction of the court that the value of the company's assets is less than the amount of its liabilities, taking into account its contingent and prospective liabilities.

. . . .

The object of s. 245 is to protect other creditors, in view of the all-embracing nature of the security. If one creditor who has been owed money for some time takes a floating charge over his debtor company's undertaking, he might do so at the expense of the others, whereas if a lender makes new monies available then ethically it is more understandable that he should be allowed in law to protect his position in respect of that new lending by taking this type of security. All floating charges are registered at Companies Registration Office, and as the charge will be advertised its creation may be noticed by an alert creditor. This means that he can take steps, if he wishes, to put the company into liquidation to protect his own position before s. 245 ceases to apply. However, any payment made by the administrative receiver to the debenture holder out of floating asset realizations before liquidation may not be reclaimed by the liquidator, the court holding that such a payment was valid as a payment by the company's agent (the administrative receiver) in discharge of its obligations (*Mace Builders (Glasgow) Ltd* v. *Lunn* (1986)).

It may be noted in passing that under the Companies Act 1929 this hardening period was six months, but in the 1948 Act the period was extended to twelve months. Now it is twelve months for an existing creditor, but two years if that party is a connected person.

Understandably, limited companies are reluctant sometimes to give a floating charge because if the company is having liquidity problems or there is any question of insolvency then it could well find itself under increased pressure from its creditors as a result, when they see the advertisement of the registration of the security.

None the less, banks have found themselves better protected than might at first sight appear to be the case, when they take a floating charge to secure an existing lending on *current* account. In that event the Rule in *Clayton's Case* operates in favour of the bank, for, as turnover passes through the current account, credits repay the unsecured debt at the date when the charge was given, and debit turnover creates a new advance subsequent to the creation of the floating charge and in consideration for the charge, and so the overdraft turns over and the floating charge becomes a valid security for all or part of the new borrowing. This principle was first accepted in *Re Thomas Mortimer Ltd* (1925). There, the company borrowed from National Provincial Bank and in January 1924 it gave the bank a limited debenture for £50 000 when the overdraft was £58 000. Shortly afterwards Thomas Mortimer Ltd was placed into liquidation. In the meantime the bank account, in summary form, appeared as follows:

1924		*Debit*	*Credit*	*Balance*
January	Balance b/f			Dr. £58 000
	Payments in		£40 000	Dr. 18 000
	Payments out	£50 000		Dr. 68 000
March	Floating charge valid for new monies:			£50 000

The principle was followed in the Court of Appeal in *Re Yeovil Glove Co. Ltd* (1964). Of course, a floating charge would be valid if the lending were made on loan account in consideration for the giving of security, but for one year a floating charge would not safely secure an existing advance on loan account. Also, it must be remembered that a floating charge will not be available to support any guarantee liabilities of the company until the twelve months has passed. This means that in a group situation, where there are cross-guarantees between the companies, secured by debentures incorporating floating charges, if and when consideration is being given to the appointment of an administrative receiver, upon a debenture which is less than one year old, the validity of the floating charge must be examined against the turnover in each company's *own* account.

The claims of preferential creditors

The second disadvantage of the floating charge is that under s. 40 Insolvency Act 1986 in an administrative receivership, and under s. 175 Insolvency Act 1986 in a liquidation, preferential creditors such as PAYE, VAT, etc. must be paid in priority to the holder of the floating charge out of the floating-asset realizations.[77] This means that when the floating charge is being valued it is important for the lender always to ascertain the extent of preferential creditors and to deduct the total of such creditors from the written-down value of the floating assets. It is only the floating charge which is disadvantaged in this way and the holder of a fixed charge is not so affected. Consequently, if the debenture incorporates a fixed charge over land and perhaps debtors, then these assets will not be subject to the claims of preferential creditors.[78] It can be seen therefore that this is one reason why the giving of a fixed charge over book debts has become of value to the lending banker.

Subsequent fixed charges

Another disadvantage of the floating charge is that a company may create a fixed legal or equitable charge subsequently over the assets which have been charged by way of the floating charge and, if it does so, the basic legal position is that such a fixed charge would have priority over the floating charge. Consequently, it is usual for the debenture document to contain an agreement between the lender and the company whereby the company undertakes not to create any subsequent mortgage or charge which would rank *pari passu* or in priority to the floating charge. This clause is then recorded on Form 395, when the floating charge is registered at Companies Registration Office pursuant to s. 395 Companies Act 1985, and this is deemed to be notice to the world of the prohibition on the creation of superior fixed charges, and thus any lender taking a subsequent fixed charge would become aware of the position as a result of his own search.

Alternatively, the protection of the floating-charge holder can be secured by asking the company to pass a special resolution authorising the giving of the floating charge and incorporating in that resolution a restriction not to create a subsequent fixed charge which would rank in priority or *pari passu* to the floating charge. As all special resolutions passed by limited companies have to

77 See Appendix I, Q. 59 (April 1983).
78 See Appendix I, Q. 59 (April 1983).

be filed at Companies Registration Office, this step will protect the floating-charge holder in the same way as did the registration on Form 395 mentioned above, for again it is notice to the world.

Understandably, there must be means available whereby a company can borrow from another source against a fixed charge over a particular asset, as for example if it were buying a factory, and were raising the money from a different lender. In such a case, the company can approach the holder of the floating charge and the latter will give his permission for priority to be given to the new lender against his specific charge. The document whereby this arrangement will be agreed is known as a deed of priority or a letter of priority and it will usually be given under seal by the new lender, the floating-charge holder, and the company, and it will set out the variation to the floating-charge holder's secured position. The asset or assets concerned might be released completely from the charge, or priority up to a certain amount might be given. It is usual in the latter event for interest and other charges to be capable of being added to the principal amount of the priority and in some instances, therefore, in a marginal situation it will be important for the holder of the floating charge to know the rate of interest on the subsequent lender's mortgage and any penal clauses, if he looks for any residual equity in the property.

Priority arrangements can also occur where two or more banks or lenders each have debentures. It must then be clear which assets serve which lender first, and whether up to a certain figure only. Where it is arranged that the proceeds of the realization of the security shall be shared equally, the term *'pari passu'* is frequently used. Alternatively, where the sharing ratio is related to the extent of their respective lendings, or commitments, the phrase *'pro rata'* will be encountered.

The position becomes complex where one lender has priority over some only of the fixed assets and some only of the floating assets, perhaps with limitations as to the priority amount, after which the other secured lender comes in. In every case the amounts involved, whether in sterling, foreign currencies, principal and/or interest, and contingent liabilities secured, must be accurately capable of calculation for the purpose of distributing or sharing realisation proceeds. For example, sometimes the priority document omits to mention how any preferential claim should be treated, and this can lead to argument if one lender has been advancing for wages but another has not.

Diminution in the value of company assets

An accurate valuation of a floating charge is difficult in any event, for while the last balance sheet figures can be taken, and prior charges and preferential creditors can be deducted, the resulting answer will be a historical figure which may bear little relation to what the debenture holder is likely to receive under his floating charge when it crystallizes. If a company goes into liquidation or a receiver is appointed, almost certainly there will have been a period beforehand of trading losses and difficulties, and during this time, almost invariably, the company will have attempted to keep going and to keep its creditors at bay by running down the size of its stock and perhaps even selling off some fixed assets. Debts will have been collected, and the losses incurred will have eroded the general asset base of the company. The lending banker therefore will value his security on a gone-concern basis and in arriving at this assessment he will make proper allowance for the nature of the business, the diminution of assets, and the prospects for the sale of what remains in a receivership or liquidation situation. It is therefore a common experience, unfortunately, when a bank looks to its floating-charge security, that the amount it recovers from the realization of the floating-charge assets through the receiver is invariably considerably less than the balance sheet figures seen earlier, which are calculated on a going-concern basis. Some lenders when looking at each asset write down the figure by a certain percentage, e.g. 40 per cent, but even so there can be no guarantee that any particular formula will be appropriate, and each company situation will be special.

Another factor to allow for, when valuing the floating charge, is the cost of realization and the expenses which will be incurred by the administrative receiver and his valuers.

A more recent problem which has been highlighted by case law is that relating to retention of title. This is where a supplier of goods to the company retains the title to those goods until they are paid for. In such a situation, the goods themselves might be in possession of the company customer and might even appear in the company's balance sheet, but they are owned by someone else, and when an administrative receiver is appointed under the debenture he finds that he is unable to deal with these assets and unable to sell them for the benefit of the debenture holder (*Aluminium Industrie Vaasen BV* v. *Romalpa Aluminium Ltd* (1976)). The terms of the retention-of-title contract might appear in a specific contract or in an invoice and sometimes the purchasing company itself is unaware of the terms upon which the goods have been supplied. Of course, the opposite can be true, in that if the company in which the administrative receiver is appointed has sold its goods on retention of title terms, it is possible that the administrative receiver might be able to recover such items from the purchaser, if he has not paid for them or will not pay.

Different types of retention of title clauses are used in trade and in two cases subsequent to the Romalpa decision the position has been somewhat alleviated for the debenture holder. In *Re Bond Worth Ltd* (1979) the company manufactured carpets and in that process used an acrylic fibre which it bought from Monsanto Chemical Co. This fibre was mixed with other materials in the carpet-manufacturing process and generally received several treatments before the completed carpet emerged. Receivers were appointed by Bond Worth's debenture holders and Monsanto claimed contractual rights to the fibre and the proceeds of sale of the carpets under the terms of trade which had been extended by confirmation notes issued by Monsanto when it accepted orders. The receivers applied to the court for directions as to the construction and effect of that contract and it was held that there was no simple reservation of title clause in the contract and therefore that the Romalpa principle did not apply. It was said that title had passed on delivery of the goods to Bond Worth, and that if Monsanto had any rights then these could be by way of trust or as a security. The court did not accept the trust argument, as Bond Worth had been enabled to use the fibre in its own business for its own benefit. Thus Monsanto's only claim could be by way of a security and the court saw that, in effect, Monsanto had attempted to create a floating charge over the fibre as security for any monies outstanding to it. Bond Worth had been constituted a trustee over the assets for the purpose of that security. However, as the floating charge had not been registered at Companies Registration Office the charge failed, and the receivers for the appointing debenture holders were entitled to the fibre, and the sale proceeds of the carpets, to distribute in accordance with their statutory duties.

In *Borden UK Ltd* v. *Scottish Timber Products Ltd* (1979) Borden produced a resin which was sold to Scottish Timber Products Ltd which was a company manufacturing chipboard. Scottish Timber mixed the resin with a hardening material and with wood chippings, to manufacture the chipboard. A receiver was appointed to Scottish Timber by its debenture holders, and Borden claimed that, as £320 000 was due to them for resin supplied, they were entitled to trace their rights to the monies coming into Scottish Timber's hands, when it was trading, and in receivership, under the terms of the trading agreement between the two companies. They also claimed that the chipboard was charged to them as security. In the Court of Appeal it was found that there was no fiduciary relationship nor any bailor/bailee relationship between Borden and Scottish Timber under the contract, which had allowed Scottish Timber to use the resin before it was paid for. Moreover, that contract had not given Borden any rights to the manufactured chipboard and consequently neither the end product, the chipboard, nor the proceeds of sale of the chipboard, was a security for the supplier of the resin. The Court recognized the great problem which would arise in practice in following the tracing argument where goods are mixed in a manufacturing process and took the view that where two separate suppliers find their products mixed by the purchaser then any tracing rights are lost when those products have lost their identity.

In *Henry Lennox (Industrial Engines) Ltd* v. *Grahame Puttick Ltd* (1983) a retention-of-title clause in a contract was upheld, as the goods supplied by the seller could still be identified and separated from those of the buyer. These goods were motor engines which were fixed by bolts into diesel generators; they were not changed in any way and each was still identifiable by a serial number.

Following futher examination of the problems created by reservation of title clauses and 'mixed' goods in *Clough Mill Ltd* v. *Geoffrey Martin* (1984) the following picture emerges from case law over the last 10 years or so.

A seller can retain his title to his goods after delivery provided that those goods are still capable of being identified in their original state, but once they lose their separate identity by being changed or by becoming part of something else the right of retention is lost. However, if they are merely fixed or attached to something else without any alteration and if they can be detached without damage they will not have lost their separate identity and title can be retained. When goods lose their separate identity the clause will operate as a charge on the new goods in the supplier's favour, but as such must be registered at Companies Registration Office, assuming private individuals or partnerships are not involved.

Where the supplier knows that his goods after being supplied will be on-sold, his rights will extend to the sale proceeds, but in that event the proceeds must be kept on a separate account. The seller's rights may extend either by way of retention, or, dependent on the wording of the contract, as a charge.

It must be remembered therefore that assets shown in a company's balance sheet could be subject to retention-of-title agreements, and, when valuing the debenture, allowance should be made not only for this but also for the more complex problems which can arise for the receiver, if appointed. The latter's whole approach to the receivership can be affected by the extent of the retention-of-title position. He will find himself uncertain as to whether he can safely deal with stock, for example, in the company's warehouse, and will not know whether he can continue using it in manufacturing processes, or whether he exposes himself to an action for conversion if he does so. Thus his decision whether to continue trading, or close down the business, becomes more difficult, and frequently he has to enter into very urgent negotiations with the suppliers of the stock. Moreover, he finds it difficult to calculate his potential profits, should he decide to trade on while seeking a purchaser for the business. As has been seen, he can also find himself involved in complex legal cases when proceedings are brought against him.

Prior charges

In addition to the effect of retention-of-title clauses in connection with assets when valuing a debenture, care must be taken to ensure that any relevant entries on the liabilities side of a balance sheet are deducted from the asset valuation. For example, a property might be entered in the balance sheet at its cost, or current valuation, but a mortgage on that factory, to an outside lender, might be shown on the liabilities side.[79] Similarly, plant and machinery, motor vehicles etc. could be subject to hire purchase agreements, and the extent of those must be ascertained and deducted to see if there is any equity in the asset; frequently this is not the case. Of course, where the bank has given priority to another lender, it will be more aware of the position. Thus for

79 See Appendix I, Q. 48 (September 1981).

example, if it has allowed the company to factor its debts then it will be aware that the entry for debtors in the balance sheet should be excluded from the valuation of its floating charge or debenture, as invariably the factoring company takes a first charge over the balance of debtors outstanding at any one time, and rarely does any equity arise in that connection.

Action by execution creditors

When a company is in financial difficulties, it is possible that writs will be issued against it, and that some of its creditors will have obtained judgment. These creditors can enforce their judgment by levying exection over company assets and the bailiff might then seize and sell stock, to the disadvantage of the debenture holder, unless the latter is alert and intervenes by appointing the administrative receiver. To guard against this possibility, the directors of the company should be questioned whether any creditors have obtained judgment, and, if so, whether satisfactory arrangements to settle the debts have been agreed. It must be remembered that whereas County Court judgments are advertised, High Court judgments which involve larger sums are not advertised, and to that extent the degree of risk is greater. In addition to judgment creditors, if property is rented, and rent is in arrears, the landlord is able to levy distress and need not obtain judgment beforehand. In all these cases, if the distress or levy is completed, and the assets are seized and sold without the bank knowing, or before the charge can be crystallized and an administrative receiver can be appointed, then the outside creditor is entitled to retain the proceeds of his levy. Similarly, if that creditor has served a garnishee order on a third party owing monies to the company and the garnishee order has been made absolute, it is too late for the receiver to intervene.

Costs

Before an administrative receiver is appointed, it is possible that the debenture holder will require legal advice and this can be costly. Moreover, the administrative receiver himself will incur expenses in carrying out his duties, and he will of course also require his own remuneration, based either on a percentage of realizations or on another formula, such as a time cost basis, agreed with the debenture holder. Occasionally, the administrative receiver will continue trading while he assesses the business and, if so, he aquires his own trade creditors and naturally these will have to be paid off. If his trading is carried on at a loss, then those losses will have to be covered from the eventual realizations in the administrative receivership. Thus if the administrative receiver finds himself unable to sell the business as a going concern, he will have to close it down, dismiss the employees and sell the assets piecemeal. This will involve professional valuation of assets and the costs of auctions, and it can be seen therefore that the outgoings in a administrative receivership may be very heavy before monies become available for the debenture holder. There is a further risk for the administrative receiver, and the debenture holder, in that it will be remembered that preferential creditors must be paid ahead of the debenture holder in respect of floating-asset realisations. No problems arise if the administrative receiver closes down the business in the early days, but if he trades on, and uses floating assets which are lost in the trading process, by the incurring of losses, so that ultimately he finds himself unable to pay the preferential creditors as at the date of his appointment, then he becomes personally liable to those preferential creditors (*Westminster City Council* v. *Haste* (1950)). Moreover, it was held in *Inland Revenue* v. *Goldblatt and another* (1972) that the administrative receiver is under a duty to pay the preferential creditors, and if he fails to do so both he and the debenture holder are liable to them. In that case the administrative receiver knew or ought to have known that there were preferential creditors and it was inferred that the debenture holder also knew and that he therefore was liable as a constructive trustee.

VALUATION EXAMPLE

Z Ltd manufactures textile machinery parts. The trading position is known to be deteriorating and the bank has asked the directors to produce a statement of affairs, as it wishes to assess the likely value of its debenture security, should an administrative receivership become necessary. The directors produce the following figures:

Assets		
Freehold and leasehold properties		£220 000
Goodwill		80 000
Plant and machinery		90 000
Motor vehicles		35 000
Stock of goods, parts etc.		160 000
Debtors		85 000
		670 000
Less: Liabilities		
Directors' loans	£70 000	
Preferential creditors	45 000	
Trade creditors	140 000	
Bank	315 000	
		570 000
Represented by issued capital		£100 000

With total assets shown as being worth £670 000 against a bank borrowing of £315 000, and preferential creditors only amounting to £45,000, the bank considers itself fully secured on a going-concern basis.

However, further questioning of the directors, and an assessment of the individual items in the balance sheet on a gone-concern approach, reveal that the position is nothing like as good, as will now be described.

Fixed charge

Properties These comprise three units. One is freehold, and was bought for £180 000 some six years ago, and has been included at cost in the statement of affairs. No recent professional valuation has been undertaken, but the branch know it is situated in an area which has become an 'industrial wasteland', and there are several factories there unoccupied which have been up for sale for many months. Vandalism is becoming a feature, and similar problems could be encountered with Z's unit if the business were shut down.

The other two units are leasehold, and the leases will be forfeit upon a liquidation or receivership. Annual rentals total £80 000 and there are arrears for the past two quarters. The bank feels it must discount the value of £40 000 put on these leases by the directors. The bank therefore extends a valuation of £100 000 on a forced-sale basis for the properties.

Goodwill This has been included in the balance sheet for many years and represents the value which the company attributed to its position in the trade and special know-how, in respect of the machinery parts it manufactures. Some patents have been filed, but it is unlikely that in a shut-down situation any value would be realised.

Debtors The bank has a fixed charge over book debts, and the directors, upon request, produce an age-related list of their major customers who owe amounts over £5 000. Collection seems, in the main, to be fairly well up to date, but you consider it prudent to bring the figure of £85 000 in at 75 per cent for gone-concern purposes, knowing the difficulties that a receiver could meet with counter-claims etc. Valuation therefore is £63 750.

Valuation of fixed charge

Properties	£100 000
Goodwill	nil
Debtors	63 750
	£163 750

Floating charge

Plant and machinery This has become somewhat out of date, because of technological changes, and is unlikely to be worth much at auction. For forced-sale valution purposes the bank assesses it at 33⅓ per cent of the figure shown, which was taken from the company's last balance sheet by the directors. Valuation is therefore £30 000.

Motor vehicles The directors confirm there is no outstanding hire-purchase on these, and upon seeing a list of the cars involved you agree that £35 000 should be realized.

Stock This represents manufactured units and unprocessed materials, and is a major item; you know it is specialized. One of the reasons for the company's present difficulties is the recession in the textile industry and reduction in orders. It may well not be easy to realize in a receivership. Upon being questioned the directors state that reservation-of-title agreements cover materials valued at £60 000. The bank considers it prudent to extend a valuation of 40 per cent of the remaining value, viz.

$$£160\,000 - £60\,000 = £100\,000 \text{ at 40 per cent} = £40\,000.$$

Preferential creditors You question the directors closely as regards the breakdown of the figure of £45 000 and learn that PAYE and VAT arrears have been included. You are satisfied that the figure is not significantly understated, but remind the directors that in a receivership or liquidation these creditors will be paid first out of floating-assets realizations. While the bank will have a preferential claim for wages advanced, it appears that this may be academic as, even on a forced-sale basis, floating-asset sales should be sufficient to meet all preferential creditors, including the bank whose maximum claim could only be £32 000, being £800 per employee, of which there are 40.

Valuation of floating charge

Plant and machinery	£30 000
Motor vehicles	35 000
Stock	40 000
	105 000
Less: Preferential creditors	
(excluding bank)	45 000
	£60 000

Valuation of debenture (gone concern)

Fixed charge	£163 750
Floating charge	60 000
	223 750
Less: Estimated receivership costs and remuneration, say	20 000
	£203 750

TYPICAL BANK DEBENTURE FORM

As has been noted, the usual bank debenture form will incorporate a specific fixed charge over certain company assets, and a floating charge over the remainder. The charge form will usually include some or all the following provisions:

(*a*) That the security is available for all liabilities of the company whether alone or jointly, and whether for principal advances or for contingent liabilities on bonds, guarantees or otherwise.

(*b*) The charge will be expressed to be a continuing security to overcome the effect of the Rule in *Clayton's Case*.

(*c*) The company will covenant to pay all monies secured on demand and s. 103 Law of Property Act 1925 will be excluded so that the bank's power of sale and ability to appoint an administrative receiver becomes enforceable immediately upon default. In addition, the bank's rights to appoint an administrative receiver will be covered for any adverse situations which might arise, such as the presentation of a petition against the company for liquidation, or the appointment of an administrator, or should a receiver be appointed over any part of the company's assets or undertaking by a third party. Also, if a levy of execution is carried out by the sheriff or distress by a landlord, or if the company ceases business or stops making payment generally to its creditors, if it fails to make agreed interest payments, or if it attempts to dispose of the whole of its assets or undertaking in a way inconsistent with the normal course of business, then the debenture holder will be entitled to appoint an administrative receiver.

(*d*) A first specific charge will be granted by way of legal mortgage on the scheduled mortgaged premises and a first specific equitable charge on all other company premises owned both now or at any time in the future. The company will undertake to deposit with the bank the title documents of any property acquired and to execute a legal mortgage if called upon to do so.

(*e*) A fixed charge over the company's present and future book and other debts will be created, and the company will undertake to pay all such monies received into its account with the bank, and agree not to assign, sell or factor these without the consent of the bank.

(*f*) A fixed charge over goodwill, patents, trade marks and the uncalled capital of the company will be granted.

(*g*) Thereafter the debenture will grant the bank a floating charge over all other property and assets of the company and its undertaking.

(*h*) The company will covenant that it will not create any fixed charge which would rank in priority or *pari passu* with the floating charge.

(*i*) Some bank forms incorporate a covenant whereby the company agrees that it will maintain a certain ratio of assets cover to the level of its borrowing, and undertakes that it will inform the bank if this falls below the specified level. The right to appoint an administrative receiver may arise if this covenant is breached.

(*j*) The company will undertake to advise the bank or any accountant appointed by the bank of any information relating to the business of the company at any time as required by the bank.

(*k*) The company will covenant to keep all buildings and fixed and movable plant and other fittings and implements in a good state of repair and to keep the company assets adequately insured with a reputable insurance company, acceptable to the bank. It will covenant to pay all premiums regularly and on their due date. If the company fails to do so, the bank will be empowered to insure as necessary and to recoup the cost by debiting the company's account, or through its security when it is enforced.

(*l*) It will be stated that when the security has become enforceable the bank may appoint any person or persons as administrative receiver or receivers, to act jointly or severally, either under seal or in writing. The administrative receivers will be expressed to be the agent of the company who will be solely responsible for their acts. An administrative receiver will be given power to take possession of the mortgaged premises and to collect all assets and undertake their sale and take any legal action in the name of the company as necessary. He will be empowered to carry on the business and to manage it, as he thinks fit, and to employ the company's workforce in larger or smaller numbers as necessary, and generally to do all things which the company is capable of doing.

(*m*) The debenture form will state that the bank will not be liable for the administrative receiver's acts or defaults either before the company is placed in liquidation or subsequently.

(*n*) One clause will deal with the administrative receiver's right to remuneration, out of the realization proceeds of the company's assets. This may be expressed as a percentage of such funds (e.g. 5 per cent) or may give the debenture holder the right to agree any other rate with the administrative receiver. It may be said that this remuneration and all other costs shall be payable before any distribution to the debenture holder or to preferential creditors.

(*o*) There will usually be a clause stating that any notice which it is necessary to serve on the company, such as demand to repay, may be served at the company's registered office and that such notice shall be deemed to be served whether or not it is accepted or returned. It is usual for the notice to be capable of being given under hand and under the signature of any manager, or director, of the bank.

Most of these clauses are self-explanatory and, while a debenture document is usually lengthy, the object is to give full freedom and protection for both the bank and the administrative receiver (see Fig. 10.1).

A modern debenture may just refer to the statutory powers in Schedule 1 of the Insolvency Act 1986 which devolve upon the administrative receiver, except in so far as any are excluded.

TAKING THE SECURITY

As with any company security, when taking a debenture the bank must consult the company's memorandum and articles of association. In the memorandum it must be ensured that the purpose of the lending is consistent with the objects clause and that the company has power to borrow; in the case of a trading company there is an implied power to borrow and charge security. The articles of association should be examined to see whether there are any restrictions on the directors' delegated powers. Here the security clerk should look to see if there are any monetary limitations on the borrowing powers and whether the directors are enabled to give the security, a debenture, without any further formalities – such as the permission of members in general meeting. It will be necessary to ensure that a quorum of disinterested directors was present when the necessary resolutions were passed, if the articles so require. If, however, the company has adopted article 84 of Table A Companies Act 1948, or Article 94 Table A Companies Act 1985, even if a director is personally interested in the giving of the security his presence may be counted for quorum purposes and he may vote.

If the debenture incorporates a legal mortgage over land in addition to the floating charge, it will be necessary for the bank to carry through all the usual steps in connection with the perfecting of the legal mortgage over the land.

In connection with the debenture itself, the security requirements will be:

(*a*) The copy of the board resolution agreeing to give the security is obtained. (Some banks do not take board resolutions and prefer to rely on the Rule in *Turquand's Case*, and simply accept the debenture duly sealed by the company and witnessed by the directors and/or secretary. This is because the danger with any resolution is that it may recite the purpose of the borrowing or security and, if so, the debenture might not then be available for other liabilities of the company to the bank as a continuing security.)

(*b*) The bank's standard form of debenture is completed accurately and if any land is to be legally mortgaged this is usually specified on a schedule. The charge form is sealed by the company in accordance with its articles of

This Debenture made the   day of   19

BETWEEN

                                                        LIMITED

whose registered office is at

(hereinafter called "the Company") of the one part and BANK OF CYPRUS (LONDON) LIMITED of 27-31 Charlotte Street London W1P 4BH (hereinafter called "the Bank") of the other part **WITNESSETH** as follows:—

1.   The Company hereby covenants with the Bank that the Company will on demand in writing pay or discharge to the Bank all moneys and liabilities matured or unmatured whether actual or contingent which are or may at any time hereafter be or become from time to time due owing or incurred to the Bank by the Company or in respect of which the Company may be or become liable to the Bank on any current loan or other account or otherwise in any manner whatsoever including the amount of any note or bill made accepted endorsed discounted or paid and of any liability under any guarantee or indemnity or other instrument whatsoever given or assumed by the Bank for or at the request of the Company (in all cases whether alone or jointly with any other person and whether as principal or surety) and all commission discount and other banking charges including legal costs (as between solicitor and own client) and disbursements and any expenses incurred by the Bank in relation to this Debenture or any other security held by the Bank for the same indebtedness or in enforcing the same together with interest compounded quarterly to the date of repayment at such rate as may be agreed from time to time between the Company and the Bank or according to the usual practice of the Bank as well after as before any demand made or judgment obtained hereunder.

2   The Company as beneficial owner hereby charges all its property and undertaking whatsoever and wheresoever both present and future as a continuing security with the payment and discharge of all moneys and liabilities hereby covenanted to be paid or discharged by the Company and so that such charge shall be:—

(i)   a charge by way of legal mortgage over all the freehold and leasehold property of the Company the title to which is registered at H.M. Land Registry and which is described in the Schedule hereto together with all fixtures and fixed plant and machinery from time to time thereon;

(ii)   a charge by way of legal mortgage over all other freehold and leasehold property now vested in the Company (whether registered at H.M. Land Registry or not) together with all fixtures and fixed plant and machinery from time to time thereon;

(iii)   a first fixed charge over:—

    (a)   the goodwill of the Company;

    (b)   all future freehold and leasehold property of the Company together with all fixtures and fixed plant and machinery from time to time thereon;

    (c)   all and any interests of the Company in land and the proceeds of sale thereof;

    (d)   the uncalled capital of the Company;

    (e)   all stocks shares and other securities now or hereafter owned by the Company;

    (f)   all book debts and other debts and claims (including insurance claims) now and from time to time due or owing to or vested in the Company;

(iv)   a first floating charge over all other the undertaking and assets of the Company both present and future but so that the Company shall not without the consent in writing of the Bank create any mortgage or charge upon and so that no lien shall in any case or in any manner arise on or affect any part of the said undertaking and assets either in priority to or pari passu with the charge hereby created and further that the Company shall have no power without the consent of the Bank to part with or dispose of any part of such undertaking and assets except by way of sale in the ordinary course of its business. Any debentures mortgages or charges hereafter created by the Company (otherwise than in favour of the Bank) shall be expressed to be subject to this Debenture.

3.   The Company shall subject to the rights of any prior mortgagee deposit with the Bank and the Bank during the continuance of this security shall be entitled to hold all deeds and documents of title relating to the Company's freehold and leasehold property (and all insurance policies relating thereto) for the time being and the Company shall on demand in writing made to the Company by the Bank at the cost of the Company execute a valid legal mortgage in such form as the Bank may require of any freehold or leasehold property owned by it from time to time and also any other document which the Bank may from time to time think requisite for the purpose of further securing the payment or discharge to the Bank of the moneys and liabilities hereby secured.

4.   During the continuance of this security the Company shall:—

(i)   furnish to the Bank copies of the trading and profit and loss account and audited balance sheet in respect of each financial year of the Company and its subsidiaries forthwith upon the same becoming available and not in any event later than the expiration of six months from the end of such financial year and permit such person or persons as the Bank may from time to time designate in writing to examine at all reasonable times all books accounts and documents relating to its business and to investigate its affairs and to furnish such person or persons with all such information as he or they may require;

(ii)   maintain the aggregate value of the Company's book debts (excluding debts owing by any subsidiary of the Company) and cash in hand as appearing in the Company's books and of its stock according to the best estimate that can be formed without its being necessary to take stock for the purpose at a sum to be fixed by the Bank from time to time and whenever required by the Bank obtain from the Managing Director of the Company for the time being or if there shall be no Managing Director then from one of the Directors of the Company and furnish to the Bank a certificate showing the said aggregate value;

(iii)   until such time as the Bank shall determine such agency collect as an Agent for the Bank the book debts and other debts and claims hereby charged and pay into the Company's account with the Bank all moneys which it may receive in respect of such debts and claims and not without the prior written consent of the Bank charge or assign the same in favour of any other person or purport to do so and if so required by the Bank execute a legal assignment to the Bank of all or any such debts and claims in such form as the Bank shall require;

(iv)   forthwith notify the Bank of the acquisition of any freehold or leasehold property by the Company.

5.   (a) The Company hereby covenants with the Bank:—

(i)   that the Company will keep all buildings and all fixtures and fittings plant machinery and other effects in good and substantial repair and in good working order and condition and will maintain all such insurances as are normally maintained by prudent companies carrying on similar businesses and in particular will insure and keep insured such of its property as is insurable with an insurance office or underwriters nominated in writing and if so required through brokers appointed by the Bank against loss or damage by fire and such other risks as the Bank may from time to time require in their full replacement value for the time being and if so required by the Bank in the joint names of the Company and the Bank and if not so required the Bank's interest as mortgagee shall be noted on the policy or policies so effected;

(ii)   that the Company will pay all premiums and other moneys necessary for effecting and keeping up such insurance immediately on the same becoming due and will on demand produce to the Bank the policy or policies of such insurance and the receipt for every such payment.

(b) If the Company shall make default in keeping such buildings fixtures fittings plant machinery and other effects in good and substantial repair and in good working order and condition or in effecting or keeping up such insurances as aforesaid the Bank may repair and keep in repair the said buildings and other property or any of them (with liberty for that purpose by itself or its agents to enter upon the freehold and leasehold property of the Company) or may effect or renew any such insurance as aforesaid as the Bank shall think fit.

(c) The Bank shall be entitled to be paid the proceeds of any such policy of insurance (other than in respect of employers' or public liability) and the Company hereby irrevocably instructs the insurer in respect of any such policy to pay such proceeds to the Bank and undertakes to the Bank to issue such further instructions to that effect as the Bank may require.

(d) All moneys received on any insurance whatsoever (other than as aforesaid) shall as the Bank requires be applied either in making good the loss or damage in respect of which the money is received or in or towards discharge of the moneys for the time being hereby secured.

(e) The Company will permit any authorised representative of the Bank at all reasonable times to enter upon any part of the freehold and leasehold property of the Company and of any other property where the Company may be carrying out any contract or other works.

6.   (a) At all times during the continuance of this security the Company will discharge all liabilities which may be incurred by the Company under any of the covenants agreements or obligations contained in or imposed by any lease or tenancy affecting the whole or any part of the freehold and leasehold property of the Company which may have been or may be granted or entered into by the Company or its predecessors in title and all actions losses damages and costs whatsoever in consequence of any claim by any tenant or occupier of the whole or any part of such freehold and leasehold property or any other person or company arising out of any defect in or want of repair to such freehold and leasehold property or any part thereof or out of any failure to perform any such covenant or obligation and in the event of the Company failing upon the request in writing of the Bank to discharge any such liability as aforesaid the Bank may settle liquidate or compound or contest such claim (as it may think fit) and expend such moneys as the Bank may deem necessary for that purpose.

(b) The Company will at all times during the continuance of this security deliver to the Bank the counterparts of or if the same are held by a prior mortgagee copies (certified by the Company or a responsible officer of the Company) of all leases or agreements for tenancy subsisting in respect of any part of the freehold and leasehold property of the Company.

(c) The Company will if so directed by the Bank issue instructions to any tenant of its freehold and leasehold property or any part thereof to pay all rents to the Bank.

7   During the continuance of this security the Company will pay and keep the Bank indemnified against all rates taxes duties charges assessments and outgoings whatsoever (whether parliamentary parochial local or of any other description) which shall be assessed charged or imposed upon or in respect of the freehold and leasehold property of the Company or any part thereof and will on demand produce to the Bank the receipt for every such payment and if the Company shall at any time refuse or neglect to make any such payment or to produce the receipt therefor to the Bank on demand then and in any such case the Bank may pay the same.

8.   The Company will within seven days of receipt thereof give to the Bank a copy of any notice or order or proposal for a notice or order given issued or made by any planning or other authority body or person whatsoever which in any way relates to or affects the freehold and leasehold property of the Company or any part thereof and will if so required by the Bank produce to it the original such notice order or proposal and will take all reasonable and proper steps to comply with such order or notice without delay and will at the request of the Bank make or concur with the Bank in making any objections or representations against or in respect of any such notice or order or proposal for a notice or any appeal against any such order as the Bank may deem expedient and will pay to the Bank any compensation received as a result of any such notice or order.

9   The Company will at all times observe and perform and ensure the observance and performance by any other person or company at any time occupying the freehold and leasehold property of the Company or any part thereof of all restrictive and other covenants to which the same or any part thereof may from time to time be subject all obligations on the part of the Company in any lease or tenancy agreement all building regulations and all restrictions conditions and stipulations for the time being affecting the same or any part thereof or the mode of user or enjoyment of the same and provide to the Bank on request such evidence of such observance or performance as the Bank shall require and within three days will deliver to the Bank any notice or proceedings served by any landlord and relating to any alleged breach of the terms of the relevant lease or tenancy.

10   The Company will not without the Bank's previous consent in writing create or purport or attempt to create any mortgage charge or encumbrance on the freehold and leasehold property of the Company or any part thereof nor in any way dispose of the equity of redemption thereof or any interest therein.

11.   (a) The Company will not erect or make any building erection improvement material change or addition on or to the freehold and leasehold property of the Company or any part thereof nor make any material change in the user thereof or of any part thereof nor make any application therefor nor proceed in accordance with any permission therefor without in any such case the previous written consent of the Bank.

(b) Subject as aforesaid the Company will apply to the Local Planning Authority as defined by the Town and Country Planning Acts for any necessary permission for any of the aforesaid matters and will give to the Bank notice of such permission if granted within seven days of the receipt of the same.

(c) Where at the date hereof or at any time during the continuance of this security the freehold and leasehold property of the Company or any part thereof is intended to be developed or is in the course of development the Company will proceed diligently and to the satisfaction of the Bank and any competent authority with such development in all respects in conformity with the planning and bye-law consents relative thereto.

(d) The Company will not do or omit or suffer to be done or omitted any act matter or thing in on or respecting the freehold and leasehold property of the Company or any part thereof which shall contravene any of the provisions of the Town and Country Planning Acts.

(e) The Company will execute and do at the expense of the Company all such work and things whatsoever as may now or at any time during the continuance of this security be directed or required by any national or local or other public authority to be executed or done upon or in respect of the freehold and leasehold property of the Company or any part thereof or by the owner or occupier thereof.

(f) The Company will on request produce to or provide for the Bank such documents or information relating to the freehold and leasehold property of the Company or the development thereof as the Bank shall require.

12   The Company will duly observe and perform the provisions of every offer letter and/or loan or other agreement which has been or may now or at any time hereafter during the continuance of this security be issued by the Bank to the Company.

13.   The Company shall not without the previous written consent of the Bank be entitled to exercise any of the powers of leasing or of agreeing to lease or of accepting surrenders conferred on mortgagors whether by the Law of Property Act 1925 or otherwise.

14   This security shall not be considered as satisfied or discharged by any intermediate payment of the whole or part of the moneys hereby secured but shall constitute and be a continuing security to the Bank notwithstanding any settlement of account or other matter or thing whatsoever and shall be in addition to and shall not operate so as in any way to prejudice or affect the security created by any deposit which may have already been made with the Bank of any title deeds or any other documents or any other securities which the Bank may now or at any time hereafter hold for or in respect of the moneys and liabilities hereby secured or any part thereof.

15.   The Bank shall in the event of its receiving notice that the Company has encumbered or disposed of the property hereby charged or any part thereof be entitled to close the then current or loan or other account or accounts (as the case may be) of the Company or any of them and to open a new account or accounts with the Company and no money paid in or carried to the credit of the Company in any such new account shall be appropriated towards or have the effect of discharging any part of the amount due to the Bank on the said closed account or accounts at the time when it received such notice as aforesaid and if the Bank does not in fact open such new account or accounts it shall nevertheless be treated as if it had done so at the time when it received or was affected by such notice and as from that time all payments made by the Company to the Bank shall be credited or treated as having been credited to such new account or accounts and no such payments shall operate to reduce the amount due from the Company to the Bank at the time when it received or was affected by such notice but this clause shall not prejudice any security which apart from this clause the Bank would have had for the discharge by the Company of liabilities incurred after that time.

16.   A demand for payment or any other demand or notice under this security may be made or given by any director manager or officer of the Bank or of any branch thereof by letter addressed to the Company and sent by ordinary pre-paid post to or left at the registered office of the Company or its last known place of business and shall be deemed if posted to have been made or given at 10 a.m. on the day following the date of posting.

17.   The restrictions on the right of consolidating mortgage securities which is contained in Section 93 of the Law of Property Act 1925 shall not apply to this security.

18.   The statutory power of sale shall be deemed to arise and be immediately exercisable at any time after any moneys owing on this security shall have been demanded without regard to section 103 of the Law of Property Act 1925 (which section shall not apply to this security or any sale made pursuant hereto) AND on any sale by the Bank the Bank may (i) sell the fixtures and machinery comprised in the freehold and leasehold property of the Company or any part thereof either together with the property to which they are affixed or separately and detached therefrom and/or (ii) sell the property hereby charged or any part thereof for a price payable with or without interest by instalments over such period and in any such manner as the Bank may think fit.

19-   (a) At any time after the Bank shall have demanded payment in respect of any moneys or liabilities hereby secured or if requested by the Company the Bank may appoint by writing any person or persons (whether an officer of the Bank or not) to be a receiver and manager or receivers and managers (hereinafter called "the Receiver" which expression shall where the context so admits include the plural and any substituted receiver and manager or receivers and managers and so that where more than one receiver and manager is appointed they may be given power to act jointly and/or severally) of all or any part of the property hereby charged;

(b) The Bank may from time to time determine the remuneration of the Receiver and may remove the Receiver and appoint another in his place;

(c) The Receiver shall (so far as the law permits) be the agent of the Company (which shall alone be personally liable for acts defaults and remuneration) and shall have and be entitled to exercise all powers conferred by the Law of Property Act 1925 in the same way as if the Receiver had been duly appointed thereunder and in particular by way of addition to but without hereby limiting any general powers hereinbefore referred to (and without prejudice to the Bank's powers) the Receiver shall have power in the name of the Company or otherwise to do the following things namely:—

(i)   to take possession of collect and get in all or any part of the property hereby charged and for that purpose to take any proceedings (including proceedings for the winding up of the Company) as he shall think fit;

(ii)   to carry on and manage or concur in carrying on and managing the business and any activities of the Company or any part thereof;

(iii)   to borrow money from the Bank or others on the security of the property hereby charged or otherwise;

(iv)   to sell let or lease or concur in selling letting or leasing and to vary the terms of terminate or accept surrenders of leases or tenancies of the property hereby charged or any part thereof in such manner and for such term with or without a premium with such rights relating to other parts thereof and containing such covenants on the part of the Company and generally on such terms and conditions (including the payment of money to a lessee or tenant on a surrender) as he in his absolute discretion shall think fit and without prejudice to the generality of the foregoing any such sale may be for cash (payable in a lump sum or in such instalments with or without interest as the Receiver may think fit) shares stock or debentures or other valuable consideration and any such shares stock or debentures shall ipso facto become charged to the Bank on the terms hereof so far as applicable and the Receiver shall have the power to execute a formal legal charge thereof in favour of the Bank in such form as it may require;

(v)   to promote or concur in promoting a company to purchase the property hereby charged or any part thereof on such terms as he shall think fit;

(vi)   to make any arrangement or compromise which he shall think fit;

(vii)   to make and effect all repairs improvements and insurances as he shall think fit;

(viii)   to appoint managers officers contractors and agents for all or any of the aforesaid purposes upon such terms as to remuneration or otherwise as he may determine;

(ix)   to do all such other acts and things as may be considered to be incidental or conducive to any of the matters or powers aforesaid and which he lawfully may or can do;

PROVIDED NEVERTHELESS THAT the Receiver shall not be authorised to exercise any of the aforesaid powers if and insofar and so long as the Bank shall in writing exclude the same whether in or at the time of his appointment or subsequently.

20.   The statutory powers of sale leasing and accepting surrenders exercisable by the Bank hereunder are hereby extended so as to authorise the Bank whether in its own name or in that of the Company to grant a lease or leases of the whole or any part or parts of the freehold and leasehold property of the Company with such rights relating to other parts thereof and containing such covenants on the part of the Company and generally on such terms and conditions (including the payment of money to a lessee or tenant on a surrender) and whether or not at a premium as the Bank in its absolute discretion shall think fit.

21.   The Company hereby irrevocably appoints the Bank and the Receiver jointly and also severally the Attorney and Attorneys of the Company for the Company and in its name and on its behalf and as its act and deed or otherwise to execute seal deliver and otherwise perfect any deed assurance agreement instrument or act which may be required or may be deemed proper for any of the purposes hereof.

22.   All powers of the Receiver hereunder may be exercised by the Bank whether as Attorney of the Company or otherwise and whether or not the Receiver shall have been appointed.

23.   In no circumstances shall the Bank or the Receiver be liable to account to the Company as a mortgagee in possession or otherwise for any moneys not actually received by them respectively.

24.   Any moneys received under the powers hereby conferred shall subject to the payment of any claims having priority to this Debenture be paid or applied in the following order of priority:—

(a) in satisfaction of all costs charges and expenses properly incurred and payments properly made by the Bank or the Receiver and of the remuneration of the Receiver;

(b) in or towards satisfaction of the moneys outstanding and hereby secured;

(c) as to any surplus to the person or persons entitled thereto.

Fig.10.1   *(contd)*   287

25. All costs charges and expenses incurred hereunder by the Bank and any receiver appointed by the Bank and all other moneys paid by the Bank in perfecting or otherwise in connection with this security or in respect of the property hereby charged including (without prejudice to the generality of the foregoing) all moneys expended by the Bank under clauses 5 (b) and 7 hereof and all moneys advanced or paid by the Bank to any Receiver for the purposes set out in clause 19 hereof and all costs of the Bank of all proceedings for enforcement of the security hereby constituted or for obtaining payment of the moneys and liabilities hereby secured (whether or not such costs charges expenses and moneys or part thereof would be allowable upon a party and party or solicitor and own client taxation by the Court) shall be recoverable from the Company as a debt and may be debited to any account of the Company and shall bear interest accordingly and shall be charged on the property hereby charged.

26. The Company hereby certifies that this Debenture does not contravene any of the provisions of its Memorandum and Articles of Association.

27. (a) If the freehold and leasehold property of the Company or any part thereof is not registered under the Land Registration Acts 1925 to 1971 no person shall during the continuance of this security be registered under the said Acts as proprietor of the same without the consent in writing of the Bank and upon any such registration the Company shall forthwith deliver to the Bank all Land Certificates relating to the same.

(b) If the freehold and leasehold property of the Company or any part thereof is or becomes registered under the Land Registration Acts 1925 to 1971 the Company hereby applies to the Registrar for a restriction in the following terms to be entered on the register of the title relating to it:—

"Except under an order of the Registrar no disposition by the proprietor of the land is to be registered without the consent of the proprietor for the time being of the charge hereby created".

28. In this Debenture where the context admits:—

(a) the expressions "the Company" and "the Bank" include their respective successors in title and assigns.

(b) the expression "the Town and Country Planning Acts" shall mean and include the Town and Country Planning Acts 1971 to 1977 and references thereto or to any other statute include any Act or Acts for the time being amending or replacing the same and any instruments orders rules or regulations for the time being in force issued under or by virtue thereof

IN WITNESS whereof the Common Seal of the Company has been hereunto affixed the day and year first before written

THE SCHEDULE above referred to

(Registered Land)

County and District (or London Borough)	Title No.(s)	Address of Property

THE COMMON SEAL of the Company)
was hereunto affixed pursuant)
to a Resolution of the Board)
of Directors in the presence of:—)

Director

Secretary

(registered in England No................................)

THIS RELEASE made between Bank of Cyprus (London) Limited of the one part and the above-named Company of the other part WITNESSETH that the Bank as Mortgagee hereby releases the property comprised in the before written Debenture from all moneys and liabilities thereby secured

As Witness our seal this   day of   19

THE COMMON SEAL of BANK OF)
CYPRUS (LONDON) LIMITED was)
hereunto affixed in the)
presence of:—)

Director

Secretary

Fig. 10.1   *(contd)*

DATED   19

                    LIMITED

              to

BANK OF CYPRUS (LONDON) LIMITED

Debenture

Fig.10.1   *(contd)*

association and the affixing of the seal is witnessed as required, by a director or directors and/or the company secretary.

(c) The date of the charge form should be the day on which it is sealed.

(d) The debenture is a security which requires registration at Companies Registration Office within twenty-one days of its creation if it is to be valid against the company's creditors and/or a liquidator. The details of the debenture are therefore entered on Form 395 by the branch security clerk or the solicitor acting and this form is lodged at Companies Registration Office. It is on this form that mention is made of the restrictive clause in the debenture prohibiting the company from granting any fixed charge which will rank ahead or *pari passu* with the floating charge.

(e) It is usual to search at Companies Registration Office both before and after the giving of the security to ensure that there are no charges outstanding beforehand, and then to ensure that the bank's charge has been properly registered and that no other charges have intervened.

(f) The debenture is returned by Companies Registration Office to the bank with an ink stamp affixed showing that registration has been effected. Also, the Registrar issues a certificate of registration. It was because it held this document, and because of the provisions of (now) s. 401(2) Companies Act 1985 which states that 'the certificate is conclusive evidence that the requirements of this chapter as to registration have been satisfied', that the bank's security was held to be good in the circumstances of *Re C. L. Nye* (1970).

(g) The company will exhibit its fire policy and it should be ascertained that this is adequate to cover all assets at current or replacement value and also any loss of profits arising as a result of a fire.

(h) The bank will give notice of its interest to the insurance company and should seek an acknowledgement; usually this is done by the insurance company returning a duplicate of the notice to the bank duly marked to that effect.

(i) Suitable diary notes should be taken to ensure that the premium receipts are exhibited annually, and that at all times the cover of the insurance is adequate to meet current values. The insurance level should always be assessed in conjunction with the company's last balance sheet, and also its more recent trading picture, taking into account the effects of inflation and rising prices and values, and any other assets acquired.

(j) The debenture can then be valued, conservatively, taking into account all the factors which were examined on pp. 279-282.

In connection with valuation and the taking of a debenture from a recently incorporated company, the ruling in *Re Simms* (1930) should always be remembered. There, the bank had allowed overdraft facilities to the new company against the security of a debenture. The company had been formed to take over the business of a sole trader and it had acquired all the assets and liablities of that individual, Mr Simms. When Mr Simms's creditors learned that he had transferred the assets and business to the company, without their 'permission', they pressed for payment of debts due to them and Mr Simms was made bankrupt. His trustee in bankruptcy then took steps to recover the assets transferred to the company, and sought a declaration that the transfer was void (as a fraudulent conveyance under the law then current. Now he would seek to have the transaction set aside as one at an undervalue (see Chapter 9)). He was successful, and in consequence all the assets held by the company had to be returned to the trustee in bankruptcy. Lloyds Bank therefore, although still holding their debenture, in fact had little more than a worthless piece of paper.

While these circumstances were special, should there be any possibility of a similar situation arising, where the business of a trader is being transferred to a limited company, it is wise for the bank to ensure either that the private or partnership creditors have been paid before the transfer of assets takes place, or alternatively that they have agreed to the proposed transfer – possibly by accepting substituted claims against the company. Everything will of course depend upon the circumstances involved, and where the bankground is entirely sound and the possibility of bankruptcy does not exist then the bank need not be concerned, and to pursue enquiries of the creditors or to raise such a matter with the individual could be embarrassing.

ENFORCEMENT OF THE DEBENTURE

The usual remedy under a debenture is to appoint an administrative receiver, although, in addition, the debenture holder may, if he prefers, sue the company on its covenant to repay the monies lent, and he may recover judgment for the advance and interest and costs. Also, as with an unsecured liability, the debenture holder could petition the court for the company to be wound up.

The debenture holder may also sell or transfer his debenture to a third party for a cash or other consideration, or if land is mortgaged by way of legal charge then all the usual remedies in that respect apply and he could apply to the court for foreclosure, which would vest the title to the property in the debenture holder, irrespective of the value of the property charged or the amount of the debt. The debenture holder may also sell the land as mortgagee.

A prerequisite of any action and especially the appointment of an administrative receiver is for the bank to be able and to make demand for the monies due and secured. The terms of any facility letters and whether they have been breached are crucial. It is not sufficient for a letter to say that monies are repayable on 'normal banking terms' without going on to say what those terms are. Several cases have been brought against banks in recent years alleging that demand has been made in error and hence the appointment of the administrative receiver was illegal, viz. *Cryne* v. *Barclays Bank* (1985). It is for reasons of safety therefore that banks prefer to receive a request from the company to appoint under their debentures. However, one case in their favour was *Bank of Baroda* v. *Penessar* (1986) where it was held that the fact that the demand letter did not specify the sums due did not in itself vitiate the demand made.

Enforcement of a debenture is usually effected by appointing an administrative receiver who must be a licened insolvency practitioner, and his appointment is made in writing either under seal or under hand (see Fig 10.2). This document will recite, briefly, the nature of the debenture and its date and perphaps the events leading to the right to appoint an administrative receiver. The administrative receiver is named and his appointment takes effect from the time when he receives the instrument of appointment and not when he takes up his duties. He or his authorized agent must accept his appointment before the end of the business day next following, and he or his agent must confirm in writing to the appointor within seven days. The administrative receiver's appointment must be registered at Companies Registration Office within seven days of the date of his appointment pursuant to s. 405 Companies Act 1985. The effect of the appointment of the administrative receiver is to suspend the authority and powers of the directors, although they remain in office. They are required to produce a statement of affairs relating to the company and give this to the administrative receiver.

The administrative receiver's obligation is to his debenture holder, even if he is expressed to be the agent of the company in the debenture. This relationship of agency ends, however, if the company goes into liquidation. A problem for the bank in that event was seen in *American Express International Banking Corporation* v. *Hurley* (1985), where, because of constant communication between the receiver and the bank, with the receiver seeking the bank's approval of his intended actions, the bank was held liable as principal, the receiver being the bank's agent. The administrative receiver takes on statutory duties, the most important of which is to pay the settled claims of preferential creditors out of floating-asset realizations, before passing monies over to the debenture holder (s. 40 Insolvency Act 1986). The main preferential debts are those in respect of value added tax referable to the period of six months immediately before the administrative receivership, income or corporation tax due but not exceeding one year's assessment. An important preferential claim will be that of any employee in respect of his wages or salary, not exceeding £800, in respect of work carried out in a period not exceeding four months prior to the administrative receivership. Under the provisions of Schedule 6 of the Insolvency Act 1986 the debenture holder may subrogate to the claims of an employee if he has advanced money to pay the wages or salaries.

Subject to these duties and the need to sell assets at the true market price, in respect of which the administrative receiver will instruct professional valuers and estate agents to advise him, he has no duty to attempt to rescue the

We, Practice Bank plc
and under the provisions of a Mortgage Debenture

and charge dated   15th April 1970

given by Alfa Ltd.

DO HEREBY APPOINT John Lewis

OF Messrs Lewis, Parker & Co., 17 High Street, Town

AS ADMINISTRATIVE RECEIVER of the undertaking property
and assets of the above named company compromised in and
charged by the said charge so that the Administrative
Receiver may exercise all the powers thereby conferred.

For and on behalf of
Practice Bank plc

ADVANCES CONTROLLER

DATE

This Appointment was received by me at 11.15 a.m. on

3rd April 1987 and accepted by me at 11.15 a.m. on

3rd April 1987 I hereby confirm my acceptance of

my appointment.

J.Lewis

Fig.10.2   *Instrument appointing an administrative receiver*

company or to realize monies for the unsecured creditors. Usually the administrative receiver will continue trading for a short while, to assess the position, and to attempt to obtain offers for the business as a going concern, but care must be taken in case losses are made or continued, and a close-down of the business may become necessary. The assets will then be sold off piecemeal, and it is likely that they will not realize the same price as they would have in a sale of the business as a going concern. Monies realized from the sale of assets must be used in the following order:

(a) the costs of realization,

(b) the administrative receiver's remuneration,

(c) preferential debts,
(d) the debenture holder.

It must be remembered, however, that preferential creditors only take out of the floating-asset realizations, and they have no right to monies recovered from fixed-charge realizations.

The general rule concerning an administrative receiver's or any receiver's duty of care can be found in *Cuckmere Brick Co. Ltd* v. *Mutual Finance Ltd* (1971), dealing with the position of a mortgagee who enters into possession of property with a view to sale. Such a mortgagee has a duty to obtain the best price which the circumstances permit. In *Latchford* v. *Beirne* (1981) the court had to examine as a preliminary issue whether a receiver owed any duty to a guarantor in realizing assets. It found that the receiver had no greater duty to the guarantor than to the debenture holder. However, in *Standard Chartered Bank Ltd* v. *Walker and another* (1982) the decision in the Latchford case was not viewed favourably and Mr and Mrs Walker, joint and several guarantors for £75 000, were granted a right to appeal against a judgment entered against them by the bank in respect of the guaranteed company debt outstanding after the receivership. Their case was that the bank had interfered in the receiver's actions, and they claimed that it had wanted a quick sale of assets. These were of a specialized nature, and the Walkers alleged that there had been insufficient advertising by the receiver, and that, in the event, the sale took place at the wrong time of year, when inclement weather reduced the attendance at the auction. The court did not accept that the receiver owed no duty of care to the guarantors and criticized the clause in the guarantee form which purported to allow the bank to realize any securities in any manner, as it thought expedient. It was said that such terms were unreasonable and would be invalid under the Unfair Contract Terms Act 1977.

If, when the debenture holder has been repaid, the administrative receiver is in possession of surplus funds or assets, he must hand these back to the company, acting through its directors, or, if the company has been put into liquidation, he will hand over to the liquidator. Quite frequently, a company is put into liquidation shortly after an administrative receivership, so that the liquidator can safeguard the interests of the unsecured creditors, although in a normal administrative receivership his position involves little more than that of taking a watching brief, and he must wait until the administrative receiver has discharged his duties. The administrative receiver files his receipts and payments account at the Companies Registration Office each year, where it can be seen by unsecured creditors.

Now under the provisions of the Insolvency Act 1986, s. 48, an administrative receiver must publish notice of his appointment and within twenty-eight days of his appointment send such notice to all creditors. Within three months he must send to all creditors a report on the events leading to his appointment, advice of the disposal of any company assets, the amount due to the debenture holder and the amount if any likely to be available to the other creditors. The unsecured creditors may also establish a creditors' committee to receive information from the administrative receiver, but it cannot interfere in his actions.

DISCHARGE OF DEBENTURE

Where the bank agrees to set aside a debenture which has been granted by a company it is not essential for the form of charge to be returned to the company or for the company to be given a form of release. However, companies frequently like to have some form of documentation, in which event a simple letter stating that the debenture has been released may be given to the company, or the debenture form may be endorsed to that effect and signed by an officer of the bank, thereafter being returned to the company. Of course, the charge must be removed from the register of charges at Companies Registration Office and usually this is left to the company to carry out by filing a memorandum of satisfaction using Form 403a.

If any land is charged within the debenture then the usual requirements dealing with the discharge of a mortgage over land should be carried out in accordance with the procedures necessary for the appropriate title.

CHAPTER 11

Bank Security Forms

Naturally bank security forms vary, depending upon the type of the security being taken and, of course, will also differ where a legal charge is being taken, as opposed to an equitable charge. Some banks have documents which are very long and are couched in legalistic language, which, perhaps, it may be claimed are difficult for a chargor to understand unless he takes legal advice. Other banks use shorter forms, and presumably find in practice that they are not experiencing difficulties by reason of this in the courts. The latter might claim that the brevity and clarity obtained has been of benefit. Whatever the approach, an examination of all forms, side by side, will show that many clauses are similar in effect, as they attempt to deal with general principles and protections which the banks, through their experiences and upon legal advice, have come to realize are necessary.

All bank charge forms are therefore drawn very widely to attempt to cover a variety of situations and potential problems, and herein lies an element of danger, for the actual circumstances under which a security is given may not exactly fit all the concepts in the charge form. In such a situation, the terms of the form will have been varied, and in consequence it will be important not to rely on the security form in respect of its wider stated powers. For instance, if Mr X gives a mortgage specifically to secure Mr Y's borrowing of £20 000 on loan account for a single purpose, it will not be possible to rely on the usual clause in the form stating that the security was given for all lendings past, present and future.

In considering security forms, and their clauses, it is first necessary for us to define some of the terms we will use, for whatever the security's nature – that is, for example, whether it is a mortgage over land or an assignment of a life policy – the charge form will have been drawn up either to secure the liability of the person giving the security or to secure the liability of another party, the borrowing customer. We will refer to the first type as a *direct* form and this will secure the liability of the chargor, as when he himself is the borrower.

The second type of a form will be called a *third-party form* and it will secure the liability of a person other than the chargor, as for example when A mortgages his house as security for a borrowing by B.

Where security is given by a guarantor to support his guarantee we will refer to *supporting* security, which we will expect to be given on a direct form of charge. Because it is on this form it will also secure any liability of the chargor on his own accounts.

However, the reader should realize that each bank has its own expressions in this area, so it is important to understand the principles involved and not just the terminology, which can vary. For example, some banks call third-party securities collateral securities, while others use the term 'collateral' as a noun denoting any security given by a borrower himself or a third party. To make the position even more obscure, some banks use the term 'collateral' when referring to security given on a direct form of charge in support of guarantee liabilities. Also, and really to confuse the issue, one or two banks use forms which while they are third-party forms (in our definition), given by a third party to secure the liabilities of a different borrower, *also* secure any liability to the bank of the chargor himself on his own account(s)! Even worse, under the Consumer Credit Act 1974 all chargors of security are referred to as the 'surety' even though they may be the borrower(s) themselves, and therefore giving direct security.

Bearing these points in mind, the student reader should have no difficulty in understanding our terminology in this book, but as a keen banker he will, it is hoped, also wish to relate the principles examined to the forms in use in his own bank. In doing so he should also note how clauses used in his office are the same as, or perhaps slightly different from, those we shall briefly speak about here.

To summarize therefore for the purposes of this book:

DIRECT FORM OF SECURITY

This is used when A is the borrower and A is giving the security. It would also be the one chosen where A is a partner in the firm of A B C & Co., and where, being severally liable by way of the mandate, any security given by him for his own liabilities would thus secure the partnership borrowing. Similarly, if A is in joint account with D, and they have each undertaken severally liability, the security would cover A's obligations to the bank on that account.

Also the form is used where A is already a guarantor for the liability of A Ltd and supports his guarantee with tangible security, such as an assignment over a life policy.

THIRD PARTY FORM OF SECURITY

This is used when A gives a charge over his life policy to secure a borrowing of B.

It would also be the form chosen where A B C & Co., a partnership, borrow, and the bank takes an assignment over a life policy in the name of A, to secure that advance only. A guarantee is of course a type of third-party security *par excellence*.

TYPICAL CLAUSES IN BANK CHARGE FORMS

To assist the reader's understanding, the symbol D will be placed against the clause heading where the clause is found in a direct form of charge: the symbol T will indicate that the clause is applicable only to third-party forms. D & T will mean that the clause is common to both forms.

In this chapter we will not look at clauses which relate to a specific type of security (e.g. an equitable mortgage over shares), and such clauses will be explained in the relevant later chapter dealing with that security. In other words, here we will look only at clauses common to all types of charge, whatever the actual nature of the security itself.

(1) Parties (D & T)

In the direct form the mortgagor will be securing his own liabilities; it will be necessary only therefore to enter his full names and his address, although the latter is not essential.

In the third-party form it will be necessary to enter the full names of the party whose liabilities are secured and his address and the full names and address of the chargor.

(2) The liabilities secured (D & T)

The liabilities secured will be described in a detailed list attempting to cover all likely banking situations. These are frequently referred to as actual, or contingent liabilities, joint or several, past, present or future, on current or any other account, alone or jointly, on bill of exchange, promissory note, guarantee or indemnity and include interest, commission and costs in taking and realizing the security. The expression 'banking facilities' is adequate to include foreign exchange contracts (*Bank of India* v. *Trans Continental Commodity Merchant Ltd and Patel* (1983)).

Contingent liabilities remain secured even when the principal debt has been repaid and in such circumstances a bank may retain its security in case these crystallize. For example, a call might be made upon the bank under a performance bond, in which case it would in turn call upon the customer and look to the security lodged if he did not pay (*Re Rudd & Son Ltd re Fosters & Rudd Ltd.* (1986)).

The clause may well be drawn so that it refers to '*all monies* owing at any time whether on . . .'. In this way difficulties are avoided with the powers of consolidation granted to a mortgagor under s. 93 Law of Property Act 1925, although, especially in land mortgages, the provisions of that section are often specifically excluded additionally, in a later clause in any event. Often the clause is extended at this point (although it may be included separately by some banks) into what is known as the 'whole debt' clause. This means that a third party's security or a guarantor's liability, although perhaps limited in monetary terms (see clause 6) is security for the whole borrowing(s) or balance of accounts etc. By expressing the security in this way, it remains in force after the limited amount is paid. Hence, the third party cannot exercise his rights of subrogation against the principal debtor until the bank is fully repaid, nor can he prove in the principal debtor's bankruptcy.

(3) Continuing security clause (D & T)[80]

All securities are expressed as continuing securities. This prevents any claim in law that the security was granted to cover a borrowing which on a fluctuating account has been repaid by credits into the account since the security was given, albeit that the account is still overdrawn as other cheques have subsequently been paid. In other words, by the use of this phrase, any attempted reliance by an obstructive chargor or guarantor on the operation of the Rule in *Clayton's Case* is avoided.

(4) The consideration clause (D & T)

Where the charge is under seal this clause is not essential, but it is frequently inserted. It will speak of the bank having agreed to lend money to the customer, or to continue to lend money or to give the customer further time in which to meet his existing liabilities. In consideration for such matters the chargor will grant security specified in the form.

(5) Joint and several clause (D & T)[81]

The joint and several clause will state that where the charged property is held jointly in two or more names the covenants and agreements entered into by each chargor will be several as well as joint, and will explain that reference to one party in the wording in the form is to be read as reference to them all and vice versa.

The clause is often drawn so as to secure the separate liability of each chargor, whether the security is in joint names or not.

(6) The limitation clause (D & T)

This is invariably found in a third-party form of charge, and occasionally in direct forms too. Basically it restricts the monetary amount recoverable under the security. The amount is inserted at the time when the security is executed and is usually expressed in a figure, e.g. '£10 000 together with interest, commission, costs and charges'. This means that if a property is worth £40 000 and a first mortgage is held then the bank will only be able to recover the amount secured, £10 000, and any costs relating to the sale, together with interest which has accrued since demand was made on the mortgagor to pay under the mortgage.

The interest rate applicable will be clearly stated.[82] This may be a formula linked to the bank's base rate – such as 2 per cent above base rate – or it may

80 See Appendix I, Q. 53 (September 1982).
81 See Appendix I, Q. 53 (September 1982).
82 See Appendix I, Q. 43 (April 1981).

be linked to Bank of England minimum lending rate. With old bank forms referring to 'Bank Rate', no problems will arise, for although 'Bank Rate' was suspended in the early 1970s and was replaced by Bank of England minimum lending rate, there is case law accepting that for these purposes the two are the same.

The formula might also be expressed to be the same rate as has been agreed or paid between the borrower and the bank.

The limitation 'amount' can be deleted if the chargor does not intend to limit his liability, and the security is then available for all the liabilities of the borrower without a ceiling. Clearly, it is highly desirable for this amendment or deletion to be authenticated by the chargor, preferably by way of his full signature and not by mere initials.

It is worth remembering here that where a security is given *in support* of a limited guarantee liability it is essential to record in the bank's books that the total amount recoverable will be the amount of the guarantee, and not the value of the supporting security *and* the guaranteed sum. Various combinations of security situations can arise and the intention of the parties must be certain at the outset and the understanding of the bank security officer clear, so that no costly mistakes are made, whereby the lending officer is led to believe he has more security than is really the case, or which will enable valid defences to be raised if legal proceedings are taken later.

Examples

(a) Customer Smith: Dr £50 000   Security = guarantee by Jones, limited to £20 000,

                                              supported by deeds value £40 000.

                                              Total security value £20 000.

(b) Customer Smith: Dr £50 000   Security = guarantee by Jones for all advances,

                                              supported by deeds value £40 000.

                                              Total security value = £50 000 (deeds can be fully relied upon).

(c) Customer Smith: Dr £50 000   Security = guarantee by Jones, limited to £20 000,

                                              plus deeds by Jones—charge limited to £10 000.

                                              Total security value = £30 000.

In this third case it is vital to be able to show the court, if necessary, that the deeds were lodged as *additional* security and not just to support the guarantee.

(*d*) Customer Smith: Dr £50 000 Security=mortgage by Smith limited to £40 000 (property worth £60 000).

In this fourth case the bank could recover only £40 000 under its mortgage. (It might, however, before the property is sold, have obtained judgment in the courts against Smith for the full monetary debt due (£50 000) and enforced this by obtaining a charging order through the court against the property. Effectively the bank would then have an unlimited second mortgage which would overcome the monetary restriction in the direct form of charge. Action such as this would not be possible with third-party security as such a party would have no liability to the bank as principal borrower.)

(7) Personal covenant to repay upon demand (D)

This is applicable only to direct securities but reinforces the contract between the borrowing customer and the bank that the borrower will repay on demand. It strengthens the bank's hands should it wish to sue for a money judgment upon default in repayment. It also clearly shows when the adverse effects of the Limitation Act 1980 start to run against the lender in respect of his security. In other words, the bank has six years (memorandum of deposit) or twelve years (security under seal) after demand, before his right of action in law dies (*Lloyds Bank Ltd* v. *Margolis* (1954)). (In respect of a guarantee the clause was held to be effective in *Bradford Old Bank Ltd* v. *Sutcliffe* (1918).)

(8) Service of demand (D & T)

As the demand process is so important because the power of sale flows from it, the mechanics are invariably set out in detail, in such a way that all foreseeable circustances which could create problems are avoided.

A typical clause will state that the demand notice should be in writing, addressed to the chargor at the address last known to the bank, and in the case of a limited company at its registered office or any business premises. Usually the clause will state that service may be made by post or by hand, and will be effective whether or not it is accepted or whether or not it is returned by the postal authorities or refused by the addressee or anyone on his behalf.

The clause will state that any written notice may be signed by 'an officer of the bank' or a 'manager' or 'controller'. Sometimes agents, such as solicitors, are empowered to act on the bank's behalf.

(9) Conclusive evidence clause (D & T)

This will state that a certificate given under the hand of a bank official stating the amount due on the security shall be conclusive evidence in any legal proceedings of that amount. The object of the clause is to prevent any dispute as to the amount of the debt and it was found to be effective in *Bache & Co. (London) Ltd* v. *Banques Vernes et Commerciale de Paris* (1973). Whether such a clause would be upheld today under the provisions of the Unfair Contract Terms Act (1977) as meeting the test of 'reasonableness' would be likely to depend on the overall circumstances, which if needing examination would probably militate against the prime object of its inclusion, that is to prevent debate.

(10) Agreement as to when the power of sale arises (D & T)

Under s. 103 Law of Property Act 1925 a mortgagee's ability to sell the mortgaged property arises only after demand has been made on the mortgagor to meet his liability or redeem his security and he has defaulted for three months. Similar provisions exist under section 109 as to when a receiver for rents can be appointed. This time delay could be very disadvantageous, hence it is avoided by the provisions of the section being excluded from all bank charge forms and a lesser period is substituted.[83] Typically this is 'forthwith', 'on demand', or 'after seven days'.

The clause may be extended to say that as well as selling, the mortgagee may transfer his security, but this is propably implied and its absence does not seem to cause problems for banks who make no reference to the alternative method of obtaining repayment.

(11) Protection against loss of priority (D & T)

A lender's 'position in the queue' can be adversely affected if he fails to stop a fluctuating current account, when he receives notice of a later charge, or similar event which would bring the operation of the Rule in *Clayton's Case* into play to his disadvantage. In an attempt to avoid the consequences of failure to stop the account(s) secured and the loss of priority, some banks incorporate a clause in their charge forms based on that used by the plaintiff bank and accepted by the court in *Westminster Bank Ltd* v. *Cond* (1940). This case concerned a guarantee and the clause read:

> In the event of the guarantee being determined . . . by demand in writing by the bank, it shall be lawful for the bank to continue the account with the principal, notwithstanding such determination, and the liability of myself . . . for the amount due from the principal at the date when the guarantee is so determined shall remain, notwithstanding any subsequent payments into or out of the account by or on behalf of the principal. . . .

Clauses based on this are drawn to cover the omission of stopping the account(s) and usually state that the bank will be deemed to have carried out this step and also opened a new account, even though it has not done so. In such form the clause has not been tested in court. Naturally, however, its efficacy would only extend to cover priority at the date notice of determination or notice of a later charge was received, and could not be relied upon to protect the priority of a bank which advanced additional funds after

83 See Appendix I, Q. 39 (September 1980).

receipt of a further charge. Where there has been an exchange of letters of priority, however, these considerations will obviously not be material.

(12) Security to the bank to pass to any successor upon bank's change of identity (D & T)

This clause states that while a security is expressed to be in favour of ...... Bank, it shall remain as security for any successor to that bank's title, as might occur upon an amalgamation or an assignment of the security. Its effectiveness was seen as recently as 1983 in *First National Finance Corporation Ltd* v. *Goodman.*

(13) Changes in the constitution of the parties comprising the principal debtor (T)

The object of this clause is to ensure that a guarantor or third party cannot escape liability because there has been a change in the constitution or identity of the parties originally defined under the term 'principal debtor'. Thus, if a partnership is secured, and there are changes in membership, the guarantee will continue to apply and will secure the liability of the firm as constituted by the members at the time when the guarantee is determined.

(14) Clause giving rights of lien and set-off (D & T)

This type of clause seeks to give the bank a right of lien over any articles or monies coming into its hands, belonging to the chargor, in the course of its banking business, and seeks to cover items lodged even for safe custody, which would normally be outside the usual contract of security.[84] It purports to give a right of set-off over a balance in one person's account which would not normally be available for set-off under the usual rules.

A clause to this effect is quite unrelated to the nature of the security granted, and as such its use may now not be suitable, except perhaps in the case of a guarantee. In many instances where the chargor acts without the benefit of legal advice, it is hard to see how such an unconnected covenant could be regarded as 'reasonable', under the provisions of the Unfair Contract Terms Act 1977.

(15) Additional security clause (D & T)

This clause states that the security deposited is additional to, and not in substitution of, any other security held. Its objective is clear, but despite its presence, particularly in third-party forms and guarantees, it will still be vitally important for the banker to be sure that this is the real intention of the chargor and that the surrounding circumstances when the security is given do not later suggest that the opposite was the case, for then, despite the presence of the clause, difficulties could be expected at realization time.

84 See Appendix I, Q. 40 (September 1980).

(16) Security to be valid, despite want of authority by the borrower (T)

Some banks include a clause seeking to give protection in those situations where the borrower is acting beyond its authority – as for example when a limited company or its directors act *ultra vires*. The clause will state that, despite this, the security from the third party is still to be valid. It will often cover the difficult position which might arise where the borrower is an unincorporated association which cannot be sued in law, or where the borrower is a minor, when the security will be expressed as an indemnity under which the chargor assumes primary liability for the debt himself and for which his security will be valid.

(17) Right to release/vary other security held or the accommodation granted to the debtor (T)

This clause applies only to third-party security, or security lodged in support of a guarantee. It gives the bank right to release any security lodged by the debtor himself or by a co-surety, without affecting the liability of this chargor or surety. (By the term 'surety' we mean a guarantor or any depositor of any security for the liabilities of the borrowing customer.) In other words, while that party personally will be in a weaker position because the bank will have less security to rely on, and his rights of contribution or subrogation will be less valuable, nevertheless he will not be able to avoid being fully liable on the document which he has signed. This clause therefore overrules the common law position under which, in its absence, the surety would be discharged.

The clause is often also worded so as to keep the surety liable, where any other security has been realized, and he cannot avoid liability in those circumstances by claiming that the other security has been sold at too low a price.

In *Barclays Bank Ltd* v. *Thienel and another* (1978) two of three joint and several guarantors sought to avoid liability on the grounds that the bank had sold property charged to it by the principal debtor at too low a price, and that as a consequence they, the guarantors, were being asked to make up a shortfall which should not have existed.[85] The court ruled on a preliminary issue that the guarantors' rights all depended upon the terms of the guarantee document. This included a clause stating:

> You are to be at liberty without thereby affecting your rights hereunder at any time and from time to timé (whether before or after any demand for payment made by you under or any notice of determination of this guarantee or receipt by you of any notice of any disability or incapacity of the undersigned) to refuse or grant (as the case may be) further credit to the principal, to renew any bills of exchange or promissory notes for any period and to compound with, give time for payment or grant other indulgences to the principal or to any obligant on bills of exchange or

85   See Appendix I, Q. 43 (April 1981).

promissory notes or otherwise or to accept *compositions from* and make *any other arrangements* with the *principal or any persons liable to you in respect of securities held or to be held by you,* to give up, modify, exchange or abstain from perfecting or taking advantage of or enforcing any securities, guarantees or other contracts or the proceeds of any of the foregoing and to discharge any parties *thereto and to realize any securities in such manner as you may think expedient.*

Taking these terms into account the court ruled that the guarantors could not escape liability on the grounds they were asserting.

However this decision was criticized in *Standard Chartered Bank Ltd* v. *Walker and another* (1982) on grounds that the clause was 'unreasonable' and could now be void in certain circumstances under the terms of the Unfair Contract Terms Act 1977.

The clause is also worded so that the bank can vary its contract with the borrower at any time without reference to the surety, enabling the bank to compound or settle for a lesser sum in appropriate circumstances, such as under a scheme of arrangement.

(18) Agreement not to take security from the principal debtor (T)

The object of this covenant by a third-party chargor or guarantor is clearly to keep whatever other security the borrower might possess available for the bank should it require it. Often the clause will state that if the surety does take such security in breach of these terms he will be deemed to hold it in trust for the bank. However, the reader might well think that this clause, too, could now be suspect and perhaps ineffectual under the provisions of the Unfair Contract Terms Act 1977, particularly as the customer can always in any event charge his free assets to any other party, hence the value of the restriction is limited. Certainly, if the security were given by the principal debtor to the third party in respect of an entirely separate matter, then it is felt that in the present day the courts would look closely at the covenant in the guarantee or third party form of charge. Fortunately, in the author's experience, the number of situations encountered where a surety has taken security from the debtor customer have been few and far between.

(19) Agreement not to sue or prove in competition with the bank (T)

This clause is included to maximize any benefit for the bank that it might hope to achieve in legal proceedings, or when lodging a proof of debt in its customer's estate in bankruptcy. Clearly, the fewer in number and amount of outside claims, the greater the potential return for the bank.

The clause prevents a surety whose liability was for a limited sum, and whose property has been sold, from exercising his rights of subrogation or contribution until the bank has been fully repaid, as the security is also said to apply to 'the ultimate balance' due to the bank.[86] Thus it enforces the Rule in *Re Sass* (1896), applicable in bankruptcy proofs, which is discussed in greater depth in Chapter 15.

(20) Bank's rights after release of security in event of a preference (T)
This clause will state that if the principal debtor should become bankrupt, go
into liquidation, administration or enter into a voluntary arrangement and
should any prior payments to the bank by him be judged to have been a
preference, then the bank will still be able to look to the surety for the full
amount of his liability, even if it has in fact discharged his security or agreed
to settle for a lesser figure. In other words, it seeks to reinstate the position
which existed before the preference took place. Of course, if, say, a property
has been released from mortgage and sold or remortgaged, those rights may
not in practice be of much value to the bank. These provisions have now been
superseded to some extent, as the Insolvency Act 1986 s. 342 gives the court
power to make an order restoring the position to what it was previously.

Some banks extend their clause to give them a right to retain the third
party's security for six or even seven months after the bank has been repaid by
the customer himself, and in this way seek to remain in possession of the
security until the danger of bankruptcy, liquidation, or company
administration and a preference claim have passed.

CHAPTER 12

Land as Security

INTRODUCTION

At one time land was not regarded favourably as security and while it still has disadvantages, in this century it has become a major item against which substantial sums of money are lent either on a first or subsequent charge. Adequate attention must always be given to valuation, however, and to maintaining a safe margin between the amount of the advance and the present-day value of the property. We may not agree entirely therefore with George Rae, in whose memory the annual prize for the top marks in the Practice of Banking Papers is awarded by the Institute of Bankers, but we can still recognize an element of truth in the approach in his book *The Country Banker* (1885) when he includes second mortgages in a chapter entitled 'Securities which are not Security'! Times and practices have certainly changed in this area, but even so the safety of an advance against land and property security will depend upon a careful assessment, skill and common sense: the lending banker is warned never to trust without question a mere figure in his security ledger, when relying on deeds security for cover.

A charge over land will give the mortgagee rights not only to the land itself but also to any property built on it. This means, for instance, that if land is mortgaged by a builder who is erecting houses for sale, the bank's charge will automatically encompass these newly built houses, without the need for any further action. Moreover a mortgage over land, as well as gripping the buildings built or to be built, will also cover any growing crops, trees, and anything put up on or attached or fixed to it, although chattel items may retain their identity as chattels and may not become part of the real estate.

Except in the case of farm land, or land with planning permission for development, it is mainly the property erected on the land which contributes to the major part of its value; hence business premises, such as shops and factories, and domestic dwelling houses are the most commonly encountered 'securities'. Of these the value of dwelling houses is the most readily ascertained, the banker being guided by amounts paid for similar properties in the area and any surveyor's report which may be available. Consideration must of course be given to whether or not the property is freehold or leasehold and to its state of repair. Valuation of commercial property is more difficult and its specialized nature must be kept in mind to maintain an adequate margin between the amount of the advance and the value, in case a forced sale should become necessary.

Certain legislation also affects the value of land as a security, such as that contained in the Rent Acts. These give security of tenure in respect of furnished lettings which fall within the ambit of the various Rent Acts, and prevent a sale of the property with vacant possession. Enquiries should be made at the outset, before accepting the security, as to whether or not the property is let or is owner occupied.

Properties on which local authority improvement grants have been given are also subject to restrictions and the banker should establish if the property offered as security is subject to any disadvantages as a result.

Local authority development plans for the area should also be checked, as any compulsory purchase order pending, or usage of the property for purposes inconsistent with those authorized, could seriously affect its security value.

In the case of farm land, charges can be created under the Agricultural Holdings Act 1948 which will rank in priority to an existing mortgage. These charges can arise on the termination of a lease and provide compensation for a tenant who has improved the property. Another point for a mortgagee of farm land to remember is that he will be unable to evict a tenant with an agricultural tie.[87]

The matrimonial home

Perhaps the most important legislation, however, is that governing the rights of occupants of the matrimonial home, for such properties so frequently represent a bank's main item of security. In recent years the courts have increasingly recognized that while title might only be held in the name of one party, that person might mortgage the home in order to borrow monies for a personal or business venture; such action could lead to disaster for the other party to the marriage if the mortgagee had to sell the home upon a failure to repay.

This was why in 1967 the Matrimonial Homes Act was passed and it gives a spouse, either the husband or the wife, who has no legal title in the matrimonial home, a means of protection, by filing a Class F land charge (in the case of unregistered land), or by lodging a notice (when the land is registered title). (Notices were formerly cautions but changed upon the passing of the Matrimonial Homes and Property Act 1981.) An entry gives either spouse a right to occupy the property, whatever the wishes of the other, and similar rights against any mortgagee who has taken a charge after the entry. Prospective mortgagees will be aware of the entry following their search at the Land Charges Register or District Land Registry and bankers will not usually proceed further then, without a written agreement from that spouse that the bank's charge will none the less have priority.[88] This is because it would not be possible otherwise for the mortgagee to obtain vacant possession and hence he would, in practice, not be able to sell his security. When notice of this type of charge is received, after the advance has been made, a lending on current

87 See Appendix I, Q. 54 (September 1982).
88 See Appendix I, Q. 42 (April 1981).

account must be stopped, as otherwise the Rule in *Clayton's Case* will operate against the mortgagee who would find his charge ranking behind the Class F charge or notice, after the subsequent turnover had 'repaid' the original advance.

However, even if an entry under the Matrimonial Homes Act 1967 is not made, a bank's position as mortgagee will still be weak in circumstances where only one spouse has mortgaged the property and the other has not consented or charged his/her interest.[89] Indeed the position is virtually identical, as a sale with vacant possession will not be possible. This follows recent case law which highlighted a previously little-known section of the Land Registration Act 1925, and even though the two cases dealt with registered title, in practice it is felt that the position would be no different with unregistered land, as a mortgagee is aware of the occupancy of the property by the other spouse at the time when the charge is taken and can be presumed to know the other spouse's prior equitable interests.

The two cases were *Williams & Glyn's Bank Ltd* v. *Boland* (1980) and *Williams & Glyn's Bank Ltd* v. *Brown* (1980). In view of their importance we shall look at the facts in detail.

In the Brown case, Mr and Mrs Brown were married in 1958, and in line with social customs at that time, both continued working and earning money, which they pooled. In 1960 they bought their first home, and six years later they moved house, and a second property was bought in the husband's sole name, with a mortgage from a building society. In 1973, the husband and a company Saunhurst Productions Ltd borrowed from Williams & Glyn's Bank and Mr Brown guaranteed the company's liabilities. He also executed a legal mortgage to the bank over the matrimonial home, although he did not tell his wife about this. The bank registered their charge, and in accordance with normal procedures received a warning from the Land Registry which stated *'Enquiries should also be addressed to any persons in occupation of the land or buildings as to their rights of occupation and to whom rent (if any) is paid'*. However, again in accordance with banking practice at that time, no enquiries were made either of the wife or the husband.

Mr Brown and the company became substantially indebted to Williams & Glyn's Bank, who some years later sought a possession order over the property to recover the monies owing. Their action was not defended by the husband, but Mrs Brown sought to remain in possession, by virtue of her alleged half-share interest in the property.

In the case of the Bolands, the marriage took place in 1959, both worked, and in 1961 a property was purchased in joint names. In 1969 they moved house, but the second property was purchased in the husband's sole name, although the wife did not realize this. Mr Boland formed a company, Epsom Contractors Ltd which borrowed from Williams & Glyn's Bank, and, as

89 See Appendix I, Q. 55 (September 1982).

director, Mr Boland gave his guarantee, supporting this with a second mortgage over the matrimonial home. Again, the bank made no enquiries of the wife. The business failed, went into liquidation, and £55 000 was owed to the bank. Williams & Glyn's Bank sought possession of the property and Mrs Boland resisted the action claiming a half-interest in the house.

In the Court of Appeal it was said that a wife who contributes money or money's worth obtains a proprietary interest in the matrimonial home by way of trust imposed on her husband, even though title is taken in his sole name. The trust extends to contributions in respect of the purchase, and improvements. The Master of the Rolls was of the view that the trust was not only in respect of the proceeds of sale, but of the house itself and he went on to examine this concept as it affected a purchaser for value, such as a mortgagee. In the case of unregistered title, he said the purchaser's position depended on whether he had notice or not of the other party's equitable interest, but he decided the cases before him under the provisions of the Land Registration Act 1925, as both titles were over registered land. Unanimously, the Court held that the wife's interest was a 'minor interest', capable of being over-ridden by a sale of the trustees for sale, but that it was also an 'over-riding interest' under section 70(1)(g) of that Act. This section protects 'the rights of every person in actual occupation of the land or in receipt of the rents and profits thereof, save where enquiry is made of such a person and the rights are not disclosed'. It was held that the wife was clearly in 'actual occupation', and it was common ground that no enquiries had been made. Lord Denning, Master of the Rolls, stated *'If a bank is to do its duty, in the society in which we live, it should recognize the integrity of the matrimonial home. It should not destroy it by disregarding the wife's interest in it – simply to ensure that it is paid the husband's debt in full – with the high interest rates now prevailing. Monied might must, in this Court, give way to social justice'.*

These rulings were followed in the Lords, on legal grounds, although Lord Scarman referred to the social implications of the case. He recognized that in following the Court of Appeal, the beneficial interest of a married woman in the matrimonial home would be strengthened. His view was that the courts should not *'flinch, when assailed by arguments to the effect that the protection of her interest will create difficulties in banking or conveyancing practice'.* He believed the difficulties to be exaggerated and that banks, existing to provide a public service, should adjust their practice if it were socially necessary.

It will be remembered that in these cases the wives had *not* registered cautions under the Matrimonial Homes Act 1967 (Class F charges in the case of unregistered land), giving rights of occupation, and these were said to be separate protections available for a deserted wife.

The implications of the decision are very far-reaching, and refer not only to matrimonial situations. All lenders are affected by the decision, not only banks, for the principles of the cases may well extend to business properties which are shared, and affect mortgages over them. Many questions now arise, such as: 'What is a bank's position, when lending on current account, if persons go into actual possession of the mortgaged security and acquire an equitable interest? Does the banker need to initiate enquiries before paying each cheque, in case his secured position is postponed behind the interests of this person, through the operation of *Clayton's Case?*' This is surely impracticable!

At present, banks and other lenders taking new securities are now making detailed enquiries of the mortgagor whether or not the land is registered or unregistered; and whether matrimonial property is involved or not, consideration is being given as to whether a physical inspection of the property, as opposed to a mere external valuation, will be necessary. Mortgagors are now asked to reply to written enquiries concerning all occupants, and the extent of their equitable interest, if any, and should names be revealed, these parties are then requested to postpone their interests, or to mortgage them to the bank, after taking independent legal advice. The practical problems, and expense created, are considerable, and add to the charges that are levied when security is taken.

Each situation must be looked at separately, however, for the facts can vary. For instance in *Midland Bank Ltd* v. *Farmpride Hatcheries Ltd and Willey* (1980), the bank was granted a possession order over fifty acres of unregistered farm land and a manor house, charged by way of legal mortgage by the company. Mr Willey, who with his wife was a director of the company, had sought to claim that his family's occupation of the manor house, which was on a twenty-year rent-free licence, ranked ahead of the bank's charge, which was subject also to their rights under the Boland decision. His argument was that the bank had had constructive notice of his licence, and that they should have made enquiries into the basis of his occupation. The court held that when the bank had been discussing the company mortgage with him as director, Mr Willey had had ample chance to disclose and explain his own position and had failed to do so; he was therefore estopped from later seeking to set up a defence. The court distinguished the case from a situation where an employee lived on company property under a service tenancy, and who would obviously not necessarily be aware of the negotiations between the company and its mortgagee.

More recently and somewhat surprisingly the Court of Appeal took a view opposite to that in the Boland and Brown cases when hearing *Midland Bank Ltd* v. *Dobson* (1985). The bank was there granted a possession order in respect of property mortgaged by Mr Dobson in whose sole name the title was vested. The court ruled Mrs Dobson had no right of occupation against the bank as she had no equitable interest, not having contributed to the purchase of the matrimonial home some thirty-two years previously when the property was bought. (Monies had been put up by Mr Dobson and his mother, who had died by 1985). Whilst subsequently Mrs Dobson had contributed from her earnings to the family budget, and had carried out the usual housewifely chores and had performed maintenance and decorating tasks, these facts did not pursuade the court that she had acquired an interest in the property subsequently.

ADVANTAGES AND DISADVANTAGES[90]

In normal times land and property tend to be stable in value, even though short-term variations occur, and over the longer period appreciation of prices in line with inflation is seen. Unlike other securities, land can always be used productively (to grow food), although mortgagees never seem to think of this attribute!

However, property is not an easy security to realize, especially if it is a domestic home, occupied by the mortgagor and his family. Resort to the courts is then usually necessary, in order to obtain a possession order, and no mortgagee likes to evict the occupants in order to obtain vacant possession. Adverse publicity for the mortgagee can therefore arise occasionally. Even when possession is obtained, it is necessary to find a purchaser, and vacant property can deteriorate rapidly if the market is not buoyant. Estate agents' costs and legal costs will need to be incurred in realizing the security and these, although usually recoverable under the terms of the charge, will mean that the forced sale value of the property will almost certainly be less than the open market value placed on the property in happier times; sometimes the difference is quite dramatic and can result in a bad debt being incurred if the lending was too generous in relation to the property value.

To value a property can be a difficult exercise, except where it is a domestic house, similar in size and location to others in the same road, which have changed hands recently. However, specialized domestic property may not appeal to many potential purchasers and the price obtained may consequently prove to be low.

It is particularly hard to value commercial property, such as factories and offices, and while professional agents may be used, the crux of any situation from the bank's point of view is what the property will fetch when times are bad, and the business has been closed down. Often industrial premises may only be suitable for the trade which has been carried on previously, and this can restrict the degree of interest shown when the property is put on the market for sale.

If a tenancy is created after the bank's mortgage, this can have a detrimental effect upon the valuation of the security, if it has previously been valued as owner-occupied property, and a sale has been envisaged with vacant possession. Usually, it is a term of the mortgage that any tenancy created after the mortgage will be void as against the mortgagee, unless the latter has consented to the tenancy in writing. While this means that if a mortgagee encounters such a situation where an unauthorised tenancy has been created

90 See Appendix I, Q. 42 (April 1981).

then he should, ultimately, in law be able to obtain vacant possession, the legal costs incurred will in themselves adversely affect the value of the security. However there is is always a risk that in court the mortgagee will be deemed to have accepted the tenancy, if he had notice of it, and then to be 'estopped' from claiming vacant possession.

Certainly if the tenancy existed at the time the charge was taken, then it will not be possible to obtain vacant possession, and the property will only be saleable as investment property, at a consideration much less than the vacant-possession figure. With this in mind, it is clearly important to ensure that any valuation carried out initially is on the correct basis, i.e. as owner-occupied property, or subject to lettings.

Another demerit of this type of security is that land is expensive to mortgage, as solicitor's costs are invariably incurred, and, in the case of registered title, Land Registry fees have to be paid if a registered charge is to be obtained.

Finally, there is a greater chance of technical irregularity, because of the complexities involved in the legal nature of the security, and the various interests which can arise.

LEGAL ESTATES

Two types of legal estate can be encountered, freehold and leasehold.

Freehold

This is the estate in fee simple, absolute in possession, and is the best legal estate which can be held. In consequence, freehold property is more attractive than leasehold property to an owner and to a mortgagee.

Leasehold

This refers to a term of years absolute granted by the freeholder to the lessee upon declared terms. The value of the leasehold estate or interest to the lessee, and hence the mortgagee, will depend upon the original terms of the lease, and the unexpired portion of the term of years. Thus, a short-term lease (for example one for seven years) would be unlikely to have much, if any, value in itself, and even medium-term leases may not be good security. Leases of 99 years, or 999 years, are much better propositions, and the latter term is little different, in practice, from a freehold interest. Even a ninety-nine year lease, where most of the period is unexpired, may be regarded as almost as good as a freehold title, especially if it carries only a small ground rent payment of say £10 per annum.

Generally, however, short-term and medium-term leasehold properties are not attractive to banks as security and while occasionally a 'premium value' can arise at certain periods in the term of the lease (where, for example, the originally agreed rent has become out of date through the incidence of inflation, and there is no rent-review clause), usually, in a situation where the bank looks to its security, it will be found that arrears of rent payments have built up, and these will be a first deduction from the sale proceeds. Invariably, before the lessee or his mortgagee can sell or assign the lease, the consent of the freeholder or head lessee will be required, and clearly this will not be forthcoming while rent remains unpaid. Usually therefore it has to be arranged for the mortgagee to pay the rent arrears to prevent the lease being forfeited, or for the back rent to be paid out of the sale proceeds, and on this condition the consent to an assignment is granted. A lease is really a wasting asset, and its value as security to the bank will, among other things, very much depend upon the length of time which it has still to run. A twenty-one year lease, for example, with, say, nineteen years expired, will virtually be worthless in security terms.

Also, in the event of bankruptcy or liquidation, a clause in the lease will usually state that the lease is then forfeit and that the landlord has an immediate right of re-entry. While there are provisions for relief for a mortgagee, under s. 146 Law of Property Act 1925, the number of instances where resort to this section would be worthwhile is few. Such relief would probably only be granted by the court if the bank were prepared to pay arrears and future rents and assume all the other responsibilities of the lessee, which could be extremely onerous. Unless there were prospects of an immediate sale at a good price, the bank would be unlikely to want to risk getting itself into such a position, and in consequence might even prefer to give up its security.

Invariably, in a realization situation, because of the bankruptcy or liquidation of the customer, any goodwill attaching to the business will have long since been lost, and therefore any figure for this should be excluded when a valuation of the lease is being made for security purposes.

SOLE OR JOINT TITLES

Title to freehold or leasehold land can be held either solely or jointly. Since 1926, however, it has not been possible for the legal estate in land to be held by two or more persons as tenants in common, and this means that where there are two title holders the land is held by them as joint tenants, and the bank need not concern itself about proportionate rights, although these will exist as equitable rather than legal interests, under the trust which they hold for each other. Indeed, when one of two joint tenants dies the title passes to the survivor, and all that is then necessary is to place a copy of the death certificate with the deeds. The survivor need not recharge the security.

Occasionally a bank finds itself with a mortgage given by only one of the two joint tenants; this may be because the other has refused to sign the charge form or even because the signature of the second party has been forged. This occurred in *First National Securities Ltd* v. *Hegarty and another* (1984), when the court had to decide what protection, if any, this gave the bank, which held a mortgage on which the husband had signed for himself and forged his wife's signature. It was held that the charge, although purporting to be a *legal* charge, was not such, but was rather a valid equitable charge over the husband's beneficial interest in the proceeds of sale of the property. The husband and wife held the property as joint tenants upon statutory trust over the legal estate in the property. The act of mortgaging by the husband had severed any beneficial joint tenancy and converted the title holders into tenants in common of their beneficial interest in the proceeds of sale. Consequently, the mortgage was effective as an equitable charge over the husband's beneficial interest in the proceeds of sale, as his own signature on the mortgage document was sound.

However, where one of two joint title holders lodged the deeds without executing a mortgage form (although he did sign an agreement undertaking to create a mortgage), the court held that he had no power to bind his co-joint tenant, and when she sought the return of the deeds to her this was approved (*Thames Guaranty Ltd* v. *Campbell* (1984)). It follows from this case that, where title is in two or more names, and should one party purport to create a change merely by depositing the deeds without signing any mortgage form, it is essential to obtain some form of written acknowledgement from the other joint tenant or tenants confirming that the act is authorized, to prevent later dispute.

LEGAL MORTGAGE

Under the Law of Property Act 1925 legal mortgages can only be effected in one or other of the following ways: first by a charge by deed expressed to be by way of legal mortgage, and second by the granting of a lease of the land for a term of years absolute subject to a proviso for 'cesser on redemption', i.e. that upon repayment the term ceases.

The first method by way of legal mortgage gives the lender the same protection, powers and remedies that apply when the mortgage is taken by lease or sub-lease and it applies to both freeholds and leaseholds, when the same wording can be used. It is the more usual method employed in bank charge forms.

The second method applies also to freehold land and leaseholds, both of which can be mortgaged in similar style. With leasehold land a sub-lease of at least one day less than the terms vested in the grantor is taken. However one disadvantage of this method when it is used for leasehold title is in that the consent of the landlord is required in those cases where the lease contains a covenant restricting the right to sub-let or assign, although often permission is also required, when the charge is expressed to be by way of legal mortgage.

A legal mortgage gives the mortgagee superior rights to those given by an equitable mortgage. For instance, provided a legal mortgagee has no knowledge of any other interests outstanding or existing at the time when he takes his charge, his security will rank ahead of those interests, should they in fact exist. This means that should an unknown party appear later and claim that he has an interest in the property, perphaps because he put up money to facilitate the purchase, or perhaps because he has some beneficial interest under a trust, his claim can be defeated in law. Of great value is the fact that at realization time it is not necessary with a legal mortgage to obtain a court order for sale and provided a property is vacant then it can be sold, and conveyed or transferred to a purchaser, when the mortgagee's power of sale has arisen by calling in the security by service of a suitable notice on the mortgagor.

EQUITABLE MORTGAGE

Equitable mortgages are usually created by the deposit of the title deeds or land certificate relating to the property with *or without* a memorandum of deposit. An equitable charge on the land could be created by deed, or by writing under hand, without deposit of the title deeds or land certificate, but this would only be seen where the bank most exceptionally took a second or subsequent equitable mortgage on property. Usually second and subsequent charges are taken by way of legal mortgage.

An equitable mortgage is sometimes taken on a memorandum of deposit under seal, incorporating a clause that the borrower will complete a legal mortgage on property, when called upon. However, should he fail to do so then this specially drawn *sealed* memorandum of deposit grants the bank an irrevocable power of attorney, appointing a bank official or its nominee as attorney to sell or grant leases on the property and/or to give the bank a legal mortgage. Alternatively, it is drawn as a declaration of trust under which the mortgagor declares that he holds the property in trust for the bank and authorizes his own removal and appointment of a new trustee, as directed by the bank. These provisions enable the bank to carry out an easy sale without resort to court and are not affected by the mortgagor's subsequent death or bankruptcy.

The mortgagee can act directly under these powers or can create a legal mortgage in his own favour and then proceed. This 'intermediate' step becomes necessary if there are subsequent mortgagees who will not be repaid from the sale proceeds which will be insufficient. Such parties could refuse to release their charge, thus preventing completion of the sale, if the bank sold as attorney for the mortgagor. Where it sells as mortgagee, the bank can overrule any attempt by the later mortgagees to frustrate the sale and this gives the bank a free hand, subject to its obtaining a fair price.

The disadvantage of an equitable charge is that if there are any existing equitable interests at the time when the bank takes its charge then the earlier equitable interests will rank ahead of the bank. There is an old maxim, 'Where the equities are equal, the first in time prevails'. Also, unless the equitable mortgage is under seal with a power of attorney clause, it will be necessary in every case, whether there are occupants in the mortgaged property or not, for the bank to go to court and obtain a court order for sale. This is costly, and allows the mortgagor an opportunity to be obstructive if he so wishes.

THE EQUITY OF REDEMPTION

Nothing in a mortgage can bar the mortgagor's right to redeem his mortgage, but the right can be lost when the mortgagee sells under his statutory power of sale, when a decree for foreclosure is made absolute, or when the mortgagee has been in possession for twelve years. Although a mortgage cannot be made irredeemable, it is acceptable for the mortgagee to insist that redemption be postponed for a reasonable period. Upon redemption a mortgagor will take his property free from all claims by the mortgagee (*Noakes & Co. Ltd* v. *Rice* (1902)).

REMEDIES IN THE EVENT OF FAILURE TO REPAY – LEGAL MORTGAGES

Sue on the personal covenant to repay

The bank, as mortgagee, may sue its customer on his covenant as mortgagor to repay the principal and interest on demand. This may of course prove worthwhile only when the debtor has funds and pressure may well be required to compel him to part with these. This is in fact a remedy which would be available even if no security were held.

Sale of property

The statutory power of sale arises as soon as the legal date for repayment has passed and the mortgage debt has not been paid. Under s. 103 Law of Property Act 1925, the power may however not be exercised until:

(*a*) notice requiring payment of the money has been served on the mortgagor and he has failed to pay it after the expiration of three months from service of the notice;

(*b*) interest is in arrears and unpaid for two months after becoming due; or

(*c*) the mortgagor has broken some provision in the mortgage deed other than the covenant for repayment of the mortgage money and interest.

The power of sale arises only when the mortgage money has become due, but bank mortgage forms state that the monies secured by the mortgage are to be deemed to become due on demand, and the provisions of s. 103 are excluded, so there is no need to wait three months before selling the property.

As the charge is by way of legal mortgage, an application to the court for an order for sale will not be necessary, unless the security covers a regulated agreement under the Consumer Credit Act 1974 and provided there are no persons resident in the property, and no chattel assets remain, then the bank may proceed to contract and convey, as soon as a purchaser is found at a 'fair and reasonable' price, for it will be able to give vacant possession to the purchaser. It must be remembered, however, that if the property is occupied then it will be necessary first to apply to the court for a possession order, and if, then, the occupants will not peaceably give up vacant possession, a return to the court will be necessary for powers to evict. Naturally most mortgagees, including banks, are sorry and reluctant to have to take such steps, and the opportunity would usually be given to the mortgagor for him to sell the property himself voluntarily, in the first instance.

However, if the bank has possession, or takes possession, it will then usually instruct professional and well-qualified estate agents to act for it to find a purchaser, and a sale may proceed either by private treaty or by public auction. The bank will rely upon its professional advisers as to the price which it asks and accepts, and its only duty to the mortgagors is to ensure that the open market price is obtained.

An example of the effect of a failure of this duty was seen in *Cuckmere Brick Co. Ltd* v. *Mutual Finance Ltd* (1971). Here the finance company exercised its power of sale over a plot of land, but failed to advertise the fact that planning permission was held for the building of flats on the land. This planning permission had the effect of making the land more attractive to a purchaser, and more valuable. The finance company was sued by the mortgagors for negligence, and was unable to succeed in its counter-claim for the monies still owing.

However, it was held in *Bank of Cyprus (London) Ltd* v. *Gill* (1979) that there is no obligation on a mortgagee, when selling, to await an upturn in the property market, if it is depressed. The security in this case had been a hotel which had been closed down, and the court agreed that there was no obligation on the mortgagee to keep the business running, pending the sale.

It is usual for the bank to ask the estate agent to recommend an acceptance of an offer in writing, so that it can show that it has carried out its duty of care, should the mortgagor demur. Thereafter, the bank will convey as mortgagee, but of course the mortgage to the bank is not released, and a separate conveyance or transfer (if registered title) is sealed.

Generally, fixtures pass to the mortgagee whether they were in position when the mortgage was taken or whether they were added later. Trade machinery is usually excluded and also fixtures belonging to third parties under an agreement which allows them to remove these, such as a hire purchase contract.

If, after a sale as mortgagee, the bank finds it is in a position of having surplus funds, before these are handed over to the customer it is essential to search the Land Charges Register in the case of unregistered land, to see whether a later mortgage has been created, of which the bank has no knowledge, by direct notice from that mortgagee. If the search is clear, then the surplus proceeds may be handed to the mortgagor against his written receipt, except in those cases where rights of subrogation, or contribution arise. (In the case of registered land a search is strictly unnecessary, because the bank should have been kept notified by the registrar of any subsequent entries, so long as the bank's charge is expressed to cover further advances, and the land certificate will have been brought up to date by the solicitor acting in the sale.)

Subrogation is usually said to mean 'standing in the shoes' of another person as, for instance, where a guarantor has met his liability, prior to the sale of the customer's property by the bank following which there is then a surplus. The guarantor then becomes entitled to a refund of some or all of his monies; that is, he subrogates to the surplus sale-proceeds up to the amount of his payment, and to the extent that these monies are not required by the bank.

Rights of contribution arise between co-guarantors or co-sureties, where each has made a payment, of whatever amount, in respect of their liability. If the bank, overall, has a surplus, these funds must be held to the order of the paying sureties, and it is usual not to become involved in *pro rata* distributions, but to seek the written instructions in writing from all interested parties as to how the monies should be distributed. In the absence of agreement, surplus funds can be paid into court.

Appointment of receiver

This power arises under the Law of Property Act 1925 and becomes exercisable upon precisely the same events as the power of sale. A receiver is often appointed where a property is let and a sale is not immediately likely. He is deemed to be the agent of the mortgagor, who is solely responsible, therefore, in law, for his acts and defaults, although in practice, the number of instances where the receiver does not assume actual day-to-day responsibilities is rare. He is appointed by the bank executing and delivering to him a written or sealed instrument of appointment.

Often the receiver is merely a receiver for rents, and the man chosen is usually a qualified estate agent. His duty is to collect the rents payable by tenants, and to grant new leases, when the old ones fall in. However, he is likely to assume onerous obligations and responsibilities for the property, such as fire insurance, repairs and general upkeep, and before appointing a receiver for rents the bank will ensure that, over all, the exercise will be worth while with a net return after the receiver has taken his commission, which is usually 5 per cent of gross receipts. The appointment of a receiver is often considered in those cases where the bank has a block of flats or portfolio or tenanted properties in mortgage, and is not able to find a purchaser in the short term. In such a case, while the property is advertised, the receiver will be able to manage the property, and collect the rents. Each situation must of course be considered on its merits, after a detailed report, and the number of appointments encountered in practice is fairly small.

A right to take possession of the land mortgaged and grant leases
The bank as mortgagee can go into physical or constructive possession of the land. It then grants a lease, and any rent collected must be applied in satisfaction of the claim for principal and interest. Banks seldom take this course of action because of the onerous responsibilities associated with it, as effectively they then become the landlord.

If the mortgagor has been occupying the property himself, the mortgagee must obtain possession through the courts and evict him before enjoying the leasing powers conferred by the Law of Property Act 1925.

Right to foreclose
Foreclosure is a legal proceeding whereby, whatever the size of the debt and the value of the security, the title to the property is ordered to be transferred to the mortgagee, and so the mortgagor loses his right of redemption of the mortgage and his interest in the property. An order for foreclosure *nisi* can only be obtained from the court. Before granting such an order the court will invariably give the mortgagor time to repay the sums owing, but when the order becomes absolute the mortgagor's rights to redeem his property are extinguished, and title passes to the mortgagee. The courts are reluctant to grant an order of foreclosure and will usually direct that the property be sold, as theoretically the mortgagee could, by foreclosure, obtain a property worth £50 000 in discharge of a borrowing of only £20 000.

The term 'foreclosure' tends to be used very loosely in relation to sale of a property by a mortgagee, and this is wrong. Banks hardly ever resort to foreclosure but they do sell property in security and use the proceeds to repay the borrowing secured.

REMEDIES OF EQUITABLE MORTGAGEE

Under hand
The mortgagee may sue on the debt or seek a court order for sale. If the borrower has undertaken in one of the mortgage covenants to execute a legal mortgage when called upon to do so, yet fails, the court's assistance is necessary to allow the mortgagee to sell the property or take possession.

Under seal
Sometimes an equitable mortgage is taken under seal, and then the mortgagee is in a much stronger position. Section 101 Law of Property Act 1925 expressly provides that the power of sale and power to appoint a receiver are available to mortgagees whose mortgages are by deed, so that so far as remedies are concerned, the equitable mortgagee by deed is in very much the same position as a legal mortgagee, except that he has no power to enter into possession of the mortgaged property.

REMEDIES OF A SECOND OR SUBSEQUENT MORTGAGEE

The remedies available to a second mortgagee are similar to those of a first mortgagee and could, in theory, be pursued independent of, but subject to, the prior claims of the first mortgagee against the sale proceeds or the income collected. It is *not* necessary for a second mortgagee to pay off the amount outstanding on the first mortgage *before* exercising his power of sale, although clearly it will be sensible for a second or subsequent mortgagee to be entirely certain, before becoming involved in all the promblems of obtaining vacant possession and selling the property, that in the final analysis there will undoubtedly be sufficient monies remaining, after costs, and after discharge of the prior charge(s) to make the whole exercise worthwhile from his own point of view.

Second mortgages are discharged in the same manner as first mortgages.

BANKS' MORTGAGE FORMS

Legal and equitable charges

It is recommended that the reader, especially a student, should now refer again to Chapter 11, where we examined the type of clauses which are invariably found in all bank mortgage forms, whatever the nature of the security. These clauses will be found in the standard legal or equitable mortgage form used for taking a charge over land, but additionally there will be other clauses in the land mortgage forms (Fig. 12.1) which cover matters specific to this type of security. These will be as follows:

The property upkeep and insurance clause Under this the mortgagor will undertake to keep the mortgaged premises in a good state of repair and to insure them against possible loss by fire to the full value of the property. He agrees that he will effect the insurance with an insurance company acceptable to the bank and covenants that he will pay premiums on policies promptly and then exhibit the premium receipts. The clause usually goes on to state that if the mortgagor should fail to maintain the necessary repairs then the bank is empowered to carry out the work and to recover the cost from him or through the mortgage. It also is desirable to stipulate whether any monies received under an insurance policy, whether effected by the mortgagor or by the bank as mortgagee, are to be applied towards making good the damage, or are to go towards repayment of the debt secured by the mortgage.

The agreement not to create or surrender leases We have seen how important it is, when valuing property, to know who is in occupation and to consider the effect of this on the ability to sell the property. It is obviously vitally important therefore that nothing can be done in law by a mortgagor to detract from this value, as would happen, for example, if property originally

This Legal Charge made the   day of

19   BETWEEN

of

(hereinafter called "the Mortgagor") of the one part and BANK OF CYPRUS (LONDON) LIMITED of 27-31 Charlotte Street London W1P 4BH (hereinafter called "the Bank") of the other part **WITNESSETH** as follows:-

1.   The Mortgagor hereby covenants with the Bank that the Mortgagor will on demand in writing pay or discharge to the Bank all moneys and liabilities matured or unmatured whether actual or contingent which are or may at any time hereafter be or become from time to time due owing or incurred to the Bank by the Mortgagor or in respect of which the Mortgagor may be or become liable to the Bank on any current loan or other account or otherwise in any manner whatsoever including the amount of any note or bill made accepted endorsed discounted or paid and of any liability under any guarantee or indemnity or other instrument whatsoever given or assumed by the Bank for or at the request of the Mortgagor (in all cases whether alone or jointly with any other person and in whatever style name or form and whether as principal or surety) and all commission discount and other banking charges including legal costs (as between solicitor and own client) and disbursements and any expenses incurred by the Bank in relation to this Legal Charge or any other security held by the Bank for the same indebtedness or in enforcing the same together with interest compounded quarterly to the date of repayment at such rate as may be agreed from time to time between the Mortgagor and the Bank or according to the usual practice of the Bank as well after as before any demand made or judgment obtained hereunder.

2.   The Mortgagor as beneficial owner hereby charges by way of legal mortgage the property described or referred to in the Schedule hereto (hereinafter called "the Mortgaged Premises") as a continuing security with the payment and discharge of all moneys and liabilities hereby covenanted to be paid or discharged by the Mortgagor

3.   (a)   The Mortgagor hereby covenants with the Bank:-

(i)   that the Mortgagor will keep all buildings from time to time on the Mortgaged Premises and all fixtures and fittings in or upon the Mortgaged Premises in good and substantial repair and decorative condition and insured with an insurance office or underwriters nominated in writing and if so required through brokers appointed by the Bank against loss or damage by fire and such other risks as the Bank may from time to time require in their full replacement value for the time being and if so required by the Bank in the joint names of the Mortgagor and the Bank and if not so required the Bank's interest as mortgagee shall be noted on the policy or policies so effected:

(ii)   that the Mortgagor will pay all premiums and other moneys necessary for effecting and keeping up such insurance immediately on the same becoming due and will on demand produce to the Bank the policy or policies of such insurance and the receipt for every such payment.

(b)   If the Mortgagor shall make default in keeping such buildings in good and substantial repair or in effecting or keeping up such insurances as aforesaid the Bank may repair and keep in repair the said buildings or any of them (with liberty for that purpose by itself or its agents to enter upon the Mortgaged Premises) or may effect or renew any such insurance as aforesaid as the Bank shall think fit.

(c)   If there shall be any other policy of insurance covering any of the buildings on the Mortgaged Premises against any such risks as aforesaid the Mortgagor will hold such policy and any sums received thereunder in trust for the Bank and will pay any such sum to the Bank on demand

(d)   The Bank shall be entitled to be paid the proceeds of any policy of insurance covering any of the buildings fixtures or fittings on the Mortgaged Premises and the Mortgagor hereby irrevocably instructs the insurer in respect of any such policy to pay such proceeds to the Bank and undertakes to the Bank to issue such further instructions to that effect as the Bank may require.

(e)   All moneys received on any insurance whatsoever in respect of loss or damage by fire or other insured risk to the Mortgaged Premises or any part thereof shall as the Bank requires be applied either in making good the loss or damage in respect of which the money is received or in or towards payment of the moneys for the time being hereby secured.

(f)   In any case in which any lease or agreement for tenancy (either now subsisting or hereafter made by the Mortgagor) in respect of the whole or any part of the Mortgaged Premises contains a provision for suspension of rent in the event of damage by fire and/or other insured risks the Mortgagor will keep such rent insured against suspension to the full value thereof and all moneys which may be received by virtue of any such insurance shall be paid to the Bank in or towards discharge of the moneys for the time being hereby secured

(g)   The Mortgagor will permit any authorised representative of the Bank at all reasonable times to enter upon any part of the Mortgaged Premises.

4.   (a)   At all times during the continuance of this security the Mortgagor will discharge all liabilities which may be incurred by the Mortgagor under any of the covenants agreements or obligations contained in or imposed by any lease or tenancy affecting the whole or any part of the Mortgaged Premises which may have been or may be granted or entered into by the Mortgagor or his predecessors in title and from and against all actions losses damages and costs whatsoever in consequence of any claim by any tenant or occupier of the whole or any part of the Mortgaged Premises or any other person or company arising out of any defect in or want of repair to the Mortgaged Premises or any part thereof or out of any failure to perform any such covenant or obligation and in the event of the Mortgagor failing upon the request in writing of the Bank to discharge any such liability as aforesaid the Bank may settle liquidate or compound or contest such claim (as it may think fit) and expend such moneys as the Bank may deem necessary for that purpose.

(b)   The Mortgagor will at times during the continuance of this security deliver to the Bank the counterparts of or if the same are held by a prior mortgagee copies (certified by the Mortgagor or a responsible officer of the Mortgagor) of all leases or agreements for tenancy subsisting in respect of any part of the Mortgaged Premises.

(c)   The Mortgagor will if so directed by the Bank issue instructions to any tenant of the Mortgaged Premises or any part thereof to pay all rents to the Bank.

5.   During the continuance of this security the Mortgagor will pay and keep the Bank indemnified against all rates taxes duties charges assessments and outgoings whatsoever (whether parliamentary parochial local or of any other description) which shall be assessed charged or imposed upon or in respect of the Mortgaged Premises or any part thereof and will on demand produce to the Bank the receipt for every such payment and if the Mortgagor shall at any time refuse or neglect to make any such payment or to produce the receipt therefor to the Bank on demand then and in any such case the Bank may pay the same

Fig.12.1   *Legal mortgage over land*

6.　　The Mortgagor will within seven days of receipt thereof give to the Bank a copy of any notice or order or proposal for a notice or order given issued or made by any planning or other authority body or person whatsoever which in any way relates to or affects the Mortgaged Premises or any part thereof and will if so required by the Bank produce to it the original such notice order or proposal and will take all reasonable and proper steps to comply with such order or notice without delay and will at the request of the Bank make or concur with the Bank in making any objections or representations against or in respect of any such notice or order or proposal for a notice or any appeal against any such order as the Bank may deem expedient and will pay to the Bank any compensation received as a result of any such notice or order.

7.　　The Mortgagor will at all time observe and perform and ensure the observance and performance by any other person or company at any time occupying the Mortgaged Premises or any part thereof of all restrictive and other covenants to which the Mortgaged Premises or any part thereof may from time to time be subject all obligations on the part of the Mortgagor in any lease or tenancy agreement all building regulations and all restrictions conditions and stipulations for the time being affecting the Mortgaged Premises or any part thereof or the mode of user or enjoyment of the same and provide to the Bank on request such evidence of such observance or performance as the Bank shall require and within three days will deliver to the Bank any notice or proceedings served by any landlord and relating to any alleged breach of the terms of the relevant lease or tenancy.

8.　　The Mortgagor will not without the Bank's previous consent in writing create or purport or attempt to create any mortgage charge or encumbrance on the Mortgaged Premises or any part thereof nor in any way dispose of the equity of redemption thereof or any interest therein.

9.　　(a)　The Mortgagor will not erect or make any building erection improvement material change or addition on or to the Mortgaged Premises or any part thereof nor make any material change in the user of the Mortgaged Premises or any part thereof nor make any application therefor nor proceed in accordance with any permission therefor without in any such case the previous written consent of the Bank.

(b)　Subject as aforesaid the Mortgagor will apply to the Local Planning Authority as defined by the Town and Country Planning Acts for any necessary permission for any of the aforesaid matters and will give to the Bank notice of such permission if granted within seven days of the receipt of the same.

(c)　Where at the date hereof or at any time during the continuance of this security the Mortgaged Premises or any part thereof are intended to be developed or are in the course of development the Mortgagor will proceed diligently and to the satisfaction of the Bank and any competent authority with such development in all respects in conformity with the planning and bye-law consents relative thereto.

(d)　The Mortgagor will not do or omit or suffer to be done or omitted any act matter or thing in on or respecting the Mortgaged Premises or any part thereof which shall contravene any of the provisions of the Town and Country Planning Acts.

(e)　The Mortgagor will execute and do at the expense of the Mortgagor all such work and things whatsoever as may now or at any time during the continuance of this security be directed or required by any national or local or other public authority to be executed or done upon or in respect of the Mortgaged Premises or any part thereof or by the owner or occupier thereof.

(f)　The Mortgagor will on request produce to or provide for the Bank such documents or information relating to the Mortgaged Premises or the development thereof as the Bank shall require.

10.　　The Mortgagor will duly observe and perform the provisions of every offer letter and or loan or other agreement which has been or may now or at any time hereafter during the continuance of this security be issued by the Bank to the Mortgagor.

11.　　The Mortgagor shall not without the previous written consent of the Bank be entitled to exercise any of the powers of leasing or of agreeing to lease or of accepting surrenders conferred on mortgagors whether by the Law of Property Act 1925 or otherwise.

12.　　The Bank shall be at liberty from time to time to give time for payment of any bill of exchange promissory note or other security which may have been discounted for or received from and for account of the Mortgagor by the Bank or on which the Mortgagor shall or may be liable as drawer acceptor maker indorser or otherwise to any party thereto or liable thereon as the Bank shall in its absolute discretion think fit without in any manner releasing the Mortgagor or affecting the security hereby created and it is hereby expressly agreed that all such bills of exchange promissory notes and or other securities shall be collateral security only for payment of the moneys hereby secured and shall not constitute or be deemed to constitute payment thereof.

13.　　This security shall not be considered as satisfied or discharged by any intermediate payment of the whole or part of the moneys hereby secured but shall constitute and be a continuing security to the Bank notwithstanding any settlement of account or other matter or thing whatsoever and shall be in addition to and shall not operate so as in any way to prejudice or affect the security created by any deposit which may have already been made with the Bank of the title deeds or any other documents relating to the Mortgaged Premises or any other securities which the Bank may now or at any time hereafter hold for or in respect of the moneys hereby secured or any part thereof.

14.　　The Bank shall in the event of its receiving notice that the Mortgagor has encumbered or disposed of the Mortgaged Premises or any part thereof be entitled to close the then current or loan or other account or accounts (as the case may be) of the Mortgagor or any of them and to open a new account or accounts with the Mortgagor and no money paid in or carried to the credit of the Mortgagor in any such new account shall be appropriated towards or have the effect of discharging any part of the amount due to the Bank on the said closed account or accounts at the time when it received such notice as aforesaid and if the Bank does not in fact open such new account or accounts it shall nevertheless be treated as if it had done so at the time when it received or was affected by such notice and as from that time all payments made by the Mortgagor to the Bank shall be credited or treated as having been credited to such new account or accounts and no such payments shall operate to reduce the amount due from the Mortgagor to the Bank at the time when it received or was affected by such notice but this clause shall not prejudice any security which apart from this clause the Bank would have had for the discharge by the Mortgagor of liabilities incurred after that time.

15.　　A demand for payment or any other demand or notice under this security may be made by any director manager or officer of the Bank or of any branch thereof by letter addressed to the Mortgagor and sent by ordinary pre-paid post to or left at the address of the Mortgagor as given in this security or the last known place of business or abode of the Mortgagor (or if the Mortgagor is a company at the option of the Bank to or at its registered office) and shall be deemed if posted to have been made or given at 10 a.m. on the day following the date of posting.

16.　　The restriction on the right of consolidating mortgage securities which is contained in Section 93 of the Law of Property Act 1925 shall not apply to this security.

17.　　The statutory power of sale shall be deemed to arise and be immediately exercisable at any time after any moneys owing on this security shall have been demanded without regard to section 103 of the Law of Property Act 1925 (which section shall not apply to this security or any sale made pursuant hereto) AND on any sale by the Bank the Bank may (i) sell the fixtures and machinery (other than trade machinery as defined in Section 5 of the Bills of Sale Act 1878) comprised in the Mortgaged Premises or any part thereof either together with the Mortgaged Premises to which they are affixed or separately and detached therefrom and/or (ii) sell the Mortgaged Premises or any part thereof for a price payable with or without interest by instalments over such period and in

Fig.12.1　*(contd)*　　　323

any such manner as the Bank may think fit.

18.   (a)   At any time after the Bank shall have demanded payment in respect of any moneys or liabilities hereby secured or if requested by the Mortgagor the Bank may appoint by writing any person or persons (whether an officer of the Bank or not) to be a receiver and manager or receivers and managers (hereinafter called "the Receiver" which expression shall where the context so admits include the plural and any substituted receiver and manager or receivers and managers and so that where more than one receiver and manager is appointed they may be given power to act jointly and/or severally) of all or any part of the Mortgaged Premises;

    (b)   The Bank may from time to time determine the remuneration of the Receiver and may remove the Receiver and appoint another in his place;

    (c)   The Receiver shall (so far as the law permits) be the agent of the Mortgagor (who shall alone be personally liable for his acts defaults and remuneration) and shall have and be entitled to exercise all powers conferred by the Law of Property Act 1925 in the same way as if the Receiver had been duly appointed thereunder and in particular by way of addition to but without hereby limiting any general powers hereinbefore referred to (and without prejudice to the Bank's powers) the Receiver shall have power in the name of the Mortgagor or otherwise to do the following things namely:-

(i)   to take possession of collect and get in all or any part of the Mortgaged Premises and for that purpose to take any proceedings as he shall think fit;

(ii)   to commence and/or complete any building operations or other development on the Mortgaged Premises or any part thereof and to apply for and obtain any planning permissions building regulation approvals and any other permissions consents or licences in each case as he may in his absolute discretion think fit;

(iii)   to borrow money from the Bank or others on the security of the Mortgaged Premises or otherwise;

(iv)   to provide such facilities and services for and grant such licences to tenants and generally to manage the Mortgaged Premises in such manner as he shall think fit;

(v)   if the Mortgaged Premises are leasehold to vary the terms of or surrender any lease and or to take a new lease thereof or of any part thereof and generally on such terms as he shall think fit and so that any such new lease shall ipso facto become charged to the Bank on the terms hereof so far as applicable and to execute a formal legal charge over any such new lease in favour of the Bank in such form as it may require;

(vi)   to sell let or lease or concur in selling letting or leasing and to vary the terms of terminate or accept surrenders of leases or tenancies of the Mortgaged Premises or any part thereof in such manner and for such term with or without a premium with such rights relating to other parts thereof and containing such covenants on the part of the Mortgagor and generally on such terms and conditions (including the payment of money to a lessee or tenant on a surrender) as he in his absolute discretion shall think fit;

(vii)   to make any arrangement or compromise which the Bank or he shall think fit;

(viii)   to make and effect all repairs improvements and insurances as he shall think fit;

(ix)   to appoint managers officers contractors and agents for all or any of the aforesaid purposes upon such terms as to remuneration or otherwise as he may determine;

(x)   to do all such acts and things as may be considered to be incidental or conducive to any of the matters or powers aforesaid and which he lawfully may or can do;

PROVIDED NEVERTHELESS THAT the Receiver shall not be authorised to exercise any of the aforesaid powers if and insofar and so long as the Bank shall in writing exclude the same whether in or at the time of his appointment or subsequently.

19.   The statutory powers of sale leasing and accepting surrenders exercisable by the Bank hereunder are hereby extended so as to authorise the Bank whether in its own name or in that of the Mortgagor to grant a lease or leases of the whole or any part or parts of the Mortgaged Premises with such rights relating to other parts thereof and containing such covenants on the part of the Mortgagor and generally on such terms and conditions (including the payment of money to a lessee or tenant on a surrender) and whether or not at a premium as the Bank in its absolute discretion shall think fit.

20.   The Mortgagor hereby irrevocably appoints the Bank and the Receiver jointly and also severally the Attorney and Attorneys of the Mortgagor for the Mortgagor and in his name and on his behalf and as his act and deed or otherwise to sign seal deliver and otherwise perfect any deed assurance agreement instrument or act which may be required or may be deemed proper for any of the purposes hereof.

21.   All powers of the Receiver hereunder may be exercised by the Bank whether as attorney of the Mortgagor or otherwise.

22.   In no circumstances shall the Bank or the Receiver be liable to account to the Mortgagor as a mortgagee in possession or otherwise for any moneys not actually received by them respectively.

23.   Any moneys received under the powers hereby conferred shall subject to the payment of any claims having priority to this Deed be paid or applied in the following order of priority:-

    (a)   in satisfaction of all costs charges and expenses properly incurred and payments properly made by the Bank or the Receiver and of the remuneration of the Receiver;

    (b)   in or towards satisfaction of the moneys outstanding and hereby secured;

    (c)   as to any surplus to the person or persons entitled thereto.

24.   At any time after payment in respect of any moneys or liabilities hereby secured has been demanded and any part thereof remains unpaid the Bank may as agent of the Mortgagor remove and sell any chattels on the Mortgaged Premises and the net proceeds of sale thereof shall be paid to the Mortgagor on demand and the Bank shall not have the right to retain or set off such proceeds of sale against any indebtedness of the Mortgagor to the Bank.

25.   All costs charges and expenses incurred hereunder by the Bank and any receiver appointed by the Bank and all other moneys paid by the Bank in perfecting or otherwise in connection with this security or in respect of the Mortgaged Premises including (without prejudice to the generality of the foregoing) all moneys expended by the Bank under clauses 3 (b) and 5 hereof and all moneys advanced or paid by the Bank to any Receiver for the purposes set out in clause 18 hereof and all costs of the Bank of all proceedings for enforcement of the security hereby constituted or for obtaining payment of the moneys and liabilities hereby secured (whether or not such costs charges expenses and moneys or part thereof would be allowable upon a party and party or solicitor and own client taxation by the Court) shall be recoverable from the Mortgagor as a debt and may be debited to any account of the Mortgagor and shall bear interest accordingly and shall be charged on the Mortgaged Premises.

26.   Where the Mortgagor is a company the Mortgagor hereby certifies that this Charge does not contravene

    Fig.12.1   *(contd)*

any of the provisions of its Memorandum and Articles of Association.

27.   (a)   If the Mortgaged Premises or any part thereof is not registered under the Land Registration Acts 1925 to 1971 no person shall during the continuance of this security be registered under the said Acts as proprietor of the Mortgaged Premises or any part thereof without the consent in writing of the Bank and upon any such registration the Mortgagor shall forthwith deliver to the Bank all Land Certificates relating to the same.

(b)   If the Mortgaged Premises or any part thereof is or becomes registered under the Land Registration Acts 1925 to 1971 the Mortgagor hereby applies to the Registrar for a restriction in the following terms to be entered on the register of the title relating to it:-

"Except under an order of the Registrar no disposition by the proprietor of the land is to be registered without the consent of the proprietor for the time being of the charge hereby created".

28.   In this Deed where the context admits:-

(a)   the expressions "the Mortgagor" and "the Bank" include their respective successors in title and assigns;

(b)   if there are two or more parties hereto of the first part the expression "the Mortgagor" shall throughout mean and include such two or more parties and each of them or (as the case may require) such two or more parties or any of them and shall so far as the context admits be construed as well in the singular as in the plural as in the singular and all covenants charges agreements and undertakings herein expressed or implied on the part of the Mortgagor shall be deemed to be joint and several covenants charges agreements and undertakings by such parties and in particular this security and the covenant in clause I hereof and the remaining covenants charges agreements and undertakings herein contained or implied shall extend and apply to any moneys owing or liabilities incurred by any of such parties to the Bank whether solely or jointly with each other or with any other person and references to the Mortgagor shall where the context permits mean and include any one or more of such parties as well as such parties jointly;

(c)   the expression "the Town and Country Planning Acts" shall mean and include the Town and Country Planning Acts 1971 to 1977 and references thereto or to any other statute include any Act or Acts for the time being amending or replacing the same and any instruments orders rules or regulations for the time being in force issued under or by virtue thereof.

IN WITNESS whereof the Mortgagor has executed this Deed under seal the day and year first before written.

THE SCHEDULE referred to

(Short description of the Mortgaged Premises)

ALL THAT freehold/leasehold property situate at and known as

comprised in the following document(s):-

County and District (or London Borough)	Land Certificate(s) Title No. (s)

Date	Description (conveyance, lease, etc.)	Parties

Fig. 12.1   *(contd)*

SIGNED SEALED and DELIVERED

by the said ....

....

in the presence of

SIGNED SEALED and DELIVERED

by the said ....

....

in the presence of

SIGNED SEALED and DELIVERED

by the said ....

....

in the presence of

(Where the Mortgagor is a company or companies)

THE COMMON SEAL OF ....

.... LIMITED

(registered in England No ....) was hereunto affixed in the presence of:-

Director

Secretary

THE COMMON SEAL OF ....

.... LIMITED

(registered in England No ....) was hereunto affixed in the presence of:-

Director

Secretary

Dated   19

THIS RELEASE made between BANK OF CYPRUS (LONDON) LIMITED of the one pa
and the within named Mortgagor of the other part WITNESSETH that the Bank as Mo
gagee hereby releases the Property comprised in the within written Legal Charge fro
all moneys and liabilities thereby secured.

As Witness the seal of the Bank this   day of

THE COMMON SEAL of
BANK OF CYPRUS (LONDON) LIMITED }
was hereunto affixed in the presence of:

Director

Secretary

TO
BANK OF CYPRUS (LONDON) LTD.

Legal Charge
OF

326   **Fig.12.1**   _(contd)_

mortgaged by owner-occupiers were found later to be occupied by tenants who had been granted security of tenure by the mortgagors. The bank would not then be able to obtain vacant possession in order to sell.

Hence, as under s. 99 Law of Property Act 1925, a mortgagor has the power to grant agricultural or occupational leases, subject to certain conditions, for a period not exceeding fifty years and building leases for any term up to ninety-nine years, and may accept a surrender of any lease, if his object in doing so is to grant a new lease within his statutory powers, it is vital for the bank's position as mortgagee to exclude the mortgagor's rights under this section of the Act. Consequently, a clause is included in the mortgage deed withdrawing this power to grant leases, unless the prior written consent of the bank is given.[91] (There is however one exception to this in that, under the Agricultural Holdings Act 1948, the statutory power of a mortgagor in possession to grant a lease of agricultural land cannot be excluded and such a lease would be binding on a mortgagee.)

The case of *Dudley and District Benefit Building Society* v. *Emerson* (1949) illustrates the value of this clause. There a borrower had mortgaged his house to the building society under a deed which contained a clause that expressly excluded the statutory powers of the mortgagor to grant leases. In fact, *subsequently*, the borrower granted a weekly tenancy of the house to a person who took possession. The borrower failed to maintain his repayments under the mortgage and the building society started legal proceedings to obtain possession. However, the tenant claimed that he could not be evicted as the tenancy was subject to the Rent Restriction Acts. The case went to the Court of Appeal, where it was held that while the tenancy granted by the mortgagor conferred a good title as between him and the tenant, this was not the case as against the mortgagee.

It follows from this that a lending banker should always question a mortgagor who has just bought premises, to ensure that they have not been let to a tenant on or before the date of execution of the mortgage. Particular care should be exercised where the mortgagor is known to live at another address, as by that implication it might later be claimed that the bank knew that the property was, or was to be, the subject of a tenancy, for if a property is let *at the time* when the mortgage is given, the bank will not then be able to obtain vacant possession, in reliance on the ruling of the case described above.

Equally important is the need for a bank not to do anything which would lead to a claim that even in the absence of prior written agreement the bank was still bound by a tenancy that had been created because it was estopped by its conduct in relying on its mortgage[92] (see page 339 regarding 'Occupants').

The agreement to keep covenants This clause is a routine clause, sometimes omitted, whereby a mortgagor agrees that he will perform his

91 See Appendix I, Q. 41 (April 1981).
92 See Appendix I, Q. 41 (April 1981).

obligations to his lessor, in the case of leasehold land, as set out by way of covenants in his lease. As those covenants are present in the lease which will be deposited by the mortgagor, no real benefit is derived by their inclusion in the mortgage form.

The exclusion of the power of consolidation clause[93]   At common law, and prior to the Conveyancing Act 1881, a mortgagee of two or more properties could treat the securities as jointly charged for repayment of the whole debt. Hence a mortgagor could not repay one without redeeming them all; in other words, the mortgagee could 'consolidate' his securities. This right was abolished by the Act of 1881 which was re-enacted in s. 93 Law of Property Act 1925: it allows a mortgagor who is redeeming one mortgage to do so without payment of any sums due under any separate mortgage granted by him. To overcome any possible difficulty for the bank as mortgagee by a mortgagor repaying one advance and calling for the return to him of a security worth more than that advance, yet leaving the bank still lending on another account secured by an unsatisfactory or inadequate property, a clause is sometimes included in the mortgage deed with excludes the statutory right given to the mortgagor by s. 93. However, many banks do not bother to cover the point in their forms of charge as these are drawn up as security for 'all monies owing on all accounts. . .' and hence in effect the bank is 'in the driving seat', or in control, in all such situations.

Certificate that the charge does not contravene any provisions of a company's memorandum and articles of association   This clause is frequently included in mortgages over land, and is used to obviate the need for a separate resolution to this effect when the security is granted over registered title by a limited company. In either form the resolution is necessary to satisfy the land registrar before he will issue a charge certificate.

Bank's consent required before mortgagor can create a further mortgage   Not all banks incorporate a covenant to this effect in their mortgage forms, but the reason for its inclusion is obviously to strengthen the bank's control over its security and to afford a means whereby it is kept advised of attempts to deal with the land before, and not after, the event. If the covenant is broken, that does not necessarily mean that the later mortgage is void, as the restrictive agreement is only between the bank and the mortgagor. It might mean in a converse situation, however, where the bank is attempting to obtain a second charge behind a lender incorporating such a clause in his security, that that lender, if not approached beforehand or if he has refused to grant permission, will not acknowledge notice of the bank's later charge.

93 See Appendix I, Q. 45 (September 1981).

UNREGISTERED LAND

Title deeds

Title to unregistered land is represented by the title deeds, which may be several documents showing all dealings in the land over a long period of time, or may be just a few documents and appropriate searches, as in the case of a short-term lease recently created by the freeholder. Invariably, when mention is made of 'deeds', it is title to unregistered land that is referred to, and, strictly, the term should not be used for a land certificate representing a registered title at HM Land Registry.

Deeds are usually accompanied by a schedule, which is a list that helps any party needing to inspect them, as he can then quickly check whether any documents are missing, especially if a receipt has to be given, as when a bank accepts the deeds for safe keeping or as security.

A typical schedule is shown in Fig 12.2. The reader should note the chain of title, and also released mortgages. The abstract is a document prepared by a solicitor reciting past transactions, necessary when the documents covering those transactions are not present in the deeds, perhaps because they have passed to other parties when part of the land has been sold off. These should always be 'marked' or initialled.

The conveyances are documents transferring the freehold title to another party on the date shown and the assent is a conveyance by an executor, acting in the deceased title holder's estate, transferring title to the beneficiary under the will.

An assignment would be the name given to the document transferring a leasehold interest.

The schedule also shows searches at the Land Charges Department, carried out on the occasion of each conveyance or mortgage and also searches in the local land charges register to ascertain the position on planning permissions and other possible local orders affecting the property.

Banks will often obtain a report on title from solicitors but in straightforward cases sometimes they can satisfy themselves. When deeds are checked at the branch they should show a good root of title going back at least fifteen years and a chain of title in respect of all subsequent transactions in the property; each deed should describe the property clearly and each must have been correctly executed. If there is any doubt that the title might have become a registered title an enquiry can be made at the local Land Registry to ensure that this is not so, but registration is normally indicated by the Land Registry stamp on the last document.

Priority of mortgages over unregistered land

Priorities may be defined, rather simply, as the order in which parties interested in the land or proceeds of sale are able to assert their rights or take the amount to which they are entitled upon a sale, or other dealing.

```
Schedule of Freehold Deeds and Documents relating to 54 Brandon Avenue  Town

1929                      ABSTRACT OF TITLE

10th January 1929         CONVEYANCE        -Mary Bucklow to David Bradford

20th May 1934             CONVEYANCE        -David Bradford to Ann Slater

20th May 1934             MORTGAGE          -Ann Slater to Townshire
                                             Building Society

10th October 1949         RELEASE           -Townshire Building Society to
                                             Executors of Ann Slater

1949                      SUPPLEMENTAL ABSTRACT OF TITLE

10th Nov. 1949            ASSENT            -Executors of Ann Slater deceased
                                             to Walter Lewis

10th Nov. 1949            MORTGAGE          -Walter Lewis to Seaside
                                             Building Society

14th April 1952           SUB-MORTGAGE      -Seaside Building Society to
                                             Practice Bank Ltd.
                                             (release endorsed 21st August
                                             1959).

12th February 1969        RELEASE           -Seaside Building Society to
                                             Walter Lewis

21st February 1969        CONVEYANCE        -Walter Lewis to Tony Brewis

17th May 1969             MORTGAGE          -Tony Brewis to Homes Building
                                             Society

10th July 1978            SECOND MORTGAGE   -Tony Brewis to Practice
                                             Bank Ltd.

VARIOUS SUNDRY SEARCHES AND PAPERS
```

Fig.12.2   *Schedule of deeds – unregistered land*

The general rule, under s. 97 Law of Property Act 1925, is that priorities are determined by whichever comes first, either possession of the title deeds with no notice of other interests at that time, *or* the date of registration of a charge at the Land Charges Department. Section 97 states:

> Every mortgage affecting a legal estate in land made after the commencement of this Act, whether legal or equitable (not being a mortgage protected by the deposit of documents relating to the legal estate effected) shall rank *according to its date of registration* as a land charge pursuant to the Land Charges Act 1925.

Thus, under the Land Charges Act 1925 a puisne mortgage or a general equitable charge is void as against a subsequent mortgagee, unless it has been registered in the land charges register before the subsequent mortgage.

A first mortgagee of unregistered land in possession of the deeds need not therefore register his charge to rank 'first in the queue'. When taking his charge he must however search the land charges register at the Land Charges Department, Plymouth, to ensure that no mortgage or interest has been registered before him, for if that is the case then he will rank after it. If, when taking a mortgage, the deeds are missing then this is constructive notice of a prior charge.

Second or third mortgages which are created without the deposit of the deeds must be registered at the Land Charges Department to determine the order of their priority, but not so as to make the mortgage valid. In the case of a legal mortgage registration will be as a 'puisne' mortgage; in the case of an equitable mortgage it will be as a general equitable charge. The date of registration, not the date of the mortgage, is the important date which determines the priority.

After he has searched, a prospective mortgagee should get his mortgage executed within the protective period shown on the official search (fifteen working days), as he will not then be affected by any entry made in the land charges register in this period, unless that entry is made in pursuance of a priority notice already lodged by the other party. However, there is an apparent conflict between the statutes giving effect to this rule (s. 4 Law of Property (Amendment) Act 1926 and s. 94 Law of Property Act 1925), as some authorities believe that an entry by another party between the search and the date of the mortgage could be effective and give priority in certain instances. Bankers therefore always ensure that a further search is made on the day the mortgage is signed, or immediately afterwards, to guard against having lost priority. There is no case law to clarify matters, so ideally they should not lend on current account until that further clear search has been seen.

Bankers could, however, lodge a priority notice to protect themselves, although this procedure is not at all common. This is done by lodging a priority notice at the Land Charges Department at least fourteen days before the creation of the mortgage. If an application to register the mortgage is then presented within twenty-eight days of the submission of the priority notice referring to that notice then registration will take effect as if it had been made at the time when the mortgage was created.

Normally, however, bankers simply search again after execution of their mortgage so that they can ensure that, if they are first mortgagees, no other charge has been recorded between their first search and the execution of the mortgage. If they are second or subsequent mortgagees then they search again for the same reason and also to ensure that their charge has been correctly registered and ranks in the order which they anticipated.

To summarize, therefore, the first mortgagee of unregistered land is *usually* in possession of the deeds, having searched the Land Charges Department to ensure that no one ranks in front of him. He does not register his charge.

Subsequent mortgagees will not hold the deeds and will register a C(i) (puisne legal mortgage) or C(iii) (general equitable charge), depending on the nature of their charge, and this registration determines their order of ranking after the first mortgagee, whose existence is known or presumed, because of the absence of the deeds. Direct notice is given to the earlier mortgagees which fixes their monetary priority, unless they have an obligation to make further advances.

Searches and land charges register charges

The index of the land charges register at the Land Charges Department is one of names, and it is necessary to search against the full name and all known addresses for the person concerned, usually by post. The certificate of the result of search (Fig 12.3) will not give sufficient details of any prior charge which appears still to be outstanding and office copies of the entry (Fig. 12.5) can be obtained on application, to obtain full particulars and to ensure that the information refers to the person the searcher is concerned with. Searches should be present with the deeds, being part of the chain of title, and the mortgagee or his solicitors may need only to search against the name of the mortgagor and the person who conveyed to him.

The registers at the Land Charges Department cover pending actions, such as those in bankruptcy or liquidation, e.g. a petition, plus writs and orders made, such as a bankruptcy order or winding up order, or a charging order granted to a judgment creditor. They also cover annuities and deeds of arrangements. Land charges themselves are divided into classes denoted as A, B, C, D, E, and F. The entry is made against the name of the proprietor, not agianst the property, and a request for search should quote full names, descriptions and addresses of the mortgagors, or other party. Charges in classes C, D and F are of prime importance to the banker, although if other entries appear he will ask a solicitor to advise on the consequences. Common entries encountered are:

Class C

(i) Puisne mortgages,[94] these are legal mortgages not protected by the deposit of the deeds, and are usually second or subsequent charges.

(ii) A limited owner's charge; an equitable charge in favour of a tenant for life or other statutory owner acquired by discharging certain liabilities, as would happen where someone has paid death duties in respect of the estate in which his interest lies.

(iii) A general equitable charge; an equitable mortgage which is not protected by deposit of title deeds.

(iv) An estate contract; this is a contract to create or convey a legal estate, and might for example be registered by a party who has an option or contract to purchase.

94 See Appendix I, Q. 33 (April 1980).

FORM K18

LAND CHARGES ACT, 1972.
CERTIFICATE OF THE RESULT OF SEARCH

CERTIFICATE No.		CERTIFICATE DATE	PROTECTION ENDS ON
1279814	PAGE 0001	13 DEC 1983	06 JAN 1984

It is hereby certified that an official search in respect of the undermentioned particulars has been made in the index to the registers which are kept pursuant to the Land Charges Act, 1972. The result of the search is shown below.

PARTICULAR SEARCHED		
COUNTY OR COUNTIES		63

NAME(S) / Particulars of Charge	PERIOD	Fees £
ANTHONY NORMAN * WHEELER *	1979-1983	.50
(1) F NO. 90293 DATED 4 MAY 1979 (2) 98 NEW ROAD (3) TOWN (4) LOAMSHIRE		
(1) C(I) NO. 254175 DATED 7 DEC 1979 (2) 98 NEW ROAD (3) TOWN (4) LOAMSHIRE		

– – – – – – – – – END OF SEARCH – – – – – – – –

APPLICANT'S REFERENCE	APPLICANT'S KEY NUMBER	AMOUNT DEBITED	£	0.50
SEC/JCW				

Practice Bank plc
1 High Street
TOWN

Any enquiries concerning this certificate
to be addressed to
The Superintendent
Land Charges Department.
Burrington Way,
Plymouth, PL5 3LP

IMPORTANT
PLEASE READ THE NOTES OVERLEAF.

Fig.12.3 *Land charges register – certificate of result of search*

334

B. Securities for Advances

Fig.12.3 *(contd)*

Class D

(i) Charges in favour of the Inland Revenue in respect of capital transfer tax/inheritance tax.

(ii) Restrictive covenants which restrict the use of the land. However, those made between a lessor and lessee would not be recorded here.

(iii) Equitable easements, such as a right of way.

Class F[95] A charge affecting the matrimonial home by virtue of the Matrimonial Homes Act 1967. The rights of occupation given to a spouse by the Act are a charge on the estate, and the charge is registrable. The rights are binding on a subsequent mortgagee, unless they are waived, and have been discussed fully above.

Lost priorities

A mortgagee of unregistered land, who has taken the deeds or registered his charge at the Land Charges Department and made the necessary searches, need not periodically search for further charges. Indeed, if he could not rely on his priority as it stood, the banker as mortgagee would have to search every time he paid a cheque, and that would be an impractical situation.

Priority can be lost, however, where notice of a subsequent charge comes to the attention of the lender, usually by way of specific advice from the new lender or a judgment creditor who has obtained a charging order. This lost priority occurs where the bank is lending on a current account, the balance of which is fluctuating, for there, under the operation of the Rule in *Clayton's Case*, old borrowings are constantly being repaid and new ones being created. If action is not taken upon receiving notice of the creation of another charge then the bank's priority will become postponed behind that of the later lender who will move ahead of him.[96] This means that if a bank is lending on current account secured by mortgage, and the customer subsequently grants a second or subsequent mortgage elsewhere, the current account should be stopped as soon as notice of the second mortgage is received, thus ensuring that the Rule in *Clayton's Case* does not operate against the bank. Failure to break the account will result in the reduction, and possible postponement, of the full amount secured by the mortgage, behind the amount lent by the new lender, as a result of credits being paid into the current account and debits creating a new debt (*Deeley* v. *Lloyds Bank Ltd* (1912)). In this case the bank sold a property under its powers as mortgagee, and the amount realized was just sufficient to repay the bank's advance. Earlier, however, Mrs Deeley had been given a mortgage after that to the bank, and she had given notice of it to Lloyds. The bank, however, had failed to stop the customer's current account at that point, and upon the sale, Mrs Deeley claimed priority over the bank's charge and was successful in her action to recover the proceeds of the sale ahead of the bank.

A similar stop on the account should be made when notice of a Class F charge under the Matrimonial Homes Act 1967 is received, for if not, the holder of the Class F will eventually rank ahead of the bank by the operation of *Clayton's Case* on the fluctuating account.

However, where a lending is made on loan account, these considerations do not apply, as no new debt is created, and consequently it is safe to allow the loan account to continue to operate on the basis that the only entries will be credits reducing the debt, and interest entries which will be fully secured.

Following the Boland decision (a registered land decision), it might be thought that to be 'safe' from the dangers that might arise if a new person takes up occupancy and starts to contibute to the upkeep of the house, a bank should stop a fluctuating account when it learns of this. In practice, the 'art' of dealing with overriding interests has not yet grown to such a degree of perfection, and could be difficult to implement in practice.

95 See Appendix I, Q. 33 (April 1980).
96 See Appendix I, Q. 58 (April 1983).

In case they should fail to stop a current account secured by a mortgage when they receive notice of a later charge, many banks have introduced a clause into their mortgage forms which purports to protect them and retain the priority position as it would have been if they *had* stopped the account and opened a new one. The effectiveness of such a type of clause (see Fig. 12.1 clause 14) was upheld in *Westminster Bank Ltd* v. *Cond* (1940).

Thus the bank will be affected by subsequent charges only when it knows of them, and this is why notice is usually sent direct by the later mortgagee. That notice will ask how much is secured by the bank's charge, so that the later mortgagee can value his security and it will ask if there is any obligation on the part of the bank to make further advances which would rank ahead of his mortgage.[97] The answer here, as far as most banks and their charge forms are concerned, is that no such obligations will exist.

Occasionally the subsequent lender will agree with the bank and the customer that whatever the position at the time of notice the bank can have priority up to a certain amount; a letter of priority will then be given and should be placed with the deeds.[98] In such cases the bank must remember that once that amount is exceeded it will rank after the later lender and it will only be able to recover more under its mortgage if the property sells for sufficient to clear the bank's first secured amount and the lending of the second mortgagee. In other words, if there is sufficient 'equity' remaining, the bank will become the effective 'third mortgagee', although there is no need for a new charge to be executed in favour of the bank.

The letter of priority, or deed of priority as it is sometimes called, may be executed by the two mortgagees and the borrower, although sometimes it consists merely of a letter from one lender to the other, reciting the charge dates and giving a brief description of the mortgaged property for identification purposes. The letter or deed then contains the agreement not to look to the security over and above a certain amount. Invariably, however, the first secured lender is empowered to look also for all his interest, commission, costs and other charges associated with the taking and realization of the security. Letters of priority, of course, apply to situations involving both registered and unregistered land.

Similar considerations apply if the bank receives notice that a charging order has been granted against property in mortgage. This is equivalent to another mortgage granted by the court to a judgment creditor over assets belonging to his debtor, the bank's mortgagor. If the amount of the debt is shown in the notice the bank will be able to calculate the extent of any equity remaining, but if the charging order was made under s. 9 or s. 10 of the Drug Trafficking Offences Act 1986, until such time as the defendant is convicted and a confiscation order is made this will not be known, although clearly the amounts could be substantial.

97 See Appendix I, Q. 45 (September 1981).
98 See Appendix I, Q. 58 (April 1983).

In all cases when notice of a charging order is received the account secured should be broken. Charging orders are not restricted to land, and may be made over life policies or stocks and shares.

Perfecting the mortgage

In taking a first mortgage over freehold unregistered land, whether by way of a legal charge, or an equitable charge, the branch securities officer will need to attend to the following points, some aspects of which we have discussed earlier in greater depth.

Security step A: valuation It is essential that all property offered as security should be inspected and valued either by a bank official or by a professional estate agent and surveyor, who visits personally, and not simply by relying on what the deeds say and what the customer claims is the value. In the case of domestic property, the current vacant possession valuation can usually be fairly accurately ascertained by the banker, but where specialized or commercial property is concerned professional valuations are desirable. It must be remembered that the valuation of the security will be affected not only by the condition of the property, its location, access, and local authority plans for the area, but also by its present terms of occupation. The only real way to know what a property is worth is to 'test the market', either by advertising it for sale or by putting it up for auction. It is, of course, not possible to do this when a property now occupied and bought some years ago is offered for mortgage! Where the property has just been acquired, the recent consideration will give a useful guide, but even so, for mortgage valuation purposes care should be taken. During the property slump in the mid-1970s, many a lender found that he had been deceived by the price paid for land and property in the earlier boom years, as a result of which he had lent well over the realistic value of his security.

It is important to identify the property from the deeds, and to ensure that all the property as seen is in fact covered by the title offered in mortgage. The author once encountered a situation where a golf course was mortgaged to a lender, but when the lender had need to resort to his power of sale to recover his money, he discovered to his horror that the land in mortgage only covered part of the course, in fact only seventeen of the eighteen holes, and the club house was not included!

If the bank is offered a tenanted property as security, then the valuation is likely to be very much less than the value if it were only owner-occupied, and will be dependent, among other things, upon the covenants in the lease and upon its terms.[99] The reason for this is that the property would only be of interest to an investor in property, were it to be offered for sale, and the investor would base his price on the income obtainable from tenants – less the

99   See Appendix I, Q. 54 (September 1982).

costs of any upkeep which is his responsibility under the lease. The net income multiplied by a number of years (perhaps five or so), plus, perhaps, a premium if vacant possession is likely in the not-too-distant future, gives an indication of the value although this can vary with movements in interest rates, and the attraction of property as an investment from time to time.

We have seen that where a tenancy is created *after* the bank's mortgage and without its consent the bank will be able to obtain vacant possession and evict the tenant. Problems can arise, however, where the tenant claims that the bank became aware of the situation and did nothing to protect itself at that time, and has therefore become estopped or prevented from seeking possession later. This could be so where the bank has accepted rent into the account,[100] or knows that his mortgagor lives at another address. Also, of course, if a Class F charge has been registered by a spouse, ahead of the bank, then it will never be able to obtain vacant possession as against that person, unless the spouse waives his or her interest.

Security step B: occupants   The banker should always ensure who is in occupation when the property is charged, that is whether it is owner-occupied property or whether there is a tenant. The position in law is that if the property is tenanted at the time when it is mortgaged then the mortgage will be subject to the prior rights of occupation of the tenant (*Universal Permanent Building Society* v. *Cooke* (1951)). Where, however, the property is not subject to a tenancy at the time of mortgage, and a tenancy is granted subsequently without the mortgagee's consent as required by the mortgage deed, then that tenancy is void as against the mortgagee (*Dudley and District Benefit Building Society* v. *Emerson* (1949)).

Equally important, these days, is consideration of the repercussions of the Boland decision (*Williams & Glyn's Bank* v. *Boland* (1980)). Although that case concerned registered land, the implications for unregistered title are such that much the same considerations apply. Put simply, if the title is vested in one person's name (e.g. Mr Smith) but another party (e.g. Mrs Smith) has contributed to the purchase, and is in occupation at the time of the mortgage to the bank, then she (he) will have rights which override the bank's mortgage rights to vacant possession (even though a Class F charge has not been registered).

Since this decision, banks have made careful enquiry as to who occupies a property offered for mortgage and seek to obtain a waiver or charge from any party or parties who could obstruct a later sale by the bank as mortgagee. In the case of old security taken before 1979 they try to obtain a waiver or charge upon the renewal of borrowing facilities, but this is not always possible. Some banks ask the mortgagor to sign a form stating who is in occupation of the property offered for mortgage, and this goes on to state that the mortgagor will inform the bank of any changes as and when they occur.

100 See Appendix I, Q. 41 (April 1981).

When considering the question of who occupies a property offered for mortgage, the banker should not think that he is only concerned with domestic property. Very similar considerations apply to company premises, and often in group situations it will be found that a subsidiary is in occupation of a property the title to which is in the name of another subsidiary or the holding company. Sometimes an entirely unrelated company may be in occupation, the only link being the family shareholding. Clearly these situations can lead to difficulties if the title-holder company fails and the bank looks for a sale to repay its lending to that company.

Security step C: report on title Most banks ask a solicitor to undertake this duty and the deeds are then sent to him against his standard undertaking to hold them to the bank's order and to return them upon request. Any defects, or possible defects in title, should thus be brought to the bank's attention, and the effect of the security should be carefully noted and considered.

The report will include a description of the property and its tenure, the name of the estate owner, and will go on to say whether or not the title is good and marketable and unencumbered. If there are any statutory orders affecting the property these should be mentioned, as should any local authority plans revealed in local land charges searches.

Should the solicitor make any mistake which later turns out to be costly to the bank, it will be able to seek compensation from him or the Law Society for negligence.

Security step D: execution of the mortgage
(a) *Completion of details.* The correct bank mortgage form must be selected for use and it should be completed showing the name(s) of the mortgagor(s) in full and, if third-party security, the name of the account secured.

If the mortgage is to be limited in amount the maximum figure for which it will be enforceable must be inserted, and upon the mortgage being signed the mortgagor may 'initial' or 'sign' in the margin to show that the limitation was present at that time. This avoids any subsequent claim that the clause was blank and was later completed at the wrong level by the bank.

Details of the property to be charged will be entered on the mortgage schedule by one of three methods: by listing the deeds, by referring to the last conveyance or assignment, or by describing the property by quoting from the deeds.

The mortgage form should be dated as to the day on which it is executed. While it is important to insert the correct date on a mortgage (particularly with company securities in view of the registration necessary at Companies House), the date is not an essential part of a mortgage and the mortgage takes effect from the date of its delivery, even when the mortgage is dated and that date is not the date on which delivery takes place (*Goddard's Case* (1584)).

A copy of the completed form is now often given to the mortgagor who acknowledges this.

(b) *Signature*. The charge should be executed under seal by the mortgagor(s), private individuals signing alongside an affixed wafer-seal or LS sign.

The charge form must not be sent out to the mortgagor(s) and he should attend at the branch to sign it, or, if that is not possible, at a local branch or his own bankers who will have been asked to explain matters to him. Any further explanation which he requires must of course be answered, although if the security is third-party security it will be necessary to have the customer's consent, if any of the enquiries relate to the customer's personal affairs, as otherwise there could be a breach of secrecy. As regards the terms of the charge form, it is important that any misunderstanding by the chargor is corrected, and that he is not misled in any way, for unfortunately mortgagors often seem to seek to avoid liability later by saying that they had not understood what they were signing.

Before this stage is reached, consideration should have been given as to whether the mortgagor should receive the benefit of independent advice from his own solicitor, and the factors in the banker's mind here will revolve around whether the chargor fully understands the purport of what he is doing. In the case of a woman the same considerations apply as for a man, although the added possibility of undue influence by her husband must be taken into account, if the security is being given for him, or a business with which he is associated. If there is any doubt in the banker's mind then independent legal advice should be offered, and if the recommendation is not accepted it is advisable for that fact to be recorded, contemporaneously, in the bank's records, so that this can be demonstrated to a court at a later date, if necessary, should the mortgagor claim that he/she did not have independent advice (true) and the he/she did not know it could be taken (untrue). If advice from a solicitor is required, the solicitor should be chosen by the mortgagor, and not the bank, although the bank can suggest names if the mortgagor wishes.

Sometimes the mortgagor banks at another branch or bank, and in those cases it is acceptable for him to sign the charge form at his own branch (if independent advice is not required). Care should be taken, however, to ensure that the witnessing branch is properly instructed and that it does not mislead the mortgagor in any way.

(c) *Witnessing*. It is not legally necessary for a mortgage to be witnessed, but to avoid later dispute a bank officer or the mortgagor's solicitor will invariably append his signature and state the capacity in which he signs.

Security step E: land charges register searches We have seen how priority of mortgages is established in the case of unregistered land, and where the bank is taking a first mortgage the land charges register search which is

FORM K15

LAND CHARGES ACT 1972

APPLICATION FOR AN OFFICIAL SEARCH
NOT APPLICABLE TO REGISTERED LAND

Application is hereby made for an official search in the index to the registers kept pursuant to the Land Charges Act 1972 for any subsisting entries in respect of the under-mentioned particulars.

Payment of fee
(see note 3 overleaf)

EITHER

Insert a cross (X) in this box if the fee is to be paid through a credit account

OR

affix stamps in this space

For Official Use Only	IMPORTANT:	**Please read the notes overleaf before completing this form.**		
STX		NAMES TO BE SEARCHED (Please use block letters and see note 4 overleaf)	PERIOD OF YEARS (see note 5 overleaf)	
			From	To
	Forename(s)			
	Surname			
	Forename(s)			
	Surname			
	Forename(s)			
	Surname			
	Forename(s)			
	Surname			
	Forename(s)			
	Surname			
	Forename(s)			
	Surname			

COUNTY (see note 6 overleaf)

FORMER COUNTY

DESCRIPTION OF LAND (see note 7 overleaf)

FORMER DESCRIPTION

Particulars of Applicant (see notes 8, 9 and 10 overleaf)		Address for despatch of certificate This Box must be Completed with Branch Address
Key Number	Name and address	
2497071		

Branch

Applicant's reference :   Date

FOR OFFICIAL USE ONLY

Fig.12.4   *Land charges register search – Form K15*

NOTES FOR GUIDANCE OF APPLICANTS

The following notes are supplied to assist you in making the application overleaf. For further information on procedures for making applications to the Land Charges Department, see the booklet (36 pages) "Computerised Land Charges Department: a practical guide for solicitors", obtainable from any bookshop of Her Majesty's Stationery Office.

1. **Effect of search.** The official certificate of the result of this search will have no statutory effect in relation to registered land (see Land Registration Act 1925, s.59 and Land Charges Act 1972, s.14).

2. **Bankruptcy only searches.** Form K16 should be used for Bankruptcy only searches.

3. **Fee payable.** A fee is payable for each name searched. If you have been granted a credit account, you may ask for the fee to be debited to your account. Otherwise, you must affix Land Registry adhesive fee stamps for the appropriate sum in the fee panel provided overleaf. These stamps can be purchased from any head post office or from a sub-post office where the demand is sufficient to warrant stocks being held. Cheques and postal orders are not usually acceptable (but see the guide referred to above).

4. **Names to be searched.** The forename(s) and surname of each individual must be entered on the appropriate line of the form. The name of a company or other body should commence on the forename line and may continue on the surname line (the words "forename(s)" and "surname" should be crossed through). If you are searching more than 6 names, use a second form.

5. **Period of years to be searched.** The inclusive period to be covered by a search should be entered in complete years e.g. 1968-1975.

6. **County Names.** The name of the county borough must not be given as the name of the county. Searches affecting land within the Greater London area should state "Greater London" as the county name. ANY RELEVANT FORMER COUNTY SHOULD ALWAYS BE STATED (see the guide referred to above for list of county names).

7. **Land description.** It is not essential to provide a land description but, if one is given, any relevant former description should also be given (see the guide referred to above).

8. **Key number.** If you have been allocated a key number, please take care to enter this in the space provided overleaf, whether or not you are paying fees through your credit account.

9. **Applicant's name and address.** This need not be supplied if the applicant's key number is correctly entered in the space provided overleaf.

10. **Applicant's reference.** Any reference must be limited to 10 digits, including any oblique strokes and punctuation.

11. **Despatch of this form.** When completed, send this application to the address shown below, which is printed in a position so as to fit within a standard window envelope.

THE SUPERINTENDENT,
LAND CHARGES DEPARTMENT,
SEARCH SECTION,
BURRINGTON WAY,
PLYMOUTH, PL5 3LP.

(see note 11 above)

Printed in England by Trafford Press, Doncaster and published by Her Majesty's Stationery Office
5p or 25 for £1 (exclusive of tax)
Dd4475.16 K8000 3 77   ISBN 0 11 390179 8

Fig.12.4   *(contd)*

effected on Form K15 (Fig. 12.4) against the name of the mortgagor and all his known addresses should be returned marked 'No subsisting entries'. The first search will be carried out before the charge is executed and upon its return the protective period will be shown (fifteen working days), during which time the bank may take its mortgage and no other entries will meanwhile be placed on the register. Thus the search should be made shortly before the execution of the document, as the protective period will run from the date of the search.

However, as noted, banks are cautious about the effectiveness of the protective period when they lend on current account, and consequently as a general practice they search again on the day the mortgage is given or immediately afterwards. This is often done irrespective of whether the advance is on current account or loan account; some banks omit the first search before the signing of the mortgage, and search only after the mortgage is executed. This practice requires caution to ensure that the lending is not made before a clear search has been returned.

If any entry is disclosed upon searching (Fig. 12.3), full details should be obtained by seeking an office copy of the entry, using form K19.[101] Thereafter the mortgagor can be interviewed to explain the position, if necessary, and if an earlier mortgagee is revealed then it will be essential to give him notice of the bank's charge and to ascertain how much is owing to him. The mortgagor's authority addressed to the mortgagee may be required in order to facilitate this.

Security step F: search in local land charges register This search, using Form LLCI, can be carried out before or after the execution of the charge.

If any entries are revealed the solicitor acting for the bank and local estate agents can be asked to advise on the implications on the security, and can make further enquires of the local authority.

The registers are kept at the local authority offices and comprise charges acquired by statute by any local authority, as for example in respect of money spent on making up roads. If not registered before completion of a purchase, entries are void against the purchaser of a legal estate in the land affected. Charges in the register are registered against the properties and not person's names.

Also shown here will be any local authority plans for the property, planning permissions and restrictions. Of particular danger would be a pending compulsory purchase order; any such entries can adversely affect the value of property in mortgage to the detriment of the lending banker, and might make the property very difficult to sell at a later date.

---

101 See Appendix I, Q. 33 (April 1980).

Security step G: fire insurance   It is obviously most important that there should be adequate insurance cover against fire and other risks covering the buildings, and that the policy has been taken out with a reputable company. The policy is usually lodged with the mortgagee, and is examined to ensure that it covers all the required contingencies. Sometimes, after perusal, the customer is allowed to retain the policy. The amount of the cover must of course be adequate for the full reinstatement cost of the property, in the event of loss by fire, plus a percentage to cover architect's fees and the cost of removing rubble.

The value of the land is usually excluded from these considerations, but, equally, it is important that inflation is taken into account, and that the overall cover is updated sufficiently from time to time.

In a second-mortgage situation there is a tendency for the later mortgagee to find that the insurance cover is inadequate, only purporting to cover the first mortgagee and that amount borrowed, and such situations must not be allowed to remain uncorrected.

If a property is under-insured, then the principle of 'average' may apply, in the event of a claim arising, and the insurance company may not pay the full amount of the policy, deeming that the insured has assumed a proportion of the risk himself.

Notice of the bank's interest must be given to the insurance company, and an acknowledgement requested in writing. Diary notes are then taken to ensure that the premium is paid regularly, usually annually, and that the premium receipt is exhibited. Companies which are members of the British Insurance Association have agreed that when a policy is not renewed they will inform the bank and hold it fully covered as mortgagee until such time.

In the case of private dwellings below a certain value (£100 000 in 1987) some banks and some insurance companies have entered into an arrangement whereby notice need not be given to the insurance company, although the policy needs still to be examined by the bank.[102] The arrangement between the two is that the bank will be covered in the event of loss, up to the amount of the policy, despite not having given notice.

Mortgages over leaseholds: additional security steps

Security step H: consent of lessor   Where title is held by way of a lease, it will be necessary for a prospective mortgagee to examine the document very carefully and in particular to note whether it is necessary for the lessor to grant permission for the creation of any mortgage or assignment. With a long-term lease this may not be the case, but with short-term leases, up to say twenty-one years, it is fairly common to see this right reserved in the covenants in the lease document. In the event that permission is required (and for this purpose, a lease while silent about mortgages, but requiring consent

102   See Appendix I, Q. 57 (April 1983).

for an assignment, is usually viewed as requiring consent, so as to ensure that the bank's security could not be challenged later), the mortgagor or bank should write to the lessor and obtain his consent in writing. This permission is then placed with the mortgage and deeds.

Security step I: notice to lessor Later, after the mortgage has been executed, written notice is given, informing the lessor of the creation of the mortgage, and an acknowledgement in writing is obtained. This notice is sometimes given whether or not prior permission is set out as a condition in the lease.

Security step J: rent receipt exhibited Another requirement with leasehold charges is that the rent receipt, evidencing payment on the due date, must be exhibited to the bank by the mortgagor from time to time. This is essential at the outset when the security is taken but is equally important throughout the duration of the security. A diary note should therefore be taken to ensure that all future rent receipts are exhibited (e.g. quarterly or annually), and the branch records must be marked appropriately on each occasion. (It should be noted that some *freehold* properties in parts of England are subject to a perpetual rent charge, or chief rent, and if so then evidence of payment there too is necessary.)

Security step G: fire insurance (amended procedure) The fire insurance position may be different with a leasehold security for, perhaps, the mortgagor may not be responsible for this himself, the duty falling on the lessor. It is necessary therefore for the security clerk to peruse the lease to see what is said and who is responsible, and then to liaise with the freeholder, head lessor or lessee, as appropriate, to obtain details of the cover currently in force. It may be that the lease will specify the use of a particular insurance company. Thereafter, matters will proceed as in respect of freehold unregistered land.

Second or subsequent mortgages of unregistered land: additional security steps

Second legal mortgages of freehold land or property can be created either by a charge expressed to be by way of legal mortgage or by the granting of a lease for a term longer by one day than that granted to the first mortgagee. A second legal mortgage over leasehold land is created by a sub-lease for a term longer by one day than that granted to the first mortgagee, or by a charge by way of legal mortgage as for a freehold.

A second mortgage is a charge over a property which is already subject to one mortgage.[103] As with a first mortgage, a later mortgagee must examine the

103 See Appendix I, Q. 61 (September 1983).

title, but dispensation is sometimes exercised where the first mortgagee is a respectable institution such as a building society, where it should be safe to rely on the work it will have undertaken. In other cases the deeds will have to be sent by the first mortgagee to the bank's solicitor, against his undertaking to hold them to the first mortgagee's order, for the purpose of inspection and return. The bank's solictor will then be able to examine them and report upon title to the bank, as in the case of a first mortgage.

Except where the prior mortgagee is a well-known bank or similar institutional lender, it is desirable to see a copy of the mortgage form, so that any terms which might have disadvantageous repercussions for the bank as subsequent lender are known. These could, for example, include terms for a higher rate of interest to apply when a mortgage has been in default for a specified period, and if so then the bank's 'equity' might be less than it believes.

It will also be necessary, by searching the land charges register, to ensure that no other charge has been registered since the first mortgage was created, for any other *registered* charge would rank in priority to the mortgage offered to the bank, and the bank would then be a third mortgagee. (It will be remembered that it is the date of registration not the date of the mortgage which is important.)

In other words, attention must be given to security steps A to G inclusive, in the case of freehold land, and to security steps A to J in the case of leasehold land. However, slightly amended procedures will be necessary for two steps, as outlined below, with two further steps being taken in addition to those already listed.

Security step A: valuation (amended procedure)   The value of a second-mortgage security will depend upon all the usual factors, and also the amount outstanding on the prior charge. It will be very desirable to allow an adequate margin, as arrears building up on payments to the prior mortgagee can erode the equity, that is, the difference between the value of the property and the amount secured by the prior charge.

For example, consider a property worth £23 000, on which the first mortgage outstanding amounts to £15 000. On paper the equity is £8000, but upon a forced sale by one of the mortgagees, almost certainly, because there will be arrears of unpaid interest (say £1500 for one year), legal costs in obtaining possession (say £500), and solicitors' and estate agents' costs in respect of the sale transaction (say £2000), the real worth of the security will be reduced to only £4000 to the second mortgagee.

This type of situation can be far worse when the property is highly valued, for example say at £100 000, with a first mortgage of, say, £90 000 outstanding. Although the equity is then £10 000, the factors mentioned in the first example will almost certainly mean that there is nothing at all left for the subsequent mortgagee upon a forced sale.

Security step G: fire insurance (amended procedure) The fire policy
may be held by the first mortgagee or other party (e.g. head-lessor in the case
of leasehold land), in which case details should be obtained from him, and
consideration should be given to ensure that the cover is adequate to reinstate
the premises at current costs if they are destroyed or damaged. If the
mortgagor holds the policy he should be asked to let the bank examine it.

As with a first mortgage, notice of the bank's interest should be given to the
insurance company and an acknowledgement should be obtained, except
where domestic property up to £100 000 is involved and the insurer and the
bank are participants in the special arrangement for such properties.

In addition the following two steps must also be taken:

Security step K: registration on land charges register The bank as
second or subsequent mortgagee must protect its own priority by registering
the legal mortgage as a land charge Class C(i), that is as a puisne mortgage, on
the land charges register.[104] Should the mortgage be an equitable mortgage
then the registration would be as a general equitable charge, Class C(iii).

Registration is effected by way of Form K1 (Fig. 12.5). It is usual to search
again later to ensure that the bank's charge has been correctly recorded.

Security step L: notice to prior mortgagee(s) After taking his charge, a
second mortgagee should give notice to the first mortgagee, in writing (Fig.
12.6), requesting an acknowledgement of his notice and a note of the amount
outstanding.[105] It is usual also to ask if the first mortgagee has received notice
of any other subsequent mortgage. Usually, the chargor's written authority
addressed to the other mortgagee(s) will be required, to enable the other
mortgagee to disclose the mortgagor's affairs to the bank. The bank will also
enquire as to whether the first mortgagee has any obligation to make further
advances. This is necessary because of the provisions of s. 94(1) Law of
Property Act 1925 which gives a mortgagee a right to tack on to his existing
mortgage any further advances he might make, and in those circumstances
those lendings would rank in priority to the bank's second mortgage, whether
legal or equitable, even if they were made after the first mortgagee had
received notice of the bank's charge. The section provides for priority of such
advances, provided the mortgagee had no notice of the subsequent mortgages
at the time when the further advances were made by him, or whether or not
he had such notice, where his mortgage imposed an obligation on him to make
such further advances. Of course an arrangement can always be made with
other lenders by a priority agreement, and the section also provides for this. It
is fairly rare to find that there is an obligation in a prior mortgage to make
further advances and often the provisions of s. 94(1) are excluded from the

104 See Appendix I, Q. 41 (April 1981).
105 See Appendix I, Q. 63 (September 1983).

PAYMENT OF FEE

EITHER
Insert a cross (X)
in this box
if the fee is
to be paid through a
credit account
OR
affix Land Registry
fee stamps

LAND CHARGES ACT 1972   **FORM**   **K1**

APPLICATION FOR REGISTRATION OF A LAND CHARGE

(Form K2 must be used for a Land Charge of Class F).

IMPORTANT: PLEASE READ THE NOTES OVERLEAF BEFORE COMPLETING THE FORM

Application is hereby made for the registration of a Land Charge in respect of the following particulars.

PARTICULARS OF CHARGEE(S)	Name(s) (in full) Address(es)	*(Continue on form K10 if necessary)*
PARTICULARS OF CHARGE	Enter (1) the date of and full names of the parties to instrument creating the charge OR (2) If class A or B, state relevant Act and Section OR (3) If neither of the above, state short particulars of effect of charge	
	Enter Class and Sub-Class of Charge (see note 4 on reverse)	Class............ .... Sub-Class............... If application is made pursuant to a Priority Notice please state its official reference number ....
PARTICULARS OF LAND AFFECTED	County District Short Description	
PARTICULARS OF ESTATE OWNER	Forename(s) Surname Title, Trade or Profession Address	FOR OFFICIAL USE ONLY

PARTICULARS OF APPLICANT(S) SOLICITOR(S)

If no solicitor acting the name and address of the applicant must be supplied

KEY NUMBER	NAME AND ADDRESS			
		1	2	3
		* C		
		4	5	6
Solicitors' reference:				

I/We certify that the estate owner's title is not registered at the Land Registry.

SIGNATURE OF SOLICITOR OR APPLICANT ....   Date ....

Fig.12.5   *Form K1 – registration of land charge, office copy*

NOTES

Form Completion	1.	Please complete the form in BLOCK LETTERS in writing or typewriting using black ink not liable to smear. No covering letter is required and no plan or other document should be lodged in support of the application. If the application is not made by a practising solicitor it must be accompanied by a statutory declaration on form K14.
Fee	2.	The prescribed fee should be paid either by the use of an authorised credit account or by affixing Land Registry fee stamps (available at Head Post Offices). Postal orders and cheques should only be used for payment in the circumstances described in the "Practice Guide" which is available from the address printed in the box below.
Chargee's Name(s)	3.	Please give the full name(s) and address(es) of the person(s) entitled to the benefit of the charge and on whose behalf the application is made.
Class and sub-class of Charge	4.	The following are the relevant classes and sub-classes of land charge (see Land Charges Act 1972, s.2).

Class A
Class B
Class C (I) (puisne mortgage)
Class C (ii) (limited owner's charge)
Class C (iii) (general equitable charge)
Class C (iv) (estate contract)
Class D (I) (Inland Revenue charge)
Class D (ii) (restrictive covenant)
Class D (iii) (equitable easement)

FORM K2 SHOULD
BE USED FOR A
LAND CHARGE OF
CLASS F.

County	5.	County borough names must not be given as the county. If the land referred to in the application lies within the Greater London area, then "GREATER LONDON" should be stated as the county name.
Short Description	6.	A short description, identifying the land as far as may be practicable, should be furnished.
Estate Owner	7.	Please give the full name, address and description of the estate owner as defined in the Law of Property Act 1925 against whom registration is to be effected. A separate form is required for each full name. Enter forename(s) and surname on separate lines. The name of a company or other body should commence on the forename line and may be continued on the surname line (the words "Forename(s)" and "Surname" should be deleted).
Key Number	8.	If a key number has been allotted this MUST be supplied.
Solicitors' Reference	9.	Any reference should be limited to ten digits (including oblique strokes and punctuation).
Despatch of form	10.	The completed form should be signed and despatched to the address shown below.

THIS FORM IS DESIGNED FOR USE WITH A STANDARD WINDOW ENVELOPE

THE SUPERINTENDENT
LAND CHARGES DEPARTMENT
REGISTRATION SECTION
BURRINGTON WAY
PLYMOUTH PL5 3LP

Printed in England by Wiltshire (Bristol) Ltd., and published by Her Majesty's Stationery Office
1½p net or 25 for 30p net (exclusive of tax)
Gp 1664 Dd 504446 K 24,000 8/73   ISBN 0 11 390165 8

Fig.12.5   *(contd)*

mortgage. For instance, in the case of the bank's own mortgage, the section is frequently excluded, and it should be appreciated that while bank mortgages are usually expressly stated to be a containing security for advances made and to be made (to overcome *Clayton's Case*), this of itself does *not* constitute *an obligation* to make future advances.

BANK OF CYPRUS (LONDON) LIMITED

27 31 Charlotte Street
London W1P 4BH
Telephone:
01-637 3961
Telegraphic Address:
Cyprobank
London W1P 4BH
Telex:
22114 Cybanc G

Your ref.:   Our ref.

NOTICE OF SECOND CHARGE

Dear Sir(s)

Re:

WE HEREBY give you Notice that by a Legal Charge dated
              and made between
on the one hand and BANK OF CYPRUS (LONDON) LIMITED on the other
hand, the above mentioned property was charged to us by way of
Second Charge.

We should be grateful if you would acknowledge receipt of this
Notice by signing a copy of this letter and returning it to us
without delay.

Yours faithfully
BANK OF CYPRUS (LONDON) LIMITED

Registered Office
27/31 Charlotte Street
London W1P 4BH
Registered Number
652394 (London)

Fig.12.6   *Notice to prior mortgagee*

Mortgages over land by a limited company

Many additional important security steps become necessary when the mortgagor is a limited company, revolving around the requirements of the Companies Acts, as to the registration of the charge at Companies House, and the necessity to ensure that the company and the directors have power to give the security. These aspects have been examined in Chapter 9. Summarized, they involve:[106]

(a) A search at Companies House and the Land Charges Register, to see if any prior charges have been registered, such as a floating charge, or other mortgage which would rank in priority to the bank's charge.

(b) A perusal of the memorandum and articles of association, to ensure that the necessary powers are present, both for the company and the directors and that the purpose for which the advance is granted is consistent with the main objects of the company, especially if the security is for the liabilities of a third party. Consideration must also be given then as to whether it is in the general interests of the charging company so to pledge its assets (the doctrine of commercial justification). If there is any doubt then legal advice should be obtained, for if there is a lack of commercial justification the security might be set aside.

(c) Ensuring that if the articles of association specify the number of directors necessary to form a quorum at directors' meetings, this aspect is satisfactory. It will also be necessary to check whether interested directors are enabled to vote.

Assuming all is well, a copy of the resolution passed by the board of directors, authorising the giving of the security in the form exhibited to the meeting, may be obtained and it should be placed with the security papers. Usually this resolution will be certified as a true copy by the chairman of the meeting.

After execution the charge must be registered at Companies House, within twenty-one days of its creation, as otherwise it will be void against a liquidator and creditors.[107] Some time after the bank's charge has been registered, a further search is usually made to ensure that the bank's charge has been correctly registered.

Sub-mortgages

Great care should be taken to distinguish a sub-mortgage from a second or subsequent mortgage. A sub-mortgage is a 'mortgage of a mortgage', and can be legal or equitable, except that if the mortgage to be mortgaged is equitable then the sub-mortgage must necessarily also be an equitable one. In practice the use of sub-mortgages is not often encountered, although occasionally small building societies borrow temporarily from banks and lodge their deeds

106 See Appendix I, Q. 61 (September 1983).
107 See Appendix I, Q. 41 (April 1981).

securities by way of sub-mortgages as cover. A sub-mortgage would arise in the following way. A, the customer, has lent money to a party, known as B, and has taken a mortgage from B over B's house. Now, some time later, A is short of funds himself, but he is reluctant or legally unable to call in the mortgage he holds from B. Consequently he goes to his bank to borrow, and offers the bank a sub-mortgage as security, so that the bank will have all the protection and rights A had under his mortgage from B. B's mortgage to A therefore becomes the bank's security.

As security, sub-mortgages suffer from the practical disadvantage that whatever the underlying value of the property, the sum recoverable is restricted to what remains due from the original mortgagor: as this is usually subject to periodic reduction by instalments (as for example with a building society mortgage) it is difficult for a sub-mortgagee to maintain control over the security margin, and the value of his security must be written down *pro tanto*, whenever a payment is made by the original mortgagor.

The remedies available to the bank as sub-mortgagee, on default by the customer, are either to sue the sub-mortgagor (the customer), or to sell or assign the mortgage debt. If the head mortgagor (the original borrower) is also in default, the bank will be able to exercise the powers conferred on the head mortgagee (the customer) by the terms of the original mortgage.

It would be coincidental if both mortgagors were in default, and it would be more usual just to find that the bank's customer had failed to make repayment; this means that where the original mortgagor is up to date with his payments of capital and/or interest, the bank will not be able to sell the property to obtain repayment of the customer's borrowing.

The holder of a sub-mortgage can therefore never be in a better position in respect of his security than the person who took the original mortgage. Consequently if, when the original mortgage steps were carried out, there was an error or omission, the bank as sub-mortgagee will have a defective security which it may not be able to rely on. For example if Zeta Ltd charged a factory to Mr A who failed to register the charge at Companies Registration Office, any sub-mortgage given by Mr A will be of no value in the event of the liquidation of Zeta Ltd, as the original charge would be void.

In taking a sub-mortgage as security, therefore, it is essential both to carry out the necessary new security steps and also to ensure that all the appropriate original security steps have been correctly taken with the head mortgage.

As well as reviewing the original security carefully to ensure that it is entirely sound, the bank, as sub-mortgagee, will have to carry out the following security steps to perfect its own charge:

Security step A: valuation (see p.338) In addition, it must be remembered that the maximum value of the sub-mortgage will depend wholly on the amount outstanding on the original charge *or* the value of the property, whichever is the lesser. As the original mortgagor pays off his debt the value of the sub-mortgage must be regularly reduced in the bank's records and adequate diary notes should cover this.

Security step B: occupation (see p.339)

Security step C: report on title This step will involve the need for the bank's solicitors to peruse the title of the head mortgagor and the perfection of the customer's mortgage given by him.

Security step D: execution of the sub-mortgage form (see p.340)

Completion of details A special form of sub-mortgage will be used and completed with details stating the parties involved. The schedule will then be filled in describing the mortgage granted to the sub-mortgagor, which in turn should refer to the property in question. The sub-mortgage should then be signed and witnessed.

Security step E: land charges register searches As the land we are considering is *unregistered title*, step E will be necessary, and searches will be made against the names of the head mortgagor and the customer. If it is found that the original mortgagor has created a second charge, then the bank's security will depend for its priority on the priority position of the sub-mortgagor, which should be checked. As he is probably not lending on a fluctuating account there should be no need to be concerned with *Clayton's Case*. However, in examining title the bank's solicitors should give consideration to all the circumstances and implications of the head mortgagor's creation of a second mortgage.

Security step F: search in local land charges register One such search should be present with the original mortgage papers but needs to be repeated, to ensure that the position in respect of local authority plans has not changed.

Security step G: fire insurance The bank should be satisfied as to the adequacy of the cover in existence and give notice of its interest to the insurance company; an acknowledgement must be received.

Security step M: notice to head mortgagor Written notice is given to the original mortgagor and he must acknowledge this, stating the amount owing on his charge. Often this notice will incorporate the bank's request and the head mortgagor's undertaking in reply that he will in future make all mortgage payments direct to the bank. If this is not included in the notice form, then, as it is a vital part of the control of the security, the step must be carried out separately.

Thereafter whenever monies are received, the value of the security in the bank's records must be written down accordingly, to the lesser sum then remaining secured, and due to be paid.

DISCHARGE OF MORTGAGES OVER UNREGISTERED LAND

Legal mortgages

There are two methods available for the discharge of legal mortgages: first a receipt may be annexed to, or endorsed on, the mortgage deed, signed by the mortgagee and stating the name of the person paying the money. This operates as a surrender, or a reconveyance of the mortgage to the mortgagor, and formally discharges the mortgage. The same wording may be used for both freeholds and leaseholds and it makes no difference whether the mortgage was created by legal charge or by a long lease, or in the case of leaseholds by a sub-lease. Most bank mortgages have a standard form of receipt already printed on the back of the mortgage awaiting completion at the appropriate time.

The released mortgage is then placed with the deeds, which are forwarded to the customer, or his solicitor, against a receipt. However this must not be done where the bank has notice of the existence of a later chargee, unless that party agrees (as in the course of a sale). Thus where the bank is repaid and is giving up its first mortgage, it must pass the deeds and the released charge form to the second mortgagee. However, in the case of the bank itself being a second or subsequent mortgagee, the released mortgage should be sent to the mortgagee who hold the deeds.

If the property is in course of sale, it is better practice not to release the mortgage before the sale proceeds are received, although the deeds themselves can be sent out to the solicitor acting against his undertaking on the bank's own form. This will be either to hold the deeds to the bank's order, and to return them upon request (inspection only), or to hold them to the bank's order pending the sale and to remit the net sale proceeds, 'being the sale price of not less than £x, less only those reasonable costs incurred in the sale'. These would include the estate agent's costs and the legal fees relating to the property transaction.

A mortgage may also be discharged by an endorsement on the mortgage made under seal as a reconveyance of the property to the mortgagor, or by a separate deed of release. This method of discharge by way of reconveyance or release is appropriate where the whole of the sum secured by the mortgage is not being repaid, or where not all the land is being released from the charge.

Where the release is that of a legal mortgage unsupported by the deposit of title deeds, that is a puisne mortgage, the entry at the land charges register must be removed by sending Form K11 (Fig. 12.7) to the Department.

Equitable mortgages

The discharge of an equitable mortgage can be effected by a simple receipt, or by the mere cancellation of the memorandum of deposit, which is often

Important: Please read the notes overleaf before completing the form	**Form K11** *(Use Form K13 for a Class F Land Charge)* Land Charges Act 1972 APPLICATION FOR CANCELLATION OF AN ENTRY IN THE REGISTER	**FEE PANEL** If the fee is to be debited to your credit account put a cross (X) in this box ☒ If not affix Land Registry fee stamp(s) in this space *(See Note 1 overleaf)*
Enter full Name(s) of Applicant(s) *(See notes 2 and 3 overleaf)*	**PARTICULARS OF APPLICANT(S) ENTITLED TO THE BENEFIT OF THE ENTRY**	

Delete words in *italics* which are not applicable	**CERTIFICATE**
	I We as *solicitor(s) acting* for the above-mentioned applicant(s) hereby apply for cancellation in the register as shown below
	
	I We certify that
	  a) *The applicant(s) is are the person(s) entitled to the benefit of the entry and is are named as the chargee(s) in the original registration*
	  b) *The applicant(s) is are the successor(s) in title to the original chargee(s) and evidence of the applicant's title is enclosed*
	  c) *The application is made pursuant to an order of the Court directing vacation of the entry and an office copy of the order is attached*
	  d) *The restrictive covenants protected by the under-mentioned entry are the covenants discharged by the order of the Land Tribunal, an office copy of which is attached*
	
	Signature of Solicitor Applicants Date
	(or attested seal of company)
	
	Address

Delete (a) or (b) as appropriate	**PARTICULARS OF THE ENTRY** Please cancel the under-mentioned entry as to OR (a) the whole (b) the following part Being part of the land affected by the original registration	

Delete words not applicable	LAND CHARGE (Class Sub Class	Insert below number and date of the original registration
	PENDING ACTION WRIT OR ORDER DEED OF ARRANGEMENT ANNUITY	Official reference no Date of registration *(See note 4 overleaf)* DAY MONTH YEAR

(See note 5 overleaf)	**PARTICULARS OF ESTATE OWNER** Forename(s) SURNAME	**FOR OFFICIAL USE ONLY**

KEY NUMBER **2497071** *(See note 6 overleaf)*	Enter Name and Address of Applicant	NAME AND ADDRESS FOR DESPATCH OF ACKNOWLEDGEMENT ▬▬▬▬▬▬▬▬ This Box must be Completed with Branch Address	COUNTY

		1	2	3
Branch XXXXXXX *reference* *(See note 7 overleaf)*			C	
		4	5	6

Fig.12.7   *Form K11 – removal of land charges register entry*

retained at the branch with obsolete security forms. The deeds can be dealt with on the customer's written instructions – that is, he can authorize them to be sent to his solicitors against their receipt or he can instruct the bank to place them in safe custody. He may of course wish to take them away himself, in which case he will sign a schedule of the deeds as having received them all.

If the mortgage has been made without the deposit of the deeds then the registration at the land charges register will need to be cancelled, again using Form K11.

Fire insurance After release of any mortgage, the insurance company should be advised that the bank has no longer any interest in the policy covering the property.

Inspection of title deeds
Title deeds should only be released to a solicitor against his undertaking, on the customer's authority. They must never be released to the customer himself, although the latter may inspect them in the presence of a bank officer. If, very exceptionally, the bank is prepared to release them to the customer for inspection, a C(i) (legal mortgage) or C(iii) (equitable mortgage) must be registered beforehand to preserve priority, in case the customer charges them elsewhere!

Release of part security
Although the release of part of the security in a *legal* mortgage is effected by a separate deed reciting the land released, as the discharge cannot be made on the mortgage deed, in the case of an *equitable* mortgage, which does not create a legal estate or interest in favour of the bank, the part release can be effected simply by giving the borrower a suitably worded letter (Fig. 12.8). This system is particularly easy where the borrower is a highly reputable house builder, to whom the bank is happy to lend against only an equitable mortgage over his building land. As the houses are built and become ready for occupation, they can be conveyed to the purchaser by the builder's solicitors, who will only need a short letter of release from the bank. If, however, the land had been charged by way of legal mortgage, it would be necessary for the bank to join in and seal the release and conveyance upon each sale.

Transfer of mortgage
If the bank is repaid by a third party, not the borrower, then the Law of Property Act 1925 provides that a receipt on the mortgage operates 'as if the benefit of the mortgage had by deed been transferred to him', unless it is otherwise expressly provided. Alternatively the bank can transfer its mortgage to that party by way of a separate deed. In either case, except where there are specific exclusions, the third party will have all the rights embodied in the bank's charge. It is therefore rare for a bank to agree to a transfer of its security in this way, although where a guarantor pays off the principal debtor's liabilities, under his rights of subrogation, as paying surety to stand in the bank's shoes, he will be entitled to take a transfer of any deed security charged by the principal debtor to the bank.

To _____ .

Property known as _____

_____

(being the land shown and edged
blue on the plan attached)

We PRACTICE BANK plc hereby confirm that we have released the above mentioned
property from the equitable charge to the Bank dated_____

For and on behalf of
PRACTICE BANK plc

_____

Advances Controller

Fig.12.8 *Release of part of land from equitable charge*

REGISTERED LAND

For the student, registered titles are easier to understand than unregistered land and much of the land in England is now held with this State-guaranteed title.

The HM Land Register which is held at several different District Registries around the country serving specified areas is entirely separate from the land charges register at the Land Charges Department, Plymouth, about which we have been reading when examining unregistered land as security; it is vital not to confuse the two.[108] Registered land has the attraction of a simplified system of transfer, and title is evidenced merely by a land certificate, hence large packets of deeds are unnecessary.

As well as being generally voluntarily registrable, in many areas of the country unregistered land has been compulsorily registrable there for some years. In such areas unregistered land acquires a registered title with a land title number at the District Land Registry either when there is a disposition of the freehold upon a sale, or a new lease of forty years or more is being created. Additionally, when a lease is being assigned which will have forty years or more to run from the date of the assignment, in a compulsory area registration is required. This applies also when a lease of twenty-one years or more is in

108 See Appendix I, Q. 57 (April 1983).

course of creation, if the freehold or superior leasehold interest has itself already been granted a registered land title.

There are four types of registered title, as follows.

Absolute title

This category consists mainly of freeholds and as such they represent the best possible title. Leaseholds are only given an absolute title where the Land Registry has examined the freeholder's title. However, although an absolute title is granted, this will nevertheless be subject to any overriding interests (e.g. occupational rights of the 'Boland' type) and minor interests (e.g. beneficiaries' interests under a trust of which he has notice).

Good leasehold title

In this case the title of the leaseholder is guaranteed, but there is no guarantee as to the right of the freeholder to have granted the lease. Again, the title is subject to any overriding or minor interests.

Qualified title

Registered titles of this type are rarely encountered, but they arise in the two cases mentioned above, where the Land Registry has examined the title derived through the deeds, but where because of some defect, or the absence of documents, it is unable to give an absolute title or good leasehold title as indicated. The old title deeds are therefore usually retained with the land certificate in these cases.

Possessory title

Here the proprietor's title is guaranteed only in respect of those dealings which take place after registration; the first applicant for registration does not have a guaranteed title until ten years have elapsed in the case of a leasehold and fifteen years in the case of a freehold. Again, the old pre-registration title deeds should have been retained with the land certificate. Possessory titles are not often met, but where they are, the bank's security is technically weaker. The writer has encountered several possessory titles in and around the south coast of England near Brighton.

The land certificate

When a registered title is granted, the Land Registry issues a document evidencing title, which is known as a land certificate (Fig. 12.9), and this includes copies of entries on the records at the Land Registry. This land certificate is divided into three parts:

The property register   This section will show the land title number, e.g. ABC 123456, and will describe the land shown and described in a plan of the title filed at the Registry. A copy of the plan appears in the land certificate.

Fig.12.9 *Land certificate*

B. *Securities for Advances*

NOTICE

The last date entered below is the last date on which this land certificate was made to correspond with the register to which it relates. Vendors should supply this date to purchasers when furnishing them with a copy of the **subsisting** entries on the register pursuant to Section 110 of the Land Registration Act, 1925, as it must be quoted to the Registry by them when applying for official searches in Form 94.

Dates when this land certificate was made to correspond with the register	Dates when this land certificate was made to correspond with the register	Dates when this land certificate was made to correspond with the register	Dates when this land certificate was made to correspond with the register

SEARCHES AND INSPECTION OF THE LAND

This land certificate is the best possible evidence as to the entries in the register up to the date last above mentioned.

1. It may be sent at any time to the Land Registry, London, or to a district Land Registry as appropriate to be officially examined and (where necessary) made to correspond with the register without fee. A registered proprietor proposing to deal with the land is, therefore, in a position to afford conclusive evidence as to the entries in the register up to date.

2. To enable intending purchasers to ascertain without attendance at the Registry whether any entry has been made in the register subsequent to the last date entered above, they may with the authority of the registered proprietor apply in Form 94 for an official search to be made. That form is obtainable from H.M. Stationery Office or through any law stationer and it must be lodged by post. The certificate of the result of official search will state whether or not a subsequent entry has been made. No fee is payable.

3. Under Rule 1 of the Land Registration Rules, 1930, as amended by Rule 1 of the Land Registration Rules, 1936, where a purchaser has applied for an obtained an official certificate of the result of search in Form 94, any entry which is made in the register after the date of the certificate and before an application is made for registration by the purchaser of the instrument effecting the purchase (and is not made pursuant to a priority notice or mortgage caution entered on the register before the certificate is issued), shall be postponed to the application by the purchaser, provided such application

    (a) is in order under the Acts and Rules;

    (b) is delivered at the proper Office (that is, at the Land Registry, London, or to the appropriate district Land Registry) before that Office is opened or deemed to be opened on the fifteenth day after the date of such certificate;

    (c) is accompanied by such certificate which shall be retained in the Registry; and

    (d) affects the same land or charge as the postponed entry.

4. Intending purchasers should inspect the land for the purpose of ascertaining its precise boundaries and whether there are any rights of way, light, drainage or other overriding interests to which it is subject. Enquiries should also be addressed to any persons in occupation of the land as to their rights to such occupation and as to whom rent (if any) is paid.

Fig. 12.9 *(contd)*

The date of filing will be mentioned and the address of the property, and it will also name the administrative area, or parish. In the case of leasehold property, the term of the lease is described (Fig. 12.10).

H.M. LAND REGISTRY

<table>
<tr><td>Edition 1
opened 14.8.1965</td><td>TITLE NUMBER SO19834
This register consists of 2 pages </td></tr>
</table>

A. PROPERTY REGISTER

containing the description of the registered land and the estate comprised in the Title

ADMINISTRATIVE AREA (County, County Borough, etc)	PARISH OR PLACE
SOUTHUMBERLAND	OLDCASTLE

The Freehold land shown and edged with red on the filed plan of the above title registered on 14 August 1965 known as 97 Acacia Gardens, together with a right of way over the part of the driveway at the side not included in the title.

NOTE 1:-The land edged and numbered in green on the filed plan has been removed from this title and registered under the title number or numbers shown in green on the said plan.

NOTE 2:-There is appurtenant to the land in this title the following right reserved by the Transfer dated 12 March 1971 referred to in Entry No.4 of the Charges Register:-

"EXCEPT AND RESERVING to the Transferor for the benefit of the Transferors' retained land the full and free right to the uninterrupted passage and running of water and soil through the drains and sewers now existing or within 21 years hereafter to be constructed in or under the land hereby transferred."   (15.4.1971)

The land is now in the County of Southumbria, Oldcastle District. (15.1.1969)

B. PROPRIETORSHIP REGISTER

stating nature of the Title, name, address and description of the proprietor of the land and any entries affecting the right of disposing thereof

TITLE ABSOLUTE

Entry Number	Proprietor, etc.	Remarks
1.	PERCY BYSSHE SHELLEY, of 97 Acacia Gardens, Oldcastle, Southumberland, Steel Erector, registered on 14 August 1965.	Price paid £4250
2.	ROBERT BROWNING, Sales Representative, and ELIZABETH BARRETT BROWNING, his wife, both of 97 Acacia Gardens, Oldcastle, Southumbria, OL3 7PJ., registered on 15 January 1979.	
3.	RESTRICTION registered on 15 January 1979:-No disposition by one proprietor of the land (being the survivor of joint proprietors and not being a trust corporation) under which capital money arises is to be registered except under an Order of the registrar or of the Court.	

Any entries struck through are no longer subsisting

Fig.12.10 *Land certificate – property register, proprietorship register, charges register*

B. Securities for Advances

TITLE NUMBER   SO19834   SPECIMEN

C. CHARGES REGISTER

Page 2

containing charges, incumbrances, etc., adversely affecting the land and registered dealings therewith

Entry number	The date at the beginning of each entry is the date on which the entry was made on this edition of the register.	Remarks
1.	14 August 1965–The part of the driveway at the side included in the title is subject to rights of way.	
2.	14 August 1965–CHARGE dated 12 July 1965 registered on 14 August 1965 to secure the moneys including the further advances therein mentioned.	
3.	PROPRIETOR–HIGH STREET BANK LIMITED of 44 High Street, Oldcastle, Southumberland, registered on 14 August 1965.	
4.	15 April 1971–A Transfer of the land edged and numbered SO22463 in green on the filed plan dated 12 March 1971 by Percy Bysshe Shelley to John Keats contains the following covenant by the transferor:– "The Transferor hereby covenants with the Transferee and his successors and assigns as owners for the time being of the land hereby transferred that he the Transferor will not at any time use the land remaining in title number SO19834 or permit the same to be used for any purpose other than as the site for a single private dwellinghouse with the usual garages outbuildings and appurtenances."	
5.	15 January 1979–CHARGE dated 18 December 1978 registered on 15 January 1979 to secure the moneys including the further advances therein mentioned.	
6.	PROPRIETOR–WEYFORD BUILDING SOCIETY of Society House, The Avenue, Weyford, Blankshire, registered on 15 January 1979.	

The proprietorship register   This details the type of title and the name, address and description of the registered proprietor; also shown is the date of registration. The consideration or price paid upon a transfer of the property used to be shown, but this is no longer so. However, any matters affecting the registered proprietor's ability to deal freely with the land are also recorded in this section of the register, and all restrictions appear here, together with any bankruptcy or liquidation matters pending (Fig. 12.10).

The charges register   This section shows all the covenants and leases created, and if a legal or equitable mortgage has been created then this will be recorded. A legal mortgage will appear as a registered charge, while in the case of an equitable charge the notice of deposit will be recorded (Fig. 12.10).

Searches in respect of registered land

There are several District Land Registry offices throughout the country, and to ensure that the particulars in a land certificate, which is a copy of the entries in the Registry records, are up to date, the land certificate must be submitted to the appropriate Registry to be written up, as and when necessary. It is possible also to obtain an office copy of the register using Form A44 (Fig. 12.11), but this procedure is more usually restricted to use when a second or subsequent mortgage is being created as, with a first charge, it is easier to submit the land certificate itself.

Alternatively, an official search may be carried out, calling for details of all adverse entries on the register since the date entered on the form. This date should be either the date on which an office copy of the subsisting entries in the register was issued or the last date on which the land certificate or charge certificate was compared with the land register. This search can only be carried out with the authority of the registered proprietor, or his solicitors, which must be given on Form 201. The search is usually carried out by post, as opposed to personally, and Form 94A is used (Fig. 12.12). This search in addition to giving the information required, also extends priority over intervening entries if a mortgagee, having searched, then registers his charge within thirty working days of the date of the search certificate. An official search exonerates the person searching from the responsibility for any error made, whereas a personal search, while possible, would not afford this protection. Moreover, in order to obtain the protective period, a person making a personal search would need to enter a priority notice under the land registration rules and this is avoided with the postal search on Form 94A.

Priorities in respect of registered land

Priority of mortgages and interests in registered title depend not upon the date of mortgage but upon the date of entry at the Land Registry, except in the case of any minor or overriding interests – such as those under s. 70 Land Registration Act, e.g. 'Boland'-type occupational rights. As explained above, an intending mortgagee can obtain a period of protection, however, by carrying out a search, which gives him thirty working days in which to obtain and register his mortgage.

After an interest has been recorded, should there be a subsequent attempt to make a further entry at the Land Registry, then s. 30 Land Registration Act 1925 enacts that:

> When a registered charge is made for securing further advances, the registrar shall before making any entry on the register which would prejudicially affect the priority of any further advance thereunder, give to the proprietor of the charge at his registered address notice by registered post of the intended entry, and the proprietor of the charge shall not, in respect of any further advance, be affected by such entry, unless the advance is made after the date when the notice ought to have been received in due course of post.

Form A44 HM Land Registry

Application for Office Copies[1]

Numbers in brackets relate to notes overleaf.

.... District Land Registry.[2]

I/We ....

(Use BLOCK LETTERS)

hereby apply for the office copies specified below

and I/We declare that

(Please enter X in the appropriate box)

☐ I am/We are the registered proprietor(s)

☐ I/We act as solicitor(s) for the registered proprietor(s)

☐ the written authority of the registered proprietor(s) (or his solicitors) to inspect the register is enclosed.

PAYMENT OF FEES[3]

If by Land Registry fee stamp(s) affix here.

If by either of the following methods, enter X in the appropriate box.

credit account ☒

cheque or postal order ☐

FOR OFFICIAL USE ONLY

PARTICULARS OF ACCOUNT HOLDER[3]

Key Number	Reference
2497071	

Title number [4]	
County and district (or London borough)	
Short description of property	
Full name(s) of registered proprietor(s)	

Please state in the appropriate box(es) the NUMBER of copies required

A	Complete set[5] with Title plan	C	Register entries	E	Form 102[6]
B	Complete set with form 102	D	Title plan	F	Document(s) referred to on the register as filed[7] Specify here or state "all" ....

a) Where you have requested a form 102 certificate and an estate plan has been approved, enter the the plot number(s) in the space opposite.
b) Where no estate plan has been approved a plan MUST be lodged in duplicate.[8]

(a) Plot number(s) [   ]

(b) The certificate is to be issued in respect of the land shown ....on the attached plan.

OFFICIAL USE FEE DEBITED

£   p

If you are aware that an application is in the course of registration in respect of the above title and you require office copies back dated to the day prior to the receipt of that application, enter YES in the box opposite [9]

[   ]

Signed ....   Telephone No. ....   Date ....

Reference ....

Please enter above using BLOCK LETTERS the name, address and reference to whom the office copies are to be sent.

FOR OFFICIAL USE ONLY

ITEM	NUMBER	FEE DEBITED	
		£	p
Complete set			
Register Entries			
Title Plan			
Form 102 certificate			
Document(s)			
TOTAL FEE DEBITED			

Fig.12.11 *Form A44 – application for office copies*

Form 94A   H.M. Land Registry   Land Registration (Official Searches) Rules 1981

Application by Purchaser[1] **for Official Search with priority in respect of the WHOLE of the land in a title**

(Numbers in brackets relate to notes overleaf.)

.... District Land Registry[2]

The attached duplicate must also be completed (A carbon copy will suffice).

(For an official search of part of the land in a title, use form 94B).

FOR OFFICIAL USE

County and district (or London borough)	
Title number[3]	
Enter full name(s) of the registered proprietor(s)[4]	
Application is made to ascertain whether any adverse[5] entry has been made in the register since the date shown opposite being EITHER the date on which an office copy of the subsisting entries in the register was issued OR the last date on which the land or charge certificate was officially examined with the register.	
Enter full name(s) of the applicant(s) *(i.e. purchaser(s) lessee(s) or chargee(s))*	

I/We *as solicitors acting for*[6] the above mentioned applicant(s) certify that the applicant(s) intend(s) to:-

(Enter X in the appropriate box opposite)

- [ ] **P** purchase
- [ ] **L** take a lease of
- [ ] **C** lend money on the security of a registered charge on

the WHOLE of the land in the above title

A   WHERE A SOLICITOR IS ACTING FOR THE APPLICANT(S)

I/We certify that I/We hold the duly signed written authority of (or of the solicitor(s) for) the above mentioned registered proprietor(s) to inspect the register of the above title OR that I/We also act as solicitor(s) for the registered proprietor(s).

Indicate this by entering X in the box

A

B   WHERE A SOLICITOR IS NOT ACTING FOR THE APPLICANT(S)

The duly signed written authority of (or of the solicitor(s) for) the registered proprietor(s) to inspect the register of the above title accompanies this application.

Indicate this by entering X in the box

B

Key number[7]	
	Signed: ....
	Date: ....
	Telephone number
	Reference

This panel must be completed using BLOCK LETTERS and inserting the name and address to which the official certificate of result of search is to be sent.

Fig.12.12   *Form 94A – search at land registry*

FOR OFFICIAL USE ONLY			Dated	No. of copies
Prepare office copies of:				
Register				
Filed plan/GM Negative Positive Tinted				
Deed dated	Marked with title	No. of pages	No. of plans	Tinted	Untinted	No. of copies

Deed dated	Marked with title	No. of pages	No. of plans	Tinted	Untinted	No. of copies

Drafted by ....   Despatched by ....

Date ....   Date ....

NOTES FOR GUIDANCE OF APPLICANTS

1 Full information on all aspects of applications for office copies is set out in Practice Leaflet No. 13 which is obtainable without charge from any district land registry.

2 The application should be sent to the district land registry serving the area in which the land is situated. A list of addresses of the district land registries is set out below.

3 The fees payable are set out in the current Land Registration Fee Order and also in Practice Leaflet No. 13. In special cases, an enquiry by telephone can be made of any district land registry. Cheques or postal orders should be made payable to "HM Land Registry". Where an applicant, who has been granted credit facilities, wishes to pay by monthly credit account he must also complete the "Particulars of Account Holder" panel. Any reference should be limited to ten digits (including oblique strokes and punctuation). Failure either to supply the credit account details or to send the prescribed fee with this application will usually mean its return to the applicant.

4 A separate application form must be used for each title number in respect of which copies are required.

5 A "complete set" of office copies comprises copies of (a) the entries in the register (b) the title plan (or a certificate in form 102) and (c) any document referred to on the register as being filed in the Land Registry.

6 This is a simpler and quicker alternative to obtaining an office copy of a large title plan for the purpose of a sale or other transaction affecting only a part of the land in the registered title.

7 Mortgages and leases. Original mortgages and leases are not filed in the Land Registry. Where copies are filed, office copies of the filed copies will not be issued save in response to a special request by letter showing why a copy cannot be obtained from the person who holds the original.

8 Any plan accompanying this application must be drawn to a suitable scale (generally not less than 1/2500) and supplied in duplicate. The plan must show by suitable marking the extent of the land affected and, where necessary, figured measurements should be entered on the plan to fix the position of the land by tying it to existing physical features depicted by firm black lines on the plan of the registered title.

9 If there is a pending application and you are applying for an office copy in connection with a further transaction it is possible for negotiations to proceed on the strength of a back-dated office copy of the register which can be brought up-to-date in effect by making a non-priority official search in form 94C in which the date of that office copy is entered as the date for the commencement of the search; a fee under the current Land Registration Fee Order is payable for an official search of this type. The certificate of result of search will reveal details of the pending application for registration and will state officially (if such be the case) that it is in order but has not yet been completed by entry on the register. If negotiations proceed on this basis, and assuming that your prospective transaction is a transfer, lease or charge, the normal search in form 94A or 94B can be made as usual immediately before the completion of the transaction. **If a back-dated office copy is not required, your application for office copies will be held until the completion of the pending application for registration.**

ADDRESSES OF DISTRICT LAND REGISTRIES

District Land Registry	Address	Telephone No.	Telex Call No
Birkenhead	76 Hamilton Street, Birkenhead, Merseyside L41 5JW	051-647 5661	628475
Croydon	Sunley House, Bedford Park, Croydon CR9 3LE	01-686 8833	917288
Durham	Aykley Heads, Durham DH1 5TR	0385 61361	53684
Gloucester	Bruton Way, Gloucester GL1 1DQ	0452 28666	43119
Harrow	Lyon House, Lyon Road, Harrow, Middx, HA1 2EU	01-427 8811	262476
Lytham	Lytham St Annes, Lancs. FY8 5AB	0253 736999	67649
Nottingham	Chalfont Drive, Nottingham NG8 3RN	0602 291111	37167
Peterborough	Aragon Court, Northminster Road, Peterborough PE1 1XN	0733 46048	32786
Plymouth	Plumer House, Tailyour Road, Crownhill, Plymouth PL6 5HY	0753 701234	45265
Stevenage	Brickdale House, Danestrete, Stevenage, Herts. SG1 1XG	0438 4488	82377
Swansea	37 The Kingsway, Swansea SA1 5LF	0792 50971	48220
Tunbridge Wells	Tunbridge Wells, Kent TN2 5AQ	0892 26141	95286
Weymouth	1 Cumberland Drive, Weymouth, Dorset DT4 9TT	03057 76161	418231

Printed in England by Beeston Printers Limited, Beeston, Nottingham and published by Her Majesty's Stationery Office

Dd 718800 C3000 9/81   20p net, 25 for £2.25 net, or 100 for £8.10 net (exclusive of tax)   ISBN 011 390244 1

Fig.12.12   *(contd)*

Form 94D H.M. Land Registry   Land Registration (Official Searches) Rules 1981

This page is to be completed only by H.M. Land Registry

Official Certificate of the Result of Search

It is hereby certified that the offical search applied for has been made with the following result:

Since................................19......

N.B. — To obtain priority[9], the application for registration in respect of which this search is made must be delivered to the proper office at the latest by 11 am on the date when priority expires.

NOTES

(1) "Purchaser" means any person who, in good faith and for valuable consideration, acquires or intends to acquire a legal estate in land, so it includes a lessee or a chargee but not a depositee of a land or charge certificate. An official search made by such a depositee or by any person other than a "purchaser", as so defined, should be made in form 94C and a fee is payable.

(2) The application should be sent to the district land registry serving the area in which the land is situated. A list of addresses of the district land registries is set out on page 4 of this application form.

(3) A separate form must be used for each title number to be searched.

(4) The name(s) of the registered proprietor(s) should be entered as they appear on the evidence of the registered title supplied to the applicant. If there has been a change of name(s) the new name(s) should also be entered in brackets.

(5) Any entry made in the register since the date of commencement of this search but subsequently cancelled will not be revealed.

(6) Where no solicitor is acting delete all or some of the words in italics as appropriate to the particular situation.

(7) This should be restricted to a maximum of 10 digits including oblique strokes and punctuation.

(8) Where a key number has been allocated it should be used.

(9) The period of priority reserved for the registration of the disposition protected by the official search certificate will be shown either by a stamp impressed in the result of search above or on a separate computer printed result.

(10) Where a first registration is pending, an official search certificate cannot be issued unless and until the first registration of the title to the land affected has been completed.

(11) Fuller information about the official search procedure is contained in Practice Leaflet No. 2, entitled "Official searches of the Register", and Practice Leaflet No. 7, entitled "Development of registered building estates" which are obtainable free of charge from any district land registry.

Fig.12.12   *(contd)*

Thus where the bank has a registered charge, the registrar is obliged to give the bank notice of any attempt for further entries to be placed on the register, such as a second mortgage or a caution, or inhibition appertaining to bankruptcy proceedings (Fig. 12.13).

By s. 5 Law of Property (Amendment) Act 1926, the following subsection has been added to s. 30 of the Land Registration Act 1925:

> Where the proprietor of a charge is under an obligation, *noted on the register*, to make a further advance, a subsequent registered charge shall take effect subject to any further advance made pursuant to the obligation.

But, as we have seen, banks do not normally have an obligation to make a further advance. The provisions mean that a subsequent mortgagee need not necessarily himself give notice of his charge to the first mortgagee, for this party should hear from the Land Registry, but nevertheless it is invariable practice for a later mortgagee to give notice, and to enquire how much is secured by the earlier charge. Whatever his source of notice, a lender on fluctuating current account must then stop the account(s) to prevent *Clayton's Case* operating to the detriment of this priority, unless he is prepared to rely on the protection of the *Westminster Bank Ltd* v. *Cond* (1940) decision if there are such provisions in this mortgage form[109] (see Chapter 11).

Taking a first legal mortgage over registered land – freehold or leasehold

A legal mortgage is effected by the mortgagee becoming registered as the proprietor of the charge, and his name will then appear in the charges register. Prior to the execution of the mortgage, the land certificate will have been brought up to date, and an official search will have been carried out, giving the protective period during which the mortgage must be executed and registered.

After it has been signed or sealed the legal mortgage *and a certified copy*, together with the land certificate, are forwarded to the Land Registry with a completed form A4. They are accompanied with payment of the scale fee, and a certificate from the bank as to the reliance that is placed on the charge. This will either be the value of the property or the amount of the advance, whichever is the lesser. Copies of the charge and the land certificate are retained at the Registry, and the mortgagee is then issued with a charge certificate (Fig. 12.14) with the mortgage form itself stitched inside this. The charge certificate, like the land certificate, shows the property register, the proprietorship register, and the charges register where the mortgagee's name has been entered.

Naturally, all the other security steps necessary to perfect the security must be carried out, apart from those which relate specifically to unregistered land.

109　See Appendix I, Q. 45 (September 1981).

B17A

The Manager
Practice Bank plc
Seatown Branch

Please reply to the above address.

Date .... 18 Jan 1980 ....

NOTICE pursuant to s.30 Land Registration Act 1925 of an entry in the register by way of notice or caution.

County and district
(or London Borough) ...... HILLINGTON ....

Title No. ...... LBX 1279548 ....

Property ...... 9 OLD ROAD, S... .WN ....

....

Proprietor(s) of land ...... JAMES SCOTT ....

....

Mortgage account no. ....

The Chief Land Registrar hereby gives notice that pursuant to an application made by
Messrs. STANLEY SMITH, Solicitor ....

of ...... 14 SOUTH STREET, SEATOWN ....

.... (Solr's ref: ...... SS/79/AB/FEA ....) the following entry by way of

(1) *Delete as appropriate*

(1) *[notice under section 49 of the Land Registration Act 1925]*
[caution under section 54 of the Land Registration Act 1925] has been made in the register:

(2) *Strike out if not appropriate*

(2) *Note: The nature of the interest protected by the caution is stated to be:*

If and so far as the making of the above entry in the register may prejudicially affect the priority of any further advances made by you under the charge dated ...... 28.2.75 ...... registered in your favour against the above-mentioned title, notice of the entry is required to be served on you pursuant to section 30, subsection (1) of the Land Registration Act 1925, a copy of which is set out overleaf.

It is important that any change in your address for the service of notices should be notified to the above District Land Registry stating the title number.

Revised 2/80

Fig.12.13 *Notice from land registrar under section 30 of later dealing*

The following is a copy of Section 30 of the Land Registration Act, 1925 as added to by Section 5 of the Law of Property (Amendment) Act, 1926:

"(1) When a registered charge is made for securing further advances, the registrar shall, before making any entry on the register which would prejudicially affect the priority of any further advance thereunder, give to the proprietor of the charge at his registered address, notice by registered post of the intended entry, and the proprietor of the charge shall not, in respect of any further advance, be affected by such entry, unless the advance is made after the date when the notice ought to have been received in due course of post.

(2) If by reason of any failure on the part of the registrar or the post office in reference to the notice, the proprietor of the charge suffers loss in relation to a further advance, he shall be entitled to be indemnified under this Act in like manner as if a mistake had occurred in the register; but if loss arises by reason of an omission to register or amend the address for service, no indemnity shall be payable under this Act.

(3) Where the proprietor of a charge is under an obligation, noted on the register, to make a further advance, a subsequent registered charge shall take effect subject to any further advance made pursuant to the obligation."

Your attention is directed to rule 313 of the Land Registration Rules, 1925 of which the following is a copy:

"(1) Every notice sent through the post shall, unless returned by the Post Office, and in the absence of evidence of its actual delivery, be deemed to have been received by the person addressed within seven days of its issue, exclusive of the day of posting, and the time fixed by the notice or taking any step thereunder is to be calculated accordingly."

The reference to registered post contained in subsection 1 of section 30 above must now be read as including a reference to the recorded delivery service by virtue of section 1 of the Recorded Delivery Service Act, 1962.

This means that attention must be given to such matters as local searches, valuation and fire insurance covered earlier.[110] Normally, however, a report on title from a solicitor may be waived, unless the land certificate actually makes a mention of an overriding interest or a minor interest, when advice as to the implications will be required. Also, should the charges register detail complicated restrictive covenants etc. a solicitor should be asked to comment.

With leasehold title, the additional steps described when we considered the formalities for unregistered land will apply here too. Thus the lessor's permission to create the mortgage may be required and notice to him of the charge will need to be given and his acknowledgement obtained. The mortgagor will be asked to produce the last rent receipt and a diary note will be taken to ensure that this aspect is checked on regularly. As regards the fire insurance position, the bank will need to examine the lease to see whose duty it is to insure and will then approach that party for details of the current insurance. It should be satisfied that the cover is adequate and then give notice and obtain an acknowledgement from the insurance company.

Notice of deposit procedure using a legal mortgage form

This is an alternative method of obtaining a mortgage over registered land used by some banks, in reliance on s. 66 Land Registration Act 1925 which states that a *lien* can be created over registered land by the deposit of the land certificate with a third party. This is effectively the equivalent of an equitable

110 See Appendix I, Q. 57 (April 1983).

SPECIMEN

H.M. LAND REGISTRY

Land Registration Acts, 1925 to 1966

CHARGE CERTIFICATE

TITLE NUMBER: Entry number in the Charges Register:

This is to Certify that a charge for the moneys within mentioned has been registered at H.M. Land Registry against the Title number referred to above. The charge or an office copy thereof, together with an office copy of the entries in the register relating thereto, and a plan of the land affected by the registration are within. Under rule 264 of the Land Registration Rules, 1925, these documents are, for the purposes of section 68 of the Land Registration Act, 1925, deemed to be contained in this certificate.

Under section 68 of the Land Registration Act, 1925, this certificate shall be admissible as evidence of the matters contained herein and under section 64 of the said Act it must be produced to the Chief Land Registrar on every entry in the register of a disposition by the registered proprietor of the charge and on every transmission thereof.

Consequent on the registration of the said charge the land certificate has been deposited and is retained at H.M. Land Registry pursuant to section 65 of the said Act.

WARNING

1. No endorsement, note, notice or entry made in this certificate other than those officially made at H.M. Land Registry shall have any operation.

2. All persons are cautioned against altering, adding to or otherwise tampering with this certificate or any document annexed thereto.

Fig.12.14 *Charge certificate*

NOTICE

The last date entered below is the last date on which this charge certificate was made to correspond with the register. Vendors should supply this date to purchasers when furnishing them with a copy of the **subsisting** entries on the register pursuant to section 110 of the Land Registration Act, 1925, as it must be quoted to the Registry by them when applying for official searches in form 94.

Dates when this charge certificate was made to correspond with the register.

SEARCHES AND INSPECTION OF THE LAND

This charge certificate is the best possible evidence as to the entries in the register up to the date last above mentioned.

1. It may be sent at any time to the appropriate District Land Registry to be officially examined and, where necessary, made to correspond with the register without fee. A registered proprietor proposing to deal with the land or charge is therefore in a position to afford conclusive evidence as to the entries in the register up to date.

2. To enable intending purchasers to ascertain without personal attendance at a District Land Registry whether any entry has been made in the register subsequent to the last date entered above, they may with the authority of the registered proprietor apply in form 94 for an official search to be made. That form is obtainable from H.M. Stationery Office or through any law stationer and it must be lodged by post. The certificate of the result of official search will state whether or not a subsequent entry has been made. No fee is payable.

3. Under rule 1 of the Land Registration Rules, 1939, as amended by rule 1 of the Land Registration Rules, 1936, where a purchaser has applied for and obtained an official certificate of the result of search in form 94, any entry which is made in the register after the date of the certificate and before an application is made for registration by the purchaser of the instrument effecting the purchase (and is not made pursuant to a priority notice or mortgage caution entered on the register before the certificate is issued), shall be postponed to the application by the purchaser, provided such application:

    (a) is in order under the Acts and Rules;

    (b) is delivered at the proper office (that is, at the appropriate District Land Registry) before that office is opened or deemed to be opened on the fifteenth day after the date of such certificate;

    (c) is accompanied by such certificate which shall be retained in the Registry; and

    (d) affects the same land or charge as the postponed entry.

4. Intending purchasers should inspect the land for the purpose of ascertaining its precise boundaries and whether there are any rights of way, light, drainage or other overriding interests to which it is subject. Enquiries should also be addressed to any persons in occupation of the land as to their rights to such occupation and as to whom rent (if any) is paid.

GENERAL INFORMATION

APPURTENANT RIGHTS AND PRIVILEGES

Under rule 251 of the Land Registration Rules, 1925, the registration of a person as proprietor of land vests in him together with the land, all buildings, erections, fixtures, commons, hedges, ditches, fences, ways, waters, water courses, liberties, privileges, easements, rights and advantages whatsoever, appertaining or reputed to appertain to the land, or any part thereof, or at the time of registration demised, occupied, or enjoyed therewith or reputed or known as part or parcel of or appurtenant to the land or any part thereof.

CERTAIN PROVISIONS OF THE ACT AND RULES AS TO CHARGES

1. Section 27 (1) of the Land Registration Act, 1925, provides that a registered charge shall, unless made or taking effect by demise or sub-demise, and subject to any provision to the contrary contained in the charge, take effect as a charge by way of legal mortgage.

2. Section 28 of the Act provides that:

    (1) Where a registered charge is created on any land there shall be implied on the part of the person being proprietor of such land at the time of the creation of the charge, unless there be an entry on the register negativing such implication:

        (a) a covenant with the proprietor for the time being of the charge to pay the principal sum charged, and interest, if any, thereon, at the appointed time and rate; and

        (b) a covenant, if the principal sum or any part thereof is unpaid at the appointed time, to pay interest half-yearly at the appointed rate as well after as before any judgment is obtained in respect of the charge on so much of the principal sum as for the time being remains unpaid.

Fig.12.14   *(contd)*

charge, as far as the Land Registry is concerned. However, the customer is asked to execute the bank's usual form of *legal* mortgage, but thereafter the bank does not proceed to the full stage of registering its charge and obtaining a charge certificate, i.e. the legal mortgage is held 'off the register' for the time being. This 'quasi-legal' procedure is cheaper for the customer, as Land Registry fees are not then payable, for the bank protects its position by lodging a notice of deposit of the land certificate using Form 85A (in duplicate) (Fig. 12.15). This form is sent to the District Land Registry together with the land certificate, which is then returned with the bank's interest noted in the charges register operating as a notice. (It is possible even to omit sending up the land certificate, in which case the notice of deposit will be effective, but perhaps at the customer's request, the land certificate will not then show the entry).

After notice of deposit has been given, should there be any attempt later by the customer to give another mortgage, or enter into a dealing, or if prejudicial entries are to be recorded at the Land Registry, then the bank will normally receive notice from the registrar, and it may then proceed to register its charge within fourteen days, thus obtaining a full legal mortgage. However if it did not do this it would still maintain its priority ahead of the new party (subject to any effect *Clayton's Case* might have on an unstopped fluctuating account). In other words, if the bank were lending in reliance only on a notice of deposit security, but did not take any steps to register its charge on learning, say, of the granting of a charging order against the property (the equivalent of a second mortgage granted to a creditor by the courts), it would retain its priority as against that other party, but might, however, later experience greater difficuty in selling as mortgagee, because it would not have a legal mortgage (for Land Registry purposes). As will be appreciated, the other party will have notice of the bank's interest recorded by way of notice of deposit and his priority will rank after that (*Barclays* v. *Taylor* (1974)).

Effectively, therefore, under the notice of deposit procedure the bank possesses its legal charge form with all the advantages of the clauses in that, but for Land Registry purposes a cheaper equitable charge has been created, which can later be turned into a registered charge in case of need. For instance, as mentioned, it would be usual for the bank to register its charge prior to selling as mortgagee.

The notice-of-deposit procedure is particularly useful where property is being bought by the customer using funds advanced by the bank, but when the land certificate will not be immediately available. Notice of *intended* deposit on Form 85C may then be given ahead of the transaction and the bank will be protected as soon as title is transferred. Similarly, in the case of a first registration of title, a notice of *intended* deposit can be given on Form 85B, as the delays in the production of the land certificate frequently extend to several months on these occasions.[111]

111 See Appendix I, Q. 34 (April 1980).

B. *Securities for Advances*

Form 85A

H.M. Land Registry

Land Registration Acts 1925 to 1971

Notice of deposit of land certificate or charge certificate

(Rule 239, Land Registration Rules 1925)

For official use only		
Date of registration	Application number	Pending dealings

This form must be completed in duplicate (see page 3). See also the notes on page 2.

County and district
(or London borough)..

Title number ....

Property ....

....

Registered proprietor(s) of land [*or charge nod.......*] ....

....

1   I/We, having accepted the land certificate [*or charge certificate no............*] of the title above mentioned by way of lien as security for money, hereby apply for the following notice to be entered in the charges register:

(1) In BLOCK LETTERS, enter full name and postal address of the body or person with whom the certificate is deposited

Notice of deposit of land certificate [*or charge certificate nod.......*] with ....

(1)..

....

....

2   This application is made by:

BLOCK LETTERS

Name ....

Address ....

....

Solicitor's reference.. Telephone number.....................

Signature of
applicant or solicitor(s)...

Date...

Fig.12.15   *Notice of deposit – Form 85A*

Equitable mortgages

An equitable mortgage to cover the borrower's own liabilities may be created by the mere deposit of the land certificate at the bank with the intention of creating a charge.

However, it is desirable also to get the mortgagor to execute a form of equitable mortgage over registered land or to execute a memorandum of deposit, for the clauses in these forms will strengthen the bank's position.

A third-party form of charge is of course essential where the mortgagor is not the borrowing customer, as the mere deposit of the land certificate would not then suffice. In all cases, however, the notice-of-deposit procedure will be utilised.

Second mortgage of registered land

A second or subsequent mortgage over registered land must always be by way of a legal mortgage, and thus the bank will have a registered charge. The 'quasi-legal' procedure is not possible.

The method employed is to obtain an office copy of the land certificate from the District Land Registry by applying on Form A44. (The actual land certificate will of course be held by the Registry.) Then, later, a search can be made using Form 94A to ensure no other entries have been made in the interim, and to obtain the thirty working days' statutory protective period. The legal mortgage is then executed within that period, the schedule in the charge form being completed, with reference to the land title number, and to details of the prior mortgage. Again, the charge form, a certified copy, form A4, and the scale fee, are forwarded to the Land Registry, and a certificate of second charge is issued, similar in design to a charge certificate.

It should be noted, however, that technical difficulties can arise if the first mortgagee has not registered his charge, but is merely on notice of deposit;[112] in those instances, the subsequent mortgagee would not be able to obtain a certificate of second charge, and might need to ask his solicitor to register a caution, to obtain some sort of protection. Usually, however, it is possible to persuade the first mortgagee to register his charge, if only by offering to pay the costs involved!

All the usual other formalities required for a second or subsequent mortgage will be necessary, such as notice to the prior mortgagees, notice to the fire insurance company and local land charges searches.

Sub-mortgages over registered land

The method used to obtain a sub-mortgage over registered land is relatively simple:[113] the charge certificate evidencing the customer's security should be obtained from him, and after searching at the Land Registry on Form 94A, to ensure there have been not further adverse entries, the bank's standard form

112 See Appendix I, Q. 47 (September 1981).
113 See Appendix I, Q. 49 (April 1982).

of sub-mortgage should be executed.[114] This, and a certified copy, together with the charge certificate should then be forwarded to the Land Registry, with the requisite fee, so that a certificate of sub-charge can be issued to the bank.

It would also be possible for the notice-of-deposit procedure to be used (Form 85A) referring to the deposit of the charge certificate, but this method is rare.

The usual steps appertaining to sub-mortgages, mentioned under unregistered land, should also be carried out, apart of course from the land charges register search which applies only to unregistered title.

Mortgage by limited company over registered land[115]

In addition to the many matters needing attention when company security is taken, registration of the mortgage within twenty-one days must of course be effected at Companies Registration Office. As the Land Registry will need sight of the certificate of registration at Companies Registration Office before proceeding to register the bank's charge on the land register, the Companies Registration Office matter should be attended to first.

Should the time limitations present practical problems (twenty-one days from creation of the charge for registration of the mortgage at Companies Registration Office and thirty working days since the date of the official search for registration of the charge within the protected priority period of the Land Registry), it will be found that the Land Registrar will be very helpful if he is approached in the following way: the banker sends him *a certified copy* of the charge, the completed form A4 for registration of the charge, and the appropriate fee, with a covering letter explaining that the actual charge form is at Companies Registration Office for registration at present, but undertaking to forward that actual charge form to the Land Registry as soon as it has been returned.

Also the Land Registry will require a certificate from the company's secretary to the effect that the charge does not contravene the company's memorandum and articles of association. This may be by way of a separate document dated concurrent to the mortgage or later, or it may be covered by a clause in the actual form of mortgage.

Incidentally, it should be noted that a fixed legal charge over land, incorporated within a debenture, will always be a registered charge.

Discharge of mortgage

Registered charge   A registered charge is released by use of Form 53 which requires sealing by the bank (Fig. 12.16). In some instances dispensation has been given by the Land Registry for an equivalent form to be used, which

114   See Appendix I, Q. 60 (April 1983).
115   See Appendix I, Q. 34 (April 1980).

Form 53
H.M. Land
Registry

Oyez Publishing
Limited
Oyez House
237 Long Lane
London SE1 4PU
a subsidiary of
The Solicitors'
Law Stationery Society
Limited

F21525.24-8-73
✱ ✱ ✱ ✱

*No Land Registry fee
is payable.*

DISCHARGE OF REGISTERED CHARGE(1)

(Rule 151, Land Registration Rules, 1925)

to be accompanied by the charge certificate

(1) *Where the proprietor of the charge
is a company or corporation, form 53
(Co.) should be used.*

County, County borough or ⎱ LOAMSHIRE
London borough ⎰

Title number...... ABC 12349

Property ...... 17 West Hill

...... TOWN

(2) *In BLOCK
LETTERS, enter full
name and address
of the proprietor of the
charge. In the case
of co-proprietors, both
or all should join in
and the form should be
amended throughout
as necessary.*

Date......19...... I(2) PRACTICE BANK

plc of PALATINE ROAD, TOWN

...... hereby admit

that the charge dated the...... 24th ......of...... August ......, 19......,

and registered on the...... 20th ......of...... October ......, 19......, of which

(3) *Strike out the
words in italics if
discharge is of the
whole of the charge.
If a discharge of
part of the money
only is intended,
substitute for italics,
" to the extent of
£   ".*

I am proprietor has been discharged(3) *as to the land shown and edged with red*

on the accompanying(4) plan signed by me, being part of the land comprised in the

title above mentioned.

(4) *This plan must
be based on the official
title plan giving
figured dimensions
not only of the land
affected but also tying
it to physical features
shown by firm black
lines on the official
title plan.*

Signed by the said......

PRACTICE BANK plc

in the presence of

Name......

Address......

......

Description

or occupation......

Signed by the said......

in the presence of

Name......

Address......

Description

or occupation......

(*Reproduced by kind permission of the Solicitors' Law Stationery Society.*)

Fig.12.16 *Form 53 – discharge of registered charge*

may simply be signed by a bank manager. Whichever form is completed, the form and the charge certificate are forwarded to the Registry. In the case of a first mortgage the land certificate is usually returned to the proprietor, but a request can be made for it to be sent to the bank, after which it can be given to the mortgagor against his receipt, or dealt with on his instructions, such as placing in safe custody. In the case of a second mortgage, the Land Registry merely acknowledges to the bank that its charge had been deleted.

Withdrawal of notice of deposit   The form of withdrawal (Form 86) is an additional part of the origianl form used to lodge notice of deposit on Form 85a, 85b or 85c, and to remove the bank's interest it is completed and forwarded, together with the land certificate, to the District Land Registry (Fig. 12.17). The land certificate is then returned to the bank, and upon reference to the charges register section it will be seen that the entry, which referred to the notice of deposit, has been ruled through. Again the land certificate may be given to the customer against his receipt. As the bank's form of legal mortgage or memorandum of deposit (if used) is not part of a chain of title it is usually merely marked 'cancelled' by the bank and retained with old security forms at the branch.

Sale by bank as mortgagee

No major differences in procedure arise upon a sale by a mortgagee of registered land, as opposed to a sale of unregistered title. However, the document which passes title to the purchaser will be a transfer in place of the conveyance or assignment which would be drawn up for unregistered title; this transfer will have to be sealed by the bank as vendor.

THE USE OF SOLICITORS' UNDERTAKINGS

In the course of his duties, the branch securities officer will have many contacts with firms of solicitors, especially in respect of mortgages over land and property. The standing and reputation of these firms will become known to him, but on some occasions he will be asked to rely on the word of an unknown firm and in those circumstances it will be essential to obtain a good reply to a status enquiry from the firm's bankers before exposing his own bank to risk.

Fortunately default by solicitors is rare, but should a bank have a bad experience it will usually be able to have resort to the Law Society's compensation fund if loss is incurred. In most cases this will arise because the solicitor has been in breach of his duty of care, or has failed to fulfil his undertaking. It is therefore equally important for the branch securities officer not only to obtain a good status report, but also to ensure that he instructs the solicitor precisely in what is required by the bank, so that the responsibility of the solicitor is clear. This is particularly so when the solicitor is acting for the customer or mortgagor, and, for the sake of convenience, is asked concurrently

Form 86
H.M. Land Registry

Land Registration Acts 1925 to 1971

Withdrawal of a notice of deposit or intended deposit of land certificate or charge certificate[1]
(Rule 246, Land Registration Rules 1925)

County and district
(or London borough) ....

Title number ....

Property ....

....

I/We [2] ....

....

....

....

hereby apply to withdraw from the register the notice of [intended] deposit of the **accompanying** land certificate

[*or charge certificate no.* ....].

Signature(s) of
applicant(s) [3] ....

Date...

Notes

1   The relevant land or charge certificate must accompany this application which should be sent to the district land registry serving the area in which the land is situated. If in doubt as to the proper office, consult Explanatory Leaflet No. 9 available from any district land registry. Postage must be prepaid on all mail.

2   In block letters, enter the full name(s) and postal address(es) of the body or individual(s) where the certificate was deposited.

3   This application must be signed **personally** by the person(s) entitled to the lien created by the deposit or by his/their successors in title. In the case of a company or corporation, the signature of a responsible officer on its behalf will be sufficient. This includes, in the case of a bank, the signature of a branch manager.

Printed in England by Trafford Press, Doncaster and published by Her Majesty's Stationery Office
10p each or 25 copies for £2 (exclusive of tax) Dd.597547 K1160 4 79 GP 1168 ISBN 0 11 390072 4

4

Fig.12.17 *Notice of deposit – withdrawal*

to advise or assist the bank in obtaining its security, as might happen, for example, upon a property being acquired by the client which is forthwith to be mortaged to the bank that has put up all or part of the purchase monies.

Suppose the client is a limited company and the property is bought and the mortgage executed, but there are then delays for some good reason in forwarding the documents to the branch. During this period neither the solicitor nor the bank has registered the charge at Companies House. In such circumstances who will be to blame? Was it made clear to the solicitor that the bank relied on him to protect the bank's interests fully? What did his undertaking say?

Generally, a solicitor will be very careful about what he commits himself to, in an undertaking, and he will be unwise if he agrees to do something which, in the event, it may transpire he cannot, as it was never within his own full power to do because this depended also upon the prior action of some other party. This is why a solicitor will rarely undertake to pay a specific sum from the proceeds of a sale of property until contracts are exchanged, and even after that stage an undertaking may be worded as conditional upon the successful completion of the transaction.

A solicitor's undertaking may be enforceable even though it is not a contract, and a solicitor may face disciplinary action by the Law Society in certain circumstances. It has been said that the onus on the solicitor as to the standard of his professional conduct is greater than the strict legal requirements.

As far as banks are concerned, many undertakings will be in the form of an obligation to pay to them monies of an unspecified or specified amount, perhaps with a lower limitation (e.g. 'not less than £10 000'), or to obtain and forward documents of title, perhaps including an executed mortgage. Whatever its nature, the undertaking should be read most carefully and the bank officer must be entirely happy that he can rely on it as doing what he wished it to do.

The London clearing banks entered into an arrangement with the Law Society some years ago, whereby the two parties agreed the nature and form of solicitors' undertakings which should be used, so that no dispute would arise in those exceptional cases where default occurred and the banks had to resort to the Law Society's compensation fund. These banks invariably therefore insist on these standard forms being used and they will not accept an undertaking merely embodied in a letter from the solicitor, even if on headed paper.

Solicitors' undertakings cover the following most common circumstances under which their use is necessary.

Release of deeds/land certificate for inspection and return

Deeds in mortgage should never be released to the customer himself, although of course he could respect them at a branch while supervised by a bank officer. Usually, however, if for some reason it is necessary to refer to them – as when drainage rights or obligations in respect of boundary fences need to be examined – they should be forwarded on the written authority of the customer to his solicitor (on whom a good report is held) for the purpose of inspection, against his undertaking to hold them to the bank's order and to return them upon being requested to do so in the same condition, unencumbered. The schedule of the deeds and documents released will be prepared and this should be receipted by the solicitor, if it is separate from the undertaking. It is advisable for the bank to retain its mortgage form in such circumstances, although of course in the case of registered title and with a registered charge this will be bound up inside the charge certificate and must therefore be sent to the solicitor. Some banks make a practice of retaining the last conveyance and supplying a photocopy only. All these procedures guard against loss of priority and loss of its security by the bank, and should anything untoward happen they give the bank recourse to the compensation fund.

Release of deeds/land certificate upon sale or remortgage[116]
Here again the customer's written authority will be necessary before the deeds/land certificate/charge certificate can be forwarded to the solicitor acting. If the purpose is to repay the bank or reduce reliance on the bank borrowing by a remortgage then the bank will wish to know the amount involved and that the commitment of the new lender is firm. If the intention is that the bank is to remain secured it may postpone its charge, in which event the bank's mortgage will not be released. In the event of a sale of the property, before proceeding the bank will wish to know what price has been obtained for the property in question, and especially whether contracts have been exchanged at that figure. If not, the first type of undertaking (inspection and return) may be more appropriate at this stage, but if contracts have been exchanged then the solicitor will be able to undertake that, if completion ensues, he will pay the net sale proceeds, less only the costs relating to the sale, to the bank without any other deductions. His undertaking may state that this sum will amount to 'not less than £. . . . . ' with a realistic estimated figure being inserted. More usually it will refer simply to the known sale price and say that deductions will only comprise estate agents' costs and legal costs and possibly any deposit that has been paid, if the solicitor does not hold that. The undertaking will say that the documents will be returned to the bank in the same condition if the sale is not completed, or at any time should the bank so require.

After completion, and after receiving the net sale proceeds, the bank will release its mortgage form under seal, or in the case of a registered charge it will seal Form 53. Where it was only on notice of deposit, that notice will be

116 See Appendix I, Q. 38 (September 1980).

withdrawn from the Land Registry after completing the bottom half of the form which will be sent to the solicitor acting. The mortgage may be forwarded to the solicitor if he requires it, or it may just be marked 'cancelled' and placed with obsolete securities at the branch.

The type of undertaking described above is sometimes used in bridging or bridge-over transactions, where the bank has a mortgage over the property being sold. The bank's position as mortgagee could arise through an earlier charge or simply because the deeds or land certificate are passed through its hands at this time – a highly desirable step – giving it an equitable charge or lien; in such circumstances there will be no mortgage form to release.

Bridge-over transactions involve the bank in lending money to enable the customer to acquire title to a second property pending repayment from a sale of the first, or pending refinance from one source or another. In such a case a further form of undertaking could also be used, as now described.

Undertaking to use monies advanced to acquire title to property[117]

This amounts to an undertaking not just to acquire title, but to obtain a good and marketable title, to use the funds only for that purpose, and to hold the deeds/land certificate upon completion to the order of the bank, to whom they will then be forwarded. It may extend to obtaining a (legal) mortgage in favour of the bank from the purchaser, concurrent with the transfer of title into his name.

In some instances the bank may only be taking a second mortgage, behind another lender, in which case an amended form of this type of undertaking will be necessary. However, the solicitors may well be asked beforehand to confirm that the monies to be advanced by the first mortgagee are available and that they have seen written confirmation of this fact (and not a mere indication in principle or something not so certain!).

Undertaking used in connection with bridging finance

In fact it is more usual to see another type of form (Fig. 12.18) specifically relating to bridge-over transactions. This special form incorporates a variety of clauses designed to cover all possible combinations of bridge-over transactions and those not applicable with be struck out. Often a bank will rely merely on undertakings and never have possessed the title documents itself; on other occasions it will be releasing property already in mortgage,[118] in others the new property may form new or additional security.[119]

Some bridge-over transactions will be agreed by a bank before contracts for the sale of the existing property are exchanged, perhaps because there is no sign of a purchaser at that stage. These are called open-ended bridgers and clearly involve a much greater degree of risk for the lending bank. In such a

117　See Appendix I, Q. 38 (September 1980).
118　See Appendix I, Q. 61 (September 1983).
110　See Appendix I, Q. 61 (September 1983).

Name and address of solicitor	To _____
	_____
	I/We hereby irrevocably authorise and request you to give an undertaking in the form set out below and accordingly to pay the net proceeds of sale after deduction of your costs to
Authority to be signed in duplicate by the client(s)	Practice Bank plc _____ Branch
	Dated _____
	Signed _____

To Practice Bank plc _____ _____ Branch

If you provide facilities to my/our client _____
for the purchase of the Freehold/Leasehold property (the new property)
_____ (Description of Property)
pending the sale by my/our client of the Freehold/Leasehold property (the existing property)
_____ (Description of Property)

I/We undertake

1   that any sums received from you or your customer will be applied solely for the following purposes

*Delete words in *italics* as applicable

 *   (a)   *in discharging the present mortgage(s) on the existing property.*
     (b)   in acquiring a good marketable title to the new property
           (subject to the mortgage mentioned below.)
     (c)   in paying any necessary deposit legal fees costs and disbursements in connection with the purchase.

The purchase price contemplated is £ _____ gross.

I/We are informed that a sum of £ _____ is being advanced on mortgage by
_____

The amount required from my/our client for the transaction including the deposit and together with costs disbursements and appointments is not expected to exceed £ _____

2 To hold to your order when received by me/us the documents of title of the existing property pending completion of the sale (unless subject to any prior mortgage(s)), and/of the new property (unless subject to any prior mortgage(s)).

3 To pay to you the net proceeds of sale of the existing property when received by me/us.

The sale price contemplated is £ _____ and the only deductions which will have to be made at present known to me/us are:

Fig.12.18 *Solicitor's undertaking re bridge-over transaction*

(i)   the deposit (if not held by me/us)

(ii) the estate agent's commission

(iii) the amount required to redeem any mortgages and charges which so far as known to us at present do not exceed £ _____

(iv) the legal fees costs and disbursements relating to the transaction.

(v)

Deductions to be made from net proceeds of sale other than as shown above must be specifically mentioned.

4 To advise you immediately of any subsequent claim by a third party upon the net proceeds of sale of which I/We have knowledge.

Signature _____

Date_____ _____

Fig.12.18   *(contd)*

case great care must be taken with margins, the valuation of the property not yet sold and a realistic assessment of the prospects for sale. In particular, the impact of interest accrual on two mortgages running concurrently must be borne in mind. Banks much prefer closed bridgers – that is those where contracts have been exchanged for the sale of the existing property, as in those cases the timing of the end of the transaction – the completion date – is certain.

In some bridging transactions the bank will be asked first to advance the deposit monies required when contracts are exchanged for the purchase of the new property. Usually this sum is 10 per cent of the purchase price. (It is usual for the contract to stipulate that such monies will be forfeited to the intended vendor, if the purchaser fails to complete.) Later the bank will lend the balance of the consideration, i.e. the other 90 per cent of the purchase price.

Sometimes bridging transactions are organized differently and the bank will advance monies to enable the mortgage on the house, which is to be sold, to be paid off. This can mean that the deeds become free and are available to the bank as security pending the sale. Also, as repayment is to flow from the sale proceeds this is a neater way of handling matters. However, it may well involve the bank in lending more than does the other method, as the customer may well need also to rely on the bank to lend that proportion of the price of the new property which is not being advanced by, say, his building society. This element will represent that part of the 'equity' arising ultimately when the old property is sold which the customer intends to introduce into the new house.

The example of the form of undertaking used in these situations shown in

Fig. 12.18 should be examined carefully by the student reader, as bridging transactions are very common in the branch banking scene.

In concluding our examination of the use of solicitors' undertakings we should remember that in all cases the customer's authority should be obtained before matters proceed. Also, it is highly desirable, where the situation is one when the bank is to benefit by the receipt of monies to which is was not previously entitled, that a written authority addressed to the solicitor should be obtained, couched in *irrevocable* terms. On the basis of this authority the solicitor will give his undertaking, and the advantage to the bank will be that, in case of need, it will be able to claim that it has an equitable assignment over the funds. This could be very useful should bankruptcy proceedings have intervened between the date of the authority and the date set for completion.

Students, having read this chapter on land as security, may now find reference to Appendix II helpful.

CHAPTER 13

Life Policies as Security

ADVANTAGES AND DISADVANTAGES

Although, apparently, in the early days of joint stock banking, life policies were not well regarded as security, this is not the case today, and they form a large proportion of securities taken for small personal bank advances or to support guarantee liabilities; they have many advantages.

Life policies are simple and cheap to charge, and when a legal mortgage has been taken they are readily realizable. Moreover, provided premiums are paid when they are due, the bank can expect the surrender value of a life policy to increase steadily during the time it is lodged with it. On the other hand, if the premium is not paid there is a risk that the policy might lapse, but in most instances the assurance company will give notice to the assignee before cancellation and it is more usual, in fact, in those circumstances for an automatic loan to come into operation and for the surrender value to be reduced by the amount of the unpaid premium. It is the fact that a policy has a readily ascertainable value in the form of a cash figure which can be obtained upon its surrender, which makes the security so attractive. This surrender value can be readily discovered by an enquiry to the assurance company, and can be updated on a regular basis; thus the bank is always aware of the amount it is likely to receive in a realization situation. The formalities associated with surrender are few, and simply by completing the necessary papers from the assurance company and providing the charge form and policy, and any prior assignments, the bank will receive the assurance company's cheque which is certain to be met within a few days. Indeed, most British insurance companies may be regarded as being as financially sound as many banks themselves, although caution is necessary with some of the less well-known companies, who have from time to time got into difficulties. Usually, however those companies have not been involved in the life assurance side of insurance business.

The life policy is a particularly attractive and useful form of security where the bank is lending to any individual whose financial worth is not strong, but where the lending is justified because of the individual's personal skills or the contribution which he can make to his company. There, although the surrender value may be negligible in relation to the advance, death cover ensures that if the individual dies, and his services are lost to his company or firm, nevertheless the bank can be repaid out of the capital value of the policy. Again, where the bank is lending against a reversionary interest which is only contingent, and it is necessary for the remainderman to outlive the life tenant

386

if monies under the reversionary interest are to pass to the mortgagee, the provision of life cover in the form of a policy charged additionally as security, and of sufficient capital value, will ensure that the bank is repaid, if the remainderman predeceases the life tenant (see p.472)

There are, however, one or two risks in taking life policies as security, and the main one has been touched upon in that the customer might be financially unable to continue meeting the premiums, as and when they fall due. However, under the terms of their charge, banks are usually empowered to debit the customer's account with the cost of premiums to keep the policy alive, although each such situation will need to be assessed carefully. This is because, with high interest rates applying, the amount of the overdraft could increase more rapidly than the surrender value of the policy and the exercise would not be worth while, except where the death benefit cover is worth protecting because of the health of the assured. However, it is usually possible for a life policy to be converted into a paid-up policy, and in that case no further premiums are payable and the policy retains a certain but reduced value until the maturity date.

In the financial crisis of the mid-1970s some insurance companies decided to reduce the surrender values of their policies below the level at which these had earlier been quoted, and while that period of history may now be regarded as exceptional, the incident served to show a risk. Nevertheless, even in those times many large and reputable companies who had already quoted surrender values to assignees, such as banks, were prepared to stand by those figures if the bank could state that it had advanced funds in reliance on their earlier figure.

Another point to bear in mind in considering the attractions of this type of security is that naturally an assignee cannot acquire rights under an assignment of a policy which would be better than those of the assured. As a contract of life assurance is a contract *uberrimae fidei* (of the utmost good faith) there is therefore a danger, albeit remote, that if there has been any misrepresentation or non-disclosure to the assurance company in the proposal form, the policy might later be cancelled, when the true facts come to light. Moreover, if the policy contains conditions which the life assured does not comply with, then the company will have a right to refuse payment upon a claim being made. However, where a bank as assignee has given notice of its interest in the policy, reputable insurance companies tend not to disclaim the policy. Nevertheless, for example, this means that a bank should examine a policy carefully to see whether it will be payable in the event of death by suicide. Normally it will find that, because of the inclusion of a protective clause, assignees for value, such as a bank, will still be able to recover, should the assured die as a result of sane or insane suicide.

There is, however, a general legal principle that where a person insures his life and commits suicide while sane, his personal representatives cannot recover the proceeds of a life policy from the assurance company and even if the policy provides for payment in the event of suicide committed while the person was sane, this appears to make no difference. An illustration of this is the case of *Beresford* v. *Royal Insurance Company Ltd* (1938), which was taken to the House of Lords, where the decision was based on the following facts. Major Rowlandson took out a life policy for £50 000 and the assurance company agreed that this sum would be paid to his executors or assignees upon his death, even should he die by sane or insane suicide, but only if one year had elapsed since the start of the contract of assurance. A few years later Major Rowlandson shot himself a few minutes before the expiry time for renewal of the premium on the policy. His administratrix claimed the capital value of the policy, but the assurance company pleaded that as the assured had died by suicide the policy was void. The House of Lords upheld this view, pointing out that a provision by an insurance company for payment in the event of suicide while sane was contrary to public policy. However, it must be remembered that suicide is now no longer a crime in English law following the passing of the Suicide Act 1961, and it is felt that Lord Atkin's statement in the Beresford case is still applicable, that an assignee of a policy which provided for payment on sane suicide would be protected. As mentioned, in fact many policies have clauses stating that innocent assignees will not be affected by a clause precluding payment of the capital value to the beneficiary or his estate should the assured die by his own hand.

Another disadvantage with a life policy is the possible adverse publicity which might be occasioned to the bank if it needs to surrender the policy, so depriving the beneficiary of the death cover. This would apply also should the bank look to the capital value upon the death of the life assured, to the exclusion of his dependants. However, such publicity is far less than that occasioned by the realization of domestic property.

Another technical disadvantage with a life policy is that the proposer must have had an insurable interest in the life of the assured, and if for any reason this did not exist then the policy would have been wrongly issued. In the case of reputable British insurance companies, however, it can be assumed that an insurable interest exists and that the matter has been thoroughly and properly investigated by the insurance company before the policy was issued. This is an area which is unlikely in practice therefore to cause any problems to the bank as assignee. Nevertheless, it may be noted that insurable interests exist where an individual takes out a policy on his or her own life, or where a man insures the life of his wife, or a wife insures the life of her husband. A creditor has an insurable interest in the life of his debtor and a limited company can insure the life of its directors or employees, as may any other employer. Also, in a long civil trial, where the costs incurred have been heavy, and where it would be neccessary to start the hearing again, should the judge die, the plaintiffs and/or defendants may insure the life of the judge! The writer recalls this being done in the *Selangor* trial in 1968.

TYPES OF POLICIES

The two types of policy usually offered as security are the endowment policy and the whole-life policy and either type may have been issued 'with profits' or 'without profits'. Profits are the bonuses declared by the assurance company, and usually, if the policy is 'with profits', the premium payable will be higher than for a policy issued without these benefits. It is usual to see the surrender value increase more rapidly in the case of a 'with profits' policy and the amount received at maturity or upon the death of a life assured will be more than the capital value of the policy, if the bonuses have been allowed to accumulate.

Endowment policies are policies which mature at a fixed future date, for example at age sixty of the life assured, or upon that person's earlier death. Endowment policies are therefore slightly more attractive as security than whole-life policies, which do not become payable until the life assured dies. As will be appreciated, with an endowment policy, the capital value, with or without bonuses, is certain to pass to a bank as assignee on a known date or sooner, and this can help the bank in any decision necessary as to whether or not it should pay premiums to keep the policy in existence. With a whole-life policy, if the bank continued to pay premiums, there would be no guarantee that such a commitment would cease in the foreseeable future.

Banks are occasionally offered industrial life policies as security and usually the capital value of such policies is fairly small. Historically, premiums on policies of this type have been paid weekly or monthly to a collector who calls personally for the money. The terms under which industrial policies are issued usually place restraints on assignment, and they are therefore not really suitable as security, although in a situation where the bank's money is at risk and the bank is looking for any possible security available to bolster a weak position, it might well take any assignment and give notice, even though the assurance company might not acknowledge matters. Each such policy should therefore be carefully examined to see what its particular terms are and, in some instances, assignment might be possible. In view of the way in which premiums are paid, the proposer will hold a premium receipt book issued by the insurance company and as amounts are paid entries will be made in the book by the collector. Consequently, if a bank takes a charge over an industrial policy it will be necessary for the premium receipt book to be exhibited from time to time, so that the bank can ensure that the premiums are indeed being paid.

Another type of policy is one having a capital value which decreases as time passes. These are known, occasionally, as mortgage protection policies and are used in connection with house purchase advances made by building societies or insurance companies themselves. The amount assured is reduced annually, as the mortgage debt, which they seek to cover, is gradually repaid. At the end of the period the policy may well have no value left in it, although sometimes at the end of the term there is a small sum payable. In the latter case the premiums charged are higher. Banks might be interested in taking an assignment over either type of policy so as to have the benefit of the death cover, or the comfort that a capital value could be payable in due course, when the mortgage loan is repaid and the policy matures.

In recent times there has been a movement to link the value of life assurance policies to investments in unit trust units and a proportion of the premiums paid are invested in that way. Consequently the value of the policy for surrender purposes or upon maturity is linked to the value of the units acquired and it may not be so easy to estimate its worth as security, as the market price of the unit trust units will fluctuate. The assignment over the policy is taken in the normal way, however, and the assignor should be asked to produce the premium receipts from time to time to enable the bank to see how many units have been allocated to the policy; by reference to the financial press it will then be possible to calculate the approximate surrender value.

Some policies are issued creating a trust in favour of a beneficiary other than the policy holder, the most usual policy being those issued subject to s. 11 Married Woman's Property Act 1882. Under this, a trust arises in favour of the beneficiary where a policy is proposed by a husband on his own life in favour of his wife or his children, or where a policy is proposed by a wife on her own life in favour of her husband or children. In these cases it is necessary both for the proposer and the beneficiary to assign the interest in the policy, and consideration will be necessary as to whether the beneficiary should receive independent advice or not.[120] The charge will only be possible where the beneficiaries are specifically mentioned by name and, in the case of children, are no longer minors. Even so, because of possible technical problems which can arise and also the possibility of adverse publicity, banks will hesitate to accept some trust policies as security.

DUPLICATE POLICIES

Clearly, it is desirable that the policy document should be the original one issued by the life assurance company, and a bank will hesitate to take an assignment over a duplicate policy, for the implication of such a situation would be that possibly problems could arise upon surrender or maturity because of a claim by a third party who sought priority, as he held the original. The failure of the assignor to produce the original policy would in fact have been constructive notice of an earlier assignment, and a clear warning is seen in *Spencer* v. *Clarke* (1878). There the assignee was told by the assignor that he had left the policy at home by mistake, whereas he had in fact already created an equitable assignment over the policy and the earlier assignee had relied upon possession of the policy for his security. He had not given notice of his charge to the assurance company, although the second

120   See Appendix I, Q. 44 (April 1981).

assignee, who held not even a duplicate policy, did give notice of his charge. When the issue came to be examined as to who was entitled to rights under the policy, the court held that the second assignee had had constructive notice of the earlier charge, because the policy could not be produced at the time he took his assignment, and therefore his priority ranked behind that of the earlier assignee.

In *Newman* v. *Newman* (1885) it was held that where an assignee had notice of a previous assignment, although the assurance company had not been advised, the second assignee could not obtain priority over the prior assignment by giving notice of his charge ahead of the other assignee. This was so despite the fact that the Policies of Assurance Act (1867) states that priority of an assignment is regulated by the date on which notice is received by the insurance company.

THE BANK'S FORM OF LEGAL ASSIGNMENT OVER LIFE POLICIES

In addition to the standard clauses used in all security forms (see Chapter 11), a legal assignment of a life policy to a bank (Fig. 13.1) will usually include the following agreements and covenants:

(*a*) There will be an undertaking by the assignor that he will pay all premiums on their due dates, and will hand the receipts to the bank; he will agree that, should he not do so, the bank will be empowered to pay the premiums and to charge the cost to him, by recovering these monies through the security or by debiting his account.

(*b*) As well as excluding s. 103 Law of Property Act 1925 (see Chapter 11) the bank's power of sale will be extended to include a right to *surrender* the policy immediately after failure to meet a demand to pay (or after fourteen days or some similar period).

(*c*) The bank will agree that when the liabilities have been repaid it will reassign the policy to the assignor but as his expense.

TAKING A FIRST LEGAL ASSIGNMENT[121]

Security step A: examination of the policy When perfecting its security the bank should first examine the policy carefully to see that it is issued by a reputable, well-known company. The bank will expect the amount assured to be stated in sterling and to be payable in the United Kingdom so that there is no added risk of exchange rate fluctuations. The policy should also be examined to see if there are any special conditions or restrictions which might apply, and which would vitiate it or reduce its value. For example, travel by aircraft might be excluded, or in the event of death following engagement in motor sports the policy might become void. There could also be restrictions

121 See Appendix I, Q. 44 (April 1981).

S.3. *Assignment of Life Policy (Individual).*

I,

of

as beneficial owner assign to BANK OF CYPRUS (LONDON) LIMITED ("the Bank") the
Policy mentioned in the Schedule hereto TO HOLD by way of mortgage and as a continuing
security for all my liability to the Bank on current account or otherwise.

I agree as follows:-

1.   "Liability" includes indebtedness, sole, several or joint, in respect of advances, bills, promissory
     notes, guarantees, interest, commission, banking or legal charges, and expenses.

2.   I will keep up the Policy and produce the premium receipts to the Bank. If I fail to do so
     the Bank may pay what is due and charge the amount against me.

3.   ·The Bank shall have immediate and unrestricted power of sale and, instead of selling, ma
     surrender the Policy.

4.   The Bank shall have a lien on all stocks, shares, securities and property of mine from time to
     time held by the Bank, whether for safe custody or otherwise, and on all monies from time to
     time standing to my credit with the Bank on any account whatever.

In witness whereof I have hereunto set my hand and seal the day and year hereunder written.

SCHEDULE

Office in which Policy effected	Number of Policy	Sum assured. Add "with profits" if applicable

Particulars of any Documents forming part of Title
to the above-mentioned Policy

Date of Document	Short description

Signed, sealed and delivered

this   day

of   19   (LS)

in the presence of

Signature ....

Address ....

....

Description ....

Fig. 13.1   *Life policy mortgage form*

on payment following the suicide of the life assured, although in practice, as we have seen, a bona fide assignee for value is unlikely to suffer upon any breach. Nevertheless, while suicide is no longer a crime and therefore the policy cannot be vitiated on grounds of it being against public policy, the principle could be invoked that any loss deliberately caused by the assured person might not be recoverable.

Security step B: age of life assured The policy should then be examined to see whether or not it states that the age of the life assured has been 'admitted', meaning that evidence of the date of birth has been seen by the assurance company. The statement to this effect might appear by way of endorsement on the policy, or by a separate letter accompanying the policy. If age has not been admitted (and so in consequence the possibility exists that the date of birth might have been wrongly stated, leading to the policy being declared void upon a claim being made or an adjustment in the amount paid under the policy to a figure appropriate to the premiums paid for a person of the correct age), steps should be put in hand to obtain the life-assured's birth certificate and to exhibit this to the assurance company, so that a suitable endorsement can be issued and retained with the policy. Certain insurance companies have special arrangements with the clearing banks so that, in respect of their policies, issued prior to October 1968, even though age does not appear to have been admitted, the bank as assignee can proceed in safety.

Security step C: identify the assignor(s) The policy should next be examined to see whether it has been issued for the benefit of one named party only, in which case the charge will simply be taken from him. However, in the case of a trust policy, the assignments will need to be executed by the trustee and the beneficiary, possibly with independent advice.

Security step D: execution of the assignment The bank's form of mortgage is a legal assignment and the schedule to this should be completed naming the assurance company, the amount insured, the date of the policy and its number. The life assured is also usually mentioned.

The charge form should be dated on the day of execution and should be signed by the assignor, with his signature being witnessed by a bank officer or his solicitor, if separate advice is taken. Naturally, if the amount secured is limited to a specific figure then this should be inserted before the charge form is signed.

Security step E: notice to the assurance company Under the Policies of Assurance Act 1867 an assignee can sue in his own name provided written notice of the assignment is given to the assurance company.

Accordingly, a standard form of printed notice is despatched in duplicate

(Fig. 13.2). The insurance company is asked to acknowledge receipt of the notice on the duplicate form which is returned to the bank and then kept with the security papers, that is the life policy and the assignment form. With some companies, a small fee (not more than 25 pence) may be payable at this stage, and this point can be ascertained by reference to the *Bankers' Almanac*.

Another reason for giving notice is that priority of assignments depends upon the time of receipt of notice by the assurance company. However, if the bank is aware of an earlier assignment of which notice has not been given or where the bank is on constructive notice of an earlier assignment, as in *Spencer* v. *Clarke*, the bank cannot obtain priority ahead of these parties simply because it gives written notice first.

Security step F: enquiries of the assurance company   When notice of the bank's charge is given, the assurance company will be asked to state whether it itself has any charge over the policy, or whether it has received notice of any other charge granted to a third party.

If the reply should state that the company had received notice of assignments which have been reassigned, it will then be important for the bank to ensure that those assignments and reassignments, and any other papers which form part of the 'chain of title' to the policy, are lodged with the bank and retained alongside the policy and the bank's mortgage. All these documents will be required for production should the bank wish to claim the maturity proceeds or surrender value of the policy.

Security step G: ascertain the surrender value   The surrender value should be discovered by writing to the assurance company separately, and diary notes should then be raised in accordance with the bank's particular practice so as to update this information from time to time; this is often done annually or every three or four years. Usually, before a policy is charged, a banker will want to assess the likely surrender value to decide whether it will be worth while accepting the policy into security, and if the customer cannot produce evidence from the company then the banker will be able to make some form of reasonable guess by reference to the amount of premiums paid since the policy was issued. While in the first two or three years these premiums are usually allocated towards meeting the expenses of the issue of the policy, and no surrender value can be expected to arise on the policy, thereafter it is reasonable to work on the basis that approximately two-thirds of the premiums paid will be reflected in the current surrender value. On top of this, further value will have accrued through bonuses declared on a 'with profits' policy.

Security step H: production of premium receipts   The assignor should be asked to produce receipts for premiums paid and the bank will encourage him, if he is a customer and not a third-party assignor banking elsewhere, to

S.5

BANK OF CYPRUS (LONDON) LTD.

Date

The Secretary,

Dear Sir,

We hereby give you notice that by deed dated the
day of   19
                                                    of

has assigned to this Bank all that Policy of Assurance
No.   dated the   day of
        19   for the sum of £   on the life
of   .
together with all moneys assured by or to become payable under
the said policy.

Please acknowledge receipt of this notice on the duplicate
attached and state if any prior charges on the Policy have been
registered in your books.

The fee of   is enclosed.

Yours faithfully,

Manager

Received Notice of Assignment of which the above is a duplicate.
No prior charges have been registered in our books.

Signature

Fig.13.2   *Notice of assignment of life policy to assurance company*

make future payments by standing order or direct debit. This mean that it will
not be necessary for the bank to insist on seeing premium receipts in the
future, as it will be able to monitor the safety of its security through its
internal standing order or direct debit payment records and the customer's
account. However, if this cannot be arranged, or the assignor banks elsewhere,
careful diary notes must be made to ensure the premium receipts are exhibited
annually or at other appropriate intervals.

If there are any unpaid premiums when the policy is charged, the bank
should examine the policy to see whether arrears of premiums are to be
automatically applied as a deduction from the surrender value and used as a
loan by the assurance company towards meeting the costs of the premium. It
will be important, of course, to ensure that the policy does not lapse upon
non-payment of a premium.

Certain assurance companies have, however, undertaken to advise the London clearing banks when premiums are unpaid.

SECOND OR SUBSEQUENT ASSIGNMENTS

While second or subsequent assignments to a bank are rare, there is nothing technically to prevent these being taken as security, and, if there is any 'equity' in the surrender value after allowing for the amount secured by the first assignment, there can be some attraction in the appropriate circumstances.

The procedure is exactly the same as for a first assignment, although the bank will of course not hold the life policy, and it might be necessary therefore for the bank to examine the policy at the offices of the first assignee, or at least to obtain full details from him. The bank's charge form is completed in the usual way, although the schedule in which reference is made to the policy will also make mention of the details of the prior assignment.

The bank must also give notice of its assignment to all prior assignees, as this will determine the account of that lender's priority and ensure that if he comes into possession of any surplus funds, upon maturity or surrender, he will pass these to the bank. The bank will enquire as to the amount secured by the earlier assignments, and when this amount is deducted from the quoted surrender value, the bank will know the 'equity value' of its security.

Occasionally the bank itself, being a first assignee, might receive notice of a subsequent charge over the policy, and if so, and if its lending is on current account, this must be stopped to avoid the application of the Rule in *Clayton's Case* whereby priority would be lost through continued credit and debit turnover.

Later, when the bank's advance has been repaid, it will be necessary for the assignment to be reassigned and for the policy and the reassignment, together with any earlier released assignments, to be passed to the later assignee. Similarly, there is an obligation on the bank to account to that subsequent assignee, if it comes into possession of funds surplus to its own requirements upon maturity or surrender.

ASSIGNMENTS BY LIMITED COMPANIES

Where a limited company is the proposer of a life policy, possibly taken out on the life on one of its directors or a valued member of staff, the company may charge the policy as security for its liabilities provided it is the beneficiary. The same security steps are necessary as with a charge by an individual, but additionally the bank must examine the company's memorandum of association to see that the company has power to give security for the purpose for which it is required, and the assignment must be given in accordance with the company's articles of association within the ambits of any limitations imposed. It will be necessary to see that a disinterested quorum, if required, is present and that the directors voting on the resolution may do so (see Chapter 9). A copy of the resolution to charge the policy as security should be placed with the assignment and the assignment should be executed under seal by the company. Where there is any deficiency in the ability of the directors to act, a resolution from the company in general meeting should be taken and a copy of this should also be placed with the assignment. The assignment does not need registering at Companies Registration Office. The granting of security by a limited company is examined in greater depth on pp. 219-239.

EQUITABLE ASSIGNMENT OF LIFE POLICIES

An equitable assignment will arise if a policy is lodged as security with the bank by the borrower without any written form of assignment. In such event it is most desirable for an interview note of the transaction to be made concurrently, to avoid any later arguments or claim that the life policy was only lodged for safe keeping. In any event the policy should be entered into the bank's security ledger. It would of course not be possible for a third party to secure the liabilities of the customer in this way without a charge form, as such an intention and contract is similar to a guarantee and under the Statute of Frauds 1677 must be evidenced in writing.

Any equitable assignment is strengthened when, at the time the policy is lodged, a memorandum of deposit is also completed as evidence of the transaction, incorporating clauses similar to those seen in the form of legal assignment.

The bank should always give notice to the assurance company of the creation of an equitable charge, for while there is no statutory requirement for the company to accept notice of an *equitable* interest, this step ensures that the bank has priority over any previous assignees who have taken an assignment and not given notice, provided of course that the bank has no notice, constructive or otherwise, of the existence of the prior charge.

If notice of the equitable assignment is not given, and other equitable assignees have also not given notice, priority will depend upon the date of the charge, and it will not matter whether the equitable charge were given in writing or simply by way of deposit.

An equitable charge of a life policy suffers from the usual defects of this type of charge, the most important of which is that if there are any other equitable interests existing then the 'first in time prevails'. In practice what is more likely to be a problem is that the bank will need to obtain a court order before it can obtain the proceeds of the policy.

REALIZING THE SECURITY

Upon the death of the life assured, or at the maturity of an endowment policy on its due date, the assignee will obtain the necessary papers from the assurance company for completion, so as to be able to claim the benefits under the policy. Accordingly the bank as assignee will then forward the completed claim form, the life policy, all previously released assignments and bonus notices and its own charge form to the insurance company and will ensure that the proceeds are directed to itself. In the case of the death of the life assured, a copy of the death certificate should accompany the bank's papers.[122] Frequently, where a policy is about to mature, the assurance company will approach the bank before the due date, but in all instances the bank should itself have a careful diary note in its security records to ensure that the matter is not overlooked.

Should it become necessary to look to the policy before maturity, because of the failure of the customer to repay, the bank will need to ensure it has a power of sale by calling in the borrowing and it should write to the assurance company to obtain the necessary form to enable the policy to be surrendered. The same documentation as has been described above should then be sent to the assurance company to claim the monies.[123]

If the customer himself agrees to the surrender of the policy, then it may be that he will be able to complete the necessary documentation, but the bank must ensure that the surrender proceeds are remitted direct to it and not to the assignor.[124] Circumstances such as this could arise where the customer knows he cannot reduce his borrowing from other sources, and agrees to a voluntary surrender. As the bank will be prepared to continue to conduct the account, it is inappropriate to call in the borrowing (to obtain a power of sale when the customer fails to repay), hence the co-operation of the customer is helpful. Alternatively, to avoid calling in the borrowing, but to give the bank a right to surrender the policy, the customer could simply agree in writing and sign a letter to the assurance company and another to the bank authorising them both to go ahead.

An alternative course to surrender is for the bank to sell the policy by transferring it to another assignee for an agreed consideration. In practice, this step is uncommon, although there is a specialist market in London where life policies can be auctioned, and in certain instances it is just possible that the amount obtained at auction might be greater than which would be obtained by surrender of the policy to the issuing assurance company.

The surrender or sale of a life policy does of course deprive the beneficiary of the protection of the life cover, and, understandably, it is a course which will be regarded as a last resort. It is possible that as an alternative the

---

122 See Appendix I, Q. 56 (September 1982).
123 See Appendix I, Q. 39 (September 1980).
124 See Appendix I, Q. 47 (September 1981).

assignor might be able to arrange to raise a loan on the policy from the insurance company itself, in which event the loan, while less than the surrender value, might be adequate for the bank's purposes and might be taken to repay or reduce the bank advance, thus preserving the capital value for the beneficiary. The bank could then release its assignment, or enter into a priority agreement with the customer and the company whereby it would retain its security, effectively as a second charge, the value of which might build up in the course of time as the new loan is repaid and/or as premiums are paid and the surrender value of the policy grows.

Should the bank's charge be by way of an equitable assignment only, it will be necessary upon the death of the assignor to seek the assistance of his executors or administrators to obtain the maturity proceeds, as they will be required by the assurance company to join in the receipt. Where a policy matures that has only been equitably assigned to the bank, it will probably be necessary for the beneficiary to sign the insurance company's papers to facilitate the collection of the maturity proceeds.[125] Again, the bank should ensure that the proceeds are mandated direct to itself and are not allowed to pass to other parties. Also, as we know from examining securities generally, if the co-operation of an assignor or his personal representatives cannot be obtained and only an equitable assignment is held then it will be necessary for the bank to obtain a court order for sale, which will involve attendant expense and difficulties.

RELEASING THE ASSIGNMENT

The forms of assignment used by banks invariably have a form of release and reassignment on the last page, and should the security no longer be required then this form is completed, and the assignment is then *sealed* by the bank, following which the assignor will be asked to give a receipt for the charge form and the policy. Naturally, the documents cannot be released to the assignor if the bank has had notice of a second charge, and in that event the released form of assignment and the policy should be sent to the later assignee. The bank must also, in both cases, give notice to the assurance company that it is no longer interested in the policy.

Where the policy has been charged by way of equitable charge under a memorandum of deposit, no specific release is necessary, and the memorandum may simply be marked 'Cancelled' and it and the policy can be delivered to the assignor. Again, the insurance company should be advised of the ending of the bank's interest. In some cases, where notice of the bank's charge might not have been given to the insurance company, no harm would result in the bank retaining its memorandum of deposit, and in its delivering only the policy to the assignor against his receipt.

125 See Appendix I, Q. 58 (April 1983).

CHAPTER 14

Stocks and Shares as Security

ADVANTAGES AND DISADVANTAGES

Stocks and shares held in a joint stock company are still a fairly common form of security lodged by private customers to secure their borrowings, and although the extent to which shares are held by private individuals in the United Kingdom declined in the middle of the twentieth century, it is now on the increase again, fostered by the Government's programme of 'privatization'.

A holding is represented by a share certificate, but this merely evidences title and gives no rights in itself. Often, of course, the shares are quoted on the Stock Exchange, and indeed most shares charged to banks fall within this category. Generally, as a type of security, shares have many attractions to a bank for they can be handled quickly and cheaply with a minimum of formalities and banks often have standard printed transfer forms ready in their main branches so that registered securities can be transferred out of the holder's name and into the name of the bank – or more usually that of its nominee company – without delay, thus effecting a legal mortgage.

Bearer securities have the additional advantage for the bank in that they are fully negotiable instruments, and the bank can therefore technically obtain a better title, as mortgagee, than that held by the person from whom it takes delivery. Thus the bank obtains a legal mortgage, quickly and merely by delivery; transfer forms are not necessary, and these bearer bonds can readily be sold, if required, without the co-operation of the customer.

More frequently, however, merely an equitable mortgage is taken over registered shares, by the deposit of the share certificate with the intention of creating a security. The lodgement may be with or without an accompanying memorandum of deposit. Either way the security steps are few and it is not necessary for the bank to instruct a solicitor to investigate the holder's title to the security. If the shares are quoted and trading is active, valuation can be made quickly by reference to the financial columns in the daily press, although, if dealings are infrequent, a glance at the Stock Exchange daily official list will still show the price at which they last changed hands. Alternatively, an enquiry through the branch's stockbrokers can be made to ascertain the price at which a current dealing could be transacted. In normal times it would be reasonable to expect the value of shares to be relatively stable, but over a longer period, or when markets are volatile, as was the trend in the 1970's and early 1980s, it is important to allow for booms and slumps, and changes in fashion, and also to allow for wider margins, and a spread of risk in a share portfolio.

Where the shares represent holdings in companies which are not quoted on the Stock Exchange, it is of course then very difficult to value the security realistically, and problems arise in realizing the shares, should the customer fail to repay.

Quoted shares are normally easy to sell in a realization situation, particularly where the bank has taken a legal charge and the shares are registered in its own name. Buyers can quickly be found through the medium of a stockbroker, and challenges to the bank based on an argument that it has under-sold the security can usually be dealt with easily, as, unlike with property, there is a ready point of reference, so as to be able to demonstrate the market price at and around the time of sale. The expenses associated with a sale as mortgagee are small, although these increase if the bank only has an equitable charge and has to seek a court order for sale if the customer will not co-operate. Stockbrokers' commission, however, is far less than the expenses of realizing deeds security through estate agents and solicitors.

Also, in the vast majority of cases when a borrowing has been repaid as arranged, the security can be returned to the chargor with the minimum of formalities.

PROBLEMS WITH EQUITABLE CHARGES

However, most mortgages over stocks and shares are taken by way of equitable charge. Consequently, when they are taken in that way, they are subject to all the usual disadvantages of equitable charges.[126]

One of the biggest dangers with any equitable charge is that there could be a prior equitable interest in existence at the time when the bank takes its security, and in that event the earlier interest will take precedence over the bank's charge. There is an old legal maxim which states 'Where the equities are equal, the first in time prevails'.

To illustrate the effect of this rule, we can imagine a situation where Mr X, a trustee, holds share certificates in his capacity as trustee, but that the certificates, as is common, merely show him as the registered proprietor of the holding, with no mention of the trust element. Clearly, Mr X would hold these shares on behalf of the beneficiaries, and their interests, which would be equitable, would rank prior in time to those of any equitable chargee, such as a bank to whom Mr X might fraudulently attempt to give security for any personal borrowing on his own account.

In such a situation, even should the bank become aware of the true position later, it would not be possible for it to overcome the effect of the rule by taking a transfer of the shares into its own name as legal mortgagee, for although normally, if a legal mortgage is taken it overrides equitable interests, this is only so when there is no knowledge, at the time of the legal charge, that prior equitable interests exist.

126 See Appendix I, Q. 51 (April 1982).

All this can be seen in the decision in *Coleman* v. *London County and Westminster Bank Ltd* (1916). There the bank held an equitable charge over debenture stock but was unaware that this was held by the chargor in trust for other persons. However, later, the bank learnt of the existence of the beneficiaries, and at that stage it took a transfer of the debentures into its own name and registered them, becoming the proprietor under a legal charge. Thereupon the beneficiaries brought an action to have the bank's charge set aside and in this they were successful, on the grounds that the bank had been well aware of the prior equitable interest when it took its legal mortgage.

Looking at another disadvantage of an equitable charge over shares, we will recall that customers are frequently unco-operative in realization situations and hence, if the depositor will not sign a sale order and execute the transfer document, the equitable mortgagee must apply to the court for an order for sale, unless it holds a blank transfer and is prepared to rely on it. This is a transfer stating the name of the company and amount of stock, signed by the mortgagor, but lacking the name of the transferee; it is executed at the time when the memorandum of deposit and share certificate is lodged, with the intention that it be completed, as and when necessary, upon default in repayment. However, this practice has fallen out of favour with certain banks, but, if used, it does have the advantage of avoiding legal costs and the opportunity for defences to be raised.

As under an equitable charge the proprietor remains the registered shareholder on the company's register, any communications in respect of scrip issues (the allotment of more shares, free, in proportion to the number held) or a rights issue (the right to buy more shares, usually at a favourable price, in proportion to the number already held) are sent to him. The customer may therefore receive these without the bank's knowledge, unless the security clerk is alert and sees the issue of the shares mentioned in the financial press. If so, the bank should then call upon the mortgagor to deposit the additional shares as security, for invariably there is a term in the standard memorandum of deposit under which the mortgagor has undertaken to deposit any such bonus shares with the bank. Of course, the mortgagor may chose to ignore this covenant and the bank could find itself with only the original holding, but with a market price which is reduced following the scrip or rights issue. In theory the bank could then resort to the courts for an Order of Mandamus or an injuction to have the new shares lodged, but this is rarely done, if at all, although if substantial monies were at stake it would be worth consideration.

It is of course always possible that with an equitable charge the customer might be able to obtain a duplicate certificate and sell his holding, and if so then the bank could be left high and dry, for the title required by the purchaser of the shares would be good against the bank. The only way the bank could protect its position against this happening, is by serving a stop notice – formerly known as a notice in lieu of distringas – upon the company. This is obtained by filing a sworn affidavit at the Supreme Court, asserting the bank's equitable charge; the affidavit and order is then served on the company. The effect is that the company must then give the bank eight days' notice of any attempt by the registered holder to transfer the shares, and so the bank will be able, in that period, to obtain an injunction from the court, restraining the company from registering the transfer. Stop notices are rarely used, other than in exceptional circumstances, as for instance where the bank might fear that the depositor is about a transfer a substantial holding fraudulently. Consequently, any action in this respect is more likely to take place when the bank is seeking to recover its money, having called in the advance, and stop notice procedure is unlikely to be taken at the outset, when the shares are first being lodged as security.

There is another way in which protection might be obtained when an equitable charge is taken, although this practice has dropped out of use with quoted shares; it is, however, still used with unquoted stock, or partly paid shares. The procedure is that written notice is given by the bank, in duplicate, to the company or its registrars, informing them that a holding of shares has been lodged as security by a shareholder. They are requested to acknowledge the notice and it is expected that they will mark their records, so that they will refer then to the bank in the event of receiving a transfer form for registration. However, most companies reply to the bank's notice stating that they cannot accept it, and refer to s. 360 Companies Act 1985 precluding them from noting any trust, whether expressed, implied or constructive, on their registers in respect of a company's shares. Nevertheless, some advantage can be gained, for, unofficially, the company may note its other records and upon an attempted dealing, or should the registered holder attempt to obtain a duplicate share certificate, it might then make enquires.

Another advantage is that should the shareholder become indebted personally to a company which under its articles of assoc iation has a lien on its own shares as security for such a debt, then this lien might not be effective against the bank's equitable charge, if the shareholder's personal debt became due after the company received the bank's notice. Thus, while monies due at the time of notice might be secured by a lien over the shares, the lien will not apply to any subsequent indebtedness. This is the rule in *Bradford Banking Co. Ltd* v. *Henry Briggs Son & Co. Ltd* (1886). There the bank had taken shares as security by way of an equitable charge and given notice to the company, who in their reply had advised the bank that the shareholder was indebted to them and that under their articles of association they had 'a first and permanent lien upon all shares held by him'. However, the shareholder's debt to the company increased after the time of this notice, and in due course the court was asked to rule upon the question of priorities. Matters reached the House of Lords where it was held that while the company had priority for the amount outstanding at the time when it received notice from the bank, it could not claim a lien in priority to the bank in respect of those advances made subsequently.

However, as a company cannot claim a lien over its own fully paid shares when it has a quotation on the Stock Exchange, because the rules of the Exchange preclude this, the practice of giving notice to a company of the granting of an equitable charge to the bank is dying out, for by far the vast majority of stocks and shares held by banks as security fall within this category. Where shares in a non-quoted company are offered as security, the position could, of course, be different.

PROBLEMS WITH LEGAL CHARGES

Where the shares have been transferred into the bank's name, the bank as legal mortgagee and registered holder will receive the dividends which it can credit to the customer's account, but of course it will also receive all other letters, reports and circulars from the company, and it has an obligation, then, to ensure that these are forwarded to the customer. Consequently, administration work expands to ensure that the customer is kept up to date.

Another danger for a bank is that where it presents a transfer for registration it impliedly represents that the signature of the transferor is genuine and it is liable to indemnify the registering company should it suffer any loss as a result of acting on the transfer.

In *Sheffield Corporation* v. *Barclay* (1905) the Corporation were presented with a transfer instrument sent to them by Barclays Bank, and this purported to be signed by the two registered holders in favour of a Mr Barclay, as the nominee for Barclays Bank Ltd. One of the signatures on the transfer was genuine, but the other had been forged, and in due course the holder whose signature had been forged obtained a judgment in the courts against the Corporation, which had to reimburse him with a new holding in the stock. The Corporation then looked to the bank which resisted the claim, but lost, on the grounds that in sending the transfer for registration it had impliedly represented that the instrument was genuine and thus had become liable to indemnify the Corporation against the loss which it had incurred.

More recently in *Yeung & Another* v. *Hongkong & Shanghai Banking Corporation* (1980) a firm of stockbrokers acted as agents for one of their clients, who handed them a stolen share certificate together with a transfer document apparently bearing the true owner's signature, although this had in fact been forged. The stock represented by the certificate was a holding in the Hongkong and Shanghai Banking Corporation and the bank acted upon receipt of the stock transfer form and made over the shares to the name of another holder. The bank held a specimen signature of the true owner, but when acting upon the transfer it did not check the signature, although had it done so it could possibly have spotted the forgery.

An action was brought by the stockbrokers to claim relief from the principle established in *Sheffield Corporation* v. *Barclay* (1905), but it was held that the default by the bank in not checking the signature was not sufficient reason to prevent the bank from relying on the implied indemnity which it took from the stockbrokers with the transfer, when the latter had impliedly warranted that the signature was genuine. This implied indemnity was present although the stockbrokers had acted as agents.

Athough partly paid shares are not encountered as frequently now as formerly, when they are taken as security the bank could find itself having to put up the money for calls if the shares are registered in the bank's name, and even where an equitable charge is held, if the customer is unable to find monies to meet the call. In such a situation, to preserve the existing value of the security, rather than see the partly paid shares cancelled, the bank might have to lend additional funds. Moreover, even in a situation where the customer himself finds the cash, it could mean that he has less money to meet his repayments to the bank under the agreed repayment programme and that there are adverse repercussions in that respect.

Technically, too, although rarely in practice, the bank exposes itself to a risk in taking a legal mortgage over partly paid shares, for although it might have released the shares it still remains liable for calls for the next twelve months: this would occur if the company went into liquidation and the liquidator was unsuccessful in getting the current shareholder to meet a call. The liquidator could then turn to the list of 'B contributors' – those who had been registered proprietors within the preceding twelve months.

Another problem encountered is where a director of a limited company holds the shares as part of his qualification holding under the company's articles of association. In such a case it may not be possible for the shares to be transferred into the bank's name, as the articles may require the director to hold a certain number of shares to be qualified to act. Also, articles may not allow a public company to be a member of a private company. In these cases it is necessary, therefore, to take an equitable charge only.

THE CHARGE FORM – MEMORANDUM OF DEPOSIT

Whether a legal mortgage is taken or an equitable charge, it is desirable for the bank to have the customer sign a memorandum of deposit, although both types of charge can of course be created without such documentation – a legal mortgage merely by the transfer of the shares into the bank's name, and an equitable charge simply by deposit of the share certificate (*Harrold* v. *Plenty* (1901)). The memorandum of deposit, however, strengthens the bank's hands considerably, and of course where third-party security is concerned it is essential.

Banks usually have two types of memorandum of deposit which they use in the case of share security. One is drawn up specifically to cover only the one or two holdings which are lodged at the time the form is signed, while the other is a more general form, which covers any shares which come into the bank's hands from time to time, whether lodged as security or even for safe keeping. This general form is more appropriate where the depositor changes his shareholdings fairly frequently, as it avoids the need to take a new memorandum of deposit upon each occasion. It is therefore very suitable for use by a private individual with an active portfolio, or for use by stockbroker customers. (However, in the case of stockbrokers it would be usual to find the deletion of any clause charging shares lodged in safe keeping, for they prefer to be able to hold certain portfolios entirely free from claims by the bank as mortgagee.)

The student reader should now refer again to Chapter 11, where we examined the type of clauses in bank charge forms which are common to every type of security. These will again be found to be present when a typical bank memorandum of deposit form is inspected (Fig. 14.1), although additionally there will be other clauses which particularly deal with matters which are specific to stocks and shares. These latter clauses will now be considered.

Statement of ownership
By this clause the chargor states that he holds the shares in his own beneficial ownership, and not as a trustee or on behalf of any other person, but as we have seen, in the event of there in fact being a prior equitable interest, the statement would seem to have little practical value, other than, perhaps, causing the chargor and the bank to stop and think at the time they are lodged! Many banks therefore omit it. If used it might state that the shares are free of charge or any prior encumbrance.

Agreements regarding bonus shares
Here the chargor undertakes to lodge with the bank any bonus shares he might receive (as when only an equitable charge is taken). He agrees that such further shares issued to him will be a security in accordance with the terms of the charge he has signed earlier, and confirms that he will meet all calls or instalments falling due. Often this clause also deals with the bank's right to act appropriately when it is the registered shareholder under a legal mortgage and so receives any bonus shares. Thus the bank will be authorized then to sell any shares received under a rights or scrip issue, or to take up any rights at the expense of the chargor, either with or without prior or subsequent reference to him.

Extension of security
The security may be said to extend to all dividends and interest payments arising out of the share security, and to apply to all shares issued by way of bonus, scrip or rights issue. The bank will be authorized to vote in any way, at its own discretion, where it becomes the registered shareholder and receives papers from the company seeking the views of its members.

S.7

Stocks, Shares and Securities—Advances, etc., to Depositor(s)

TO BANK OF CYPRUS (LONDON) LIMITED

I/We have deposited with or transferred to the Bank or its nominees the Stocks, Shares and Securities mentioned in the Schedule hereto ("The Scheduled Securities").

I/We jointly and severally agree with the Bank as follows:—

1. The Bank is to hold the Scheduled Securities by way of mortgage and so that the Scheduled Securities (including all interest, dividends, bonuses, rights and benefits arising therefrom or attaching thereto) shall constitute a continuing security for all my/our liabilities to the Bank on current account or otherwise.

2. I/We have good right and title to mortgage the Scheduled Securities to the Bank, and will execute any further documents which may be required for vesting the Scheduled Securities in the Bank or its nominees or in any purchaser from the Bank.

3. "Liabilities" include indebtedness, sole, several or joint, in respect of advances, bills, promissory notes, guarantees, interest, commission, banking or legal charges, and expenses.

4. I/We will provide such additional security or make such cash payments as the Bank may require from time to time to maintain a satisfactory margin of security.

5. I/We will pay off on demand all or any of my/our liabilities to the Bank.

6. In case I/we shall fail to pay off all or any of my/our liabilities on demand, the Bank shall have immediate and unrestricted power of sale over the Scheduled Securities.

7. A demand hereunder shall be made in writing signed by an officer of the Bank. Such a demand may be addressed to me/us at my/our address(es) last known to the Bank, and a demand so addressed and posted shall be effective 24 hours after it is posted, notwithstanding that it be returned undelivered, and notwithstanding the death of the addressee, addressees or any of them. Such a demand made on some or one of us or on my/our personal representatives (if any) shall also be effective, whether or not a like demand is made on the other or others (if any).

8. In respect of my/our liabilities to the Bank, the Bank shall have a lien on all stocks, shares, securities and property of mine/ours, or of any one or more of us, from time to time held by the Bank, whether for safe custody or otherwise, and on all moneys from time to time standing to my/our credit, or to the credit, of any one or more of us, on any account whatever.

9. On any release to me/us out of this security the Bank shall not be bound to return the identical Stocks, Shares or Securities mentioned in the Schedule hereto but I/we will accept Stocks, Shares or Securities of the same class and denomination, or any other Stocks, Shares or Securities which then represent the Scheduled Securities.

Fig.14.1   *Memorandum of deposit over shares*

B. *Securities for Advances*

THE SCHEDULE

Dated   ......   19 ......

Witness(es)   Depositor(s)

(1)   Signature   (1)   Signature

      Address

      Description

(2)   Signature   (2)   Signature

      Address

      Description

(3)   Signature   (3)   Signature

      Address

      Description

Fig.14.1   *(contd)*

Agreement to grant a legal mortgage

This clause is quite straightforward: the mortgagor agrees that, whenever he is called upon to grant a legal charge over the shares deposited by way of equitable mortgage only, he will do so. In practice, of course, as it happens he may not, but at least the bank could then seek an order for performance from the court, if it wished; it is more likely, however, to go for a straightforward order for sale, and this is why the clause is ommitted by some banks.

Power of attorney clause

Some banks incorporate a power of attorney clause in their memorandum of deposit covering equitable charges, and if so then the form must be executed under seal, and a release by the bank must also be under seal. The bank is appointed attorney of the mortgagor, and in this way, while the shares remain registered in the name of the customer, the bank can if necessary sell the shares in its capacity as attorney, as a means of realizing its security. Consequently, the need to resort to the court for an order for sale is avoided. The power of attorney clause could also include powers enabling the bank to create a legal mortgage in its own favour, and if the bank did this and became the registered proprietor as legal mortgagee it would be able to sell the shares, and override any objections raised by a later mortgagee, who could possibly prevent the bank from selling as the attorney of the chargor.

Completion of blank transfer

Such a clause would declare that the mortgagee can complete the necessary details in any form of signed but undated transfer given to the bank at this time or any future time. It is included to avoid any later claim that the bank had no right to complete the form in the way it did to facilitate a sale of the shares.

Return of shares to the chargor

A protective clause used by some banks governs the return of the shares to the chargor, who agrees at the time of deposit that upon release he will accept shares representing equivalent stock. Under these provisons there is no obligation on the bank to transfer the actual stocks or shares which were mortgaged. This aspect was more important when shares were numbered, and nowadays it is often omitted.

Margin of cover

Occasionally the chargor undertakes to maintain a specific margin of cover in the form of shares, in relation to the particular advance at any one time, and this means that if the borrowing escalates, or the value of the portfolio drops, then the bank is justified in calling upon the chargor for further security. Upon his failure to do so it can call in the advance or sell the existing security.

TAKING A LEGAL MORTGAGE OVER REGISTERED SHARES

Most stocks and shares issued by British companies and the Government are in registered form. The owner's name is entered in the register of members or stockholders, after which he is supplied with a certificate which is evidence of his title, showing the amount of stock or the number of shares held, and their particular class, such as, for example ordinary shares or preference shares. Any transfer of a holding is effected by the registered owner signing a transfer form and this is forwarded to the company or its registrars with the old share certificate, usually by the firm of stockbrokers, when there is a market dealing. The transferree is named in the transfer document, but he does not need to sign the transfer form and in due course he will be issued with a new certificate which is evidence of his title.

Consequently, when the bank takes a legal mortgage, after the share certificate has been carefully examined, to ensure that the holding purports to be in the name of the chargor and that there is no evidence of trust noted, the method employed is identical, as the stocks or shares are simply transferred into the bank's name, or that of its nominee company, usually for a nominal consideration. When the lending is repaid the shares are transferred back into the name of the transferor.

As we have seen, a memorandum of deposit is frequently also taken when a legal charge is involved, because of the value of the clauses in that document. This should be signed by the chargor, and witnessed by a bank officer, or the chargor's solicitors, if independent advice is required. If there is a schedule in the memorandum of deposit it should be carefully completed, specifying the number and type of shares lodged in whatever company, although where a general memorandum of deposit covering all stocks or shares coming into the bank's possession is used then no schedule needs to be filled in, and details of the holding need only be entered in the bank's internal security register, and amended upon any changes.

The bank should then value its security by reference to the lower of the two prices quoted (the selling price) in the financial press. It is usual for share security to be regularly revalued each six months, or more frequently when there are periods of volatile market conditions, and share prices generally are falling.

It may be noted that the company, or the Government, is not concerned as to the relationship between the transferor and the transferee. The company, or Government, will therefore deal entirely with the registered holder, and all letters, reports and dividends will be sent to the registered holder. Hence the bank, as legal mortgagee, should keep records to ensure that dividends are credited to the correct customer's account (or suspense account if third-party security is involved), and that receipt of notices of company meetings are sent on to the transferor promptly, as are also any annual reports. Of course the transferor will not be entitled to attend meetings, but unless there is an agreement to the contrary the mortgagee under a legal charge could attend and vote in whatever way he wished. In practice, a bank rarely becomes involved and does not attend members' meetings, although in a 'take-over battle' it may wish to seek the views of the transferor or its own brokers.

If the company declares a scrip issue and issues bonus shares, the new shares will be issued in the bank's name. Similarly, if a rights issue is declared, an allotment letter will be sent out in the bank's favour, and the bank will then usually need to consult with the chargor, to see whether he wishes the rights to be sold or taken up. However, where a memorandum of deposit has been signed, the bank will probably have also been given the power to deal with the matter on its own initiative, should that prove necessary.

Where a bank takes up the shares issued under a rights issue, even though it does not hold a memorandum of deposit, it is felt that nevertheless it will be entitled to add the cost involved to the principal sum secured in those cases where the security has been lodged by the customer for his own liabilities. Otherwise, in the case of third-party security, the bank would need to debit a suspense account and would need to look for clearance of this from the chargor, by agreement or upon the shares being sold. In *Waddell* v. *Hutton* (1911) (a Scottish case) it was held that a mortgagee who had not given the chargor the opportunity to subscribe for new shares issued was liable to him in damages, after those shares had appreciated in value to his detriment.

TAKING AN EQUITABLE MORTGAGE OVER REGISTERED SHARES

In this case the shares remain registered in the name of the depositor, but the share certificate is lodged with the bank, usually with supporting evidence that the lodgment was by way of security in the form of the execution of the memorandum of deposit. However, if the customer simply handed over a share certificate with the intention of creating a charge, this would amount to the creation of an equitable mortgage for his own liabilities, whether as borrower or in support of a guarantee liability. It must be remembered, however, that a third party could not secure the liabilities of the customer, simply by handing a share certificate to the bank, as there would have to be written evidence before the bank could sue (s. 4 Statute of Frauds 1677). It was held in *Harrold* v. *Plenty* (1901) that the mere deposit of a certificate with the intention of creating a charge is an effective equitable mortgage of a shareholding. In that event it is desirable for an interview or similar note to be made concurrently, to be referred to, if necessary, at some future time should there be any dispute.

After the deposit of the shares, and after they have been valued, practice varies from bank to bank, some then giving notice to the company in which the holding is held. However, as we have seen, frequently this acknowledgement is returned unaccepted, but with a covering letter to the effect that the company is precluded from noting any trust on its records under the provisions of s. 360 Companies Act 1985. Some banks therefore omit this formality.

Other banks obtain a blank transfer at this stage – that is, one which is undated and unstamped but signed by the stockholder, albeit leaving the name of the transferee blank. These banks can then complete this into their own name or into the name of purchaser, when they sell the shares, and in this way they avoid the need to go to court for an order for sale.

SHARES CHARGED BY A LIMITED COMPANY

Where the shares are charged by a limited company the usual precautions necessary in taking a security from a limited company apply.

Usually thereafter the board will be required to pass a suitable resolution, and a certified copy of this authorising the officials of the company to sign the bank's memorandum of deposit will be given to the bank. It is unusual for a company to be required to act under seal, but if that is the case then the securities clerk must ensure that matters proceed in that way.

Before taking the charge, a search should be carried out at Companies Registration Office, to see whether the company has given a debenture incorporating a fixed or floating charge, for if so then such a charge could rank ahead of the bank, particularly if the floating charge has the usual restriction precluding the creation of subsequent fixed charges which would rank ahead in priority.

It is *not* necessary for the bank's charge over shares held by a limited company, whether by legal or equitable mortgage, to be registered at Companies Registration Office, as this type of security is one of the *exceptions* to those requiring such action under s. 396 Companies Act 1985.

MORTGAGE OVER BEARER SECURITIES

Bonds, scrip issues, share warrants and debentures can be issued in bearer form by overseas-based undertakings and in that case the issuer does not keep a record of the name of the owner. The most common form of bearer bonds are those issued by overseas governments. Ownership changes when these bearer bonds are transferred by delivery to another person who then becomes the owner. In consequence, bearer securities are said to be fully negotiable, and it is possible for the new holder to acquire a better title than that of the transferor, provided he takes in good faith, without notice of any defect in the title of the transferor, and for value, thus meeting the requirements of s. 29 Bills of Exchange Act 1882. As the company or government issuing the stock is not aware of the identity of the owner at any one time, sheets of coupons are attached to the bearer bonds or share warrants, and when a dividend or interest payment is declared the coupon is cut off and submitted by the holder to the issuer, who then makes payment of the dividend to the claimant.

At one time, it was necessary in the United Kingdom for all bearer securities to be lodged with an authorized depository, but following the suspension of the Exchange Control Act 1947 in this area this requirement no longer applies, and bearer bonds can be held by private individuals. In consequence, it is prefectly acceptable for a bank to receive bearer bonds from a private customer and to take them into security.

The manner in which bearer bonds are charged is known technically as a pledge, and not a mortgage. A pledge arises when documents of title are delivered by one person to another to be held as security, with an express or implied undertaking by the pledgee that the property, which is the subject of the pledge, will be returned to the owner when the advance has been repaid. Where, however, a debt is not met, the pledgee may sell the item pledged to obtain repayment. This type of charge occurs often with produce, but a pledge over bearer bonds is a superior security to a pledge over merchandise, because of the fully negotiable attributes of the bearer securities.

The method by which the bank obtains its security over bearer bonds is simple. No transfer form is required, and no stamp duty is payable. The security clerk will ensure that the bond is undefaced and correctly stamped and that all the relevant unmatured coupons accompany the bond itself. It is then handed to the bank to hold as security. Usually, the customer will also be required to execute the bank's form of memorandum of deposit giving its usual protections, including the power of sale upon the customer's failure to repay on demand.

In *London Joint Stock Bank Ltd* v. *Simmons* (1892) the bank lent money to a stockbroker and as security he lodged with the bank bearer bonds which had been issued by a foreign government. In truth, the bonds belonged to one of his clients and he had no right to charge them to the bank. Later the stockbroker disappeared, and the bank sold the bearer bonds to obtain repayment. In an action before the court, it was held that the stockbroker's client had no right as against the bank to the value of the bonds, as, because these were negotiable instruments, and the bank had taken them in good faith and for value, it had a superior title. This is of course an old case, and while the principle of law will still remain true, there must be doubt as to whether, on ethical grounds, a bank would wish to rely on its bearer security in such a situation obtaining today. Much would obviously depend upon the circumstances and the amount involved; mention is made of the possible doubts surrounding such a security, however, in similar circumstances, to ensure that any reader does not automatically consider his position entirely safe and watertight. In the late twentieth century, influences other than strictly legal ones are of increasing importance in day-to-day commercial practice.

AMERICAN AND CANADIAN SECURITIES

Some shares and stock in American and Canadian industrial companies are quoted on the Stock Exchange in Great Britain, and the share certificates are treated as bearer securities, although they are not fully negotiable by transfer and delivery, as are the bearer bonds which we have been discussing above. In these cases the registered holder is named on the face of the certificate, but on the reverse of the certificate there is usually a form of transfer coupled with a power of attorney, and once this has been signed in blank the shares become treated as bearer securities and are transferred by mere delivery of the certificate. It is then possible for a holder to register his own name in the records of the company by forwarding the certificate at any time. Usually this is done through use of the power of attorney and an attorney acts in America or Canada, which are the only places where the transfers can be recorded.

Although not fully negotiable, by usage such share certificates have acquired an attribute which has been described as 'quasi-negotiability' but it must be remembered that a holder cannot sue in his own name until he has been registered with the company.

Many such share certificates are registered in 'marking names', and to constitute a good delivery on the Stock Exchange the shares have to be in a 'good marking name' and to be endorsed correctly. Reference to a Stock Exchange Year Book will show those names which are regarded as 'good marking names' among firms of stockbrokers and finance houses. When taking these types of shares in security, therefore, a bank will wish to be certain that they are registered in a 'good marking name' before proceeding. It will be appreciated that dividends are paid to the 'marking name', and in consequence it is necessary for security clerks to take note of advertisements mentioned when dividends have been declared, and thereafter to claim the dividend from the 'marking name' recipient.

When a bank is offered certificates which are not registered in a 'good marking name', steps should be taken to ensure that this position is rectified without delay, as clearly it takes a little time to have the title transferred; meanwhile the shares are not readily saleable.

To effect a good security, the share certificate is lodged with the bank, and the bank's usual form of memorandum of deposit is signed by the chargor. In practice, if the shares are in a 'good marking name' then the bank's security is probably almost as goods as with a legal mortgage over bearer bonds, but there is no recent case law which gives any guidance as to whether, should any prior equitable interest exist, this would be overruled by the bank's charge, taken in good faith and without knowledge of that prior equitable interest.

However, where a firm of stockbrokers lodged quasi-negotiable share certificates to secure advances to them, and it subsequently transpired that the shares belonged to one of their clients, the court held that, as there had been nothing to put the bank upon enquiry, the client was estopped or prevented from obtaining a better title to the securities as against the bank. This case was *Fuller* v. *Glyn Mills, Currie & Co.* (1914) where the stock concerned was Canadian Pacific Railway Stock registered in the name of Mr Harmsworth who had endorsed the form of transfer on the reverse of the certificate. When the firm of stockbrokers became the subject of bankruptcy proceedings the client's efforts to recover the shares were unsuccessful, but the court took into account the fact that he had left the certificates with the stockbrokers in such a condition as to convey a representation to any person who took the shares from the stockbrokers in good faith, that they, the stockbrokers, had an authority to deal with them. They were of course not in a 'marking name', so the case does not help directly in an assessment of 'quasi-negotiability'.

Naturally, where a bank has caused the shares to be registered in the name of the bank's own nominee company, or marking name, it has an unassailable legal title. Where, however, the shares have been left in the depositor's name, although endorsed, the presence of any prior equitable interest could cause problems for the bank despite the decision mentioned above.

UNIT TRUSTS

There are now many unit trust units issued by professional investment management companies and these represent a proportionate share in a portfolio of stocks or shares which the managers have power to vary from time to time. The value of the portfolio, less costs and management fees, is divided into units and each confers upon the holder an indirect interest in the general portfolio which is maintained and managed by professionals. Certificates representing the number of units held, and naming the holder, are issued by the managers, although the actual shares held in the portfolio are invariably lodged with trustees on behalf of the unit-holders. Dividends are declared from time to time and the managers report to the unit-holders upon their investment changes and policy over the preceding accounting period.

The reverse side of these unit trust certificates usually makes provision for the holder to renounce his interest in the units and consequently, if the bank wishes to take a legal mortgage, this form of renunciation can be signed and the bank or its nominee company can be registered as the holder, in which case a certificate is issued in the bank's name or that of its nominee company, in due course.

More usually an equitable charge is taken, and the reverse of the certificate is signed by the depositor, thus enabling the bank, should the need arise, to sell the holding and transfer the shares without difficulty. The method employed upon a disposal is for the units to be sold back to the managers at the published buying-back or 'bid' price and the certificate is then forwarded to the managers. An equitable charge over unit trusts suffers from the usual disadvantages of an equitable charge, although it is the practice of banks to give notice to the managers of the charge, but they may not acknowledge it. Valuation is easy, as unit trust prices are quoted daily in the press.

An increasing trend is for a proportion of premiums in connection with life assurance to be invested in unit trust units and in this event if the bank is taking a charge over the life policy it should proceed normally, although when it values its security it will need to know the number of units which have been acquired so that it can then ascertain the current value of the units by reference to the financial press and to the company's statement as to the number of units acquired.

ALLOTMENT LETTERS

Whenever a company makes a rights issue or scrip issue, the entitlement to the new shares is shown, in the first instance, on a letter of allotment, which is sent to the registered holder of the primary shareholding. Should the shareholder not wish to take up the shares under a rights issue, as more cash needs to be put up, he will sign the form of renunication which is part of the documentation he has received. The 'rights' themselves are quoted on the Stock Exchange frequently *at a premium*, and thus they can be sold for immediate value. In this way the renounced allotment letters become transferable virtually as bearer documents. They are therefore very suitable to take as security from the transferee or even the allottee if he has taken up the rights himself, although it is important for the security clerk to note in his diary the latest date for payment of any calls and the last date for registration at the company's registrars or its registered office. All monies are sent to the company's registrars accompanied by the allotment letter which is quickly returned, duly receipted. Normally the bank will require a customer's authority to take these steps, and this will incorporate the right to debit his account. In appropriate circumstances, all this might have been granted by a clause in the memorandum of deposit, if signed.

When the time for registration arrives, the allotment letter should be sent for registration into the name of the last transferee, or the bank's nominee company, if a legal charge is required. It is important then for the bank to ensure that all the shares mentioned in the allotment letter have been fully paid.

In due course, in exchange for the fully paid allotment letter, a share certificate is issued. Sometimes, however, where the original shareholder has taken up his rights, it is not necessary for the allotment letter to be lodged with the company, and after a certain date it becomes valueless; the new share certificate is then issued to the original allottee, a point which the security clerk must watch, so as not to find the bank's position prejudiced.

GILT-EDGED SECURITIES

These are loan stocks, nicknamed 'gilts', issued by HM Government. They are quoted on the Stock Exchange, and carry various interest rates and maturity or repayment dates; all these factors influence the current price.

Generally, they tend to be more stable in value than industrial shares, although the gilts market can be a specialized and difficult one in which to predict price movements.

The method of charge is identical to that of quoted shares, and an undated 'blank transfer' can be completed to assist realization, if that is the practice of the bank.

NATIONAL SAVINGS CERTIFICATES AND PREMIUM SAVINGS BONDS

These Government-issued securities are not quoted on the Stock Exchange and are not capable of transfer into the bank's name; thus a legal mortgage cannot be obtained over them. However, an equitable charge created by depositing the certificates or bonds is possible with or without an accompanying memorandum of deposit. Notice of the charge cannot be given to the Director of Savings, as he will not accept it. This means that a holder, so minded, could obtain duplicate certificates and fraud could occur. Happily, such experiences are exceptionally rare. However, as evidence of means, both savings certificates and premium bonds are lodged as security, from time to time.

In the case of national savings certificates, when taking the security the bank will need to see the Holder's Registered Card which will show the customer's number and his signature, and these details can be checked with the numbers on the certificates. Concurrent with the deposit, the customer is also usually required to sign a repayment form, on which will be listed the number of the national savings certificates and their date of purchase. This means that the bank can retain this, undated, and, should realization of the holding become necessary, the certificates can then be forwarded to the Director of Savings, with this form, incorporating a signed irrevocable authority for the proceeds to be sent to the bank.

With premium savings bonds, there is no indication on the bond as to ownership and obviously great care is necessary. Should the bonds have been bought from the bank it will be possible, from internal records, for the true owner to be identified, but otherwise this is not so with those bonds issued in the early years of the scheme. More recently, a holder's registered card showing his number has been issued, as with national savings certificates, and the registered number is quoted on the bonds. Even so, there is no guarantee that the depositor is entitled to the holding and these securities should be viewed with caution.

UNQUOTED SHARES

Not all shares of public limited companies are quoted on the Stock Exchange, and shares in private companies clearly have no such advantage. However, banks are offered shares in non-quoted companies as security from time to time, and while the procedures will be the same as with registered quoted shares, these shares have inherent disadvantages when it comes to valuation or realization.[127]

Frequently, also, it is not even possible at the outset for the bank to obtain a legal mortgage, as the company will not accept the bank, a public limited company, as a registered holder, although since the Companies Act 1980 there have been relaxations in the restrictions on membership of private companies. Often the shares belong to a director of the company and to transfer the shares out of his name might deprive him of his qualification holding necessary under the company's articles. Moreover it could well be, in any event, that such a director would not wish his co-directors to know that he is borrowing from a bank and has lodged the shares as security.

Upon realization, should the bank be able to find a purchaser, it is even possible that the company might not be prepared to accept that person as a member, for often the articles of private companies give the directors power to decline transfers at their discretion, or the articles state that the shares must first be offered to the existing shareholders or directors upon any dealing.

As will be understood, it is extremely difficult to value unquoted shares, for while the chargor may be able to tell the bank the price at which he acquired the shares, or the bank might be able to ask the company secretary the price at which the shares were last valued for probate purposes, or at which they last changed hands, this is not entirely satisfactory. The bank could, if it wished, assess the value of the shares by studying the company's last balance sheet, and, assessing the assets at a realistic level, it could then deduct the liabilities and relate the resultant figure to the issued share capital. Alternatively, it could value the shares by reference to the rate of dividend declared, or the earnings yield, relating these figures to the figures for similar companies quoted on the Stock Exchange. In practice, however, these steps are rarely taken and shares in private companies are accepted for what they are worth, it being recognized that upon the need to realize them the bank will be extremely fortunate to turn them into cash. It may be noted, however, that following the passing of the Companies Act 1981 it is possible now for companies to buy their own shares, and in the right circumstances this might be a method open to the bank to obtain redemption (s. 162 Companies Act 1985).

Consequently, shares in private companies can only at best be regarded as evidence of means, and there is certainly no point in taking them as security behind a guarantee where the shareholder is a director of the borrowing

127 See Appendix I, Q. 51 (April 1982).

company concerned. In such a case, should the bank need to seek repayment from the company which proves unable to meet its commitment then clearly the shares themselves would have no value.

RELEASE OF SHARES FROM SECURITY

The precise mechanics of retransfer or redelivery of the shares to the chargor will depend upon the particular nature of the share itself, and the type of charge – legal or equitable – held by the bank. Obviously, with an equitable charge the steps are simple: the memorandum of deposit (if any) can be marked 'cancelled' and placed to obsolete records within the bank, and the share certificate can then be given to the shareholder against a suitable form of receipt. If notice of the charge had been given to the company, then the company should of course be advised of the end of the bank's interest, even if originally the notice had been 'refused'; this is likely to apply only to situations involving private limited companies.

With a legal charge, the memorandum of deposit will again be placed to 'obsolete securities', but a full retransfer into the name of the original holder will be necessary, by the use of a stock transfer form, which, when completed, needs lodging with the company's registrars, together with the now 'old' share certificate in the bank's name. After a few weeks the new certificate will be sent to the bank or to the chargor, if arrangements have been made to that effect.

REALIZATION OF SHARES AS MORTGAGEE

When a borrowing becomes unsatisfactory the bank must call in its lending before it can realize its security. Moreover, if the security has been lodged by a third party then it will be necessary to give notice of its intent to that surety, and to afford him the chance to redeem his security at the current market value, or a lesser figure if the charge is limited in amount and the value of the holding exceeds that figure.

As the provisions of s. 103 Law of Property Act 1925 are always excluded, it will not be necessary for the bank to allow three months to elapse after demand, and more usually the security becomes realizable immediately, or at least after a brief interval of perhaps seven or fourteen days, dependent on the precise terms of the charge form.

Legal charge

With a legal mortgage and quoted shares, the bank can readily instruct its stockbrokers to sell all or sufficient shares on the market, although in some instances, dependent on market conditions, it may prefer beforehand to obtain its stockbrokers' recommendations as to whether to retain the shares for the time being, in the expectation of a hardening of the price. Such a course has the risk that prices will fall in the interval however!

Transfer into the name of the purchaser is achieved in a similar fashion to that employed when the bank took its security, with the use of a stock transfer form, or mere delivery in the case of bearer bonds.[128]

Equitable charge

Usually the bank will first try to enlist the co-operation of the chargor,[129] or, in the case of his death or bankruptcy, that of his executor or trustee in bankruptcy, to get the shares sold voluntarily, but if unsuccessful it will need to proceed on its own. Unless the bank then has a power of attorney clause in its memorandum of deposit, or holds an undated but otherwise completed 'blank transfer' form on which it is prepared to rely in circumstances other than death, where it will no longer apply, it will be necessary to go to court to obtain an order for sale before shares charged by an equitable mortgage can be realized. This, of course, is costly and time-consuming, and among other things allows the chargor the opportunity of raising defences, spurious or real, as to why the security should not be sold. However, assuming these difficulties are overcome, matters can than proceed in a fashion similar to when a legal charge is held, the court order being produced to the company's registrars as evidence and authority for the transaction. The memorandum of deposit, if held, is placed to obsolete security papers marked 'cancelled' or 'sold'.

---

128 See Appendix I, Q. 47 (September 1981).
129 See Appendix I, Q. 47 (September 1981).

CHAPTER 15

Guarantees

ADVANTAGES AND DISADVANTAGES

Of all the securities taken by banks probably the guarantee is the easiest to complete, as the formalities associated with it are the least.[130] There is therefore less risk of technical irregularity, although special care must be applied when taking a guarantee from a limited company.

Because of the terms incorporated in the usual form, a bank is normally able to take legal action against a guarantor as soon as demand has been made on him and he has failed to pay. Indeed, because the guarantee document is also drawn up as an indemnity, it would be possible to make demand on the guarantor without calling upon the principal debtor, but in practice this step is rarely taken and normally demand is made on the customer as principal debtor first, and then on the guarantor after the customer has failed to meet his obligations.

A guarantee is of course only worth as much as the person who has given it, but it can be supported by other security, and where this is so the bank is in a much safer position. This supporting security should be taken on the direct form of charge expressed to secure all the guarantor's liability to the bank, as these will include his own borrowings and the guarantee liability.

Whether it is supported or not, a guarantee is a third-party security and so it can be ignored when proving a debt in the estate of the principal debtor, the borrower.

When a bank is lending to a limited company it is particularly desirable to have taken a guarantee from the directors, even if they are men of small means, for in this way they become more personally associated with the need for the company to repay the bank, and they are less likely to walk away from a difficult situation if one develops. Also, in a situation where the bank is lending to the company against the security of a debenture, the directors might be more interested in ensuring that there is no depletion of assets, leaving themselves, as well as the bank, exposed as guarantors.

However, a guarantee has several disadvantages, and, somewhat cynically but with an element of considerable truth, it has been said that the guarantee is the easiest security to take, but the most difficult to realize; clearly no third party will be happy at having to pay monies to meet obligations which should have been settled by another person, the principal debtor. The Wilson Committee, which sat from 1977 to 1980 to study the working of the City and

130 See Appendix I, Q. 51 (April 1982).

financial institutions heard suggestions that the legal implications of personal guarantees were not always properly understood,[131] and suggested that a formal code of practice could perhaps be set up.

Unfortunately, legal proceedings are frequently necessary to encourage a guarantor to face up to his obligations and to meet his liabilities and this means that costs and lengthy litigation can be incurred, during which time, if the guarantee is not supported, the guarantor might be in a position to salt away his assets beyond the reach of the bank. Even where a guarantor is a good customer in his own right and it might be thought that the guarantee is 'undoubted', this may not necessarily be the case and if, as guarantor, the individual becomes difficult, the bank may then be reluctant to upset further the good relationship which existed previously. Such a guarantee, once described as 'undoubted' or 'good', because of the wealth of the guarantor, might in fact be of little practical value if, at the time when reliance is necessary, the bank does not wish to call on him or to pressurize him if he will not pay.

Occasionally, the publicity arising out of a case where the bank has sued a guarantor can result in further difficulties in other situations and the risk of an adverse precedent in court proceedings can be worrying. An example of these problems was experienced in the years immediately following the decision in *Lloyds Bank Ltd* v. *Bundy* (1975), when many guarantors' solicitors sought to avoid liability because independent advice had not been given to their guarantor, although the guarantor knew full well what obligations he had entered into. Also, the proceedings in the case of *Williams & Glyn's Bank Ltd* v. *Barnes* (1980) illustrated the way in which a bank can find itself facing heavy counter-claims to its writ seeking judgment. Indeed, in that case there was a challenge to the whole basis of a bank being able to call in an overdraft.

DEFINITION AND FEATURES

A guarantee is defined in the Statute of Frauds 1677 as 'a written promise made by one person to be collaterally answerable for the debt, default, or miscarriage of another'.

There are therefore three parties involved in the guarantee situation, although only two are in a contractual relationship arising out of the guarantee document, the creditor and the guarantor. The party who is owed the money, or whose rights are protected, is known as the creditor and the person owing him the money, or who is under an obligation to him, is called the principal debtor. The guarantor, or surety as he is sometimes called, therefore assumes a secondary liability and in effect says to the creditor: 'If the principal debtor does not meet his liabilities to you, then I will (but only up to £x if there is a limitation in the amount)'.

There are similarities between a contract of guarantee and a contract of

131 See Appendix I, Q. 43 (April 1981).

indemnity, but the difference is that an indemnifier assumes primary responsibility himself and in effect he says to the creditor 'I will see that you are paid'. The distinction is important, for whereas a guarantee to be enforceable must be evidenced in writing under the provisions of s. 4 Statute of Frauds 1677, this is not the case with an indemnity and an indemnity given orally would be enforceable, although understandably it might be difficult to prove to a court that such a contract had been entered into.

In point of fact, nearly all bank guarantee forms are drafted in such a way that not only do they constitute a contract of guarantee, but they are also an indemnity. The advantage of this is that it gives the bank rights against the party signing, even though the bank might find itself with no rights which it could exercise against the principal debtor, for in such circumstances a contract of guarantee alone would be unenforceable. In other words, enforcement is not dependent upon the efficacy of the contract between the creditor and the principal debtor.

One example of a situation where a guarantor might be able to avoid liability were the form not drawn also as an indemnity, is that where the principal debtor is a minor. As we have seen, any lending made to a minor is irrecoverable, under the provisions of the Infants Relief Act 1874, although this position may change if the Minors Contracts Bill 1986 becomes law (see Chapter 2).* Another example would be where a limited company has borrowed money for a purpose outside the scope of its memorandum of association. Both such situations would normally discharge the guarantor, but with the guarantee form drafted additionally as an indemnity no problems should be encountered by the bank.

Guarantees may be executed by hand, or under seal, but if by hand they must be supported by consideration. This is usually recited in one of the early clauses of the guarantee form, although it is not essential to do so, and in its absence the guarantee is still enforceable (s. 3 Mercantile Law Amendment Act 1856). The consideration usually given by a bank is of course the loan of money to the principal debtor, or the agreement to continue to allow borrowing facilities for a further period of time.

A guarantee may be a specific guarantee given for one particular lending, usually on a loan account, as for example when the bank agrees to lend money so that the customer can buy a yacht: as security it takes a guarantee from the customer's friend who stresses that it is only this transaction he is securing. In such a case, it would be unlikely that a special guarantee document would be drawn up and usually the bank's standard form would be used. Undoubtedly, this would be expressed to be a continuing guarantee for all liabilities or transactions and it would therefore be important for the bank in such circumstances not only to lend on loan account, but also to note its security records most carefully, as this type of guarantee must be lapsed as soon as the borrowing is repaid. Moreover, it would not be good security for any other

* Minors Contracts Act 1987 effective from 9 June 1987.

concurrent borrowing by the customer. There are parallels here with a guarantee given for a regulated agreement under the Consumer Credit Act 1974 (see Chapter 8).

The usual form of guarantee is the continuing guarantee, and this is drawn in such a way that it covers all liabilities at any time, past, present or future, outstanding to the bank from the principal debtor; the form will refer to the 'ultimate balance' owing and fixed at the date of determination. Because there is a danger that a guarantor might forget that he has an outstanding contingent liability to a bank in respect of a guarantee that he has given, it has become the practice of some banks in recent years to write to the guarantor from time to time, to remind him that the liability is outstanding; the guarantor is asked to acknowledge the notice by signing it and returning it to the bank. The advantage of this practice is that if there is any doubt as to the position then it should come to light at an earlier time. However, it is important for the bank to ensure that the acknowledgement has not been amended or varied in any way, and that the covering letter, if any, does not modify the terms of the continuing guarantee contract.

OBLIGATIONS TO INTENDING GUARANTOR[132]

A contract of guarantee is not a contract *uberrimae fidei* (of the utmost good faith), but there are parallels between it and a contract of life assurance. The difference is that neither the borrowing customer nor the bank is under any duty to disclose material facts to the prospective guarantor which might affect his decision whether or not to enter into the security. This is important from the bank's point of view, where it must also be remembered that the bank is under a duty of secrecy to its customer, and could not, in any event, discuss that customer's affairs with a prospective guarantor, without the customer's prior authority. If any discussion is required, or likely, it is usual for the customer to be present at the interview between the bank and the prospective guarantor, and at the commencement of the interview for the customer to be asked to indicate that he has no objection to his affairs and financial business being discussed openly.

No responsibility falls on the bank, therefore, to give or volunteer any information concerning the customer's account, either as it stands at the present, or in the past. However, the guarantor must not be misled, for if he is then the guarantee will be voidable at his option, and the bank could find itself unsecured if it called upon him to pay. Consequently, when the bank has its customer's authority to disclose, it must answer any question accurately, and if, in any discussions or correspondence, it becomes apparent that the intending guarantor is under a misapprehension, then he must be corrected. If the bank does not have its customer's authority to disclose, and it

132   See Appendix I, Q. 43 (April 1981).

becomes apparent that the guarantor might be misled, then naturally before the bank takes matters further it will approach its customer so that there is no breach of secrecy.

The case of *Cooper* v. *National Provincial Bank Ltd* (1946) is an important one on this aspect of guarantee security. There Mr Cooper gave two guarantees to the bank, but claimed later that he was not liable on those documents, because the bank should have disclosed to him, when the guarantees were signed, that the customer's husband was an undischarged bankrupt and was signing as an agent on the customer's account. Cooper also sought to avoid liability by saying that the bank account had been operated unsatisfactorily in the past, as cheques had been drawn when there were no covering monies, and these had subsequently been stopped by the drawer. The court did not accept these defences, and held that there is no obigation on the part of the bank to disclose information about the customer's account, and the guarantees were good security.

There is not even any obligation to explain the maximum liability under the guarantee or its terms and effects if the prospective guarantor is a stranger to the bank (*O'Hara* v. *Allied Irish Banks Ltd and another* (1984), although where he is a customer the position may be different (*Lloyds Bank* v. *Bundy* (1975).[133] In a case concerning a land mortgage it was held that where a bank takes it upon itself to advise the chargor about the nature and effect of a mortgage in favour of the bank it is under a duty not to mis-state the effect negligently, and in particular, if the mortgage covers further advances that must be explained (*Cornish* v. *Midland Bank plc* (1985)).

It can be seen, therefore, that a stranger-guarantor would only be able to escape liability if material factors had been misrepresented to him by the bank either in the course of negotiations directly, or possibly by the bank acquiescing silently to something said or written which clearly showed that the guarantor was under a misunderstanding. The misrepresentation might be innocent or fraudulent; it is more likely to be the former.

A case of interest here is that of *MacKenzie* v. *Royal Bank of Canada* (1934), which was a Privy Council decision upon appeal. Mrs MacKenzie succeeded in avoiding her liability on a guarantee given to that bank, because when she had executed the guarantee document at the bank it had inadvertently been misrepresented that the transaction was a way in which she could obtain the return of certain shares which earlier she had lodged as security. Lord Atkin said 'A contract of guarantee, like any other contract, is liable to be avoided if induced by material misrepresentation of an existing fact, even if made innocently'.

One aspect of this case was that part of the documentation concerning the transactions was a form signed by a solicitor which said that he had given independent advice to Mrs MacKenzie. In fact, the solicitor had not given such advice; the charge forms had been signed at the bank and the bank had subsequently asked Mrs MacKenzie to obtain the signature of her solicitor to the form. It is clear therefore, that if there is a need for independent advice then this must be taken *before* the transaction, and must not just purport to have been taken, by drawing up subsequent documentation to that effect.

A guarantee may also be rendered voidable by undue influence or duress. Undue influence exists where the party taking an obligation is unable to exercise his or her own free will. This may arise because of the relationship in which he stands with the other parties, particularly the principal debtor. Undue influence is presumed to exist where there is a close association, such as that between a patient and his doctor, or between a priest and a member of his church. It can be particularly relevant where a wife is asked to guarantee her husband's account or that of a business in which he is involved, although here much will depend upon whether the wife is a business woman herself.

Clearly it would be very risky for the bank to give the security document to the customer for him to arrange for it to be executed by a guarantor with whom he stood in a fiduciary relationship. A bank should always therefore deal directly with the party giving the guarantee or third party charge or that party's own solicitors. Indeed in all such cases, to ensure that the guarantor cannot later avoid liabiltiy if he or she is called upon to pay, a bank will insist upon the intending guarantor taking independent advice from his or her own solicitor, and usually an endorsement is made upon the guarantee document, or a side letter is added, signed by the solicitor, to the effect that he has explained the meaning of the document and the implications of the liability to the guarantor, who has understood. It should be noted here that the choice as to which solicitor to use lies entirely with the intending guarantor, and while banks frequently have local firms of solicitors who act for them, if the intending guarantor asks for a solicitor to be chosen, dependent upon the circumstances, it might not be wise to direct them to a firm which regularly acts for the bank. Certainly, if the intending guarantor has his or her own solicitors then they are the ones which the bank would expect to be used.

In addition to these situations where there is a close relationship between the borrower and the guarantor, it is possible that in certain instances a special relationship could exist, also or alternatively, between the prospective guarantor and the bank. This can arise where the prospective guarantor is also a customer of the bank and relies entirely or mainly on the bank for advice in financial matters. In such a sutuation there could clearly be a conflict of interests for the bank, for on the one hand it would be anxious, presumably, to obtain the security, while on the other it might perhaps be thought that it ought to be advising the intending guarantor that it is not in his interest to give the guarantee. It would be essential in such a situation to require the guarantor to take independent advice. Failure to obtain this brought unfortunate consequences both to the bank concerned and the banking industry generally following the decision in *Lloyds Bank Ltd* v. *Bundy* (1975).

The facts were as follows. Mr Bundy was an elderly man, a former farmer, not possessed with much financial acumen, and his home, Yew Tree Farm, was his only asset of note. He had an acount at a branch of Lloyds Bank where his son also banked, as did a plant hire company of which the son was a director and shareholder. This company was borrowing from the bank. In 1966, Mr Bundy senior gave Lloyds Bank a guarantee for £1500 to secure the company's borrowing and in support he created a legal mortgage over Yew Tree Farm. Unfortunately, the company's business was not successful and as justification for continuing its support the bank sought additional security. In consequence, in May 1969 the assistant branch manager and Mr Bundy junior visited Mr Bundy senior at his farmhouse. The bank representative suggested to Mr Bundy senior that he might like to give an additional guarantee and a further charge over the property for £6000 and Mr Bundy senior said he was ready to help his son's business in this way. The assistant branch manager, who had taken the security documents to be the meeting, left them with Mr Bundy senior so that they could be considered, and so that advice could be taken. Mr Bundy senior sought this advice from his own solicitor, but was told by the solicitor that he should not commit himself beyond £5000 in respect of his son's business, as that would be about half his assets, the propety then being valued at approximately £10 000. Nevertheless, despite this advice, Mr Bundy senior signed the further guarantee and mortgage, which were witnessed by the assistant branch manager. The guarantor's contingent liability now totalled £7500.

Once again the company failed to retrieve its trading position and despite there being an increased overdraft facility, this line of finance was proving to be inadequate; the bank dishonoured cheques. The son, however, still felt that the problems were temporary and when a new assistant manager arrived at the branch he took him to meet his father. This meeting was held shortly before Christmas 1969, when the new banker took with him a fresh form of guarantee and mortgage in the anticipation that an increased commitment would be given by Mr Bundy senior. He explained to the old farmer that the bank would continue to allow the company to operate with an overdraft up to the existing limit of £10 000, but that to do so the bank needed his guarantee for £11 000 coupled with an additional charge over Yew Tree Farm for £5300, bringing the total mortgages on the farmhouse into line with the contingent liability on the new guarantee. Thereupon, at the meeting, Mr Bundy senior executed the documents which were witnessed by the assistant branch manager; no legal advice was taken.

In May of the following year, a receiving order in bankruptcy was made against Mr Bundy junior and the company ceased to trade. To recover the company borrowing, the bank sought possession of Yew Tree farmhouse and brought proceedings for possession so that they could evict the occupants. While succeeding in the county court, upon Mr Bundy's appeal the bank lost, and the guarantee dated 17 December 1969 and the legal mortgage of that date were declared null and void. It will be remembered, that a new guarantee had been taken in the December, and as this was the prime security, taken in substitution and not in addition to the earlier guarantees, the bank was therefore completely unsecured.

In reaching their decision, the appeal judges found that there had been an inequality of bargaining power in the situation obtaining when the December 1969 securities were taken. They defined this as being when one party is 'grievously impaired by his needs or desires, or ignorance, or infirmity, coupled with influences or pressure brought to bear on him for the benefit of another'. The court found that there was a relationship of trust and confidence between the guarantor and his bank manager and noted that while it was not wholly material to their decision the fact that the father was in account as customer in his own right was not irrelevant to their decision. It was held that there had been a conflict of interest on the bank's part and that in the light of the overall circumstances there had been undue influence, thus rendering the securities voidable at the surety's option. Moreover, the court was unhappy with the consideration extended by the bank and found this inadequate, as no increased facilities had been granted to the company, and the overdraft had merely been continued at the same level for a further period of time.

This decision received considerable publicity, and for some time subsequently it was not uncommon for guarantors who were also customers to seek to avoid their liability on grounds of the Bundy decision. Many of those defences failed, however, as other courts distinguished the Bundy decision as special and were ready to give judgment in the bank's favour against a guarantor, even though he was a customer, when he was a person entirely capable of understanding the purport of the commitment into which he had entered. Thus, for example, in *National Westminster Bank* v. *Scarisbrick* (1976) (unreported) Mr Justice Crichton saw the giving of a guarantee by a director of the company in which he was the major shareholder as a straightforward commercial transaction, even though he was a customer. He saw the facts of the Bundy case as quite exceptional and found no defence for Mr Scarisbrick on those grounds.

Banks' positions have been further improved by the decision in *National Westminster Bank* v. *Morgan* (1985). Here the House of Lords held that in order for a security to be set aside on a later claim of undue influence, the transaction had to be shown as being at the time it was entered into, manifestly disadvantageous to the surety. The relationship between the two parties (bank and surety) would have to be such that the surety was dominated by the bank. It was said that the doctrine of undue influence arising out of a fiduciary relationship was 'that it is right and expedient to save persons from being victimized by other people', and it was 'to protect people from being forced tricked or misled in any way by others into parting with their property'.

Clearly, therefore, in an ordinary banking situation this will not arise.

In examining this area of void or voidable guarantees, the bank, provided it is unaware of the situation, will not find itself in difficulties if, between the borrower and the guarantor, matters are represented to be other than what they really are. If a guarantor has any quarrel on these grounds, his action lies against the principal debtor, although usually clauses in the guarantee contract will preclude him from taking any steps until such time as the bank is fully repaid.

The danger of misrepresentation was clearly seen in the old decision of *Carlisle and Cumberland Banking Co* v. *Bragg* (1911), where because of bad banking practice the borrowing customer was allowed to take the guarantee document to his guarantor for signature, and so fraud was facilitated. When he produced the guarantee form to Mr Bragg, the borrower indicated that it was an insurance document, and so the guarantor signed it under a mistake of fact. When the guarantor defended an action brought by the bank, the court held that he was not liable, as 'his mind had not run with his pen', when he signed. Thus he was able to rely on the doctrine of *'non est factum'* – that is that the signing was not his act. However, this case decision was overruled in 1970 in *Saunders* v. *Anglia Building Society*, where it was said:

> Whenever a man of full age and understanding, who can read and write, signs a legal document which is put before him for signature – by which I mean a document which, it is apparent on the fact of it, is intended to have legal consequences – then, if he does not take the trouble to read it, but signs it as it is, relying on the word of another as to its character or contents or effect, he cannot be heard to say that it is not his document. By his conduct in signing it he has represented to all into whose hands it may come, that it is his document; and once they act upon it as being his document, he cannot go back on it and say it was a nullity from the beginning.

After a guarantee has been signed, no further disclosure should be made to the guarantor, apart from answering his question at any time as to the extent of his liability. This will depend upon the balance of the borrower's account, if the guarantee is for a limited amount, and in that case, if the borrowing is in excess of the guarantee the guarantor should be informed that his guarantee is relied on fully. However, if the borrowing is below the amount of the guarantee or is for an unlimited amount, the guarantor may be advised effectively of the balance of the account which is secured.

COMMON LAW RIGHTS AND PROTECTION OF A GUARANTOR

Before we remind ourselves of the usual clauses in bank guarantee forms it will help our understanding of the reason for them, if we examine a guarantor's common law position, which would exist were there not the special agreements in the guarantee document. It will already have been appreciated that the law seeks to protect a guarantor strongly, and in addition to being able to escape liability in the circumstances discussed above, in common law a guarantor would have rights against the borrower (the principal debtor), the bank (the creditor) and against any co-guarantors or co-sureties (another guarantor or depositor of security).

For instance, in common law, as against the borrower, if and when he is called upon to pay, a guarantor may petition the court for an order that the debt be paid by the borrower which would expunge any liability he had. Such an event is unlikely. However, also, when a guarantor meets his liability, or part of it, in common law he has an immediate right of action against the borrower to recover the sum paid and this right extends to lodging a proof in the borrower's bankruptcy or deceased estate. He may do this in the creditor's name or his own name, particularly where he has taken an assignment of the debt from the creditor.

The guarantor is also entitled to take advantage of any right of set-off or counterclaim which exists between the borrower and the creditor and he may use this right as a defence if sued by the creditor.

As against a bank a guarantor's most important right is that of subrogation, and when he pays off the guaranteed amount he is entitled to subrogate to all the rights and securities of the bank. Thus unless he were restricted by covenants in the guarantee form he would be entitled to any securities lodged by the borrower himself, or any securities lodged by co-guarantors or co-sureties (s. 5 Mercantile Law Amendment Act 1856). These rights could clearly be prejudicial to the bank if the guarantee were for an amount less than the total liability of the borrower.

As against his co-guarantors or co-sureties, a paying guarantor is entitled to reimbursement on a *pro rata* basis and this is so even if separate guarantees have been signed, or the guarantee is a joint and several one, and it is a right exercisable irrespective of the date of the documents. Also, where a third party is liable as surety, for example by the deposit of deed security, but he is not a guarantor, the paying guarantor's rights extend against that surety and the security. These rights of contribution are available whether or not a guarantor knew of the existence of the other guarantees or security at the time he undertook his obligation and extend into a situation where perhaps another guarantor or surety has recovered securities from the principal debtor, or creditor; the latter may then be made to share the benefit of those securities with the other paying co-guarantors or sureties.

CLAUSES IN BANK GUARANTEE FORMS

The standard form of bank guarantee (Fig. 15.1) is drawn widely to give the bank the strongest possible rights and protection, and, until the bank is repaid in full, to deprive the guarantor of those common law rights which he could exercise to the bank's disadvantage.

The reader is asked at this point to refer again to Chapter 11 where an examination of typical clauses in standard charge forms was undertaken.

Guarantee

To: BANK OF CYPRUS (LONDON) LIMITED (hereinafter called "the Bank")

1.   IN consideration of the Bank's giving time credit facilities or accommodation to

(hereinafter called "the Principal") I/we the undersigned (hereinafter called "the Guarantor") hereby guarantee and undertake on demand in writing to pay or discharge to the Bank all moneys and liabilities matured or unmatured whether actual or contingent which are now or may at any time hereafter be or become from time to time due owing or incurred to the Bank by the Principal or in respect of which the Principal may be or become liable to the Bank on any current loan or other account or otherwise in any manner whatsoever including the amount of any note or bill made accepted endorsed discounted or paid and of any liability under any guarantee or indemnity or other instrument whatsoever given or assumed by the Bank for or at the request of the Principal (in all cases whether alone or jointly with any other person and in whatever style name or form and whether as principal or surety) and all commission discount and other banking charges including legal costs (as between solicitor and own client) and disbursements and any expenses incurred by the Bank in relation to any of the matters aforesaid or the recovery of any moneys due hereunder or keeping the Principal's account or which are otherwise recoverable by the Bank from the Principal and/or the Guarantor together with interest compounded quarterly to the date of repayment at such rate as may be agreed from time to time between the Principal and the Bank or according to the usual practice of the Bank as well after as before any demand made notice of determination given or judgment obtained (including any further advances made by the Bank to the Principal and any other liabilities of the Principal to the Bank arising during the period of notice referred to in Clause 2 hereof)

PROVIDED THAT the total amount recoverable hereunder shall (if the Schedule hereto shall have been completed but not otherwise) not exceed the sum stated in such Schedule and in addition the interest (on such sum or such less sum as shall be due and owing) charges costs and expenses above referred to accruing due to the Bank from the Principal before or after the date of demand or expiration of the said notice as the case may be and not debited to the Principal's account at such date.

2.   THIS Guarantee shall be a continuing guarantee to the Bank notwithstanding any settlement of account or other matter or thing whatsoever but may and shall be determined (save as hereinafter provided) and the liability hereunder crystallised (except as regards unascertained or contingent liabilities and the interest charges costs and expenses above referred to) at the expiration of three months after the receipt by the Bank from the Guarantor of notice in writing to determine it but notwithstanding determination as to one or more of the Guarantor (being more than one) this Guarantee shall remain a continuing security as to the other or others and in the event of the death of the Guarantor (being an individual) the liability of the legal personal representatives of the estate of the Guarantor shall continue until the expiration of three months' written notice by such legal personal representatives to determine this Guarantee.

3.   FOR all purposes of the liability of the Guarantor to the Bank hereunder (including the liability of the Guarantor for interest) every sum of money which may now be or may hereafter from time to time become due or owing to the Bank as aforesaid by the Principal (or which would have become so due or owing were it not for the bankruptcy or winding up of the Principal) shall be deemed to continue due and owing to the Bank by the Principal until the same shall be actually paid to the Bank notwithstanding the bankruptcy or winding up of the Principal or any other event whatsoever and in case of the death of the Principal all sums which would have been due or owing as aforesaid to the Bank by the Principal if the Principal had lived until the time at which the Bank shall have received actual notice of his death shall for all purposes of this Guarantee be deemed included in the monies due and owing to the Bank by the Principal.

4.   IN the event of this Guarantee's being determined (whether by notice given by the Guarantor or in the case of an individual by his legal personal representatives or by the Bank or by this Guarantee's ceasing from any cause whatsoever to be a continuing security) the Bank may continue its account(s) with the Principal and the liability of the Guarantor in respect of the amount due from the Principal at the date when the determination becomes effective shall not be released or diminished by such determination or by any dealings in the account(s) subsequent to the date of such notice or the date on which this Guarantee ceased to be a continuing security.

5.   THIS Guarantee shall not be affected by any failure of the Bank to take any security or by any defect in or invalidity of any security given or to be given to the Bank by the Principal or by any co-surety or by any disability incapacity or lack of or limitation on the borrowing or other powers of the Principal or by want of authority of any agent director officer or other person appearing to be acting for the Principal in respect of the Principal's liabilities and where by reason of any such matter moneys advanced by the Bank to or for the benefit of the Principal are not recoverable from the Principal they shall nevertheless be recoverable from the Guarantor as sole or principal debtor and shall be repaid by the Guarantor on demand in writing.

6.   THE Bank shall be at liberty without thereby affecting its rights hereunder at any time and from time to time (whether before or after any demand for payment made by the Bank under or any notice of determination of this Guarantee or receipt by the Bank of any notice of any disability or incapacity of the Guarantor) to refuse grant or renew (as the case may be) further credit to the Principal to hold over renew or give up in whole or in part any bills of exchange promissory notes mortgages charges or liens for any period and to compound with give time for payment or grant other indulgence to the Principal or to any obligant on bills of exchange or promissory notes or otherwise or to accept compositions from and make any other arrangements with the Principal or any persons liable to the Bank in respect of such securities as aforesaid held or to be held by the Bank to give up modify exchange or abstain from perfecting or taking advantage of or enforcing any such securities as aforesaid guarantees or other contracts or the proceeds of any of the foregoing and to discharge any parties thereto and to realise any securities in such manner as the Bank may think expedient.

7.   THE Bank shall in respect of the liability of the Guarantor hereunder have a lien on all stocks shares securities and property of the Guarantor which or the certificates of title to which are from time to time held by the Bank whether for safe custody or otherwise and on all moneys from time to time standing to the credit of the Guarantor with the Bank on any account.

8.   NOTWITHSTANDING payment to the Bank by the Guarantor or any other person of the whole or any part of the amount recoverable hereunder the Bank alone may until its claim against the Principal is fully satisfied pursue such claim and prove and receive dividends in the Principal's bankruptcy or winding up in respect thereof.

9.   THIS Guarantee shall be in addition to and shall not be in any way prejudiced or affected by any other guarantee (including any other guarantee signed by the Guarantor) or any collateral or other security now or hereafter held by the Bank for all or any part of the liabilities of the Principal nor shall any such guarantee or security or any lien to which the Bank may be otherwise entitled or the liability of any person not a party hereto for all or any part of the liabilities of the Principal be in any way prejudiced or affected by this Guarantee. And all money received by the Bank from the Guarantor or the Principal or any person liable to pay the same may be applied by the Bank to any account or item of account or to any transaction to which the same may be applicable or at the option of the Bank to a separate or suspense account without any intermediate obligation on the part of the Bank to apply the same or any part thereof in or towards the discharge of the liabilities of the Principal.

Fig.15.1   *Guarantee*   431

10   No assurance security or payment which may be avoided under any enactment relating to bankruptcy or liquidation and no release settlement discharge or arrangement given or made in reliance on any such assurance security or payment shall prejudice or affect the Bank's right to recover from the Guarantor and any security held by it for the liability of the Guarantor hereunder to the full extent hereof as if the same had never been granted given or made and the Bank shall notwithstanding any assurance security or payment be entitled to retain any such security for so long as it shall in its absolute discretion deem necessary in order to protect its rights hereunder

11   THE Bank shall be at liberty without any notice to or further or other consent from the Guarantor to apply or transfer any money now or at any time hereafter standing to the credit of the Guarantor upon current deposit or any other account with the Bank in payment or in part payment of any such sums of money as may now be or hereafter may become due or owing to the Bank from or by the Guarantor hereunder and whether such liability shall be actual or contingent and the Bank may refuse payment of any cheque bill note or order drawn or accepted by the Guarantor or upon which the Guarantor may be otherwise liable and which if paid would reduce the amount of money standing to the credit of the Guarantor as aforesaid to less than the amount of any such sums of money as aforesaid Provided that where the liability is contingent the Bank may determine the amount to be retained against such liability and any such determination shall be conclusive and binding on the Guarantor.

12   SO far as may be necessary to give effect to the provisions of this Guarantee the Guarantor waives in favour of the Bank all rights which but for this waiver the Guarantor might exercise or enforce against the Bank or the Principal to the intent that as between the Bank and the Guarantor the Guarantor shall be deemed to be a principal debtor in respect of the liabilities of the Principal to the Bank

13   A demand for payment or any other demand or notice under this Guarantee may be made or given by any director manager or officer of the Bank or of any branch thereof by letter addressed to the Guarantor and sent by ordinary prepaid post to or left at the address of the Guarantor as given in this Guarantee or the last known place of business or abode of the Guarantor (or if the Guarantor is a company at the option of the Bank to or at its registered office) and shall be deemed if posted to have been made or given at 10.00 a m on the day following the date of posting

14   WHERE there are two or more persons included in the expression "the Guarantor" the liability of each of them hereunder shall be joint and several and every agreement and undertaking on their part shall be construed accordingly and the Bank shall also be at liberty without thereby affecting its rights hereunder at any time and from time to time at its absolute discretion to release discharge compound with or otherwise vary or agree to vary the liability under this Guarantee of or make any other arrangements with any one or more of such persons and no such release discharge composition variation agreement of arrangement shall prejudice or in any way affect its rights and remedies against the other or others of such persons

15   IN this Guarantee where the context admits "the Guarantor" means and includes every person liable hereunder (including all partners in a firm) or any one or more of them and his or their legal personal representatives and any other party lawfully acting on behalf of every such person and "the Bank" includes its successors and assigns and any company in which the business of the Bank shall become vested to the intent that this guarantee shall constitute a continuing security in favour of any such company as if it has been expressly named herein instead of Bank of Cyprus (London) Limited

16   THIS Guarantee shall at all times remain the property of the Bank

IN WITNESS whereof the Guarantor has executed this Deed under seal the   day of   19

THE SCHEDULE above referred to
Maximum principal sum recoverable hereunder (Clause 1)

Words   Pounds

Figures £

SIGNED SEALED and DELIVERED by   )
)
of

)
in the presence of:—

Signature: . . . .

Full name (block capitals) . . . .

Address: . . . .

        . . . .

Occupation: . . . .
SIGNED SEALED and DELIVERED by   )
)
of

)
in the presence of:—

Signature: . . . .

Full name (block capitals) . . . .

Address: . . . .

        . . . .

Occupation: . . . .

Fig.15.1   *(contd)*

SIGNED SEALED and DELIVERED by

of

in the presence of:—

Signature: . . . .

Full name (block capitals) . . . .

Address: . . . .

. . . .

Occupation: . . . .

SIGNED SEALED and DELIVERED by

of

in the presence of:—

Signature: . . . .

Full name (block capitals) . . . .

Address: . . . .

. . . .

Occupation: . . . .

THE COMMON SEAL of . . . .

of . . . .

was hereunto affixed in pursuance of a Resolution of the Board of Directors
in the presence of:—

. . . . Director

. . . . Secretary

Registered in England No.

I/We and each of us hereby acknowledge receipt of a copy of the above Guarantee.

. . . .

DATED   19

Fig.15.1   *(contd)*

A guarantee is a third-party form of charge and when one is perused it will be found that all the clauses (numbered 1 to 20) apply except clause 7 (the personal covenant of the debtor to repay) and clause 10 (the exclusion of s. 103 Law of Property Act 1925 regarding the power of sale). Clearly these two clauses are not relevant.

Additionally, a bank guarantee will include the following:

Determination clause   The guarantor agrees to give *written* notice of any determination of the guarantee and confirms that such a notice will not take effect until the expiration of a period of time, typically one month or three months, from when the bank receives the notice. It is said that even upon his death his executors or administrators must give a similar period of notice (but see p. 450).

The object of this clause is to enable the banker and his customer to reorganize their positions and to allow time to decide how to deal with the future conduct of the account. If this leeway were not available, it would be necessary for the banker to stop the customer's account immediately; clearly this could have practical disadvantages.

Continuation of account   This clause will state that after a notice of determination has been received and has become effective, the bank may continue *an* account for the principal debtor and that credits to that account will not reduce or extinguish the liability of the guarantor as at the date of determination.

Guarantor's monies to suspense account   Here the guarantor confirms that any monies paid by him may be placed to a suspense account or bank realized security account. It is often coupled with the clause stating that such monies need not be taken into account in any proof in the principal debtor's bankruptcy. In this way it underlines the ruling in *Re Sass* (1896), the circumstances of which were that Sass was borrowing from National Provincial Bank and his overdraft reached £755. As security the bank had a guarantee for the 'whole debt', but with the monetary liability recoverable from the guarantor limited to £300 and interest. A receiving order in bankruptcy was made against Sass and when the guarantor was called upon to meet his liability he paid £303 which the bank credited to a suspense account. Thereupon, the bank submitted a proof in the bankrupt's estate for the balance of the overdraft, £755. This proof was rejected by the trustee in bankruptcy who claimed that the proof should be reduced by the amount paid by the guarantor, £303. However his claim was overruled in court, where it was held that the bank's proof in the sum of £755 should be admitted for dividend purposes.

Guarantee is the bank's property   A clause is usually included stating that the bank may retain the guarantee document at all times, whether before or after demand is made on the guarantor. The object of this is to retain for the bank the written evidence of all those rights which it holds under the specially drawn guarantee contract. This means that if a paying guarantor asks for the paid guarantee to be cancelled and handed to him, it is usual for the bank to decline, and to refer him to this clause in his guarantee. Naturally, if he wants a receipt for the monies paid the bank will oblige, although the wording of the receipt must be very carefully phrased, so as not to negate any clauses in the guarantee itself.

JOINT AND SEVERAL GUARANTEES[134,135]

Bank forms of guarantee, signed by two or more persons, are invariably drawn in such a way that each party contracts to be both jointly and severally liable. In the absence of a clause referring to several liability, the liability would be joint and there would be disadvantages to the bank's secured position in that case. Formerly, the main disadvantage of joint liability only was that there was only one right of action against the parties and if one guarantor were omitted from an action then the bank would not then have been able to sue the other guarantor(s). However, that rule, seen in *Kendall* v. *Hamilton* (1879) has been abolished by the Civil Liability (Contribution) Act 1978, section 3, and it is now possible to sue a party whose name has been omitted from the original writ.

The principal advantage to the bank of several liability is that it can sue each guarantor separately for the full nominal amount of the guarantee and in doing so it can ignore any monies or contributions received from co-guarantors; it may also sue the guarantors in any order it wishes. The bank is clearly in a much stronger position where it takes a guarantee in joint and several terms from Mr A and Mr B, limited, say, to £20 000, rather than taking two separate guarantees for £10 000 each, one from Mr A and the other from Mr B. Under the former security the bank could sue Mr A and recover £20 000 from him if Mr B were a man of straw. In the second case, if and when the bank had discovered that it was not worth suing Mr B, it had turned to Mr A, the maximum it could recover would be £10 000.

The joint and several clause is particularly useful in bankruptcy situations as there the bank is able to prove for its debt in each guarantor's separate estate and also in their joint estate, should there be one, and in this way it can maximize its recovery through the dividends received, athough naturally it must not retain more than one hundred pence in the pound overall.

A further advantage of several liability is that if one guarantor has an account in his own name operating in credit, then the bank might be able to exercise a right of lien or set-off over that balance in respect of the several guarantee liability. Often a clause in the guarantee document will allow the bank to appropriate the monies and dishonour cheques drawn in reliance on the balance.

When taking a joint and several guarantee from two or more parties, it is usually advisable to ensure that each one appreciates that he will be fully liable as an individual for the full extent of the guarantee and that there is no question of his simply undertaking to contribute a share of the liability. This is a common defence and argument used by joint and several guarantors when they are called upon to pay, and it is helpful in refuting such arguments if the bank officer can say that it is his invariable practice to have explained the

134 See Appendix I, Q. 33 (April 1980).
135 See Appendix I, Q. 42 (April 1981).

nature and extent of the liability when the guarantee was executed, although this is not essential.

Also, when taking a joint and several guarantee it is important to remember that the security does not become effective until it has been executed by all the parties who are intended to be guarantors. Until the last signature is added, the guarantee is no security at all, and no reliance should be placed upon it.

This unsecured position can be seen clearly if the case of *National Provincial Bank of England Ltd* v. *Brackenbury* (1906) is examined. There, the bank was lending to Brewers and Maltsters Machinery Manufacturing Co. Ltd and sought a joint and several guarantee from Mr Brackenbury, Mr Brown, Mr Hazlehurst and Mr Johnson. The first three guarantors signed, but Mr Johnson was ill, and died before the bank was able to obtain his signature to the guarantee document. However the bank relied on its security and later called upon the three guarantors, who had signed, to pay the amount owed. As this was not forthcoming, the bank sued Mr Brackenbury, but he defended the action on the grounds that he had been released from liability, because the bank had not obtained the signature of the intended fourth guarantor, and had relied on the security without seeking his, Mr Brackenbury's, permission. As we have seen, the courts are very keen to protect the rights of guarantors, and in assessing this situation they took into account the fact that Mr Brackenbury's position had been weakened and prejudiced by the absence of a signature from Mr Johnson, for among other things Mr Brackenbury had no rights of contribution against Mr Johnson's estate, and had a greater proportional liability, *vis-à-vis* his co-guarantors, than would have been the case if Johnson had signed.

The moral of this decision is clear, and to depart in any way from recognized practice in obtaining the signatures of all intending parties is fraught with danger. It might be possible, in similar circumstances, to protect the position, if those guarantors who had signed were to agree in writing, subsequently, that they were still liable on the guarantee document, despite the fact that another intended guarantor had not joined in. However, as will be appreciated, the correspondence and explanations necessary here could lay that practice open to problems, and it would be much simpler and safer for a *new* guarantee form to be prepared and executed.

Similar principles as in the Brackenbury decision were seen in *James Graham & Co. Ltd* v. *Southgate-Sands and others* (1985), where the signature of the third joint and several guarantor was forged, although this did not become apparent until the company attempted to enforce the security. The court held that all guarantors were free from liability.

It should be remembered that as the courts are anxious to protect contribution rights, it is also very important that when one of a number of guarantors signs a guarantee document he should not be allowed to vary the terms in any way, for if he does so then he and all the other guarantors will be discharged from liability (*Ellesmere Brewery Co. v. Cooper* (1896)). Nevertheless, once the guarantee has been signed, the bank is usually in a position of being able to release any one or more guarantors from liability or to release their supporting security without reference or permission from the other guarantors, because of the way its form is drawn. The danger of not having such a clause in the guarantee was seen in *Barclays Bank Ltd* v. *Trevanion* (1933). There the bank held a joint and several guarantee for £10 000 from three parties to secure a lending to a limited company. When the company borrowing seemed at risk, the bank looked to the three guarantors and came to arrangements with two of them whereby each agreed to pay £500 or a slightly higher figure if the payent were made by instalments over a period of three years. The company debt was in excess of £3000 and the bank sought to make similar arrangements with the third guarantor, Mr Trevanion, but he would not agree, and so the bank started proceedings against him. When he defended these the court did not accept the bank's claim for judgment, for in the absence of any clause in the guarantee document enabling the bank to enter into a composition or to release other guarantors, the court could not see that the bank had any right to retain its rights against the third guarantor. It was said by the judge:

> In my view, when they released two, they altered the contract between themselves and the third guarantor in such a way as to prevent it being enforceable. They deprived him of his rights of contribution against his co-sureties and I think that they did something that released him from his bargain *altogether*.

A further danger associated with joint and several guarantees can arise where there are subsequent changes in the security structure or parties involved. This was seen in *Ford & Carter v. Midland Bank Ltd* (1979), illustrating the great care needed with a 'group' situation, often encountered when another limited company becomes a subsidiary of a holding company, alongside other companies who are already involved in a cross-guarantee structure. In this case a holding company, Wilson Lovatt & Sons Ltd, and its subsidiary Magna Plant Ltd, executed a joint and several guarantee in favour of Midland Bank in February 1964. Later, in 1967, three other companies joined the group, and to ensure that these companies became liable for the liabilities of the first two, and that the first two became liable for any debts or liabilities arising in the name of the three further companies, all five companies executed a memorandum which was endorsed on the original guarantee. This was signed by two officers of each company after a resolution had been passed by each company stating:

> For the above consideration and also in consideration of your making or continuing advances in like manner to either or both of us we hereby agree to be bound to you by the terms of the foregoing agreement as if we had signed the said agreement simultaneously with Wilson Lovatt & Sons Limited and Magna Plant Limited to the intent that we and each of us and they and each of them shall be and become mutually responsible as guarantors for each others' indebtedness to the Bank.

In July 1969 Ford & Carter Ltd was acquired and was brought into the group. Its name was added to the memorandum and it assumed the liabilities mentioned, with two officers signing pursuant to a board resolution. *However, on this occasion no other resolutions or signatures were obtained from the existing five companies.*

In December 1969 two more companies were acquired and the same practice as in July of that year was carried through again, *with the existing six companies not being required to sign anything.* In the same month Ford & Carter Ltd gave Midland Bank a floating charge expressed to secure its own borrowings and to be available in support of any guarantee liabilities.

In February of 1971 the board of Ford & Carter Ltd resolved to request Midland Bank to appoint a receiver although its own bank account was in credit and the liability to the bank arose only through the guarantee structure for other companies in the group. The receiver was appointed and he proceeded to realise assets of the company. About one year later, a liquidation having ensued, the liquidator wrote to the bank and suggested for the first time that the guarantee given by Ford and Carter Ltd might not be valid; in July 1973 he issued proceedings against the bank and the receiver.

The liquidator's case was brought on the grounds that the mutual guarantee, in respect of which Ford & Carter Ltd had assumed liabilities to the bank, was null and void, through the failure of the bank in the documentation to obtain a like liability by the existing companies for the debts of Ford & Carter Ltd. Hence it was argued that if this was correct then the receiver had been appointed by mistake, both on the part of the bank and on the part of the board of the company when it requested the appointment by resolution. The liquidator sought repayment of all monies collected by the receiver and moreover claimed damages for trespass from the time that the receiver became aware of his possible position.

In defence the bank sought to show that the mutual liabilities of the first five companies arose through the document of October 1967 which, the bank claimed, indicated that those companies accepted liability for any member of the Wilson Lovatt Group which might later be brought in, with the approval of its chairman or finance director. This argument was rejected, as was also the argument that what had been done in July and December 1969 had been done not only on behalf of Ford & Carter Ltd but also by the agency of the financial director of Wilson Lovatt, with whom negotiations had taken place. This argument had been accepted by the majority of the Court of Appeal and the House of Lords when referring to it spoke of its attraction because it corresponded with commercial reality, the group being treated as one. The individual companies, it was said, would undoubtedly have been ready to join in any proper arrangement which the finance director had recommended. However, finally the House of Lords did not accept this, separating *intention* from what was *actually done.* This highest court in the land accepted that the finance director had been the spokesman for the individual companies but took the view that *the formalities had been left to the bank.* The bank had decided on an amended memorandum, mistakenly, despite what it had done in 1967, and therein lay its fault.

Bankers and company directors frequently encounter situations similar in general outline to that seen in this case, where a group is expanding and creating new subsidiaries or acquiring existing companies which are brought into the group structure.[136] An existing cross-guarantee and debenture structure exists and it is desired to bring in the new subsidiary so that it assumes full liability for the existing borrowing and liabilities of the holding company and the subsidiaries, and the parent and other subsidiaries become liable for the debts and liabilities of the newly acquired or created company. Such developments and the paper work involved are sometimes thought to be a nuisance both for the bank and the older company because of the need to prepare and excute new securities on a regularly recurring basis, but this case clearly emphasizes that short cuts are not to be recommended and can have disastrous consequences if taken.

The decision emphasizes the great need for care in any documentation relating to securities, particularly where existing securities are amended or varied by ancillary documents or endorsed memoranda. It may be noted however that, by implication, the House of Lords accepted that the memorandum endorsed in 1967 which was executed by all five companies (i.e. the two existing companies and the three further companies which were brought into the group) was an acceptable practice when done properly. This case was lost because later, upon a further acquisition, not all the existing companies executed the further memorandum which was endorsed, that only being executed by Ford & Carter Ltd when the new company was brought in, in July 1969, and the two further companies in the December of that year.

This judgment did not indicate that there is a need for entirely fresh forms of guarantee to be executed where a new company comes into a group situation, although this has been and continues to be the practice of some banks despite the disadvantages of the paper work involved and the possibility that any new security might become subject to the provisions relating to liquidation which might apply to any new security substituted for an older one.

To summarize, it can be seen that the standard form of joint and several guarantee used by a bank needs to have been drafted most carefully, because in common law the rights of guarantors, as against each other, and as against the principal debtor, are strictly maintained and protected, and if in practice therefore anything is done outside those rights, which is not permitted by the contract in the guarantee, then the whole guarantee will be rendered void, and the bank will not be able to recover from any of the parties who have signed. Over the years, however, building on experience, specially drafted clauses

136 See Appendix I, Q. 48 (September 1981).

have been regularly incorporated to free the banker's hands and to facilitate flexibility coupled with safety.

Death of one joint and several guarantor

Yet a further advantage to the bank is that if the liability were only joint, under the rule of survivorship should one of several joint guarantors die, his liability, and that of his estate would cease, whereas when he and his estate are separately liable, this rule does not apply. Usually to enable it to fix the liability in money terms, the bank will have included a clause in its guarantee form requiring the executors to give notice to the bank of their intention to determine the liability. Where such notice is received, the remaining guarantors would remain liable for any further monies lent in reliance on the guarantee and strictly a new guarantee is not necessary. However, if the account secured is a current account overdrawn, it will be necessary to stop it at the expiration of the notice, to prevent *Clayton's Case* working against the bank for the benefit of the executors, if not the other guarantors.

Notice to determine a joint and several guarantee

Normally, however, in the absence of death, there is a clause incorporated in a joint and several guarantee requiring all such guarantors to give notice of determination before the notice is effective. In practice, if the bank received notice of determination from one joint and several guarantor it would, almost certainly, as a matter of prudence, arrange for an early meeting between all guarantors and the bank, possibly also with the borrowing customer present, so that a new arrangement could be made for the ongoing operation of the account, with a clear and legally enforceable position obtaining, in respect of the liability of the guarantors. In such a case, the bank might rely upon its strict rights and require notice from all guarantors, or it might regard the notice given by the one guarantor as effective in the circumstances. It might for instance be possible to arrange for new security to be provided, perhaps in the form of a fresh guarantee given by the remaining guarantors for monies to be lent in the future on a new account.

Because a notice of determination does not usually take effect until after one month or three months (dependent upon the terms of the form) there is usually plenty of time to rearrange matters so that the borrower is not inconvenienced.

Mental incapacity of a joint and several guarantor

Where the bank receives notice that one of the joint and several guarantors is mentally ill to the extent that he is unable to manage his own affairs, as would undoubtedly be the case if a receiver under a court of protection order had been appointed, then the bank should stop the customer's current account, if overdrawn, to retain the liability of the guarantor and to prevent the operation of the Rule in *Clayton's Case*. In the case of *Bradford Old Bank Ltd* v.

Sutcliffe (1918) there was no clause in the guarantee form giving the bank any added rights in a situation where a guarantor became insane (as the term then was), and this is usually still the prevailing position. Thus, while all guarantee forms deal with what should happen upon the death of one guarantor, they are usually silent as regards the position in the event of mental incapacity.

So, upon notice of the mental incapacity of the guarantor, the customer's account is broken, and a new account is opened for future transactions. It would seem that it is possible to continue to look to the remaining guarantors for the lending on the stopped account and also any fresh lending made on a new account, subject of course to any maximum liability of the guarantee. However, the point has not been tested, and in practice the bank might well feel it safer and prudent to interview the sane guarantors and the customer and to reach a clear and certain situation regarding future advances – possibly with the provision of a new guarantee from the remaining guarantors.

Bankruptcy proceedings involving a joint and several guarantor

Upon learning that a petition has been presented against a joint and several guarantor, or that a bankruptcy order has been made, the bank should stop the customer's account, if it wishes to retain its claim in his estate in bankruptcy. Failure to do so may again make the account subect to the operation of the Rule in *Clayton's Case*, whereby the claim against that guarantor's estate would be lost by subsequent turnover. The only protection would iie if the bank had a clause in its guarantee form similar to that seen in *Westminster Bank Ltd* v. *Cond* (1940).

If the bank decides to prove in the bankruptcy, it may of course do so for the full amount secured by the guarantee document, and in so doing it would not prejudice its right to claim for a similar sum against the other co-guarantor(s). In some situations it might be that the financial standing of the remaining guarantors is such that the bank will be prepared to release the bankrupt's estate and look only to the solvent guarantors, but before doing so it should examine all the surrounding facts carefully.

GUARANTEES BY PARTNERSHIPS

When a bank requires a guarantee from a firm it is its invariable practice to obtain the signature of all the partners in the firm to the guarantee form, which will be drawn to cover their joint and several liability. This overcomes the situation which would apply otherwise, namely that, in law, a partnership is only jointly liable for its debts. However, the position upon the death of one partner would be slightly different even if only a joint guarantee and been taken, for in that event the partner's estate becomes severally liable for the debts of the firm after the payment of his private debts out of the estate assets (s. 9 Partnership Act 1890)

Banks do not accept the signature of one partner as a guarantor on behalf of his firm, although it would be possible to proceed in that way if the partner were authorized in writing by all his partners to give the guarantee. However, it is simpler and safer to obtain the other partners' signatures to the guarantee form.

The only other circumstances in which, possibly, a bank might accept the signature of one partner on behalf of his firm is where it is part of the partnership's normal business to give guarantees, and this is covered in the partnership agreement.

The reason for banks' caution and practice here lies in the wording of s. 5 Partnership Act 1890. This states that:

> Every partner is an agent of the firm and his other partners for the purpose of the business of the partnership; and the acts of every partner who does any act for carrying on in the usual way business of the kind carried on by the firm of which he is a member bind the firm and his partners, unless the partner so acting has in fact no authority to act for the firm in the particular matter, and the person with whom he is dealing either knows that he has no authority, or does not know or believe him to be a partner.

It can be seen from this that a partner has no implied authority to bind a partnership by giving a guarantee, unless it is part of the normal business of that firm.

Where a new partner is introduced he will not be bound by the old guarantee unless he so agrees in writing, perhaps by executing a new guarantee with his co-partners upon joining the firm.

GUARANTEE FOR A PARTNERSHIP

Where a guarantee is taken for the liability of a firm from an outside party, the usual form of bank guarantee form will state that the guarantee will remain binding despite any changes in the composition of the firm, through the retirement of a partner and/or the introduction of another.

From time to time the author has seen some bankers take a guarantee from the partners themselves, when lending to a partnership. This is a dangerous practice, as all partners are fully liable for the debts of the firm, unless one or other is a limited partner, which is rare. There is no advantage in taking such a guarantee, and indeed, where it is limited in amount, the full rights of the bank to recover all the borrowing from the partners could be prejudiced, as this would conflict with the mandate form and the principle that each partner is liable for all partnership debts.

GUARANTEE BY A MINOR

At the time of writing a person under eighteen years of age cannot give a legally enforceable guarantee, and should he do so he cannot even ratify the contract after he has attained his majority (Infants Relief Act 1874, sections 1 and 2). However, the position will be different if the Minors' Contracts Bill (1986) becomes law and readers should refer to Chapter 2 'Minors' in this respect.

GUARANTEES FOR THE BORROWING OF A MINOR OR UNINCORPORATED BODY

If a bank is unwise enough to lend money to a minor, under the present law it will be unable to sue him for recovery if he will not repay voluntarily (s. 1 Infants Relief Act 1874), for the contract is void. Unfortunately, the bank would be no better placed if it had taken a guarantee to secure his liabilities, for there can be no effective guarantee where there is no debt enforceable against the principal debtor, as in such circumstances the guarantor's rights of subrogation would be prejudiced. This unhappy position was realized and suffered by Coutts & Co. in their case, *Coutts & Co.* v. *Browne-Lecky and Others* (1947). The background to this case was that the bank had allowed Brown-Lecky, a minor, to overdraw his bank account, relying on a guarantee given by two persons of mature years. When the bank called upon them to pay and instigated proceedings, they defended, on grounds that they could not be liable for a debt which itself was unenforceable against the borrower. This argument was accepted by the court, where it was said: 'It would certainly seem strange if a contract to make good the debt default or miscarriage of another – which is the classic definition of a guarantee – could be binding where, by statute (in this case the Infants Relief Act 1874), the loan guaranteed is, in turn, made absolutely void'.

This decision created a problem for banks, but it has been overcome by guarantee forms now being drawn in such a way that they constitute not only a contract of guarantee but also an indemnity. The difference, as we have seen, is that under an indemnity the persons signing assume primary responsibility, and so recovery is possible from them even though, in law, it might not be possible to recover from the principal debtor.

This type of clause is also useful when banks lend to unincorporated bodies or associations, as these cannot be sued for recovery of money lent. Again, under the indemnity, the 'guarantors' are legally liable.

However, all this may be different if the Minors Contracts Bill becomes law (see Chapter 2).*

GUARANTEES BY WOMEN

It is an offence under the Sex Discrimination Act 1975 to treat women in any different manner from men on grounds of sex alone, and therefore no special considerations apply if a guarantee is to be taken from a woman.

In *Quinn* v. *Williams Furniture Ltd* (1980) a retailer arranged a credit sale

* Minors Contracts Act 1987 effective from 9 June 1987.

for Mrs Quinn, but insisted on having a guarantee by her husband. It was later admitted that had the other facts been identical, and the hirer been a man, a guarantee would not have been required; the transaction was held to have been an offence under the Sex Discrimination Act 1975.

However, when in a banking situation a guarantee is taken from a woman, the bank should consider carefully whether there is any possibility of undue influence in a situation where it is to secure the liabilities of her husband or the liabilities of a limited company or partnership with which he is associated. This consideration, however, is one which could equally apply in the converse situation and what the bank needs to take into account, in making its decision, is whether there is any possibility of duress or undue influence, or whether there is any doubt about the woman understanding completely the purport of the document she is to sign and the liability which she is assuming. If independent advice is not taken, and duress or undue influence is present, then the guarantee would be voidable and the bank could experience difficulty when it called upon the guarantor to pay.

However, in those cases where the intending woman guarantor is a business woman or a professional woman, or perhaps even a director or secretary of a limited company, *and* it is quite clear that she is well aware of what she is doing, perhaps because she is active in the business, and not merely a nominee, then the bank need not insist on independent advice.

In other instances, where it might be felt that there is a lack of financial acumen and an over-readiness to follow the husband's request, then independent advice should be insisted upon. If for any reason the prospective guarantor will not take independent advice, despite strong recommendations to that effect from the bank, then this fact should be carefully noted in the bank's records, for, should the guarantor seek later to escape liability if called upon to pay, on grounds that she was not independently advised, then the bank will be able to show to the court that it did everything possible on its part to ensure that she was guided independently.

Even so, there would be no certainty that the bank would succeed in court, and it is clear from an old ruling that protection of the guarantor ranks high in the minds of the judiciary. In *Bank of Montreal* v. *Stuart* (1911), a Privy Council decision, the female guarantor successfully defended the bank's action. In judgment it was said:

> The evidence is clear that in all these transactions Mrs Stuart, who was a confirmed invalid, acted in passive obedience to her husband's directions. She had no will of her own. Nor had she any means of forming an independent judgment even if she had desired to do so. . . . It may well be argued that when there is evidence of overpowering influence and the transaction brought about is immoderate and irrational, as it was in the present case, proof of undue influence is complete. However that may be, it seems to their Lordships that in this case there is enough, according to the recognized doctrine of Courts of Equity, to entitle Mrs Stuart to relief.

A solicitor had been present at the meeting when Mrs Stuart had signed the guarantee, but he was there acting for the bank and Mr Stuart, and he was himself associated with the company whose borrowing was being secured, as he was an officer and shareholder. Of him, the court felt that he should have approached Mrs Stuart and then, if she had not accepted his advice, he should have approached Mr Stuart and insisted to him that Mrs Stuart was independently advised by her own solictor. The court then said:

> If that was an impossibility owing to the implicit confidence which Mrs Stuart reposed in her husband, the solicitor ought to have retired from the business altogether and told the bank why he did so.

GUARANTEE BY A LIMITED COMPANY

In every case, when taking a guarantee from a limited company, the bank should examine the company's memorandum of association to see whether or not power is given for the company to give guarantees. While a trading company has an implied power to borrow money and to give security for its own business, a power to give guarantees cannot be implied, even in a group situation where there is a parent – subsidiary relationship. The wording in the memorandum should be precise and clear, and in the event of doubt the bank might ask the company to amend its memorandum. However, it was held in *Re Friary Holroyd and Healy's Breweries Ltd* (1922) that the phrase 'to subsidize or assist' in the memorandum was sufficiently clear to cover the giving of a guarantee.[137] It could be that a bank would prefer, even today, not to rely on such wording, and certainly it should not rely on the general words, which usually, in an all-embracing phrase at the end of the objects clause in the memorandum, purport to enable the company to do all or any thing which is 'desirable incidental or conducive to the performance or attainment of the objects of the company'.

Next, the articles of association must be examined to ascertain whether there is any limitation as to amount or restriction on the manner in which the directors may act. Guarantee obligations must be included in the calculation of the amount presently 'borrowed' by a company and if the directors' borrowing powers are limited then there is a potential danger here if the granting of a guarantee would cause that amount to be exceeded. Remedial action will then be necessary as has been discussed in detail in Chapter 9.

Usually, unless there are specific provisions in the company's articles of association, the guarantee may be executed either under hand or under seal. Some banks prefer guarantees to be sealed, and do not take a resolution in support of that action, relying on the Rule in *Turquand's Case*. Others are happy for a guarantee to be signed by a director(s) and/or secretary in accordance with a resolution passed by the board. A copy of the resolution is

137 See Appendix I, Q. 64 (September 1983).

filed with the guarantee document, and if this method is used then the resolution should refer to the specific form of guarantee which was produced at the board meeting, as this obviates any possibility of it later being claimed that the director or secretary who signed the guarantee incurred liabilities which were greater than those considered to be involved by the board.

There are, however, circumstances where, even if the guarantee is under seal, some banks still require a resolution. In particular this arises in connection with the problems associated with the doctrine of commercial justification, which were discussed on page 223. Such a resolution passed by the board and authorizing the giving of a guarantee will also refer to the fact that the directors have considered the transaction and agree that it is one which is in the interests of the company. The object of this is to facilitate reliance on the decision in *Charterbridge Corporation* v. *Lloyds Bank Ltd* (1969), should the guarantee ever be attacked by an outside party, such as a liquidator.

Interested directors

Another aspect requiring thought, when taking a guarantee from a company, is the position of the directors who attend at the board meeting and vote on the resolution, for the bank needs to consider whether they might be personally interested in the giving of the security on behalf of the company and, if so, what restrictions, if any, apply under the articles of association in that case. The problems involved and the decision in *Victors Ltd* v. *Lingard and Others* (1927) were discussed in detail in Chapter 9, to which the student reader is recommended to refer again at this point.

Finally, for the avoidance of any doubt, it is stressed that guarantees given by limited companies do *not* require registration at Companies Registration Office, but certain securities lodged in support of a guarantee liability do, if they are charges over items mentioned in section 396 of the Companies Act 1985.

TAKING THE SECURITY[138]

Security step A: enquiries as to the guarantor's means   Despite the difficulties which might arise later in realizing a guarantee, at the outset the bank will wish to be reasonably confident that the guarantor has the means to pay, if he is called upon to do so. If he is a customer in his own right his financial position is likely to be fairly well known to the bank, and from the conduct of his account and other information available, it should be relatively easy for the bank to form an accurate assessment. However, where he is not known it will be necessary for the bank to ascertain the name of the guarantor's bankers and to make an enquiry of them, by way of a status

138 See Appendix I, Q. 33 (April 1980).

opinion request, as to his general standing and sufficiency as a guarantor for a specified amount. In the case of joint and several guarantors the amount mentioned in the enquiry should be the full amount of the guarantee, and no apportionment should be made, as the bank may need to look to that one guarantor for the full amount of the liability. It would however be usual to mention that the enquiry is on the person concerned as a joint and several guarantor.

A reply to a status enquiry is usually recorded on a card or in the security register. The opinion is of course updated from time to time, as the bank will need to ensure that this is not weakening, for should it do so then the bank might need to review its whole approach to the advance.[139] Usually, updating is carried out on a six-monthly or twelve-monthly basis, based on diary notes raised at the outset.

Security step B: independent legal advice The circumstances under which separate advice is necessary have been discussed earlier and if the bank feels that the person giving the security should have the benefit of this, it must be obtained from his or her own solicitors, not from the bank's solicitors. Some banks ask the solicitor concerned to attest the guarantee document with words to the effect that he has explained the purport of the document to his client who understood it, although the point might alternatively be covered in correspondence which will be retained with the guarantee.

If, despite the bank's advice that the guarantor should take legal advice he or she is not prepared to do so, then the bank must consider whether it is prepared to proceed with the lending, or, if it is already committed, all it can do is to make careful written notes of the circumstances and ensure that these are kept, so that should a defence be raised, in due course, based on the absence of legal advice, the bank will be able to show that the purport of the document and the liability was explained to the guarantor, that separate independent legal advice was strongly advised, but that despite this, the guarantor would not approach his/her own solicitor.

Security step C: execution of guarantee form Guarantee forms should normally be executed on the bank's own premises or at the guarantor's own solicitor's offices. Certainly they should never be sent out to the borrowing customer or to the guarantor requesting either of them to arrange for signature, for considerable difficulties could arise if reliance on the guarantee became necessary. The position is slightly different, of course, where the guarantee document is to be sealed by a limited company, in which case it will be sent to the company directors or secretary, and the company's seal will be impressed and witnessed by its officers in accordance with the company's

---

139 See Appendix I, Q. 63 (September 1983).

Articles of Association. Usually, however, when it is signed at the bank, the form will be witnessed by a bank official, who will know the identity of the person signing it; some banks make a practice of always making an interview note of the circumstances so that these can be recalled later if necessary, and evidenced to a court.

If it is impracticable for the guarantor to call at the account holding branch then the guarantee form may be sent to the guarantor's own bank, with a letter of request that the bank should witness the signing of the guarantee by their own customer. The guarantee form is then returned to the bank which is to be secured.

Naturally, the full names of the party or parties whose liabilities are to be secured should be inserted before the form is signed, as should also the figure in respect of any maximum amount. Often the guarantor will be asked to initial, or sign, against this figure to indicate his acceptance.

The standard form of bank guarantee should never be amended, except under the special guidance of the bank's solicitors in exceptional circumstances. The danger of adding to a guarantee form, or amending it, was illustrated in *Westminster Bank Ltd* v. *Sassoon* (1926). There Mrs Sassoon, the guarantor, wished to limited the liability as to time, and so a clause was added to the guarantee document stating 'This guarantee will expire on 30 June 1925'. The account of the borrower was overdrawn on that date so the account was stopped and in October 1925 the guarantor was called upon to pay. However, she then claimed that she had no liability at all after 30 June 1925 and defended the bank's legal action. The bank claimed that the intention behind the amendment to its standard form had only been to safeguard Mrs Sassoon from being liable for any advances made after 30 June, and that was why they had stopped the account, preserving the liability as at that date. Fortunately, because of surrounding evidence the bank won its case, but there was a very clear warning here of the danger of amending charge forms, as the wording used can be dangerous and capable of more than one interpretation.

DETERMINATION OF GUARANTEE

Demand by bank

As a guarantor is only secondarily liable, when a borrowing is unsatisfactory it is usual to call upon the customer to repay in the first instance, and then, if he defaults, upon the guarantor(s). If the guarantee is for an unlimited sum, then the amount called in will be the amount owing by the customer at that date, including all accrued interest and charges. However, if the guarantee is limited in amount, then that limitation must not be exceeded in the notice (Fig. 15.2). Joint and several guarantors will each be asked to pay the full amount of the guarantee. A clause in the guarantee form usually allows the

```
TO _____  _____ DATE_____

OF _____
```

We, Practice Bank plc hereby DEMAND payment of the sum of £ _____ ,
(words) (_____)
FORTHWITH, being the amount due to us by you on a guarantee dated _____
in respect of the liabilities to the Bank of _____

For and on behalf of
Practice Bank plc

```
_____
```
MANAGER

Fig.15.2   *Call-up notice for guarantee*

service of notice by post, to the last known address, and often the notice is deemed to be effective, even if it is undelivered or returned to the bank.

Once a guarantee has been called in, no further debit transactions should be allowed on the accounts secured, as these could vitiate the effect of the notice. Should legal action against a guarantor be necessary it must be remembered that this will be a statute-barred six years after demand has been made, unless, in the meantime, the right of action has been revived by a written acknowledgement, or a part payment under the guarantee (*Bradford Old Bank Ltd* v. *Sutcliffe* (1918).

Any payments received from a guarantor are usually placed to a suspense account, or a securities realized account as it is sometimes called, to preserve the bank's full claim against its borrowing customer in the event of his bankruptcy (*Re Sass* (1986)).[140]

Where a guarantor does not discharge his liability at once, interest will run against him at the rate specified in the charge form, and to the extent that *this* interest is eventually paid a guarantor may be entitled to a bank interest certificate for taxation purposes, although whether this will enable him to obtain tax relief will depend upon Finance Act legislation current at the time. The guarantor is not entitled to a certificate in respect of interest debited to the principal's debtor's account, as this becomes part of the principal capital sum immediately it is added (*Holder* v. *Inland Revenue* (1932)).

140 See Appendix I, Q. 35 (April 1980).

Notice by guarantor or his personal representative

It is usual for the guarantee form to include a clause whereby the bank is entitled to a period of written notice before fixing the guarantor's liability at his own request. The period is commonly one month, or three months, and it enables the bank to continue the operation of the account in the meantime. The customer can be interviewed, and, hopefully, arrangements can be made for alternative security to be lodged. However, it is most important to take a diary note, as soon as notice of determination is received, so that the customer's account is stopped after the requisite time has elapsed. At that time, if other arrangements have not been made, a new account should be opened which will be operated in credit. At the expiry of the notice, the bank should write to the guarantor advising him of the amount of his liability, although no doubt it will have acknowledged his notice earlier and then reminded him that the exact extent of his obligation was not capable of quantification until the notice had run its requisite time.

A guarantor may provide cash at any time in respect of his liability, and, if received, this should be held in a suspense account, even though, if his notice is running, the full extent of his liability may not be apparent. Where the guarantee is for a limited amount tendered in full, the monies should still be placed to a suspense account.

When a guarantor has given notice in writing to determine his liability, it is not necessary for the bank itself to call upon him to meet his liability, during the period while the guarantor's notice is running. If therefore the bank merely treats the guarantor's notice as a means of crystallizing the amount recoverable under the guarantee upon the expiry of the notice then the guarantor remains liable for this sum, and the bank can serve notice upon him to pay this crystallized amount at any time within the next six years. Occasionally a guarantor has sought to avoid liability on grounds that as the bank did not call upon him to pay before his notice expired he has been discharged (*National Westminster Bank Ltd* v. *French* (1977)), but this is not so.

Death of guarantor

Notice of the death of a guarantor, not the fact of death, would in common law determine the guarantee liability, but there is usually a clause in the guarantee form requiring written notice from the legal personal representatives acting, to determine the liability, and again, often one or three months' notice is necessary. Despite this, in practice, efforts are usually made with the executors and the customer to reach an arrangement sooner, but the bank will preserve its right to look to the executors to settle the liability out of the realizations of the estate assets. Again, any monies received should be held on a suspense account. The position is different, however, where supporting security is held behind the guarantee, as it is then considered advisable to stop the customer's account as soon as notice of the guarantor's death is received.[141]

If the guarantee is a joint and several guarantee, and only one guarantor has died, there is frequently a clause retaining the deceased's liability, and allowing the bank to continue to look to the other guarantors for future advances. However, reliance is not always placed on this clause, and a new guarantee from the remaining parties may be taken for fresh advances made on a new account, dependent upon the circumstances.

Insolvency or mental incapicity of a guarantor

Upon learning that a petition or bankruptcy order has been made against a guarantor, the customer's account should be stopped. The same applies if the guarantor is a limited company, and a petition for liquidation is presented, a winding up order is made, or an administrative receiver is appointed under a debenture. Similarly if a petition for an administration order is presented, or an administration order is made by the court against a guarantor company, the account secured must be stopped. If a voluntary arrangement is proposed and a supervisor is appointed, again the account should be stopped.

The bank would then lodge its claim for the amount guaranteed at that date, and would place its dividend to a separate suspense account. Meanwhile, a new account could be operated for the customer, against any remaining security or additional security, although clearly an early interview with the customer will be essential.

Similar principles apply in the event of the mental incapacity of the guarantor, and the customer's account should again be stopped. It is important for the bank to be certain that the guarantor is incapable of conducting his own affairs, either by obtaining verification from his medical advisers or by seeing that an appointment of a receiver under a court of protection order has been made, or that an enduring power of attorney has been certified by the court as applicable to the circumstances obtaining.

Death of a joint account holder

Where one party to a joint account dies, and the account is overdrawn, any guarantee will not be a good continuing security for the liabilities of the remaining debtor, and the joint account should be stopped to preserve the bank's rights against the estate of the deceased party, against the remaining party to the account and against the guarantor. Whether the bank would wish to call in the guarantee at that point in time will depend upon the overall background and situation, and whether the bank expects to be repaid by the deceased's executors from his estate.

---

141 See Appendix I, Q. 56 (September 1982).

GUARANTOR'S RIGHTS OF SUBROGATION AND CONTRIBUTION

Where a guarantor makes full repayment of the customer's debt (as happens when he is an unlimited guarantor, or when the amount of a limited guarantee is the same or more than the total facilities afforded to the customer), then he is entitled to take over all the securities lodged with the bank by the customer (s. 5 Mercantile Law Amendment Act 1856). This is called his right of subrogation. A guarantor is also entitled to take over the principal debtor's securities if he voluntarily pays in full a debt which is in excess of the amount specified in the guarantee – that is he pays more than he needs to.

Where the guarantee is joint and several, and contributions have been made by several parties, or where separate guarantees are held, or even where monies have been recovered under a guarantee and also through security lodged by a third party, not necessarily a guarantor, then each party will have his own right of subrogation. This could mean that it will be difficult to calculate in monetary terms the extent of those rights, and also, perhaps because of arrangements between the parties themselves, known or unknown to the bank, matters will be complex. In such circumstances the bank will usually prefer to receive an authority, in writing, from all parties concerned, instructing it as to how the customer's security should be transferred. The important thing is ensure that these securities are not released to the customer or just to one paying guarantor.[142]

If, exceptionally, the paying guarantors or sureties are prepared to allow the bank to release the security to the customer then their agreement in writing should be obtained to prevent any future dispute.

Similarly, where a customer's debt has been repaid in full, and security remains from a co-guarantor, or co-surety, the paying guarantor's rights will extend to this security by way of his rights of contribution.[143] Thus, the security lodged by the other parties should not be released, and again it is desirable for the bank to obtain the specific authority in writing of all interested parties, as to the disposal or transfer of the security.[144] If there is any dispute, the bank should not become involved, and should not prejudice any party's rights. In the last resort, in the absence of agreement, the security may be lodged in court.

DISCHARGE OF THE GUARANTEE DOCUMENT

Occasionally, having paid up under a guarantee, the guarantor will request the delivery of the guarantee document to him, but it is more normal for this to be retained by the bank, in view of the many rights which still remain under the various clauses – for instance the clause enabling the bank to return to the

---

142   See Appendix I, Q. 35 (April 1980).
143   See Appendix I, Q. 62 (September 1983).
144   See Appendix I, Q. 35 (April 1980).

guarantor, if it transpires there has been a preference in the form of reductions to the customer's borrowing which have relieved or reduced the guarantor's liability.

Sometimes a bank will be prepared to give a simple receipt for the amount received or to supply a copy of the guarantee document or even a letter of acknowledgement of monies paid, although in the latter event legal advice may well be taken beforehand.

Usually, however, the guarantee form remains with the bank, undefaced although the entries are struck out of the bank's security registers. Many banks in fact have a clause in their forms stating that the guarantee remains the bank's property at all times, and if so, this helps prevent argument.

REPAYMENT BY PRINCIPAL DEBTOR

When the borrower has repaid his debt and there are no other liabilities outstanding which would be secured by the guarantee, the guarantee can be set aside, if it is not intended to look to the security at any time in the future.[145] This would be particularly important if the guarantee had been given only to cover a specific lending, for to retain it in the bank's records could lead to misunderstandings in the future and the bank might think it was secured when the opposite was the case.

Often, however, where the principal debtor is a regular borrower, and where the guarantee is expressed as a continuing security for all past present and future liabilities, then it will be retained in the security register and will cover future advances.

Some banks might feel it desirable and equitable to remind the guarantor of his continuing obligations, if there is a delay between one lending being repaid and another one taken, and at least this approach avoids any misconceptions and future disputes.

PREFERENCES

Claims that the bank and guarantor have been preferred sometimes arise in bankruptcy or liquidation situations, the trustee, liquidator or administrator bringing proceedings pursuant to ss. 340/341 in bankruptcy and ss. 239/240 (Companies Act 1985) in liquidation or company administrations.

It is, of course, so easy for a customer who is in financial difficulties to use what limited funds he has to reduce his borrowing, so as to relieve his guarantor, before his failure, which he sees coming, but an alert insolvency practitioner will soon spot this from the trend in the account (see *Re M. Kushler Ltd* (1943)). These matters have been discussed fully on pp. 181-183 and 256-257.

145   See Appendix I, Q. 40 (September 1980).

CHAPTER 16

Specialist Securities

AGRICULTURAL CHARGES

Under the provisions of the Agricultural Credits Act 1928, it is possible for a farmer to give security over his farming stock and other agricultural assets, but only to a bank. Moreover, the security can only be made available for his own borrowing or his personal liabilities as a farming partner; it may not be used to support any guarantees. However, if the bank has undertaken a bond or guarantee liability on behalf of the farmer then it could look to an agricultural charge to recoup any monies it had to pay.

An agricultural charge may be either a fixed charge or a floating charge. If fixed, it will specify certain farming stock and other agricultural assets belonging to the farmer at the date of the charge and scheduled in the charge form. Even so, in the case of livestock, any progeny which may be born after the date of the charge, or any agricultural plant which is substituted for the plant specified in the charge, will be caught by the fixed charge (s. 5(3)).

If the charge is a floating charge over farming stock and agricultural assets generally, these will not be scheduled but will invariably be set out in a clause in the charge form, taking wording from the act. Section 5(4) states 'the property affected by a floating charge shall be the farming stock and other agricultural assets from time to time belonging to the farmer, or such part thereof as may be mentioned in the charge'.

It is also possible for the charge to be drawn as a combination of a fixed charge and a floating charge:

The Agricultural Credits Act 1928, s. 5(7), defines farming stock as:

Crops or horticultural produce, whether growing or severed from the land, and after severance whether subjected to any treatment or process of manufacture or not; livestock, including poultry and bees, and the produce and progeny thereof; any other agricultural or horticultural produce whether subjected to any treatment or process of manufacture or not; seeds and manures; agricultural vehicles, machinery, and other plant; agricultural tenant's fixtures and other agricultural fixtures which a tenant is by law authorized to remove. 'Other agricultural assets' means a tenant's right to compensation under the Agricultural Holdings Act 1923 for improvements, damage by game, disturbance or otherwise and any other tenant right.

It should be noted therefore that the farm land itself, whether it be freehold or leasehold, cannot be charged in this way, and to create a security a mortgage is necessary.

Also, the alert reader will have seen that, unlike the floating charge which can be created by a limited company under the Companies Acts, the agricultural charge, whether fixed or floating, does not capture debts due to the farmer. Consequently, monies due from the Milk Marketing Board, and non-farming assets such as life policies, also need to be charged separately.

The Act defines a farmer as any person, other than an incorporate company or society, who either as tenant or owner of an agricultural holding cultivates the holding for profit. Agriculture is said to include horticulture and the use of land for any purpose of husbandry inclusive of keeping or breeding livestock, poultry or bees, and the growth of fruit, vegetables and the like.

Priorities
Under the provisions of s. 8, the priority of agricultural charges ranks as follows:

(*a*) In relation to one another, the time at which the first is registered at the Agricultural Credits Department of the Land Charges Department determines the priority.

(*b*) If a floating charge has been given to a bank, any instrument creating a fixed charge on any property comprised in the floating charge will be void as regards the property caught by the floating charge. Moreover, a bill of sale covering assets encompassed by the floating charge is void to that extent.

(*c*) Where a farmer has given a mortgage over farm land which he owns, perhaps to an outside lender such as an insurance company or finance house, and later executes an agricultural charge to his bank over his crops and farming stock, the bank's rights under the agricultural charge over the crops have priority over those of the mortgagee of the land, whatever the dates upon which the charges were given.

(*d*) Section 8(7) states that an agricultural charge shall be no protection in respect of property included in the charge, which but for the charge would have been liable for distress for rent, taxes or rates. Distress is the right of the landlord as creditor to enter into the property and seize and sell assets to recover monies owed to him.

Under s. 8(5), if a farmer who has given an agricultural charge has a bankruptcy order made against him on a petition presented within three months of the execution of the charge, and he is later adjudged bankrupt, then, unless it is proved that he was solvent immediately after creating the charge,

> the amount which but for this provision would have been secured by the charge shall be reduced by the amount of the sum so owing to the bank immediately prior to the giving of the charge, but without prejudice to the bank's right to enforce any other security for that debt or to claim payment thereof as an unsecured debt.

It should be noted that *Clayton's Case* does not operate in favour of the bank in respect of an overdraft existing at the time of creation of the charge, as there is no case law similar to the decisions in *Re Thomas Mortimer* (1925) and in *Re Yeovil Glove Co. Ltd* (1964) which refer only to a floating charge given by a limited company and s. 245 Insolvency Act 1986. To illustrate this: if Farmer Giles's current account were overdrawn £10 000 on 1 January when he gave his bank an agricultural charge and a bankruptcy order were made against him on 4 April based on a petition presented on 21 February, the agricultural charge would only secure £2500 if the borrowing had increased to £12 500 by the date of the bankruptcy order. The only exception would be if it could be proved that the farmer was solvent immediately *after* the giving of the charge, which seems unlikely. The bank would of course be able to prove as an unsecured creditor in the bankruptcy in respect of the remainder of the overdraft (£10 000), being the balance at the date when the agricultural charge (fixed or floating) was created.

Advantages and disadvantages

An agricultural charge is easy and cheap to execute, with few formalities, and is a particularly suitable security for tenant farmers to give, as they might have no other assets, most of their wealth being tied up in their farm. Also, it is a useful supporting security for a bank to take from a farmer who has got into financial difficulties, even if he owns the freehold of his land.

A very useful facet of the security is that it enables a bank to act quickly in the event of problems arising on the farm, which could put the value of the security in jeopardy, as under the powers in the charge, if the farmer should die, become mentally incapacitated, or have a bankruptcy order made against him a receiver can be appointed quickly and he will be able to take over control. This can have considerable practical advantages for all parties concerned, not only the bank, especially if there are no other near relatives who would be able to carry on managing a business which by its very nature needs close daily attention.

An important technical advantage of the agricultural floating charge is that if a subsequent fixed charge is created it will not have priority over the agricultural floating charge, and provided a farmer does not have a petition in bankruptcy presented within three months of giving the security to the bank the bank's position is safe.

However, there are naturally disadvantages, the biggest of which is that when reliance needs to be placed upon the charge by the appointment of a receiver, it will invariably be found that the farm has become run down and the assets have been dissipated, so that the value of the charge will be very much less than expected. This should not really be a surprise, for a moment's thought will show that where the bank needs to appoint a receiver to recover its lending the background is likely to be one where the farming customer has been making losses, and with strained finances he has been unable to maintain the numbers of his livestock or cultivate his land as well as might have been hoped. Indeed, he could have been taking animals to market for sale, so as to be able to raise cash to pay his pressing creditors.

Another factor on the 'down-side' is that the costs involved in an agricultural receivership can be heavy, for it will be necessary for the receiver to continue to run the farm for a while and he will have outgoings in the form of wages and also need to appoint specialized valuers and managers to ensure that the assets are properly sold.

Additionally, it must be remembered that the farming stock can be subject to distress action by a landlord to recover unpaid rent, or can suffer a levy carried out by a bailiff on behalf of a judgment creditor. If these steps are taken before the intervention of the bank, in the form of the appointment of the receiver, all or some of the farm stock will be lost. Also, preferential creditors must be paid in priority to the bank out of realizations, after a receiver has been appointed.[146]

Another problem at the outset, when the charge is taken, is that while there is no official publication of the creation of the charge (indeed it is unlawful under the Agricultural Credits Act 1928 to publish any list of agricultural charges, and the names of farmers who have created them), the event can become known in the locality, and in consequence a farmer might find that his supplies of foodstuffs, or his credit, are cut off. Moreover, if he is in severe financial difficulties his creditors might take bankruptcy proceedings to render the agricultural charge void.

The bank's charge form

If the charge is a fixed charge, the charge form should be completed by scheduling the assets concerned, but where a floating agricultural charge is taken the form merely refers to the 'farming stock and the other agricultural assets which belong to the farmer from time to time'. As these are defined in the Agricultural Credits Act 1928, they become the subject of the security.

It is usual to find a clause in the charge form stating that the floating charge will become a fixed charge upon certain events, such as the making of a bankruptcy order against the farmer, the death or mental incapacity of the farmer, or the dissolution of the partnership in which he is a member. Other incidents set out in the form which would trigger this effect are a composition or arrangement made by the farmer with his creditors, a distress or execution levied against the farming stock, or the cessation of farming by the farmer. Often the bank's form will also state that the failure of the farmer to observe and perform any covenants in the charge form will be an event which will crystallize the floating charge.

The most important 'trigger clause', however, is that referring to the service of a notice upon the farmer stating that one of these events has happened, or simply the service of notice to repay. When the farmer defaults after such

146 See Appendix I, Q. 44 (April 1981).

demand has been made, the charge forthwith becomes fixed and a receiver may be appointed. Sometimes the charge form will have been drafted in such a way that service of a further notice in writing is necessary, after the farmer has failed to repay, this second notice advising the farmer that the floating charge has crystallized and has become a fixed charge.

The covenants usually mentioned in the form are those in respect of the agreement to insure all the farming stock caught by the charge with a reputable insurance company acceptable to the bank. Here the farmer undertakes to pay all premiums regularly and to pay any monies received under his policy to the bank.

Another covenant is that the farmer will keep the property and farming assets in a good and proper state of repair and condition, and that he will undertake to manage his farm in a husbandmanlike fashion. He will agree that whenever he sells any farming stock subject to the agricultural charge he will pay the proceeds into his bank account and/or apply those proceeds to buying further farming stock or agricultural assets by way of replacement. In this way, in theory, the value of the charge should be maintained.

Taking the security[147]

The bank's standard form of fixed or floating agricultural charge must be signed by the farmer or farmers who are borrowing from the bank and it is important to ensure, early on, that these people are identified properly. Usually the audited accounts are the best guide, but sometimes enquiries will have to be made, for the arrangement in the family could be loose, as for example where a son has succeeded in business to his father, or where he might recently have joined in partnership with his father. It does not necessarily follow, for instance, that if the title to the land is in one name, the farming business is only being carried out by that person. Only if the charge is a fixed one will it be necesary to schedule the assets caught, and otherwise the charge will simply need dating and witnessing by the bank officer, or the farmer's solicitor, if independent advice has been taken.

As we have seen, agricultural charges rank in priority in accordance with the time that they are registered at the Agricultural Credits Department at the Land Charges Department. It is usual, therefore, before the bank's form of charge is signed, for a search to be made on Form AC6 to see if any prior charges have been created. If one is revealed an office copy of the entry can be obtained by using Form AC5. However, no period of priority is granted by the search, during which time the bank's charge could be taken and registered, and therefore it will be necessary always to search *after* the bank's charge has been registered to ensure no other bank has intervened. This is why some banks only search afterwards and not beforehand.

The bank's own agricultural charge must be registered within seven working

147 See Appendix I, Q. 44 (April 1981).

days of its execution by using Form AC1 and, as this form requires the signature of the farmer and the bank, it is important to remember to obtain the farmer's signature, conveniently at the time when the charge form is signed. Form AC1 when submitted to the agricultural credits register must show the amount secured, and this can be stated as the balance outstanding on any loan account, or, if the borrowing is on current account the security clerk may simply write in the words 'a fluctuating current account'. All addresses must be shown. Should the farmer later commence farming at a new address, it will be necessary to search against that address, and to register the bank's charge additionally, using Form AC7.

As regards insurance, the farmer should be asked to produce his insurance policy covering the farming stock and assets, as the bank will wish to ensure that cover is adequate and with a reputable company. Notice is then given by the bank to the insurance company concerned and an acknowledgement of the bank's interest is obtained. It is of course important to check that premiums have been paid to date, and, preferably, arrangements should be made for the farmer to pay future premiums by way of standing order or direct debit.

The valuation of an agricultural charge can be carried out by examining the assets scheduled in the farmer's audited accounts, care being taken not to include debtors or life policies and to make allowance for any preferential creditors. However, a better and more up-to-date assessment can be obtained by walking the farm[148] with the farmer and abstracting what is known as a 'farmer's statement of means' or 'farmer's balance sheet' (Fig. 16.1). If this exercise is carried out at the same time each year a useful comparison can be obtained, as obviously, with certain types of farming, because of the seasonal nature of the trade it could be confusing to abstract figures at different seasons. In any event, much will depend upon the honesty of the farmer, as his assets can easily be transferred out of the bank's reach and the proceeds of sale used to pay other creditors. Moreover, the farmer could, if he were unscrupulous, 'borrow' animals and livestock so that upon a visit to the farm it would appear to be better stocked than in reality it is. Fortunately, such events are rare.

Realization of the security

The bank realizes its security by exercising its right to appoint a receiver, when any of the events mentioned in the charge form giving rise to such a right arise. Usually, the bank will serve notice to repay, and upon the farmer defaulting, a receiver, who will probably be an accountant or valuer having a specialist knowledge of farming matters, will be appointed by a letter of appointment.

The receiver is empowered to take possession of all the farming assets and to sell them, or to carry on, or manage the business. By the terms of the

148 See Appendix I, Q. 63 (September 1983).

PRACTICE BANK plc
FARMER'S STATEMENT OF MEANS

NAME OF FARMER George Giles _____ DATE 4th April 19..

Green Farm _____

LAND OWNED (Acres) _____ LAND RENTED (Acres) 150 _____

(cost per annum) £ _____ 6,200 _____

FARMING STOCK	Number	Item	Value	
LIVE:	92	COWS	x £500 =	46,000
	32	STIRKS	x £250 =	8,000
	1	BULL	x £650 =	650
	33	CALVES	x £50 =	1,650
				56,300
STOCKS:	900 BALES OF HAY x £1			900
	500 TONS OF SILAGE x £22			11,000
	WHEAT			—
	BARLEY			—
				11,900
MACHINERY:	TRACTOR, WAGONS, MILKING			26,400
			sub-total	94,600

OTHER ASSETS   MONIES DUE FROM DEBTORS:

	Milk Marketing Board	7,000
	Others	8,500
		15,500

TOTAL ASSETS   110,100

LESS AMOUNTS DUE

Agricultural Mortgage Corporation	NIL
Trade Suppliers	16,300
Bank	72,000
Hire-Purchase	3,000
Others	NIL
	91,300

CAPITAL   £18,800

Fig.16.1   *Farmer's statement of means*

charge form, he is usually deemed to be the agent of the farmer, but despite this his prime duty is to obtain repayment for the bank and he can disregard any claims made by the unsecured creditors, although he will need to consider what rights the preferential creditors have, if any. It should be noted carefully that, before a receiver sells any farming assets, there must be an interval of five clear days after he has been appointed as receiver, unless the agricultural charge form used by the bank states otherwise (s. 6(1)(b) Agricultural Credits Act 1928).

Understandably, the receiver need only sell sufficient farming stock to be able to repay the bank, after meeting the costs involved and his remuneration, and should a surplus arise this can be paid over to the farmer. The receiver is under no obligation to sell any particular asset or assets and it is important to ensure that the farmer himself does not become too closely associated with the receiver and able to dominate his operations. Nevertheless, the receiver may well value the farmer's knowledge and experience, and each situation must be treated on its merits, albeit with care.

Release of charge

When the bank has been repaid, or when in the ordinary conduct of an account it is requested to release an agricultural charge, Form AC3 should be filed at the agricultural credits register. It is usual for the agricultural charge form itself to be retained by the bank and placed with its old or obsolete security forms. If a receiver has been appointed, it is possible that he may request a release, and if so, a simple letter or document to this effect can be given, although it is not in fact essential. The insurance company should be advised that the bank is no longer interested in the policy.

GOODS AND PRODUCE AS SECURITY

Produce loans are usually only encountered in large commercial towns and ports, and even there only at branches of banks which are known by tradition to specialise in such lendings. In this way local expertise is built up, and the branch concerned has a regular knowledge of the people engaged in the trade and is able to make a sound judgment that it is dealing with an undoubted party.

Advantages and disadvantages

The main attraction of a produce advance to the lending banker is that it is self-liquidating, as when the goods are sold the sale proceeds are received into the account, thus repaying the borrowing. As the bank will normally undertake such advances only for undoubted customers it is rare to meet any problem associated with the ownership of the goods and so complications with title, which can be experienced with other types of security, are avoided. Nevertheless, a risk does exist that if the customer himself is not entitled to the property which is pledged then the bank cannot obtain a good security.[149]

149 See Appendix I, Q. 52 (April 1982).

An attraction of the security is that the charging formalities are easy and few costs are incurred. However, control on an ongoing basis can involve detailed paperwork, and the branch needs to keep careful records in respect of each consignment of goods; for instance, ledgers will have to be maintained showing the location of the goods and it will be necessary to take regular opinions on the warehousekeepers and the purchasers, to ensure that while the goods are stored on behalf of the bank, and later are released for sale, full trust can be placed in the parties involved. Even so, where a warehouseman's charges have not been paid, he will be entitled to a lien over the goods and this will be superior to the security of the bank, unless exceptionally, he has agreed to waive his right of lien in the bank's favour.

There are other disadvantages associated with this type of security, the most important perhaps being that accurate valuation of many goods is difficult, although if the prices are shown in a financial or trade journal then control is naturally facilitated. Some goods might be perishable, and in those cases the bank could suffer a heavy loss if the customer, or for that matter the bank in a realization situation, were unable to dispose of the produce. Understandably, the prices of some produce fluctuate quite widely and although the lending banker will take an adequate margin of security against the amount lent, in a particularly weak market this margin can soon be eroded. Other disadvantages associated with the security are the costs incurred for insurance and storage, and while these are of course mainly the customer's responsibility, should he be unable to meet them then the bank will need to pay them itself in order to protect its security.

Sometimes, because of the nature of the trade or the product, the goods will be stored in a warehouse on the customer's own property and clearly in such a situation if the customer has a key he might be able to gain access to the goods, or he might be able to obtain a duplicate key, even though the original has been lodged at the bank. As we have seen, however, these types of loans are granted only to undoubted customers and although fraud can be facilitated by such arrangements, fortunately it is rarely encountered.

It is this question of trust and the possibility of fraud which is crucial to the whole advance and the safety of the security, for at some point in time the actual physical possession of the goods will move out of the bank's control and the goods will be with the customer or a third party. Clearly, if fraud is intended, this is the stage at which it can most easily be carried out, and while the technical risks can be protected by the party to whom the goods are released being asked to undertake that he then holds them in trust for the bank, the fact remains that an unscrupulous person could sell them and abscond with the proceeds.

In our chapter on debentures and floating charges we considered the problems created by the rights of unpaid vendors to retain title to goods which have not been paid for, and we examined the extension of this principle through the Romalpa decision and other cases. The same problems can be encountered with security stored in a warehouse and pledged to the bank, thus rendering the security of considerably less value than thought, and perhaps even worthless.

Sometimes, where the goods in security are stored in a warehouse which also contains similar goods, and should the bank's security not have been segregated, it can be very difficult to identify the bank's security. Upon the failure of the business, disputing claims can arise as to which goods belong to the secured creditor and which belong to the trustee in bankruptcy or liquidation – or even possibly an investor client of the customer as might happen with wines etc.

Types of charge
There are three methods by which goods and produce can be charged as security, and while the first two methods are mentioned here for sake of completeness it is by way of the third method, the pledge, that banks invariably proceed.

The other methods are mortgage and hypothecation. Under a mortgage, the legal property in the goods is transferred to the mortgagee by a deed, but no delivery, actual or constructive, of the property need take place. In fact, the mortgage arises under the Bills of Sale Acts and by virtue of s. 9 of the 1882 Act such a mortgage must be strictly in the prescribed form to be valid and must be registered within seven days of its execution. However, in view of the measure of publicity associated with this form of security and the stigma which the granting of a bill of sale has acquired over the years, a charge by way of mortgage over goods is not acceptable to customers.

Under hypothecation neither actual nor constructive possession of the goods is obtained by the lender, nor is there any transfer of title to the property. Hypothecation must not be confused with a pledge, although frequently the term is used loosely to apply to that method of charge.

As stated, banks take a charge over goods and produce by way of a pledge, and this arises when possession of the goods, actual or constructive, is delivered to the pledgee. Usually the legal transaction is evidenced by a written document, but strictly the actual pledge is created when the lender agrees to advance monies against the security of the goods. Frequently a general letter of pledge is used, but this makes it clear that the security does not arise until there has been an actual or constructive delivery of the goods to the lender and it obviates the need for further documents in respect of future transactions.

Charge form
Usual clauses seen in a bank's form are those stating that the security is a general letter of pledge which will cover all present and future goods that are delivered into the possession of the bank or its agents, and indicating that the pledge will arise whether the goods pass physically or only 'constructively' by

way of documents of title. The pledge will incorporate the usual continuing security clause, to overcome the operation of the Rule in *Clayton's Case* in respect of advances on current account, although invariably produce advances are made on loan account, often with a separate loan being raised in respect of each consignment. The pledge will be expressed to cover the customer's past, present and future liabilities to the bank, whether actual or contingent, and will cover the bank's interest charges and expenses associated with the conduct of the account, and the costs involved in relation to the protection of the security at any time. The bank will be given a power to sell its goods in security, usually after the customer has failed to repay upon receiving notice calling in the advance. The pledgor will covenant with the bank that he will pay all insurance premiums and storage charges in connection with the goods or produce and any rent charges due to warehouse-keepers or other persons; he will agree that the bank is not to be responsible for any loss which might arise in any dealing with the goods at any time, whether such loss arises before or after the bank intervenes to sell on its own behalf.

Trust receipt

It must be remembered at all times that despite the wide terms of the pledge letter it is the actual or constructive possession of the goods themselves which is important. Consequently, when it is necessary for the goods to be released by the bank, so that a sale can go ahead, the customer will be asked to execute a further document, known as the trust receipt or trust letter. The purpose of this used to be the technical one of overcoming the reputed ownership provisions in s. 38 Bankruptcy Act 1914. However, under the Insolvency Act 1986 the assets falling into the debtor's estate are more simply defined as being 'all assets belonging to or vested in the bankrupt at the commencement of the bankruptcy' (s. 283), so clearly assets held on trust are excluded. Hence it might be argued that the trust receipt procedure is no longer necessary, but that said, most banks have retained its use. Consequently, should the customer have a bankruptcy order made against him while he is in possession of the goods, his trustee in bankruptcy will not now be able to claim and realize them. Moreover, a person's position as a trustee is not automatically revoked by the making of a bankruptcy order and the intervention of bankruptcy creates no technical problem. In practice, of course, it might make the bank wish rapidly to assume direct control of the goods in case they, or the proceeds of sale, are dissipated wrongly!

The terms of a trust letter will incorporate an acknowledgement by the customer that the bank has security rights over the goods and over the proceeds of sale when they arise. The customer will then undertake to hold the goods and the sale proceeds in trust for the bank and also any insurance monies which might arise under any policies covering loss. He will undertake to pay the proceeds of sale and insurance monies to the bank. As trustee, he will covenant to store the goods carefully and adequately, and keep them insured in their full value with a reputable insurance company and to pay premiums on the due dates. He will agree to return any goods or produce which are not sold to the bank or the warehouse keepers on the bank's request or authority. If the bank requires the monies which will arise out of the sales to be paid direct to the bank then the trustee will agree to arrange for authorities addressed to the buyers so authorising and arranging matters.

It will be appreciated that it is at the point in the transaction when the bank has to lose physical control of the goods that the risk of fraud or misfeasance is greatest and it is for this reason that produce advances are considered only suitable for entirely trustworthy customers.

An example of the sort of problem which can arise where the customer is dishonest and acts in breach of his trust can be seen from the case of *Lloyds Bank Ltd* v. *Bank of America National Trust and Savings Association* (1938).[150] There Lloyds Bank had lent £57 000 to its customer Strauss & Co. Ltd on a produce loan; it took its usual form of security, later releasing documents of title to the goods against the customer's trust receipt. The customer, then acting fraudulently, lodged the documents of title with the Bank of America National Trust and Savings Association as a means of obtaining further finance. Shortly afterwards the company failed, was placed in liquidation, and Lloyds Bank sued Bank of America for return of the goods or their value which they claimed was their security. Unhappily for them their action was unsuccessful, the Court of Appeal ruling that under the terms relating to the release of the goods on trust the customer had been made a mercantile agent as defined within s. 2(1) Factors Act 1889 and thus Bank of Amercia in dealing with them in good faith had been able to obtain a valid pledge, and this ranked in priority to Lloyds Bank's charge. In giving judgment it was said that, while every aspect of commercial dealing cannot be proof against the possible results of frauds, there was no doubt that the business methods which were used in this and similar cases were very convenient and would continue to be used, because the whole basis of commerce and business rests upon honesty and good faith, and it is rare that dishonesty or bad faith intervenes and undermines established practices.

However, the case serves to underline the fundamental concept of the produce loan that the customer must be of an undoubted standing, and that the bank should not be lulled into a sense of false security simply because transactions of this nature have been carried on for a long time. Thus, if the customer's financial state is changing and there is any sign of pressure, it will be prudent to consider whether future requests for produce advances or release of the goods into the customer's hands as trustee can be considered on exactly the same basis as previously.

150 See Appendix I, Q. 52 (April 1982).

Security steps

The formalities necessary to take the general letter of pledge and to perfect it are few and simple.[151] The bank's standard document is dated, signed by the customer and witnessed by a bank officer. The goods themselves, if they are to be lodged with the bank (which is unusual), are taken and placed carefully in the bank's strongroom. More usually, they will be located in a warehouse and will be retained there, but in the bank's name, with a warehouse warrant issued in favour of the bank or a warehouse receipt endorsed in the bank's favour. The bank will give attention to the insurance question and the policy should be examined and will need to cover the risks associated with the particular produce. The bank will wish to see the last premium receipt and to be assured that cover is adequate. As usual, careful diary notes will be taken to ensure that any future premiums due are properly paid without delay and that the premium receipt at that time is again exhibited to the bank. The bank will give notice to the insurance company of its interest and an acknowledgement in writing will be obtained, usually on a duplicate of the notice. Clearly, it will be important to know that the warehouse keeper is reputable, and status opinions will be taken. The bank will wish to ensure that any charges due to the warehouseman have been paid to date and receipts must be exhibited. If regular rent payments are agreed, then careful diary notes are necessary to ensure that receipts for the rent are shown to the bank when payment has been made.

Control of produce advance

It is essential with produce lending for the bank to keep detailed records concerning each lending, relating to each consignment or commodity. Usually lendings are made on a loan account or separate loan accounts and in this way it is possible to ensure that the particular advance is repaid when the goods are sold.

Careful valuation is necessary and an adequate margin is needed at all times, and this means that the security clerk should take into account changes in market prices for the commodity and the possibility of the goods perishing.

Inspection of the goods themselves, when they are held in warehouses, must be made from time to time by a bank representative, even though satisfactory status reports are held on the warehousemen, the customer and the buyers. If at all possible, these inspections should be made without any advance warning, as in that way, should there be any attempt at fraud, the ability to cover up will be avoided. Occasionally, inspections have been the start of the revelation of a widespread fraud, but fortunately in practice such occurrences are rare and commerce proceeds on the basis of trust.

---

151 See Appendix I, Q. 52 (April 1982).

Other documents encountered in produce loans

It is beyond the scope of this book to deal in depth with the detail of foreign trade or the many and varied situations which can arise where imports and exports are carried out under letters of credit or other arrangements. However, mention of the following documents which could be encountered in produce loan situations will be helpful.

Warehouse-keepers' warrants Warehouse-keepers' warrants are of two types, namely those which are issued under private Acts of Parliament and those that are issued outside of such an Act and which are not documents of title. In the case of goods represented by warehouse-keepers' warrants not issued under an Act of Parliament, it is usual, when the goods become the subject of the bank's pledge, for a new warrant to be made out in favour of the bank. This is done by forwarding the dock or warehouse-keepers' warrant to the warehouse-keeper with a transfer order.

In the case of warehouse-keepers' warrants issued under an Act of Parliament, reference is necesary to the terms of the statute such as the Trafford Park Act 1904 or the Port of London (Consolidation) Act 1920. The question of whether the title to the goods can pass by transfer of the warrant is complex, but in the case of the last-mentioned statute it appears that the warrants are virtually fully negotiable because a transferee can obtain a better title than the person passing the document to him.

Warehouse-keepers' receipts These documents are merely receipts stating that goods have been received and are held in the warehouse; they are not documents of title, nor can they be transferred by endorsement. Consequently once again, it is necessary for transfer orders or delivery orders to be made out, authorising the warehouse-keeper to hold the goods or deliver them to a named third party.

Delivery orders These are the authorities addressed to the warehouse-keeper authorizing the goods which are stored in the bank's name in the warehouse to be delivered to the customer, after he has executed the trust letter. Consequently, the warehouse-keeper has authority to release the goods which he is holding for the bank, and the customer can proceed to make arrangements with his purchaser. It is unusual for a delivery order to be issued by the bank in favour of the customer's purchaser, although in special circumstances, where the customer is completely undoubted and extremely highly valued, the bank may agree, exceptionally, to such a request, particularly where the purchase monies are handed over when the goods are delivered, and payment is made by way of a bank draft or certified cheque.

Bill of lading In respect of goods which have been imported the bank will be particularly concerned with the document of title to the goods which is known as the bill of lading. The other two important documents are the invoices and the insurance policy, although other papers may be required under import rules and any exchange control regulations which are in force at the time.

The bill of lading is issued by the shipowner or his agent and this evidences the receipt on board of the goods and their shipment. It confirms the contract under which the goods are to be transported and it is a document of title to the goods or produce while they are at sea, and until such time as they are delivered to the consignee or parties taking from him under his order or assignment. Usually bills of lading are drawn in sets of three, and, to prevent problems which would arise from them all being lost at the same time, they are mailed separately. The goods are however delivered to the person who first presents a valid bill of lading and therafter the duplicate bills of lading becomes void. When the bank takes a pledge over goods 'constructively', it will need to have a full set of clean on-board bills of lading drawn to order, endorsed in blank, and marked 'Freight paid'. Under special circumstances the bank might be prepared to relax its requirement that it receive 'clean' bills and prepaid freight, although indemnities might well be called for to allow matters to proceed. A bill of lading is described as 'clean' when there are no qualifying clauses inserted in it which would in any way indicate that the goods were not in a proper state or order when they were received on board for shipment. If there are such qualifying reservations the bill of lading is described as 'foul' or 'dirty'.

A bill of lading is quasi-negotiable and is transferable if it is drawn in favour of a named person 'or to his order or assigns', although in the absence of such wording a shipowner will not be able to deliver the goods to any person other than the named consignee with safety. Bills of lading are transferred by endorsement and delivery or simply by delivery where the title is blank. The act of transferring the bill of lading constitutes the delivery of the goods, but usually the bank will ensure that no other person has a copy of the bill of lading which might perhaps be used to obtain possession of the goods. A bill of lading is described as only being quasi-negotiable because a holder for value does not obtain a good title from the transferor if the transferor's title is defective, whereas under full negotiability the transferee acting in good faith and without notice of defect in the title of the transferor would acquire a better title than the person from whom he took. However, a bona fide holder for value acquires the right to receive the goods free from the seller's right of lien, as might be the case, for instance, where the original seller of the goods had not received payment from his purchaser, but a third party who had acquired rights to the goods subsequently could not be prevented by the original unpaid seller from taking delivery. In such a case the original unpaid seller would have no right of lien or right of stoppage *in transitu*, although the shipper would have a right of lien over the goods until all the freight charges had been met.

Supplier's invoice This document is issued and signed by the supplier of the goods and it will show the nature and type of the goods and their value. The price basis could be shown as c.i.f. or f.o.b., etc.

Insurance policy The insurance company will issue its policy in favour of the shipper and if the bank is concerned in the transaction the policy must be endorsed by the shipper in blank, so that the bank will have recourse to the insurance policy proceeds, should there be any loss or damage to the goods or produce while they are in transit. Clearly, it will be important for the bank to read the detailed terms of the policy to ensure that they meet expected requirements and that the cover is adequate. Sometimes a bank is willing to accept an insurance certificate instead of an insurance policy, although an insurance certificate will not be accepted by the insurance company as evidence of entitlement to payment under the policy, and in the event of a claim arising it is necessary for the actual policy to be produced.

Examples of produce loan situations

Produce stored in a warehouse on behalf of the bank Where a situation such as this is entailed and the bank has hired the use of the warehouse with the object of storing the goods in its own name, clearly the situation is as good as it can be. Naturally the standing of the warehouse-keeper will be important and the general locality and quality of the warehouse, but these are matters which can be checked to the bank's satisfaction.

Produce stored in a public warehouse Again in these cases the location of the property and the report on the warehouseman are critical. The goods will be stored in the name of the bank and a warehouse-keeper's warrant will be issued in the bank's favour. Should an earlier warrant have been issued in the customer's name, it should be endorsed in favour of the bank and the bank will exchange this for a warrant in its own name, although in this way the bank technically becomes liable for warehouse-keeper's charges. In practice, however, it would wish to ensure that these were paid to protect its security.

Produce stored at the customer's own warehouse or factory Such a state of affairs is very unsatisfactory from the bank's point of view and should be avoided if at all possible. However, where the customer is unwilling, or perhaps unable to remove the goods which are pledged, at least they should be stored separately from other items belonging to the customer and they should be segregated in a separate room or shed which must be locked with the bank's name marked on the door. The bank should have control over the room by possession of the only key and the bank should make a note of the circumstances in its internal records to evidence the transaction. It would be prudent for a schedule of the goods or produce stored on the bank's behalf to be drawn up, and signed by the customer, for retention by the bank.

Goods or produce in the hands of a third party   The goods or produce which are pledged to the bank might, in certain circumstances, be in the possession of a party such as a dyer or packer or processer, and if so, it will be necessary for a written acknowledgement to be obtained from that party that he is holding the goods as bailee for the bank. As a prerequisite, the third party concerned is certain to require a letter from the bank's customer so that he can give the undertaking to the bank. This undertaking and acknowledgement should include a clause that he holds the goods free from lien, for if not, and if there are any debts due by the customer to the processer or packer then the bank, in the absence of such a clause, could meet problems if the third party tried to exercise his right of lien and retained the goods until such time as he were paid.

We have seen that where the goods were previously held by a warehouse-keeper on behalf of the customer, a new warrant will be issued in favour of the bank. Usually the original warrant in favour of the customer is endorsed and a letter is sent to the warehouse-keeper together with a form of transfer so that the new warrant can be issued. Delays should not arise, but there might be circumstances where the bank would wish to have an acknowledgement from the warehouse-keeper that he holds the goods as bailee for the bank in the meantime.

Goods or produce under import and export trade   Where the bank grants produce advances for an importer or an exporter it is rare for the physical possession of the commodity to come into the bank's possession or into the possession of a warehouse-keeper on its behalf, and usually possession arises through constructive delivery only. In fact this is a much more common method of obtaining security over produce and goods, particularly when the goods are held abroad or are in transit at sea.

The two most common ways used in banking situations arise from the use of the documents of title. Under s. 1(4) Factors Act 1889 documents of title are defined as including any bill of lading, dock warrant, warehouse-keeper's certificate, or warrant or order for the delivery of goods or any other document used in the ordinary course of business as proof of possession or control of the goods, or authorizing, or purporting to authorize, either by endorsement or by delivery, the possessor of the document to transfer or receive goods thereby requested.

In dealing with documents of title so defined, the requirements of s. 4 Bills of Sale Act 1878 relating to registration are expressly excluded and hence no problems or reluctance on the part of the customer to proceed are encountered in that regard.

The constructive delivery arises where the documents of title are delivered to the bank and in respect of bills of lading it is accepted that, as they are the only documents of title, if they are pledged then the goods themselves are also pledged.

CHARGES OVER INTERESTS IN WILLS, TRUSTS AND SETTLEMENTS

Advantages and disadvantages

Although not often taken as the primary security at the outset of an advance, except where the mortgagor has nothing else to offer, a charge over an interest in a will, settlement or trust can be a useful security. The amount involved can be substantial, and to that extent an effective mortgage of the interest, however it arises, can enable the lending banker to advance funds at a level to which he might not have been prepared to go against less valuable, but more usual, types of security. Also, where in a risk situation the bank is looking for anything which will bolster up its position, then a charge over an interest in a will or trust could make the difference between an ultimate loss and full recovery. However, as the beneficiary's interest – which may be in respect of a capital sum or income – is usually an equitable one, the bank's security will be equitable also, and it will therefore be subject to all the disadvantages of that type of charge. Moreover, as the law concerning trusts is complex, there is a greater risk of a technical irregularity in the background. For instance, where the interest arises through a will, or an intestate estate, it will be important for the bank to ensure that the beneficiary's interest has not been, nor is likely to be, challenged by other members of his family under the provisions of the Inheritance (Provision for Family and Dependants) Act 1975.

The value of the security may be difficult to assess accurately, and it could depreciate if the trust is badly administered. For instance, where the charge is over the income derived under a trust, obviously there is also a risk that the amount paid could fall, dependent on the nature of the capital assets concerned, or on interest rates, and to this extent such a charge is a poor security.

In particular, where the charge is over a capital fund in a trust which will only pass to the beneficiary at some time in the future, it can suffer from the same risks, but also might become non-existent if the beneficiary's interest depends on him surviving the life tenant, who is deriving the benefits for the time being, and the beneficiary pre-deceases the life tenant. This type of interest is known as a reversionary interest, and the ultimate beneficiary is called the remainderman.

It must be noted that if the trust is a protective trust, a beneficiary is precluded from charging his interest or selling it, and then the giving of a charge is totally unsuitable. Indeed, in such a case the beneficiary would lose all rights to the property; the need for legal advice can therefore be seen as paramount in many instances.

Mortgage by a remainderman[152]

Most charges taken by banks over interests in trusts are in fact over those of a remainderman under a reversionary interest, and in all such cases it is vital for the bank to determine at the outset whether the remainderman has an absolute interest or only a contingent interest. In the first case, the bank will ultimately benefit from its security, but where the remainderman's interest is only contingent no property will pass to him or the bank if he fails to survive the life tenant. In the latter case, the bank must insist on adequate life cover as additional security.

To take and perfect the security, the bank will firstly have to examine the trust instrument, almost certainly with the benefit of professional advice from a solicitor, to ensure that there is a chargeable interest and that there is no restriction on its being mortgaged. The nature of the estate will need very careful investigation, and the market valuation of any properties or other assets will need to be assessed.[153] This can be complicated, and a professional valuation may be necessary. It could be that the trustees will have power to vary the assets in the trust from time to time, and in consequence the bank may need to renew this formality on a regular basis. Another factor of interest to the bank where the trust derives from a deceased's estate is whether all the inheritance tax falling due to be paid has been met and whether therefore the value of the remainderman's interest is capable of being accurately quantified. In some cases the tax position can be very complex and further deductions from an assessment of a remainderman's interest are possible.

In examining the nature of the interest which is to be charged and its value it will be vital for the bank to ensure that there are no restrictions in the trust upon the remainderman charging his interest, and of course also to enquire about any prior charges which might already have been created in favour of third parties, or the trustees themselves, who might have advanced money.

Enquiries will then need to be made as to the age and health of the life tenant, for in this way it will be possible to estimate approximately how long it might be before the remainderman receives his benefit.[154] Indeed even after the security has been taken, regular enquiries to see if the life tenant is still living will be necessary.

Assuming after all these enquiries that the bank is prepared to proceed, the bank's standard charge form should be executed and witnessed in the presence of a bank official or the customer's solicitor. The form rarely includes any clauses which are special to this type of security and the schedule is easily completed by a simple reference to the interest in the will or trust, suitably identified as to the parties and its date. Written notice of the charge should then be given to the trustees, and their acknowledgement in writing should be obtained, for under s. 137 Law of Property Act 1925 the priority of charges

152   See Appendix I, Q. 36 (April 1980).
153   See Appendix I, Q. 63 (September 1983).
154   See Appendix I, Q. 63 (September 1983).

will rank in the order of time in which written notice is first received by the trustees. The notice will request the trustees to undertake to pay all monies which become due to the remainderman to the bank. Some trustees may have power to appoint a trust corporation to receive notices, and this may be endorsed on the trust instrument. In any event, the trustees should be asked if they have nominated a trust corporation to act and, if so, notice of the bank's charge should of course be given to the trust corporation and the usual acknowledgement should be obtained from the corporation. It will of course be important to have ascertained that the trustees are men of integrity and, if they are unknown, status opinions on them from their bankers should be obtained.

Realization

If the bank needs to realize a mortgage over a reversionary interest then the bank's power of sale must have arisen, and usually this will come about upon the customer failing to repay his borrowing on demand. As with all bank charges the need to wait three months is avoided, as s. 103 Law of Property Act 1925 is excluded. It is possible sometimes for the interest to be sold, usually by auction, on a specialist market in London, but the price obtained is often discounted and is unlikely to reflect the full pecuniary interest of the remainderman; because of this, the security should be written down and valued cautiously for advance purposes at the outset, with due allowance being made for the costs of realization involved.

When a purchaser is found the sale will take effect by way of an assignment to him of the bank's charge, and a special document will have to be drawn up by solicitors to effect this. The bank will hand its mortgage, unreleased, to the purchaser and it should then give notice to the trustees of the transfer it has effected.

Release

If a charge over a reversionary interest is no longer required by the bank, the charge form can be released under seal, and given to the chargor, or, if he wishes, it can be sent to the trustees, with an advice note that the bank is no longer secured.

If, however, the trust falls in, so that the benefit passes to the remainderman, the bank will receive the monies or assets from the trustees and will give a receipt for them. The charge form may then be set aside, but the bank should consider the possible need to obtain a mortgage from the beneficiary over the property as the legal estate will now vest in him; further advice from the bank's solicitors may be necessary in the particular circumstances.

Mortgage by a life tenant

There are obvious disadvantages in taking a mortgage from a life tenant, as it would become valueless on his death. However, if for special reasons the bank decides to proceed, it will invariably require a life policy to be taken out as additional cover, giving further protection.

In taking the security it will again be necessary to examine the trust deed in detail, and professional advice from a solicitor may well be necessary. The value of the life interest will be quantified, as far as this is possible, and the bank's standard charge form will be executed, under which the customer will assign his interest to the bank. The bank will then give notice in writing of the charge to the trustees, and will seek their written acknowledgement. An enquiry should be made of the trustees, as to whether they have notice of any other charges, or have made an advance themselves against the trust property. The bank will also ask for an undertaking that all future payments due to the beneficiary will be paid direct to the bank, and in all these respects procedures follow identically with a charge over a reversionary interest. It is therefore mainly in the valuation aspect that the security differs, the interest of a life tenant usually being a right to occupy or use property during his own lifetime, or to derive the income from it. In this last respect there could be some attraction to a bank in taking a charge, if only as a means of ensuring that monies, paid to the customer on a regular basis by the trustees, are received straight into the bank account.

Realizing the security

To realize the mortgage, the bank will need to ensure that it has an effective power of sale, and this is achieved by calling upon the mortgagor to repay his debt. However, a sale of a life interest could prove very difficult to achieve, as it is likely that only a speculator would be prepared to pay much, remembering that the income would cease upon the death of the life tenant. An offer to assign any additional life-policy cover could make a sale more likely. Again, a sale by auction on the specialist market would be the way ahead. The only other alternative for the bank would be to receive the income paid for the remainder of the life tenant's life, meanwhile not allowing his account to operate, so that some reduction, or possibly even full repayment, is eventually achieved.

Release

When the bank no longer requires its security, the charge form may be released under seal, and then given to the life tenant or the trustees, the latter in either event being told that the bank is no longer interested in the security.

Where a life tenant dies and the income ceases, the charge may simply be placed to obsolete documents within the branch.

ASSIGNMENT OF DEBTS AND CONTRACTS

These securities are only encountered occasionally, as bankers will usually look for more acceptable items. However, an assignment of a debt due from a specified debtor or an assignment of the benefits to be derived under a contract can be of benefit in the right circumstances. For example, when a building contractor wishes to borrow and has no other security to offer, he could assign his contract with the party for whom he is to carry out the work, and in this way, provided he meets his part of the deal and the employer is financially sound, the monies due will pass then to the bank. A charge over a contract is also used where bankers are lending to a farmer who sells his milk output to the Milk Marketing Board, and receives a monthly payment in settlement.[155] To ensure that these monies are sent direct to the bank a charge over the Milk Marketing Board's contract is taken. Another situation could be in a bridge-over, where it could be possible to take a charge over the proceeds of a property sale after contracts have been exchanged. Surprisingly, the method is hardly ever employed in that area.

Where a charge is taken over an existing specific debt or rights under a contract, it will protect the bank against a claim by a trustee in bankruptcy to those monies, unless of course it is technically defective or the trustee can show that the granting of the charge was a preference of the bank. However, a charge expressed to be given over book debts generally would be void unless registered under the Bills of Sale Act 1878. As the reader will know, banks do not take securities which need registering there, as it is thought that the stigma would damage a customer's name and credit.

Advantages and disadvantages

The security is easy to take, as the usual form of a charge is short, with few clauses, and will be worded in such a way as to create an absolute assignment, and not an assignment by way of charge only. There are also few formalities necessary in order to perfect the security.

However, the assignment can only cover a debt which is rightly due to the customer, and, while ostensibly the amount concerned might appear definite, in practice it can become the subject of counter-claims by the debtor, who might exercise a right of set-off, or allege bad workmanship or breaches of contract. Not infrequently, therefore, disputes arise between the customer and the party owing the money (the debtor), and litigation becomes necessary to recover the monies; in such cases, it can be a long time before a decision and judgment is reached, and by then the debtor's financial position may have worsened, making recovery unlikely. Moreover, the risk of the debtor's inability to pay exists, even if there is no dispute and this means that his financial strength is obviously an important factor in assessing and relying on the security. Consequently, a good banker's opinion on the debtor is an essential part of the protective security steps.

155 See Appendix I, Q. 60 (April 1983).

Legal assignments of existing debts

To comply with s. 136 Law of Property Act 1925 a legal assignment over a debt already due to the customer must be in writing, signed by the assignor. Thereafter the bank must give written notice to the debtor.

Equitable assignment of debts

An equitable assignment of an *existing* debt is unlikely to be acceptable to the bank, but it would arise in those instances where the assignment is not in writing, or where notice has not been given to the debtor.

An equitable assignment suffers from inherent disadvantages, the main one being that the bank cannot sue the debtor in its own name, and in consequence it has to rely on its customer's support in any action in the courts to recover the monies due, by bringing the proceedings in his name. If he will not agree to this then it will be necessary to join him in, as a co-defendant with the debtor.

There can be no legal assignment of a future debt, but it is possible to charge monies which will become due under a contract at a future date, and, as such, an assignment takes effect as an equitable charge, upon which an action for specific performance can be brought. Obviously, if the monies are not due at the time of the charge then the bank will be dependent upon the customer carrying through his part of the contract or deal, so that the monies become payable in due course.

Security steps

Where a bank takes an assignment over a contract, it is to the monies due under that contract to which the bank looks. It is therefore prudent for a copy of the contract to be lodged, and for this to be perused carefully, so that the bank's rights as assignee are known. The copy contract will also show any rights which the third party might have, in the event of default by the customer in performing his part of the contract, or whether any monies due can be retained for a period. In some cases the contract, might specify that it is only assignable after permission has been granted by the third party.

The bank's standard form of legal assignment of a debt or contract is then completed, identifying the debt or contract rights by reference to the parties involved. The date of the contract and its number should be inserted if they are known, as is the case with an assignment over a Milk Marketing Board contract. The charge form is then dated, signed by the customer, and witnessed by a bank officer or the customer's own solicitor, if independent advice is taken.

As soon as possible thereafter the bank should give notice, on the bank's standard form, in duplicate to the debtor, and he should be asked to acknowledge the notice by signing and returning the copy. In addition he will be asked to confirm the amount of the debt and to say whether he has any set-off himself, at the time of receiving notice. The bank will also ask the debtor to state whether he has had notice of any prior charge and will ask him to given an understanding to pay all monies due to the assignor to the bank as assignee.

If the debtor is unknown a banker's opinion should be obtained on him as to his ability to pay and his general trustworthiness; consequently, it is necessary to ascertain the identity of his bankers. This status report will be renewed from time to time, if the period involved is long.

While it may not always be appropriate to consider the question of insurance, with some contracts – for example a building contract – it will be important to ensure that the builder is adequately covered by insurance and that notice of its interest in the policy is given to the company concerned by the bank.

Notice to the debtor

The reasons for giving notice are both legal and practical, for clearly the debtor should be made aware of the assignment so that he will pay monies to the bank. From the legal point of view, written notice is necessary to enable the bank, should it wish, to sue the debtor in its own name, as legal assignee, under s. 136 Law of Property Act 1925. If notice in writing is not given, however, the assignment takes effect only as an equitable assignment. More importantly, priorities are determined by the time when the debtor receives notice, and if the bank did not give notice then it could rank behind another assignee, who takes his security without notice of the bank's charge and gives his notice to the debtor first.

Another reason for the formality is that as against the assignee the debtor can only exercise his rights of set-off or counter-claims as they exist at the time when the notice is received. Thus he cannot set off any claims which arise subsequently against the monies due in respect of the assignment.

If notice is not given to the debtor, and if he acquires rights of set-off against the customer after the date of the assignment, he will be enabled to exercise those rights in equity as against the assignee. Also, if notice is not given to the debtor then the bank will not be able to claim against him if in error he pays the monies due direct to the customer, for understandably no right can fairly be claimed against him, in respect of a transaction of which he was completely unaware. However, if the debtor disregards the notice and still pays the customer and not the bank as assignee then the bank could sue the debtor and recover the funds paid away.

Assignments by limited companies

An assignment of a debt granted by a limited company will be given under seal or under hand by directors authorised in accordance with the company's memorandum and articles of association. Such a charge must be registered within twenty-one days of its creation, pursuant to s. 395 Companies Act

1985, as otherwise it will be void against a subsequently appointed liquidator, administrator or the company's creditors.

The leading case on this subject is *Re Kent and Sussex Sawmills Ltd* (1947). In this the bank's company customer had a contract with a Government department to supply and cut timber. The bank became concerned for its lending, but agreed to continue the facility, provided monies due to the company were paid direct to the company's bank account. A short letter was written by the company to the Government department saying:

> With reference to the above-mentioned contract, we hereby authorize you to remit all monies due hereunder direct to this company's account at Westminster Bank Ltd, Crowborough, whose receipt shall be your sufficient discharge. These instructions are to be regarded as irrevocable unless the said bank should consent to their cancellation in writing, and are intended to cover any extension of the contract in excess of 30 000 tons if such should occur.

The bank forwarded the letter to the department and obtained an acknowledgement. A year later the company entered into another contract and precisely the same steps were taken. In 1946 the company went into liquidation at which time monies were due to it under the two contracts. The bank claimed these funds, but the liquidator disputed its rights, and the matter was settled by the court. It held that the two letters constituted charges on the company's book debts, and as such should have been registered pursuant to (as it then was) the Companies Act 1929. As they had not been, the charges were void for want of registration at Companies Registration Office. The bank lost £30 000, due under the defective assignment.

However, in *Siebe Gorman* v. *Barclays Bank Ltd* (1978) it was held that an absolute assignment was not a mortgage with an equity of redemption, and as title had passed absolutely, registration was not necessary. Despite this, banks continue to ensure that assignments of debts and contracts by a limited company are registered at Companies Registration Office. Indeed, they go to these lengths when a company charges a credit balance in one of its bank accounts as security, or gives the bank a lien or letter of set-off over such monies, just in case a liquidator should challenge the bank's rights to retain monies in such an account. This applies even where monies are lodged specifically to cover a contingent liability, which might, for example, arise under a bond which the bank has entered into on their or another party's behalf.

Irrevocable authority to a solicitor to give his undertaking

When a customer's solicitor is acting for him, and monies will be obtained and become payable by the solicitor to the customer, it is possible for the bank to ensure that those funds come to the bank by obtaining the customer's irrevocable authority in writing addressed to the solicitor, authorizing him to pay the monies to the bank. This letter should usually be taken in duplicate, one copy being retained by the branch, so that the original, in the form of the instructions to the solicitors, can be forwarded as constituting their client's instructions to give an undertaking to pay those monies to the bank. Such an instruction takes effect as an equitable assignment, if the monies are not yet payable, or a legal assignment, if the debt already exists, and they are good as security against a trustee in bankruptcy, although it might be necessary to argue the point with him!

Release

Upon the monies being received from the debtor, the charge form may be cancelled and placed with the bank's obsolete documents. If, for some reason, the security is no longer required before the monies are paid, then the charge must be reassigned by the bank and the debtor should be informed that the bank is no longer the assignee. If the assignment has been given by a limited company then it will be necessary for the company to remove the entry at Companies Registration Office by filing the usual memorandum of satisfaction on Form 403(a).

Realization

As we have seen, a legal assignment enables the bank to sue the debtor in its own name, and recovery can be achieved only by negotiation, legal proceedings and enforcement of a judgment if matters go that far. Clearly, therefore, realization can be costly and in the final analysis much will depend upon the identity of the debtor and his ability to pay, and whether he has any good grounds for counter-claim or set-off against the customer himself, or, under the contract, is entitled to retain funds for a specified period, during which he can see whether the work carried out is entirely satisfactory.

In the case of an equitable assignment, the bank would need to have the co-operation of its customer, or join him in proceedings, so that it could sue in his name. This might increase costs, but the same legal processes as with a legal assignment would then be followed.

Past Examination Questions
Set by the Institute of Bankers

1. Today, Monday 21 April, you receive in the morning post a garnishee order made on 18 April naming your customer Percy Wilde as the judgment debtor and attaching all monies due by the bank to him. This is the first intimation of the garnishee that you have had. The judgment creditor is named as A. B. Limited and the debt is for £1,892.17, plus £15.20 costs.

Percy Wilde's current account is credit £427.11 and a copy of his account for the last few weeks, with narratives, is shown below.

P. Wilde

Date		Dr.	Cr.		Balance
1 April	Balance fwd.			Dr.	33.10
2 April	Cheque		98.40	Cr.	65.30
9 April	Jones	17.02		Cr.	48.28
10 April	At Town Branch		111.17	Cr.	159.45
	Brown	32.28		Cr.	127.17
11 April	Cheque		201.01	Cr.	328.18
14 April	Taylor	131.07		Cr.	97.11
18 April	Cash		230.00	Cr.	427.11

In this morning's in-clearings are two cheques drawn by Percy Wilde, both dated 14 April. The first is for £110 in favour of A. B. Limited and the second is for £40 drawn under his cheque card in favour of Tony Hilton & Co. There is also a bank giro credit for £200, comprising cash £100 and a cheque for £100, paid in at your Town Branch on 17 April.

What action would you take? Give full reasons for your answer.   [17]

(April 1980)

2. Twelve months ago you opened a joint deposit account for Patricia Bradly and Peter Smith. The bank's usual form of mandate was signed, incorporating joint and several liability and instructions that withdrawals should only be allowed against the signatures of both parties. The account was opened with a transfer from Patricia Bradly's current account which was already maintained at your branch, and subsequently the only transactions have been credits, in the form of cash, received over the counter.

Miss Bradly explained, when the joint account was opened, that Mr Smith was her fiancé and that the deposit account was a 'savings' account to assist them to set up home when they married. You took no further reference on Mr Smith at that time.

Miss Bradly has now called to see you, and says that her engagement was broken off three months ago, that Peter Smith has now married somebody else, and she has lost contact with him. She says that all the funds in the joint account have been provided by herself, and she asks you to transfer the balance of £1050 to her current account to enable her to issue a cheque to a travel agent, as she is taking a long holiday abroad to recover from her experience.

(*a*) How would you deal with her request? Give reasons for your answer.
[11]

(*b*) Would your approach be different, if, when the account was opened, you had omitted to take a mandate? [3]

(*c*) Would your approach be different if all the entries in the deposit account had been by way of internal transfer from Miss Bradly's current account? [2]

[Total marks for question – 16]
(*April 1980*)

3. Two months ago your customer, Christopher Robbings, was admitted to a mental hospital; shortly afterwards you received a Court of Protection order referring to him, and appointing his son Harold Robbings as receiver. The order referred only to his current account, which was credit £1502, and enabled you to obtain a discharge from the receiver for this sum. Upon Harrold Robbings' instructions you transferred the balance to an account opened in his name styled 'Harrold Robbings – receiver for Christopher Robbings'. Christopher Robbings also had a deposit account credit £10 000, and items in safe custody at the branch.

Today, you received a letter from Harold Robbings' solicitors, informing you of Christopher Robbings' death. They ask you to release to them the balances of all the accounts, and to forward the items in safe custody, to facilitate a valuation for probate purposes.

(*a*) How would you deal with this situation? [9]

(*b*) How would you have dealt with matters if the letter from the solicitors had informed you of the death of Harrold Robbings, the receiver, and had contained no request? [8]

[Total marks for question – 17]
(*April 1980*)

4. Peter Dawson opened his account at your branch in his university days. He is now a qualified electrical engineer aged 29. Five years ago, upon the death of his parents, he inherited a detached house where he lives with his

wife. In 1975 he set up a small business, Peter Dawson (Electrical) Limited, with bank assistance and his cash inheritance. He charged the deeds of the house to secure the borrowings on his own accounts and in support of his guarantee for the company.

Peter Dawson's own account is conducted satisfactorily, and the business, whilst having initial difficulties, now appears to be trading profitably. However, it is under-capitalized, and you feel that there is a need for longer-term permanent capital. You have therefore advised Mr Dawson to raise a mortgage against his house, and inject the funds into the company, saying that you would then either release or postpone your charge.

Today you have received a status enquiry on Dawson as to his general financial standing and trustworthiness and ability to meet monthly mortgage instalments of £102 over 20 years.

(a) What considerations would you have in mind before replying?   [10]

(b) Draft a suitably reply.   [3]

(c) Would your approach be different if the accounts were unsatisfactory and you had called in all borrowings?   [3]

[Total marks for question – 16]

(*April 1980*)

5.   Mr J. Tollpuddle, a solicitor and a good customer of yours, has recently introduced to you Mr A. Brown, who, with his partner Mr B. Green, intends to form a limited company to take over the business of their partnership which operates under the trade name Colours. Mr Brown and Mr Green wish to use the opportunity to change bankers, and you are offered the account of the company, Colour Designs Limited. Mr Brown says that the account would be conducted in credit, and you are asked if you could supply specially printed cheques, with the trade name Colours across the top of each cheque, and the same trade name in the usual place as drawer. The company is anxious to retain this established trade name and to derive the benefits of publicity from its use.

You are required to set out the formalities necessary to open and conduct the new account, and to comment, with reasons, on how you would deal with Mr Brown's request.   [16]

(*September 1980*)

6.   About 9 years ago, John Stratt, a wealthy influential customer of the bank of which you are manager, had a disagreement with your predecessor, as a result of which he ran down his balance, and stopped using his current account, leaving a balance of £14 in it. Thereafter the account remained dormant. In 1978, shortly after your appointment as manager, this balance was transferred, in accordance with the bank's practice, to dormant accounts in the bank's central accounting system, and the account at your branch was closed.

You have only just ascertained this history, following receipt of a letter from a firm of solicitors acting for John Stratt, who are claiming damages against the bank in respect of a status report given by you to another bank two months ago. At that time, your clerk could not trace the account of John Stratt in the branch's records and the reply to the status enquiry which asked about his general standing and trustworthiness was 'J.S. does not have an account at this branch'.

(*a*) What is the bank's position and how would you reply to the solicitor's letter? [10]

(*b*) What would the position have been had John Stratt drawn a cheque for £14 in favour of a third party and this had been dishonoured with the answer 'No Account'? [7]

[Total marks for question – [17]
(*September 1980*)

7. Donald Buckley opened his account with you some years ago when he was an articled clerk with a firm of accountants. It became overdrawn and on making enquiries you discovered that Buckley had left the firm and was a casual labourer on building sites. However, the overdraft was repaid, and the account continued to operate in a small way.

Four months ago, Buckley paid in to his account a cheque for £323 in favour of Ye Olde Breade Shoppe, endorsed for that firm by James Flour. Your cashier asked Buckley about the cheque, and he replied that he was assisting Mr Flour on the financial side of the business, with a view to entering into a partnership later on. Subsequently eight further similar cheques were paid in.

You have now been served with legal proceedings by solicitors acting for a Mr William Dough, claiming damages for conversion of nine cheques totalling £2200. Mr Dough states that he is an equal partner with Mr Flour in the firm of Ye Old Breade Shoppe and that he has been defrauded by his partner who passed the partnership cheques on to Mr Buckley, his accomplice. Mr Flour and Mr Buckley have now disappeared.

What is the bank's position? Give reasons for your answer. [17]
(*September 1980*)

8. Your customer Bill has conducted an active, satisfactory current account for the last twelve years. Three months ago he wrote asking you to cancel his monthly standing order in favour of his wife Betty, who maintains a separate current account at your branch. Bill explained that he and Betty had separated and that a divorce was pending.

Unfortunately this letter was not acted upon, and it now transpires that £600 has been transferred to Betty's account in error.

Bill has received his statement each month, but Betty's has not been despatched during this period. The balance on Betty's account is now credit £320, and on Bill's account credit £78.

What is the bank's position as regards both Betty and Bill? What action would you take? Give full reasons for your answers.   [16]

(September 1980)

9.   How would you deal with the following situations? Give reasons for your answers.

(*a*)   Mr Michael Warner opened his current and deposit accounts 18 months ago. Shortly afterwards, he wrote giving strict instructions that you should not answer any enquiries, including requests for bankers' opinions, which you might receive. Whilst you were surprised at this, you agreed, in view of the substantial balances on the accounts.

Today, you have received a letter from the Inland Revenue asking you to supply a copy of all bank accounts in Mr Warner's name for the period 1979 – 1981 to date. It asks you to forward all paid cheques to them. You are also asked to supply a list of all securitites held by the bank for Mr Warner in that period.   [8]

(*b*)   A local firm of accountants writes to you, saying that they act as auditors for your customers Black's Building Supplies Limited. They ask you to supply a certificate of balance as at 31 December 1980, and to list all direct and third party security held by the bank. You are also asked to state if there are any contingent liabilities outstanding to the bank.

Your researches show that the company was overdrawn £5607 at the year end, and that as security you hold an unlimited guarantee by the director Joseph Black, supported by a first mortgae over the deeds of his house, valued at £24 000. Black's Building Supplies Limited guarantees Black's Properties Limited in the sum of £10 000. This account with your branch was in credit on 31 December, 1980.   [9]

[Total marks for question – 17]
(April 1981)

10. (*a*)   John Hope, a retired man, has maintained small accounts with your branch for many years. Today, with credit balances of £37 on the current account and £313 on the deposit accounts in his name, you receive a visit from Mrs Hope, who tells you that her husband died two weeks ago in hospital.

She says she knows he has left no will and, as his estate is very small, she has been advised that she need not take out letters of administration. She asks you to transfer the balances in her deceased husband's name to her account, which you ascertain is maintained at a local branch at you bank.

How would you proceed? Give reasons for your answer.   [8]

(*b*)   As manager of your branch, you have recently noticed a considerable increase in turnover in the account of your customer Stella Stephenson, and, on seeing her in the branch yesterday, you spoke to her. She said that the family had been having a difficult time as her husband's business had collapsed some months ago, but they were overcoming their problems and she was taking an active part in the business which was now in her name. Mrs Stephenson hastened to assure you that she did not expect to need to borrow, but that if she did, she would call and see you before hand, so that you could take her guarantee.

How would you react to the situation? Give reasons for your answer. [8]

[Total marks for question – 16]
(*April 1981*)

11. Tower Tubes Limited has a current account, which usually operates in credit, and a loan account, which is being reduced by transfers of £500 on the sixth day of each month. Whilst the transfers to the loan account are up to date, the current account has become overdrawn, and from time to time you have to return cheques. As security, you hold a legal mortgage over the company's freehold factory premises and an unsupported guarantee for £20 000 by two directors.

Today, 27 April 1981, you have received a letter from a firm of accountants, countersigned by the directors, addressed to all creditors, saying that the company is insolvent and cannot continue in business. The letter gives notice of two meetings, to be held in 21 days' time, of shareholders and creditors, at which it will be proposed that the company be placed in liquidation, and that Mr Dick of their firm will be proposed as liquidator. Today's ledger balances are current account £423 credit; loan account £7513 debit.

(*a*) What action will you take now, and in the period before the meeting?
[8]
(*b*) Assuming the resolutions are then passed, what steps will be necessary to protect the bank's position?
Give reasons for your answer. [9]

[Total marks for question – 17]
(*April 1981*)

12 (*a*) Mr Silver, a valued customer, calls to say that he is going abroad for three months, and that he wishes his son, John, to be able to operate his account, should the need arise, whilst he is away. Mr Silver is a widower, and he says that John will continue to board at this local public school in his absence. Whilst John is unknown to you, you are aware that he is aged 15.

How would you deal with Mr Silver's request? Give reasons for your answer. [6]

(*b*) George and mary Ruskin have a joint account at your branch, operating under the bank's usual mandate form, incorporating joint and several liability, and authorizing you to pay cheques on the signature of either. Recently Mary Ruskin drew a cheque for £960 in favour of a local furrier, but before it was presented you received a visit from George Ruskin who countermanded payment. He said that he was not going to allow his wife to buy a fur coat out of his earnings when other items were needed for the family. You duly returned the cheque with the answer 'payment stopped' when it was presented three days ago.

Today, Mary Ruskin calls to see you, in some distress. She says that there are disagreements over money, but that the funds in the account have all been provided by her and the cheque must be paid on re-presentation. The balance on the account is £1908 credit.

How would you deal with this situation? Giver reasons for your answer.

[10]

[Total marks for question – 16]
(*April 1981*)

13. (*a*) Mr Walsh, whose account is overdrawn, calls on a Friday to see you, as manager of the branch, to discuss the future operation of his account. This interview takes longer than expected, and it ends thirty minutes after closing time. As he is being shown out of the bank. Mr Walsh remembers that he wanted to pay in a crossed cheque for £1530 in his favour, drawn by another customer of your branch, Mr Martin. You ask your cashier to accept the credit slip and cheque and Mr Walsh then asks if the cheque is paid, and is told that it is.

After he has left, however, it is discovered that the final entries in the branch books for that day have been put through on the computer and no further entries are possible. It is therefore decided to hold over the credit slip and cheque until the following business day, which is a Monday.

During the weekend, Mr Martin is killed in a road accident and you read of this in the morning newspaper before you arrive at the branch on Monday morning.

What is the bank's position and what action would you take on your return to the office? Give reasons for your answer. [11]

(*b*) You are the manager of the Town branch of Alpha Bank Ltd. A Miss Tree, who was previously unknown to you, tenders £180 for the credit of her account at the City branch of the Beta Bank Ltd, comprising a cheque for £50, and £130 in cash. The cheque is drawn on the City branch of Beta Bank by L. Drew and is in favour of Miss F. Tree, the account holder named in the bank giro credit tendered.

Miss Tree asks if the funds will reach her account more quickly if she pays in at another local branch of Beta Bank Ltd. She says that it is important for the money to be in her account as soon as possible because she has issued a cheque today and does not want it to be dishonoured. City branch is one hundred miles away from your Town branch.

How would you reply? Give reasons for your answer   [5]

[Total marks for question – 16]

(*September 1981*)

14. Two years ago your customer, Mary Madden, was admitted to a local mental hospital for treatment. Her current account then stood at £413 credit. Shortly afterwards, Mr Ian Madden, her husband, who was known to you, called and, at his request, you transferred the balance of Mary Madden's account to a new account in his name, which he undertook to use to pay for hospital costs and other expenses, including some debts outstanding in Mary's name.

Recently, Mary Madden has fully recovered her health and, through her solicitors, is now suing for divorce on grounds of cruelty which, she claims, occasioned her mental breakdown. This morning you have received a letter from her solicitors referring to the monies which were formerly in Mary Madden's account. The solicitors claim that the monies were not used by Mr Madden for the purposes he mentioned when he gave his undertaking to the bank. The solicitors say that the bank had no authority to deal with the monies in the way it did, and they seek reimbursement for their client. Upon consulting your records, you see that there is a credit balance of £505 in Mr Madden's private account, and a credit balance of £27 in the new account which was opened two years ago.

What is the bank's position, and what action would you take? What points would you consider before drafting a reply to the solicitors' letter? Give reasons for your answer.   [17]

(*September 1981*)

15. You were instructed in a letter from your customer, Alec Brown, who has had an account with you for five years, to transfer the balance on his account to his account at the Seaside Branch of South Bank Ltd, a competitor. Hoping not to lose the account, which usually carries balances of around £20 000, you wrote to Alex Brown, asking him to call and see you to discuss the transfer of his account, and you expressed the hope that any dissatisfaction with your services could be corrected and that he would change his mind. There was no reply and, as a result, the transfer of the balance to South Bank was delayed.

At the end of 14 days, an irate Alec Brown calls to say that he is astounded that the bank has not acted on his authority and, having consulted solicitors, he intends to sue you for not carrying out his instructions without delay. He explains that he had been engaged in a transaction to buy some land and that, by prior arrangement with the vendor's solicitors, he had asked South Bank

Ltd, with which he had had an account for several months, to confirm to the solicitors that it held sufficient monies on his account to complete the transaction. As a result of your inaction, South Bank had been unable to give this confirmation. Mr Brown further states that he had fed the account at South Bank Ltd from several sources, and it was never his intention to close the account with you; he merely instructed you to transfer the balance. Now, he says, he will certainly close the account at your office, and will sue you for damages. He had expected to make a profit of £100 000 in the property transaction, and he claims that restitution of this sum will be part of his proceedings.

Required:

(a) Comment on the bank's position and say how you would have handled Mr Brown's original request. How will you proceed now? [12]

(b) Would the position have been different if Mr Brown's letter had been delayed in the post and had been received at the branch two days ago but had not been acted on when Mr Brown called? [4]

[Total marks for question – 16]
(*September 1981*)

16. How would you deal with the following situations which you notice in the branch to which you have just been appointed manager? Give reasons for your answers.

(a) Flowers Ltd, market gardeners, operate a current account in substantial credit, and the two directors keep good balances on their own current and deposit accounts. You have noticed that the company regularly pays into its account unendorsed cheques in favour of Flowers (Seeds) Ltd, and on making enquiries you are told that Flower (Seeds) Ltd, is a wholly owned subsidiary of Flowers Ltd, but it does not have an account in its own name at your bank. [10]

(b) Two months ago, your predecessor called in the borrowing of Mr and Mrs Mitchell at £10 019. An interview note shows that, when Mr Mitchell called subsequently, your predecessor agreed to accept repayment at the rate of £200 per month, provided £7000 was provided within three months, with the monthly instalments commencing immediately.

You have now received a letter from Mr Mitchell, enclosing the cheque for £7000, your bank being named as payee. The drawer is Mitchell Products Ltd, and the cheque is signed by Mr Mitchell as director. The cheque is drawn on another of your bank's branches, and you ascertain by telephone that the account is sufficiently in credit to enable the cheque to be paid upon presentation. [17]

[Total marks for question – 17]
(*September 1981*)

17. Zeta Ltd has had an account with your branch since 1960, when the company was first formed to take over a partnership of builders which had also banked at the branch. In the 1960s and 1970s the company's business expanded, but recently the nature of its operations has changed and it is now engaged only in running a hotel at a seaside holiday resort. The directors are Mr Black and Mr White.

In January 1982 Alpha Ltd was formed as a subsidiary of Zeta Ltd, and, like its parent, was incorporated under the Companies Act 1948 and adopted Table A. The company provides catering services and the account is also at your branch. A loan of £10 000 was made to Alpha Ltd in January of this year against the unlimited guarantee of Zeta Ltd, supported by a legal mortgage over the hotel.

Overdrafts of up to £10 000 are now appearing on Zeta Ltd's account. You are an assistant manager of the branch and your newly appointed manager speaks to you about the borrowing position generally in the light of Zeta's latest balance sheet figures, which are summarized below, together with the opening statement of affairs for Alpha Ltd. The manager refers to the possibility that Zeta may be trading illegally and you agree that this may be so. You draw his attention to another problem facing the bank and you discuss the steps that now need to be taken to protect the bank in these circumstances.

ZETA LTD

Balance Sheet as at 31 December, 1981

	£		£
Issued capital	25 000	Freehold property	80 000
Reserves	30 000	Fixtures and fittings	17 000
Profit and loss account	24 000	Stock	18 000
Loans from directors	17 000	Debtors	6 000
Sundry creditors	19 000	Cash	2 000
Bank overdraft	8 000		
	£123 000		£123 000

ALPHA LTD

Opening Statement 13 January, 1982

	£		£
Issued capital	20 000	Fittings etc	5 000
		Motor vehicles	10 000
		Cash	5 000
	£20 000		£20 000

Required:

(*a*) A statement of the problems facing the bank, and the reasons for them.

[7]

(*b*) Notes setting out possible solutions to the problems and indicating the steps the bank should take. [10]

[Total marks for question – 17]
(*April 1982*)

18. Mr Sprout, a local grocer, has had a current account with you for about 18 months, since he bought his business from a former customer of yours. However, you have not been very satisfied with the account. Unauthorized overdrafts have frequently been taken, and there have been delays in regularizing the account, despite letters which you have sent to Mr Sprout asking him to adjust matters.

Mr Sprout has also frequently complained about the bank's services, claiming that he is kept waiting at the counter and that his statement is sent late. Last Christmas you interviewed Mr Sprout, and told him that he must operate his account in credit in the future. This was because you felt there was some risk in lending to him, as his business did not appear to be prospering, with the turnover considerably less than it had been when your former customer owned the shop.

Today, 19 April, Mr Sprout has called to see you, and he complains that you have charged interest to his account as at 31 March in respect of the last quarter. He says that since he saw you in December, he has kept the account in credit, and has regularly paid in on the day when cheques drawn have been presented for payment, so that his account has never been overdrawn in 1982. He adds that many of the cheques he pays in are drawn by his customers against their cheque guarantee card. Mr Sprout also says that the commission charge of £32.50p. is excessive; that when he opened the account he did not agree to pay a commission charge; and he disputes your right to debit his account without his authority.

Required:

How would you handle this interview, and what considerations would you have in mind, both now and for the future? [16]
(*April 1982*)

19. At the branch at which you are the manager, you have the valued account of Televideo Ltd, which is a main dealer for an international television and video recorder manufacturer. Televideo Ltd has many retail outlets, and its shares are quoted on the stock exchange. You are lending to three of the company's directors against the security of their holding in Televideo Ltd.

At the beginning of last month, one of these three directors called to discuss the company's future and the changes to its banking arrangements necessitated by the Companies Act 1980. He told you that the company was about to form a subsidiary which would finance the sales of television sets and video recorders on credit, and he asked you what the bank would require to enable it to open an account for the new company. He mentioned that when all the formalities had been completed, the subsidiary would seek some working capital from the bank.

Required:

A tabulated account of the matters which you would have had to cover in your discussions with the company director, stating what action you would have taken and why. [16]

(April 1982)

20. (*a*) Mr Tom Cutler, one of your customers, calls to tell you that he is in financial difficulties and that a petition in bankruptcy has been presented against him in the High Court by one of his creditors. Your researches show that Mr Cutler is associated with the undermentioned accounts and that there are transactions in the day's work as shown.

Accounts

(*i*)   Tom Cutler and Mary Cutler (either to sign) £217 credit

(*ii*)   Cutler, Bates & Co. Ltd £3,417 debit. Security: joint and several guarantee £10 000 by Tom Cutler and Bill Bates, supported by legal mortgage value £20 000 by Bill Bates.

Transactions

(*i*)   Cheque for £117 presented through the general clearing, drawn on the joint account by Mary Cutler.

(*ii*)   Cheque for £28 presented through the general clearing drawn by Cutler, Bates and Co. Ltd, signed by Tom Cutler.

What action would you take? Give reasons for your answer [8]

(*b*) One of your customers, Eric Jones, calls and tells you that he is in financial difficulties because of a large bad debt that he has incurred. He says that he asked a local accountant, Mr J. Young, to act for him under a deed of arrangement which he has executed on his solicitor's advice.

Mr Jones's account is overdrawn by £480, you have no security, and you refuse his request to withdraw a further £100.

Later in the day, Mr Young calls and asks you to open an account in respect of Mr Jones with two cheques for £532 and £128 drawn by P. Oates and R. Hay in favour of Mr Jones.

Mr Young asks you agree to his withdrawing £100 for Mr Jones's use for living expenses.

Describe the actions and steps you would have taken during the day and say how you would handle Mr Young's request. Give reasons for your answer. [9]

[Total marks for question 17]
(April 1982)

21. (*a*) Your customer, Mr Bull, is a director of a building company M. Bull Ltd and he maintains good credit balances in his joint account with his wife. He has a portfolio of quoted shares.

This morning he telephones to ask you to sell on his behalf 400 shares in Redrag plc, the share certificate for which is held by you in safe custody.

Required:

Notes of all the steps necessary to process this customer's instructions through to a satisfactory conclusion, and an indication of the risks involved. [9]

(*b*) Harry Goat has a locked tin box in safe custody at your branch and he sends his secretary to the bank with a letter authorizing her to have access to the box in order to list the contents. Subsequently Mr Goat alleges that the secretary removed a valuable diamond ring from the box and that she has now disappeared. Mr Goat claims that the bank is liable for restitution and damages.

What points would you consider in dealing with this claim? Do you think it might succeed? [7]

[Total marks for question – 16]
(September 1982)

22. You are the manager of Country branch of Alpha Bank, a member of the London Bankers' Clearing House. The account of Mr Hutton, one of your customers, regularly appears on your morning computer print-out of irregular accounts. He has borrowing limits of £3000 on his current account and £8000 on his loan account and you have warned him that these limits must be strictly adhered to, as otherwise you will have to return cheques.

On this morning's print-out, the balances as at the close of business last night are shown as current account £3502 debt and loan account £8000 debit. You ask your clerk to produce all yesterday's vouchers, so that you may see the entries which have caused this position. Shortly after the bank has opened for business, your clerk tells you of five items debited in yesterday's general clearing:

(*a*) a crossed cheque in favour of A. Morris for £179, dated 13 September 1982;

(*b*) a crossed cheque in favour of L. Brown for £41, dated 18 September 1982, with Mr Hutton's cheque card number 127864 on the reverse.

(*c*) a crossed cheque in favour of J. Johnston for £68, dated 19 October 1982;

(*d*) a direct debit for £39 in favour of Living Assurance;

(*e*) an open cheque in favour of D. Ring for £69, dated 19 September 1981.

He also informs you that, at the counter today, a Mr Miller has just tendered a bank giro credit for his account at Town Branch for £200. This credit is made up of cash and a crossed cheque for £100 drawn by your customer, Mr Hutton, and dated 13 September 1982. Mr Miller has asked if the cheque is paid.

Your clerk suggests that all items be dishonoured. Bearing in mind that you do not wish to increase the bank's exposure, how would you reply to him and what instructions would you give? Give reasons for your answer.   [17]

(*September 1982*)

23. (*a*) Mary Penn, a well-known journalist on a national newspaper calls to see you and informs you that she has recently married Tony Pencil, another journalist. She says, however, that she will wish to continue to write her books and articles under the name by which she is now well known, and she tenders for collection for her account three cheques: one for £340 in favour of Mary Penn, one for £89 in favour of Mary Pencil, and one for £180 in favour of Tony Pencil, endorsed by him.

What action would you take? Give reasons for your answer.   [9]

(*b*) Some nine months ago, Mr Hill transferred his account to the Country branch of your bank, where you are manager, from your Town branch. This transfer took place when he retired from a stockbroking firm and moved to a house in the country.

Today Mr Hill calls to see you, and says that he has lost a share-certificate for 500 ordinary shares in Zeta plc which, he says, are quoted at 120 pence on the Stock Exchange. He adds that it will be necessary for him to obtain a duplicate from the company and, having written to Zeta plc's registrars, he has been asked to obtain an indemnity from his bankers before they will issue a duplicate certificate. He produces the document they have sent him, and asks you if you will execute this on his behalf.

How would you deal with this situation? Give reasons for your answer.

[8]

[Total marks for questions – 17]

(*September 1982*)

24. Albert Black, an engineer, executed a power of attorney in favour of Tony White last March, when he went to Hong Kong on business. The power of attorney was expressed to be irrevocable for a period of 12 months. Black has both a current and a deposit account with you, and you hold a portfolio of shares and a locked tin box in safe-custody on his behalf. The

bank omitted to take the usual form of third-party mandate, but Mr White was given a specially prepared cheque book.

Recently there have been three developments as follows. State, with reasons, how you would have dealt with each of these successive developments.

(*a*) In July, Mr White asked you to supply a list of items held in safe custody on Mr Black's behalf. [6]

(*b*) In August, in error you credited a remittance for Albert Black from Hong Kong to the account of Anthony Black, and subsequently dishonoured a cheque for £320 drawn by Tony White as attorney for Albert Black, with the answer 'refer to drawer – please re-present'. This cheque was paid on its second presentation when the error came to light.

Mr White is now claiming compensation for damage to his credit. [5]

(*c*) Mr Black returned unexpectedly to the United Kingdom last week and wishes to operate his account again on his own. [5]

[Total marks for question – 16]
(*September 1982*)

25. (*a*) Homes' Ltd is a house-building company whose accounts have caused considerable difficulties for the bank over the last year. The current account has been overdrawn by more than the agreed amount, and instalments in respect of term loan account facilities can now be passed each month only at the expense of the current account. Recently, interest and commission charges were passed to the current account at the end of the March quarter, further increasing the borrowing. However, the bank holds a debenture given as security in 1981, and considers itself fully secured.

The accounts are now due for report to your head office advances control and, as manager, you wish to recommend that the borrowing should be called in and a receiver appointed. However, when you discuss matters with your assistant manager, he suggests that it may not be legally possible to proceed as you wish, for he says he remembers hearing of a case a few years ago where a bank's action in calling in borrowings was challenged, and a substantial counterclaim for damages was made.

Required:

Comment, with reasons, on the points which the assistant manager has in mind. [9]

(*b*) Peter Smith's account has been regarded as very unsatisfactory for some time, and he has recently taken to drawing cheques and then telephoning you to stop payment to avoid their being dishonoured with the answer 'Refer to drawer'. By these means, and by your own strict control, the account is now kept in credit, but balances overnight never exceed £50.

As manager, you wish to see the account closed as soon as possible. How would you proceed? Give reasons for your answer. [8]

[Total marks for question – 17]
(*April 1983*)

26. John Steel, aged 35, who has maintained a satisfactory current account at your branch for several years whilst working as a surveyor for a nationally known firm of estate agents, calls to tell that he is about to set up as an estate agent on his own. He also introduces his wife, Rita, whom he has married recently, and says that he will want his private account to be in their joint names in future but the business accounts will be his sole responsibility, although his wife will be employed on clerical duties.

In conversation you learn that Rita Steel had an unfortunate experience 12 years ago when she was in partnership with her father, as their business failed and the partnership was made bankrupt. She says this is why she never wants to go into business herself again.

Mr Steel asks you to make arrangements for all the necessary new accounts to be opened, and Mrs Steel asks if she can be given a cheque guarantee card now.

Required:

Notes, with reasons, on the matters and procedures you would discuss at this interview. State how you would deal with your customers' requirements. Give reasons for your answer. [16]

(*April 1983*)

27. (*a*) Through an article in your local newspaper you have recently learned of the death of Miss Dorothy Penny, an elderly spinster who had been one of your customers at Country branch for over 30 years and who had been well known throughout the locality for her charitable works. Shortly afterwards, a Mr Alan Penny calls and tells you that he is Miss Penny's brother and he believes he is the sole executor appointed under her will.

Your researches have shown that Miss Penny's accounts carried the following balances at the date of the newspaper article:

Current account £7017 credit
Deposit account £10 000 credit

In safe custody is a sealed envelope marked 'Will', share certificates, and a sealed envelope marked 'diamond ring'.

Mr Penny, who tells you he is a customer at Town branch of your bank, asks for the will and also asks to be allowed to take away the ring so that it can be valued.

State how you would proceed. [11]

(*b*) Three months later, at Town branch, Mr Penny's account is overdrawn well in excess of the agreed limit and the manager is aware that Mr Penny's business is not prospering. Cheques have been dishonoured. With his overdraft at £6049 debit, Mr Penny calls and pays in a cheque for £7000 drawn on an account at Country branch, styled 'Alan Penny, executor of Dorothy Penny'.

As manager of Town branch, state how you would deal with this transaction. Give reasons for your answer. [6]

[Total marks for question – 17]
(*April 1983*)

28. (*a*) Wood and Stone Ltd, a large engineering company, has banked with you for five years. You have supported it with borrowing facilities from time to time, to help to finance work-in-progress, against a legal mortgage over the company's land and buildings. For the last few months the account has been operating in credit.

A week ago, one of your clerks took a telephone call from the company secretary, instructing the bank to stop payment of a cheque for £20 000, drawn in favour of Z Ltd, a building company which was in the course of erecting a new factory on your customer's land. This cheque was a stage payment under the terms of the contract. Unfortunately, your clerk suffered an accident in the office shortly after taking this call and, as a result, the message was not recorded. On the following day, the cheque was presented in the clearing and was paid. The letter from the company confirming the telephone call has only just been received, and the company mentions that the reason for its stopping the cheque is that Z Ltd has had a receiver appointed by its bankers.

What is the bank's position? What steps must now be taken in the best interests of the customer and the bank? [8]

(*b*) Your good customer, Edward Parry, called three days ago and requested a draft for £2500 in favour of Mr M. Andrews, mentioning that he was buying Mr Andrews' car, and that the latter would release the car only against a banker's draft. You were happy to assist, and issued a draft in favour of M. Andrews, crossed 'Not negotiable'.

Today, Mr Parry has called again, and he tells you that he left his briefcase on the train after last visiting you, and that the draft was inside it, together with his cheque book. The briefcase has not been found, and he asks you if you will stop payment of the draft and issue a duplicate.

What action would you take, and why? What other considerations would you have in mind? [8]

[Total marks for question – 16]
(*April 1983*)

29. (*a*) Drake Ltd manufactures industrial goods and employs a workforce of some 50 people. Five of these have small deposit accounts at your branch, which is situated about half a mile away from the factory premises.

Today, you have received a letter from the company secretary saying that it has been agreed that in future all the workforce will be paid by transfers into a bank account, and those who do not have accounts with you already have agreed to open accounts at your branch, where the company account is maintained. A list of names is appended to the letter, and the company secretary asks you to return the copy marked to show those persons who already have accounts with you. He also asks you to send any necessary papers to him to facilitate the opening of the other accounts.

What reply would you send to the letter and what arrangements would need to be put in hand? [8]

(*b*) Brian Speed, a second-hand car dealer, paid a cheque for £420 into his account last week and, since he had been known to you for some years, your assistant manager allowed him to draw out £450 in cash, although the balance of his account before these transactions was only £50 credit.

Today the cheque for £420 has been returned with the answer 'Payment countermanded by order of drawer'.

What action would you take to protect the bank as fully as possible in these circumstances? [8]

[Total marks for question – 16]
(*September 1983*)

30. You are the manager of Town Hall branch. Rags Ltd, clothing manufacturers, have been your customers for five years, with increasing reliance on borrowing facilities over the last 18 months. Initially you were content to rely on the unlimited guarantee of the two directors but last April, in view of increasing strain on the account, you asked for more security and were offered a mortgage debenture incorporating a fixed and floating charge which you took and valued at £120 000.

This afternoon, 19 September 1983, it has come to your notice, following the return of your clerk from holiday, that, during the period when his job was done by a relief clerk, there was mention in a head office circular dated 12 September 1983 that a petition for winding up had been presented against Rags Ltd on 10 September 1983. A computer print-out shows that on 10 September 1983 the balance of the account was £65 213 debit. It is now £69 513 debit, after the payment of a cheque for wages for £7100, a cheque for £510 in favour of the Electricity Board, and a credit comprising cash and cheques totalling £3310. All entries were made last week.

What instructions would you give your clerk on learning of this matter and what are the dangers for the bank in the present situation? [17]

(*September 1983*)

31. John Smith, a solicitor in sole practice, conducts his business accounts and private accounts at your branch, the ledger balances of which at close of business last night were as follows:

John Smith – Office account: current account £1030 credit
John Smith – Clients account: current account £8216 credit
John Smith & Mary Smith (his wife): current account £502 credit
John Smith: Deposit Account: US $1000 credit
John Smith re Tom Smith (his son): savings account £82 credit

Mary Smith has a sole account: current account £89 credit.

In this morning's post was a special presentation by Zeta Bank of a cheque for £330 in favour of A. Short drawn on the joint account. Ten minutes after you opened for business Zeta Bank enquired by telephone if the cheque was paid and was told that it was.

One hour later you received a telephone call from your head office saying that a garnishee order *nisi* had just been served on them naming John Smith and Mary Smith as judgment debtors for £12 213 and costs.

Required:

State what action you would take in respect of the accounts. Give reasons for your answer.   [16]

Note: For the purposes of this question, US $1.50=£1.00.

(*September 1983*)

32. How would you deal with the following situations? Give reasons for your answers.

(*a*) Dick Barton, the son of Mrs Barton who died three months ago, calls concerning his mother's affairs. Mrs Barton had a current account at your branch (£313 credit), which was stopped on notice of death. Dick Barton asks for this balance to be transferred into his account at Seaside branch, together with the balance of a deposit account in respect of which he produces a pass book showing a balance of £210.

You discover that this deposit account is not now open and, according to your records, it was closed five years ago by a withdrawal which appears not to have been entered in the pass book. When you tell him this Mr Barton doubts your statement, and you cannot produce the voucher to show him, since your bank retains such items for only three years.   [6]

(*b*) You receive a letter from one of your customers, Dee & Co. Ltd, asking if another of your customers, Ellis & Co. Ltd, are good for trade credit of £1000 per month. Both customers are electrical engineers and you have seen cheques passing between them in the past.

Ellis & Co Lld have been established 50 years and have an annual turnover of £2 million. They are borrowing from you on current account up to £600 000 against the security of a debenture incorporating fixed and floating charges. Recently, however, following the death of the managing director and because of trading losses in the recession, your head office has become increasingly concerned at the position and will consider appointing a receiver upon the next report due from you in six weeks' time.   [11]

[Total marks for question – 17]
(*September 1983*)

33. You have agreed to lend your customers Fuller & Company Limited £10 000 on overdraft, against the security of a joint and several guarantee for £10 000 from the two directors, Alan Apple and Alison Pear. The guarantee is to be supported by a legal mortgage over Alan Apple's freehold residence, which he values at £45 000, and on which property he tells you he took a building society mortgage of £9000, and lodged the deeds with the society, when the property was purchased seven years ago.

(*a*) You are required to set out the procedure for taking the guarantee and protecting the bank's position fully in that respect.   [6]

(*b*) When carrying out the security formalities in respect of the mortgage over the property, a search at the Land Charges Register has been returned showing the following entries:

    (i) Class Ci   Number 95957   Dated 17 November 1973
    (ii) Class F   Number 31174   Dated 28 November 1977

What do these entries mean, and how do they affect the bank's position? What action would you take on receipt of the search, and how much would you deal with the position generally?   [10]

[Total marks for question – 16]
(*April 1980*)

34. Your customer, John Donovan, who has banked with you for seven years, called two months ago to inform you that on his accountant's advice he was to turn his business into a limited company. He said that the company would require overdraft facilities of up to £20 000, and as a director he was prepared to give his guarantee. You agreed to his request, provided that the deeds of 79 West Hill were charged in addition. The company was in the process of acquiring this property and planned to carry on its future trading at that address.

Matters subsequently progressed satisfactorily, the company's account was opened, and the director's guarantee taken. However, delays have now developed in respect of the company mortgage, as the land in question was, until now, freehold unregistered title, but, on this transaction, the title is to be registered at the Land Registry for the first time. The land certificate has not yet been received by the company's solicitors.

The company now wishes to use its overdraft facilities to the full, but you are not prepared to make them available with only the director's guarantee as security.

How would you deal with the situation? Give full reasons and explanations for your answer, and indicate all the steps you would take.   [17]

(April 1980)

35. Three years ago you agreed overdraft facilities of £27 000 for your customer Peter Overland. As security you were given a first mortgage over his domestic property, the deeds of which were in the name of his wife. His son and his brother, who both worked for him in the business, gave their joint and several unlimited guarantee. The property was then valued at £20 000.

The business has not succeeded, and with the overdraft at £34 000 you called in the borrowing five months ago, when a dramatic fall in the turnover in the account led you to suspect that another bank account was being used. Overland reduced the borrowing to £21 000 but, as he would not offer any further satisfactory proposals, you called upon the guarantors in the sum of £21 000. A letter was received from Overland's son, offering to pay £6000 without interest by monthly instalments over two years, and Overland's brother offered £15 000 at once, provided the bank would release him from all liability. This the bank agreed to do, and the monies were received and dealt with in the usual way. You also accepted the son's offer.

Now, two months after these arrangements were made, a letter has been received from a firm of solicitors acting for Mrs Overland, asking you to forward the deeds to them, as the house is to be sold. The letter says that the solicitors understand that arrangements have been made with the other members of the family as to repayment, and the deeds are not required as security. You reply that day. The next day you are advised by telephone that a receiving order has been made against Peter Overland.

(a) As manager how did you reply to the solicitor's letter, and what considerations did you have in mind?   [12]

(b) Upon receiving written confirmation from the Official Receiver, how would you reply to his questions as to the amount owing and the security held? What considerations would you have in mind?   [5]

[Total marks for question – 17]

(April 1980)

36. Your customer Timothy Small, age 31, qualified as a solicitor a few years ago. After gaining suitable experience with several firms, he joined the firm of Pegden and Hayward last year as a junior partner and introduced

£5000 into the firm by way of capital. At the same time he transferred his account to you from one of your other branches.

Mr Small now has the opportunity of increasing his stake in the partnership, owing to the unexpected retirement through ill health of Mr Hayward, and, as manager of the branch, you have said that you will consider assisting him with a loan of £20 000, repayable out of his share of the firm's profits over 7 years. However, Mr Small has no security to offer other than his revesionary interest in a will trust. Subject to satisfactory replies to your enquires you will be prepared to accept this. When you discuss the proposition with your security clerk, he asks you to explain the nature of the charge and to advise him how he should proceed to take the security and complete all the necessary protective formalities, as he has not encountered such a situation before.

How would you reply? [16]

(April 1980)

37. Rags Limited, clothing manufacturers, maintains an overdrawn current account and a loan account at your branch against the security of an unlimited joint and several guarantee by the two directors. Control of the borrowing has proved difficult.

Last March the directors called with their audited accounts as at 31 October 1979, which showed a loss of £15 000 for the previous year's trading on turnover of £150 000. However, they assured you that this was because of one particular line of stock which had been difficult to sell, and they believed that they were again trading on a profitable basis. You therefore agreed to continue the overdraft facilites of £10 000 fluctuating on current account, and £13 000 on loan account reducing at £1000 per month, subject to further security in the form of a debenture incorporating a legal mortgage over the company's freehold factory and a floating charge over all other assets. This security was received on 8 March 1980.

The account continued to give trouble, and on 15 September 1980, with the balances at debit £21 000 on current account and debit £7000 on loan account, the company went into creditors' voluntary liquidation. Today you have received a letter from the liquidator claiming that:

(a) the company security is invalid, as it was taken within the last year;

[10]

(b) the giving of that security was a fraudulent preference, and is void on those grounds;

[3]

(c) as the directors were personally interested in the giving of the debenture, it is also void on those grounds.

[4]

What has the liquidator in mind in respect of each of his claims, and what matters will the bank need to investigate to determine if he is correct?

[Total marks for question – 17]

(September 1980)

38. Alan Spark, an established customer, is currently borrowing £10 000 on overdraft, as a working capital facility for his electrical sales and repair business. As security you have a legal charge over the deeds of his small freehold workshop premises, valued in your books at £18 000.

He has recently called you to tell you that he is retiring and that his two sons, who already have a partnership account with you, will be acquiring the premises for their own carpentry business. Shortly afterwards the sons call and you agree to lend them £15 000 on loan account to facilitate the purchase at £24 000, on the understanding that the deeds will be legally charged by them at the same time as the completion of the purchase.

How would you proceed so that the bank is fully protected throughout these transactions:

(a) when the solicitor, who acts for both parties, writes and asks you to forward the deeds so that sale and purchase can go ahead;

(b) when, ten days later, you are asked to send a bank draft for £24 000? [16]

(*September 1980*)

39. Peter Clogg, a retired company director, has a limit of £2500 on his current account, but with the borrowing at £3246 the account became inactive ten months ago. There was no response to your letters and last July you called in the borrowing. Again there was no response and as you held a legal charge by Clogg over a life policy, nominal value £10 000, with a surrender value of £3200, you surrendered the policy.

Now, seven weeks later, you have had a visit from Mr Clogg's son, Donald, who tells you that his father died in hospital last week and that he is named as executor in the will which is in safe custody. Mr Clogg asks you to let him have the will, and also a stamp collection which is in safe custody, so that he can have it valued for probate purposes. He enquires about the life policy and is astounded to learn that the bank has surrendered it. He claims that, as sole beneficiary, he has, by your action, been deprived of the capital value which would have accrued to the estate upon his father's death. He further states that, had the bank enquired, they would have learnt that his father was seriously ill in hospital. Mr Clogg, who is a legal executive with a firm of solicitors, says that in any event the bank should have given three months' notice before realizing the security, and he threatens action as executor and sole beneficiary.

Required:
Giving full reasons:

(a) Outline the bank's position in respect of Mr Clogg's claim that the life policy had been wrongly realized. [4]

(b) Describe the procedure which the bank would have followed in surrendering the life policy. [8]

(c) State how you would have dealt with the request to hand over the will and the stamp collection. [4]

[Total marks for question – 16]
(*September 1980*)

40. (a) Two years ago you lent Raymond Brown £2000 to assist with the purchase of a motor car. Repayment was promised by equal monthly instalments over three years from drawings out of a plumbing business run by Brown and his father, Simon Brown. The partnership account is with another bank, and as Raymond Brown's account was only recently opened you asked for a guarantee from his father for £2000, to be supported by the land certificate for his house, which you agreed to hold without formal charge.

You have recently seen in the *Gazette* a county court judgment against Simon Brown for £181. However, the son's borrowing has been reduced as promised and now, with twelve months' instalments still outstanding, the son has called and repaid the loan early. He asks you to write to his father indicating that the guarantee has ceased and to forward the land certificate with your letter.

How would you deal with these requests? Give reasons for your answer.
[8]

(b) Jack and Jean Bean, the proprietors of a grocery business, operate a joint overdrawn account, and recently it has been necessary to return cheques to keep the borrowing within the agreed limits. You hold no charged security, but in safe custody is the land certificate in their joint names in respect of their shop and living premises.

You have received a letter from Jack Bean, saying that he is raising a mortgage and asking you to forward the land certificate to his solicitors, Giant & Co.

How would you proceed?

Would your approach be different if Jack and Jean Bean were guarantors for the facilities which you had allowed on an account styled Jack Bean Ltd? [9]

[Total marks for question – 17]
(*September 1980*)

41. Because of sickness, the work of the securities section in the branch of which you are manager has fallen behind. However, a new clerk, Mr Smart, has been appointed and, in dealing with outstanding correspondence, he draws your attention to the following items:

(a) A letter, dated three months ago, from your customers Peacock Limited, who borrow up to £100 000 net on three accounts against the security of a first mortgage over their freehold factory premises valued in your books at £250 000. The letter reads: 'We are writing to advise you that we have recently arranged for Messrs Seagull Limited to occupy part of our factory premises and outhouses at an annual rent of £5600. This will be paid quarterly and when it is received will you please credit our number 2 account under advice to us'.

No action has been taken on this letter, and this is the first time that you have heard of the matter. [9]

(*b*) A letter, dated six weeks ago, from your customers Squirrel Limited, enclosing a sealed legal mortgage form and a copy of a resolution by the directors, in respect of a second mortgage to the bank over its leasehold unregistered land at 4 Nutkin Road. This company is borrowing £30 000 on loan account and no action appears to have been taken on this matter. [7]

As manager, how would you react in each case and what instructions would you give Mr Smart? Give reasons for your answers.

[Total marks for question – 16]
(*April 1981*)

42. Deansgate Supplies Limited have banked with you for three years, and you know that the company has accounts with competitor banks.

At a recent interview you agreed to lend the company £30 000 repayable over 5 years, to assist with the building of an extension to their existing factory premises, provided adequate security was lodged.

The two directors accepted your need for security, but said that they were anxious to retain a degree of flexibility in case they should need to borrow from their others bankers in the future. Consequently they would give you only either a first mortgage over the company's existing leasehold land and buildings, valued at £40 000 in the company's last balance sheet, or their joint and several guarantee for £30 000 supported by two second mortgages, equity £20 000 in each, over their matrimonial homes, title to which is in their sole name in each case. They say that they will in any event agree to postpone their loans of £10 000 each to the company in favour of the bank.

Required:

Tabulate the attractions and disadvantages of each of the securities offered, and say what further information you might require, if any, to enable you to reach your decision. [17]

(*April 1981*)

43. (*a*) Your, customer Alan Lander is overdrawn £4000 and you have called on him to provide security. He telephoned last week to say that the only security available was a guarantee from his friend and business associate John Jones, and that Mr Jones will call to see you shortly. In fact, John Jones is already known to you, having been a customer himself for five years. He is the

director of Jones Building Supplies Limited which banks at another of your branches. You consider him good for the liabiltiy.

In due course, when John Jones calls, he mentions that when he was first approached by Alan Lander he had some reservations about signing a guarantee, but he now realizes that it is only a formality and he is therefore happy to sign. He mentions that he owes Alan Lander £5000 in respect of some sub-contracted work he has recently completed.

How would react to this situation, and what action would you take? Give reasons for your answer [7]

(*b*) Bricks Limited ceased trading last year, but was not placed in liquidation as it had no assets apart from a plot of building land in mortgage to the bank. With the assistance of estate agents, the bank sold this land for £20 000, which left a residual borrowing of £5000. The bank then called upon the guarantor, Joseph Wood, to meet this liability, and informed him that interest would continue to accrue on his liability until repayment.

Today you have received a letter from him saying that he cannot understand how he has any liability to the bank. He says that if legal proceedings are taken he will dispute the claim on the grounds that he is no longer associated with the company as he resigned as director six months ago, when the bank took it upon itself to sell the company's asset. In any event, he alleges, the bank has sold the land for too low a price, and if it had obtained £25 000, the valuation in the company's balance sheet, the bank would have been fully repaid. He goes on to say that he never agreed to pay interest, and was not allowed to consult his solicitor when he executed the guarantee in 1974.

What is the bank's position, and how would you respond to Mr Wood's letter?

Give reasons for your answer. [9]

[Total marks for question – 16]
(*April 1981*)

44. David Scott farms 836 acres of land, which he rents at £17 000 per annum from Lord Snooty. His account has been regularly overdrawn over the last five years, with the figures increasing in the last twelve months.

As manager, you ask Mr Scott to call and see you and bring his own up-to-date figures for the business. Mr Scott explains his problem to your satisfaction and you feel able to continue your support, provided that adequate security is given. Mr Scott then agrees to give you an agricultural floating charge, and an assignment over a life policy, shown in his own draft figures which he has brought with him and which are set out below. You notice, however, that this policy is drawn up under the provisons of the Married Women's Property Act 1882.

Required:

Tabulate all the steps necessary to take the securities, so as to protect the bank fully at all times. You should indicate the value of each item of security, as you would enter it into your records, giving reasons for your answer, and add any further comments which you feel may be pertinent.

D. SCOTT – FARMER

Liabilities	£	*Assets*	£
Loans	10 000	Livestock	3 000
Rent due	4 250	Harvested crops	78 000
Mercants, seedsmen	29 250	Growing crops	18 600
Tax	7 000	Stores, foodstuffs, fertilisers	9 000
Life policy premium arrears	400	Machinery/tractors	10 500
Other creditors	12 100	Car	3 000
Bank	50 000	Debtors	29 400
		Life policy £25 000	
	113 000	surrender value	1 500
Capital	40 000		
	£153 000		£153 000

[17]

(April 1981)

45. Your customer, Percy Scott, is borrowing from your bank and as security you hold a first legal mortgage over his freehold house, St Agnes, which you value at £40 000. Your arrangement with Mr Scott is that his current account facility is £10 000, fluctuating on overdraft to 31 December 1981, when it will be reviewed in accordance with the bank's standard annual arrangement with him. There has been strain on the account recently, and you have found it necessary to dishonour the occasional cheque to control his borrowing.

Mr Scott also guarantees Great Scott Ltd in the sum of £30 000, the company having a loan account and a current account. The loan account facility is being reduced by £1000 per month, with interest being debited quarterly to the current account.

Two months ago, on 20 July 1981, when the borrowings were:

Percy Scott	£9 739 debit
Great Scott Ltd	
Current account	£413 credit
Great Scott Ltd	
Loan account	£25 000 debit

you received notice from Diddy Bank Ltd that it had taken a second mortgage dated 10 July 1981 over St. Agnes. The balances of all the accounts on 10 July 1981 were:

Mr Percy Scott	£10 201 debit
Great Scott Ltd	
Current account	£3 100 credit
Great Scott Ltd	
Loan account	£26 000 debit

Diddy Bank asked you to acknowledge notice of their charge and to state the amount secured by your mortgage. They also asked if you had powers of consolidation, and whether your mortgage imposed an obligation to make further advances. You replied appropriately, taking the necessary action in the branch.

Now, on 20 September 1981, you have received a notice from the Land Registry stating that pursuant to s. 30 Land Registration Act 1925 a creditor's notice and bankruptcy inhibition have been registered against the title of the proprietor. The notice refers to land title No. BZ 42055, and you hold a charge certificate over this title, which is St Agnes. The bankruptcy inhibition referred to is a petition.

Later the same day, Mr Scott calls and seeks to withdraw a share certificate for 2000 ordinary shares in the Z. Co. Ltd, which you hold in safe custody in his name. He says that he requires these shares to make arrangements with one of his business creditors, who is pressing for payment.

Required:

(*a*) Notes on the action you would have taken on 20 July 1981, with reasons. [5]

(*b*) A draft reply to Diddy Bank Ltd [5]

(*c*) Comments on the action necessary on 20 September 1981, with reasons, and suggestions as to the practical manner in which you could deal with the situation. [7]

[Total marks for question – 17]

(*September 1981*)

46. Mr Kay has a current account and a loan account at your Country branch, and there is a also a joint account maintained in his name and that of this wife. The last account operates under a joint and several mandate, with either to sign. Country branch has agreed borrowing facilities of £2000 in Mr Kay's loan account and this is being reduced at £100 per month. Repayments are up to date. Occasionally, small borrowing facilities have been allowed on the joint account without prior arrangement.

As security, the bank holds one thousand shares in Zee Ltd, lodged by Mr

Kay on a memorandum of deposit, securing all his liabilities to the bank. The balances on the accounts are:

Mr Kay: current account	£213 credit
Mr Kay: loan account	£1400 debit
Mr and Mrs Kay: current account	£250 debit

You are the manager of Country branch, and during your absence on holiday the bank notices in the financial press that dealings in the shares of Zee Ltd have been suspended. A worried assistant manager writes to Mr Kay mentioning this, and saying that he has consequently stopped all the accounts after transferring Mr Kay's credit balance in reduction of the joint account. The same day he dishonours a cheque for £110, drawn by Mr Kay on his current account with the answer 'Refer to drawer'.

You return to the office on the day following these events and, when perusing the files, you notice the action that has been taken.

What action would you take, and what advice would you give your assistant manager? Give reasons for your answer. [17]

(September 1981)

47. (*a*) You have agreed to lend to your customer, Mr Kirby, £12 000 on a fluctuating account, to help with working capital for his tailoring business. As security you have asked Mr Kirby for a legal mortgage over his domestic property, which Mr Kirby now values at £30 000. However, when the property was acquired by Mr Kirby, he was assisted to the extent of £10 000 by a friend, with whom he lodged the Land Certificate as security. The friend, Mr A. Smith, acting on his solicitor's advice, lodged a notice of deposit at the Land Registry, to protect his position.

Are there likely to be any special problems with the security offered, and, if so, what can be done to overcome them? Give reasons for your answer. [11]

(*b*) Miss Sutton's account has not been operated to your satisfaction recently, and with the borrowing having increased to £787 you have asked her to call and discuss matters, although you are fully secured by a legal charge over a life policy, with a surrender value of £310, and a legal charge over industrial shares quoted on the Stock Exchange and valued at £610.

When Miss Sutton calls, she volunteers to sell the shares and surrender the life policy to effect repayment, and she undertakes to conduct her account in credit thereafter.

How would you respond, and how would you proceed to ensure that the bank is repaid? [5]

[Total marks for question – 16]
(September 1981)

48. The Alphabet Group of companies (A Ltd, the holding company, and B Ltd and C Ltd, wholly-owned subsidiaries) have been your customers for many years and you have extended borrowing facilities ranging up to £1 million from time to time against unlimited cross-guarantees from each of the three companies in the group, supported by debentures, incorporating fixed charges over property and floating charges over all assets. You last valued the break-up value of the three debentures at £1.9 million.

The group have now decided to acquire all the share capital of Z Ltd, for £500 000, and, at the same time, the group will be restructured. A Ltd will remain as the holding company, but the main company office and factory premises valued at £750 000 will be transferred into the name of B Ltd from A Ltd, and a mortgage of £400 000 will be raised on this property from a merchant bank, who have asked you to agree to their being first mortgagees. Z Ltd's property, valued at £100 000, will be transferred to B Ltd.

Trading will be conducted through C Ltd and Z Ltd, and these companies intend to factor their book debts, which amount to approximately £130 000 and £80 000 per month respectively.

To assist with the acquisition and with continued expansion, your branch has been asked to lend £1.2 million to A Ltd as working capital. Subject to Z Ltd coming into the same security arrangements as the other companies in the group, you are prepared to help.

What steps will be involved in the security rearrangement, and what aspects should receive special attention, if any? Detail your answers for each company and the group generally. Give reasons for your answers.   [16]

(September 1981)

49. You are the securities officer at Country branch, 1 High Street, and your manager has just passed you a copy of an interview note which he has made. This reads:

Lionel Moffatt. I have agreed in principle to set up a loan of £6000 repayable by monthly instalments over three years, to assist customer with the purchase of a new motorized caravan. Interest is to be debited to his current account. He agreed to give security but has few assets at present. However, five years ago he lent his company, Moffatt Confectioners Ltd (who have an account at our Town Branch), £15 000 to enable it to acquire its third retail outlet, next door to us here at 3 High Street. He holds a charge certificate and he will do all that is necessary so that this security covers us.

Action: Securities Officer – please discuss security with me and let me know all the steps necessary to protect the bank. Are there any special points we should check before this lending is set up?

Required:

Notes on the action you would take, with reasons.   [16]

(April 1982)

50. Footsies Ltd, shoe manufacturers, are borrowing approximately £500 000 net from you on four accounts, viz:

No. 1 account £310 000 debit   (current account stopped on 1 January 1980 on death of guarantor).

No. 2 account £43 000 credit   (active current account opened 1 January 1980).

No. 3 account £117 000 debit   (active current account opened 14 April 1980).

Loan account £90 000 debit   (opened 10 June 1979 to assist with purchase of new factory – reducing at £10 000 per month by transfers from No. 2 account).

As security, you hold an unlimited guarantee dated 18 January 1976 from Ivor Foote, who died on 31 December 1979. You also hold a mortgage debenture dated 28 Feburary 1975 from the company incorporating a legal mortgage over one freehold factory, a specific equitable charge over all other real property, and a floating charge over all other assets.

The company has been incurring heavy losses in the recession and, upon your recent application to head office, the advances controller stipulated that continued support would only be given provided the company gave a supplemental fixed charge over its book debts and agreed to the opening of a wages and salaries account.

As manager you have passed head office's reply to your new security clerk, Mr Sim, for action, but he approaches you saying that he does not understand why head office want another charge over book debts. He asks what steps will be necesary to complete this security and also to open and operate the wages and salaries account. He also asks why this new account is required when the company has four accounts already.

How would you reply? Give reasons for your answer.   [17]

(April 1982)

51. In 1977 Mr Volt and Mr Amp formed a limited company, Sparks Ltd, to develop and manufacture electronic instruments. Mr Volt and Mr Amp became directors and each held 40 per cent of the equity capital. The private and company accounts are all at your branch, and are overdrawn. As security for the company borrowing, you hold an unlimited joint and several guarantee given by Mr Volt and Mr Amp in 1977. For Mr Volt's own borrowing (agreed in 1980) and liabilities generally you were given a share certificate over 17 500 shares in Sparks Ltd in Mr Volt's name, lodged without any other documentation. Mr Amp secured his borrowing when you first granted an overdraft in 1976, by handing you a life policy for £25 000, payable at death.

Mr Volt recently called to see you and said that the shares of Sparks Ltd were to be introduced into the unlisted securities market, with a view to the further expansion of the company. He expected the company's borrowing to be reduced over the next six months from a number of sources. However, he asked you to agree to increase his own borrowing so that he could buy 10 per cent of Mr Amp's shares. You concurred. These shares would also be lodged with you as security.

Required:

(a) Tabulated notes on the nature, advantages and disadvantages of the various forms of security held by the bank prior to the recent interview with Mr Volt. [14]

(b) Notes on any differences in the bank's security which would result from the development mentioned by Mr Volt. [3]

[Total marks for question – 17]
(*April 1982*)

52. Your customers, Tom Plum and Alan Pear, traded as Golden Fruits and were importers of tinned fruit until they went into bankruptcy recently. Two years ago, when they had the opportunity of supplying a large supermarket chain on a regular basis, you advanced monies to them as the supermarket insisted on taking six weeks' credit between delivery of supplies and payment. The tinned fruit was to be imported from several European countries and you were told that the overseas exporters required early payment. Because of the amounts involved you called for security, but the only security the partners could give was a charge over the stocks of goods themselves held from time to time in warehouses to the order of the partnership. You accepted this position and took the usual steps to perfect your security.

Now, however, following the failure of the firm, you have heard from another bank with which, unknown to you, Golden Fruits had an account. Finance Bank Ltd claims to have a charge over a consignment of tinned fruit which you believed formed part of your security. These goods have been inadvertently released from the warehouse and pledged to Finance Bank Ltd.

A German supplier has also written claiming that two of his consignments to Golden Fruits had not been paid for, and that he is therefore entitled to either the tinned fruit or the sale proceeds.

Required:

(a) A statement, in note form, of the steps originally taken by the bank to perfect its security. [7]

(b) Comments on the bank's position in respect of the claims which have now arisen. [9]

[Total marks for question – 16]
(*April 1982*)

53. (*a*) Babar Ltd is borrowing £50 000 from you against the security of a debenture, given on 3 February 1979, which incorporates a fixed charge over its land and buildings and a floating charge over all other assets.

At an interview with the directors, you learn that the company is proposing to enter into a factoring agreement with Ledger Factors Ltd in order to assist its cash flow. The directors inform you that part of the arrangement will be that Babar Ltd will assign its existing and future book debts to Ledger Factors Ltd and the factors will in future carry out all the company's book-keeping and the collection of monies due to it.

How would the bank's position be affected, and what arrangements would you make? [8]

(*b*) Mr Biggs, a company director, whose account is held at another branch of your bank, calls to execute a guarantee document at your branch in respect of the liabilities of his wife. Mrs Biggs is borrowing £7000 on current account, and has given you a memorandum of deposit over shares quoted on the Stock Exchange and valued at £2500. The guarantee which Mr Biggs has agreed to give is for £5000 and is in the bank's standard form.

In your presence, Mr Biggs reads the security form, and then asks you what the following clauses mean, and how they affect his position in this case:

(*a*) 'Where this guarantee is executed by two or more persons the covenants and agreements expressed herein are joint and several.'

(*b*) 'This guarantee shall be a continuing security and shall be determined only in writing by three months' notice of such intent being given to the bank by the guarantor or his personal representative, although the bank shall be at liberty to determine the guarantee at any time it requires.'

(*c*) 'This guarantee applies to the ultimate balance owing by the principal debtor to the bank and until paid the guarantor will not be entitled to any security held by the bank in respect of the liabilities of the principal debtor, nor will the guarantor be entitled to exercise any rights as surety in competition with the bank.'

How would you reply? Give reasons for your answer. [8]

[Total marks for question – 16]
(*September 1982*)

54. Chipmics Ltd is a computer consultancy agency incorporated two years ago, which banks at your branch. The director and secretary are Mr Roscoe and his wife respectively and the company trades from their home address, 1 Elm Lane. The company has prospered but, because some of its customers are slow to pay, it requires occasional overdrafts of up to £8000. Provided there is adequate security, the bank is prepared to help.

Unfortunately, 1 Elm Lane is fully mortgaged, and the company has no suitable assets of its own to charge. However, Mr Roscoe has a good friend and neighbour who runs a market gardening business in the name of Smiths

Plants Ltd which adjoins 1 Elm Lane. Mr Roscoe says that Smiths Plants Ltd is prepared to guarantee Chipmics Ltd and that the three acres of market-garden land can be mortgaged to the bank, but he is uncertain whether the land is in the name of Smiths Plants Ltd or is owned by Mr Smith himself.

You are the securities officer at the branch, and your manager asks you to let him have your observations on the acceptability of the security offered, together with a note of any special aspects which need consideration. How would you respond? [16]

(September 1982)

55. Mr Elliott, a wealthy customer, is borrowing £4000 on a loan account which you arranged so that he could have his house extended. The loan is being reduced at £200 per month and, when it was granted in 1978, you were given a first legal mortgage by Mr Elliott over the deeds of his house which is now shown in your security register as being worth £75 000. Mr Elliott is a director of Sunderland & Co. Ltd, which also banks with you, and which, from time to time, borrows against Mr Elliott's unlimited guarantee. Recent audited accounts for this company have shown that in the last 12 months it traded at a loss, although its capital base is still considered by you to be adequate for the lending of £40 000 on an occasional basis which you have permitted in the past.

Today, you have received a letter from Mr Elliott saying that he wishes to transfer the deeds of his house into his wife's name, and he asks you to forward these to his solicitors, Whiffle and Co., so that this can be arranged. You are prepared to agree, but wish the bank to continue to remain secured by the guarantee and the deeds.

Required:

Notes on the considerations you would have in mind regarding your security. What would be the likely sequence of events, and how would you ensure that the bank was fully protected at all times? [17]

(September 1982)

56. Roses Ltd is borrowing £4000 from you on a fluctuating overdraft and, as security, you hold an unlimited joint and several guarantee by Mr Rose and his wife supported by a legal charge from Mr Rose over a life policy for £10 000 on his own life. The policy has a surrender value of £2300. Mr Rose is a director of the company and Mrs Rose is the secretary and a director.

You have just learnt that Mr Rose has been killed in a car accident.

Required:

(*a*) Comments on the action you would take to protect the bank's secured position, and other steps you would put in hand over the next few weeks.

[13]

(b) A note of any differences in procedures which would now apply if the life policy had been taken out by the company on Mr Rose's life. [4]

[Total marks for question – 17]
(September 1982)

57. You are the officer in charge of the securities section of your branch of Telford's Clearing Bank plc and you have a new trainee clerk, Miss Gordon. She is engaged in taking a second mortgage over the house of one of your customers, Paul Fillington. The house is at 17 Rose Lane, Sutton, Surrey, land title number: LX 127 946 and it was brought for £95 000 two years ago with the help of a building society mortgage.

Miss Gordon approaches you for help, saying that she has searched the Land Charges Register, and the search has been returned with the answer 'No subsisting entries – Protection expires 30.4.83'. She asks you why the first mortgagee's name does not appear on the search, and what the entry means. Miss Gordon also refers to the fire insurance position, mentioning that she understands that for domestic property no action is necessary by the bank.

What would you tell her and why? [16]
(April 1983)

58. (a) Your head office has agreed to lend Gamma Ltd £200 000 on fluctuating overdraft to help it with the development of houses on a small estate. However, the local authority requires a bond in respect of roads and sewers, in case the builders should fail to complete this work to the authority's satisfaction, and the bank has agreed to assist by providing a bond. This is drawn in the form of a guarantee in favour of the local authority with a maximum liability of £50 000 by the bank. Your head office wishes your branch to obtain a counter-indemnity from the company.

State how you would proceed, and the advantages of taking the counter-indemnity proposed by your head office. [4]

(b) Peter Trueman will be aged 60 on 1 May next when a life policy for £5000 (plus profits) in his favour will mature. He lodged this policy as security and signed a memorandum of deposit on 17 January, 1973.

Peter Trueman's account is now overdrawn by £6600, and you wish to see repayment out of the policy monies.

State how you would ensure that this happens. [4]

(c) Mary Mills, a professional cook and writer, is borrowing £3000 on overdraft, and for security she handed to you two years ago the deeds of her leasehold flat, valued at £19 000. To simply matters, no papers were signed at that time. Last year the bank was given notice by Alpha Finance Co. of a second charge for £12 000, but your new securities clerk only placed this letter with the deeds and took no other action. This fact has just been discovered.

State the bank's position and say what steps you would now take. Give reasons for your answer. [8]

[Total marks for question – 16]
(*April 1983*)

59. Shoes Ltd maintains an account with your branch of Brown's Bank plc and also an account with a competitor, Zeta Bank plc. The account at your branch is fed mainly by transfers from Zeta Bank and you have extended unsecured overdraft facilities in view of good connections with the directors and partly in the hope of obtaining all the company's business.

To your surprise, on 3 April, Zeta Bank appointed a receiver under a debenture which they took in 1981, and which incorporated a fixed charge over the company's factory and a floating charge over all other assets. It transpires that Zeta Bank has no preferential claim.

A copy of the statement of affairs is produced below, together with a copy of the company's account at your branch since July.

Required:

(*a*) A calculation of Brown's Bank's preferential claim in the receivership.

(*b*) A statement of what Brown's Bank's preferential claim would have been if a wages and salaries account had been opened in October 1982.

(*c*) Assuming that the realization agreed exactly with the figures in the statement of affairs and Brown's Bank's preferential claim is accepted in full by the receiver, a statement of:

(*i*) Brown's Bank's loss;

(*ii*) the position of Zeta Bank.

Give brief reasons for all your calculations [17]

SHOES LTD

Statement of Affairs as at 3 April 1983

Liabilities	£	Assets	£
Preferential creditors	35 000	Factory	50 000
(excluding banks)		Plant and machinery	10 000
Creditors	115 000	Stock	10 000
Brown's Bank	25 000	Debtors	5 000
Zeta Bank	75 000		
			75 000
		Deficiency	175 000
	£250 000		£250 000

SHOES LTD - BANK STATEMENT

1982			Debit £	Credit £	Balance £
July	1	Balance b/f			Dr. 30 312.—
	2	Gas Board	210.17		Dr. 30 522.17
	4	Rates	2008.29		Dr. 32 530.46
	17	Cheques		8 010.98	Dr. 24 519.48
	28	Wages and salaries	8016.42		Dr. 32 535.90
Aug.	9	Electricity	507.19		Dr 33 043.09
	28	Wages and salaries	8102.19		Dr. 41 145.28
Sept.	2	Transfer from Zeta Bank		15 000.—	Dr. 26 145.28
	28	Wages and salaries	8016,42		Dr. 34 161.70
Oct.	10	Long Transport Ltd	3814.76		Dr. 37 976.46
	28	Wages and salaries	7810.50		Dr. 45 786.96
	30	Cheques		7 248.10	Dr. 38 538.86
Nov.	11	Gas Board	529.18		Dr. 39 068.04
		Transfer Zeta Bank		15 000.—	Dr. 24 068.04
	28	Wages and salaries	7606.03		Dr. 31 674.07
Dec.	10	Cheques		3 111.14	Dr. 28 562.93
	28	Wages and salaries	8010.54		Dr. 36 573.47
		Interest	4002.18		Dr. 40 575.65
		Commission	50.—		Dr. 40 625.65
1983					
Jan.	10	Transfer Zeta Bank		15 000.—	Dr. 25 625.65
	17	Electricity	1637.39		Dr. 27 263.04
	28	Wages and salaries	7648.28		Dr. 34 911.32
Feb.	10	Mays Computer	4310.43		Dr. 39 221.75
	28	Wages and salaries	6582.94		Dr. 45 804.69
March.	3	Cheques		5 804.69	Dr. 40 000.00
	10	Transfer Zeta Bank·		15 000.—	Dr. 25 000.00

(April 1983)

60. (a) Pipes Ltd, one of your customers, is owed £50 000 by an associated company, Copper Ltd, and, as security, in 1979 it took a mortgage over Copper's factory and three acres of land, total value £100 000.

Over the last two years you have been lending to Pipes Ltd on current account, against a legal charge over your customer's security from Copper Ltd. Your charge has been registered at the Land Registry. The present balance on the current account of Pipes Ltd is £69 812 debit, against an agreed overdraft limit of £70 000 expiring on 30 June, 1983.

However, Copper Ltd has just written to tell you that it has sold the factory and land for £70 000. You are asked to forward your security to their solicitors. Drain and Co., to enable the completion of the sale to take place in one month's time.

Required:

How would you deal with this request, and what considerations would you have in mind? What would the bank's position be, assuming that the sale takes place? [12]

(*b*) George Childs is a dairy farmer with a herd of 200 cows. In view of recent problems on his account, you are no longer prepared to extend the unsecured facilities allowed to him over the last five years and he agrees to give you a charge over his contract with the Milk Marketing Board.

Required:

Notes on all the steps necessary to take and perfect this security. [5]

[Total marks for question – 17]
(*April 1983*)

61. For several years you have extended overdraft facilities to your good customers, Pinetree Ltd, ranging up to £80 000 on occasions, against the security of deeds of the factory premises at Oldsway from which they trade. Title to this factory was at one time in the name of John Pinetree (present director and guarantor) when he traded as an individual before the incorporation of the company. Upon the formation of the company in 1978, he simply became a trustee of the property for the company, thereby avoiding costs which would have arisen in a conveyance of the title. You retained your first mortgage from John Pinetree and ensured that you were fully protected as regards the company's interest.

The company now intends to move to new premises at 1 New Street, and you have agreed to certain rearrangements of the bank's security. The old factory will be sold for £90 000 and a new one will be bought by the company for £120 000. Pinetree Ltd have arranged a long-term loan of £60 000 from Mercury Finance plc, who will hold the deeds, and the bank will be given a second mortgage by the company over this new factory at 1 New Street. There will be a delay of one month between the completion of the two transactions to enable Pinetree Ltd to move all their business without difficulties, and you have agreed to provide the additional short-term bridging facilities.

Required:

Prepare a brief note, in *tabulated form*, of all the steps involved in this rearrangement to ensure that the bank will be fully protected throughout.

[17]
(*September 1983*)

62. Plantpot Ltd ceased to trade eighteen months ago, and the bank called in the borrowing with outstanding balances of £19 300 on its loan account, and £432 credit on its current account. There were no assets, apart from your security, which consisted of a legal mortgage over the deeds of the company's shop premises, valued at £30 000 in your books. You also have a guarantee given by Mr Plant for £10 000, and a guarantee for £5000 from Mr Pot.

Mr Plant's guarantee is supported by an assignment over a life policy for £3000, with a surrender value of £498, and Mr Pot supported his guarantee by handing you a share certificate in Seeds plc, whose shares are quoted on the Stock Exchange. You valued this holding at £1200.

After the company ceased trading, you waited to see if it would be put into liquidation but, as no steps were taken, the bank eventually instructed its own estate agents, and sold the shop for £20 000, less legal and other costs of £2010. In the meantime, you had called in the guarantees, and Mr Plant and Mr Pot commenced making payments of £200 each on the first day of each month with effect 1 June 1982. These payments have been maintained regularly.

On 10 September 1983, following receipt of the net proceeds for the sale of the shop, Mr Plant called to see you, and he asked if you would pay over to him any surplus monies in your hands, and also return his life policy to him, together with the cancelled guarantee.

Required:

(a) A short arithmetical statement setting out the bank's position in monetary terms. [3]

(b) A statement of how you would deal with Mr Plant's request, and what considerations you would have in mind. [8]

(c) A tabulated statement of how the position would have changed and how your handling of Mr Plant's request would have differed if the guarantors had made the same payments but the bank had sold the shop for the figure originally shown in its books. [5]

[Total marks for question – 16]
(*September 1983*)

63. Your new securities clerk at North Street branch shows you the diary for today in which the following entries appear and asks your advice:

(a) 'Account: P Wit – Enquire if Mrs D. M. Wit is still living. Obtain details of assets in estate.'

(b) 'Account: I. Long Ltd – Obtain opinion on I. Long.'

(c) 'Account: L. Tooth – Has Home Building Society replied to our letter?'

(d) 'Account: M. Sinclair Ltd – Has Peter Bolton signed guarantee yet?'

(e) 'Account: Y. Hartley – send her quotation regarding costs of taking security.'

(f) 'Account: H. Mole – Arrange for manager to walk his farm.'

You consult the securities records and find in the sundries securities register that Peter Wit charged his reversionary interest in the estate of Malcolm Wit on 10 September, 1978. Harry Mole gave the bank an agricultural floating charge dated 17 May, 1979.

In the guarantee register, on the page for I. Long Ltd, you see that Issaac Long gave a guarantee for £15 000 on 20 April 1980. On the page for M. Sinclair Ltd, a joint and several guarantee for £5000 by Peter Bolton and Peter Brown is recorded in pencil only, and no entry appears in the column for the date of charge.

Your deeds register shows that you are in the process of taking a second mortgage from Lionel Tooth over his house at 17 Oak Avenue.

There are no entries under the name 'Y. Hartley'.

Required:

Your explanation to the clerk as to why his predecessor made the diary entries and your instructions on how to proceed.

Set out your answer in tabulated form and give reasons for your views.

[17]

(*September 1983*)

64. Red Ltd holds 30 per cent of the issued share capital of Pink Ltd, and both companies have accounts with you. Red Ltd manufactures paint, and Pink Ltd is a retail outlet for 10 per cent of Red's production

Your branch has been asked to lend Red Ltd £300 000 and Pink Ltd £25 000. Red Ltd will give you a legal mortgage over its factory and will guarantee Pink's account for all advances.

You are assistant manager of the branch, and your manager shows you Red's last balance sheet and asks you to look into the question of borrowing and charging powers in conjunction with a copy of the company's memorandum and articles of association. You notice that Red was incorporated in 1972, under the Companies Act 1948 and adopted Table A in full. There is no mention of guarantees in either the memorandum or the articles of association, but the company is able to 'subsidize or otherwise assist' any subsidiary company.

Required:

Prepare a brief note for your manager covering the points which he asked you to examine, and make any neccessary recommendations.

520 *Appendix I*

RED LTD

Balance Sheet as at 31 December 1982

	£		£
Capital (Authorised		Land and buildings	400 000
£750 000) Issued	500 000	Plant and machinery	170 000
Reserves	200 000	Investment in Subsidiary	50 000
Debenture	60 000	Stock	300 000
Director's loan	130 000	Debtors	150 000
Hire purchase	40 000	Bank	10 000
Trade creditors	150 000		
	£1 080 000		£1 080 000

[16]

(September 1983)

A Student's Guide to Land Mortgage Analysis

For every question the student should choose one entry from each line. In this way it is possible to break the question up into sections, and to comment, as required, on what is relevant. This system helps the student's understanding, and prevents omissions.

a		*b*
FIRST	—	SUBSEQUENT

c		*d*
LEGAL	—	EQUITABLE

e		*f*
DIRECT	—	THIRD PARTY

g		*h*
MORTGAGE	—	SUB-MORTGAGE

i		*j*
FREEHOLD	—	LEASEHOLD

k		*l*
REGISTERED	—	UNREGISTERED

m		*n*
SOLE NAME	—	JOINT TITLE

o		*p*
INDIVIDUAL(S)	—	LIMITED COMPANY

q		*r*
OWNER-OCCUPIED	—	TENANTED

EXAMPLE

Question

Two years ago John Ham, your customer, lent his friend George Stamp's company £60 000, to enable it to acquire the freehold of the premises from which it had traded for the past five years. The total cost of this acquisition was £80 000 and at the time the freehold deeds were legally charged to John Ham as security for his loan.

Your customer is an electronic engineer and he now wishes to borrow £100 000 from you to facilitate the expansion of his own business into new computer markets. He produces a cash flow forecast which satisfies you that he will be able to repay the advance over two years, and subject to his legally charging the mortgage deeds as security you will assist.

Required: Detail all the steps and precautions you will take to perfect this security and to protect the bank.

Analysis:

Letters

a c e h i l m o q

Explanation of analysis: This question is about a first legal direct sub-mortgage over freehold unregistered land held under a mortgage by a sole party as an individual; title to the land in question is in the name of a limited company, which occupies the property itself.

Index